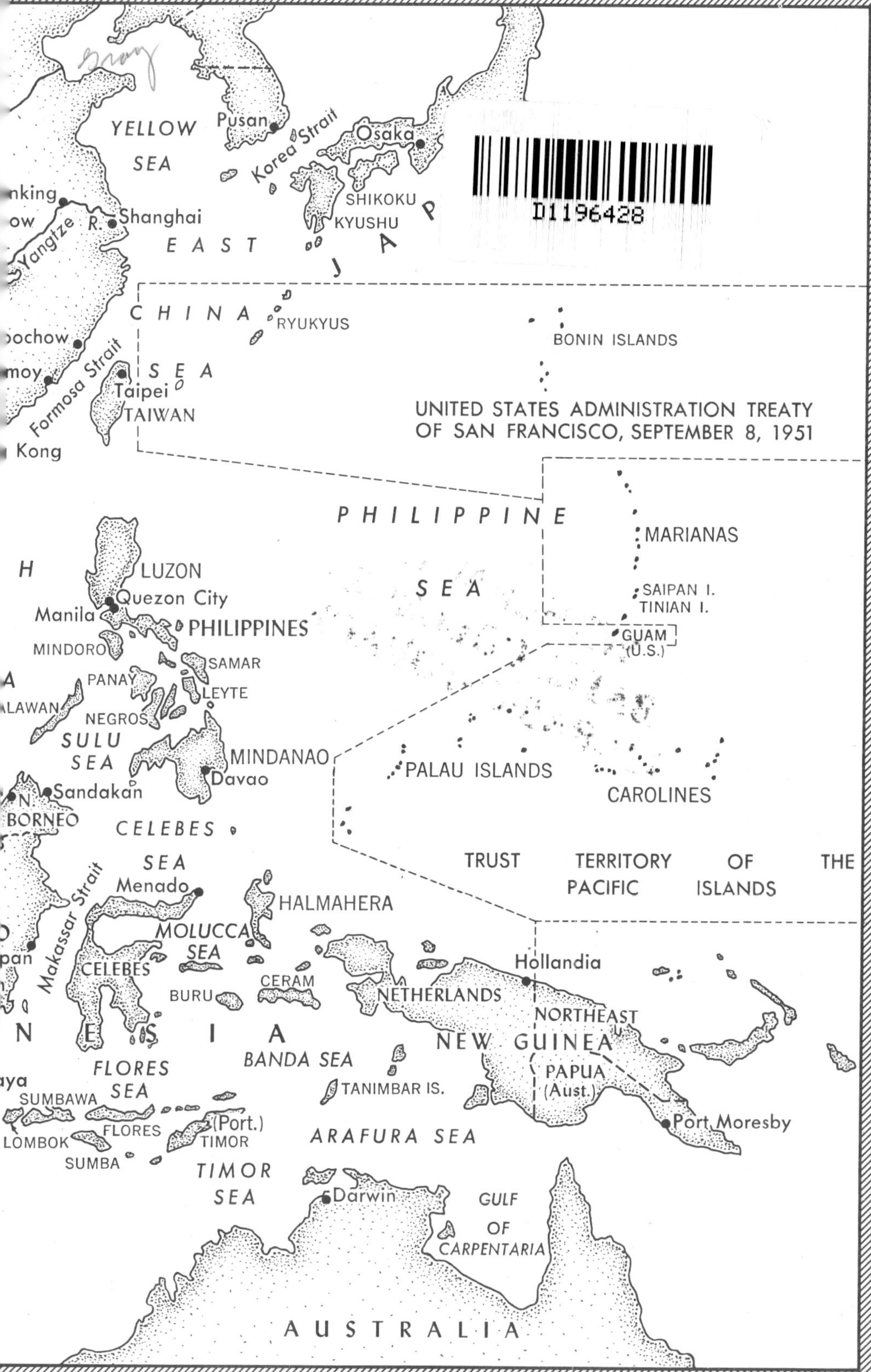

YELLOW SEA
Pusan
Korea Strait
Osaka
SHIKOKU
KYUSHU
JAPAN
nking
ow
Yangtze R.
Shanghai
EAST CHINA SEA
RYUKYUS
BONIN ISLANDS
oochow
moy
Formosa Strait
Taipei
TAIWAN
Kong
UNITED STATES ADMINISTRATION TREATY OF SAN FRANCISCO, SEPTEMBER 8, 1951
PHILIPPINE SEA
MARIANAS
SAIPAN I.
TINIAN I.
GUAM (U.S.)
LUZON
Quezon City
Manila
PHILIPPINES
MINDORO
SAMAR
PANAY
LEYTE
LAWAN
NEGROS
SULU SEA
MINDANAO
Davao
PALAU ISLANDS
CAROLINES
Sandakan
N. BORNEO
CELEBES SEA
TRUST TERRITORY OF THE PACIFIC ISLANDS
Menado
Makassar Strait
HALMAHERA
MOLUCCA SEA
CELEBES
BURU
CERAM
Hollandia
NETHERLANDS NEW GUINEA
NORTHEAST
PAPUA (Aust.)
BANDA SEA
TANIMBAR IS.
Port Moresby
FLORES SEA
SUMBAWA
LOMBOK
FLORES
SUMBA
(Port.) TIMOR
TIMOR SEA
ARAFURA SEA
Darwin
GULF OF CARPENTARIA
AUSTRALIA

The DIPLOMACY of SOUTHEAST ASIA: 1945-1958

The DIPLOMACY of SOUTHEAST ASIA: 1945-1958

By RUSSELL H. FIFIELD
PROFESSOR OF POLITICAL SCIENCE
UNIVERSITY OF MICHIGAN

HARPER & BROTHERS, *Publishers*, NEW YORK

The DIPLOMACY of SOUTHEAST ASIA: 1945-1958

F-H

Library of Congress catalog card number: 58-8354

To

Ramon Magsaysay

Late President of the Philippines

CONTENTS

MAPS

PREFACE

A new pattern of international relations has emerged in Southeast Asia since the end of the Second World War in 1945. The Philippines, Burma, Indonesia, Cambodia, Laos and Vietnam, actually partitioned into two states, have joined Thailand in the family of sovereign nations. The independence of the Federation of Malaya in August, 1957, reduced the colonial territory to Singapore, British Borneo, and Portuguese Timor. And even in the case of Singapore, self-government came in 1958. West Irian or Netherlands New Guinea remained a special case, a subject of bitter controversy between Indonesia and the Netherlands. The relations among the states of Southeast Asia and between them and the world present a unique opportunity to describe and analyze a new phase of international politics in a strategic part of the globe.

The period from 1945 to 1958 generally represents the formative years in the determination of foreign policy by the new states of the area. By 1958 territories, having emerged from dependence upon the mother country, had in most cases made a basic adjustment as sovereign states to her. They had in the majority of instances reached settlements with Japan arising from her occupation of the area in the Second World War. They had taken a basic policy position toward the cold war dividing the Western world led by the United States and Great Britain and the Communist world led by the Soviet Union and the People's Republic of China. Thus the Federation of Malaya upon receiving independence found herself in a world far more stabilized than that existing in 1945. Thailand for her part had been successful in diplomatically rehabilitating herself after Japan's defeat and in adjusting to the new frame of international politics.

Equally important is the fact that by 1958 the basic foreign policy of key outside powers toward Southeast Asia had crystallized. Communist China, independent India, emergent Japan, and a watchful Australia were exerting their influence in varying degrees of intensity from Rangoon to Manila to Djakarta. The United States, Great Britain, France, and the Netherlands had adjusted for better or for worse to the loss of all or most of their possessions in Southeast Asia. The potential power occasioned by the Eurasian alliance of the Soviet Union and the People's Republic of China or by the Western-orientated alliance of the Manila Pact signatories reached to the very heart of the region.

By 1958 seven states of Southeast Asia had become members of the United Nations—the Philippines, Burma, Thailand, Indonesia, Laos, Cambodia, and the Federation of Malaya. Divided Vietnam shared with the two Germanys and the two Koreas the disadvantages of nonmembership in the world organization. To the states of Southeast Asia the United Nations with over a decade of experience behind it had begun to reveal its basic elements of strength and weakness. Also by 1958 the forces working for and against regionalism in the area had been given an opportunity to manifest their strength.

The participation of Southeast Asia was widespread in different international activities outside the United Nations. Instances are the Bandung Conference, the New Delhi Conference on Indonesia, the Asian Relations Conference at New Delhi, the Baguio Conference, the Japanese Peace Conference at San Francisco, the Geneva Conference on Indochina, and the Simla Conference. Further evidence is found when the Colombo Plan, the Panch Shila, and the Colombo Powers are considered.

The Korean War from 1950 to 1953 and the Indochina War from 1946 to 1954 were international conflicts that came to affect in a real sense Southeast Asia. The United Nations war effort in Korea and the colonial aspect of the Indochina struggle contributed among other considerations to preventing the region from being truly neutral in the bloodshed. From the overall aspect of the cold war the area by 1958 represented a mirror of world politics—the pro-Western, the pro-Communist, and the uncommitted approaches to foreign policy.

As international politics is dynamic, change is the order of the day. But the author is convinced that the period from 1945 to 1958 is sufficiently distinctive to merit special consideration. It is doubtful, barring a global conflict, if any other similar duration of years will be as formative in the foreign policy of the states concerned.

Moreover, most of the Asian leaders who have guided the international destinies of the countries during different parts of the period under consideration are still living. They are often the George Washingtons and the Simón Bolívars of today. Their viewpoints can still be given, lending authority to the study of the comparative foreign policy of the states of the area. In many cases these leaders are the living embodiment of the spirit of the times in their part of the world. In the years to come the diplomacy of the period can be analyzed with the advantage of greater perspective but there may be lost some of the personal element so important in understanding international relations.

The author has chosen to organize the body of his data around the countries of the area rather than around broad topics like nationalism, specific organizations like the Southeast Asia Treaty Organization, the states that influence the region like India, or important events like the Bandung Conference. In other words, the focus is on the countries of Southeast Asia with such factors as the policies of outside powers and the impact of international conferences woven into the chapters. Quite naturally there is a stress on Asian relations. At the same time, in the interests of overall coverage, the first part of the book includes a consideration of the background of independence and the final part deals with regionalism and with Southeast Asia in the United Nations.

Emphasis in the study is placed upon the description and analysis of the political aspects of international relations. Domestic politics is considered in so far as it directly relates to foreign policy. The author has tried to build up a bibliography that the reader can use for further study. He has followed a policy of quoting in the text key passages of important documents.

It would be impossible to list all the people who have assisted in one way or another in the preparation of this book. The author is grateful to the staff in the law and general libraries of the University of Michigan, the Orientalia Division of the Library of Congress, and the library in the Department of Foreign Affairs in the Philippines. He has profited among other meetings from attendance at the Conference on South and Southeast Asia under the auspices of the School of Advanced International Studies in the summer of 1955, the Conference on Human Values in Social Change in South and Southeast Asia and in the United States under the U.S. National Commission for UNESCO in Ann Arbor in the spring of 1956, and the Brookings Institution National Seminar at Lake Forest in the early summer of 1949.

Professors in Southeast Asia at the University of the Philippines, Silliman University, University of Manila, University of Indonesia, University of Malaya, Chulalongkorn University, and the

University of Rangoon, as well as at the University of Hong Kong and National Taiwan University have given assistance. Individuals with the Indian Council of World Affairs, the Pakistan Institute of International Affairs, the Siam Society, Academia Sinica, the Cornell Research Center in Bangkok, the Asia Foundation, the Michigan State University Vietnam Technical Assistance Project, and the American Universities Field Staff have aided in the research. Professors Amry Vandenbosch, George McT. Kahin, and John F. Cady suggested people for the author to see in parts of Southeast Asia. In Ann Arbor a number of students from the Philippines, Indonesia, Burma, Thailand, and Vietnam have helped.

On the government level the author is grateful to officials in the United States Department of State, the Canadian Department of External Affairs, the Office of the Commissioner-General for the United Kingdom in South-East Asia, and the Office of the Commissioner for New Zealand in South-East Asia. A large number of Americans in official capacity in Asia, associated with embassies, the United States Information Agency, Military Assistance Advisory Groups, and the International Coöperation Administration, have given the author some of their valuable time. Individuals with the United Nations in New York and the Economic Commission for Asia and the Far East in Bangkok as well as the resident representatives of the Technical Assistance Board in Burma and the Philippines have helped. Officials from the International Commissions for Supervision and Control in Laos and Cambodia have given their assistance.

A large number of political leaders in Southeast Asia including the late President Ramon Magsaysay, President Sukarno, Prime Minister U Nu, Field Marshal Pibul Songgram, President Ngo Dinh Diem, and Tengku Abdul Rahman have given their viewpoints to the author in conversation. Letters have been received from Prince Norodom Sihanouk of Cambodia and Prince Souvanna Phouma of Laos. Embassy officials in Washington have been considerate. Outside Southeast Asia but in neighboring countries interviews have included Chiang Kai-shek and Mohammed Ali and letters Jawaharlal Nehru and R. G. Casey. The detailed list of interviews, discussions, and correspondence in the Appendix indicates a stress on Asians.

In his travels in the Philippines, Indonesia, Burma, Thailand, Laos, Cambodia, Vietnam, and Malaya the author has received many kindnesses from people in all walks of life. Indeed, it would have been difficult to gather information without their coöperation. In terms of financial assistance, the author acknowledges his gratitude to the United States Educational Foundation in the Philippines and the University of Michigan's Horace H. Rackham School of Graduate Studies.

As for any errors in judgment or unintended mistakes in facts, the author accepts responsibility.

R. H. F.

Ann Arbor, Michigan
January, 1958

The DIPLOMACY of SOUTHEAST ASIA: 1945-1958

I. *The Setting*

In the international politics of the present century Southeast Asia has reflected the dominant forces of the times. Almost entirely divided by the beginning of this period among the Western powers under various types of direct and indirect colonial rule, the region was subject to decisions in vital matters from distant metropolitan capitals. Nineteenth-century imperialism, even with its idealistic aspects, produced a political, and in many respects, an economic, social, and cultural pattern that did not possess the elements of permanence. Its greatest foe was the nationalism of the twentieth century, reaching a climax in the creation of sovereign states with many untried approaches to domestic and international problems.

Although the First World War officially involved all Southeast Asia except the Netherlands East Indies, the great battles of the conflict were far removed. In contrast, Southeast Asia was a theater of operations in the Second World War, the Japanese overrunning the entire area in the months following their attack on Pearl Harbor and the forces of the United Nations later driving them out in certain countries, notably the Philippines and Burma. After the end of the war Southeast Asia came to be a vital region in the struggle between the Communist and Western forces of the world.

As is often the case in other areas, the region called Southeast Asia has not been defined to the satisfaction of all. At the present time the political area is most commonly considered to include on the mainland of Asia the Union of Burma, the kingdoms of Thailand, Laos and Cambodia, Vietnam, and the Federation of Malaya while the insular parts consist of the republics of Indonesia and the Philippines, technically the State of Singapore, the crown colonies of Sarawak and North Borneo, the Protected State of Brunei, and the Portuguese overseas territory of Timor. For political purposes Netherlands New Guinea or West Irian may be considered in Southeast Asia although geographic and ethnological reasons exist for excluding the territory. On the other hand, Taiwan belongs more fittingly to Northeast Asia along with China, Japan, and Korea, and Ceylon may be more conveniently classified in South Asia with India and Pakistan.

From the strictly geographical viewpoint Southeast Asia, although not a natural unit, is reasonably well defined. The Indo-Chinese or Indo-Pacific peninsula is separated from the rest of the mainland of Asia by a mountainous barrier rarely affording terrain favorable to migration except in northeast Vietnam along the Gulf of Tonkin. The islands fringing the peninsula to the south, southeast, and east are more related to the mainland of Asia than to Australia southeast of Indonesia or to the Trust Territory of the Pacific Islands east of the Philippines. The Japanese have significantly referred to the whole region as Nan Yo and the Chinese as Nan Yang, both meaning "Southern Seas," while some Indians have called it Further India. Within the area itself a number of rivers like the Irrawaddy in Burma, the Chao Phraya (Menam) in Thailand, and the Mekong in Indochina have provided avenues of passage while in the insular territories of the Philippines and Indonesia the proximity of many of the islands has facilitated movement. Nevertheless, Southeast Asia is a region of great distance, extending over an area larger than Europe.

Geography and politics have combined on the international level to make Southeast Asia one of the most strategic areas of the world. The Strait of Malacca between Sumatra and Malaya is a strategic gateway between the Pacific and Indian oceans. In contrast to the Panama and Suez canals, which are man-made, the Strait of Malacca is a natural gateway. Not without reason did Singapore, located at the southern end of Malaya, become a base of considerable importance in the "geostrategy" of Southeast Asia. Although its significance has been reduced as a result of the events of the Second World War when the Japanese captured the base and as a consequence of the development of nuclear and thermonuclear weapons, Singapore is still an important key to the defense of the region. In another respect, the land and sea pattern in Southeast Asia, peninsular and insular, has provided the natural facilities for movement from continental Asia to Australia. The "Near North" is an expression often used by Australian writers to describe the geographic relationship of their Commonwealth to Southeast Asia. The peninsular part of the area, it should further be noted, is very important in an air age, Bangkok, for instance, having one of the most strategic and modern airports in Asia.

Southeast Asia as a whole is underpopulated although certain areas like Java in Indonesia, Central Luzon in the Philippines, and the Red River delta in Vietnam suffer from overpopulation. The existence, nevertheless, of considerable territory in the region capable of sustaining a much larger population exerts to some degree an influence on outside states in South and Northeast Asia where the pressure of the people upon the land is frequently marked. The total population of Southeast Asia is between 150 million and 185 million people increasing by over 20 million each decade. In contrast, Communist China has about 600 million, India around 380 million, and Japan around 90 million.

The linguistic and religious complexity of the area is indicative of the various forces that have molded the region. Malayo-Polynesian languages are generally spoken in Indonesia, the Philippines and Malaya; Burmese and Siamese belong to the Tibeto-Chinese family; in parts of Burma, Malaya, Thailand, and Indochina the people speak Austro-Asiatic languages. Indians, Chinese, Arabs, and Europeans have obviously added to the linguistic complexity. At the present time a large number of government officials in Southeast Asia, apart from the states of Indochina, are fluent in English, now the language of diplomacy.

In terms of comparative religion, Indonesia and the Federation of Malaya are predominantly Moslem, the Philippines Christian, and Burma, Thailand, Cambodia, and Laos Buddhist. Vietnam is basically Buddhist though like China with strong Taoist and Confucian elements. Hinayana Buddhism is prevalent in Burma, Thailand, Cambodia, and Laos while Mahayana Buddhism is common in Vietnam. The Christians of the Philippines are predominantly Roman Catholic although various Protestant faiths are present. Christians outside the Philippines are chiefly restricted to the Europeans and to Asians in certain localities like communities of Karens in Burma, of Vietnamese in Vietnam, and of Menadonese in northern Sulawesi. Indians now living in Southeast Asia are largely Hindus in religion although some are Moslems. The religious imprint of Hinduism is still preserved in the island of Bali in Indonesia. In the field of international relations the various religious groupings in Southeast Asia, especially the Moslem, Buddhist, and Roman Catholic, have ties with states outside the area of similar religious conviction.

The ethnological composition of the people of the region is complex, reflecting the centuries of migration into or through the Indo-Pacific peninsula. The existence of many minorities in the area raises difficult problems comparable to those found in the

Balkans. The Union of Burma, for instance, is politically named to indicate the effort of the government to establish a union of the different peoples of the country. To some extent the former United States of Indonesia under a federal government reflected more accurately the politico-geographical needs of all the people than the present unitary Republic of Indonesia. The more articulate Asians of the region, it should be noted, are revealing a greater consciousness of, and pride in, their heritage.

The basic population of Southeast Asia is Indonesian or Austronesian, the result of two major waves, the Proto-Malays and Deutero-Malays, roughly between 2500 and 1500 B.C. These peoples pushed earlier inhabitants into more remote areas, a process that has been frequently repeated on the peninsula. In the latter case three subsequent invaders merit special attention in view of their impact in Southeast Asia today. The Annamites, probably originating in Nan Yueh embracing Kwangsi, Kwangtung, and the Red River delta area of Tonkin, gradually advanced southward along the coast of Indochina, defeated Champa, pushed Khmer jurisdiction westward, and expanded into Cochin China. The Thai-Shan-Lao people moved down the Menam, Mekong, and Salween valleys from their home in Nan Chao on the Kwangtung-Yunnan plateau, occupying as they went the plateaus of eastern Burma and Laos, defeating the Mons and Khmers in the Menam basin and establishing the state of Siam. To the west the Burmans penetrated the Irrawaddy valley, defeated the Pyus who were also Tibeto-Burmans, and later conquered the Mons in southern Burma. The rivalry between Siam and Burma, Cambodia and Vietnam, and Siam and Cambodia had historic roots long before the advent of the Western powers in Southeast Asia. As for the insular part of the region, the Indonesian population was more isolated from the migrations in the peninsula. Nevertheless, some of the national leaders of today recall the time when previous empires in the area included parts of Indonesia, the Philippines, and Malaya.

Indians, Chinese, Arabs, and Europeans have contributed to the culture of the region, helping to produce the contrasts of today. At various times between the first and fifteenth centuries A.D. Indian-influenced states such as the kingdoms of Funan, Champa, and Angkor, and of the Mons and Burmans, rose and fell on the mainland while the kingdoms of Srivijaya, the Sailendras, of Singosari and Majapahit followed a similar process in the islands. The Indian cultural impact was expressed in the propagation of Buddhism and Brahmanism in Southeast Asia, in the flowering of art and architecture as revealed today in the monumental ruins at Angkor in Cambodia and Borobudur in Java, in the extension to the region of Sanskrit, and in the application of the Hindu concept of kingship, law, and administration at a number of royal courts. At the same time it should be added that the Indian cultural impact tended to be centered in the capital of the kingdom around the group that is sometimes called today the élite.

In contrast to the Indian influence, the Chinese was more political and commercial, less religious and cultural. Chinese emperors generally considered the states of Southeast Asia vassals who, since the second century B.C., on occasion sent missions with tribute to the capital of the Middle Kingdom. As Western concepts of sovereignty were not involved, the vassals in Southeast Asia were independent, free to war among themselves without directly involving the Chinese emperor. The list of vassals who recognized the Son of Heaven varied from time to time depending upon the expansionist policies of the Chinese rulers, the vicissitudes of power politics in Southeast Asia, and the force of tradition in the various royal courts.

The interests of the Chinese in the region were closely tied to the expansion of trade through or around the area to India, the Middle East, and Europe. Most of the Chinese, settling in Southeast Asia during these centuries, were merchants who took little part in politics. Only in Tonkin when Chinese rule was direct over a long period of time did the people become Sinicized. Here the impact on the language, religion, and culture of the Annamites was pronounced. Moreover, as the Annamites pushed south into Annam and then into Cochin China, the Chinese emperors extended their influence.

By the end of the fourteenth century A.D. Islam had become a significant cultural factor in Southeast Asia. Although the Arabs and Persians, trading along the coasts of Malaya and the East Indies, had carried the new religion with them, widespread conversion to Islam in the area did not occur until Indian merchants, especially those from Gujerat, became active in the propagation of the faith. It was much easier for Indians than for Arabs and Persians to convert the people, for the former, as indicated, had a long record of experience in cultural expansion. Malacca, strategically located in southwest Malaya across from Sumatra along the Strait of Malacca, became by 1500 not only the center of trade in Southeast Asia but also a great and important spearhead in the expansion of Islam.

The political history of Malacca was drastically altered in 1511 when the Portuguese captured the great entrepôt. The demand for spices in Europe and their availability in the East Indies had increased the interests of the Europeans in Southeast Asia. With the rise to power of the Ottoman Turks, who captured Constantinople in 1453, the search for a sea route to the Spice Islands or Moluccas became increasingly more urgent. The Vasco da Gama age in Asian history—if the analysis of the Indian diplomat and writer, K. M. Panikkar, is followed—began in May, 1498, with the arrival of the Portuguese squadron at Calicut in western India.

After establishing command of the Indian Ocean in the naval battle at Diu in 1508 and thereby securing the sea route from the Cape of Good Hope, the Portuguese under Viceroy Affonso d'Albuquerque secured Malacca as their main base in Southeast Asia. Since the Portuguese were motivated in Asia by considerations of commercial expansion and not of territorial aggrandizement, the pattern of conquest centered around the development of a few fortified bases facing the sea, strategically located to assist in the preservation of Portuguese sea power and to command key markets and trade routes. As a result, the Portuguese were not primarily interested in the hinterland behind their bases, and the masses of Asians for their part were not deeply influenced by the newest invaders in Southeast Asia. Until the nineteenth century when new economic conditions would favor extensive territorial expansion, successive European invaders in most cases would tend to follow in varying degrees of emphasis the Portuguese pattern.

The Spice Islands in the East Indies were a goal not only for the Portuguese but also for the Spanish. In fact, European rivalries were transferred to Southeast Asia which in turn provided fuel for the controversies. Seeking a route to the East Indies not monopolized by Portugal, the Spanish under Ferdinand Magellan sailed westward across the Atlantic, through the straits near the tip of South America, then across the Pacific where they discovered the Philippines in 1521. On the shores of Mactan off Cebu in the central Philippines Magellan lost his life through intervention in a local conflict. The Spanish expedition, however, sailed on to the Moluccas, then across the Indian Ocean, around the Cape of Good Hope and back to Spain. Apart from the first circumnavigation of the globe, the voyage opened the way for the rivalry between Spain and Portugal in the Moluccas as well as for Spanish settlement in the Philippines.

As for the Asians, the Filipinos consider Lapu-Lapu, the local chieftain whose followers killed Magellan, a national hero, while some Indonesians have insisted, despite the denial of the Filipinos, that Magellan died in Indonesia.

The Treaty of Saragossa in 1529 between Spain and Portugal provided for the sale of the former's interests in the Moluccas to the latter. Although the Spanish in 1545 made another effort to defeat the Portuguese in the islands, they later directed their efforts to the Philippines where, in 1565, they established a permanent settlement in Cebu. Expanding northward, the Spanish made Manila six years later the headquarters of their regime in Luzon and the Philippines. As in the case of the Portuguese, the Spanish were interested in the spread of Christianity and in the restriction of Islam. Since Islam was more firmly entrenched in the Indies and was only expanding into the southern Philippines, the Spanish had a considerable advantage in converting the Filipinos to Roman Catholicism. In this Asian country the European impact in terms of religion and administration came to be strong.

Meanwhile the Dutch, by securing a foothold in Java and getting control of the Sunda Strait between Sumatra and Java in 1602, were in a position to threaten the Portuguese in Southeast Asia both in the Moluccas and Malacca. At the same time the Dutch were forced to cope with the English, who sought to establish and maintain a commercial empire in the Indies. European politics involving the Spanish, Portuguese, Dutch, and English was clearly reflected in the rivalry of the Dutch and English East India companies in Southeast Asia. The Dutch emerged as victors in the Spice Islands after establishing footholds at the expense of the Portuguese and successfully challenging the English. In 1623 the execution by the Dutch of ten Englishmen at Amboyna quickened the end of English power in the Indies and encouraged the concentration of commercial efforts in India. In 1641 Malacca, long the citadel of Portuguese power, fell to the Dutch, who now controlled the Strait of Malacca. From their headquarters at Batavia, renamed from the old Jacarta, the Dutch came to exercise effective rule over Java and to control a large island empire that would last for some three centuries.

The English, however, had not given up hopes of commercial expansion in Southeast Asia. Although they had relinquished their factory at Bantam in northwestern Java in 1682 they established one at Bencoolen in southwestern Sumatra three years later. A number of efforts to establish other factories in insular Southeast Asia failed, but the stimulus of the China trade coupled with the influence of Francis Light helped to induce the English Company in 1786 to found a settlement at Penang, a strategic island on the Strait of Malacca off northwest Malaya. The events of the Anglo-Dutch war between 1780 and 1784 had already led to the destruction of the Dutch trade monopoly in the Indies. The long contest between the French and the English from 1793 to 1815, furthermore, enabled the latter to take over Malacca in 1795 and to occupy Java from 1811 to 1816. Three years later Stamford Raffles, apprehensive about the future of the English position in Southeast Asia, established a settlement at Singapore, destined to become the center of British influence in the area. It was not until 1824, however, that the British and the Dutch in a treaty defined the sphere of influence of the former in the Malay peninsula and of the latter in the Indies. The Dutch accepted the British claim to Singapore and exchanged Malacca for Bencoolen. As a result the interests of the English East India Company in Malaya were now concentrated in Singapore, Malacca, and Penang, all strategic positions on the trade route to China.

In peninsular Southeast Asia north of the Kra Isthmus Europeans whether as traders or adventurers were not able up to the nineteenth century to establish the footholds that they did in the island areas. Siam and Burma were left to fight each other in the west or Annam and Siam in the east. The Europeans were rivals in the area but their governments or trading companies were not prepared to conquer the Asian kingdoms. In so far as possible responsible Europeans wanted to divorce trade from politics although some of the Asian rulers were eager to receive Western aid against their neighbors. As the years of the nineteenth century passed Western colonial policy would greatly change in the area.

The basic economy of Southeast Asia is agricultural, centered around the peasant family in the myriads of villages. Since practically the entire area, divided by the equator, has a tropical climate, subject to the monsoons, many similarities are found in the human response. About nine-tenths of the people engaged in earning a living are farmers or fishermen. Approximately two-thirds of the area devoted to sedentary agriculture is occupied by subsistence farmers, cultivating for the most part their staple crop of rice. Commercial agriculture in terms of farming for cash on a large scale is a comparatively new aspect of the occupational pattern.

In the production of rice commercial agriculture has achieved a position of great importance. As a result of this type of farming, Burma, Thailand, and Indochina became the only rice pool in the world from which countries like China, India, and Japan purchased supplies. If both commercial and subsistence production are counted, 65 percent of the cultivated area in Burma has been devoted to rice, 95 percent in Thailand, and 85 percent in Indochina. Rice production was decreased in Southeast Asia during the Second World War, and recovery in some areas after the Japanese surrender was retarded because of civil strife. Thailand was most fortunate, having in 1939-1940 an estimated 8.8 million acres of rice producing 2.86 million metric tons of clean rice and ten years later 12.4 million acres with 3.7 million metric tons. In contrast, Burma, which suffered both from devastation during the Second World War and civil turmoil after it, had in 1939-1940 an estimated 12.8 million acres of rice producing 4.73 million metric tons and ten years later 9.0 million acres with 2.9 million metric tons. By 1950-1951 about three-fourths of the rice areas in Lower Burma had been restored to production. In Indochina 14.7 million acres of rice produced 4.00 million metric tons in 1939-1940 and ten years later the figures were 12.0 and 3.6 respectively. In Southeast Asia as a whole 51 million acres in 1952 produced some 19 million tons of clean rice.

It is obvious that the rice bowl of peninsular Southeast Asia, apart from Malaya, is a factor of considerable importance in international relations. The addition of this area to the economy of neighboring states like China or India would assist in the solution of a number of problems facing the governments in Peking and New Delhi. In terms of export figures, Burma sent abroad 2.50 million metric tons of clean rice in 1940 and 1.29 in 1951, Thailand 2.00 and 1.55 in the same years, and Indochina 1.40 and .31. At the same time, however, the other areas in Southeast Asia must be considered. In 1940 the Netherlands East Indies imported .06 million metric tons of clean rice, Malaya .70, and the Philippines .11. Efforts to be self-sufficient in rice production are being made in the deficit areas.

Among the other commercial crops rubber is the most important, although tea, coffee, sugar, palm oil, coconut, and cinchona should be mentioned. Before the Second World War 90 percent of the world's rubber came from Southeast Asia, and the figure has not declined. Some 6 million acres are devoted to rubber, Malaya and Indonesia being the most important producers. Indonesia, for instance, in 1954 produced around 750,000 tons. The markets for rubber exist outside Southeast Asia, especially in the United States, and the price of the product on the world market has important effects on the areas specializing in its production. The development of synthetic rubber, greatly accelerated during the Second World War, raises a serious question about the ultimate future of rubber in Southeast Asia.

In the world economy tin is the most important mineral produced in the region. Before the last war over 60 percent of the world's supply came from Malaya, the Netherlands East Indies, and Thailand. Smelting tin at Penang and Singapore is in itself an important industry. Although mining tin has made a relatively slow recovery, almost 100,000 tons were produced in 1950. As in the case of rubber the markets are largely in the West, and their stability is problematical.

Petroleum is the basis of the other mining industry of considerable importance, 3.6 percent of the world's production in 1938 coming from the region. This figure was relatively small but it represented practically the only petroleum produced in the monsoon area. Before the last World War the most important single producer was the Netherlands East Indies followed by British Borneo and Burma in about equal position. By 1951 the output of petroleum was 12 million tons, Indonesia and British Borneo being the important producers. In 1955 the former alone produced 11.8 million tons and Brunei 5.3.

Iron ore is mined to some extent in Malaya and the Philippines, but in 1938 only 1.3 percent of the world's total came from the former and .6 percent from the latter. In 1954 Malaya produced 1.23 million tons and the Philippines 1.42, a large amount being exported to Japan. The output of bauxite in 1938 was 7 percent of the world's total in the Netherlands East Indies and 1.5 percent in Malaya. In 1954 Indonesia produced 173,000 long tons and in 1955 Malaya over 200,000. The proportion of the world's production of tungsten in Southeast Asia in 1938 was 22.1 percent with Burma supplying 17 percent, Malaya 3 percent, and Indochina and Thailand the remainder. Since the war Burma's production of tungsten has dropped; in 1954 she produced 443 tons of concentrates. Apart from Tonkin, Southeast Asia suffers from a lack of good coal, an important aspect in an analysis of power resources. At the same time the possibilities of using water power are great but little realization of the potential has yet occurred.

Although certain minerals are very significant in export, their impact so far on the life of the people as a whole is very limited. Only a relatively small number of individuals are employed in the relevant industries, and the mining and processing are done in localized areas. World statistics in terms of mineral exports can easily be misleading if applied to the typical Malayan kampong or the Philippine barrio.

The transportation network of Southeast Asia will have to be further developed to meet the needs of the region. In 1939 the total railway mileage in the area was only 12,564. Burma and Thailand had around 2000 miles each, the Netherlands East Indies some 4500, all in Java and Sumatra, Malaya about 1000, Indochina some 1800, the Philippines about 800 and British Borneo around 100. Railway facilities in a number of countries, especially the Philippines, Burma, and Malaya, were seriously damaged during the Second World War, and after V-J Day civil turmoil interfered with transportation in Burma, Indochina, Malaya, Indonesia, and the Philippines. Navigable rivers like the Irrawaddy and Mekong have served as highways from and into the interior but here again political conditions since 1941 have often been adverse. The road pattern, it should be noted, is not extensive. Although air lines operate in the countries of Southeast Asia they are not an important factor in the economy. The transportation facilities are presently being repaired and expanded but progress is slow.

From the industrial viewpoint the region is underdeveloped. The village people have a number of domestic industries that meet family requirements calling in this respect for little if any money. Indeed, it should be stressed that the great majority of the inhabitants of Southeast Asia, though subject to pressure and change, is still basically living under a traditional village economy founded upon the subsistence principle. The mechanical industries that have developed are chiefly related to agriculture such as rice and sugar mills or have come as a result of European enterprise like modern transportation and mining. Only in Java before the last World War was there a promise of industrialization somewhat along the Japanese lines of mass production.

The achievement since V-J Day of independence in most of the region is resulting in the encouragement of local industries. The desire to manufacture at home instead of importing from abroad is strong. In the past a number of industrial processes outside the area have been based upon agricultural products exported from the region. At the present time the new governments give many indications of wanting to do the processing at home. Since the traditional markets for such goods are in Europe and the United States, while Southeast Asia is not able at present to absorb a great amount, the transfer of the processing from abroad to at home raises questions not only of local production but also of maintaining markets. At the same time a substantial amount of the manufactured goods needed in Southeast Asia will continue to be produced in the outside world. For many years the states will need foreign capital and advice to establish and expand their industries. Assistance from abroad under such auspices as the United Nations, the Colombo Plan, and the United States has been given to various projects associated with the economy of the countries. The road to industrialization in Southeast Asia is paved with difficulties but realistic analysis and careful adaptation will facilitate the process.

In the international politics of the region the most influential neighbors are the People's Republic of China and India followed by Japan and Australia in much weaker positions. Beyond these countries Great Britain, France, the United States, and the Netherlands merit particular mention. The influence of the Soviet Union is a factor of importance though possibly expressed more indirectly than directly at the present time. Pakistan's impact is growing but is still limited. In the case of all outside powers the degree of influence is not the same in every country of Southeast Asia and is subject to changes from time to time.

Within ten years of the surrender of Japan, China under a Communist government became the state with the greatest impact on the area as a whole. Through her large minorities in Southeast Asia, her boundary with Vietnam, Laos, and Burma as well as proximity to Thailand and her active role in support of the Democratic Republic of Vietnam, Communist China exerts her pressure. Allied with the Soviet Union, the People's Republic of Mao Tse-tung appears to have assumed the leadership of the Communist revolution in the region.

The reaction among the states of Southeast Asia to the Peking government is varied. In some cases the official position differs from the personal inclination of the leaders; in other instances personal and official viewpoints coincide. Basically involved is an evaluation of the capabilities and potentialities of the Chinese Communists as well as of their short- and long-range intentions in Asia and the world. This evaluation is necessarily made against a background of global rivalry between the United States and the Soviet Union involving Communist and Nationalist China. Recognition of the regime of Mao Tse-tung or of Chiang Kai-shek is a question that has divided the states of Southeast Asia.

India's impact on the area is much less than that of Communist China. Considerations of importance are the Indian minorities in Burma and Malaya and the common boundary between the Union of Burma and the Republic of India. Especially important is the personal stature of Prime Minister Jawaharlal Nehru involving his close ties with U Nu of Burma, Sukarno of Indonesia, and Norodom Sihanouk of Cambodia. The international position of Nehru has been further strengthened by India's chairmanship of the important armistice supervisory commissions set up for Vietnam, Cambodia, and Laos at the Geneva Conference on Indochina. In certain parts of Southeast Asia, however, the influence of Nehru is very limited.

The heritage of the Pacific War is still found in anti-Japanese feeling in some of the states of the region, in the long delay in liquidating the reparations problem, and in the apprehension that Japanese militarism is not dead. Nevertheless, some of the present leaders in Southeast Asia held power under the Japanese and met for the first time their Asian colleagues in conferences in Tokyo. Present Japanese diplomacy in the area is economic, for the countries of the region could make a definite contribution in helping the Nipponese solve their economic difficulties. At the same time the Japanese are the only Asians who have considerable technological skill for export. The concept of Japan as the workshop of Asia is generally opposed by the national leaders of the new states.

Although Australia is not an Asian country, she is making every effort to exert her influence in Southeast Asia. The security of the Australians, it is realized, is closely related to developments in the "Near North." The great interest of the Commonwealth government at Canberra in the Colombo Plan is an indication of concern for the area. The so-called "White Australia" policy, however, is a detriment to close ties with the peoples of the "Near North." The West New Guinea question has specifically impaired friendship between Indonesia and Australia. Although the overall impact of Australia in the region is limited, the future can well bring changes.

Among the Western powers who make up the Atlantic community of nations Great Britain and the United States are the most important in Southeast Asia. Despite her colonial empire still remaining in a part of the area, Great Britain has managed to exert far more influence among the new states of South and Southeast Asia than might be expected. This fact is all the more remarkable in the light of the decline of her power position in Asia after each of the world wars of the twentieth century. Great Britain's stature is the result of many factors: her timely recognition of Asian nationalism leading to the independence of India, Pakistan, Ceylon, Burma, and the Federation of Malaya with the later establishment of the State of Singapore, her stress on economic uplift adapted to the needs and conditions of the people, her careful attention to the viewpoints of Asian leaders like Nehru and U Nu and her contacts on a personal basis with the Asians through people like Malcolm MacDonald, former Commissioner-General in South-East Asia. British diplomacy in the region was well reflected in the role of Anthony Eden, Secretary of State for Foreign Affairs, at the Geneva Conference on Indochina. At the same time it is clear that the United Kingdom suffered a loss of prestige through military intervention in the Suez crisis late in 1956.

The United States as the most powerful of the Western countries has indicated real concern over developments in Southeast Asia twice in the present century. The first occasion was in the months prior to the Japanese attack at Pearl Harbor in 1941, when the Nipponese were expanding their foothold in the region, particularly in French Indochina. The second came after the Chinese Communist victory in 1949 when the full implications of the effect of a militant China on Southeast Asia, especially Indochina, were realized. American diplomacy in the area has been reflected in military, economic, informational, and cultural programs. Yet only in the Philippines are American ties deeply rooted. To some Asians, unfortunately, the United States stands for imperialism and militarism; to them she is also the personification of a twentieth-century Metternich. The termination of American influence in Southeast Asia, however, would be a major factor in the possible orientation of the area toward the Communist bloc of nations.

The French and Dutch impact in the region has markedly declined as a result of developments since V-J Day in Indochina and Indonesia. The partition of Vietnam in the summer of 1954 at the seventeenth parallel between the Democratic Republic of Vietnam under Ho Chi Minh to the north and the State of Vietnam under Bao Dai to the south represented a military and diplomatic defeat for France. The great weakening of the French "presence" in Asia has not been restricted to Indochina; it has also occurred in China as well as India. The concept of the French Union did not appeal as a general rule to the Asians. In the case of the Netherlands, the independence of Indonesia and the subsequent dissolution of the Netherlands-Indonesian Union have reduced the Dutch, apart from Netherlands New Guinea, Surinam, and certain of the West Indies, to a purely European status.

The impact of the Soviet Union in Southeast Asia has been greatly affected by the establishment of the People's Republic of China in 1949 and by the death of Stalin in 1953. Nevertheless, the teachings of Marx and the philosophy of Lenin, despite the outcome of de-Stalinization, remain important in the outlook of the Soviet Union under the successors of the dead Marshal. Communist objectives in Asia are directed toward the industry of Japan, the manpower of China, and the food and raw materials of Southeast Asia. As long as the Soviet Union and the People's Republic of China coöperate in world affairs, the former will have a strong influence in the Communist activities of the region but the weakening of the ties between the Peking and Moscow governments would probably work to Soviet disadvantage. After all, the Soviet Union is geographically far removed from Southeast Asia, the dominant people are Caucasians, and no Russian minorities exist in the region to be exploited. Communism as an ideology could be better perpetrated in the area by fellow Asians. At the same time the Soviet Union, as indicated by the visit and promises of Nikita S. Khrushchev and Nikolai A. Bulganin to Burma, cannot be expected to let Communist China have a completely free hand in Southeast Asia.

Within the region the independent countries themselves—the Philippines, Indonesia, the Federation of Malaya, Burma, Thailand, Cambodia, Laos and the two Vietnams—are in no current position to offer adequate defense against a powerful aggressor. Each is faced with complex political and economic problems, in all cases but one aggravated by newly won independence. Many have been forced to cope with postwar insurrections and none has been able to escape the effects of the cold war waged on a global scale. Although most of the states are members of the United Nations, the search for national security does not end in New York. At the same time the governments themselves give no indication of being willing to sanction an inclusive regional security organization, thereby strengthening individual and collective self-defense.

2. *Prelude to Independence*

The independence movement in Southeast Asia is the result of many complex forces found in the matrix of the colonial period. It was the Western powers who brought to the region the concept of nationalism, which in most cases precipitated their own withdrawal. Nevertheless, they left behind them a Westernized élite, probably less than 10 percent, which took over the reins of government. At the same time the Western powers were responsible to a large extent for the consolidation of the geographic areas found in the present pattern of states in Southeast Asia. Moreover, the concepts of national sovereignty and of the equality of states under international law in the West were opposed to the time-honored practice of vassalage in Southeast Asia, sometimes extending not to one but to a number of neighbors. The transfer of the formation of foreign policy from Western to local capitals coupled with the necessity of making numerous decisions, especially at meetings of international organizations, has brought heavy responsibility to the leaders of Southeast Asia in the international field.

The impact of the Western powers in the region was greatest during the 70-year period that began roughly around 1870. As a result of the Industrial Revolution, of the use of faster methods of water transportation and of the opening of the Suez Canal in 1869, Southeast Asia became important as a production center of raw materials needed outside the region. Although the coastal areas were valuable in previous commerce, the interior of the countries now acquired great importance. The increase in trade between China and the European powers also added to the interest in Southeast Asia. The search for raw materials and markets for manufactured goods had widespread ramifications in the political, economic and social development of the region.

In the contest for interior areas, the rivalry of the European powers became pronounced. Great Britain and the Netherlands, despite their treaty of 1824, had to reach further agreements on the East Indies. Dutch expansion in Sumatra challenged British commercial interests in the Straits Settlements while the independence of Achin in northern Sumatra, as provided in the treaty of 1824, complicated the situation. In Borneo the British occupation of the island of Labuan in 1846 and further expansion on the mainland in Sarawak, North Borneo, and Brunei conflicted with Dutch interests. In 1871 the British agreed to give the Dutch freedom of action in Achin and 20 years later the British-Dutch boundary in Borneo was defined. In New Guinea Great Britain established a protectorate over the southeastern part in 1884 and Germany over the northeastern section, but the Netherlands, subject to a small boundary modification in 1895, retained possession of the western part of the island beginning at 141° E longitude. As for Timor, a Portuguese-Dutch treaty signed in 1859 provided for the division of the island between the two colonial powers, and an agreement in 1904, though not ratified until four years later, made arrangements for the boundary. Thus the Dutch in extending rule over the East Indies established the territorial limits of their Asian empire.

The American acquisition of the Philippine Islands in 1899 under the terms of the treaty of peace ending the Spanish-American War did not involve basic territorial changes. The Spanish had already established the geographical extent of the Philippines. However, the peace treaty between the United States and Spain was not accurately drafted relative to the boundaries of the archipelago. As a result, negotiations between the governments of the two states in 1900 led to the inclusion of the Cagayan Sulu and Sibutu islands in the south and the Bashi group and others in the north, the United States paying Spain $100,000. The Spanish had previously protested British expansion into northern Borneo on the grounds that the area was tributary to the Sultan of Sulu. In 1930 a convention signed by the United States and Great Britain delimited the boundary between the Philippines and British North Borneo.

On the mainland of Southeast Asia the rivalry was focused on France and Great Britain, the former in Indochina and the latter in Burma and Malaya with both colonial powers exerting pressure on Thailand. The first Anglo-Burmese War resulted in 1826 in the British acquisition of the coastal provinces of Tenasserim and Arakan. The military activities of the English East India Company in Burma had been motivated not by the desire of territorial aggrandizement but by the need to protect the Indian frontiers against the Burmese in Arakan and Assam. In the same year the Company consolidated under one administration the Straits Settlements of Penang, Malacca, and Singapore and limited the freedom of action of Thailand in the Malay States of Perak and Selangor but made no effort to push inland and establish an administration over Malaya. In a second Anglo-Burmese War the British seized the coastal province of Pegu in 1852, thus depriving the Asian kingdom of an outlet on the Bay of Bengal. Rangoon became the center of British Burma and of Western penetration.

Meanwhile the French were developing footholds in the eastern part of the Indo-Pacific peninsula. Missionary interest in Indochina went back to the 1600's but permanent establishments were not made until the 1860's when the French hoped to tap the China trade through the Mekong and Red River valleys. National pride in French culture was closely associated with the expansion of France in Indochina. In 1862 France acquired three eastern provinces in Cochin China, and five years later she expanded her rule to the three western ones. In 1863 France established a protectorate over Cambodia. In 1883 she declared a protectorate over Annam and Tonkin, forcing China after a short war from 1883 to 1885 to relinquish her claim to suzerainty.

Great Britain was concerned over the expansion of the French in Indochina, especially since the Burmese government under King Thibaw in Mandalay was intriguing with them. After a series of incidents the British invaded Upper Burma in 1885, annexed the area, and governed Lower and Upper Burma as a province of India until 1937. China, who claimed suzerainty over Burma, accepted the British position in 1886.

In contrast to her western neighbor, Thailand was able to maintain her sovereignty partly through balancing France and Britain, who in 1896 became convinced of the need to neutralize the key area of the Asian kingdom as a buffer. Nevertheless, Thailand lost territory to both the British and the French. After reducing Perak, Selangor, Negri Sembilan, and Pahang in Malaya to the status of Protected States between 1874 and 1888, the British caused Thailand in 1909 to relinquish her claims to Kelantan, Trengganu, Kedah, and Perlis, adding them to the list of Protected States. In 1893 the French acquired from Thailand her territory on the east bank of the Mekong, bisecting the Kingdom of Luang Prabang, and made Laos a protectorate of the Third Republic. Three years later the upper Mekong Valley was established as the boundary between the British in Burma and the French in Indochina. In 1904 France took almost 8000 square miles of territory from Thailand including the rest of Luang Prabang and in 1907 another 12,000 square miles including Battambang.

The pattern of colonial government in Southeast Asia varied with the policies of the mother country. Each metropolitan power naturally placed the highest value on its own type of government and sought to transplant certain of its political institutions to the soil of its Asian colony. Complete independence was not usually the ultimate political goal, but if it became necessary, the mother country wanted its progeny to reflect the government brought from abroad. On the other hand, the indigenous leaders of the nationalist movement in Southeast Asia, though educated to a large extent in Western political theory abroad or at home, tended to interpret the political contributions of the colonial powers in the light of the Asian background. Although the impact of the West is clearly shown in many of the new states in the type of government established, the leaders are borrowing the political institutions of the West but adapting them according to their own standards of value.

In their attitudes on education and preparation for self-government the colonial powers were quite divergent, resulting in an uneven pattern of development when independence finally came to most of Southeast Asia. The United States definitely established an educational program directed at the attainment of independence for the Philippines. The setting of an actual date for the termination of American sovereignty in the archipelago was a milestone in the political development of Southeast Asia. France was concerned with the cultural assimilation of the people of Indochina believing that the creation of Frenchified Asians was an objective greatly to be sought. The concept of the cultural union of France and her possessions overseas did not provide for the development of genuine independence in Indochina. Great Britain realized that the result of her educational program in Burma and Malaya would be independence for the tropical dependencies but she hoped that self-government could be gradually won within the framework of the British Commonwealth of Nations. The Netherlands for her part sought to educate an Indonesian élite, and looked in the long run toward the establishment of a Dutch-Indonesian partnership.

As might be expected, the administrative structure of the colonial dependencies of Southeast Asia at the outbreak of the Second

World War in 1939 had a variegated appearance. British Malaya was made up of the Straits Settlements, Federated Malay States, and Unfederated Malay States, indicating different stages of territorial expansion without corresponding administrative reorganization. The Straits Settlements, consisting of Singapore, Penang with Province Wellesley, and Malacca, along with Labuan, Christmas Island, and the Cocos Islands, was a crown colony. The four Malay States of Perak, Selangor, Negri Sembilan, and Pahang, though each was a Protected State, were organized into a federation in 1896, called the Federated Malay States. In contrast, the Unfederated Malay States, Johore, Kedah, Perlis, Kelantan, and Trengganu, were simply Protected States without benefit of federal administration. Each of the nine Malay States had its own sultan or ruler who was advised by a British resident.

In British Borneo the administrative pattern was also complex. North Borneo was a protectorate administered by the British North Borneo Company; the State of Brunei under its sultan was subject to British protection; Sarawak ruled by the Brooke family was a protectorate of Great Britain; the island of Labuan, as already mentioned, was a unit of the Straits Settlements. At the highest level in Asia the governor of the Straits Settlements was also high commissioner for all the Malay States and Brunei as well as British agent for Sarawak and North Borneo.

In Burma the British pattern of administration was less complicated though involved. Under the Burma Act of 1935, effective in 1937, the distinction between Burma proper or ministerial Burma and the Frontier or Scheduled Areas was marked. In the case of the former, the territory was subject to the decisions of a British governor, a council of ministers, and a bicameral legislature. The Hill Peoples living in the Frontier Areas were under the control of the governor but not of the legislature in Rangoon. They constituted about 16 percent of the population of Burma and occupied some 40 percent of the total area of the country. Geographically the Frontier Areas comprised a large horseshoe around the central river valleys of Burma proper, while historically, with the exception of certain Shan States, the Burmans had not generally occupied the territory. British control over the highlands had come late in the nineteenth century, and even in 1939 some 7000 square miles of land were classified as unadministered.

Among the Hill Peoples of Burma the Shans, Karens, Kachins, and Chins merited the special attention of the British administrators.

Six Northern and 28 Southern Shan States were federated in 1922 under the presidency of a British commissioner. Since most of the Shan chiefs were tributary subjects of previous Burmese kings, Great Britain believed she had succeeded to the suzerain rights of the former rulers after Burma was annexed. The British commissioner for the Federated Shan States also administered through an assistant political officer the three Karenni States where lived about one-fourth of the Karens of Burma. Although these Feudatory States had paid tribute to the kings of Burma, this particular relationship was even more tenuous than that of the Shans to the same rulers. The inhabitants of the Kachin Hills and of the Chin Hills were the least organized of the people in the Frontier Areas.

In Indochina the French administered an empire based on their colony of Cochin China and their four protectorates of Cambodia, Annam, Tonkin, and Laos including the Kingdom of Luang Prabang. Under this arrangement local monarchies were maintained in Cambodia, Annam, and Luang Prabang. Although Tonkin was theoretically a protectorate, the area was in practice subject to direct rule very similar to that in Cochin China. Haiphong and Hanoi in Tonkin and Tourane in Annam were French enclaves with special statutes, and the French military administered certain frontier areas. In 1887 France established the federation of Indochina, which came to include Laos after its acquisition in 1893 and Kwangchowwan in southern China. The highest French official in Indochina was a governor general but each of the protectorates had a resident superior and Cochin China a governor. The French established a government council for the entire area as well as a council for economic and financial affairs. In effect French administration in the country was the common denominator, the withdrawal of which would reduce Indochina from a federation to a geographical expression in terms of political unity.

The Dutch in the Netherlands East Indies likewise maintained the legal distinction of direct and indirect rule. The total number of native states was 282 but only about 7 percent of the area of Java, chiefly Surakarta and Jogjakarta, had native rulers. Java in fact was the most intensively administered area in Southeast Asia under a Western colonial power. In practice the Netherlands East Indies was divided into Java and Madura on the one hand, and the Outer Territories or Islands, the rest of the possession, on the other. Exclusive of the native states, Java was split into three provinces, West, Central, and East, and in 1938 the Outer Territories were organized under three governments, Sumatra, Borneo, and the remainder called the "Great East," which included Netherlands New Guinea. In the native states the local rulers theoretically governed their people but actually the Dutch ruled behind the façade.

A governor general represented the highest executive and administrative authority in the Netherlands East Indies. In a preliminary step toward self-government a *Volksraad* or representative council came into being in 1918 consisting of Indonesians, Europeans, and resident foreign Asians. Under the Netherlands Indies constitution of 1925 the legislative powers of the *Volksraad* were strengthened. In their local government the Dutch made wide use of native "regents" in Java, employing them to a great extent in day-to-day administration. Despite the constitutional advances, the Netherlands East Indies was far removed from self-government at the outbreak of the Second World War.

In colonial Southeast Asia the Philippines presented a contrast in many respects to other areas. The Spanish administration in the archipelago, highly centralized and autocratic, followed the principle of direct rather than indirect rule. The governor general in Manila was virtually absolute in power although he was somewhat restricted by the supreme court or *audiencia* and the official enquiry or *residencia*, traditionally held at the end of his term of office. The Philippines was divided into provinces under *alcaldes mayores* who for decades held both executive and judicial powers. The provinces were subdivided for many years into *pueblos* under native *gobernadorcillos*. Along with the political administration, the Spanish impact was strengthened by the ecclesiastical hierarchy of the Roman Catholic Church reaching from Manila to the parishes and by the organization of the economy on the basis of the Spanish conception of feudal landownership. Taking advantage of a Filipino culture that had hardly been affected by Indian civilization in the past and that was not yet widely exposed to Islam, the Spanish, through their political, religious, and economic policies, Christianized and Europeanized the Filipinos to an extent not done by Western rulers in any other country of Southeast Asia.

In terms of administration the non-Christian peoples of the Philippines, especially the Moros, became a special problem for the Spanish. The latter never actually conquered the Filipino Moslems living in Mindanao and the Sulu Archipelago. Nor did the Spanish effectively penetrate into the wild mountains of northern Luzon or certain other remote areas where additional non-Christian people dwelt. The Moros and the pagan tribes were only subdued after the United States took over the Philippines. As a result, the difference in the cultural state between the Christian and non-Christian inhabitants of the Islands has been marked. It is not surprising that the hostility between the two created problems that have confronted all the governments that ruled the Philippines from Manila. To them, of course, the territorial integrity of the Islands was a common objective. Just as the American Congress was not prepared to approve the Bacon Bill of 1926 proposing the separation of Mindanao and Sulu from the rest of the archipelago and their retention by the United States, the Philippine governments in Manila have ardently sought to maintain the territorial integrity of the country.

Although the United States had to begin its political development of the Philippines from a Malay-Spanish base, the few years of American rule, 1898 to 1935, saw major changes. The concept of democracy and the goal of independence were obviously alien to Spain's system of government in her colonial empire. Despite the vicissitudes of domestic politics the Tydings-McDuffie Act of March 24, 1934, accepted by the Philippine Legislature on May 1, was a logical development of American policy. Under the procedure outlined by the measure, a Filipino constitutional convention drafted a constitution for the Islands which was certified by the President of the United States as conforming to the Tydings-McDuffie Act and subsequently approved by the Philippine electorate in a national plebiscite. The Commonwealth of the Philippines was established on November 15, 1935, for a period of ten years, July 4, 1946, being set as the actual date for the withdrawal of American sovereignty.

In 1939 when the Second World War broke out the Commonwealth was a going concern. The American governor general had been replaced by a high commissioner, and basic relations between the United States and the Philippines were regulated by an Ordinance Appended to the Constitution of the country. A Filipino president, unicameral national assembly, and supreme court functioned in Manila. In terms of administration the Islands, as of January 1, were divided into 49 provinces, 936 municipalities, 261 municipal districts and 9 chartered cities. Nine were classified as "special" provinces, having been organized in frontier territory or areas where chiefly non-Christians lived. Here the central government had greater control although the objective was to end as quickly as possible the special status. In 1936 the Commonwealth government created the office of Commissioner for Mindanao and Sulu in the Department of the Interior, abolishing the Bureau of Non-Christian Tribes. The Commonwealth leaders were eager to assimilate the cultural minorities within the nation.

The economic, social, and cultural consequences of Western colonialism in Southeast Asia cannot be removed by the assumption of the status of sovereign independence by the greater number of the countries of the area. Experience has shown that independence has many aspects, and the ending of formal ties is only one. The colonial heritage is still deeply rooted throughout most of the region.

In the development of commercial agriculture and mining, especially after 1870, the Europeans brought about important changes by making possible the employment of large numbers of Chinese and Indians. It is true that Chinese had entered Southeast Asia in varying numbers for many centuries, particularly during part of the Ming dynasty, and that they had been very active in opening up tin mines, especially in Malaya, in the first three-quarters of the 1800's, but the great numbers came with the rapid expansion of Western economic enterprise. Arriving chiefly from southern China and being entirely interested in economic gain, the Chinese immigrants, while sending remittances to their families back home, planned for the most part to return to China after they had made their living in Southeast Asia. Some of them, industriously taking advantage of the environment, gathered the necessary capital and became middlemen in the economy of the country where they resided. In certain activities such as rice milling and the retail trade, the Chinese rose to key positions. It is estimated that before the Second World War they owned 75 percent of the rice mills in the Philippines, some 80 percent in Indochina, and between 80 and 90 percent in Thailand.

With the general exception of mining, the Indian immigrants widely paralleled the Chinese in occupational activities. Although smaller in number and concentrated more in the British areas, the Indians ranged from the wealthy, moneylending Chettyars in Burma to the poverty-stricken Tamil coolies in Malaya. Like the Chinese, the Indians for the most part did not plan to reside permanently in Southeast Asia. As a consequence the Chinese and Indian immigrants in the region did not develop real ties to the country where they earned their living and did not assist in the social integration of the area. Moreover, the foreign Asians who did settle permanently in

Southeast Asia were usually divided from the indigenous people by religious and linguistic barriers.

The Chinese and Indian immigrants were an important factor in the plural society of Southeast Asia. Under the concept of this society, the indigenous people, the foreign Asians, and the Europeans generally made up separate economic, social, and ethnic segments of the population, failing to constitute an integrated and assimilated whole. As might be expected, the concept of plural society was not applicable in the same degree to all the countries of Southeast Asia. Moreover, plural societies had existed in different variations before the advent of the Western states. Nevertheless, it was the colonial powers who intensified to a degree never before experienced the pluralism of society in the area.

At the same time the Western governments pursued varying economic policies in the region, resulting too often in the creation of compartments closely tied to the mother country and not conducive to the economic integration of the area. In all cases, the development of a money economy, the introduction of Western technology and administrative processes, the construction of sea and land transportation and communication facilities as well as of other public works, the formulation of educational and public health programs, the introduction of Western legal systems, and the development of commercial agriculture and mining created a materialism that came to be both admired and scorned by many of the indigenous Southeast Asians. A Western investment of possibly $4,370,000,000 in the region before the Second World War assisted in the development of the area. Concomitants of the colonial era were a marked increase in the overall population after 1870, indigenous and European as well as resident foreign Asian, and the growth of dual foci in some of the countries, representing the commercial and traditional centers like Rangoon and Mandalay in Burma.

American economic policy in the Philippines led to the dependency of the Islands on markets in the United States for abacá, copra, and sugar. By placing the Philippines within the American tariff walls, the United States created a situation where political independence could be granted more easily than economic. The French sought to integrate the economy of Indochina into that of the Empire; handicraft industries suffered heavily but by no means were completely destroyed, and a substantial part of the rice was shipped to France. The tariff policy favored the industries of the French who almost monopolized investments. Burma was encouraged to produce rice and petroleum for India, using the income to buy British and Indian manufactured goods. Here commercial ties were intimately associated with political, for in many respects Burma came to be an economic colony of the Indian Empire of Britain. In Malaya the British placed no restrictions on foreign investments; the export of tin and rubber, especially to the United States, produced a triangular trade among Britain, the United States, and Malaya, and made the dependency the greatest dollar earner in the colonial empire. The Dutch put considerable stress on economic progress and scientific advancement. The Culture System of 1830 whereby the peasants were forced to cultivate export crops for the Dutch government on part of their land in place of the payment of taxes was abandoned in favor of a new policy of free enterprise. From the overall viewpoint the Netherlands East Indies was the most valuable colony that any power possessed in Southeast Asia and made a major contribution to the economy of the mother country. Thailand, although independent, also had an economy that was colonial, British interests being outstanding.

The economic consequences of Western penetration, especially after 1870, are seen in some of the effects on the village life of the area. Traditionally rooted in the social structure of the family and the village, the old order was challenged by the Western stress on individualism. The ownership of land by the peasant was threatened by the expanding economy, the payment of taxes in money, the growing power of the usurer, and the legal mantle of Western law. The Dutch in the East Indies took definite steps to prevent the alienation of land to foreigners and to confirm in land transactions native customary law. The British in Burma failed to prevent the rise of a big landless peasantry although in Malaya they followed for many years the policy of reserving rice growing to the Malays. In French Indochina a landless proletariat grew into significant proportions, chiefly in Cochin China, while in the Philippines the Americans inherited the Spanish structure of feudal landownership and tenancy remained widespread.

The indigenous inhabitants of Southeast Asia reaped the least from the material development occasioned by Western enterprise. For the most part they remained subsistence farmers and fishermen in their local villages. At the same time the economic activity of the Chinese and Indian immigrants under Western auspices created real tension with the indigenous people. Free competition worked to the advantage of the Europeans and the Asian immigrants threatening the conservative group institutions of the inhabitants considered natives. An expanding money economy without suitable credit facilities placed certain people at the mercy of the foreign money-lenders. If the peasant lost his land and became a seasonal worker away from his family and village, he was faced with the problem of adjusting to a new social world. In terms of law and order, Western expansion after 1870 brought more physical security to the peasant but at the same time his social security was lessened as his ties with family and village were weakened. Western enterprise created wealth in Southeast Asia but only a few of the indigenous inhabitants really shared in it.

In the cultural field Westernization involved the use of European languages and literature. The language of the given colonial power was used not only by the government and business leaders but also to a large extent by the small, indigenous, Westernized élite. Even Asian literature in many cases became patterned on that of the West. Technical skills, developed in Europe and America, were acquired through the educational process by a few of the indigenous inhabitants of Southeast Asia. Moral standards as interpreted by the West were brought by the Christian missionaries. The rise of nationalism and the winning of independence have occasioned a return to emphasis on Asian languages and literature. At the same time the leaders of the countries are eager to take advantage of the opportunities opened through Western technical training.

The Japanese conquest of Southeast Asia, placing for the first time in history all the region under the control of one imperial power, was not of sufficient duration to integrate the area into a compact whole. And even if the New Order in Greater East Asia with its Coprosperity Sphere had lasted for a century, it is probable that the Japanese would have been faced with increasingly serious political problems. As it was, the Japanese interlude in retrospect was a catalysis of the first magnitude in promoting nationalism in Southeast Asia. Not only was the imperial structure of the Western states easily destroyed by an Asian power but also the prestige associated with the white Western official almost suffered an eclipse at the hands of the Japanese. By the time Japan surrendered it was clear that the political *status quo ante bellum* could not be restored. The important question which was then raised was whether or not the colonial powers would be able to adjust to the new situation in their short- and long-range planning.

Japanese military strategy in effecting the conquest of Southeast Asia placed considerable emphasis on Indochina. By acquiring a foothold in the northern part of the area in the summer of 1940 and the southern part in July, 1941, the Japanese were in a position to put pressure on both peninsular and insular Southeast Asia. Thailand especially was subjected to Nipponese influence, being brought to a final position where a practically bloodless occupation could be made at the outbreak of the Pacific War. From bases in southern Indochina and Thailand, the Japanese believed Malaya could be successfully invaded, and the great naval bastion of Singapore taken. Burma also could be attacked from southern Thailand, and the conquest of the country effected by moving from the south to the north. Indochina did not play a direct part in the strategy of the Japanese for the conquest of the Philippines, Taiwan being the important staging area here. At the same time the Nipponese could not ignore the basic relationship between Indochina and the Philippines, for each facing the other across the South China Sea presents a flank to any power seeking to push south in this area. The economic goal of Japanese strategy in the Nan Yo was the conquest of the Netherlands East Indies with its vast petroleum resources, badly needed by the Nipponese navy. The fall of Malaya and the Philippines, it was clear, would facilitate the Japanese seizure of the Indies, the western as well as the eastern parts of the archipelago. By the virtual occupation of Indochina before the outbreak of the Pacific War, the Nipponese had destroyed what has been called the strategic entity of Southeast Asia.

Within a few months of their attack on Pearl Harbor, December 7, 1941, the Japanese had virtually completed the conquest of the Nan Yo. By a surprising series of land-sea-air operations they had accomplished with the use of no more than 400,000 troops their military objectives in Southeast Asia. Facilities in Thailand were acquired December 8 after very brief resistance and through an agreement with the Thai government; Manila fell January 2, 1942, although Corregidor held out until May 6; Singapore was in Japanese hands February 15 following only by a few weeks the fall of Hong Kong on December 25; Surabaya in the Netherlands East Indies and Rangoon in Burma were occupied by the Nipponese in March, almost at the same time. Within a brief period the Japanese had reached the boundaries of India in the northwest and Australia in the southeast.

Although the subject of considerable controversy in Tokyo, a

Greater East Asia Ministry was set up by Imperial Ordinance in November, 1942. It consisted of a general and three regional bureaus, one each for the Nan Yo, China, and Manchuria. Thailand and Indochina in the New Order had a special status: the former was an ally and the latter a political anomaly where the Japanese supported the façade of the French colonial regime. The rest of Southeast Asia was administratively divided into the Philippines, Burma, Malaya and Sumatra, Java and Madura, and Borneo with the Celebes and other Indonesian islands east of a line from the Macassar Strait to Bali. Singapore, whose name was changed to Shonan or Light of the South, became the strategic headquarters of the Nan Yo; Borneo, the Celebes, and the area just defined remained under a naval command; the other four administrative provinces were placed under the particular military officer who conquered the area.

The pressure of events caused the Japanese to alter the political structure in a number of the countries of Southeast Asia. Ostensibly in recognition of Asian nationalism, "independence" was given Burma on August 1, 1943, under a regime led by Ba Maw as Adipadi and the Philippines on October 14 under a government headed by José P. Laurel as President. The formula used was the establishment of a local government, a declaration of independence, the termination of the Japanese military administration, an alliance between Nippon and the newly independent state, and in the case of Burma an immediate and of the Philippines a much later declaration of war on the United States and Great Britain. The nationalist leaders in Burma and the Philippines, however, were generally not deceived by the nature of their "independence."

On March 9, 1945, the Japanese took over the administration of French Indochina, made Governor General Jean Decoux a prisoner, disarmed in so far as possible French forces, and restricted civilians. On March 11 Emperor Bao Dai proclaimed the independence of Annam, uniting Tonkin with it. The Japanese did not allow him to add the Vietnamese area of Cochin China until August 14. On March 13 King Norodom Sihanouk announced the independence of Cambodia, and the next month King Sisavang Vong of Luang Prabang took a similar step with respect to his kingdom in Laos. By overthrowing the façade of French rule and by allowing in the end the territorial unification of Vietnam, the Japanese created a situation in Indochina not at all conducive to the restoration of the French position.

In the Netherlands East Indies the Nipponese did not encourage the territorial unity of the area or promote an independence movement until late in the war. They were especially eager to maintain a privileged position in the country in the postwar period. As already indicated, Indonesia was divided into three separate occupations, the Japanese looking upon it in many respects as a geographical expression. The original linking of Sumatra and Malaya with headquarters at Singapore was not without logic, for the two have long been historically, strategically, and commercially related. Military events, unfavorable to Japan, influenced her in September, 1944, to make a public promise of eventual Indonesian independence. But even now the area to be included and the nature of independence were not defined. As the military situation further deteriorated, the Japanese Supreme Council for the Direction of the War decided on July 17, 1945, to grant independence to the entire Netherlands East Indies as quickly as possible, and to put in motion the necessary machinery leading to statehood. When the Indonesian nationalist leaders learned on August 15 of the Japanese surrender, they quickly completed their preparations and proclaimed the independence of the country on August 17. Technically the birth of the Republic of Indonesia was not an act of the Japanese, but they could probably have seized the nationalist leaders in Batavia and maintained control until the Allied forces arrived. As in the case in Indochina, the Japanese made a major contribution toward preventing the Dutch restoration of the *status quo ante bellum*.

In Malaya the policy of Japan was more consistent. The area was to become an integral unit of the Empire and no definite promise of ultimate statehood was made. In 1944 Sumatra was administratively separated from Malaya, being once more tied to Indonesia. Malaya herself had been divided into eight provinces with the former threefold division of the British terminated although the institution of the Malay Sultans was kept. A particularly chaotic situation existed in the country from the surrender of Japan to the arrival of British forces.

During the Greater East Asia War, as the Japanese called the Asian phase of the Second World War, efforts were made, especially after the establishment of the Greater East Asia Ministry, to utilize to the fullest the possibilities of cultural propaganda. Goodwill missions, exchanges of students, scientific and literary meetings, cultural societies, and the sending abroad of Japanese language instructors were used as vehicles. Japanese propaganda stressed the need to protect the Asiatics from the exploitation of Western imperialists and to create peace and prosperity in Greater East Asia. In the fall of 1943 a conference was convened by Japan in Tokyo with the allegedly independent countries of Greater East Asia—Thailand, the Philippines, Burma, China, and Manchukuo. Their Joint Declaration of November 5, calling for liberation from the yoke of Anglo-American domination, is not unlike the Communist theme less than a decade later.

In the economic field the Japanese Coprosperity Sphere was aimed at the creation of a self-sufficient Greater East Asia. Under the overall plan industrial power would be concentrated in Japan while the rest of the Empire would contribute raw materials and serve as a market for manufactured goods. A Bank for the Development of the Southern Areas was established with a capital of 100 million yen. A Five-Year Plan was adopted in 1942 although it was never given an opportunity to materialize. As the Japanese failed to maintain the necessary shipping in the vast Empire because of Allied attacks, economic decentralization came to be stressed in the Coprosperity Sphere. In their efforts to develop land transportation the Japanese managed to complete in October, 1943, the Thailand-Burma Railway but they gave up their attempt to unite the railroads of west and east Sumatra. Considerable hardship resulted in Japan's projects involving the redistribution of labor in Southeast Asia.

The people of the region were glad to see the end of the Japanese regime. Asia for the Asiatics had come to mean Asia for the Japanese. Numerous instances of Nipponese inhumanity such as the treatment of the fellow Asians and Western prisoners of war who built the Thailand-Burma Railway alienated public support. The destruction in some areas of Southeast Asia associated with the arrival and departure of the Nipponese forces added to the bitterness. Moreover, the economic dislocation produced to a large extent by the breakdown of trade channels first outside the region and then inside brought increasing unrest. The failure of Japan to capitalize on the nationalist movement in Southeast Asia became one of her great blunders. It would be some time in the postwar world before Nippon could win back the status she held in the region before the Second World War.

For most of Southeast Asia the road to independence after V-J Day was in many respects difficult. The heritage of the precolonial, then of the colonial, and finally of the Japanese periods precluded an easy transition to statehood. Yet the nationalists of the area considered independence a necessity and were not prepared to compromise.

In the Philippines the American promise of freedom was carried out although there were misgivings in both Washington and Manila as a consequence of the destruction produced during the Japanese interlude. When the Stars and Stripes were lowered at the Luneta on July 4, 1946, the day was to many Filipinos not only one of fulfillment but also one of sadness. A Philippine government in exile had functioned in the United States during the Japanese occupation headed first by Manuel Quezon, President of the Commonwealth, and after his death in August, 1944, by Sergio Osmeña, Vice-President under him. The American Congress in a joint resolution the previous June once more had promised independence to the Philippines and even authorized the President of the United States to advance the date, if he considered it desirable. President Osmeña returned to the Islands the following October, and the United States turned over civil administration to him in February, 1945. Actually the Commonwealth had started to exercise civil authority in areas earlier liberated from the Japanese, and even after February coöperation with the American military establishment was essential. As long as the Philippines remained a military problem, the Commonwealth had to take a subordinate position.

On April 23, 1946, a national election was held as a result of which Manuel Roxas and Elpidio Quirino, presidential and vice-presidential candidates of the Liberal Party, defeated President Sergio Osmeña and Eulogio Rodriguez of the *Nacionalista* Party. On May 28 Roxas was inaugurated last president of the Commonwealth and on July 4 first president of the Republic.

In Burma progress for a while was delayed toward the independence finally granted on January 4, 1948. In the first place, the British before the war had not advanced Burma along the path of independence to the extent that the United States had assisted the Philippines; and in the second place, the immediate postwar British policy in Burma, both political and economic, was not sufficiently progressive to meet the demands of the Burmese nationalists. As in the case of the Philippines, Burma had suffered severely from the ravages of war, but contrary to American policy in the former, the British wanted to insure economic recovery in the latter before granting eventual dominion status. It is possible that a more progressive policy would have resulted in the decision of a self-governing Burma to stay within the Commonwealth of Nations. As it was, the actual ending of the formal ties between Britain and Burma was done in an atmosphere that gave hope of coöperation in the future.

The complicated steps that led to independence reflected the vicissitudes of British and Burmese politics. In October, 1945, British military government was replaced by civil rule under Governor Sir Reginald Dorman-Smith. Controversy soon broke out between the governor and the Anti-Fascist People's Freedom League (AFPFL), the dominant and powerful Burmese political coalition, over the membership of the governor's Executive Council. Although the AFPFL was not successful in a request for 11 out of the 15 seats and therefore declined to participate at the time, it later entered a new Executive Council under an agreement reached in September, 1946, when it received a majority of the seats with the Burmese nationalist leader General Aung San as deputy chairman. By then the British Labor government in London was implementing a new policy toward India and Major-General Sir Hubert E. Rance had been appointed governor of Burma. Reaching the conclusion that another approach to the problem was imperative, Prime Minister Clement Attlee invited on December 20 a delegation from Burma to come to London and negotiate on self-government either inside or outside the Commonwealth of Nations.

Led by Aung San a Burmese mission arrived in the British capital, an agreement being concluded on January 27, 1947, outlining the steps that would lead to independence either inside or outside the British Commonwealth. As a result of the accord, events moved rapidly in Burma. The Executive Council became an interim government; a conference at Panglong of representatives from the Chin Hills, Kachin Hills, Shan States, and the Burma Executive Council reached agreement, February 12, on the principle of full autonomy of the Frontier Areas in a Union of Burma; a Frontier Committee of Inquiry reported, April 24, on the method of associating the Frontier inhabitants with the drafting of the new constitution; elections for a constituent assembly were held on April 9 although the representatives of the Frontier Areas were chosen in May; a week after the assembly met on June 10, it adopted unanimously a resolution declaring that Burma should be a sovereign independent republic outside the Commonwealth of Nations; at the end of June a Burmese delegation led by Thakin Nu went to London and agreement was reached for the exchange of high commissioners, the British recognizing the Executive Council on July 25 as the provisional government of Burma; the constitution of the Union of Burma, providing for a president, prime minister, cabinet, and bicameral parliament, was adopted by the constituent assembly on September 24; basic relations between Britain and Burma were defined in the "Nu-Attlee Treaty" of October 17 which embodied a defense agreement made the previous August 29; finally a Burma Independence Bill, bitterly criticized by Winston Churchill, passed the British Parliament and became law on December 10.

Meanwhile, on July 19, Aung San and a number of his colleagues had been assassinated at a meeting of the Executive Council in Rangoon. The country was deprived at a critical time of its outstanding leader although Thakin Nu, president of the constituent assembly, came to develop considerable stature as the successor to the highly esteemed Bogyoke. With the independence of Burma on January 4, 1948, at an exact date determined as most auspicious by astrologers, the constituent assembly became the parliament until elections could be held under the provisions of the new constitution and Thakin Nu became the first prime minister of the independent Union of Burma.

In Indonesia the road to independence was marked by bloodshed, by increasing ill will between the Dutch and Indonesians, and by the participation of the United Nations and foreign powers in the settlement of the controversy. In contrast to Burma, where the British were not prepared to use force in order to keep the country within the Commonwealth, the Dutch employed military pressure in an attempt to prevent the independence of Indonesia. American-Filipino and British-Burmese negotiations leading to statehood did not involve third powers but the Indonesian controversy became an international question of considerable importance in the councils of the United Nations and in the capitals of many Eastern and Western powers.

The surrender of Japan and the establishment of the Republic of Indonesia coupled with the delay in the arrival of British forces until September 29, 1945, created a transition period in the East Indies not conducive to the restoration of Dutch rule. Actually the British occupation only lasted until November 30, 1946, but during this time the basic controversy between the Dutch and Indonesians became more and more apparent. For practical purposes the British considered it necessary to work with the Indonesian Republican officials but as Dutch forces began to return they were able to establish themselves in various parts of Indonesia. Actually Republican strength was centered in Java, Madura, and to some extent in Sumatra while the Dutch regained possession of Borneo and the Great East.

Negotiations between the Indonesians and Dutch made little progress until the conclusion of the Linggadjati or Cheribon Agreement on November 15, 1946, under the chairmanship of Lord Killearn, British Special Commissioner in South-East Asia. Since the Linggadjati Agreement had been made in very loose terms, both sides proceeded to interpret it differently and the originally initialed accord was not finally signed with additions until March 25, 1947. Moreover, the implementation of the signed agreement led to further controversy.

On July 21 the Dutch began their first "police action" which increased the area of their control and in effect reduced the population now in Republican territory from four-fifths to two-fifths of the total for Indonesia. India, Australia, the United States, and Great Britain all failed in efforts to mediate or tend good offices in the conflict. On July 30 India and Australia separately brought it to the attention of the United Nations Security Council. On August 1 the Security Council called upon both sides to issue a cease-fire although the Dutch firmly denied the jurisdiction of the world body in what they considered a domestic problem. Cease-fire orders were issued by both contestants but the fighting continued. On August 25 the Security Council authorized the establishment of a Consular Commission in Batavia to report on the failure to carry out the cease-fire orders and of a Committee of Good Offices to function in the dispute. Consisting of three members, Australia chosen by the Indonesian Republic, Belgium by the Netherlands, and the United States by Australia and Belgium, the Committee of Good Offices arrived in Batavia in October and succeeded in facilitating an agreement between the Netherlands and the Republic signed on board the U.S.S. *Renville* on January 17, 1948. The Renville Agreement, as it was called, provided for a truce and included a statement of principles for a permanent political solution. Additional principles presented by the Committee of Good Offices were approved two days later.

Although the implementation of the truce agreement was effective, the discussion on the political settlement was not fruitful. Meanwhile economic conditions became worse. In September President Sukarno put down a Communist revolt, refusing Dutch offers of assistance. On December 19 the Dutch began their second police action, quickly seizing Jogjakarta, the Republican capital, and capturing Sukarno, Hatta, and Sjahrir, all prominent nationalist leaders. On December 24 the Security Council called for a cease-fire and the release of the political prisoners. The Netherlands replied five days later that hostilities would end in Java by December 31 at the latest and a few days afterward in Sumatra. International opposition to Dutch policy mounted: a conference of Asian, African, and South Pacific countries, convened in New Delhi by Prime Minister Nehru, made recommendations on January 23, 1949, sympathetic to the Repubic of Indonesia; and five days later the Security Council adopted a resolution urging a cease-fire, the release of the political prisoners, and the return of the Republican government to Jogjakarta, outlining a timetable for the Dutch transfer of sovereignty to a United States of Indonesia and changing the Committee of Good Offices into a United Nations Commission for Indonesia to carry out the Council's decisions.

On March 23 the Security Council passed another resolution, calling again for a cease-fire and the restoration of the Republican government and instructing the United Nations Commission to assist the Republicans and Dutch in reaching an agreement on the conditions and date for a Round Table Conference to effect a political settlement. There was widespread conviction among the states that had participated in the New Delhi Conference that the new resolution of the Security Council represented a weakening in the position of the United Nations. After long preliminary discussion in Indonesia, agreement was finally reached leading to the return of the Republican government to Jogjakarta on July 6 under leaders whom the Dutch had previously released in March and to the signing of a cease-fire accord on August 1. A Round Table Conference officially opened at The Hague on August 23, consisting of representatives from the Netherlands, the Republic, other Indonesian states, and the three members of the United Nations Commission. Following complicated negotiations, the Conference ended on November 2 with the signing of a set of documents including an instrument for the transfer of sovereignty, a statute setting up the Netherlands-Indonesian Union, and a transitional accord. The General Assembly of the United Nations approved the settlement on December 7 although the Soviet Union vetoed a resolution to the same effect in the Security Council six days later. Ratification in the Netherlands States-General was barely approved but was easily effected in Indonesia. On December 27 Queen Juliana in Amsterdam transferred sovereignty to the United States of Indonesia under President Sukarno; in Batavia, whose name was changed to Djakarta, appropriate ceremonies were held.

The struggle for independence in Indochina was the most complicated in all Southeast Asia. Here were involved a Vietnamese nationalist movement which was substantially captured by the Communists, a French colonial policy based on the concept of the French Union which certainly at the beginning did not satisfy the aspirations of the nationalists, and a willingness of both sides to fight for their objectives. Although Vietnam was the key unit in Indochina, it was not the only one, for Cambodia and Laos had to be considered. Unlike the case of Indonesia the United Nations did not take part in the controversy, despite the fact that by 1950 Indochina had become a threat to the peace of Southeast Asia and indirectly of the world. In the end an international conference at Geneva in 1954 attended by the representatives of nine governments including the Soviet Union, the People's Republic of China, the United Kingdom, the United States, and France was necessary to terminate the bloodshed.

As the result of a decision at the Potsdam Conference in 1945, Indochina after V-J Day had been occupied south of the sixteenth parallel by British forces and north of it by Chinese Nationalist troops for the purpose of effecting the surrender of the Japanese and freeing Allied war prisoners. By the time the foreign forces had arrived the Democratic Republic of Vietnam under the leadership of Ho Chi Minh had become firmly established. Although the British in their zone—Cambodia, southern Laos, Cochin China, and southern Annam—facilitated the return of the French, the Chinese in their area—most of Laos, Tonkin, and northern Annam—were inclined to work with Ho Chi Minh and the Lao nationalists. On February 28, 1946, France reached an agreement with Nationalist China for the withdrawal of the latter's troops in exchange for substantial French concessions. The greater part of the British forces had already left by the end of the previous month.

On March 6 France and the Democratic Republic of Vietnam, both probably motivated by opportunism, made a settlement involving French recognition of the latter as a "free state" in an Indochinese Federation and a French Union and Ho Chi Minh's agreement to the temporary return of French forces to Tonkin and northern Annam. Controversy soon arose about the implementation of the accord with charges of bad faith on both sides. In addition to the independence issue, the Vietnamese wanted the unification of the three Ky—Tonkin, Annam, and Cochin China—under one regime and the French were reluctant to part with their valuable colony of Cochin China. Conferences between representatives of France and the Democratic Republic at Dalat during the spring of 1946 and at Fontainebleau during the summer failed to reach agreement on basic issues. Meanwhile the French had reëstablished their dominant position in Cambodia, after the previous arrival of British and Indian as well as French troops, by an agreement made on January 7, and in Laos by an accord on August 27, the delay being partly the responsibility of the Chinese forces who did not leave Indochina as early as hoped. In Vietnam tension steadily mounted between the French and the Viet Minh of Ho Chi Minh. Finally on December 19, after a number of incidents, the latter attacked the former in Hanoi, starting a war that would not end for over seven and a half years.

During the conflict the French in Indochina were subject on the political level to the vicissitudes of politics in Paris and on the military front to bitter guerrilla warfare in tropical jungles. France had to decide whether or not to negotiate with Ho Chi Minh, and if not, to which Vietnamese leaders power, and what kind of power, should be transferred. Moreover, the transfer of power was complicated, for the French Union embodied in the constitution of the Fourth Republic did not technically come into being until the constitution was adopted in October, 1946, and soon thereafter the legal terminology and its practical application became a subject of controversy. In addition, the postwar Indochinese Federation was a concept subject to different French, Vietnamese, Cambodian, and Laotian viewpoints.

By late December, 1947, the French officially decided to do what they had been following in practice for some time, namely, to bypass the leaders of the Democratic Republic of Vietnam and to make terms with other Vietnamese nationalists. Having failed in their efforts to build up a provisional government in Cochin China that would attract the nationalists, the French looked to Bao Dai. The former emperor of Annam under the French and Japanese regimes and later Supreme Councillor to the Democratic Republic of Vietnam had left the country to live in Hong Kong. In the long negotiations with the French Bao Dai was interested in assuring the independence and unity of Vietnam in the French Union. He knew he would not win nationalist support if he accepted less than the French had given the Viet Minh in the agreement of March, 1946.

On a French cruiser in Along Bay on June 5, 1948, Bao Dai made an agreement with France under which Vietnam was recognized as an independent state in the French Union although the details were not yet defined. Earlier a provisional central government of Vietnam had been set up under General Nguyen Van Xuan with the approval of Bao Dai but it failed to attract popular support. On March 8, 1949, Bao Dai and France reached a comprehensive agreement which became the basis for the former's eventual return to his country and the establishment of the State of Vietnam. Provisions calling for the union of the three Ky were carried out and Cochin China, ceasing to be a colony of France, became an integral part of Vietnam on June 5. Nine days later an exchange of letters dated June 13 between Bao Dai and Léon Pignon, the French High Commissioner in Indochina, provided that the agreement of March 8 should come into force pending the approval of the French Parliament. Similar basic accords were made between France and Laos on July 19 and France and Cambodia on November 8.

The inauguration of the State of Vietnam on June 14 in Saigon aroused little enthusiasm among the people. The *attentistes* were not won over; Bao Dai had difficulty in forming a cabinet, Ngo Dinh Diem, for instance, a prominent Roman Catholic nationalist, refusing office partly because he believed Vietnam should have a status comparable to that of India or Pakistan. Nevertheless, as the result of the work of joint committees of French and Vietnamese, conventions for the implementation of the agreement of March 8 were drawn up and then approved by Bao Dai and Pignon on December 30. After long delay in Paris, the French Parliament finally voted in favor of the agreements with Vietnam, Cambodia, and Laos, the bill becoming law by the signature of the President on February 2, 1950. Five days later the United States and Great Britain recognized the three States in the French Union followed by a number of other powers closely tied in most cases to the Western group of nations. On the other hand, Ho recognized the People's Republic of China on January 15 and the Soviet Union along with other Communist states recognized in January and February the government of the Democratic Republic of Vietnam.

According to the agreements between France and Vietnam on March 8, 1949, Laos on July 19 and Cambodia on November 8, a four-party conference was necessary to reach accord on topics of common concern such as the navigation of the Mekong, the use of the port of Saigon, communications, customs, and immigration. Meeting in Pau, France, on June 29, 1950, the negotiators deliberated through November 27 and agreements were finally signed the last part of December. Instead of moving in the direction of a real Indochinese federation as the French had once envisaged in their postwar planning, Vietnam, Cambodia, and Laos revealed definite tendencies which were nationalistic and individualistic in their relations with one another.

As the military situation in Tonkin became increasingly dark for the French, partly because of the assistance rendered the Viet Minh by the Chinese Communists through training and supplies, General Jean de Lattre de Tassigny was appointed on December 7 High Commissioner and Commander-in-Chief in Indochina. In the same month Bao Dai reached agreement with the French for the recognition of a Vietnamese army as an independent force under his authority and the formation of a Franco-Vietnamese military committee for liaison between the French and Vietnamese forces. Although General de Lattre managed to stem the Viet Minh offensive in 1951 and to increase the morale of the French, he was not able to defeat in a decisive manner the forces of Ho Chi Minh. Meanwhile only limited progress was made in building up a Vietnamese national army and in winning popular support for the Bao Dai regime. It is true that the French had made extensive concessions to the State of Vietnam since the return of Bao Dai but many of the nationalists remained to be convinced. In November, General de Lattre was forced to return to France where he died the following January.

On July 3, 1953, France under Premier Joseph Laniel informed the governments of the Associated States that she was willing to "complete" their sovereignty and independence by handing over to them functions which she had hitherto kept. Negotiations with Laos were concluded on October 22 with a settlement whereby the kingdom in Article 1 of a treaty was recognized by France as "a fully independent and sovereign State" and in Article 2 Laos reaffirmed her participation in the French Union. A number of conventions were annexed to the treaty.

The negotiations with Cambodia were slower and more difficult. King Norodom Sihanouk in June had gone to Bangkok and later to western Cambodia, asserting that he would not return to his capital of Phnom Penh until the country had won full independence. He declared on June 24 that his kingdom would not consider itself a member of the French Union unless it received a status at least like that of Pakistan with respect to Britain. On August 29 France made a settlement with Cambodia transferring responsibilities regarding the police and judiciary, further agreements on the courts being made September 9. On October 17 representatives of the two governments reached an accord involving military responsibility, and on November 7 the king assumed it for the nation. He returned to Phnom Penh on November 8 although Cambodia's overall relationship with France awaited definition.

Formal negotiations with the State of Vietnam did not begin in 1953, for the political situation was not auspicious. In October a "national congress" that had been called by Bao Dai requested independence of the present French Union although it recommended an alliance with France. In the following month Ho Chi Minh noted that the Democratic Republic would consider French armistice proposals providing they respected the independence of Vietnam. It was not until April 28, 1954, that France and the State of Vietnam reached agreement in effect on two treaties, initialed June 4, one, a treaty of independence in which France recognized Vietnam as "a fully independent and sovereign State," and the other, a treaty of association in which France and Vietnam indicated a will to associate in the French Union. Subsequent agreements would be annexed to the treaty describing the conditions of the association. Despite the crucial battle of Dien Bien Phu that was being waged, the negotiations between the French and Vietnamese on the treaties had been long and complex, involving to quite an extent whether the liberal preamble or Title Eight of the French constitution should be the guiding principle of the Union. And in the end the treaties were not technically put into force.

The fall of Dien Bien Phu on May 7 coupled with the assumption by Mendès-France of the premiership of France on June 17 facilitated the Geneva settlement of July 20 and 21 on Indochina. In a declaration France asserted that in settling all problems associated with reëstablishing peace in Vietnam, Cambodia, and Laos, she would be guided by the principle of respecting the sovereignty and independence, the territorial integrity and unity of the three states. In another declaration France said she would withdraw her troops from any of the three states upon its request except where a bilateral agreement provided for a certain number of them at specified places for a given time. Such an arrangement had already been made with Laos but not with Cambodia. Under the terms of the Geneva settlement French military forces were withdrawn in Vietnam to south of the seventeenth parallel. Subsequent steps were taken by France to transfer the departments and public services she still retained to the State of Vietnam. As indication of the independence of Cambodia and Laos, a number of states that had previously not recognized them proceeded to do so. A similar step was not taken in as many cases with reference to the State of Vietnam because of the partition of the country and the projected national elections in 1956. Negotiations among Cambodia, Laos, the State of Vietnam and France on topics similar to those considered at Pau began in Paris on August 26 and led to new agreements on December 29 and 30, further reducing the French role and emphasizing the nationalism of each of the three Asian states.

Although in retrospect the issue in Indochina was not so simple as nationalism versus colonialism, one of the basic reasons for the decline of the French "presence" was the failure to channel effectively the nationalist forces in the area. Since the negotiations between France and the Associated States were long, complicated, and often stormy, agreements when finally made had lost much of their psychological impact. There was not the good will created as in the case of the final British pledge to Burma or the American offers to the Philippines. Independence seemed always a step away, and indeed powers were being transferred by France to the Indochinese states in 1955. Even Norodom Palace, the residence of the governors-general and commissioners-general of France in Saigon, was not turned over to the State of Vietnam until September 7, 1954. At the same time France was faced with a situation, unlike that in any other area in Southeast Asia, where the Communists, having substantially captured the nationalist movement, were able with increasing assistance from the outside to seek a military solution to the problem. Moreover, in France herself, policy was difficult to formulate, for Indochina was a long-standing controversy in domestic politics, ranging from the Conservatives who wanted to maintain the French Empire to the Communists who demanded the end of "*la sale guerre*."[1]

[1] Developments in Malaya leading to the independence of the Federation and involving the future of Singapore are considered in a chapter on Malaya.

3. *Machinery of Statehood*

The achievement of statehood marks the necessity for establishing the machinery for the conduct of international relations—the ministry of foreign affairs and the foreign service. Diplomatic recognition, the opening of missions abroad from the new state, and the setting up of embassies and legations at home from foreign countries are concomitants. Election to membership in international organizations, especially the United Nations, is a factor of prestige. A consideration, as of early 1954, of the Philippines, Burma, and Indonesia as well as of Thailand, Vietnam, Cambodia, and Laos with respect to the factors given provides an insight into the international outlook of each country. Since Thailand never lost her sovereignty she had the greatest experience in the field of foreign affairs. On the other hand, Vietnam, Cambodia, and Laos were still emerging in the international community and all Malaya at the time was a dependency.[1]

By early 1954 the Republic of the Philippines had acquired some experience in conducting foreign relations. Nevertheless, the process was still not easy, and the change on December 30, 1953, from the Liberal regime of Presidents Manuel Roxas and Elpidio Quirino to the administration of Ramon Magsaysay, a *Nacionalista,* marked in some respects a break with the past. On September 25, 1945, an Office of Foreign Relations had been created by Commonwealth Act No. 683. The day before independence, President Roxas signed a bill creating the Department of Foreign Affairs and authorizing the chief executive to organize it as well as a foreign service. Effective July 4, 1946, the act abolished the Commonwealth Office of Foreign Relations and the Office of the Resident Commissioner of the Philippines to the United States. A senior American Foreign Service officer assisted in the organization of the Philippine Depart-

[1] In the chapter on Malaya the author gives consideration as regards the Federation in 1957 to certain items covered in Chapter 3.

ment of Foreign Affairs and a training program for future foreign affairs officers of the Philippines was conducted in Washington under the auspices of the Department of State. Administrative orders in Manila have since altered the structure of the Department of Foreign Affairs.

The Magsaysay administration inherited a foreign office as organized under the Department's Reallotment Order No. 1, approved October 15, 1952. It is clear that the structure indicates degrees of importance. The Philippine Department of Foreign Affairs was organized into six offices and all but one had divisions. The Office of the Secretary of Foreign Affairs and the Office of the Undersecretary topped the hierarchy. Under the latter were the three Divisions of Coördination and Review, Protocol, and Intelligence and Research. The Board of Foreign Service Examiners and the Board of the Foreign Service were associated with the Office of the Undersecretary. The Office of Political and Cultural Affairs included the geographic units found in the Division of Eastern Political Affairs and the Division of Western Political Affairs as well as the three Divisions of United Nations and International Conferences, Cultural Activities, and International Information. An Office of Economic Affairs was organized into a Division of Agricultural, Commercial, Monetary, and Industrial Affairs and a Division of Trade Promotion and Consular Documentation. Five divisions were found in the Office of Administration and Controls—Departmental Administration including a Property and General Service Section, Foreign Service Administration, Passports and Visas, Financial Management and Controls, and Communication and Records. The Office of Legal Affairs contained the Law Division and Division of Treaties.

In the former reorganizations of the Department of Foreign Affairs the "geographical" and the "functional" units have been shifted. The predecessors of the two Divisions of Eastern Political and Western Political Affairs were the three Divisions of American, European and African, and Asian and Pacific Affairs. Especially noticeable are the administrative separation of political from economic affairs and the expansion of the latter. Cultural and legal affairs have been split, the former being placed in the political office. Despite the changes in administrative organization, coördination in the Department has been effected in so far as possible through staff meetings of ranking officials. In terms of personnel, President Magsaysay's first budget presented to Congress on February 9, 1954, requested the addition to the Department of one public and press relations officer and one messenger.

The foreign service of the Philippines was patterned to a large degree upon that of the United States. Under Republic Act No. 708, approved June 5, 1952, the service was reorganized to meet the demands of the day. Specifically there were five categories of personnel: chiefs of mission with three classes determined by the President for salary purposes, foreign affairs officers consisting of four classes in rank apart from the career ministers, foreign service staff officers and employees divided into six classes, alien clerks and employees, and consular agents and honorary consuls. The principle of the act of Congress was a career service of foreign affairs officers selected on a basis of merit, appointed by the President and confirmed by the Commission on Appointments. The foreign affairs officers could be rotated between the missions abroad and the home office.

With the victory of the *Nacionalistas* under Ramon Magsaysay the career principle was severely attacked by the new administration. It was argued that the Liberals, having controlled the government since independence, were entrenched by law in the foreign service. In addition, the pressure to find positions for political supporters of the new administration was intense. At the same time a substantial number of the Philippine diplomats had been graduated from the foreign affairs training program of the American Department of State and had established for themselves creditable records. The problem of the wise selection of diplomats is not restricted to any one country.

After the achievement of independence the Republic of the Philippines received widespread diplomatic recognition apart from the Soviet Union and the other Communist states. In a number of cases the exchange of diplomatic missions followed. In selecting a country for the purpose of establishing a mission, a new state like the Philippines makes in conjunction with another an evaluation in most cases of the present and potential importance of mutual relations. An analysis of the distribution of the missions established by the Philippines and other states in Southeast Asia reveals for each a general pattern of priority. As of early 1954 the Republic of the Philippines had embassies in the United States, Spain, and Indonesia, legations in France, Italy, Great Britain, Thailand, Argentina, Australia, Nationalist China, India, Mexico, and Pakistan, a mission in Japan, consulates general in New York City and San Francisco, and consulates in Honolulu, Los Angeles, Seattle, Chicago, New Orleans, Hong Kong, Singapore, and Agana. The Philippine embassy in Washington was a concurrent mission to the United Nations. An office of the ambassador in Vatican City was maintained although the envoy accredited to the Holy See resided in Madrid as ambassador to Spain. The minister to France was also accredited to Belgium and the Netherlands, the minister to Great Britain to Norway, Sweden, and Denmark, the minister to Australia also to New Zealand, the chargé d'affaires in Pakistan served as consul for Saudi Arabia, and the consul in Singapore also acted for the Federation of Malaya, Sarawak, and Brunei.

In the first budget President Magsaysay sent to Congress he provided for the separation of the embassy in Washington from the mission to the United Nations and he called for the establishment of a legation in the Republic of Korea and of consulates in Hamburg, Germany, and Menado, Indonesia. A vice-consulate under the consulate in Singapore would function in British North Borneo. The minister in Thailand would be accredited to Burma and the minister in India to Ceylon.

The pattern of Philippine representation is somewhat different from that of the other states in Southeast Asia. It is not surprising that two of the first three embassies were established in the former mother countries of the archipelago. The third embassy, the one in Indonesia, is an indication of the present, but perhaps even more of the potential, relations between the two republics. The establishment of four legations in Latin states—Italy, France, Argentina, and Mexico—reveals to some extent the cultural impact of Spain. The combining of the posts of chargé in Pakistan and consul for Saudi Arabia reflects the interests of the Philippines in the Moros, a few of whom become pilgrims to Mecca. At the same time it should be noted that matters of winning prestige and finding positions for Filipinos were also involved in the establishment of missions abroad, especially in some countries where the Republic has little actual interest.

The changes favored by President Magsaysay indicated the concern of the *Nacionalista* administration for the cultivation of closer ties with Asian states. On the mainland of Southeast Asia, only one Philippine legation had been established. By accrediting the minister in Thailand also to Burma, and in South Asia by accrediting the minister in India to Ceylon, the *Nacionalistas* hoped to widen their diplomatic ties. The plans to establish a consulate in Menado, Sulawesi, and a vice-consulate in Sandakan, British North Borneo, associated with the consulate in Singapore, revealed increasing Philippine concern about relations with southern neighbors. Finally the separation of the mission in Washington from that at the United Nations marked another round in a perennial Philippine problem of representation.

By early 1954 the list of foreign missions in the Philippines had grown since the first year of the Republic. Embassies were functioning in Manila from the United States, Spain, Indonesia, and Nationalist China, legations from Argentina, Australia, Belgium, France, India, Italy, Korea, Mexico, the Netherlands, Norway, Sweden, Thailand, and Great Britain, an apostolic nunciature from the Holy See had been established and a mission from Japan. The Swedish minister resided in Djakarta and the Norwegian in Bangkok. The consular list in the Philippines included Austria, Canada, Chile, Nationalist China, Costa Rica, Denmark, the Dominican Republic, Ecuador, El Salvador, Finland, Greece, Guatemala, Honduras, Indonesia, Ireland, Israel, Lebanon, Mexico, Nicaragua, Norway, Panama, Portugal, Spain, Sweden, Switzerland, Thailand, the United Kingdom, the United States, Uruguay, and Venezuela. Cuba had a consular agency in Manila, France in Cebu, and Britain had agencies in Davao, Bacolod, and Cebu.

Unlike the other states of Southeast Asia who had to run the gamut of election to the United Nations, the Philippines was a charter member of the organization. During the Second World War the Commonwealth had participated in the Pacific War Council, the United Nations Relief and Rehabilitation Administration, the United Nations Monetary and Financial Conference at Bretton Woods, the United Nations Conference on Food and Agriculture at Hot Springs, and the International Civil Aviation Conference at Chicago. The Philippines had adhered to the Declaration by United Nations on June 10, 1942, and had participated in the United Nations Conference on International Organization held in San Francisco from April 25 to June 25, 1945. The Commonwealth deposited on October 11 her instrument of ratification of the United Nations Charter.

As of early 1954 the Republic of the Philippines belonged to numerous specialized agencies associated with the United Nations. She was a member of the International Labor Organization (ILO), Food and Agriculture Organization (FAO), United Nations Educational, Scientific and Cultural Organization (UNESCO), International Civil Aviation Organization (ICAO), International Bank for Reconstruction and Development, International Monetary Fund, World Health Organization (WHO), Universal Postal Union (UPU), International Telecommunication Union (ITU), World Meteorological Organization (WMO), and the Interim Commission for the International Trade Organization (ICITO).

In contrast to the Republic of the Philippines the Union of Burma did not have as careful preparation for the conduct of foreign relations. The Ministry for Foreign Affairs in Rangoon after its establishment reflected the British influence. In early 1954 the foreign office list consisted of a minister for foreign affairs, a parliamentary secretary to the minister, a permanent secretary and a deputy secretary, a first secretary and a deputy secretary, two assistant secretaries, an officer on special duty, six third secretaries, an attaché and a private secretary to the minister for foreign affairs. Very noticeable is the organization of the Ministry with respect to Parliament, for, unlike the Philippines, Burma adopted a parliamentary type of government. Theoretically the office of the permanent secretary, as in the case of the British precedent, represents the continuing factor in Burmese foreign policy and is not partisan in scope. In terms of activities the foreign office was divided into United Nations, foreign service, cypher, foreign intelligence, political, consular, protocol, general, immigration, passport, and administration branches. Although the recruitment of competent personnel was difficult, a Burmese foreign service was established.

The Union of Burma was quickly recognized by states throughout the world. By early 1954 Burma maintained embassies in the United Kingdom, the United States, the Soviet Union, the People's Republic of China, India, Pakistan, Thailand, Indonesia, and Yugoslavia, legations in Ceylon and France, consulates general in Tokyo and Calcutta and consulates in Copenhagen, Hong Kong, Madras, Dublin, Dacca, Chittagong, and Singapore. The permanent delegation of the Union of Burma to the United Nations was associated with the Burmese Embassy in Washington under the same ranking official. The consuls in Ireland, Denmark, and Hong Kong were honorary and the consulate general in Kunming, China, was not functioning.

Especially significant in the Burmese pattern of representation abroad is the universality of the missions in terms of the international alignments characterizing contemporary world politics. Missions are maintained in the Communist and anti-Communist groupings as well as in states not aligned with either side. A country seeking to pursue a "neutral" foreign policy could have no better distribution of representatives abroad. Also noticeable is the widespread establishment of missions in Asian states east of Iran, the exceptions at the time being the Philippines, Korea, Cambodia, Laos, and Vietnam. There are very few missions in the rest of the world apart from those in the capitals of the Great Powers. The two embassies and four consular offices functioning in India and Pakistan are generally indicative of a number of problems that have their origin in the era when Burma was a part of the Indian Empire under the British. The establishment of an embassy in Yugoslavia reflects a certain ideological kinship that was evident for some time before the visit of President Tito to Burma. And the honorary consul in the Republic of Ireland is not unrelated to the interest in Rangoon arising from the drafting of the Burmese constitution somewhat along the model of the Irish constitution of 1937 and to the similar steps taken by Burma and Ireland in leaving the British Commonwealth. The Burmese government, it should be noted, was concerned over having the mission in Washington linked with that at the United Nations.

In Rangoon the list of diplomatic and consular officials varied in a few respects from the Burmese representation abroad. Embassies were maintained by the People's Republic of China, India, Indonesia, Pakistan, Thailand, the United Kingdom, the United States, the Soviet Union, and Yugoslavia, legations by Australia, Ceylon, Egypt, France, Italy, Israel, and the Netherlands and consulates by Belgium, Czechoslovakia, Denmark, Greece, Japan, Nepal, Norway, Portugal, Sweden, Switzerland, and Spain. Pakistan had a vice-consul in Akyab, Poland a trade commissioner resident in Karachi, and Hungary a commercial counselor resident in Bombay. The Italian minister lived in Bangkok and the Egyptian in New Delhi; Belgium, Denmark, Greece, Norway, Portugal, Sweden, Switzerland, and Spain were represented in Rangoon by honorary consular officials. The establishment of an Australian legation in Burma was an earnest of the Commonwealth's concern for Southeast Asia; the legations from Israel and Egypt reflected the Union's overall neutral policy in Israeli-Arab controversies; the consulate from Prague indicated the interest of Communist Czechoslovakia in Burma while the consulate of Nepal associated the Union with the Himalaya kingdom.

Burma was the first new state in Southeast Asia to be elected a member of the United Nations. On February 27, 1948, the Union applied for membership and on March 17 submitted a declaration accepting the obligations of the Charter. The Security Council on April 10 adopted a draft resolution of Nationalist China approving the admission of Burma. Argentina abstained because of lack of instructions. India and China requested that the application be placed on the agenda of the special session of the General Assembly. Nine days later the General Assembly with India, Pakistan, and Thailand speaking on behalf of the resolution unanimously elected Burma as the fifty-eighth member of the United Nations.

By early 1954 the Union was a member of ILO, FAO, UNESCO, ICAO, WHO, UPU, ITU, WMO, ICITO, the International Bank for Reconstruction and Development, and the International Monetary Fund. She was also a party to the Convention on the Inter-Governmental Maritime Consultative Organization (IMCO). In the general field of international organization the Union of Burma was an active participant.

The Indonesian Ministry of Foreign Affairs as of early 1954 was organized into directorates and sections. At the head were the minister of foreign affairs with his immediate staff, a secretary-general of the Ministry and his executive assistant, a board of advisers and its secretariat. Each of the five directorates had its chief and assistant chief with one exception. The first directorate was concerned with Asia and the Pacific, having two sections, one for Southeast Asia and the other for the Far East and Pacific; the second directorate dealt with Africa and Europe, having three sections, East and Central Africa, West Europe, and East Europe; the third directorate handled the Americas and United Nations, having one section for each; the fourth directorate was concerned with legal and economic affairs, having in this case two deputy chiefs and four sections, the legal and the treaties and agreements units being the first two, and the finance, industry, trade, and communications unit and commodities, planning bureau affairs, and international relations and foreign aid unit being the last two; the fifth directorate dealt with research and information and had one section for each.

Administrative affairs were handled in an office having four sections, covering personnel, finance, the functions of the sergeant at arms, and documents. A special consular section dealt with visas and passports, and a chief protocol officer handled problems related to his assignment. An academy for the foreign service provided training facilities, two of its divisions being concerned with Sinology and liaison.

The Ministry of Foreign Affairs in Djakarta is one of the larger foreign offices in Southeast Asia. In the geographic branches half of the six sections dealt with Asia and Africa and the other half with Europe and America. Noticeable is the fact that four sections were given to economic and legal affairs, one to the United Nations, and two to research and information. In the training of foreign service officers, Indonesia has had to start from very simple beginnings. Coöperation between the Netherlands and the Republic was not forthcoming in a training program when the former after the Linggadjati Agreement established a Far Eastern branch of the Ministry of Foreign Affairs in Batavia and asked the Republic to select applicants for the classes.

Events in the struggle for independence clouded the issue of the recognition of an independent Indonesia. As early as May and June, 1947, Afghanistan and members of the Arab League had granted *de jure* recognition to the Republic. The United States and Great Britain had given it *de facto* recognition following the signing of the Linggadjati Agreement. After the Dutch transfer of sovereignty to the United States of Indonesia on December 27, 1949, the new state was given widespread *de jure* recognition. The Soviet Union, however, delayed almost a month.

The pattern of Indonesian representation abroad is closer to that of the Burmese than the Filipino. Nevertheless, differences exist arising from varying conditions. As of early 1954 Indonesia maintained embassies in the United States, Brazil, Mexico, Canada, Great Britain, France, India, Australia, the Federal Republic of Germany, Egypt, the People's Republic of China, Pakistan, the Philippines, Burma, Syria, Lebanon, and Jordan, legations in Italy, Sweden, Switzerland, Norway, the Vatican, Portugal, Belgium, Denmark, Thailand, Saudi Arabia, Iraq, Iran, and Ceylon, consulates general in New York, Singapore, Hong Kong, and Tokyo, consulates in San Francisco, Noumea, Calcutta, and Bombay and vice-consulates in Penang and Davao. An Indonesian high commissioner was stationed in the Netherlands, a commissioner in Surinam, and a permanent delegation at the United Nations. Indonesia and the Soviet Union at the time were in the process of establishing embassies.

In some cases Indonesian envoys were accredited to more than one foreign state. A single embassy functioned for Egypt, Syria,

Lebanon, and Jordan. One minister was accredited to Norway, Sweden, and Denmark, another to Iraq and Iran, and the ambassador to the United States served in the same capacity to Mexico. On the other hand, one official did not head both the embassy in Washington and the United Nations mission.

Noticeable in the Indonesian representation abroad is the number of missions accredited to Moslem countries, a situation not existing in the other states of Southeast Asia. Unlike Burma there are no diplomatic relations with Israel. The establishment of embassies in Australia and the Philippines is indicative of problems arising from geographical proximity. Legations are maintained, it is interesting to note, in Saudi Arabia as well as the Vatican, both religious centers. With the establishment of an embassy in the Soviet Union, Indonesia follows Burma in trying to maintain missions at the capitals of all the leading powers.

In Djakarta Australia, Burma, Canada, the Chinese People's Republic, France, the Federal Republic of Germany, Great Britain, India, Pakistan, the Philippines, and the United States had embassies, Belgium, Ceylon, Egypt and the Sudan, Iran, Iraq, Saudi Arabia, Sweden, Switzerland, and Thailand had legations, the Netherlands an office of the high commissioner, the Vatican an apostolic internunciature, Czechoslovakia, Norway, and Japan consulates general, and Denmark, Finland, Greece, Portugal, and Italy consulates. As is often the case, consular as well as diplomatic functions were carried on in a number of embassies and legations.

Moslem representation in Djakarta was not so extensive as that of Indonesian in Moslem states. As of early 1954 there were actually no diplomats from Iran and Iraq in the capital despite the official status of a legation for each. Among the Arab states only Egypt and Saudi Arabia had missions in Djakarta. Noticeable also was the embassy of the Federal Republic of Germany, for in only two states of Southeast Asia did the Federal Republic at the time maintain missions.

Indonesia applied for membership in the United Nations on September 25, 1950. The following day the Security Council approved the application although Nationalist China abstained from voting in view of the Indonesian recognition of the People's Republic of China. On September 28 the General Assembly unanimously adopted a joint resolution of India and Australia calling for the admission of Indonesia. After the president of the Assembly welcomed the Republic into the United Nations representatives of 28 states expressed their approval of the decision. In replying the Indonesian delegate stressed the contributions of the United Nations to the independence of his country. Thus under favorable circumstances the Republic of Indonesia became the sixtieth member of the world organization.

With her admission to the United Nations Indonesia moved automatically from associate to full membership in the Economic Commission for Asia and the Far East (ECAFE). Her participation in other United Nations activities was expanded. As of early 1954 she belonged to ILO, FAO, UNESCO, ICAO, WHO, UPU, ITU, WMO, and ICITO. She was not yet a member of the International Bank for Reconstruction and Development or of the International Monetary Fund.

Thailand is the state with the oldest existing Ministry of Foreign Affairs and foreign service in Southeast Asia. In 1954 a royal decree reorganized the Ministry repealing a previous measure. At the head of the foreign office remained the minister of foreign affairs assisted by the deputy minister, the under-secretary and deputy under-secretary. In the office of the under-secretary were the central, consular, finance, telegraph, archives, translation, commerce, information, and passport divisions and the government offices in foreign countries unit. There were four departments each with divisions—a Department of European and American Affairs organized into general, European, and American divisions, a Department of Asian and African Affairs divided into general, Far East, and South and Southeast Asia divisions, a Department of United Nations Affairs with general, political, social, and economic divisions, and a Department of Protocol with general and reception divisions. Finally there was an office of the legal adviser.

It should be noted that in Thailand's Ministry of Foreign Affairs the Department of United Nations Affairs has the largest number of divisions of the departments—four in all—as compared with three each for the two departments concerned with geographical areas. In the case of the latter the administrative organization is less complicated than the Indonesian but more so than the Filipino.

As of early 1954 Thailand had embassies in Burma, Nationalist China, France, the United Kingdom, India, Japan, and the United States and legations in Cambodia, Laos, Indonesia, the Philippines, Switzerland, the Soviet Union, the State of Vietnam, and the Federal Republic of Germany. The consular list included representation in Brussels, Vancouver, Toronto, Copenhagen, Marseilles, Rome, Milan, Turin, Genoa, The Hague, Oslo, Manila, Macao, Oporto, Stockholm, Cardiff, Glasgow, Hull, Liverpool, Gibraltar, Malta, Hong Kong, Singapore, Penang, Boston, Chicago, San Francisco, Los Angeles, and Miami. A permanent delegation was stationed at the United Nations.

The Thai missions in Indochina in early 1954 were the only ones from the states of Southeast Asia. As has been noted, one legation was functioning in Cambodia, another in the State of Vietnam, and a third in Laos. Also in Tokyo Thailand maintained the only embassy or legation from the region. On the whole the Thai representation abroad was modest in scope with emphasis on countries where the Bangkok government had special interests. As for the consular list, by far the greater number of officials on it were honorary.

In Bangkok the United Kingdom, Burma, Nationalist China, France, India, the United States, and Japan had embassies and Australia, Belgium, Cambodia, Laos, the State of Vietnam, the Federal Republic of Germany, Denmark, Indonesia, Italy, the Netherlands, Norway, the Philippines, the Soviet Union, Spain, Switzerland, and Portugal had legations.

The consular body included representation from the United Kingdom with offices in the cities of Bangkok, Chiengmai, Songkhla, and Phuket and from Denmark, Austria, Israel, India, Italy, Norway, Sweden, Switzerland, the Philippines, and the United States. The location of two of the British consular offices was indicative of interest in the Malay peninsula.

Following a long-established policy of participating in international organizations, Thailand applied for membership in the United Nations as soon as feasible. She had been the only member of the League of Nations from Southeast Asia but, it should be added, she had enjoyed the position of being the sole country eligible in the area. When Thailand on August 3, 1946, formally sought admission to the United Nations, opposition was encountered from the Soviet Union, which noted that the Bangkok government did not have diplomatic relations with her, and from France, which was negotiating with the kingdom on the restoration of the areas in Laos and Cambodia awarded to Thailand in 1941 by an agreement in Tokyo. After a settlement of the problems satisfactory to France and the Soviet Union, the Security Council on December 12 unanimously adopted a Chinese resolution calling for the admission of

Thailand. The General Assembly three days later unanimously approved the entrance of the kingdom and on December 16 Thailand presented her instrument of adherence to the Charter. On April 28, 1947, at the first special session of the General Assembly Thailand received a formal welcome, speeches being made by India, China, and Denmark.

By early 1954 the kingdom was a member of ILO, FAO, UNESCO, ICAO, WHO, UPU, ITU, WMO, the International Bank for Reconstruction and Development, and the International Monetary Fund. In addition, Thailand was an active participant in other international activities. In many respects Bangkok was becoming the center of United Nations functions in Southeast Asia.

In contrast to Thailand, the oldest state in the region, Cambodia, Laos, and the State of Vietnam were in early 1954 the newest. As might be expected, the foreign offices and services were rudimentary, the diplomatic and consular offices set up abroad and those in Indochina being very limited. The great question of the day was recognition and associated with it the desire of membership in the United Nations.

The Associated States of Indochina had been recognized by Great Britain, the United States, Australia, Belgium, Luxembourg, New Zealand, Greece, Italy, Jordan, Honduras, Brazil, Thailand, the Republic of Korea, Spain, Ecuador, Peru, the Vatican, the Union of South Africa, Venezuela, Bolivia, Costa Rica, Cuba, the Netherlands, Paraguay, Colombia, Argentina, Liberia, Chile, El Salvador, Haiti, Nicaragua, Panama, Japan, Canada, and Turkey. On the other hand, the Democratic Republic of Vietnam had recognized the People's Republic of China and was recognized by the Soviet Union, the Democratic People's Republic of Korea, Czechoslovakia, Hungary, Poland, Romania, Bulgaria, Albania, Yugoslavia, and the German Democratic Republic.

The State of Vietnam had a high commissioner in France, an embassy in the United States, and legations in Thailand, Great Britain, Italy, and Spain. In Saigon the French had a commissioner-general for Indochina and a high commissioner to Vietnam, the United States an embassy, the United Kingdom, Australia, Italy, and Thailand legations, India, the Netherlands, and Nationalist China consulates general, and Belgium, Denmark, Portugal, Greece, Norway, Sweden, and Switzerland consulates. The Holy See was represented by an apostolic delegate. The United States, Nationalist

China, the United Kingdom, and India also had consulates in Hanoi and Nationalist China one in Haiphong. In the case of the diplomatic missions the ambassador or minister in Saigon was accredited to Cambodia and Laos with proper rank unless a separate chief of mission was stationed in Phnom Penh or Vientiane. The United States, for example, had one man as ambassador to Vietnam and Cambodia and minister to Laos. The Democratic Republic of Vietnam had missions in the People's Republic of China and the Soviet Union but foreign states did not establish permanent diplomatic embassies or legations in the Republic until after the Geneva settlement.

The Kingdom of Cambodia as of early 1954 had a high commissioner in France, an embassy in the United States, a legation in Thailand, and was in the process of sending a minister to Japan. Next on the list would be an envoy to the United Kingdom. Thailand had a minister in Phnom Penh, the United States and Great Britain each had a chargé, France a high commissioner, Nationalist China a consulate, and Japan was about to send a minister. The Kingdom of Laos had a royal delegation in France and legations in the United States, Thailand, and the United Kingdom. France had a high representative in Laos, Thailand a minister, and the United States a chargé.

Despite the establishment of missions abroad by Cambodia, Laos, and the State of Vietnam, no machinery existed as of early 1954 for bilateral diplomatic relations among the three states. The Cambodian and Laotian delegations in Saigon, for instance, were accredited to the French high commissioner and not to the State of Vietnam. It would be a question of time before the situation would be remedied.

The ministries of foreign affairs in Saigon, Phnom Penh, and Vientiane were simply organized and limited in personnel. In the case of the State of Vietnam the personnel of the foreign office included among other officials under the minister the chief of protocol, the director of political affairs, and the chiefs of economic and financial affairs, and legal, administrative, and cultural affairs. In Cambodia the Ministry of Foreign Affairs was divided into the offices of the minister, of the private secretary to the minister, of the cabinet director of the ministry, and of the chief of protocol, the offices of political affairs, economic affairs, and consular affairs, the administrative office, and the passport and visa office. The foreign ministry in Laos was organized under the minister with his chief of cabinet and chief of personnel bureau and had the office of foreign affairs with a director of foreign affairs, a chief of the administrative bureau, and a chief of the accounting bureau, and an office of international conferences with a director of international conferences, a chief of the bureau, and a secretary general of the UNESCO committee. The Ministry of Foreign Affairs of the Democratic Republic of Vietnam acquired a more permanent home with the return of the Ho Chi Minh government to Hanoi in the fall of 1954.

The State of Vietnam applied for membership in the United Nations on December 17, 1951, the Democratic Republic of Vietnam on December 27 and earlier on November 22, 1948, the Kingdom of Cambodia on June 25, 1952, and the Kingdom of Laos on June 30. Involved in the applications was the question of the degree of independence of the states concerned, and also in the case of Vietnam of a divided country under two governments. On September 19, 1952, the Security Council voted 10 to 1 in favor of admitting Cambodia, Laos and the State of Vietnam to the United Nations. The Soviet Union prevented the approval of the French proposal by three vetoes; the Security Council by a vote of 10 to 1 then opposed a Russian suggestion to consider the application of the Democratic Republic of Vietnam. On December 21 the General Assembly approved a French proposal to admit the State of Vietnam by a vote of 40 to 5 with 12 abstentions, Cambodia by 38 to 5 with 14 abstentions, and Laos by 36 to 5 with 14 abstentions. The Soviet bloc voted against the proposal and Indonesia, Burma, and the Philippines abstained. Only in December, 1955, would Cambodia and Laos gain admittance.

The two kingdoms were members, as of early 1954, of FAO, UNESCO, WHO, UPU, and ITU. The State of Vietnam belonged to all these agencies as well as ILO. WMO's membership, it might be noted, also included the Associated States. In April the Economic and Social Council of the United Nations voted, after certain technical steps, to raise the status of Cambodia, Laos, and the State of Vietnam from associate to full membership in the Economic Commission for Asia and the Far East. Although the Democratic Republic of Vietnam did not participate in the agencies of the United Nations, it was active in attending international conferences sponsored by Communists.

In the façade presented to the world the foreign policy of the states of Southeast Asia represents a complexity of motives, techniques, and activities. Although not always clearly defined, the interests of each government—political and ideological, military and strategic, economic and cultural—are motivating factors. In order to implement foreign policy, the employment of strategic and tactical approaches and the use of governmental and nongovernmental agencies, in particular the machinery of the United Nations, are evident. But it should be noted that the implementation does not always reflect a carefully conceived, ironclad plan of action. As far as the actual activities of each state in foreign affairs are concerned, they include the political as associated with diplomacy, the military as occasionally indicated by force or the threat of force, the economic as shown in trade and other matters, and the cultural. On the informational side various media are used—press and publications, radio, motion pictures, information centers, and exchange of persons—but on a somewhat limited basis.

The average person in Southeast Asia has little knowledge of, or interest in, foreign policy. Attitudes toward foreigners are often based on personal contacts. In places where boundaries have recently changed or where refugees flee from neighboring countries, the people in a given locality are more conscious of developments across the frontier. At the same time the basic public apathy should not be unexpected, for it should be stressed that communications are not adequate, literacy is very limited, language barriers are many, and standards of living are generally low. In addition, problems relating to foreign policy present a relatively new challenge. Nevertheless, events are moving rapidly in Southeast Asia, and generalizations that may be true at present may not be valid in the not too distant future. Attitude-forming groups—religious, educational, military, labor, and others—as well as political parties are active in varying degrees of intensity.

As a result of the absence of an articulate public opinion at the present time, foreign policy is largely in the hands of a few people in the capital cities. These men have a wide latitude of operation in determining policy, the decision-making process not involving considerations of public opinion to the extent that it does in the Western democracies. It should also be observed that the men in Southeast Asia who make the decisions on foreign policy have for the most part had little experience in their work and often fall back upon Western practice for precedents. Yet it would be a mistake to ignore the essentially Asian aspect of the decision-making process in the region.

In general the leaders in the states of the area are predominantly occupied with domestic problems, are not profound in their knowledge of world affairs, react to questions of foreign policy on a day-to-day basis and are extremely sensitive to any kind of foreign pressure. For purposes of expediency their public pronouncements do not always reflect personal convictions. Their ability to get accurate information on foreign developments is often hampered by the inexperience of new foreign service representatives abroad. Today, however, it is easier to remedy this situation partly in view of the experience gained at the frequent meetings of numerous international organizations covering a diversity of subjects.

Few systematic efforts are being made in Southeast Asia to stimulate a popular and unbiased interest in foreign relations. Indonesia has an Institute of World Affairs and Burma a Council of World Affairs. The former has been under the direction of the President of the University of Indonesia and the latter under the Secretary of the Rangoon Corporation. Although both are young organizations they are not very active. In the Philippines the Town Meeting of South East Asia has been holding frequent forums. Occasionally other meetings devoted to foreign affairs are held but they are not frequent. In Thailand, not to mention Vietnam, Cambodia, Laos, and the Federation of Malaya, there is little activity. Only in New Delhi does there exist in Asia an outstanding foreign relations institute—the Indian Council of World Affairs. Its scholarly approach to international problems stands in contrast to the Chinese People's Institute of Foreign Affairs in Peking.

4. *Republic of the Philippines*

The foreign policy of the Philippines is based upon close ties with the United States, adherence to the concept of regional collective security, support for genuine nationalist movements among dependent peoples, cultivation of ties with Asian neighbors not in the Communist bloc, and loyalty to the principles of the United Nations. It is a foreign policy that has both realistic and idealistic aspects, arising from a combination of two basic factors, the acquisition of independence from the United States by an evolutionary process and an evaluation of international Communism as constituting a threat to the independence and security of the Republic. Although Philippine nationalism should not be discounted, it has been channeled along lines of coöperation with the former colonial power and with the West in general. At the same time, the sympathy for dependent peoples is genuine and is a reaction to what was once a common colonial status. Loyalty to the United Nations is in some respects an effort to refute charges that the Philippines is too closely tied to the United States. It is also a reflection of Philippine idealism, of hope in the future of a world organization devoted to the betterment of mankind.

Philippine-American relations are the most important consideration in the Department of Foreign Affairs at Padre Faure in Manila. Independence on July 4, 1946, involved a complex political, military, and economic settlement, one that time and events have already begun to alter. A presidential proclamation issued by Harry S Truman withdrew American sovereignty from the Islands and recognized the independence of the Republic. At the same time a treaty of general relations was signed in Manila between the United States and the Philippines, defining in greater detail the transfer of sovereignty. A psychological step of considerable importance was the action of the American Congress permitting the naturalization

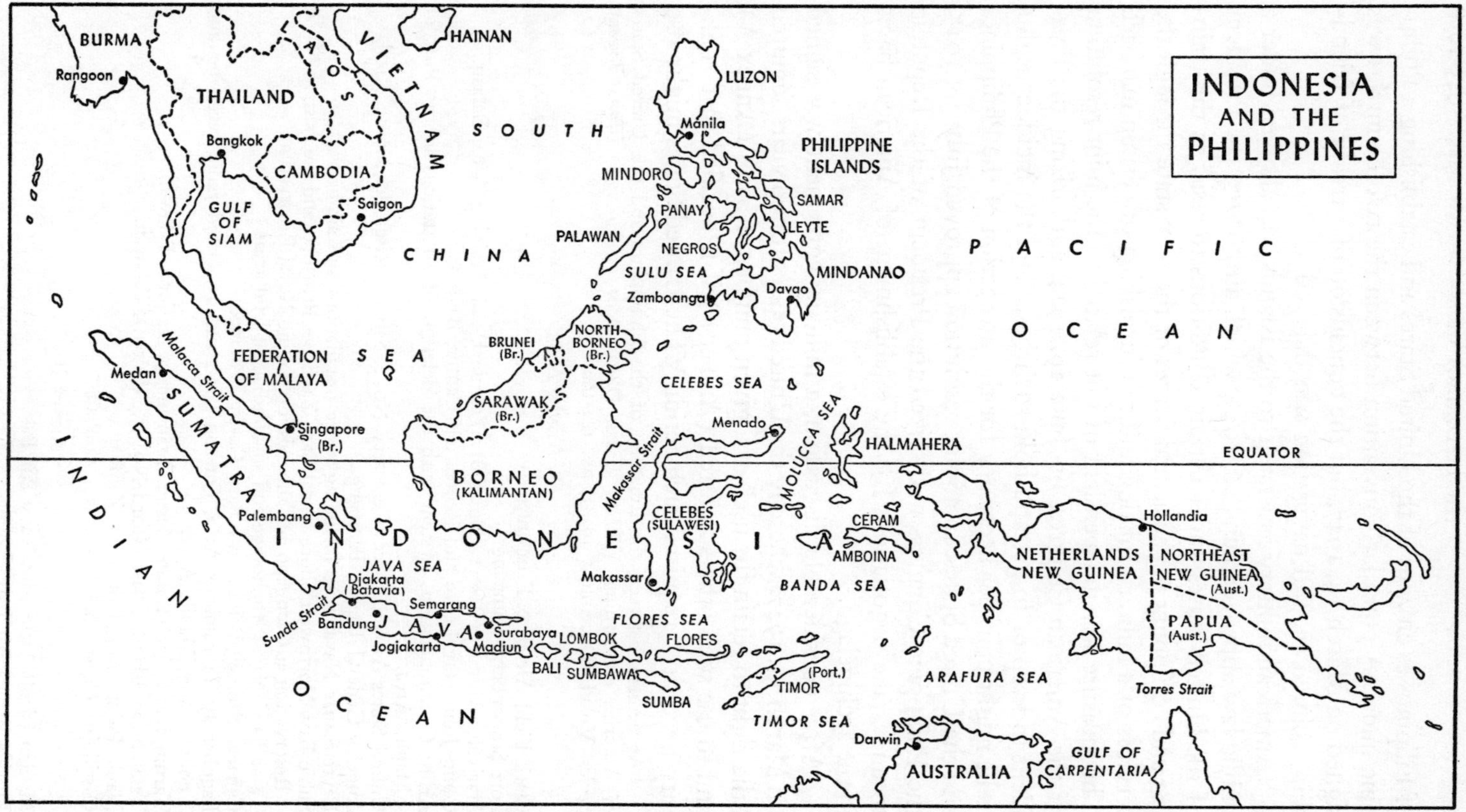
INDONESIA AND THE PHILIPPINES
BURMA
Rangoon
THAILAND
LAOS
VIETNAM
HAINAN
Bangkok
CAMBODIA
Saigon
GULF OF SIAM
SOUTH CHINA SEA
FEDERATION OF MALAYA
Malacca Strait
Medan
SUMATRA
Singapore (Br.)
Palembang
LUZON
Manila
PHILIPPINE ISLANDS
MINDORO
PANAY
SAMAR
LEYTE
PALAWAN
NEGROS
SULU SEA
MINDANAO
Zamboanga
Davao
PACIFIC OCEAN
BRUNEI (Br.)
NORTH BORNEO (Br.)
SARAWAK (Br.)
CELEBES SEA
Menado
MOLUCCA SEA
HALMAHERA
EQUATOR
BORNEO (KALIMANTAN)
Makassar Strait
CELEBES (SULAWESI)
INDONESIA
CERAM
AMBOINA
Hollandia
NETHERLANDS NEW GUINEA
NORTHEAST NEW GUINEA (Aust.)
PAPUA (Aust.)
JAVA SEA
Djakarta (Batavia)
Semarang
Bandung
JAVA
Surabaya
Jogjakarta
Madiun
Sunda Strait
Makassar
BANDA SEA
FLORES SEA
LOMBOK
FLORES
BALI
SUMBAWA
SUMBA
TIMOR
(Port.)
TIMOR SEA
ARAFURA SEA
Torres Strait
Darwin
AUSTRALIA
GULF OF CARPENTARIA
INDIAN OCEAN

of Filipinos as citizens of the United States and establishing a Philippine quota. A consular convention between the two countries was signed on March 14, 1947, but the conclusion of a treaty of friendship, commerce, and navigation was delayed.

American military assistance to the Islands was allowed under a public law approved June 26, 1946, which authorized the President of the United States under certain conditions to assist in the training and equipping of the armed forces of the new state through the services of a military mission and the furnishing of certain matériel. The measure was independent of but related to the joint resolution of the American Congress on June 29, 1944, authorizing the President to keep or to get and hold such bases and the incident rights as he might consider necessary for the protection of the Philippines and the United States. In a joint resolution approved July 28, 1945, the Philippine Congress authorized the President of the Republic to undertake negotiations for the establishment of American bases in the archipelago.

After considerable discussion, a military agreement was signed on March 14, 1947, whereby the United States for 99 years acquired "the right to retain the use" of a given number of bases (Annex A) and to use such others as listed (Annex B) if it decided that "military necessity" required such action.[1] The United States might also

[1] Agreement between the Republic of the Philippines and the United States of America concerning Military Bases, *Department of Foreign Affairs Treaty Series,* Vol. I (December, 1948), pp. 144-160.

ANNEX A

Clark Field Air Base, Pampanga.
Fort Stotsenberg, Pampanga.
Mariveles Military Reservation, POL Terminal and Training Area, Bataan.
Camp John Hay Leave and Recreation Center, Baguio.
Army Communications System with the deletion of all stations in the Port of Manila Area.
United States Armed Forces Cemetery No. 2, San Francisco del Monte, Rizal.
Angeles General Depot, Pampanga.
Leyte-Samar Naval Base including shore installations and air bases.
Subic Bay, Northwest Shore Naval Base, Zambales Province, and the existing Naval Reservation at Olongapo and the existing Baguio Naval Reservation.
Tawi Tawi Naval Anchorage and small adjacent land areas.
Cañacao-Sangley Point Navy Base, Cavite Province.
Bagobantay Transmitter Area, Quezon City, and associated radio receiving and control sites, Manila Area.
Tarumpitao Point (Loran Master Transmitter Station), Palawan.
Talampulan Island, Coast Guard No. 354 (Loran), Palawan.
Naule Point (Loran Station), Zambales.
Castillejos, Coast Guard No. 356, Zambales.

ANNEX B

Mactan Island Army and Navy Air Base.
Florida Blanca Air Base, Pampanga.

ask for the diminution or extension of the base areas under the agreement. No third state could acquire bases in the Islands without the consent of the two parties, but the Security Council of the United Nations upon call might have the use of the areas provided the Philippines and the United States were willing. A week later another accord called for the establishment of an American military mission to assist the Filipinos and for the providing of matériel. Subsequent arrangements were made whereby the Philippines received assistance under the American military aid program to certain states abroad. The Joint United States Military Advisory Group (JUSMAG) became very active in the Islands.

The significance of the agreement relative to American bases in the Asian republic should not be underestimated. By its provisions the new state was tied to the American security system in the Pacific. Neutrality was a policy that could not realistically be followed in world affairs. The American air base at Clark Field in Pampanga or the naval station at Subic Bay were locations which could become enemy targets in wartime or from which the United States might operate against hostile forces. At the same time, it should be pointed out, the Filipino people were in favor of the granting of the bases, for the Americans were in general very popular in the Islands. But, as can be expected, the location and administration of base areas, especially in a newly independent state, raise many opportunities for misunderstanding and conflict.

In the economic field the independence of the Philippines was likewise qualified. The main pillar was the Philippine or Bell Trade Act of April 30, 1946. Under its provisions trade between the United States and the Philippines was regulated for 28 years ending July 3, 1974. Three classes of goods were established. Sugar, cordage, and rice were subject to export quotas to the United States but items in a residuary class were not under this restriction. In both categories the products could enter the United States free of duty through July 3, 1954, after which they became subject to a 5 percent tariff until the end of the year. From January 1, 1955, to January 1, 1973, the tariff would increase at an annual rate of 5 percent. Cigars, coconut oil, tobacco, and buttons belonging to another

---

Aircraft Service Warning Net.
Camp Wallace, San Fernando, La Union.
Puerto Princesa Army and Navy Air Base, including Navy Section Base and Air Warning Sites, Palawan.
Tawi Tawi Naval Base, Sulu Archipelago.
Aparri Naval Air Base.

class were subject to quotas but these products could enter the United States free of duty until the end of 1954. After that date the portion free of duty was progressively reduced until the entire amount of the quota was subject to the full duty as from January 1, 1974. The annual quotas were allocated on the basis of the activities of manufacturers and producers operating in 1940. Imports from the United States were not placed on a quota basis, though following the initial period free of duty ending July 3, 1954, progressively higher tariff rates would be applied until the full Philippine duty was payable.

Other features of the Bell Trade Act also tied the economy to the United States. Provision was made for the preservation of the Philippine peso at the rate of U.S. $0.50. The fixing of the rate between the dollar and the peso as well as the free convertibility of the latter to the former and the unrestricted transfer of funds to the United States could only be altered with the approval of the American chief executive. Moreover, the operation of the Trade Act would be put in abeyance unless the constitution of the Philippines was amended within a "reasonable" period of time to give Americans under a "parity clause" the same rights as Filipinos in the development of the natural resources and public utilities of the Islands. It was only after considerable debate that the Philippine Congress approved the amendment in September, 1946, the people accepting it in a plebiscite the following March.

Controversy in the Philippines over the Bell Trade Act did not subside with the amending of the constitution. The parity clause and currency arrangement were considered an infringement on Philippine sovereignty. It was argued that the act restored a substantial part of the unbalanced economy existing before Pearl Harbor and was not conducive to the best development of the country. Although many Philippine products received immediate tariff advantages in the American market, without which they would have found it difficult to survive under the existing conditions, the transition period toward full American duties was not considered adequate. On the other hand, there were those who firmly believed the Trade Act was a satisfactory solution to a complex problem.

American economic interests in the Philippines, though important, are not of major significance. Around 35,000 United States citizens live in the Islands, excluding government personnel. In 1935 American business investments were estimated at $163,500,000 or 51.9 percent of all in the foreign business category. The inclusion of *rentier* investments would raise the American figure to about $200 million. At the end of 1954 the total investments were estimated to be $350 million and by the middle of 1956 possibly $450 million. As might be expected, the trade of the Philippines has been closely tied to the former mother country. In 1949 over 80 percent of the imports came from the latter and 70 percent of the exports went to her. The percentage of Philippine export cargo carried by American vessels amounted to 33.72. Coconut products, sugar, and Manila hemp or abacá were by far the chief exports to the United States. In 1955 the American share of the total foreign trade of the Philippines had fallen to 63 percent.

Negotiations leading to a revision of the Philippine Trade Act reached a successful conclusion on December 15, 1954. From a technical viewpoint the negotiations centered around an agreement on trade and related matters signed by the two countries on July 4, 1946, based upon the Trade Act. President Elpidio Quirino had previously written President Dwight D. Eisenhower on March 7, 1953, suggesting a reëxamination of the existing trade agreement. The American chief executive replied nine days later that his government would be willing to give consideration to specific proposals advanced by the Philippines. On May 5 the government in Manila made three proposals to the American Embassy and on July 1 the United States indicated that an executive committee would be established to study the matter. The work of the executive committee would be associated with a proposed commission to consider the foreign economic policy of the United States.

On March 22, 1954, it was announced by the United States and the Philippines that consultations would take place on the trade relations between the two countries and that both congresses would be requested to enact legislation providing for the extension of reciprocal free trade for 18 months after July 3, 1954. The necessary legislation was passed, and delegations were appointed by the two governments to conduct the negotiations, Senator José P. Laurel being chairman of the Philippine Economic Mission. The trade talks, opening formally on September 20, lasted almost three months. Although there were sharp differences of opinion, and some of the Philippine leaders believed that politicians were at a disadvantage before technicians, a compromise was reached which was referred to the respective governments for approval.

Among the terms of the Laurel-Langley agreement were the

yielding to the Philippines of control over its currency, the granting on a reciprocal basis to citizens of one state the right to do business in the other, the making of parity rights reciprocal for citizens of each country in the territory of the other, the imposing of quantitative restrictions on a reciprocal basis and the ending of the prohibition against the Philippines' having export taxes. These provisions gave the Asian republic much more independence in the economic field and helped to meet the rising tide of Filipino nationalism. Provisions were also made for increases in tariff preferences for Philippine goods going to the United States, for decreases in tariff preferences for American goods entering the Philippines, for the ending of quota allocation limitations on Philippine products subject to quotas in American markets, for increases in the duty-free quotas of Philippine products that are subject to declining duty-free quotas, for the ending of most absolute quotas on products to the United States, and for the terminating of the Philippine exchange tax and its substitution by an import levy to be gradually reduced and ended. The Philippines might also ask the Congress of the United States for an increase in the sugar quota under certain conditions. Full tariffs on each other's products would come into effect in 1974.

The actual revision of the legal basis of the trade relationship between the United States and the Philippines necessitated an act of Congress in Washington amending the Philippine Trade Act of 1946 to allow an executive agreement embodying the negotiated changes. The Philippine Congress also approved the changes. On September 6, 1955, an executive agreement containing the provisions with clarifications was signed by American and Philippine officials in Washington, entering into force on January 1, 1956. An additional agreement was reached in an exchange of notes on September 6 concerning the status based on reciprocity of Philippine and American traders and investors entering the territories of the respective parties.

In urging the Ways and Means Committee of the House of Representatives in Washington on May 16, 1955, to approve the revision, William J. Sebald, Acting Assistant Secretary of State for Far Eastern Affairs, frankly noted that the dissatisfaction in the Philippines over the Bell Trade Act had never assumed the proportions of a grave rift but there was always a real certainty that it might occur. At the signing of the executive agreement on September 6 General Carlos P. Romulo observed that the faith of the

United States in President Ramon Magsaysay was the most important factor in approval of the revision on Capitol Hill.

The Philippine Rehabilitation Act of 1946 was one of the major steps in the American program of postwar aid to the Islands. Under it an effort was made to compensate persons and firms in legitimate cases for property damage during the war, to restore and improve public services and properties, and to train Filipino technicians. Significantly no claims over $500 would be honored unless the Philippines accepted the Bell Trade Act. On January 12, 1950, it was estimated by Secretary of State Dean Acheson that the United States had given the Philippines 2 billion dollars' worth of overall assistance since V-J Day.

Despite the American economic aid and progress in urban industries and agricultural production, the financial standing of the Asian republic became increasingly grave. In the winter of 1950 President Elpidio Quirino suggested to President Harry Truman the sending of an American economic survey mission to the Islands. Although the Philippine President later tried to make the project a joint undertaking, the Economic Survey Mission under the capable leadership of Daniel W. Bell, a Washington banker and former Under-Secretary of the Treasury, was solely responsible to the President of the United States. The functions of the mission were to survey the economic situation in the country, to make recommendations by which the young republic could help itself, and to suggest ways for the United States to assist in the rehabilitation of the economy. The Bell mission arrived in Manila in July and its report was released in October.

Urging basic economic, land, and fiscal reforms by the Philippine government, the mission recommended that, conditional upon this effort, the United States should offer the new republic over a five-year period up to $250 million in carefully supervised grants and loans. In November the President of the Philippines and William C. Foster, the American Economic Coöperation Administrator in the country, reached an agreement at Baguio regarding the implementation of the Bell recommendations. As is true in all American aid programs in underdeveloped areas, a careful balance had to be made between not interfering in domestic affairs and insuring in so far as possible that the purposes for which aid is given are respected.

In a relatively new but important field of assistance the American Embassy in Manila announced in March, 1956, that Secretary of

State John Foster Dulles had told President Magsaysay that the Philippines had been selected as the site for the Asian Nuclear Center, a project proposed by the United States at the Singapore meeting in 1955 of the Consultative Committee of the Colombo Plan. The Asian Nuclear Center would serve a large region, training technicians and using its research in the peaceful uses of atomic energy for the economic and social welfare of Asians and of mankind. At the meeting of the Consultative Committee in Wellington, New Zealand, in December, 1956, the United States indicated it was willing to contribute about $20 million for the establishment of the Center, the money coming from the President's Asian regional development fund. The United States had already promised the Philippines an atomic research reactor, and coöperation in the atomic field has been the subject of bilateral agreement.

As international tension occasioned by the cold war mounted in Northeast and Southeast Asia, the leaders of the Philippines sought a formal, ironclad alliance with the United States. Concern was even expressed in Manila over the smallness of American forces stationed in Luzon and the restricted development of American bases. On January 12, 1950, Secretary Acheson reaffirmed the policy of the United States to defend the Philippines. Shortly after the Communist aggression in Korea, President Truman in his famous statement of June 27 asserted *inter alia* that American military aid to the Philippines would be accelerated and that United States forces in the Islands would be strengthened.

Negotiations relative to a Japanese peace treaty brought to the forefront the question of a mutual assistance pact between the two countries. The Philippines was very apprehensive of Japan and believed that the proposed peace terms were too lenient. A treaty of alliance with the United States would offset some of the opposition in Manila. On August 30, 1951, the two republics signed in Washington a mutual defense pact similar to one signed two days later by Australia, New Zealand, and the United States in San Francisco. Article IV, the heart of the treaty, asserted: "Each Party recognizes that an armed attack in the Pacific area on either of the Parties would be dangerous to its own peace and safety and declares that it would act to meet the common dangers in accordance with its constitutional processes."[2] Indefinite in dura-

[2] Mutual Defense Treaty between the Republic of the Philippines and the United States of America, *Department of Foreign Affairs Treaty Series*, Vol. II (January, 1953), p. 14.

tion, the pact called for consultation from time to time on the implementation of the agreement and whenever either party thought the security, territorial integrity, or political independence of one of them was threatened in the Pacific by an external armed attack. On June 23, 1954, an exchange of notes between the United States and the Philippines formally established a United States-Philippine Council for purposes of consultation.

The negotiations leading to the Southeast Asia Collective Defense Treaty or Manila Pact occasioned further assurances from the United States. The election of Ramon Magsaysay to the presidency of the Philippines had brought to power the *Nacionalista* Party. Its foreign policy spokesman had long been Senator Claro M. Recto, who had for some time raised a number of questions about the real effectiveness of the defense ties between the United States and the Philippines. At a meeting in Manila on September 4 of the Council of Foreign Ministers under the Mutual Defense Treaty Secretary of State Dulles asserted: "If the Philippines were attacked the United States would act immediately. We expect the Philippines to contribute to its own security to the exent of its capabilities. To that would be added United States air, naval, and logistical support. The United States will take all practical measures to maintain the security of the Philippines against external attack. The United States intends to maintain and use its air and naval bases in the Philippines. . . . The President of the United States has ordered the Seventh Fleet to protect Formosa from invasion by Communist aggressors. In the case of the Philippines, no specific orders are required; our forces would automatically react."[3] These viewpoints were emphasized on September 7 in a note from Secretary Dulles to Carlos P. Garcia, Secretary of Foreign Affairs. Although the Philippine government considers the Mutual Defense Treaty of 1951 more valuable than the Manila Pact, it still wanted more explicit American assurances.

On July 4, 1956, the Philippines had been a sovereign state for ten years. The special relations between the United States and the Asian republic continued in many ways but the latter was acting more and more on its own. President Ramon Magsaysay symbolized

[3] Quoted in the *Manila Daily Bulletin*, September 10, 1954. The text of a joint communiqué on the meeting asserts: ". . . Secretary Dulles said, I wish to state in the most emphatic terms that the United States will honor fully its commitments under the Mutual Defense Treaty. If the Philippines were attacked, the United States would attack immediately." Text of the Joint Communiqué Issued by the United States-Philippine Council on September 4, 1954, Malacañang, Manila, *Department of Foreign Affairs Review*, Vol. II (March, 1955), p. 28.

at the time the alliance between the two republics while Senator Claro M. Recto represented the Asian school of thought. The conflict between Magsaysay and Recto was especially bitter during the campaign leading to the off-year elections on November 8, 1955. The President, in fact, refused to allow the Senator to run on the *Nacionalista* ticket for reëlection and the latter became a "guest" candidate of the Liberals. On July 28 Magsaysay in a statement about a report that Recto would try for the presidency in 1957 said the Senator could run as the candidate of Mao Tse-tung and he (the President) as a foe of Communism and a friend of America. Recto for his part had accused Magsaysay of being a puppet of the United States. He won his seat in the Senate but was low on the list of victors, a tribute to the President's popularity.

The specific issues between the Philippines and the United States after a decade of independence for the former centered around the American bases in the Islands, the importation of Virginia leaf tobacco, the wages and benefits of Filipino workers in Guam and Wake, and American aid to the Asian republic. In an address to the House of Representatives on March 12, 1956, Congressman Pedro Lopez called attention to the rise of anti-Americanism in the Philippines. He asserted:

> If the U.S. government and people permit vested interests, like the tobacco coterie [in the United States], to carry the ball, so to speak, and daub a paint of crude mercenariness on the American mission of humanity and security in this part of the world, then they might just as well forget about their darling favorite, President Magsaysay, for under such adverse climate he will have become completely impotent to render effective help in protecting, much less advancing, American-Filipino security interests; they might just as well have the Voice of America and the USIS pack lock, stock, barrel, radio towers and printing presses,[4] and order them home, and have the carrier U.S.S. *Shangrila* [*Shangri-La*] and all other units of the Seventh Fleet sent back to Pearl Harbor, for what need do we have of the thundering jet planes, the smooth, silky radio voice of persuasion and the beautiful brochures of self-praises, if Filipino hearts no longer belong to Daddy?[5]

The problem over the American bases in the Philippines did not center around their retention. So far there has been no significant outright demand for a termination of the American bases. The

[4] A Voice of America receiving station in Baguio picks up programs from the United States and relays them to a transmitter at Poro Point for medium-wave broadcasting in Southeast Asia. The United States has facilities in Manila for printing material in a large number of Asian languages for distribution throughout Southeast Asia.

[5] Pedro Lopez speech, *Manila Daily Bulletin*, April 9, 1956.

future, however, is uncertain and the example of the fate of the British bases in Ceylon, Trincomalee and Negombo, under Prime Minister S. W. R. D. Bandaranaike is for every Filipino to see. President Magsaysay in April, 1956, observed that among the subjects related to the base areas that should be negotiated with the Americans were "the question of the ownership of the bases, the expansion of existing bases and establishment of new ones, clarification of the nature and extent of the authority of the United States government within the bases."[6] He believed the agreement on the base areas should be renegotiated but there were no problems that could not be satisfactorily settled. At the same time the President stressed that the "best time to enter upon negotiations would be in an atmosphere of mutual cordiality, shorn of emotionalism and conducive to speedy agreement."[7]

A number of developments have served to intensify Philippine sensitivities concerning the bases. In early 1954 United States Attorney General Herbert Brownell, Jr., issued a legal opinion, reminiscent of a previous American position, to the effect that the United States *could* claim absolute ownership of the bases in the Philippines, not just their use, after the transfer of sovereignty. Senator Recto wrote a detailed refutation of the Brownell thesis, claiming the Philippines owned the base lands but granted their use to the United States in the agreement of 1947. Nationalistic passions were aroused in the Asian republic. In July, 1955, two Filipinos appointed by President Magsaysay, Ambassador Felino Neri and Congressman Enrique Corpus, reported that conditions were not favorable to Filipino workers in the American Naval Reservation at Olongapo. The investigation arose from charges in a prominent Philippine newspaper. In May, 1956, President Magsaysay went to Tarlac province to investigate the impounding by authorities of Clark Field Air Base of four truckloads of manganese extracted from the United States-claimed base area by Filipino miners. In the middle of the year differences between American military personnel and Philippine authorities in Angeles near Clark Field led to the city's being placed out-of-bounds for a number of weeks to American military personnel.

On July 3 President Magsaysay and Vice-President Richard Nixon of the United States issued a joint statement in Manila indicating *inter alia* that the United States fully recognized the sov-

[6] Ramon Magsaysay interview, *Manila Daily Bulletin,* April 9, 1956.
[7] *Ibid.*

ereignty of the Philippines over the bases and that it had officially taken this position since July 4, 1946. In August formal negotiations were opened between an American and a Philippine panel. The United States in the meantime sent to Manila for transfer to the government of the Philippines the title claims and title papers of the bases. It soon developed that questions of legal jurisdiction over American military personnel for offenses committed against Filipinos within the base areas along with other items were a serious stumbling block to the successful conclusion of negotiations. The discussions were "recessed" in December. As an earnest of American interest in the security of the Western Pacific, Cubi Point Naval Air Station on Subic Bay, the largest of its kind in the Far East, was formally put into operation by the United States on July 25.

The importation of Virginia leaf tobacco into the Philippines has been a subject of considerable hard feeling. A Philippine law limits the importation of tobacco to the amount in excess of local production that the government determines necessary. The government wishes to save foreign exchange and encourage local production. A special study mission of the Committee on Foreign Affairs of the American House of Representatives in a report based on travel in a large number of states, especially in Asia, stated on March 14, 1956, that American tobacco exporters believed they had an agreement to send 9 million pounds to the Islands in 1955. While the commodity was on the way they were told that the Filipino who had made the agreement did not have the authority to do so. In the end the issue was resolved by admitting the tobacco.

A Philippine viewpoint on the controversy was presented in the speech of Congressman Lopez in the House of Representatives on March 12, 1956, when he stated that vested interests in the United States had tried to dump the tobacco whether or not the Philippines needed it or could afford it. "With a powerhouse lobby in Washington," he said, "these interests convinced an influential group of legislators in the United States congress that the tobacco industry was the victim of a doublecross from Philippine government representatives who had 'welshed' on a gentleman's agreement. . . ."[8] The Congressman noted that 6 million pounds got in without payment of tariff, 3 million pounds with payment, and efforts were being made to have the Philippines import 7 million more. Lopez accused the tobacco lobbyists in Washington of trying to prevent Congress from approving any legislation favorable to

[8] Lopez, *op. cit.*

the Philippines. This included any increase in the sugar quota allotted the Asian republic. In fact, he said that efforts were made in Washington to penalize the sugar quota of the Islands as determined by the Laurel-Langley trade agreement.

Philippine concern over the wages and benefits of Filipino laborers in Guam and Wake has not been a new development. The subject has been discussed in the Manila Congress on different occasions. It is estimated that around 13,000 Filipinos are living in Guam, some 10,000 working on military projects. In the Philippines there are charges that the salaries of Filipino workers in American businesses are discriminatory.

The American aid program to the Asian republic has been criticized both on the grounds of its amount and of its kind. Among others José P. Laurel, Jr., Speaker of the House of Representatives, has accused the United States of giving economic and military aid that is small as compared with that to some countries not so friendly to Washington. Senator Claro M. Recto has asserted that American assistance has been directed at prolonging Philippine economic dependency upon the United States by blocking industrial development. American military aid has also been criticized on grounds of being deficient. Both President Magsaysay and Vice-President Garcia defended American assistance programs in the Republic as being in the best interests of the Filipinos. Indeed, it is estimated that by the middle of 1956 total American aid since the war had risen to around $2500 million.[9] In another important step the United States on June 25, 1957, made an agreement to sell the Philippines $10.3 million worth of surplus farm products, the payment in pesos to be loaned for economic development, granted for the common defense, and used for a number of other purposes including educational exchange. Magsaysay came to look upon much of the criticism of the United States as a way of attacking himself, especially his land reform program.

The policy of the United States toward the Philippines is indicative of the *basic* objectives of American diplomacy toward all the states of Southeast Asia. These include support for political independence, encouragement of friendly relations among the countries themselves, with the United States and other members of the non-Communist world, understanding of the viewpoints and sensi-

[9] At the same time the Philippines has claims against the United States totaling over $860 million. *Official Gazette*, Republic of the Philippines, Vol. 52 (April, 1956), pp. 1909-1910.

tivities of the states of the area, and aid of various kinds when wanted and requested and when it supplements home efforts and looks toward a self-supporting basis.[10]

Secretary of State Dulles observed on March 6, 1956, that the expression of American foreign policy in Asia is found "in our active participation in SEATO, in other mutual security pacts, in our bilateral arrangements for economic aid, technical assistance, cultural exchange, in our membership in the Colombo Plan for economic development in Asia and in the United Nations Economic Commission for Asia and the Far East, and in our bilateral agreements for sharing knowledge and materials to advance peaceful uses of atomic energy."[11]

In addition to the Philippines, Indonesia, Burma, Thailand, Cambodia, Laos, and Vietnam have received help from the United States. The figures have varied from country to country and the type of assistance—economic, technical, and military—has not been uniform. A succession of United States agencies has administered in one respect or various respects the programs—the Economic Coöperation Administration (ECA), the Mutual Security Agency (MSA), the Foreign Operations Administration (FOA), the Technical Coöperation Administration (TCA) and the International Coöperation Administration (ICA). The loans of the Export-Import Bank have facilitated American policy in Southeast Asia. In 1957 the Development Loan Fund was established to assist in financing economic development. Technical assistance in the field of atomic energy is increasing and has wide ramifications. The disposal of

[10] Kenneth T. Young, "The United States and Southeast Asia," *The Department of State Bulletin,* Vol. XXXIII (November 21, 1955), p. 843. Walter S. Robertson, Assistant Secretary of State for Far Eastern Affairs, significantly observed in a speech on August 8, 1955:

"Although in American eyes no problem stands out more prominently in Asia, especially in Southeast Asia, than the threat of Communist aggression and subversion, we realize that to most of the leaders and peoples of this vast region the threat of Communism is of no more than secondary concern and that their interests and emotions are centered on such questions as 'colonialism,' 'nationalism,' and 'neutralism.' . . . What we want in Asia is what we want everywhere—a world made up of independent, responsible, democratic countries whose governments are devoted to the peaceful development of their own territory and to the welfare and personal freedom of their own people. We want this because it is the only kind of world in which the values we put above life can endure. In this picture there is no room for imperialism or colonialism, and we must continue to resist them." Walter S. Robertson, "The United States Looks at South and Southeast Asia," *The Department of State Bulletin,* Vol. XXXIII (August 22, 1955), pp. 295, 297.

[11] Statement by Secretary Dulles at Opening Session (Second Meeting of SEATO Council), March 6, 1956, *The Department of State Bulletin,* Vol. XXXIV (March 19, 1956), p. 449.

American surplus agriculture commodities under the Agricultural Trade Development and Assistance Act of 1954 is another aspect of importance. Aid is also given specifically through the Fulbright and Smith-Mundt programs based upon cultural exchange. Private American assistance is forthcoming from such foundations as the Asia, Ford, and Rockefeller. The United States Information Agency for its part through its offices in Southeast Asia tries to portray Americans at their best.

In its relations with Spain, the Republic of the Philippines, especially under the influence of Elpidio Quirino, sought to cultivate close ties. Quirino, prior to his going to Malacañang,[12] had been vice-president and concurrently secretary of foreign affairs. Although he later relinquished the portfolio, he took a deep interest in international relations and guided the foreign policy of his country. In addition to introducing the Spanish language and Roman Catholicism, Spain had left in the Islands many of the characteristics found in the Latin American states she had once ruled as colonies. Late in the Second World War, in April, 1945, Spain had broken diplomatic relations with Japan over her atrocities against Spanish subjects in the Philippines, and the Madrid government later claimed $20,278,000 for wartime losses in life and property in the Islands. In January, 1957, Japan agreed to pay Spain the equivalent of $5.5 million before the end of March.

Philippine-Spanish relations were complicated after the war by the hostility in the world to the regime of General Francisco Franco. This sentiment was indicated by the resolution of the General Assembly of the United Nations, December 12, 1946, recommending Spanish exclusion from conferences as well as from the specialized agencies of the United Nations and the withdrawal from Madrid of the heads of missions. At this particular time the Philippines did not have diplomatic relations with Spain but missions at the legation level were shortly established. After periodic discussion the General Assembly finally on November 4, 1950, adopted a resolution, one of whose sponsors was the Philippines, lifting in effect the ban on Spain. In December, 1955, the Asian republic supported the admission of Spain to the United Nations.

Beginning with a treaty of friendship signed on September 27, 1947, the Philippines and Spain further cemented their relations

[12] The first official order issued by President Ramon Magsaysay changed the spelling of Malacañan (the Philippine "White House") to Malacañang.

with a treaty on civil rights and consular prerogatives on May 20, 1948, a treaty on academic degrees and the exercise of professions on March 4, 1949, a cultural treaty on the same date, and an air transport agreement on October 6, 1951. The legations of the two countries were raised to the status of embassies on January 4, 1951. Later President Quirino visited Spain and the Spanish foreign minister came to Manila.

Basically the relations between the Philippines and Spain are cultural in nature, there being no issues to mar the friendship between the two countries. Interesting was the fact that the agreements on September 26, 1953, between Spain and the United States, the two former mother countries of the Philippines, which provided for American military facilities in Spain as well as economic and military end-item assistance from the United States, created hardly any notice in the Republic of the Philippines. The result of the Spanish-American entente, as far as the Asian country was concerned, was to place the three states—Spain, the United States, and the Philippines—in the same camp.

In contrast to the cordiality between Manila and Madrid, Japanese-Philippine relations after V-J Day were stormy for many years. Before the Second World War about 30,000 Japanese resided in the Philippines of whom around 18,000 lived in Davao where they practically monopolized the abacá production. Japanese entrepreneur investments were estimated at $25 million to $30 million. After V-J Day the Nipponese were repatriated and the Filipinos did not want to see them back. As far as the Filipinos who collaborated during the Japanese occupation are concerned, they are generally exonerated if it is believed that they acted in the best interests of the people by serving as a shield between them and the conquerors.

As a member of the Far Eastern Commission, the Philippines had a share in making policy toward occupied Japan. The new republic came to stand for a "tough" policy in any Japanese settlement. This attitude was especially reflected on the question of reparations where the Filipinos claimed about $8 billion worth, of which over $5 billion arose from damages to industrial plants and private property, and over $3 billion from a government claim for goods and services used by the Japanese during the occupation through the issuance of Nipponese military currency. Along with a "tough" reparations policy the Filipinos were greatly concerned about the possible rearming of Japan. They were fearful that a militant Nippon would once again seek to create a New Order in Greater East Asia. Nevertheless, these considerations did not prevent the resumption of trade between the two countries. And the Philippines was willing to work in the future with a nonmilitant, democratic Japan for the preservation of peace in Asia and the world.

Under the circumstances it is not surprising that negotiations for a Japanese peace treaty were carefully followed in Manila and that the proposed reparations clauses were a subject of particular interest. In the Far Eastern Commission the Philippines had pressed vigorously its claim to reparations. Although the Republic received goods valued at more than $10 million as advance reparations from Japan, the amount was only a drop that the Philippines hoped would turn into a stream. In summarizing the "fight for reparations" from 1945 to 1950, General Carlos P. Romulo, Secretary of Foreign Affairs, observed on October 10, 1951, that although his government from the beginning had followed "a consistent and unwavering policy" of seeking proper reparations, the solution to the problem had been delayed because the Allied powers involved in the controversy could not reach a compromise relative to their reparations shares and the Soviet Union had blocked American proposals to create an inter-Allied reparations committee or to call a reparations conference. Romulo noted that as a result of these failures and in view of the changing power relations in Asia, the United States had reversed its policy toward Japan, which had gradually become "a major prize in the struggle for power between the free world and the Communist world."[13]

In the latter part of 1950 the United States circulated to the members of the Far Eastern Commission an outline of the general terms which it considered appropriate in a peace treaty with Japan. Included was a proposal which, in the viewpoint of the Philippines, constituted "a total waiver of reparations properly so called."[14] In March, 1951, an American draft peace treaty was circulated although it was revised a number of times, the final revision under British-American auspices being issued on August 13. After receiving the first draft of the peace treaty, the President of the Philippines created a committee of 15 members to advise him on policy during the negotiations. Basically the Philippines sought in

[13] Address by General Carlos P. Romulo, October 10, 1951, Division of International Information, Department of Foreign Affairs, Manila, Philippines.
[14] *Ibid.*

the peace treaty to have Japan accept complete responsibility for the damage she had caused during the conflict, to make certain that a partial waiver of reparations would represent an act of compassion on the part of the victors and not a matter of right for the Japanese, and to broaden as far as possible the nature of the reparations Japan would pay.

In the negotiations the Philippine proposals in addition to the American underwent modifications. In the final treaty the Filipinos were pleased to see at least the provisions that "Japan should pay reparations to the Allied Powers for the damage and suffering caused by it during the war" and that she "will promptly enter into negotiations with Allied Powers so desiring, whose present territories were occupied by Japanese forces and damaged by Japan, with a view to assisting to compensate those countries for the cost of repairing the damage done, by making available the services of the Japanese people in production, salvaging, and other work for the Allied Powers in question."[15] The Filipinos were glad to have the adverb "presently" appear in the clause recognizing that "the resources of Japan are not presently sufficient, if it is to maintain a viable economy, to make complete reparation for all such damage and suffering and at the same time meet its other obligations."[16] The reparations part in the treaty certainly did not meet all the desiderata of the Filipinos but Romulo believed that their "positive and persistent representations" had a good effect.[17]

Although apprehension in Manila about the revival of a militant Japan was partially met by the mutual defense pact with the United States, the Asian republic was not satisfied over the absence of a prohibition on Japanese rearmament in the peace treaty.[18] The Philippines had previously suggested that the United Nations

[15] Treaty of Peace with Japan, *Record of Proceedings, Conference for the Conclusion and Signature of the Treaty of Peace with Japan*, Department of State Publication 4392, p. 319.

[16] *Ibid.*

[17] Romulo, *op. cit.*

[18] Under Article 5 the "Allied Powers for their part recognize that Japan as a sovereign nation possesses the inherent right of individual or collective self-defense referred to in Article 51 of the Charter of the United Nations and that Japan may voluntarily enter into collective security arrangements" and under Article 6, "all occupation forces of the Allied Powers shall be withdrawn from Japan as soon as possible after the coming into force of the present Treaty, and in any case not later than 90 days thereafter. Nothing in this provision shall, however, prevent the stationing or retention of foreign armed forces in Japanese territory under or in consequence of any bilateral or multilateral agreements which have been or may be made between one or more of the Allied Powers, on the one hand, and Japan on the other." Treaty of Peace with Japan, *op. cit.*, pp. 315-316.

should supervise the educational policies of Japan for 20 years and that the world organization should have the right to intervene over the same period of time to keep the supremacy of the civil over the military arm of government. These proposals were not written into the peace treaty, for the atmosphere of reconciliation was dominant in the drafting of the pact.

In evaluating their security status, however, the Filipinos noted that the mutual assistance agreement between their country and the United States was sufficiently broad in scope to include action in the case of aggression from either Japanese or Communist sources. Although the Asian republic realized the possible threat of international Communism, and even had proposed in the Japanese peace settlement the placing of Formosa under a trusteeship of the United Nations to prevent the Chinese Communists from taking over the island, the Manila government in its desire for a mutual assistance pact with the United States had been motivated chiefly by the fear of a Japanese military revival. The broader aspects of the mutual defense treaty were considered a gain.

As a result of the successful negotiation of the security pact and of the final reparations clauses, the Philippines attended the Japanese Peace Conference at San Francisco held from September 4 to 8, 1951. Exploratory conversations on reparations were conducted by Japanese and Philippine representatives at the Conference, and Secretary Romulo reported that Prime Minister Shigeru Yoshida of Japan assured him of his country's readiness "to do all that is humanly possible to repair the damage that was wrought by the Japanese Army in the Philippines."[19] Nevertheless, Secretary Romulo in his speech before a plenary session of the Conference was extremely critical of Japan, noted that the peace treaty was short in a number of respects, and concluded that "before we extend the hand of forgiveness and brotherhood, we shall await some clear sign from you [Japan] of spiritual contrition and renewal."[20] Since the Conference rules did not allow amendments to the treaty, the Philippines made the best of the situation and signed the pact.

The battle for ratification quickly began. Under the constitution of the Republic a two-thirds vote of all the members was necessary in the Senate. It was impossible to keep the issue out of partisan politics, for the opposition party, the *Nacionalista*, and the administration party, the Liberal, were bitter rivals for power. In

[19] Romulo, *op. cit.*

[20] Romulo speech, *Record of Proceedings, Conference for the Conclusion and Signature of the Treaty of Peace with Japan*, p. 233.

the off-year elections of November, 1951, the *Nacionalistas* scored impressive gains resulting in a close division of the Senate. The reparations clauses in the treaty were the principal object of criticism. Negotiations with the Japanese who sent a mission to Manila in January, 1952, under Juichi Tsushima to discuss "basic principles and working arrangements" leading to a settlement were not successful.

As the time approached for the coming into effect of the Japanese peace treaty—April 28, 1952, proved to be the date—special efforts were made by the administration in Manila to secure Senate approval. Secretary of Foreign Affairs, J. M. Elizalde, in a statement before the Committee on Foreign Relations on April 4 and again on April 23 presented the case for ratification. He stressed the need to end the state of war with Japan, the overall requirements of security in the Pacific against Communism, and the desirability of establishing normal trade relations with the former enemy. Senator Lorenzo Sumulong, Chairman of the Committee on Foreign Relations, suggested a declaration, which would have constituted a reservation, to accompany the approval of the treaty by the Philippine Senate. The American Embassy in Manila noted that in the viewpoint of the Department of State no change in the treaty could be made unilaterally and alterations would have to be accepted by all the parties before the ratification of the Philippines could be deposited.

In the latter part of 1952, the Philippine Secretary of Foreign Affairs decided to seek the good offices of the United States in the reparations controversy. According to Romulo, the Washington government had "given us formal assurances that it will use its good offices to assist us in obtaining reparations from Japan under the treaty."[21] New proposals were presented by the Nipponese mission in Manila, and in December a delegation from Tokyo led by Eiji Wajima arrived in the Philippines on its way to a conference of Japanese diplomats in New Delhi. Although the Wajima mission was not successful, discussions on the Nipponese salvage of sunken vessels in the Philippines made progress. An exchange of notes between the two Asian states on January 24, 1953, provided for a Japanese survey of the sunken vessels. On the following March 12 the Philippines and Japan made an interim agreement on the salvage of the ships but implementation was slow.

Once again the preparations for a national election, this time

[21] Romulo speech, October 10, 1951, *op. cit.*

for the presidency, all the membership of the House of Representatives, and a third of the Senate, made impossible any successful negotiations. Despite the failure of the Senate to take action in favor of the Japanese peace treaty, it should be noted that foreign policy was not in practical terms an issue in the campaign.[22] The victory of the *Nacionalistas* in November placed both the executive and legislative branches in the hands of one party. With the inauguration of President Magsaysay it fell to the *Nacionalistas* to negotiate a settlement with Japan.

Meanwhile Philippine-Japanese relations continued to function on an abnormal basis. Trade was subject to barter arrangements periodically extended. Only a temporary air traffic agreement with Japan made it possible for the Philippines to include that country in commercial airline operations. The need for a fisheries treaty existed but under the circumstances it could not be negotiated. The Philippine mission in Tokyo and the Japanese in Manila functioned under technical handicaps which could only be removed by normal diplomatic relations.

In an effort to reach a permanent settlement of the reparations controversy, the new Philippine Vice-President and concurrently Secretary of Foreign Affairs, Carlos P. Garcia, and Katsumi Ohno, Chief of the Japanese Mission, entered into discussions and reached a preliminary agreement. After a special Nipponese delegation under Shozo Murata arrived in Manila, negotiations formally began on April 17, 1954, between the two parties. The climate of the negotiations was especially unfavorable, for it was impossible to keep the discussions confidential. Senator Claro M. Recto led the opposition bloc to the Japanese proposals, and on April 21 President Magsaysay after consultation with a group of key senators rejected the Nipponese suggestions. Nevertheless, the Philippine leaders decided two days later that the points of disagreement should be referred to a conference of the reparations panels of the two participants. In a note sent to Ambassador Murata it was stated that the previous Garcia-Ohno understanding constituted "merely a starting point for the formal negotiation of a reparations agreement between our two countries."[23] On the same day Magsaysay announced that he was sending a commission to Japan to ascertain her capacity to pay reparations. He realistically noted on

[22] Russell H. Fifield, "The Challenge to Magsaysay," *Foreign Affairs*, Vol. 33 (October, 1954), p. 151.

[23] *Official Gazette*, Republic of the Philippines, Vol. 50 (April, 1954), p. cxiv.

April 27 that "there has been too much talk on this whole question of Japanese reparations. It is time to get facts and make use of those facts, without rumors, gossips, or speculation."[24] Under the circumstances it is not surprising that the Murata mission failed.

In the fall of 1954 the Philippines took the initiative in trying to reach a reparations settlement with Japan. President Magsaysay appointed Felino Neri, one of his key advisers on foreign affairs, to be in charge of the effort. On March 5, 1955, the President sent a personal message to Prime Minister Hatoyama suggesting immediate efforts to reach a solution. Three days later the Japanese leader informed the Philippine president of his agreement. During April Philippine and Japanese panels met in Tokyo, the former listing specific reparations items that were wanted and the latter considering their availability in Japan. On May 6 Ambassador Neri went to Tokyo to discuss figures and plans. Early in June he returned to Manila and reported on the results of the negotiations. On June 8 the Philippine government accepted a salvage proposal wherein a reduction of 19 percent in the cost basis of Japanese salvage services would be credited toward the reparations payment. On June 15 the Manila authorities approved the tentative reparations formula of $800 million worked out in the discussions. After the off-year elections in the Philippines in November and the further consideration of reparations in Japan, the latter on March 15, 1956, informed the former of its readiness for formal negotiations.

On May 9 the Philippines and Japan signed a reparations agreement providing for Japan to grant within a maximum of 20 years $550 million worth of reparations—$500 million in capital goods, $30 million in services, and $20 million in the form of price reduction on items the Philippines buys from Japan in normal trade outside reparations. In a separate agreement the Japanese government would expedite from private industrial sources in the nation long-term credits for capital goods, available to Philippine private enterprise, up to the amount of $250 million. With the final approval of the reparations settlement and the San Francisco peace treaty by the Senate in Manila, the way was paved for the establishment of normal relations between Japan and the Philippines. Felino Neri was sent as ambassador to Nippon.

In terms of long-range effects the reparations settlement will probably result in closer economic relations between Japan and the Philippines and their respective businessmen. At the same time it

[24] *Ibid.*, p. cxx.

should contribute to the further industrialization of the island republic and the more rapid growth of trade between it and the outside world. The share of the United States in the import market of the Philippines will decrease as a fraction of the whole but rapid economic growth and rising prosperity in the archipelago would enhance the absolute value of American trade.

As for Japan, it should be stressed that since the occupation she has sought to build her position in Southeast Asia on the basis of economic diplomacy. Prime Ministers have come and gone but this emphasis remains. Japan's outlook was well indicated in an address by Tatsunosuke Takasaki, her principal delegate at the Bandung Conference in April, 1955. He frankly observed in the forum of Asians and Africans that his country had "inflicted damages upon her neighbor nations, but ended by bringing untold miseries upon herself"; he stressed that the "new Japan is founded on peace and democracy," noting that Nippon was "one of [the] Asiatic nations whose destiny is identical with that of Asia"; he stated that his country was anxious "to contribute her share to the promotion of economic coöperation for the common prosperity of the region," and called for cultural exchange among the nations represented at Bandung.[25] "The present Conference," the Japanese delegate noted, "by promoting mutual understanding and neighborly amity among the Asian-African countries, can contribute vastly to world peace and, at the same time, accelerate the economic progress of [the] entire region."[26]

Although Takasaki spoke for Prime Minister Ichiro Hatoyama, Shigeru Yoshida, the previous prime minister, when in power, expressed similar viewpoints. In an address at the National Press Club in Washington in November, 1954, he even observed that Japan could not survive unless the free Asian nations survived and unless there were friendly coöperation and free trade among them.

On January 30, 1956, Foreign Minister Mamoru Shigemitsu told the Diet that Japan should conclude treaties of commerce and navigation with as many countries as possible, developing in particular friendship with the new states of Asia and initiating programs of coöperation in that part of the world. The Japanese Ambassador to the United States, Masayuki Tani, asserted in a speech on May 8 with reference to the role of his country in technical

[25] Address of Mr. Tatsunosuke Takasaki, Press Release, Asian-African Conference, Bandung, Indonesia.

[26] *Ibid.*

assistance to the new Asian states: ". . . Japan is the most extensively industrialized nation in Asia. We have the largest concentration of scientific and technical know-how in Asia. We have also the largest pool of managerial ability and skilled manpower. Having these, it follows that we have the capacity to contribute substantially to this great human endeavor. . . ."[27] Prime Minister Nobusuke Kishi's tour of South and Southeast Asia in the spring of 1957 and later in the year to other countries of Southeast Asia and the Southwest Pacific called attention to Japan's economic diplomacy.

The Nipponese claim that as Asians themselves they are in a position to understand their fellow Asians, and they assert that the training of foreign technicians from the same continent in Nippon is practical. At the same time Japan notes she is no longer a colonial power in Asia and the Pacific, and does not pose a military threat to any state. Prepared to render technical assistance either abroad or at home, and to help in the economic development of Southeast Asia, Japan seeks economic benefits in trade and investment.

As an island republic with well-defined boundaries the Philippines has a certain freedom of action in its neighborhood not found in the case of continental states of comparable strength located next to a potentially hostile stronger power. To the east of the Philippines is the wide expanse of the Pacific with the American trust territory of the Carolines, Marianas, and Marshalls (Trust Territory of the Pacific Islands). To the north is the Republic of China in Taiwan and to the south are the Republic of Indonesia and British North Borneo. Westward across the South China Sea is Vietnam. In view of the previous ties with Spain and the United States, the orientation of the Filipinos was so long directed toward Europe and America that upon independence it was difficult to adjust to the concept of Asian neighbors.

One of the principal tenets of the *Nacionalista* specialists on foreign policy was the cultivation of much closer ties with the Asians. The Liberal administration of President Quirino was accused of being too much interested in Western relations at the expense of Eastern. Senator Claro M. Recto has been the leader in advocating a Philippine orientation toward Asian neighbors based upon what he considers to be realistic grounds. Senator José P. Laurel has compared the Philippines to a man who is "virtually without friends in his own neighborhood although, ironically, he

[27] Masayuki Tani speech, *Japan Report*, May 15, 1956, p. 4

has among his big neighbors blood relatives with whom he and his forebears had had cordial enough dealings for a long, long time—centuries as a matter of fact."[28]

It is, therefore, not surprising that the Magsaysay administration attempted to place more stress than in the past on Asian relations. In his inaugural address the President sent "fraternal greetings" to the "Asian brothers," and in his first message on the state of the nation he observed that "as a good neighbor to the countries of Southeast Asia, we shall participate in all regional activities that will promote closer economic and cultural relations among us."[29] At the same time there is no doubt that Magsaysay's interests were chiefly in the domestic field.

Shortly after he assumed office the *Nacionalista* President was faced with a decision on the "Asia for the Asians" controversy raised by his Undersecretary of Foreign Affairs, Leon Ma. Guerrero, a friend of Senator Recto. In a speech on February 5, 1954, Guerrero observed that his country could not afford to antagonize its neighbors whose destinies were inseparable from the future of the Philippines. "If Asia," he said, "is not for the Asians, then for whom is it? For the Russians, for the Americans, for the Europeans, for the Africans?"[30] The controversy in effect came to center about American-Philippine ties. Some argued that the island republic could not strengthen its relations with Asian neighbors without weakening its position with the United States. Others believed that the future of the Philippines in the long run was inevitably associated with Asia and that the quicker this fact was realized in Manila the better it would be for the nation. The second highest official in the Republic, Vice-President Garcia, had himself in a number of speeches been calling for closer relations with Southeast Asia. He noted on January 23 that "by geographical propinquity, by ancestral ties not yet wholly forgotten, by custom, manners and even, in most respects, outlook, the Philippines belongs to this orbit."[31] It was, however, the controversy over Guerrero's com-

[28] José P. Laurel, *Bread and Freedom*, p. 68.

[29] Address on the State of the Nation by Ramon Magsaysay, January 25, 1954, *Official Gazette*, Republic of the Philippines, Vol. 50 (January, 1954), p. 86.

[30] Address Delivered by the Honorable Leon Ma. Guerrero, February 5, 1954, Division of International Information, Department of Foreign Affairs, Manila, Philippines.

[31] Speech Delivered by Honorable Carlos P. Garcia, January 23, 1954, Division of International Information, Department of Foreign Affairs, Manila, Philippines. After becoming President, Garcia thought it necessary to issue a statement on March 29, 1957, asserting that "our policy in Asia . . . cannot be adequately expressed in any single slogan." *Official Gazette*, Republic of the Philippines, Vol. 53 (April 15, 1957), p. 2124.

ments on Asia for the Asians that finally led to Magsaysay's declaration of March 10 relative to Philippine-American and Philippine-Asian relations. Noting that he and congressional leaders had agreed on the statement, the President asserted: "There is no incompatibility between the political and economic ties and solidarity of aspirations in peace and in war, which have bound our two countries [the Philippines and the United States] for more than half a century, and our warm desire to become good neighbors in Asia in a united effort, imposed by geographical propinquity and racial affinities, to achieve the general prosperity of this region. Rather, these two complementary objectives should give us that balanced foreign policy which we have lacked in the past."[32] Here is found the basis of Magsaysay's "positive nationalism." From the controversy the President learned that he could not leave foreign policy in the hands of subordinates, and from that time he took an increasingly active part in its formulation.

Although Filipinos participated in the unofficial Asian Relations Conference at New Delhi in March, 1947, the role of the Philippines at the official Asian-African Conference at Bandung in April, 1955, was far more significant. Romulo was selected to head the delegation at Bandung, partly because of his experience in conferences and his widespread personal contacts. In his opening address the chief Philippine delegate observed that all present were concerned with colonialism and political freedom, racial equality and peaceful economic growth. He praised the "basic good faith of the United States" which, he said, his country had "directly experienced," and he took a strong stand against Communism.[33] Both in the formal meetings of the delegates and in the informal discussions outside the Conference Romulo was active. To him the Bandung Conference indicated that Africa and Asia had "come of age." The Philippine delegation left Indonesia generally satisfied with the results of the meeting. At the same time members were sensitive to any criticism of their being voices of the United States.

In its relations with Nationalist China on Taiwan the Philippines has faced a number of problems. Within the latter country are some 350,000 Chinese although no figure can be accurately given. The Chinese have had an important place in the Philippine econ-

[32] Full Text of the Statement of President Ramon Magsaysay Clarifying His Administration's Foreign Policy with Reference to Asia, Issued on March 10, 1954, *Department of Foreign Affairs Review*, Vol. II (March, 1955), pp. 3-4.

[33] Opening Statement of the Honorable Carlos P. Romulo, Press Release, Asian-African Conference, Bandung, Indonesia.

omy, particularly in the retail trade, the commercial credit facilities, and the distribution of rice. Chinese investments in the Philippines may amount to more than $100 million but trade between Taiwan and its southern neighbor is not very important. Even in the years between 1934 and 1938 the share of the whole of China in Philippine foreign trade only averaged 2.9 percent of all imports and 0.7 percent of exports.

The economic position of the Chinese in the Philippines has led to a number of efforts on the part of the Filipino government to restrict the activities of the "aliens." Usually the Chinese have been able to circumvent the government efforts often with the aid of the Filipinos themselves. The *Nacionalista*-dominated Congress in 1954 passed a measure directed at the nationalization of the retail trade. The act was the subject of a strong protest from Nationalist China and was generally criticized by foreign business interests in the Philippines. Its constitutionality was brought before the Supreme Court. Another point of controversy has centered around some 3000 Chinese most of whom came from the mainland of China under temporary visas between 1947 and 1951. They do not want to return to the Communist mainland, the Taipei government does not want them in Taiwan, and Malacañang is eager to have them leave the country. The subject has entered domestic politics with charges of a 12-million-peso Chinese lobby working for their stay in the Islands.

The Republic of the Philippines has continued to recognize the Nationalist government of China. In April, 1947, a treaty of amity had been signed between the two countries. In July, 1949, Generalissimo Chiang Kai-shek visited President Elpidio Quirino in Baguio. In the United Nations the Philippines supported the Nationalist regime in its efforts to continue to represent China, and it voted in favor of General Assembly resolutions in 1951 branding Communist China an aggressor in Korea and calling for an embargo on strategic war materials to her and North Korea. At the Bandung Conference Premier Chou En-lai of the People's Republic of China told Romulo his country was willing to make a nationality agreement with the Philippines like that with Indonesia, and he invited Filipinos to visit the coastal regions of China to see if activities that might threaten the island republic were taking place.

Closely associated with the Philippine policy toward Chiang Kai-shek is apprehension over the political sympathies of the Chinese in the archipelago and the future status of Taiwan. The majority of the Chinese in the Philippines are still loyal to Nationalist China; in fact, they have a reputation of being possibly the most loyal in all Southeast Asia. Although there is a Chinese Communist organization in the Philippines and it has worked to some extent with the Communist-led Hukbalahaps, the membership is limited and the aid not extensive. Philippine officials believe that Chinese Communists are being smuggled in through the southern islands and that they are trying hard to infiltrate Chinese schools.

As regards the future of Taiwan, the Philippines considers the island a first line of defense, the United States being well aware of this attitude. The Asian republic would be most reluctant to see Taiwan fall into the hands of the Chinese Communists. Not only would a potential enemy be intrenched closer to the Philippines but also the effect on the Chinese minority in the archipelago might be very grave.

In early 1955 the Philippine attitude toward Formosa was emphasized as a result of the crisis in relations between the United States and the People's Republic of China over certain offshore islands along the mainland of China in the hands of the Nationalist Chinese. The American Congress had quickly responded to a message of President Eisenhower on January 24 by approving a joint resolution wherein the President was authorized to use armed force as he deemed necessary to protect Formosa and the Pescadores against armed attack, "this authority to include the securing and protection of such related positions and territories of that area now in friendly hands [the Quemoy and Matsu islands] and the taking of such other measures as he judges to be required or appropriate in assuring the defense of Formosa and the Pescadores."[34] On the previous January 6 the President had submitted to the Senate for approval the Mutual Defense Treaty between the United States of America and the Republic of China signed on December 2, 1954. It did not cover significantly the offshore islands.

In the Philippines President Magsaysay on February 3, ten days after President Eisenhower's message to Congress, issued a highly important statement. He asserted that "Formosa and the Philippines figure importantly in the defense pattern against aggression in this part of the world. The two countries, by virtue of their geographical proximity and respective defense commitments, have a vital stake in the resolute maintenance of this defense pattern. We can-

[34] Text of Joint Resolution on Defense of Formosa, *The Department of State Bulletin*, Vol. XXXII (February 7, 1955), p. 213.

not therefore be indifferent to the events that are transpiring in that area nor be unconcerned with the ultimate fate of the island. Our interest extends to the measures that have been taken to defend it against aggression. Formosa is vital to our national security. It must remain free and in friendly hands. For these reasons, I welcome the decision of the United States Government clarifying its stand on the Formosa question. I trust that this policy of firmness will achieve its avowed purpose of deterring further acts of Communist aggression in this area. We stand squarely behind the United States in its determination to achieve this purpose."[35]

Although the President's position was severely criticized by Senator Recto, the Congress of the Philippines endorsed it by an overwhelming vote on March 9. Recto had sought to have the Senate qualify the statement with the phrase "in the understanding that the President's stand expressed our treaty obligations."[36]

In relations with its neighbors to the south—British North Borneo and Indonesia—the Philippines has been developing a foreign policy somewhat different from that toward Taiwan although the question of security is by no means dormant. In the case of British North Borneo the problems have centered around the transfer of the Turtle and Mangsee Islands and the status of the Taganak Island lighthouse located in the former group. In addition, the Republic of the Philippines has considered making a claim to all or a part of British North Borneo on behalf of the sultanate of Sulu.

Under the provisions of the Anglo-American convention and exchange of notes, signed January 2, 1930, American sovereignty over the Turtle and Mangsee Islands was recognized by Great Britain but the British North Borneo Company was allowed to administer them unless or until the American government gave notice of its desire to assume the administration. Upon such notice the transfer should occur within one year, the United States government giving favorable consideration toward compensating the Company for its capital expenditure on the lighthouse and also providing for its future maintenance. The British were interested in the Turtle and Mangsee Islands because of their proximity to North Borneo. The center of the Turtle Islands was only 30 miles north of Sandakan, capital of the British area; the Mangsee Islands were farther to the north and west of the Turtles.

[35] President Magsaysay's Statement on U.S. Stand on Formosa, February 3, 1955, *Official Gazette*, Republic of the Philippines, Vol. 51 (February, 1955), p. 682.

[36] *Official Gazette*, Republic of the Philippines, Vol. 51 (February, 1955), p. lxxxvii.

After the Philippines received its independence the Manila government on September 19, 1946, officially informed Great Britain of its desire to take over the administration of the islands in question. The British asked the Philippines to reconsider the matter noting the need for a real police force and the importance of the lighthouse. A joint committee was established to study the situation, but after the report of the Philippine delegation, the Manila government decided to follow its original course of action and assume the administration of the islands. Although the Filipinos assured Great Britain that a proper police force would be maintained, they rejected the request that they pay for the cost of the lighthouse and that they provide for its maintenance in the future. The Manila government asserted that the lighthouse had been severely damaged in the war, that it had not been in operation since its destruction, and that the Philippines did not need its service. The government was willing to lease the site for the lighthouse to North Borneo for one peso per annum as long as the British needed and used the facility. On October 16, 1947, the Philippines took over the administration of the Mangsee and Turtle Islands without prejudice to the impasse about the Taganak lighthouse.

When the British government on July 15, 1946, changed the status of North Borneo into that of a crown colony, the Republic of the Philippines was only 11 days old. Although the British action did not go unnoticed in Manila, the government was not certain about what policy to pursue. A number of memoranda were prepared relative to the various aspects of the matter.[37] One memorandum dated September 23, 1946, written in the Division of European and African Affairs of the Philippine foreign office sketched the background of the "North Borneo Question" and suggested that the Office of Legal Affairs be asked for an opinion about a possible claim of sovereignty and its defense before the International Court of Justice. Three days later Francis Burton Harrison, former American Governor General in the Philippines, presented an ad interim exposition on the subject at the request of Vice-President Quirino who was also Secretary of Foreign Affairs. The former favored a protest to Great Britain on behalf of the Philippine government and the sultanate of Sulu. Harrison endorsed a memorandum prepared by Professor H. Otley Beyer of the University of the Philippines wherein the latter recommended that the Manila government admit the existence of the sultanate of Sulu,

[37] H. Otley Beyer collection, Manila, Philippines.

that the Moros choose a sultan, and that the Philippines protest to Great Britain for making North Borneo a crown colony. In another memorandum, dated December 8, 1946, Professor Beyer analyzed the legal aspects of the problem in considerable detail.

On February 27, 1947, Harrison in his capacity as adviser to the President of the Philippines sent to Vice-President Quirino a more definitive analysis. The former claimed that the sultanate of Sulu had had sovereignty over North Borneo since 1714 and that the proper translation of the treaty of 1878 wherein the sultan made disposition of the area would employ the word "lease" and not the expression "grant and cede" as maintained by the British. He recommended that a sultan be chosen and that he then ask the Philippine government on behalf of his sultanate to protest to Britain the absorption of North Borneo. If the British were not prepared to reconsider the matter, it should be taken to the United Nations. Meanwhile the British North Borneo Company since 1936 had ceased to make annual payments to the sultan of Sulu for the North Borneo area as the Moros could not agree on who should succeed the one who had died and the Philippine government did not press the matter. In 1939 certain heirs had sued the government of the State of North Borneo and others but without success. The British obviously consider their position in the area legally sound, and the Philippines, despite some agitation in and outside Congress, especially in 1950, has not made an important issue of the matter. In fact, on a day-to-day basis the authorities in Sandakan and Manila are much more concerned over problems relating to smuggling. In August, 1955, an agreement was signed relative to the migration, employment, and settlement of Filipino workers in the British colony.

The relations between the republics of Indonesia and the Philippines are particularly important for a number of reasons. In the first place they provided an index of the adjustment of the Philippines to Southeast Asia. With their neighbors in the island republic to the south the Filipinos have a certain opportunity that they do not have elsewhere in Asia. To some extent, although it is questionable to what extent, the Philippines can serve as an intermediary between the West and Indonesia. The long-range possibilities of an Indonesian-Philippine entente in the Pacific should not be ignored despite the impediments of the present.

The basis for Philippine-Indonesian friendship is found in a number of common factors, each being subject to limitations. The two peoples shared in many respects a common historical background before the advent of the Spanish and Americans in the Philippines and the Portuguese and Dutch in the East Indies. During the Second World War both were conquered by Japan and subjected to the New Order in Greater East Asia. Shortly after the defeat of Japan the Republic of the Philippines and then Indonesia emerged in the world community. In both cases nationalism developed against an extended colonial regime. In addition to a common historical background during certain periods, the Filipinos and Indonesians are similar in their basic linguistic and racial heritage.

Concrete evidence of amity between the two countries is shown in the treaty of friendship signed on June 21, 1951, and in President Sukarno's visit to the Philippines in the early part of the same year and President Quirino's return visit to Indonesia in the summer of 1952. Moreover, during the Indonesian struggle for independence the Philippines had supported the efforts of its neighbor. General Carlos P. Romulo took an active part in the New Delhi Conference on Indonesia in January, 1949, and the Philippines stood behind Indonesia in the United Nations. Some Indonesian officers, it might be noted, later studied in a Philippine army school.

At the same time a number of obstacles condition the friendship between the two countries. Especially troublesome has been the presence of around 6000 illegal Indonesian immigrants in the southern Philippines and of a few hundred such Filipinos in Indonesia. For centuries groups of Indonesians have moved northward for purposes of trade and of bettering their livelihood. Coming from Kalimantan (Indonesian Borneo), Sulawesi (Celebes) and Maluku (the Moluccas) and from the Talaud Islands and the Miangas (Palmas), all in Indonesian territory, the immigrants have moved into the Sarangani and Balut Islands, Jolo in the Sulu Archipelago, and Cotabato and Davao in Mindanao, all in the Philippines. Being of Malay descent, they were easily assimilated and constituted no real threat to peace and order. Nevertheless, some apprehension existed in Manila that a few of the Indonesians might be Communists and that smuggling would expand if the number of illegal immigrants grew. Philippine immigration officials have divided the Indonesians into three classes—those who have entered illegally prior to January 1, 1941, and might be entitled to legalization of residence, those who have lived long enough in the Philippines to be no longer deportable but are not yet entitled to legalization of residence, and those under technical arrest and subject to deportation. The establishment of a Philippine consulate in Menado, Sulawesi, and an Indonesian vice-consulate in Davao, Mindanao, was a step to control the immigration problem and to reduce smuggling.

Meanwhile negotiations between the Djakarta and Manila governments have sought to find a basic solution to the issue. On November 28, 1954, Filipino and Indonesian panels in Manila working on a technical level in a conference reached agreement on the problem subject to the action of plenipotentiary representatives. Opposition to the agreement, however, was encountered and the whole question had to be considered over again. Filipino legislators were concerned over the problem of precedents in an Indonesian-Philippine accord that might affect certain Chinese residing in the Islands.

On July 4, 1956, an immigration agreement of five years' duration was signed in Djakarta between the two neighboring republics. Indonesians who illegally entered the Philippines after January 1, 1946, would be repatriated by the government of Indonesia, but those who illegally came and married Filipinos before January 1, 1954, could have permanent residence in the Philippines if they so desired. Similar conditions applied to Filipinos in Indonesia. Both governments were to exchange binding estimates of illegal immigrants under their jurisdiction as of the date of the agreement. Procedures for the legalization of permanent residence were outlined. A detailed system for the control of border crossing into specific areas was provided including the use of border crossing cards.[38] The agreement, of course, was subject to the ratification of both states.

Fortunately Philippine-Indonesian relations have not been marred by the religious differences between the two peoples. Nor is there evidence of any Indonesian effort to attract the Moslem Filipinos in the southern part of the Philippines. The Moros themselves, individualistic in their outlook, give no indication of wanting to join their religious brethren in Indonesia, although they are showing a greater interest in the Islamic world. The Philippines

[38] Article VII reads:
"For purposes of this agreement, the border areas are:
Philippines: 1. Balut-Sarangani Island Group; 2. Sibtu Island Group; 3. Simanul Island; 4. Manuk Manka Island.
Indonesia: 1. Talaud-Sangi Island Group; 2. Miangas Island Group; 3. Kawio Island Group; 4. Nunukan Island."
Text of the Immigration Agreement between the Republic of Indonesia and the Republic of the Philippines, Embassy of Indonesia, Washington, D.C.

for its part has no political concern about the Indonesian Christians living in Sulawesi. Under different circumstances religion might be a serious factor of discord in the relations between Manila and Djakarta.

From the economic viewpoint the economies of the Philippines and Indonesia are basically similar and no close ties have been developed. Both countries are underdeveloped, producers of raw materials, interested in expanding industries and in need of foreign capital. Trade between the two republics has not been extensive.

In terms of security the Philippines and Indonesia face somewhat similar problems but their approach in finding a solution to them is divergent. As neighboring insular republics along the east and southeast coasts of mainland Asia, developments in either state hostile to the other would present a serious security problem. The fall of the Philippines to an aggressive power would jeopardize the northeastern frontiers of Indonesia while the southern flank of the Philippines would be exposed if the former came under the control of hostile leaders. The military association of the Philippines with the United States and the West is not appreciated in Indonesia, which has no substantial ties with either the Western or the Communist bloc of nations. Conversely the Philippines does not approve of Indonesian foreign policy, especially with reference to the Communist world.

In the West Irian or Netherlands New Guinea controversy before the General Assembly of the United Nations the attitude of the Philippines was indicative of its dilemma in foreign policy toward Indonesia. On the one hand, the Manila government is anticolonial in its outlook and wants to show sympathy for Indonesia in its efforts to acquire West Irian; on the other hand, the Philippines is aware of the security aspect of Netherlands New Guinea and is an ally of Australia in the Manila Pact. In the voting on November 30, 1954, in the First Committee of the General Assembly on the resolution, hoping the Dutch and Indonesians would "pursue their endeavors" to solve the controversy and asking them to report progress at the next General Assembly, the Philippines abstained. However, when the resolution in its three parts was considered in the General Assembly on December 10, the Philippines supported it although it did not receive the necessary two-thirds majority for adoption.

Toward Vietnam, Cambodia, and Laos the Republic of the Philippines followed for some time a somewhat cautious policy.

Disliking both Communism and colonialism, the Manila officials were in a quandary as to what to do. Despite American suggestions that the Philippines recognize the Associated States, recognition of Cambodia and Laos did not come until January 8, 1955. With the war in Indochina reaching a climax with the battle of Dien Bien Phu in 1954 the Philippines had showed increasing interest in developments across the South China Sea. President Magsaysay in a statement on April 18 indicated that he would be willing in principle to support a joint declaration with the United States "against Communist aggression in Indo-China" but that he favored in the proposed statement "an affirmation of the rights of all peoples to freedom and independence."[39]

Despite the lack of official ties for a number of years between the State of Vietnam and the Philippines, unofficial relations became relatively extensive. Filipino groups in "Operation Brotherhood" assisted the Vietnamese refugees from north of the seventeenth parallel, particularly with medical supplies. A Filipino volunteer team of doctors and nurses went to Vietnam under the auspices of the Junior Chamber of Commerce and the Red Cross of the island republic. Vietnamese groups came to the Philippines to observe certain programs in action such as the pacification and rehabilitation activities of the Manila government. In some respects the Catholics in Vietnam have received the support of the Catholics in the Philippines.

On July 14, 1955, the Philippines decided to recognize the State of Vietnam. President Magsaysay directed Vice-President Garcia as Secretary of Foreign Affairs to implement the decision at once. Magsaysay's policy was based on the considerations that Vietnam had the requirements of a sovereign and independent state, that recognition would be in fulfillment of the commitments of the Philippines under SEATO, that it would strengthen the attempt of the free countries in Southeast Asia to establish a common front against the Communist menace, and that Premier Ngo Dinh Diem's government was "deserving of support because of its success, despite great odds, in resisting both colonialism and Communism."[40] Senator Recto severely criticized Magsaysay for his decision, suggesting it was the result of American pressure.

A Philippine minister was subsequently appointed to the State

[39] President Magsaysay's Policy Statement, April 18, 1954, *Official Gazette*, Republic of the Philippines, Vol. 50 (April, 1954), pp. 1539-1540.

[40] *Official Gazette*, Republic of the Philippines, Vol. 51 (July, 1955), p. cccxiii.

of Vietnam, Cambodia, and Laos, resident in Saigon. Later in a message to the Vietnamese people Magsaysay noted that the Philippines and Free Vietnam were close neighbors in Southeast Asia; they shared a cultural, racial, and geographic affinity; and they had been called upon to bear the responsibility of defending freedom. In fact, the island republic has favored the entrance of Vietnam, Cambodia, and Laos into SEATO. Trade negotiations for the exchange of Vietnamese rice and Philippine sugar have been held, an agreement becoming effective in July, 1957. A Filipino advised on the constitution of the Republic of Vietnam. For 1956 it is reported that 49 of the 408 Vietnamese students abroad studied in the island republic. Not without reason did the vice-president, the foreign secretary, and the chief of staff of the armed forces of Vietnam attend the funeral services of President Magsaysay.

The visit of Prince Norodom Sihanouk of Cambodia to Manila in early 1956 served to direct attention to relations between the Philippines and Cambodia. In a speech to Congress on February 3 the Prince pointed to the ties between the two peoples and outlined the foreign policy of his country. Some Filipinos saw in it an outlook not unlike that of Senator Recto. The Prince had an opportunity to see the effects of American aid. He left Manila still convinced that Cambodia should pursue a foreign policy of neutrality. Subsequent relations between the two Asian states were impaired over charges and denials that Philippine officials had tried to urge the Prince to join SEATO.

In its hostile attitude toward Communism both on the domestic and international fronts the Republic of the Philippines has been consistent. No diplomatic relations are maintained with any Communist state. In 1946, it might be noted, Ho Chi Minh sent the Philippines a telegram of congratulation upon winning independence. Although the Soviet Union has never recognized the island republic, the latter has not sought to take steps that might win recognition. The USSR was severely criticized in late 1956 as a result of its military action in Hungary.

Philippine failure to recognize the People's Republic of China is of more immediate consequence in Manila. As long as the United States continues to recognize the China of Chiang Kai-shek and Formosa remains in the hands of the Nationalists, Philippine policy toward the Peking regime can be maintained. But should the Chinese Communists win Formosa or should American policy lead to the recognition of the People's Republic of China, the Philippines would probably have to change its attitude toward Mao Tsetung. The Chinese Communist press has already called for normal relations between the Peking and Manila governments. Senator Recto, for his part, has favored trade with Communist China upon her being seated in the United Nations.

In the case of the Korean War the Philippines took an active part in trying to halt the Communist aggression across the thirty-eighth parallel. Even before the outbreak of the conflict the Republic supported the early recommendations of the United Nations on Korea, participated in Korean commissions under the auspices of the world organization, and recognized the Republic of Korea under the presidency of Syngman Rhee. The Communist invasion of Korea on June 25, 1950, came as a genuine surprise in the Philippines, provoking a war scare in the country. The early public reaction was to rally behind the United States, even more than behind the Manila government. The measures of the Security Council of the United Nations in meeting the Communist aggression were quickly supported. Also welcomed was President Harry S Truman's statement on June 27 that United States armed forces, at that time sea and air, had been ordered to assist the Republic of Korea to repel the Communist aggression in the country, that the Seventh Fleet had been instructed to protect Formosa, and, as already indicated, that United States forces in the Philippines would be strengthened and American military aid to the Republic accelerated.

At first the Philippines offered to assist the United Nations effort in Korea only in terms of supplies like medicine, rice, coconut oil, and copra. Seventeen Sherman tanks and a tank destroyer, however, left the island republic for southern Korea. Many Filipino veterans and former Philippine Scouts volunteered to serve in Korea but they were informed that only Americans could enlist in the armed forces of the United States. Meanwhile, pressure mounted in Manila to send an expeditionary force to the battle front. The Quirino administration hesitated, for the Hukbalahaps constituted a serious problem at home and the government was in financial difficulties. The decision of Thailand to send troops to Korea increased the pressure on Malacañang to take similar action. In early August both the Senate and House of Representatives unanimously approved resolutions calling in effect for sending armed forces to the battle front. President Quirino took the steps to organize and dispatch a Philippine contingent to Korea. Approximately 5000 officers and men organized in regimental combat teams represented the Philippine military effort.

Throughout the war the island republic did not waver in its support of the United Nations effort in Korea. It favored General Assembly Resolution 376 (V), adopted October 7, 1950, which was considered to authorize the United Nations forces to unify Korea and which made the Philippines a member of the United Nations Commission for the Unification and Rehabilitation of Korea. The Republic voted on December 1 for the establishment of the United Nations Korean Reconstruction Agency (UNKRA). Although its military role was obviously restricted, it participated in the deliberations of the states that had armed forces in Korea. The Philippines favored the voluntary rather than the forced repatriation of prisoners of war. The Republic approved the armistice of July 27, 1953, ending the Korean fighting, and joined with the 15 other United Nations members having armed forces in Korea in a declaration on the same day that they would resist a renewal of the armed attack, the consequences of such aggression being so serious that "in all probability" the resulting hostilities would not be limited to the area of Korea. On the question of the composition of the "political conference," as envisioned by Article IV, Section 60, of the armistice, to formulate a settlement of the Korean controversy, the Philippines joined the United States in opposing the participation of India.

Vice-President Carlos P. Garcia represented the Philippines at the Geneva Conference on Korea, April 26 to June 15, 1954. Although no solutions to the Korean question were reached, the Philippines associated itself with 14 other members of the United Nations who had sent armed forces to Korea[41] in saying that the political conference at Geneva fulfilled Section 60 of the armistice agreement calling for such a gathering. The Soviet Union for its part did not agree. At the end of May, 1956, the Philippines joined with the other states in provisionally suspending the operations of the Neutral Nations Supervisory Commission in the area of South Korea until the Communist authorities carried out the provisions of the armistice agreement concerning inspection teams in North Korea.

At home the Republic of the Philippines has had to cope with Communist-led Hukbalahaps, as they are still popularly called, who

[41] The Union of South Africa had an observer at the Geneva Conference.

are determined to gain control of the government and to turn the nation into a people's republic. Should they succeed, the diplomatic revolution in Manila from the Western to the Communist alignment would parallel the change in China when Mao Tse-tung replaced Chiang Kai-shek. The election of Ramon Magsaysay to the presidency weakened the Communist movement in the Philippines, but the hard core continues to be active both in guerrilla warfare in the jungles and swamps and in the effort to infiltrate into important groups in the country. Although few supplies, if any, from the outside Communist world have reached the Philippine guerrillas, the ideological support has remained constant. Hukbalahap propaganda has reflected the usual Communist approach accusing the United States of being an imperialist power bent on starting a third world war.[42] Criticism has been directed especially at the American military bases in the archipelago. In June, 1957, President Garcia signed a bill outlawing the Communist Party in the Republic.

Relations between the Philippines and India can be termed nominal. The small Indian community of around 2000 in the former country is quite active in business but does not have at all the impact of the Chinese minority. Agreements have been made between Manila and New Delhi relative to air services and financial privileges to members of the diplomatic corps; a treaty of friendship was signed on July 11, 1952. Indeed, the nominal aspect of Philippine-Indian relations was indicated by a meeting on July 14, 1954, of Minister Mirza Rashid Ali Baig and President Magsaysay at Malacañang when the former called to present two officers in connection with the good-will visit to Manila of the naval ship *Delhi.* Magsaysay brought up the possibility of importing bulls from India to better the local breed of cattle.

Although at times Philippine leaders have indicated a certain rivalry with India in the international field, the fundamental reason for the cleavage between the two Asian republics is the alignment

[42]Jose Lava, a prominent Communist, wrote a memorandum on January 14, 1954, from Muntinglupa (a penitentiary), asserting: "As a first step, a decisive reorientation of our relationships with American imperialism must prevail. Since American imperialist exploitation and domination of our country is the main underlying cause of our basic national problems, we must achieve complete independence from the United States. Unequal relationships through which such exploitation and domination are exercised must be replaced by new relationships premised on equality and mutual respect." Jose Lava memorandum on "Basic National Problems and an Outline of Viable Solutions," January 14, 1954.

of the Manila government with the United States in the Western grouping of states and the policy of nonalignment followed by India in its relations with the so-called "power blocs." The impact of Prime Minister Jawaharlal Nehru is perhaps the least in the Philippines of any country in Southeast Asia. A number of Indian observers have taken the position that the Philippines has not yet found itself culturally at home or politically abroad, while many Filipinos consider Nehru's foreign policy unrealistic and working to the advantage of international Communism.

Philippine relations with Australia are likewise nominal although both states are allies under the Manila Pact. This apathy is largely the result of limited common ties apart from security considerations. The Commonwealth of Australia is making a definite effort to develop relations with the Philippines but results are slow in forthcoming. Trade ties are limited and the so-called "White Australia" policy is a barrier. A civil air service agreement was reached between the two Pacific countries in 1950. At the Ottawa meeting of the Consultative Committee of the Colombo Plan in October, 1954, the Philippines was welcomed as a full participant by the representatives of the other 16 members. Australian Prime Minister Robert Gorden Menzies visited Manila in April, 1957.

Philippine interest in the Middle East has been very limited but it is growing. A constant factor has been the impact of the small number of Moros who make the pilgrimage to Mecca. The Anglo-French-Israeli attack on Egypt in late 1956 was criticized in Manila but not so vehemently as in capitals like Djakarta and Rangoon. A protocol on trade relations with Egypt was signed in January, 1955, and a Philippine consulate was set up in the Arab state the following year. In 1957 the first minister to Egypt was designated, a Moro from Sulu, Pullong Arpa. Prime Minister Husseyn S. Suhrawardy of Pakistan visited Manila in May, 1957, but more in a capacity as an ally under SEATO than as a Moslem leader. The Philippines, it should be added, is establishing diplomatic relations with Israel.

In considering security on a regional basis the Republic of the Philippines has been cognizant of all the difficulties involved. In March, 1949, President Elpidio Quirino called for a Pacific Pact along the lines of the projected North Atlantic Treaty and in August before the American Senate he argued for his proposal. Nationalist China and the Republic of Korea, it was clear, favored a military defensive alliance and were sympathetic to Quirino's suggestions. But this approach was opposed by many Asian states.

The Baguio Conference held from May 26 to May 30, 1950, was not the kind of a meeting originally envisioned by President Quirino either in terms of membership or of agenda. On August 3, 1949, the President had written a letter of instructions to Carlos P. Romulo, Chief of the Philippine Mission to the United Nations, placing him in charge of establishing "a closer union among the peoples of Southeast Asia dedicated to the maintenance of peace and freedom in the region through appropriate methods of political, economic, and cultural coöperation with one another."[43] Although Indonesia, Thailand, Ceylon, Pakistan, India, and Australia joined the Philippines at the Baguio Conference, the concrete results were not significant. Romulo as Chief Delegate of the Philippines stressed in his opening remarks that the Conference was "complete master" of the agenda and "exploratory in character." He expressed the Philippine viewpoint that a permanent regional organization should be established. But in reality the effort to reach a common denominator of agreement resulted in too many platitudes.

In the "Final Act" adopted unanimously on May 30 Romulo as President of the Conference was authorized to communicate its recommendations to the participating governments and to keep them informed on the progress in carrying out the suggestions. Recommendations on social and cultural matters were general and encompassing; they were more restricted in the economic field; they were very limited on the political side. The Conference, in fact, recommended to the governments concerned that they "act in consultation with each other through normal diplomatic channels to further the interests of the peoples of the region."[44] The Baguio Conference did point up the widespread conviction that in solving the problems of South and Southeast Asia the interests of the peoples themselves should be primary.

As for a security pact, world developments were working in its favor. Although the United States was at first opposed to participation, it began to change its position. The need for a Japanese peace settlement coupled with the Communist aggression in Korea led to the signing of the Mutual Defense Treaty with the Philippines on August 30, 1951, and with Australia and New Zealand on September 1. The American security pact with Japan signed September

[43] Letter of Instructions, August 3, 1949, *The Department of Foreign Affairs Quarterly Review*, Vol. I (May, 1950), p. 34.

[44] Final Act of the Baguio Conference of 1950, *Final Act and Proceedings of the Baguio Conference of 1950*, p. 5.

8 was a significant aspect of the arrangements made by the United States in connection with the Japanese peace settlement.

As the war in Indochina grew in intensity, the question of an overall multilateral security arrangement in the Southwest Pacific, Southeast Asia, and South Asia became more pertinent. President Ramon Magsaysay stated on April 18, 1954, that he supported "any move towards establishing a NATO-type alliance provided the following conditions are met: First, that the right of Asian peoples to self-determination is respected; and second, that the Philippines be given a plain and unequivocal guarantee of U.S. help in case of attack under our Mutual Defense Pact."[45] The Geneva settlement on Indochina concluded in July led to an intensified effort on the part of a number of powers, especially the United States, to establish a security arrangement directed at stopping further Communist gains in Southeast Asia.

After careful preparation, the Philippines, Thailand, Pakistan, Australia, New Zealand, France, Great Britain, and the United States met at Manila on September 6 where their representatives approved two days later the Southeast Asia Collective Defense Treaty, the protocol to it, and the Pacific Charter. Under Article IV, Paragraph 1, of the defense pact, "each Party recognizes that aggression by means of armed attack in the treaty area against any of the Parties or against any State or territory which the Parties by unanimous agreement may hereafter designate, would endanger its own peace and safety, and agrees that it will in that event act to meet the common danger in accordance with its constitutional processes."[46] The "treaty area" was defined as "the general area of Southeast Asia, including also the entire territories of the Asian Parties, and the general area of the Southwest Pacific,"[47] excluding though not by name Hong Kong and Taiwan. By unanimous agreement Cambodia, Laos, and the territory under the control of the State of Vietnam were added by designation in a protocol to the treaty. Provision was made in the pact for consultation among the members under certain circumstances centering about a threat in the treaty area, apart from an armed attack, thus emphasizing the possibilities of subversion. Indefinite in duration, the treaty pro-

[45] President Magsaysay's Policy Statement, April 18, 1954, *Official Gazette*, Republic of the Philippines, Vol. 50 (April, 1954), p. 1540.

[46] The Southeast Asia Collective Defense Treaty, *The Signing of the Southeast Asia Collective Defense Treaty, the Protocol to the Southeast Asia Collective Defense Treaty and the Pacific Charter, Proceedings*, p. 77.

[47] *Ibid.*, p. 78.

vided for economic coöperation including technical assistance, for developing individual and collective ability to resist an armed attack and to counter subversion directed from without, for the establishment of a Council to consider matters about the implementation of the pact, and for the admission of new members or the altering of the treaty area by unanimous agreement of the others. No action in the area of a designated State or territory could be taken without the consent of the government concerned. In an understanding the United States asserted that it was thinking of "communist aggression" under Article IV, Paragraph 1, but that it would consult in the case of other aggression.

In the Pacific Charter, inspired by Magsaysay and the Filipinos, it was stated by the eight powers that "they uphold the principle of equal rights and self-determination of peoples and they will earnestly strive by every peaceful means to promote self-government and to secure the independence of all countries whose peoples desire it and are able to undertake its responsibilities."[48] Significant is the use of the words "desire" and "able" in the last clause, for they indicate a sound approach to the political development of non-self-governing territories.

Taken as a whole the agreements reached at the Manila Conference presented a partial answer to the security problem in Southeast Asia. The fact that only two states in the region were signatories to the pact, that two others, Indonesia and Burma, were not present, and that the states of Indochina could not participate in their own right weakens the collective defense of Southeast Asia as a region. Moreover, only three of the eight signatories were Asian states, leaving the great majority outside of Asia proper. Great Britain for her part, it should be pointed out, had earlier sought, in the words of Sir Anthony Eden, Secretary of State for Foreign Affairs, "a reciprocal international guarantee that would cover the [Geneva] settlement itself, and then a South-East Asian collective defence treaty to balance the existing Sino-Soviet Treaty and the close relationship which, as we know, exists between Vietminh, China, and the Soviet Union."[49] The former attempt failed, as Eden saw it, because of Communist insistence on a veto in action taken to enforce the guarantee.

[48] The Pacific Charter, *The Signing of the Southeast Asia Collective Defense Treaty, the Protocol to the Southeast Asia Collective Defense Treaty and the Pacific Charter, Proceedings*, p. 88.

[49] *Parliamentary Debates* (*Hansard*), 5th Series, Vol. 532, *House of Commons Official Report,* November 1-12, 1954, col. 929.

In the Philippines the Manila Pact was criticized at the time on the grounds that it did not have real "teeth" because of its somewhat general terminology and because of the absence of military provisions like those associated with the North Atlantic Treaty Organization. Nevertheless, the Philippines was glad to have served as host to the Conference and would have liked to have been chosen the permanent center of the envisioned organization. The treaty encountered no ratification difficulties of any consequence in Manila.

The first meeting of the Council provided by the Manila Pact met at Bangkok from February 23 to February 25, 1955, with the foreign ministers of all the participants but France present. The purpose was to implement the provisions of the treaty. It was decided that the Council, consisting of foreign ministers or their representatives, should convene at least once a year, usually in the treaty area, and reach decisions by unanimous agreement. Permanent representatives of the Council members called Council Representatives would sit in Bangkok for continuing consultation; Military Advisers to the Council would be appointed; a secretariat would be established; and subsidiary units set up. It was agreed that a message of "cordial greetings" to the "free countries" should be given the Asian-African Conference when it convened in Bandung by Thailand, the Philippines, and Pakistan as participants, and it was hoped the gathering in Indonesia would support the ideals of the Pacific Charter.

At the Bangkok meeting the Philippines reported on its experience in fighting "internal dissidence." The Republic was especially interested in a statement by Secretary of State Dulles on the peaceful uses of atomic energy and the American program of assistance to different states relative to the subject. In fact, Romulo in Washington had urged Dulles to bring up the matter at Bangkok. In his opening speech in the Thai capital, Vice-President Garcia called for a "modest but strong secretariat" for SEATO, and in his final remarks he noted that "what is all important is that the organs of the Manila Treaty are set up and start to function."[50]

In their first annual report, released on March 1, 1956, the Council Representatives of the Southeast Asia Treaty Organization indicated the progress made. In addition to the Council of Foreign Ministers meeting at least once a year, the Council Repre-

[50] Statement by Mr. Garcia, Republic of the Philippines, *The Bangkok Conference of the Manila Pact Powers*, Department of State Publication 5909, p. 36.

sentatives, it was stated, met in Bangkok usually at least once every two weeks. The Military Advisers met periodically to offer advice on common defense while their various sub-committees were busy. The Staff Planners have been especially active. Three committees operated under the control of the Council Representatives—the Committee of Security Experts to deal with certain aspects of subversion directed from outside, the Committee of Economic Experts to advise the organization on economic matters, and the Committee on Information, Cultural, Education, and Labor Activities to advise on relevant topics. A provisional Executive Secretariat provided by Thailand, headed by a Thai official, was functioning; and a Filipino served as Public Relations Officer.

The Karachi meeting of the SEATO Council, March 6 to 8, convened in the wake of the visit to Afghanistan, India, and Burma of Soviet Premier Nikolai A. Bulganin and Communist Party chief Nikita S. Khrushchev. The Russian leaders had supported Afghanistan's demands for a "Pushtunistan" territory now a part of Pakistan, and India's claims to Kashmir, also in dispute with Pakistan. In addition, the Karachi meeting was held at a time when Communist tactics were centering on penetration through economic and technical assistance, trade promotion, and political infiltration.

All the foreign ministers of the SEATO powers including the Philippines went to Karachi. In a communiqué on March 8 the Council noted the shift in Communist tactics but attributed it in large measure to the "collective security arrangements of the free nations," and did not believe the efforts were abandoned "to subvert, weaken and overthrow the political, economic and social systems which have been freely chosen by the peoples of the area."[51] The Council countered Soviet support to Afghanistan and India by noting that the treaty area under the Manila Pact extends up to the Durand Line, "the international boundary" between Afghanistan and Pakistan, thus supporting the latter's position. As far as Kashmir is concerned, the Council noted that the resolutions of the United Nations remain in force and urged an early settlement of the controversy through the United Nations or direct negotiations. Thus the Philippines as an ally of Pakistan in SEATO found itself directly involved in the "Pushtunistan" and Kashmir issues. All members of the Council were pleased with reports of developments in the Federation of Malaya toward independence within the Com-

[51] Second Meeting of SEATO Council, Communiqué of March 8, 1956, *The Department of State Bulletin*, Vol. XXXIV (March 19, 1956), p. 448.

monwealth and expressed interest in the outcome of projected discussions between Great Britain and Singapore. They noted the further extension of representative government in Cambodia, Laos, and the Republic of Vietnam. Coöperation continued in SEATO in the combat against subversive activities; in fact, this aspect was given considerable attention at Karachi.

In the organizational field the Council decided to establish a permanent working group to help the Council Representatives and a full-time Executive Secretariat, a research center service to produce reports on current Communist activities, and a cultural relations office. The public relations office would be expanded and an economic officer appointed to facilitate work in the economic aspect of SEATO activity. A common budget would provide for the costs of the organization.

The Philippines approved of the changes through the head of its delegation at Karachi, Vice-President Garcia. In his opening speech, he had stated that "SEATO must provide an effective answer not only to the threat of overt aggression but also to the rapidly developing danger of political and economic penetration and subversion of the treaty area."[52] Garcia clearly realized that Philippine foreign policy must cope with the changing order of the day.

The second annual report of SEATO was released in Manila as well as in the other member capitals on March 5, 1957, preparatory to the meeting of the Council of Ministers at Canberra, Australia, March 11 to March 13. The previous June 24 a building in Bangkok, provided by Thailand for the headquarters of the organization, had been officially opened. The annual report noted the "quiet and steady development" in the member states but warned that subversion was now the "main threat." It was pointed out that the Philippines aided some of the countries covered by the Manila Pact in training personnel for countersubversion activities. A Permanent Military Planning Staff was being set up at the headquarters of SEATO in Bangkok with Brigadier General Alfredo M. Santos of the Philippines at the head. In 1956 it was indicated that Australia offered $4.5 million for SEATO defense in terms of an economic assistance program, this being the first large one to be started specifically under the label of the organization. At the Canberra meeting of the Council of Ministers a decision was reached to appoint a Secretary-General and a Deputy Secretary-General. The

[52] Carlos P. Garcia speech, *New York Times,* March 7, 1956.

Philippines along with Thailand, Pakistan, and New Zealand would share one-third of the costs of SEATO and the other members the rest.

The island republic has been interested in military exercises in the treaty area involving different signatories of the Manila Pact. Observers were present in June, 1955, at the Commonwealth Naval Exercises in the waters between Bangkok and Singapore. Later the participating units visited the ports of Manila and Bangkok. In February, 1956, Philippine ground forces participated with units from all the SEATO powers except France and Pakistan in a joint exercise—"Firm Link"—in and around Bangkok at the invitation of Thailand. In September and October the Philippines participated in "Albatross," a maritime exercise in the South China Sea.

Vice-President Carlos P. Garcia, who represented his country at the Canberra Conference, upon his return to Manila took the oath as president of the Philippines. The tragic death of Ramon Magsaysay on March 17 in an airplane accident in Cebu brought Garcia to Malacañang. Although the new president promised to carry out the foreign policy of his predecessor, he would encounter greater difficulties. Even his election to the presidency on November 12 would not basically alter conditions. Magsaysay's popularity among the people of the Philippines gave weight to his viewpoints on foreign affairs. It is likely that his death means in the long run a weakening of Philippine ties with the United States and a greater stress on Asian solidarity.

5. Republic of Indonesia

In the realm of international relations the Republic of Indonesia is developing a foreign policy that has been officially called "independent and active." In contrast to the Philippines Indonesia seeks to follow a course that is not linked to either of the "power blocs" as the major world groupings are called in Djakarta. At the same time the Republic of 3000 islands does not favor participation in a third power bloc designed to be a counterpoise between the other two. Extending for more than 3000 miles from west to east and almost 1250 miles from north to south, the island state occupies a large area in Southeast Asia. President Sukarno in his speeches, referring to the extent of Indonesia, often uses the expression from Sabang to Merauke. "Unity Through Diversity" is the national motto of a nation of 82 million people.[1] Although Indonesian leaders are aware of the difficulties involved in their foreign orientation, they are determined to keep their "independent" outlook as long as feasible.

From the theoretical viewpoint the factors that guide foreign policy are the Five Postulates or *Pantjasila*, the acknowledged basic philosophy of the state. The *Pantjasila* is technically found in a stenographic account of a speech delivered extemporaneously by Dr. Sukarno on June 1, 1945, during the first session of the Investigating Committee for Preparation of Independence.[2] Answering his own question, "Upon what *Weltanschauung* do we intend to establish the state of Free Indonesia?" Sukarno called first for the

[1] Sutan Sjahrir, President of the Indonesian Socialist Party and former Prime Minister, has written: "The unity of Indonesia as a nation derives from a close linguistic affinity between the various groups spread over the thousands of islands, from a common history, and, to some extent, from common traditions throughout the ages and especially after the coming of the Portuguese and the Dutch in the sixteenth and seventeenth centuries." Sutan Sjahrir, "Problems the Country Faces," *The Atlantic Monthly*, Vol. 197 (June, 1956), p. 117.

[2] *Lahirnja Pantjasila (The Birth of Pantjasila), President Soekarno's Speech*, Ministry of Information, Republic of Indonesia, *passim*.

"principle of nationalism," or "the establishment of one National State based on the entity of one Indonesian soil from the tip of Sumatra right to Irian." He gave as his second principle "internationalism," adding: "But when I say internationalism, I do not mean cosmopolitanism, which does not recognize nationalism. . . . Internationalism can not flower if it is not rooted in the soil of nationalism. Nationalism can not flower if it does not grow within the garden of internationalism." For his third postulate Sukarno called for "the principle of consent, the principle of representative government, the principle of consultation." Here he noted that "for Islam, this is the best condition for the promotion of religion. . . . If we really are an Islamic people, let us work hard so that most of the seats in the people's representative body we will create, are occupied by Islamic delegates." Nevertheless, he observed that "within the people's representative body, Moslems and Christians should work as if inspired." As his fourth postulate Sukarno called for "social justice," noting "in the field of economy, too, we must create equality, and the best common prosperity." Finally as the fifth principle he sought "to set up Free Indonesia with faith in God the Almighty. The principle of Belief in God! Not only should the people of Indonesia have belief in God, but every Indonesian should believe in his own particular God."

In the preamble of the provisional constitution of the Republic of Indonesia, promulgated on August 15, 1950, the *Pantjasila* was embodied but the principles were expressed in somewhat different words and the order was changed. The "Unitary Republican State," it was asserted, is established "on the recognition of the Divine Omnipotence, Humanity, National Consciousness, Democracy and Social Justice."[3] Although the *Pantjasila* contains principles that may be somewhat difficult to apply, its influence should not be ignored in Indonesian foreign policy. Vice-President Mohammad Hatta observed in April, 1953: "No group that holds the reins of government in the Republic, no matter what its political affiliations, will be able to carry on the affairs of state if it does not strive to act in harmony with these principles."[4]

[3] *Provisional Constitution of the Republic of Indonesia*, Ministry of Information, Republic of Indonesia, p. 4. Elections began in Indonesia on December 15, 1955, for a constituent assembly of 520 members to draft a permanent constitution. Six of the seats would be reserved for West Irian and the members would be nominated by the government. On November 10, 1956, President Sukarno administered the oath of office in Bandung to the members of the assembly.

[4] Mohammad Hatta, "Indonesia's Foreign Policy," *Foreign Affairs*, Vol. 31 (April, 1953), p. 450.

The "independent" foreign policy of Indonesia has been frequently outlined during the general debate at the annual meetings of the General Assembly of the United Nations and in the yearly addresses of President Sukarno on August 17, the anniversary of the proclamation of independence. For instance, Notowidigdo told the General Assembly on November 11, 1952, that although Indonesia's refusal to support either bloc except on a given issue had been called "politically unrealistic," his government would continue to judge issues on their merits. Sunario on September 18, 1953, informed the Assembly that the independent foreign policy of his country was not one of "passive neutrality or neutral passivity." President Sukarno observed on August 17, 1952, that "cabinet has succeeded cabinet, events of various kinds have happened inside and outside the country, but our foreign policy, based upon not choosing sides and upon strengthening coöperation in Asia, has never suffered change. This policy is now known to us by the unambiguous term of *an active independent policy directed towards peace*. According to this policy, each question in foreign affairs that touches upon Indonesian interests is examined in the light of its nature and content. And what is the yardstick used to measure these questions? The yardstick is whether any action of ours in the field of foreign affairs can be reconciled with our national interests and with the spirit of the Panchasila."[5] Again on August 17, 1954, the President indicated the wish of his country to work on a friendly basis with all nations and help toward harmonious relations among the countries of the world. Vice-President Hatta for his part wrote: "Indonesia plays no favorites between the two opposed blocs and follows its own path through the various international problems. It terms this policy 'independent,' and further characterizes it by describing it as independent and 'active.' "[6]

The opposition of Indonesia to colonialism is a basic principle in the foreign policy of the country. Merdeka Palace in Djakarta is a symbol of freedom. Having won independence from the Netherlands after considerable difficulty, Indonesian leaders are eager to see the end of colonialism in the rest of the world. To them the most fundamental conflict in world politics is the struggle of dependent peoples for liberation from Western imperialist powers.

[5] "The President's Message, Hope and Facts," *Indonesian Affairs*, Vol. II (August/September, 1952), p. 17.

[6] Hatta, *op. cit.*, p. 444.

Intensely nationalistic in their outlook, the leaders of Indonesia are champions of Asian and African nationalism. Not without reason was the island republic the host for the Asian-African Conference at Bandung in April, 1955.

In the speeches of the Indonesian leaders and in the official publications of the Republic the anticolonial theme is reiterated. The controversy over West Irian has added fuel to the fire. In his speech of August 17, 1953, President Sukarno frankly asserted that as long as colonialism existed there would be no peace. "Viewed from the subjective sense," he said, "the colonial relation is one that hurts the soul of a people, while objectively it is a relation filled with internal oppositions, full of inside conflicts and an inside antithesis."[7] Subardjo told the General Assembly of the United Nations on November 15, 1951, that his government welcomed every effort by the world organization designed to encourage national independence under the provisions of the Charter. Different prime ministers of Indonesia in official statements have added their condemnation of colonialism. Ali Sastroamidjojo, for instance, asserted on August 25, 1953, that his nation with the other Asian and African countries sought to solve the colonial or semicolonial problems that hamper efforts toward world peace. Even the provisional constitution of the Republic of Indonesia, the one promulgated August 15, 1950, contains in the preamble the ringing statement: "Since independence is inherently the right of every nation, any form of colonialism in this world is contrary to humanity and justice, and must therefore be eradicated."[8]

Indonesia has taken an active part in the deliberations of the Colombo Powers, part of whose *Weltanschauung* is anticolonialism. After attending the Southeast Asian Prime Ministers' Conference or Colombo Conference from April 28 to May 2, 1954, Indonesia was host to the second session at Bogor from December 28 to December 29. In their Joint Declaration issued from Ceylon on May 2 the Prime Ministers of Indonesia, Burma, Ceylon, Pakistan, and India—Ali Sastroamidjojo, U Nu, Sir John Kotelawala, Mohammad Ali, and Jawaharlal Nehru—observed that the continuance of colonialism was a "violation of fundamental human rights and a threat to the peace of the world" and called in particular for the "right of self-determination" in the case of the peoples of Tunisia

[7] "Let Us Become the Vehicle of History," *An Address Delivered by the President of the Republic of Indonesia on the Eighth Anniversary of the Proclamation of Independence, August 17, 1953*, Ministry of Information, p. 22.

[8] *Provisional Constitution,* p. 4.

and Morocco; at the same time the prime ministers "affirmed their faith in democracy and democratic institutions" and "declared their unshakable determination to resist interference in the affairs of their countries by external Communist, anti-Communist or other agencies."[9] In relations among themselves the leaders "affirmed their adherence to the principles of respecting the sovereignty of each country and of not intervening in . . . domestic affairs." Concern was expressed over the plight of the Arab refugees in Palestine, and a satisfactory settlement of the overall problem was sought. The five prime ministers opposed "further explosions of the Hydrogen Bomb" and welcomed the efforts of the United Nations Disarmament Commission "to bring about the elimination and prohibition of such weapons." In addition, the leaders called for the representation of the People's Republic of China in the United Nations.

As the Geneva Conference on Korea and Indochina was in session, the prime ministers devoted part of their discussion to the problem of Vietnam, Cambodia, and Laos. They "proposed that France should declare . . . that she is irrevocably committed to the complete independence of Indo-China," that the United Nations should be informed of the progress of the Indochinese deliberations at Geneva, that "an agreement on a cease-fire should be reached without delay," and that a negotiated settlement should be made by the various parties concerned.[10] The conclusions on Indochina as well as the other provisions of the Joint Declaration were supported by Indonesia, for they were considered "in conformity with its active independent foreign policy."[11]

In his opening address at the Colombo Conference, Prime Minister Ali Sastroamidjojo had called for the convening of a conference, "wider in scope," of Asian and African nations to deal with common problems. The proposal was generally approved by the other leaders but the visit of the Indonesian prime minister to New Delhi and Rangoon in September produced the active support of Nehru and U Nu. A preliminary gathering of the Colombo Powers was held in Bogor to plan the projected larger conference. The joint communiqué, issued from Indonesia on December 29, defined the purposes of the Asian-African meeting and listed the

[9] The Text of the Joint Declaration as a Result of the Colombo Conference, *Indonesian Affairs,* Vol. IV (March/April, 1954), *passim.*

[10] *Ibid.*, p. 4.

[11] "The Colombo Conference," *Indonesian Affairs,* Vol. IV (March/April, 1954), p. 3.

countries in Asia and Africa to be invited. The objectives of the conference were enumerated as follows: first, to encourage coöperation among the nations of Africa and Asia; second, to discuss economic, social, and cultural questions involving them; third, to take up matters of particular interest to Asian and African peoples such as national sovereignty, racialism, and colonialism; and fourth, to view the status of Africa and Asia in the contemporary world and to consider their contribution to the promotion of peace. The prime minister of Indonesia took the position that the last objective was the most important.

Under the joint sponsorship of the Colombo Powers, 25 countries were invited to the Bandung Conference. The basic consideration in the selection of possible participants was the desire that "all countries in Asia and Africa which have independent Governments should be invited" although it was recognized that there were "minor variations and modifications" in the selection process.[12] The list included: Afghanistan, Cambodia, the Central African Federation, the People's Republic of China, Egypt, Ethiopia, the Gold Coast, Iran, Iraq, Japan, Jordan, Laos, Lebanon, Liberia, Libya, Nepal, the Philippines, Saudi Arabia, the Sudan, Syria, Thailand, Turkey, Vietnam (North), Vietnam (South), and Yemen. Absent from the list were Israel, the two Koreas, Nationalist China, the Union of South Africa, Australia, New Zealand, and the Mongolian People's Republic. In commenting on certain countries not invited, the Indonesian prime minister noted that the unanimous agreement of the Colombo Powers was necessary for favorable action. Under the circumstances Israel could not be invited whereas the Arab countries were on the list. All of the sponsoring governments, he observed with reference to China and Indochina, recognized the People's Republic, and they had a special interest in Indochina as a result of their position in Colombo on the controversy in that area. Burma and India, it might be added, wanted Israel present; both countries were more enthusiastic about the projected conference with the invitation to the People's Republic of China.

It was hoped that representation at Bandung would be on the ministerial level with either the prime minister or foreign minister of a country heading the delegation. The communiqué indicated that acceptance of an invitation did not necessarily imply recognition by a government of other participants and did not involve

[12] Joint Communiqué, *Report on Indonesia,* Vol. 6 (January, 1955), p. 2.

any obligation to accept the views at the conference of other countries unless the participant so desired. Stress was placed in the communiqué on the points that the prime ministers "were not actuated by any desire for exclusiveness in respect to the membership of the conference" and that they did not wish that "the participating countries should build themselves into a regional bloc."[13]

In convening the Bandung assembly with its final membership, Indonesia along with Burma and India was interested in finding a way of acquainting the People's Republic of China with the viewpoints of other Asian states and of giving the latter an opportunity of getting firsthand impressions of Chinese Communist leaders. Moreover, the Bandung meeting might be a factor in weakening the relations between Communist China and the Soviet Union and in producing an atmosphere less belligerent and more conducive to negotiations between Communist China and the United States.

The leaders of the Colombo Powers in their communiqué at Bogor referred to a number of subjects apart from the projected conference. They expressed "gratification at the results of the Geneva Conference on Indochina and the cessation of hostilities" and hoped that "the Geneva agreements would be fully respected and implemented by all concerned and that there would be no outside interference which would hinder their successful implementation"; the prime ministers of India, Pakistan, Burma, and Ceylon approved Indonesia's position on West Irian and hoped the government of the Netherlands would "reopen negotiations to implement their obligations under the solemn agreements concluded by them with Indonesia"; support for the "legitimate right to self-determination" of the peoples of Tunisia and Morocco was continued; a request was again made for the end of "nuclear and thermonuclear explosions for experimental purposes"; and the prime ministers called for the establishment of a committee of experts to consider economic problems of common concern.[14]

All of the countries invited to the Bandung Conference, with the exception of the Central African Federation, attended. Opening on April 18 and closing on April 24, the assembly brought together a large proportion of the leaders of Asia. In addition to the sponsoring prime ministers, such public figures as Chou En-lai, Gamal Abdel Nasser, Carlos P. Romulo, and Prince Wan Waithayakon were present. The Bandung Conference of 29 Asian-African

[13] *Ibid.*, p. 3.
[14] *Ibid.*

countries represented the three great approaches to foreign policy prevalent in the world—the Communist, the Western, and the uncommitted. Under the circumstances the decisions of the assembly in order to receive unanimous approval had to reflect basic compromises in issues relating to the cold war.

As would be expected, the President of Indonesia delivered the opening address and Prime Minister Ali Sastroamidjojo was chosen chairman of the conference. The agenda as finally approved included five headings: economic coöperation, cultural coöperation, human rights and self-determination of peoples, questions concerning countries not yet independent, and matters pertaining to world coöperation and peace. Three committees operated—an economic, a cultural, and in effect a political. A particularly troublesome controversy over procedure—whether or not opening addresses by the principal delegates should be publicly delivered or simply written and distributed—was resolved in favor of the former approach. The most serious controversy arose over the definition of colonialism, the pro-Western states desiring to condemn that of the Soviet Union as revealed by "force, infiltration and subversion" in addition to the traditional overseas imperialism of the Western powers.[15] Premiers Chou En-lai and Jawaharlal Nehru opposed such a definition with the result that a compromise was finally reached wherein it was vaguely stated that "colonialism in all its manifestations is an evil which should speedily be brought to an end."[16] Another topic of controversy concerned the alliance of certain members of the Conference with outside powers. Prime Minister Nehru observed that no Asian or African state should be a "camp follower" of either the Communist or anti-Communist blocs. In the final statement of the Conference "the right of each nation to defend itself singly or collectively in conformity with the Charter of the United Nations" was coupled with "abstention from the use of arrangements of collective defense to serve the particular interests of any of the big powers."[17]

The communiqué at the end of the Bandung Conference embraced a wide range of subjects showing basic agreement on many topics of common concern. Particularly gratifying to Indonesia was the support it received in the case of West Irian, the Con-

[15] Quoted in George McTurnan Kahin, *The Asian-African Conference*, p. 29.

[16] The Final Communiqué of the Asian-African Conference, Press Release, Permanent Mission of the Republic of Indonesia to the United Nations. See Appendix C for full text.

[17] *Ibid.*

ference urging the Netherlands to reopen negotiations with Djakarta as quickly as possible in order to implement previous Dutch-Indonesian agreements and hoping the United Nations would help the parties concerned in reaching a peaceful solution. As a Moslem country Indonesia was in favor of the statements supporting the rights of the peoples of Tunisia, Morocco, and Algeria to self-determination and independence, the rights of the Arabs in Palestine, and the case of Yemen in her territorial dispute with Great Britain. Indonesia, in fact, took the strongest position on the North African issue. The Conference adopted a declaration on the "promotion of world peace and coöperation," based upon points presented by different delegations, ranging from non-interference in the internal affairs of another nation to recogition of the equality of all countries and races. The delegates condemned discrimination and segregation, particularly in the Union of South Africa. The Conference called for a prohibition on the production of nuclear and thermonuclear weapons with an agreement among the powers concerned to begin by terminating experiments in this type of warfare. At the same time a request was included for general disarmament including an end of "all weapons of mass destruction" under "effective international control." Provisions for cultural coöperation on a bilateral basis and for economic coöperation on an enlarged scale were made. The Conference called for membership in the United Nations of a number of states, those in Southeast Asia being Cambodia, Laos, and a united Vietnam. Significant was the omission of a recommendation for the seating of the People's Republic of China in the world organization. At the same time the delegates agreed that "all nations should have the right freely to choose their own political and economic systems and their own way of life in conformity with the purposes and principles of the Charter of the United Nations."[18]

At the suggestion of Indonesia another meeting of the Colombo Powers was held, this time at New Delhi, from November 12 to 14, 1956. The prime minister of Pakistan declined to attend but Prime Ministers Ali Sastroamidjojo of Indonesia, Jawaharlal Nehru of India, U Ba Swe of Burma, and S. W. R. D. Bandaranaike of Ceylon were present. The occasion of the meeting was to consider the international situation caused by the recent Israeli, British, and

[18] *Ibid.* In December, 1957, an Asian-African People's Solidarity Conference, unofficial but Communist-dominated, opened in Cairo. It stood in contrast to the Bandung assembly.

French attack on Egypt. At the same time Russian intervention in Hungary was given careful attention.

Among the states of Southeast Asia Indonesia had taken the most active part in the international negotiations following the Egyptian nationalization of the Universal Company of the Suez Maritime Canal on July 26. Indonesia attended by invitation the London Conference of 22 powers held on the Suez problem from August 16 to 23 but joined with India, Ceylon, and the Soviet Union in not being present at the second London Conference on the controversy, September 19 to 21. On August 11 the Indonesian Parliament by a unanimous voice vote had supported the Egyptian nationalization of the Suez Canal Company, and six days later President Sukarno in his annual address commemorating the anniversary of the nation's independence called for "Hands off Egypt." He indicated that Indonesia believed Egypt would keep the canal open to international traffic. These viewpoints were expressed by Foreign Minister Ruslan Abdulgani at the first London Conference.

The Anglo-French-Israeli attack on Egypt aroused considerable hostility against Great Britain, France, and Israel and sympathy for the Egyptians in the island republic. On November 2 Parliament in Djakarta unanimously condemned the aggression and appealed to the legislative bodies in Paris and London to urge their governments to stop the attack. If the appeals of the United Nations to end the hostilities and bring about a withdrawal of the invaders were ignored, the Indonesian Parliament urged the government to consider the breaking off of diplomatic relations with Great Britain and France (there being none with Israel). Indonesian workers in the air terminal in Djakarta refused to service planes of the British Overseas Airways Corporation. On November 7 a mob attack against the British and French embassies occurred in the capital. A number of Indonesians volunteered to fight in Egypt. Soviet intervention in Hungary troubled many Indonesian leaders but did not provoke the widespread hostility evident in the Suez crisis. Nevertheless, the Djakarta government came to take an increasingly critical attitude toward Soviet policy in Hungary.

Indonesia strongly supported the resolutions of the General Assembly of the United Nations taken on November 2, 4, 7, and 24 aimed at ending hostilities in Egypt and bringing about the withdrawal of the invading forces. The island republic was willing to send three army companies to Egypt to join the United Nations police, and became, in fact, the only Southeast Asian member to have a contingent in the United Nations Emergency Force as well as the first of the countries to withdraw its unit. Indonesia joined with other Asian-African members of the world organization in sponsoring measures to establish peace in the Middle East through United Nations efforts. At one point it wanted sanctions against Israel. As for Hungary, the Indonesian delegation at the United Nations abstained on a resolution of the General Assembly on November 4 asking, *inter alia,* the Soviet Union and Hungary to allow United Nations observers to enter the latter, travel freely, and report their findings to the Secretary-General of the world organization. Later, however, Indonesia along with India and Ceylon sponsored a resolution calling in effect for the same procedure, the General Assembly on November 21 approving the resolution by an overwhelming vote. On November 9 and December 12, it should be noted, Indonesia abstained on resolutions requesting the Soviet Union to withdraw her forces from Hungary without delay.

The communiqué of the New Delhi Conference of the Colombo Powers issued on November 14 was sympathetic to both Egypt and Hungary although Great Britain and France were more severely criticized than the Soviet Union. The United Nations General Assembly resolutions of November 2, 4, and 7 on Egypt were specifically welcomed but no reference was made to the resolutions of November 4 and 9 as outlined on Hungary. Nevertheless, it was clearly stated that the prime ministers considered it an "inalienable right of every country to shape for itself its own destiny, free from all external pressures. They are of opinion that the Soviet forces should be withdrawn from Hungary speedily and that the Hungarian people should be left free to decide their own future and the form of government they will have, without external intervention from any quarter."[19] The communiqué clearly indicated the basic apprehension that aggression by strong powers against the weak menaced the peace of the world. A revival of colonialism, as the prime ministers interpreted recent events, threatened the freedom of the weak states of Asia and Africa. It is significant that after the New Delhi Conference Prime Minister Ali Sastroamidjojo visited Karachi for discussions with leading Pakistani officials, thus attempting to maintain after a fashion the solidarity of the original five Colombo Powers.

Indonesia in its attitude toward race reflects the feelings of many

[19] Joint Statement by the Prime Ministers of Burma, Ceylon, Indonesia, and India, *Burma Weekly Bulletin,* New Series, Vol. 5 (November 22, 1956), p. 263.

Asians and Africans. As is clear, Asian nationalism has among its components a certain racial aspect although emphasized in varying degrees. Fortunately Indonesia in its condemnation of racialism has not yet developed on its own part a nationalism that is primarily racial. At the same time there is a certain appreciation for the military role of the Korean and Chinese Communists against the Americans in Korea and for that of the Viet Minh against the French in Indochina.

Indonesians have not hesitated to voice their criticism of racialism, especially the *apartheid* policy of the Union of South Africa. Vice-President Hatta observed: "Talk of the brotherhood of man in a world in which racial discrimination makes possible the existence of such a policy as *apartheid* . . . indeed seems incongruous."[20] Similar criticism of the Union of South Africa has been voiced in the United Nations. Nevertheless, Indonesia did not want the Bandung Conference, despite the manifestations of racialism in South Africa, to be "a move towards international solidarity by the 'Non-Western' races against the 'Western' races."[21]

As a state where Islam is the religion of about 90 percent of the people, Indonesia is interested in coöperation among the Moslem countries of the world. At the same time the foreign policy of the Republic has not been based on considerations that are primarily religious. President Sukarno in a speech on the "National State and Ideals of Islam" on May 7, 1953, noted that "Islam is not at all opposed to nationalism. Islam does not forbid us to form a National State. But what is misunderstood is that, if you were a Nationalist, you would be an anti-religionist."[22] He had previously observed on October 24, 1951, that "we are a secular state by deliberate choice, believing that religion is a private matter between man and his Maker."[23]

Under Article 18 of the Indonesian provisional constitution of August 15, 1950, "everyone is entitled to freedom of religion, conscience and thought" although under Article 43 it is asserted that "the State is based on the belief in the Divine Omnipotence."[24]

[20] Hatta, *op. cit.*, p. 443.
[21] "INS Correspondent Interviews Indonesian Premier on A-A Conference," *Report on Indonesia*, Vol. 6 (April, 1955), p. 3.
[22] "National State and Ideals of Islam (A Speech by President Sukarno)," *Indonesian Affairs*, Vol. III (June/July, 1953), p. 47.
[23] "Towards Justice and Peace, President's Speech on the Occasion of United Nations Day, October 24, 1951," *Indonesian Affairs*, Vol. I (October/November, 1951), p. 27.
[24] *Provisional Constitution*, pp. 8, 12.

Religious organizations in Indonesia are allowed to establish contacts with similar groups abroad. A Ministry of Religious Affairs has among its functions the regulation of pilgrimages to Mecca. President Sukarno himself made one in 1955. Moslem political parties exist in the Republic such as the Masjumi or Council of Indonesian Moslem Associations, the PSII or Indonesian Islamic Association Party, and the Nahdatul Ulama or Moslem Teachers. In the first elected House of Representatives the Masjumi had 57 seats and the other two parties 53 of the total 260 seats.

It is believed in some Moslem states abroad that a Masjumi-dominated government in Indonesia would place greater stress on international ties among Islamic countries. The success of the Darul Islam movement, centering on the creation of an Islamic State of Indonesia along theocratic lines and now constituting in some respects a state within a state in a part of West Java, would certainly modify the international outlook of Indonesia.

The specific objectives of the Republic's foreign policy were carefully outlined by Vice-President Hatta as preserving the safety of the nation, getting from abroad necessary daily items and capital for various projects, strengthening international law and working toward social justice in line with the Charter of the United Nations, developing cordial relations with neighbors, and seeking coöperation among countries through the application of the ideals in the *Pantjasila*. Indonesia has made, the Vice-President said, the United Nations "the focal point of its overall policy of seeking good relations with all other nations."[25]

In an effort to find the reasons for the basic principles of Indonesian foreign policy, especially with reference to the cold war, colonialism, and racialism, certain considerations are important. As is already evident, Indonesia acquired its independence against an extended colonial background and partly at least through armed struggle. Under the circumstances it is not surprising that a strong anticolonial viewpoint developed in foreign policy. In addition, the racial aspect cannot be separated from the anticolonial, for the rulers of yesterday in Indonesia and in a large part of Asia were men of different race from the people governed. Once independence was achieved, Indonesia realized the need for peace at home and abroad in order to develop the country under the most favorable circumstances. Suspicious of Western powers as a result of its colonial heritage and still subject to their economic influence, the

[25] Hatta, *op. cit.*, p. 441.

Republic did not want to tie itself politically to them. At the same time Hatta has significantly written that his country is "bounded by the British Navy and the American Navy, which control the Indian and Pacific Oceans. But no one can say that Britain and the United States have evil designs on Indonesia. On the contrary, they are desirous of seeing Indonesia remain independent and become prosperous."[26] Since the insular republic has no common boundaries with China or the Soviet Union, Hatta has observed that "a direct threat from that direction to Indonesian independence neither exists nor is possible."[27] As a consequence many Indonesian leaders are convinced they have considerable freedom of decision in foreign policy. By not committing themselves to either the American or the Russian blocs, by opposing military alliances, and by trying to prevent the outbreak of a third world war, they believe they can best establish their identity and safeguard the independence of their country from both internal and external threats.[28]

A considerable degree of bipartisanship is evident in foreign policy. Basically the numerous political parties of Indonesia may be grouped around the three pillars of nationalism, religion, and Marxism. Although each party has its own points of emphasis, a similarity in the fundamentals of foreign policy is more often than not apparent. This similarity in a measure represents the fruits of compromise, efforts to placate various viewpoints and give the outside world the front of harmony. In addition, the cabinets of the country are dependent upon different political groupings for support in Parliament. The victory of the PKI or Communist Party of Indonesia, however, would clearly orientate the Republic toward the people's democracies.

The relations between Indonesia and the Netherlands present a contrast with those between the Philippines and the United States.

[26] *Ibid.*, p. 445.
[27] *Ibid.*
[28] In 1956 Prime Minister Ali Sastroamidjojo asserted:
"Summarizing, I would say that our active independent foreign policy is the product of the interplay of several thoughts:
"1. The historical progress towards the achievement of national independence and the problems of current growth towards emancipation in social and economic fields.
"2. The prevalence of Western economic domination in Indonesia.
"3. The desire to establish our own identity in the world.
"4. The belief that in this atomic stalemate the chances of peace would be increased if military alliances were transformed into associations of close economic coöperation and eventual technical assistance if required."
Statement on Foreign Policy, *Report on Indonesia*, Vol. 7 (June/July, 1956), p. 4.

At the beginning the concept of the Netherlands-Indonesian Union was based upon the presumption of a close community of interests between the two peoples. The failure of the Union arose from a fundamental divergence of viewpoint. In the case of the Philippines no complicated superstructure with the United States was set up, but in the case of Indonesia an effort was made to regulate relations with the Netherlands through a complex governmental arrangement.

To the Dutch, of course, the East Indies meant much more than the Philippines to the Americans. The former had between 25 and 30 percent of their invested capital in Indonesia and the economy of the Netherlands was closely tied to the Asian archipelago. Even in early 1957 over a billion dollars in Dutch private capital remained in the Indies. Much of the interisland shipping was still operated by a Dutch company. The importance of the Netherlands East Indies in world trade was an obvious asset to the mother country. The Dutch and Eurasian population living in the archipelago also constituted a factor that could not be ignored. In 1940 about 230,000 Dutch lived in the island area and in early 1957 about 46,000. Many of them were highly skilled, making a valuable contribution to the Indies. In 1949 the Eurasian or Indo-European population numbered about 100,000, the great majority keeping their loyalty to the Netherlands and finding hard times in postwar Indonesia. From the viewpoint of international prestige the far-flung and heavily populated island empire in Asia enhanced the stature of the Netherlands. In more specific terms the strategic naval base of Surabaya was of interest to all concerned with the problems of sea power in Southeast Asia and the Southwest Pacific.

The Statute of Union between the Netherlands and Indonesia, finally adopted at the Round Table Conference at The Hague on November 2, 1949, offered a basic framework for relations between the two "partners." In the negotiations the Indonesians had wanted the Union Statute to have the nature of an international treaty with voluntary coöperation by conferences of ministers from the two parties when problems of common concern needed attention. The Netherlands had supported the establishment of a Union of two sovereign states but had wanted very close coöperation through duly constituted organs uniting the two parties under the Crown. The assistance of the United Nations Commission for Indonesia was especially helpful in working out the final draft of the Statute.

Under its provisions "the Netherlands-Indonesian Union effectuates the organized coöperation between the Kingdom of the Netherlands and the Republic of the United States of Indonesia on the basis of free will and equality in status with equal rights."[29] Coöperation between the partners would "take place with respect to subjects lying primarily in the field of foreign relations and defense, and, as far as necessary, finance, and also in regard of subjects of an economic and a cultural nature."[30] All Union decisions would be taken by mutual agreement. The head of the Union would be Queen Juliana of the Netherlands and her successors; the organs would consist of ministerial conferences at least twice a year, a permanent secretariat under an alternating Indonesian and Dutch secretary-general, a Union Court of Arbitration of three Indonesian and three Dutch judges making decisions by a bare majority, and meetings of representatives from the two parliaments. High Commissioners with the diplomatic rank of ambassadors would be exchanged. Ancillary agreements referred to in the Statute covered foreign relations, defense, financial and economic relations, and cultural matters.

In the foreign relations agreement it was explicitly stated that "on the primary consideration of the principle that each of the Partners conducts its own foreign relations and determines its own foreign policy, they shall aim at coördinating their foreign policy as much as possible and at consulting each other thereon."[31] Common or joint representation abroad was allowed if both partners desired it; one party would by preference represent the interests of the other in a given country abroad if the other member of the Union did not have diplomatic representation there; both agreed not to make treaties involving the interests of the other without prior consultation; each promised technical aid to its partner upon request in the conduct of foreign relations. In an agreement relative to transitional measures, provisions on foreign affairs included a pledge by the Netherlands to promote United Nations membership for Indonesia and the former's transfer to the latter after consultation of rights and obligations arising from treaties and international agreements if and to the extent that they are applicable to Indonesian jurisdiction.

In the defense agreement each of the partners was responsible

[29] United Nations Commission for Indonesia: Special Report to the Security Council on the Round Table Conference, United Nations, Security Council, *Official Records, Fourth Year, Special Supplement* No. 6, p. 95.

[30] *Ibid.*

[31] *Ibid.*, p. 102.

for its own security and they were obligated to consult "in the event of threat of aggression" to one or both. Military missions would be exchanged and neither would accept one from a third power without consulting the other. In addition to training activities, coöperation could consist of aid in matériel and providing for necessary maintenance. Further, if one of the partners wanted to get matériel it should consult with the other about the way the latter might help. Detailed arrangements were made in a number of related agreements. A Netherlands military mission of naval, army, and air force sections would be sent to Indonesia for a duration of three years unless the agreement was previously ended or extended. The specific purpose would be to help in building and training the armed forces of the new republic and to advise on military matters. The commander of the naval base at Surabaya would initially be a Dutch naval officer responsible to the Indonesian minister of defense, sovereignty over the base being transferred to Indonesia. The Dutch navy would normally leave the Indies within a year, and the land units, if possible, in six months. Members of the Indonesian armed forces under Dutch auspices in the area would have the right to join those of the new government of the archipelago, those of the Netherlands, or return to civilian status. Their matériel could be transferred to the Indonesian authorities. Obviously the Dutch would retain no bases in the new republic.

Agreement was reached on financial and economic relations between the two partners. Indonesia pledged itself to reëstablish the privileges, rights, and concessions under the law of the Dutch regime valid when the transfer of sovereignty occurred. At the same time the Republic came to possess extensive powers to review and, if necessary, curtail foreign economic rights considered at variance with the general welfare. It would, however, resort to nationalization only if the general need demanded it and subject to due process of law and the principle of compensation. Each accorded the other commercial preferences and agreed to consult on monetary and financial matters of common concern. Indonesia took over a debt that came to be placed at around 4300 million guilders (nearly $1,130 million) but there was no lien on its revenues to insure payment. As for the Dutch civil servants in the new state, it was provided in the overall settlement that their position would be guaranteed for two years. Efforts would be made to use more and more Indonesians in business enterprises. It is noticeable that the Dutch did not acquire the right to control the Indonesian currency as the Americans did in the Philippines and that there was no "parity clause" in the Indonesian-Netherlands arrangement. In fact, it was stated in the financial and economic agreement that "foreigners of all nations will have equal rights in participating in trade with Indonesia and in the economic activity and industrial development of that country."[32]

In the cultural agreement the partners set up a joint committee of seven members from each side to develop mutual relations in science, education, and culture. Efforts would be made to promote through various means a knowledge of each other's culture and to provide, upon request, assistance such as the exchange of experts, teachers, and professors. Among other items, each of the partners would facilitate the granting of scholarships for students and research workers in the country of the other.

In anticipation of the Dutch transfer of sovereignty, the Indonesian delegations at The Hague representing the Republic and the Federal Consultative Assembly presented on October 31 to the Steering Committee of the Round Table Conference the text of a provisional constitution for the Republic of the United States of Indonesia. The Charter of the Transfer of Sovereignty stated that "the Kingdom of the Netherlands unconditionally and irrevocably transfers complete sovereignty over Indonesia to the Republic of the United States of Indonesia as an independent and sovereign State."[33] Although the ultimate status of the Residency of New Guinea was left unsettled at the time, the Charter clearly provided for the transfer of sovereignty over the rest of the area of the Netherlands East Indies on December 30, 1949, at the latest. Among the transition measures mentioned in a separate agreement were provisions for the release of the rulers of self-governing territories in Indonesia from their oaths to the Netherlands Crown and the recognition of the special position of the areas by the Republic of the United States of Indonesia. Under the principle of self-determination, any constituent state of the federation had temporarily the right to negotiate with the Netherlands and the United States of Indonesia for a special relationship.

The Dutch transfer of sovereignty to Indonesia on December 27, 1949, was followed by a series of developments that came to alter the arrangements made at the Round Table Conference. From the constitutional viewpoint the Republican leaders changed the

[32] *Ibid.*, p. 111.
[33] *Ibid.*, p. 91.

federation into a unitary state. Although all the 16 states of the federation (6 *negaras*—East Indonesia, Madura, East Java, Pasundan, South Sumatra, East Sumatra; 9 autonomous territories—Central Java, East Borneo, Southeast Borneo, Dayak, Bandjar, West Borneo, Billiton, Bangka, Riouw; and the Republic of Indonesia [itself becoming a *negara*]) had approved the provisional constitution, the Republican leaders generally looked upon the various states outside their own as artificial creations of the Dutch, constructed on the old Roman principle of *divide et impera.* On August 17, 1950, a unitary state for the entire country, called the Republic of Indonesia, was formally inaugurated. The Republic was divided into 10 provinces: North, Middle, and South Sumatra, West, Middle, and East Java, Kalimantan, Sulawesi, Maluku, and the Lesser Sundas.

Meanwhile the Netherlands-Indonesian Union began to operate. The first ministerial conference, opening at Djakarta on March 25, had on its agenda a number of items such as the setting up of the Union Court of Arbitration, the Dutch military mission, commercial and financial agreements and, of course, the case of West New Guinea. A military mission of 800, it was agreed, would be sent to Indonesia from the Netherlands; the latter granted the former a credit of 200 million guilders at 3 percent for general use and an additional 100 million guilders to pay pensions and to deliver products; commissions were set up to deal with cultural matters, judicial questions, and problems involving continued Indonesian government employment of Dutchmen. With the second ministerial conference meeting at The Hague in the latter part of November, further agreements were reached: the term of the Dutch credit previously granted was extended from July 1, 1951, to January 1, 1952; a duration of three years was set for the Dutch military mission; a new commercial accord was made and new regulations were approved about the payment of pensions. The Union Court of Arbitration had been formally set up the previous May 19.

The failure of Indonesia and the Netherlands to settle the West New Guinea controversy was a significant factor in the dissolution of the Union. On January 10, 1951, a motion by the opposition in the Djakarta Parliament calling for the abrogation of the Union was rejected by a margin of three votes. The following August Indonesia sent Dr. Supomo to the Netherlands to discuss on an informal basis an alteration in the basic agreement. On April 21,

1953, the Dutch and Indonesians agreed to end the former's military mission in the latter's country by December except for some maritime activities to be completed by the middle of the following year. One of the points in the first program of Prime Minister Ali Sastroamidjojo, whose cabinet took office on August 1, 1953, was "the acceleration in the modification" of The Hague agreements. Negotiations between the Dutch and Indonesians in the Netherlands resulted on August 10, 1954, in the signing of a protocol and exchange of notes abrogating the Union Statute and terminating the agreements on foreign relations, cultural matters, and military coöperation. Several parts of the financial and economic settlement were ended but the rest remained, subject to negotiation on new provisions. Agreements would be made on trade relations and consular matters. Ambassadors and consuls would replace high commissioners and commissioners. The Prime Minister of Indonesia significantly noted on August 16 that "the old colonial link limiting our independence has been broken."[34] The Djakarta Parliament, however, failed to approve the settlement.

Indonesia's decision on February 13, 1956, to abrogate unilaterally the Netherlands-Indonesian Union reflected the growing bitterness between the two countries. On December 10, 1955, following a statement three days before by the parties, a conference had opened at The Hague with an agenda including an Indonesian proposal for a new agreement to terminate the Union, another to replace the financial and economic agreements of 1949, the consideration of problems regarding West New Guinea, each keeping its own position on sovereignty which was not to be discussed, and other subjects either might raise to better relations. On December 13 the Conference decided to move to Geneva where a neutral atmosphere prevailed. It was indicated in a communiqué on January 4, 1956, that the three main items of dispute were the procedure of arbitrating differences in the interpretation of agreements to be concluded, the question of supremacy in case of dispute between Indonesian national legislation and treaties made by the two parties and the issue of Indonesia's recognizing the rights and concessions granted Dutch nationals by the former government of the Netherlands East Indies. The discussions were adjourned on January 7 for each party to consult its government. Both cabinets, in fact, were faced with considerable criticism regarding the negotiations. Reopening on February 7, the Conference was able to agree in

[34] *Times of Indonesia*, August 18, 1954.

principle on the abrogation of the Union and the termination of the financial and economic accords but not on the question of a provisional agreement for settling disputes before the conclusion of a permanent accord. The negotiations were ended on February 11 with a joint statement indicating no agreement on the making of arrangements for settling possible disputes.

On February 28 the provisional Parliament of Indonesia, reflecting the decision of the government, adopted a bill on the abrogation of the Union and the termination of the related agreements. President Sukarno declined to sign it, for he believed the subject matter was so important it should be approved by the newly elected Parliament when it met. A new bill with amendments was approved by this body on April 21, retroactive to February 15. Along with the annulment of all Round Table Conference agreements, the bill called for relations between Indonesia and the Netherlands "common between fully sovereign nations on the basis of international laws."[35] It was stated that "rights, concessions, licenses, and the manner [in which] Dutch companies are operated in Indonesia shall be respected if they are not in violation of the interests of a nation in reconstruction."[36] The Netherlands had vigorously but vainly protested the unilateral ending of the agreements. On May 4 it was announced that the office of the Dutch High Commissioner in Djakarta was being changed to an embassy.

Further deterioration in Indonesian-Dutch relations came on August 4 when Indonesia announced that it was repudiating its debts under the Round Table settlement to the Netherlands although not to related third parties (Australia, Canada, and the United States). In fact, Indonesian officials indicated that the island republic could demand war reparations from the former mother country. The Dutch strongly protested and compared Indonesia's actions to the recent Egyptian nationalization of the Suez Canal Company.

The arrest and imprisonment of a number of Dutch citizens in Indonesia, accused of trying to overthrow the government, have also weakened relations. In an effort to attract world attention the Dutch even issued a White Paper on the subject in June, 1955. The case of Leon Jungschlaeger, a former head of Dutch military intelligence, aroused particular concern in the Netherlands. Arrested

[35] Text of Abrogation of RTC Agreement, *Indonesian News Roundup*, Vol. II (June 2, 1956), p. 15.
[36] *Ibid.*

in January, 1954, his trial was long, only ending in April, 1956. A few days before the verdict was to be announced he died. Many Dutch consider him a martyr, for it was widely believed in the Netherlands that the charges were false and the trial unfair. The Dutch compare their resentment to the feeling in the United States over the trial and conviction of American nationals in Communist China. The Jungschlaeger case has left bitter memories in both The Hague and Djakarta. Indonesia on December 27, it should be noted, refused a Dutch request to have placed before the International Court of Justice the question of a "denial of justice" in the trial of Dutch accused of subversive activities against the island republic.

Widespread Indonesian action against the Dutch began after the General Assembly of the United Nations failed to adopt in November, 1957, a resolution supported by the Djakarta government on West Irian. On December 1 a 24-hour strike was called for the following day against Dutch enterprises; publications in the Dutch language were banned; KLM, the Dutch airline, was forbidden to operate in the island republic; all but one of the consulates of the Netherlands were ordered closed as well as the information, cultural, and military sections of her mission in Djakarta; Dutch residents were generally encouraged to leave and remittances to the Netherlands were stopped; Dutch harbor properties were taken over by the government; and Djakarta gave consideration to plans for evacuating 24,000 nationals from Holland.

The Indonesian Communists were active in the vanguard of those who took advantage of the situation to subject several Dutch firms and enterprises to "wildcat" seizures. The government took control of the firms indicating that compensation would be decided after the settlement of the West Irian issue. On December 9 similar authority was assumed for the Dutch plantation properties. It was clear that the control of Dutch property was moving into the hands of the Indonesians who were themselves divided on how to deal with the situation. As for the Dutch residing in the island republic, they were often critical of The Hague government for its Netherlands New Guinea policy. Both the Dutch and the Indonesians were paying a heavy price, the former in terms of investments and the latter in economic dislocation.

At the request of the Netherlands the permanent council of the North Atlantic Treaty Organization met on December 7 to consider a Dutch request for solidarity. At the summit meeting of the

North Atlantic Council in Paris the participants on December 19 viewed "with concern" developments in Indonesia. The Netherlands has also protested to the United Nations Indonesian actions against the Dutch in the island republic. A number of Western countries including the United States and Great Britain urged moderation in Djakarta. London rejected an Indonesian request that warships of the Netherlands be barred from Singapore. Concern was expressed in Western circles about Djakarta's announcement of sovereignty over the waters of the island state, the question of the freedom of the high seas being involved.

Indonesia for its part appealed for support to Asian and African states; India, Burma, the Federation of Malaya, Ceylon, and Pakistan were among those who favored moderation. The Soviet Union at an Asian-African People's Solidarity Conference in Cairo late in December went out of its way to support Indonesia. Djakarta indicated that if attempts to purchase arms in the United States failed the island republic would seriously turn to other countries. In view of the shipping crisis as a result of the campaign against the Dutch, the Indonesians made arrangements with Japanese shipping interests to charter vessels for use in interisland traffic. Sympathy for Indonesia came from many Malays in Malaya although the Indonesian Communist Party in December supported the Malayan Communists in not negotiating with the Federation government regarding surrender. Peking offered Djakarta a loan.

As for West New Guinea, negotiations at the Round Table Conference in the Netherlands in 1949 had resulted in a deadlock over Dutch and Indonesian claims to the area.[37] A temporary compromise was written into the Charter of the Transfer of Sovereignty whereby "the *status quo* of the Residency of New Guinea shall be maintained with the stipulation that within a year from the date of transfer of sovereignty to the Republic of the United States of Indonesia the question of the political status of New Guinea be determined through negotiations between the Republic of the United States of Indonesia and the Kingdom of the Netherlands."[38] At the first ministerial conference of the Union it was agreed that a joint commission would consider the controversy and report by

[37] The expression "West New Guinea" is widely used in United Nations documentation. "Netherlands New Guinea" is the Dutch terminology and "West Irian" the Indonesian. The author's use of the different terms does not imply any preference.

[38] Security Council, *Official Records, Fourth Year, Special Supplement* No. 6, p. 92.

July, 1950. After making the study, the commission was unable to agree and the body of its report was issued in two parts, one written by the Indonesian members and the other by the Dutch. At a ministerial conference, opening on December 4 to consider the controversy, no solution was reached and West New Guinea remained under the rule of the Netherlands.

In the liquidation of the colonial empires in Southeast Asia the appearance of a major territorial issue like West Irian is unfortunate. With an area of about 103,000 square miles, it occupies the western part of New Guinea, the northeastern section of the island belonging to the Australian trust Territory of New Guinea and the southeastern part to Australian Papua. The exact population of Netherlands New Guinea is not known but it is estimated to be around 700,000, of whom about 400,000 are under direct government control. The people are mainly Papuans, not being of the Indonesian race or culture, but like the other principal inhabitants of New Guinea, Australasians. Islam in its expansion in the East Indies did not spread beyond the Moluccas, although under the Dutch Christianity in West New Guinea came to embrace 170,000 people. The primitive culture of the Papuans has been hardly modified except along the coastal fringes of the area. West Irian has resources of oil and gold but the exact extent of these and other possible assets is not known. Despite its swamps and jungles, it is believed that the area is capable of considerable development.

The Dutch entered West New Guinea through their overlordship of the Moluccan Sultanate of Tidore, which claimed sovereignty over northwestern Irian. Asserting possession over West New Guinea in 1828, the Dutch later bought off the claims of the Sultanate of Tidore. West Irian was a part of the Residency of the Moluccas at the time of the Japanese invasion. After the Second World War the policy of the Netherlands was indicated to a degree when she joined Australia, the United States, New Zealand, France, and the United Kingdom on February 6, 1947, in organizing the South Pacific Commission whose area was then defined as embracing the non-self-governing territories of the signatories in the Pacific lying "wholly or in part south of the Equator and east from and including Netherlands New Guinea."[39] In 1952 the constitution of the Netherlands was amended to make West New Guinea a part

[39] Agreement Establishing the South Pacific Commission, *British and Foreign State Papers, 1947*, Part II, Vol. 148, p. 288. On November 7, 1951, Guam and the Trust Territory of the Pacific Islands were added.

of the kingdom. The absorption of West Irian by Indonesia, it is clear, would lead to an orientation of the area toward Djakarta.

A significant factor in the Dutch attitude toward Netherlands New Guinea has been the interest in the area of some of the Eurasians in the rest of Indonesia. In numerous cases they came to look upon Netherlands New Guinea as the answer to their hopes for a new homeland. Economic considerations in Dutch policy should also not be ignored; since the Second World War petroleum, for instance, has begun to be produced. Nevertheless, the amount of capital necessary to develop on an extensive scale the vast territory and to enable settlement by large numbers of outsiders would be great, thus raising serious questions in the field of finance for the mother country. In a consideration of a different nature, the Dutch have stressed their obligations to the indigenous people of West Irian and the eventual right of the latter to self-determination. Here a factor in progress is the work of the Christian missionary societies in the area. From the prestige viewpoint the Netherlands remains a power in the Pacific only as long as it maintains a territorial base in that part of the world.

Indonesia has based a large part of its claim to West Irian on the grounds that it was an integral part of the Netherlands East Indies. Logically, Indonesia argues, the Dutch transfer of sovereignty should not, cannot, and did not exclude any portion of the old Netherlands empire in the archipelago. In addition, stress was placed at the beginning on general nationality as a basic principle, a consideration that *inter alia* is not identical in the very broad sense with the previous argument centering upon the territory subject to Dutch control. By way of illustration, British Borneo and Portuguese Timor were not under the Dutch flag. Indonesian leaders in Djakarta have also been apprehensive lest the eastern part of the archipelago be used as a springboard against Java. A number of outbreaks after the transfer of sovereignty caused the new government of Indonesia to question the good faith of the Dutch. The winning of West Irian, moreover, has come to represent a sacred cause around which many Indonesian nationalists under the leadership of President Sukarno can rally.

The Djakarta government took the question of West Irian to the United Nations after the Netherlands refused to negotiate on the matter at the summer conference in 1954 when the two parties agreed to end their Union. On previous occasions Indonesia had protested the right of the Dutch at the United Nations to transmit annual reports on Netherlands New Guinea under Article 73 e of the Charter dealing with non-self-governing territories. Referring on August 17, 1954, to Articles 35, 10, and 14 of the Charter, Indonesia requested that the "question of West Irian (West New Guinea)" be placed on the agenda of the ninth regular session of the General Assembly for its consideration and recommendations. On September 24 the Assembly approved the inclusion of the subject and referred it to the First Committee. After considering the item from November 23 to December 1, the Committee made its report on December 4.

Although the interests of outside powers in West Irian had in many instances previously been expressed, the discussion in the United Nations brought to the forefront the international implications of the controversy. Australia, which had championed the cause of Indonesian independence, had become a staunch defender of maintaining the Dutch position in Netherlands New Guinea. During the Japanese offensive of the Second World War in Southeast Asia and the Southwest Pacific it is clear that the very security of the Commonwealth had been threatened, the island of New Guinea having greatly contributed to this situation. Unofficial Indonesian suggestions that Australian New Guinea and Papua should eventually be added to West Irian tended to create some uneasiness in Canberra. Australia came to the conclusion that a friendly Netherlands in West New Guinea was far better for the security of the Commonwealth than a neutral Indonesia. New Zealand, aware of her common security problems with Australia, supported her large neighbor in the Irian controversy. She fully realized that the stability of Southeast Asia was of direct concern to her.

Great Britain stood behind her two Commonwealth members in the Southwest Pacific. With both Malaya and British Borneo still dependencies at the time, she had an added interest in the security of Southeast Asia. France likewise opposed the Indonesian position on West Irian. Belgium, a colonial power like France, gave assistance to the Dutch cause. The United States, torn between its considerations for the Netherlands as a North Atlantic ally and Indonesia as an exponent of Asian nationalism, abstained from taking a position on the controversy.

All the United Nations members in Asia and Africa supported in the end the Indonesian case with the exception of Nationalist China, Israel, Turkey, and the Union of South Africa. Since most of the Asian-African states considered the question colonial in nature, their attitude was well defined. India took an active part in defending the Indonesian position, opposing the continuation of colonialism, as she saw it, in Asia and noting the historical, political, and geographical ties between West Irian and the rest of Indonesia. Burma also gave active support to her island neighbor. Thailand, although assuming a more passive role, favored the Indonesian case. The Communist states in the United Nations stanchly opposed the Dutch position.

Debate in the First Committee tended to be somewhat legal in nature and more acrimonious toward the end. As the *rapporteur* noted, the majority of the members believed that the United Nations was competent to argue the issue and make recommendations, but some were convinced that legal considerations prevented the world organization from dealing with the matter, and others thought the subject for political reasons should not be argued in the United Nations, since the fundamental issue was not the maintenance of the principle of self-determination but the transfer of sovereignty over an area from one state member of the world organization to another.

Indonesia on November 23 submitted a draft resolution under which the General Assembly would call upon the Dutch and Indonesian governments "to resume negotiations, without delay," invite the secretary-general to help the parties carry out the resolution and under certain circumstances authorize him to appoint a person to render good offices, and finally request the secretary-general to report on the negotiations at the next regular session of the General Assembly. On November 30, Argentina, Costa Rica, Cuba, Ecuador, El Salvador, India, Syria, and Yugoslavia submitted a joint draft resolution expressing after the preamble "the hope" in operative paragraph 1 that the Netherlands and Indonesia "will pursue their endeavours in respect of the dispute that now exists between them to find a solution in conformity with the principles of the Charter of the United Nations" and requesting the two parties in operative paragraph 2 "to report progress" at the next session of the General Assembly.[40] The joint draft resolution was approved as a whole by a vote of 34 to 14 with 10 abstentions. Indonesia as a result did not insist on a vote on its own proposal.

At the plenary session of the General Assembly on December 10 all three parts of the joint draft resolution failed to receive the necessary two-thirds majority, the chief reason being that a num-

[40] Joint draft resolution, *Yearbook of the United Nations, 1954*, p. 59.

ber of states shifted their position from abstaining to voting against the measure.[41] With considerable bitterness, Sudjarwo, the Indonesian representative, observed that "strange things indeed have happened"; he went on to conclude: "May my Government be given the strength to seek the solution [to the controversy] in a peaceful way."[42]

The question of West Irian was submitted on August 10, 1955, for the agenda of the tenth General Assembly of the United Nations by Afghanistan, Burma, Egypt, India, Indonesia, Iran, Iraq, Lebanon, Liberia, Pakistan, the Philippines, Saudi Arabia, Syria, Thailand, and Yemen. In both the General Committee and the plenary debate of the General Assembly strong opposition arose over the inscription of the question. On September 29 the General Committee by a vote of 7 to 5 with 2 abstentions recommended the inclusion of the item. In the plenary debate the Netherlands and Indonesia developed further their viewpoints on the subject. The Assembly decided by a vote of 31 to 18 with 10 abstentions to place the problem of West New Guinea on the agenda. On December 16 the same international body proceeded to adopt a resolution without objection expressing the hope that the negotiations referred to in a statement issued on December 7 by Indonesia and the Netherlands would be fruitful and that the problem would be resolved peacefully.

As the negotiations failed, Afghanistan, Burma, Cambodia, Ceylon, Egypt, India, Indonesia, Iraq, Jordan, Lebanon, Libya, Pakistan, Saudi Arabia, Syria, and Yemen on October 9, 1956, in an explanatory memorandum requested that the General Assembly give renewed consideration to the West Irian controversy. The First Committee later adopted a resolution whereby the president of the General Assembly would appoint a Good Offices Commission of three members in order to help in the negotiations betweeen Indonesia and the Netherlands leading to a solution that would be

[41] On operative paragraph 1 the vote was as follows: 34 in favor—Afghanistan, Argentina, Bolivia, Burma, Byelorussian SSR, Costa Rica, Cuba, Czechoslovakia, Ecuador, Egypt, El Salvador, Ethiopia, Greece, Honduras, India, Indonesia, Iran, Iraq, Lebanon, Liberia, Mexico, Pakistan, Paraguay, Philippines, Poland, Saudi Arabia, Syria, Thailand, Ukrainian SSR, USSR, Uruguay, Venezuela, Yemen, Yugoslavia; 23 against—Australia, Belgium, Brazil, Canada, Chile, China, Colombia, Denmark, Dominican Republic, France, Iceland, Israel, Luxembourg, Netherlands, New Zealand, Nicaragua, Norway, Panama, Peru, Sweden, Turkey, Union of South Africa, United Kingdom; and 3 abstaining—Guatemala, Haiti, the United States.

[42] United Nations, General Assembly, Ninth Session, *Official Records,* 509th Plenary Meeting, December 10, 1954, pp. 461-462.

peaceful, just, and in conformity with the objectives of the United Nations Charter. The measure was lost in the General Assembly on February 28, 1957, for it failed to receive a two-thirds majority. In the vote of 40 to 25 with 13 abstentions, Burma, Indonesia, the Philippines, and Thailand were with the majority while Cambodia and Laos abstained.

As might be expected, the issue was debated at the twelfth session of the General Assembly. A resolution sponsored by 19 states calling in effect for resumption of discussion on West New Guinea between the Netherlands and Indonesia with the possible assistance of the secretary-general passed the First Committee. The debate was acrimonious, the Soviet bloc to the embarrassment of most of the Asian-African states making the controversy a cold war issue as much as one of colonialism. It was alleged that the strategic area of West Irian was being prepared as a base for the SEATO powers. Indonesia indicated its patience was close to exhaustion, and it might seek other methods of gaining its objectives. The resolution of the First Committee failed on November 29 to receive a two-thirds majority in the General Assembly—41 in favor, 29 opposed and 11 abstaining. The Philippines at that particular time was absent. In the vote the same basic pattern was present as, for instance, in 1954 except for 11 shifts in the Latin American countries, Turkey and Liberia who abstained and, of course, the new members. In the latter category Indonesia had the support of Malaya, Laos, Japan, Ceylon, Albania, Bulgaria, Ghana, Hungary, Jordan, Libya, Morocco, Nepal, Romania, Sudan, and Tunisia; the Netherlands of Austria, Ireland, Italy, Spain, and Portugal while Cambodia and Finland abstained. The position of Cambodia was contrary to the pattern in Southeast Asia.

Meanwhile President Sukarno continued to stress the urgent need for the freeing of West Irian. On August 17, 1955, in an independence day address he said: "We must free Irian with our own strength and, God permitting, we will free Irian with our own strength."[43] Later on May 17, 1956, he told a joint session of the American Congress: "The return of West Irian is for us the remaining part of our national political aspiration. It is the final installment on the colonial debt. We see our brothers still in chains, who joined with us in proclaiming our common independence, and so our own freedom is not yet complete."[44] The

[43] *New York Times*, August 18, 1955.

[44] Address to the Congress, May 17, 1956, *The Department of State Bulletin*, Vol. XXXIV (June 4, 1956), p. 930.

second government of Premier Ali Sastroamidjojo on April 9 announced plans to create an Indonesian province of West Irian; eventually it would be given autonomous status. On August 15 Parliament approved the formation of the province. The Dutch for their part have accused the Indonesians of seeking to undermine authority in Netherlands New Guinea by encouraging raids and supporting infiltration from Indonesian territory. In June Sjahrir pointedly noted: "We long for the world to grant the justice of our case and lend us support in our controversy with the Dutch. The feeling that not only in West Irian but everywhere the Dutch are still always blocking the road to Indonesia's development and progress, especially economically, is very strong. It is, in fact, at the core of nationalist sentiment."[45]

The Japanese occupation of Indonesia was brief in duration as compared with the long period of Dutch rule. Although Indonesia later estimated that it cost the lives of about 4 million people and produced damage up to billions of dollars, the cause of national independence was in the end advanced. During the occupation Indonesians gained more experience in administration, many young people had an opportunity to train in the use of arms, the Indonesian language developed rapidly, and national leaders came to the forefront. Nevertheless, the Japanese occupation was resented and left behind it a heritage of hard feeling.

The chief issues between Indonesia and Japan in the postwar period related to reparations and fisheries. Invited to attend the Japanese Peace Conference at San Francisco in 1951 and to sign the treaty of peace, the Indonesian government under Prime Minister Sukiman decided to send a delegation without any mandate to sign the pact. During the Conference Foreign Minister Ahmad Subardjo kept close contact with Djakarta, reporting on developments that might assist the government in its final decision.

On September 6 the Indonesian leader addressed the San Francisco assembly, indicating clearly the viewpoint of Djakarta on the peace treaty.[46] He noted that his government had decided to send a delegation to the Conference only after long hesitation and that it was following a policy of "watchful waiting, until some provisions of the treaty are clarified and dealt with to our satisfac-

[45] Sjahrir, *op. cit.*, p. 120.

[46] Ahmad Subardjo speech, *Record of Proceedings, Conference for the Conclusion and Signature of the Treaty of Peace with Japan, passim.*

tion." Speaking with considerable insight, Subardjo observed that "Indonesia is occupying a position of strategic importance in the Pacific, to the extent that we can not conceive of tranquility in the Pacific without stability in Indonesia." He specifically read the amendments to Article 14 of the treaty, dealing with reparations, which his government would have liked to have inserted. The amendments included "specified conditions" under which the Allied Powers were prepared "to assume a conciliatory attitude towards Japan with the war reparations claims." Subardjo also would have preferred to amend Article 9 so that without the special approval of Indonesia, Japan or Japanese nationals could not fish in waters between and surrounding the islands of the Republic, pending the making of agreements on fishing and fisheries on the high seas. The crucial part in the speech of the Indonesian foreign minister came when he addressed three questions to Prime Minister Shigeru Yoshida: first, was Japan "prepared to pay adequate reparation to Indonesia for damages suffered by Indonesia during the Second World War in accordance with the provisions stipulated in article 14 of the Japanese Peace Treaty"; second, did Japan "agree that these reparations will be specified and the amount thereof fixed in a bilateral treaty between Indonesia and Japan, to be concluded as soon as possible after the signing of the peace treaty"; and third, was Japan "prepared promptly to enter into negotiations with Indonesia for the conclusion of agreements providing for the regulation or limitation of fishing and the conservation of fishing on the high seas between and surrounding the Indonesian Islands in order to safeguard the fish supply of the Indonesian people"?

Prime Minister Yoshida in his address to the San Francisco Conference on the evening of September 7 specifically replied to the Indonesian questions when he said: "The answer to these questions is 'Yes' since that means in our opinion a fair interpretation of articles 14 and 9 of the treaty. I hope that this answer will resolve any doubts of others as to Japan's good intentions under the treaty."[47] An exchange of notes between Yoshida and Subardjo via Dean Acheson, President of the Conference and American Secretary of State, gave further confidence to the Indonesian delegation. As a result the cabinet in Djakarta authorized the signing of the Japanese peace treaty. It is significant that the vote was badly split, ten in favor and six opposed. The Masjumi members of the cabinet who voted in favor represented a party

[47] Shigeru Yoshida speech, *Record of Proceedings, Conference for the Conclusion and Signature of the Treaty of Peace with Japan*, p. 278.

badly divided itself on the issue and the Nationalist (PNI) members reflected their party in opposing the signature. It was clear that the treaty would face extremely difficult circumstances if and when it was presented to Parliament for approval.

The three Indonesian questions asked at San Francisco and answered affirmatively by Prime Minister Yoshida raised a number of further questions, one of the most important centering around the meaning of "adequate reparation." Indonesia was eager to receive Japanese reparations in order to speed its economic recovery from the war. As in the case of the Philippines, its demands (around $18 billion in goods and services) were high and not correlated with those of other nations. The island republic also did not want to see the prewar Japanese position in fisheries restored. In addition, Indonesia realized "the dangers of Japanese economic expansion—especially if this is to be allowed once more to involve the bulk of the Japanese people being enslaved in a cheap-labour policy which sets the value of human beings too low, if it involves the wastage of natural resources, and if it involves other countries in a race to beat Japanese competition."[48]

Despite the Indonesian-Japanese agreement at San Francisco, subsequent negotiations for a long time failed to solve the basic issues between the two countries. In December, 1951, an Indonesian negotiating mission led by Dr. Djuanda, Minister of Transportation and Communications, arrived in Tokyo. Although basic differences appeared between Japan and Indonesia, an interim agreement on general principles was reached on January 18, 1952, calling for the payment of reparations in services with the preservation of Japan's economy. The accord was severely criticized in Djakarta in political and newspaper circles. Japanese Foreign Minister Katzuo Okazaki in October, 1953, while he was visiting certain capital cities in Southeast Asia, tried to start negotiations in Djakarta on reparations but met with no success. Late in the month Indonesia sent a mission to Japan to investigate further her capacity to pay. A provisional and limited reparations agreement was made with respect to the Japanese salvaging of sunken ships in Indonesian waters, a $6.5 million operation. As late as October, 1956, the Japanese had not been able to make surveys in the waters concerned, for the Indonesian Parliament had not approved the agreement.

In January, 1954, Eiji Wajima, the Japanese representative

[48] "Indonesia and the Peace Treaty with Japan," *Indonesian Affairs,* Vol. 1 (October/November, 1951), p. 6.

in Djakarta, attempted to start negotiations on the reparations issue. Now involved were around $150 million accumulated to the credit of Japan in the trade account between the two countries. Indonesia did not intend to pay the amount, for she was crediting it toward the reparations settlement. The Djakarta government in 1954 submitted a new partial reparations plan centering around Japanese aid in developing a hydroelectric power plant in northern Sumatra on the Asahan River. Negotiations between the two states continued to drag. By 1957 Indonesia was seeking outright reparations equivalent to $400 million. Mohammad Hatta discussed the subject in Tokyo in October and Prime Minister Kishi in Djakarta a few weeks later. As a result of the talks between Sukarno and Kishi in late November it was announced that a reparations formula had been found. Japan would pay Indonesia over 12 years the equivalent of $223 million in reparations; the former would give up the trade credit in her favor (now about $177 million); and Nippon would see that Japanese concerns made investments or loans up to the equivalent of $400 million over 20 years in the island republic. After the details were worked out, a formal agreement would be signed. The settlement of the reparations issue between Japan and Burma and then between Japan and the Philippines has set two precedents which exert pressure on Indonesia.

Although Japanese-Indonesian trade has continued and agreements have been made relative to it, the establishment of normal relations would facilitate matters. In an agreement reached in August, 1952, Japan would buy $40 million worth of tin, rubber, petroleum, and other items and Indonesia would purchase metal and textile products worth $55 million. The latter's debt to Japan as a consequence of trading during the occupation would be liquidated in five years. The two states exchange consuls general but Indonesia on occasion considered it necessary to impose trade restrictions on Japanese goods and Nippon came to follow a policy of cash and carry. On August 15, 1956, an agreement was reached involving Japanese processing of American raw cotton for Indonesian use.

Prime Minister Ali Sastroamidjojo in a government statement on August 25, 1953, observed that his cabinet would seek to establish normal relations with Nippon as soon as possible by means of a bilateral accord in place of the San Francisco peace treaty. Arrangements would be made relative to reparations and fisheries. In connection with the Bandung Conference in 1955 the Japanese indicated they hoped they would have an opportunity to take up mutual problems, and some discussion did occur. In 1956 plans were finalized for a Japanese-Indonesian bank to assist in the creation of different industries in the island republic, the expansion of interisland shipping, and the development of petroleum resources.

In relations with the Communist states of the world Indonesia stands in marked contrast to the Philippines. The former's policy toward the People's Republic of China, the Soviet Union, and divided Korea and Vietnam reveals an "independent" attitude in world affairs according to many leaders in Djakarta. Here it should be noted that even before the transfer of sovereignty in December, 1949, Indonesian officials had considered the question of relations with Communist states. In fact, Indonesian experience in international relations from the nationalist viewpoint technically begins with the declaration of independence on August 17, 1945.

Nationalist China was one of the Asian states that supported Indonesia in its struggle for independence. But with the victory of Mao Tse-tung on the mainland, diplomatic relations came to be established between the People's Republic and Indonesia. Communist China, however, sent a diplomatic mission to Djakarta for some months before Indonesia dispatched one to Peking. Even then there was a delay before the appointment of an ambassador from Djakarta. Although Nationalist China had the power to veto the admission of Indonesia to the United Nations she did not exercise it. Once in the world organization the island state came to support through its vote the efforts of the People's Republic to secure the representation of China. And relations between Taipei and Djakarta were further embittered by the expulsion of Tjong Hoen Nji, a prominent Nationalist Chinese supporter, from Indonesia.

Among the states of Southeast Asia the Republic of Indonesia is possibly the least concerned about the intentions of the Peking regime. One of the reasons is found in geography, the island state being the most distant of any of the countries in the region from Communist China. Intensely nationalistic, Indonesia also tends to sympathize with any Asian or African state that defies the West. In addition, the PKI has a strong position in the nation, a factor that cabinets cannot ignore in making decisions.

The large Chinese minority in Indonesia, between 2 and 3 million, is an important factor in Chinese-Indonesian relations. The

Chinese control a significant part of the economic wealth of the nation, have a key position in the trade with Asian countries, and are extremely influential in small industry and the retail trade. As of 1950 it has been estimated that less than 30 percent of the Chinese in Indonesia are *Totoks* or China-born as compared with the *Peranakans* or local-born. A number of young Chinese in the Republic (some 12,000 from 1951-1954) have been returning to mainland China to take advantage of Communist inducements with respect to furthering their education. Indonesia on February 28, 1951, announced her decision to restrict Chinese immigration to a yearly 4000 with priority to technicians and doctors. In fact, from the legal viewpoint, there has been little Chinese immigration since 1950. Undoubtedly Indonesian government leaders have been concerned over the role of the Chinese in the archipelago. In education the former are aware of the more than 900 privately supported Chinese schools with some 300,000 Chinese students. Nor can the activities of the large Chinese Communist Embassy in Djakarta and the four consulates in the country be ignored. At the same time the Chinese in Indonesia, as in the Philippines, are subject to nationalistic pressure that is often discriminating.

On April 22, 1955, Communist China and Indonesia signed in Bandung a treaty on the citizenship of the Chinese residents in the island republic. Long the subject of negotiation between the two governments as well as being an item of personal interest to Nehru, the treaty on dual citizenship is very significant, setting a precedent for other possible agreements between the People's Republic and states with substantial Chinese minorities. In essence the treaty provides for a choice by Chinese residents who have dual citizenship and who have come of age between Indonesian and Chinese citizenship within a period of two years from the time the agreement comes into effect. Article I specifically states: "The contracting parties agree that anybody with at the same time the citizenship of the Republic of Indonesia and of the People's Republic of China shall choose between the two citizenships on the basis of his or her own will."[49] Detailed provisions are made relative to various aspects, the objective being to end dual citizenship. Significant is the provision in Article XI whereby both parties will encourage their citizens residing in the other "to abide by the laws and customs of the State in which they reside and not to participate in political activities of the country in which they

[49] *Indonesian Observer*, April 28, 1955.

reside."[50] At the same time the parties "agree to give mutual protection according to the laws of the respective country, to the legal rights and interests of the respective citizens residing in the country of each contracting party."[51] Here are found in effect a Chinese pledge not to interfere in the affairs of Indonesia through its citizens residing there and an Indonesian pledge not to discriminate against the Chinese. The treaty has a duration of 20 years but can remain in force thereafter unless terminated by one of the parties on a one year's notice. It is clear that the People's Republic of China by giving up in Indonesia the traditional concept of Chinese citizenship based on *jus sanguinis* was acting on higher considerations of international interest. Nationalist sources in Taiwan denounced the Indonesian-Communist Chinese treaty as illegal.

Within Indonesia itself strong opposition to the treaty developed among the Masjumi, Socialist, Catholic, and Protestant parties as well as others. BAPERKI (Organization for Deliberation on Indonesian Citizenship), a forum largely of Chinese with permanent interests in Indonesia, criticized it. So did the Eurasians for the most part. Despite an exchange of letters between Indonesia and the People's Republic of China during the visit of Prime Minister Ali Sastroamidjojo to Peking in June, 1955, clarifying certain aspects of the settlement and providing for an Indonesian-Chinese commission on its implementation, Indonesia delayed in ratifying the pact.

Apart from the question of dual citizenship, relations between Djakarta and Peking have been somewhat nominal. On February 1, 1951, Indonesia abstained from voting on a resolution in the General Assembly of the United Nations calling Communist China an aggressor in Korea and again May 18 on another asking for a United Nations embargo on strategic war materials to both North Korea and Communist China. Nevertheless, the island state subsequently carried out the latter resolution although it declared there had been no export of such materials to the Chinese People's Republic. Some Indonesians believed the embargo was a plot engineered by the United States to reduce the world price of rubber and create a single-buyer system. Considerable publicity was given to Ceylon's export of the commodity to Communist China, especially after the slump in the market starting in 1951. Along with

[50] *Ibid.*
[51] *Ibid.*

British Malaya, Indonesia in early June, 1956, decided to end its embargo on the export of natural rubber to North Korea and Communist China. As for general trade between the island state and the Chinese mainland, it has been regulated by agreements negotiated by the two governments.

After the Bandung Conference Premier Chou En-lai paid an official visit to Djakarta where on April 28, 1955, he and Premier Ali Sastroamidjojo issued a joint statement on Indonesian-Chinese relations. They reasserted their intention to seek the realization of the objectives of the Asian-African Conference, expressed satisfaction over the recent treaty on dual citizenship, hoped to develop extensive economic and cultural relations, agreed that their countries should coöperate to strengthen their mutual understanding, declared it was "the inalienable right of the people of any country to safeguard their own sovereignty and territorial integrity" and expressed "satisfaction over the fact that Indonesia and China are living peacefully together as good neighbours on the basis of the principles of mutual respect for sovereignty and territorial integrity, non-aggression, non-interference in each other's internal affairs, equality and mutual benefit."[52] The visit of Premier Chou En-lai to Indonesia was soon followed by a trip of Premier Ali Sastroamidjojo to Communist China. Especially gratifying in Djakarta has been the strong support of Indonesia's claim to West Irian rendered by the government of Mao Tse-tung.

Among the numerous visits exchanged by Indonesian and Chinese Communist leaders in various walks of life, the state trip of President Sukarno to the People's Republic of China in October, 1956, is most noteworthy. Given an enthusiastic reception, the Indonesian chief executive was truly impressed by what he saw, especially in the domestic field. Nevertheless, he returned to Djakarta determined to maintain the independent foreign policy of his country.

Diplomatic relations between Indonesia and the Soviet Union were established only after a long delay. Problems relating to staff and finances were given by the Indonesians as an excuse for not setting up an embassy in Moscow. Actually the Communist revolt in September and October, 1948, against the Indonesian government had created suspicion of international Communism and the Soviet Union. In a government statement on August 25, 1953, Prime Minister Ali Sastroamidjojo noted that the Rondonuwu

[52] *Indonesian Observer,* April 29, 1955.

motion, approved by Parliament, calling for the opening of an Indonesian Embassy in Moscow, would "be carried into effect after the government has made preparations and provisions as best [*sic*] as possible."[53] President Sukarno in an address eight days earlier had stated that Parliament wanted an embassy set up in Moscow that year "in order that equilibrium be maintained in our diplomatic relations."[54] In 1954 ambassadors were finally exchanged between the Soviet Union and Indonesia, considerable discussion occurring in Djakarta over reports that the former wanted 40 buildings to house its staff.

Trade relations and Soviet technical assistance were the subject of negotiations between the Moscow and Djakarta governments in the latter part of 1954. Actually Indonesia concluded trade agreements and in some cases economic aid pacts with a number of Soviet satellites in Europe before taking such steps with the Soviet Union. Numerous Indonesian delegations—trade, agricultural, railway, industrial, medical, and women's—visited the Soviet Union in 1954. Especially conspicuous was the Russian exhibit at the International Trade Fair in Djakarta held during August and September. Soviet propaganda directed at Indonesia, it might be noted, has stressed Russian technical assistance to India and has tried to discredit American aid in Asia. In April, 1956, the Soviet Union offered long-term loans to Indonesia to finance important agricultural and industrial projects. On August 12 a trade agreement was finally signed whereby Indonesia would export agricultural and other products to the Soviet Union and the latter would send heavy machinery and other items to the island republic, payments being in sterling. In September an agreement was reached under which the USSR would provide Indonesia economic and technical aid valued at $100 million at a low interest rate over a long-term period. Repayment would be in pounds sterling, United States dollars, or commodities.

President Sukarno paid a state visit to the Soviet Union in late August and early September. He was given a reception the Russian leaders reserve for highly influential foreigners, a treatment in marked contrast to that the Palar mission received in Moscow in May, 1950, when it came to negotiate the establishment of diplo-

[53] Government Statement, August 25, 1953, *Indonesian Affairs*, Vol. III (August, 1953), p. 61.

[54] "Let Us Become the Vehicle of History," *An Address Delivered by the President of the Republic of Indonesia on the Eighth Anniversary of the Proclamation of Independence, August 17, 1953*, p. 21.

matic relations. In his speeches in the USSR President Sukarno outlined the foreign policy of Indonesia, called especially for the return of West Irian, and indicated he favored accepting economic aid from any source providing it had no political strings attached. In fact, a Soviet-Indonesian joint statement on September 11 issued at the end of his state visit announced, *inter alia*, the impending conclusion of the economic and technical aid agreement between the two governments. Since no American-Indonesian communiqué was issued after the visit of Sukarno to Washington, it was argued in Djakarta that the Soviet-Indonesian statement was showing partiality. The President denied the validity of the criticism.

Marshal Kliment Y. Voroshilov, Soviet chief of state, paid a formal visit to Indonesia in May, 1957. He advocated steps during his trip that would strengthen Soviet-Indonesian ties. Among these measures were the end of all colonialism, a ban on nuclear weapons tests, and nonintervention by one state in the affairs of another. He was careful to make no public reference to any ties between the PKI and the outside Communist world.

Indonesia was not a member of the United Nations when the Korean War broke out on June 25, 1950. The quick reaction of the government was to abstain from participation in the conflict. Not only was there a conviction in Djakarta that the new republic needed to divert all its energies to reconstruction, but also an inclination to look upon Korea as a pawn in the power politics of the United States and the Soviet Union. Warships involved in Korean operations were barred from possible use of facilities in Indonesia and citizens of the Republic were not allowed to volunteer for service in Korea. In view of the United Nations role in the Korean War, Indonesia was concerned about possible membership in the world organization. A formal application on September 25 with admission three days later indicated that considerations of national prestige outweighed apprehensions about involvement in Korea.

The November entrance of Communist China into the conflict aroused concern in Djakarta, for the threat of a global war was increased. Many Indonesians had looked with disfavor upon the American decision, announced June 27, to freeze the situation along the Formosa Strait by ordering the Seventh Fleet to prevent a Communist invasion of Taiwan and by requesting Chiang Kai-shek not to conduct operations on the mainland of China. Indonesia was inclined to consider the struggle between Mao Tse-tung and Chiang Kai-shek as domestic in nature. In explaining the entry of the People's Republic of China into the Korean War, Indonesia tended to interpret it as the consequence of allowing American forces to approach the Yalu River and the boundary of Communist China. Leaders in Djakarta were also quick to compare American policy in the Korean War to that during the Dutch-Indonesian conflict, especially as regards what they considered Dutch aggression.

In the negotiations at the United Nations Indonesia revealed its position on a number of questions relative to Korea. On October 7 the island republic abstained on General Assembly Resolution 376(V) which, it should be stressed, approved the Korean decisions of the Security Council taken when the Soviet Union was boycotting it and was generally viewed as authorizing the use of United Nations forces north of the thirty-eighth parallel. On December 12 Indonesia sponsored along with 12 other Asian and African states a draft resolution asking the President of the General Assembly to create a group of three persons including himself to formulate the basis upon which a satisfactory cease-fire could be effected in Korea and to propose recommendations as soon as possible to the General Assembly. Although the draft resolution was subsequently adopted, the group that was established was not able to bring peace to Korea. Also on December 12 Indonesia joined 11 other Asian and African states in a draft resolution that recommended the creation of a committee to meet as quickly as possible and make recommendations for the peaceful solution of existing controversies in the Far East. The draft resolution was not finally adopted, but it reflected Indonesia's concern over the situation in that part of the world.

Although through its abstention on resolutions passed by the General Assembly branding Communist China an aggressor and later calling for an embargo on strategic war materials Indonesia belonged to the minority, the island state continued to work for a settlement of the Korean issue satisfactory to all parties. It previously supported the creation of the United Nations Korean Reconstruction Agency, and made an ultimate contribution worth $100,000 to the fund. In general, however, the Indonesian government did not have very much sympathy for President Syngman Rhee and his administration. On December 3, 1952, Indonesia voted with 53 other states in favor of General Assembly Resolution 610(VII), which included a recommendation that force should not be employed in connection with the prisoners of war in Korea either to effect or prevent their return to their home countries. The issue of forced or voluntary repatriation, it is clear, was highly controversial in the truce negotiations.

The Korean armistice agreement of July 27, 1953, was well received in Djakarta, President Sukarno himself in an address on August 17 observing that "we enthusiastically welcome the truce. . . ."[55] On the composition of the "political conference," envisioned by Article IV, Section 60, of the armistice agreement, to formulate a settlement of the Korean problem, Indonesia took the position that both the belligerents and the nonbelligerents who were closely concerned with a settlement in the Far East should participate. The Djakarta government saw in the role of India in the Korean armistice agreement the vindication of a "so-called 'neutral' " policy. Sunario, speaking in the United Nations General Assembly on September 18, observed: "The very basis of the agreement ending the fighting in Korea rests largely on the availability of 'neutral' nations, acceptable to both sides, to perform valuable and important services."[56] In May, 1957, Indonesia and North Korea, it might be added, signed a trade agreement.

Like the Korean War the conflict in Indochina raised perplexing problems in Djakarta. After V-J Day Ho Chi Minh had made overtures to Sukarno about coöperation in the postwar period but they had not been seriously considered in Indonesia. At the same time the struggle in France's "Balcony on the Pacific" was interpreted in Djakarta as being colonial in nature. The Communist aspect of the war was subordinated to the nationalist. In many respects Indonesia saw in the efforts of the Vietnamese to win independence from France a situation comparable to its own struggle against the Netherlands. President Sukarno gave in December, 1953, his solution of the Indochina crisis: "Let the French get out."

In a significant analysis of Indonesian foreign policy, officially published by the Ministry of Information, the war in Indochina was further considered.[57] It was stated that "a scuffle between the ideals of national independence and the itch of colonialism con-

[55] *Ibid.*, p. 22.

[56] United Nations, General Assembly, Eighth Session, *Official Records*, 437th Plenary Meeting, September 18, 1953, p. 47.

[57] "The Historical and Philosophical Background of Our Independent Policy," *Basic Information on Indonesia*, Ministry of Information, Republic of Indonesia, *passim.*

tinues violently in Vietnam." The question was raised as to why the followers of Bao Dai and Ho Chi Minh were fighting since they were all "brothers of the same blood" and wanted "an independent, united, sovereign Vietnam." The answer was then given—"non-Vietnamese interests have been interwoven with those of the Vietnamese themselves." The conviction was later expressed in the analysis that "pushed back into a corner, Ho and his adherents were compelled to seek coöperation with the Soviet Bloc. . . . From what other source could Ho and his people expect support for their struggle, if the Western democratic world is ill-disposed to them?"

The question of the recognition of Ho Chi Minh's regime was debated in the Indonesian Parliament in the spring of 1950. In March a motion was introduced which sought the immediate recognition of the Democratic Republic of Vietnam. Mohammad Natsir, a prominent Masjumi leader, later introduced a counter-proposal which sought more information and urged caution on the matter. On June 3 the Natsir motion was carried by a vote of 49 to 38, a large number of the members abstaining. The international implications of the recognition of the Ho regime were obviously a deterrent to the Indonesian authorities. At the same time the island republic did not recognize the government led by Bao Dai.

As already indicated, Indonesia joined with the other Colombo Powers in making recommendations on the solution of the conflict in Indochina and later in welcoming the settlement made at Geneva. Prime Minister Ali Sastroamidjojo in his address to Parliament on August 16, 1954, observed that the latter development "gladdened the whole population of Asia." It was announced in Djakarta on April 6, 1955, that Indonesia was granting *de facto* recognition to Cambodia, Laos, and the two Vietnams and that a consulate would be set up in each of the capitals. In January, 1957, Indonesia signed a trade agreement with North Vietnam.

Among the non-Communist neighbors of Indonesia relations with India are very important. The ties between the two nationalist movements have been long-standing, the Indonesians learning in many respects from the Indians. A number of the nationalist leaders in both countries have known each other for many years; Nehru and Hatta have been friends since the Brussels conference directed against imperialism in 1927. The end of the Western colonial period in India and Indonesia led to a stress on the old cultural and historic ties between them. As Prime Minister Nehru expressed it in 1950: "Our mind tries to skip over this colonial period, to some extent, as we pick up the old threads again—the old threads that have to be picked up in a new way because new conditions have arisen."[58] He then specifically referred to India's deep interest in Indonesia and his admiration for President Sukarno. After commenting on the Indonesian leader's recent visit to New Delhi, Nehru significantly observed: "So, we become more and more intimately connected, not by formal treaties and alliances and pacts but by bonds which are much more secure, much more binding—the bonds of mutual understanding and interest and, if I may say so, even of mutual affection."[59] Indeed, the personal contacts between the leaders are a matter of considerable importance in Indian-Indonesian relations.

India took an active part in helping Indonesia win her independence. As a consequence of the first Dutch police action in the summer of 1947, India, in addition to bringing the controversy before the Security Council, banned Dutch aircraft from flying over her soil, sent a Red Cross medical unit to Republican territory, and received Sjahrir as a refugee. With the second Dutch police action in December, 1948, and January, 1949, India again imposed her ban on Netherlands aircraft and added Dutch shipping. In addition, she played host in late January to an international conference to review the Indonesian situation.

The New Delhi Conference on Indonesia met January 20-23 in an atmosphere of sympathy for the Indonesians in their struggle against the Dutch for independence. Representatives were present from Afghanistan, Australia, Burma, Ceylon, Egypt, Ethiopia, India, Iran, Iraq, Lebanon, Pakistan, the Philippines, Saudi Arabia, Syria, and Yemen and observers from Nationalist China, Nepal, Thailand, and New Zealand. The Republic of Indonesia was represented and there was an unofficial Vietnamese present. In a resolution adopted January 23 the Conference condemned the military action of the Dutch, affirmed support for the United Nations, and made recommendations to the Security Council on the settlement of the controversy. It wanted the transfer of power over all Indonesia to the United States of Indonesia by January 1, 1950. Although the Conference devoted its chief efforts to the

[58] *Jawaharlal Nehru's Speeches, 1949-1953,* The Publications Division, Ministry of Information and Broadcasting, Government of India, p. 146.
[59] *Ibid.*, p. 147.

Indonesian question, consideration was given to the establishment of machinery for future coöperation among its members within the United Nations framework. After the meeting, subsequent consultations on Indonesia were held among many of the participants in New Delhi and in the United Nations headquarters.

Since the formal independence of Indonesia the ties between India and the island republic have been specifically strengthened by a number of factors. In June, 1950, Nehru visited Indonesia repaying Sukarno's visit of the previous January. A treaty of friendship has been signed and ratified by both states, and agreements have been reached on trade relations. At meetings of the Colombo Powers the policies of the Indian and Indonesian representatives have closely paralleled. In February, 1954, there was inaugurated in New Delhi an India-Indonesian Friendship Center; in December, 1955, a cultural agreement for ten years was concluded. On a number of occasions Indonesia has shipped food to alleviate conditions in India. On colonial, economic, and cold war issues India and Indonesia very often vote alike in the United Nations. In February, 1956, the two states reached an agreement on mutual aid between their air forces for five years: Indonesian air force officers would be trained in India; equipment could be exchanged, loaned, or sold.

The Indian minority in Indonesia has not constituted a serious problem in the relations between New Delhi and Djakarta. In the census of 1930 the Indian population numbered 27,684 of which 12,654 were born in the archipelago. It is estimated that in 1952 the total figure stood at 40,000. Most of the Indians were located on Java, were making their living as small shopkeepers, and were Moslem in religion. The government of Indonesia being opposed to unrestricted immigration, efforts are made to regulate rigidly the admittance of foreigners. Cash remittances to India by Indians living in Indonesia have been allowed if the funds provide the support of refugees in India from Pakistan. A few other exceptions are also made. The Indonesian government has a policy of not discriminating against Indians resident in the country.

With Australia, Indonesia's large neighbor to the southeast, relations have varied. As one of the most active powers in support of the independence of Indonesia both in and outside the United Nations, Australia had built up a big reservoir of good will with the Republican government. The Australian Waterside Workers' Federation after both police actions declined to load Netherlands vessels. It will be recalled that the Republic of Indonesia selected Australia as its representative on the Committee of Good Offices set up by the Security Council of the United Nations. Australia likewise was active in the New Delhi Conference on Indonesia as well as in meetings subsequent to it at United Nations headquarters and in New Delhi.

The West Irian controversy has seriously marred the friendship between Indonesia and Australia. Public opinion in the Commonwealth has been aroused over the subject because of the strategic importance of Netherlands New Guinea to national defense, the conviction that the indigenous people of West Irian should decide their own future, and the desire to coöperate with the Netherlands in economic development. On the other hand, many Indonesians have become very critical of Australia and her press. A civil servant who visited the Commonwealth in 1952 wrote two years later: "News giving inflated reports about such things as starvation, internal disorder and the West Irian 'squabble' was taken as evidence that sooner or later the hungry Indonesians would swarm into the wide spaces of Australia. They [the Australians] were constantly urged to believe by their papers that a too 'backward' and 'illiterate' people like the Indonesians couldn't continue in power without causing troubles to their Australian neighbours. . . . We got the impression that the Australian people at large seemed to have acquired a wrong picture of Indonesia."[60] In debates at the United Nations on West Irian comments at times by the delegates from Djakarta and Canberra have been very acrimonious.

Australia's important role in the formulation and development of the Colombo Plan has been a positive factor in her relations with Indonesia. Having as its stated objective "Coöperative Economic Development in South and South-East Asia," the Colombo Plan in its membership has expanded from only including British Commonwealth countries in early 1950 to embracing in late 1954 a much larger area of which all of Southeast Asia except the Democratic Republic of Vietnam was a part. Indonesia sent an observer to a meeting of the Consultative Committee held at London in October, 1950, but did not become a full member until 1953. Nevertheless, it participated before then in the Technical Coöperation Scheme in 1951 and 1952. After becoming a full member,

[60] L. M. Pandjaitan, "What Australians Think of Us," *Indonesian Affairs*, Vol. IV (March/April, 1954), pp. 17-18.

the Republic began to participate in the Economic Development Programme. Within the overall framework of the Colombo Plan a number of Indonesians have gone to Australia for technical training, reducing to a limited degree the effect of the so-called "White Australia" policy.

Trade relations between Indonesia and Australia have been regulated by a number of agreements. Basically involved are Australian flour and Indonesian petroleum products. The differences between the two states over West Irian, it should be noted, have not prevented the signing of such accords. The Australian Minister for External Affairs, R. G. Casey, in stating the main points of his country's foreign policy during 1954, significantly observed at the end of the year: "We differ with Indonesia over West New Guinea, but we are determined not to allow that to obstruct our coöperation in other matters. Indeed, we have given every indication of seeking genuinely friendly and harmonious relations with Indonesia. We have every reason to want to live in harmony with our largest and closest neighbor."[61] From October 29 to November 2, 1955, Casey paid a visit to Indonesia. A communiqué, issued by the two governments, called for coöperation and noninterference in each other's affairs. Both parties kept their own views on West Irian but the matter should be dealt with by peaceful discussions; Australia would help more Indonesian students come to her country; and cultural attachés would be exchanged.

Despite the common ties of Islam, relations between Indonesia and Pakistan are not so close as those between the island republic and India. At the same time the potential exists for an entente between the two newly independent Moslem countries. Indonesia, it is evident, places more stress on its position as an Asian state than as a Moslem one. It is opposed to the creation of a purely Islamic bloc in world affairs, and prefers to work through the Asian-African group in the United Nations. Indonesia has, however, attended Moslem conferences, for instance, sending representatives to meetings of the International Islamic Economic Organization. President Sukarno visited Karachi in 1950 after he left New Delhi, and later a friendship pact was concluded between Indonesia and Pakistan. In the conflict over Kashmir between India and Pakistan Indonesia has been willing to help mediate, but its efforts have met with no success whenever it has tried. Pakistan's

[61] Statement of R. G. Casey, December 31, 1954, *Current Notes on International Affairs*, Vol. 25 (December, 1954), p. 857.

membership in the pro-Western Manila and Baghdad pacts has weakened its influence in Djakarta. And at discussions among the Colombo Powers the two Moslem countries have been at variance in their interpretation of the objectives of world Communism.

Among the states of Southeast Asia Indonesia has close ties with Burma. In many respects the foreign policies of the two republics parallel. A treaty of friendship was signed in 1951, it being Burma's first one with any state. Indonesia has supported Burma in her case before the United Nations relative to Nationalist Chinese forces in her territory and Burma has supported Indonesia in the West Irian controversy. In discussions among the Colombo Powers Burma and Indonesia have generally agreed, although the latter has been less critical of international Communism. Prime Minister Ali Sastroamidjojo visited Rangoon in September, 1954, and he and Prime Minister U Nu called for close ties between the two states. In 1955 Burma gave Indonesia a hundred tons of rice for the relief of flood victims. In accepting the gift the Indonesian Foreign Minister referred to the "close bonds of sympathy and mutual understanding" between the two countries. In November Vice-President Hatta visited Burma, and President Sukarno followed in October, 1956.

With Thailand Indonesian relations are proper but not cordial. A treaty of friendship was signed in 1954, some time after Indonesia's friendship pacts with India, Pakistan, the Philippines, and Burma. The treaty foreshadowed the making of agreements on commerce, navigation, cultural relations, consular privileges, and extradition. Thailand's alignment with the Western powers as exemplified by her adherence to the Manila Pact has not been conducive to close coöperation between Djakarta and Bangkok.

In addition to the Netherlands, Indonesian relations with some of the Western powers in Europe and America have been especially important, particularly those with France, the United Kingdom, and the United States. France became the principal obstacle to one of Indonesia's objectives, the independence of all North Africa—Morocco, Tunisia, and Algeria. Here Paris came to stand for colonialism, comparable only to the Netherlands in West Irian. Prime Minister Ali Sastroamidjojo in a policy statement to Parliament on August 25, 1953, pointedly observed: "Together with the other Asian and African countries we try to solve colonial or semi-colonial problems such as the Tunisian, Moroccan, and 'apartheid' questions. . . ."[62] In the Indonesian struggle for independence France had supported the Netherlands in the United Nations. The Arab states had favored the Indonesian Republic in its efforts for recognition.[63] In its African policy Indonesia even recognized on December 31, 1951, the King of Egypt as King of both Egypt and the Sudan. The following November the island republic allowed a "Tunisian office" to be set up in Djakarta having the goal of full independence for Tunisia from France. Treaties of friendship with Arab states like Syria and Egypt were made, following those with certain countries in South and Southeast Asia. President Sukarno visited a part of the Middle East in 1955 when he went on his pilgrimage to Mecca. In meetings of the Colombo Powers, at the Bandung Conference, and in the United Nations Indonesia has supported the cause of Morocco and Tunisia, a factor in their winning independence. In the fall of 1955 the island republic was in the majority that succeeded in placing the question of Algeria on the agenda of the United Nations General Assembly, thereby contributing to the temporary withdrawal of France from that body. Indonesia has not hesitated to continue its efforts on behalf of Algeria in the world organization.

Apart from the Suez controversy, the colonial problem has been a less significant factor in relations between Great Britain and the island state. Although the United Kingdom has favored the Dutch and Australians on West Irian, British policy in Malaya and Borneo, neighbors of Indonesia, has not been challenged in Djakarta. As regards the postwar policy of the Netherlands toward Indonesia in its struggle for independence, Great Britain was torn between the pressure exerted by Australia and India on the one hand and her ties with the Netherlands in Europe. At the time of the first Dutch police action Great Britain, though critical of the Netherlands' use of force, took the position that the controversy was domestic in nature and abstained on the Security Council's cease-fire measure of August 1, 1947. During the second Dutch police action the British supported the Security Council's resolution of December 24, 1948, calling, *inter alia*, for a cease-fire. *De facto* recognition of the Republic by the United Kingdom, as in the case of the United States, had been granted after the signing of the Linggadjati

62 Government Statement, August 25, 1953, *Indonesian Affairs*, Vol. III (August, 1953), p. 59.

63 There are about 100,000 Arabs living in Indonesia. They are active in commerce and well adjusted to the country.

Agreement but *de jure* recognition of the United States of Indonesia came with the Dutch transfer of sovereignty.

Indonesian-Malayan relations, long regulated in London and The Hague, assumed a new character with the independence of Indonesia. Moreover, as Malaya advanced to statehood, the relations of Djakarta with Kuala Lumpur and Singapore had a new frame of reference. David Marshall, Chief Minister of the Crown Colony of Singapore, visited Indonesia on a good-will mission in September, 1955. After discussion, it was agreed that Indonesia would temporarily lift its ban on the export of slab rubber to Singapore from Sumatra as soon as the details were taken care of by a working party, and would not discriminate against exports from the Crown Colony including textiles. Indonesia would also sympathetically consider allowing the import of dried fish from Singapore. The Crown Colony for its part would sympathetically work on existing difficulties over currency and payments. The decision here would rest in London. Both agreed that the Indonesian State Bank would open a branch in Singapore and that a Singapore trade commissioner would be stationed in Djakarta. A joint Singapore-Federation economic working party soon went to Indonesia and a fact-finding mission from Djakarta later went to Singapore. Nevertheless, progress was slow in implementing the accord of September, 1955.

In November Tengku Abdul Rahman, Chief Minister of the Federation of Malaya, made a highly successful trip to Indonesia. Hailed as a fellow Asian nationalist, the Chief Minister was a personal guest of President Sukarno. *Merdeka* or freedom was a frequent cry from the crowds who saw the leaders in the island state. In a communiqué issued November 14 it was stated that Indonesia and the Federation would coöperate to develop the Malayan language, *Bahasa Malayu*, and the Indonesian language, *Bahasa Indonesia*, with the aim of the ultimate fusing of the two. Education and linguistic experts and cultural and educational material would be exchanged. It was agreed in principle that technical information on agriculture would be shared including that on the cultivation and processing of rubber. Indonesia and the Federation would seek to coöperate on the international level regarding the important exports of tin and rubber. They would consult on the development of the production of tin and improve the trade relations between Penang and North Sumatra. During the visit President Sukarno promised to give moral support to the independence movement of Malaya and hoped for an eventual federation of the Moslem countries in Southeast Asia. Indonesia announced on November 14 that its consulate in Kuala Lumpur would be raised to the status of a consulate general.

It is clear that Singapore, the Federation, and Indonesia are actively engaged in evaluating their respective positions in the new framework of Southeast Asia. An entente between the Federation and Indonesia is quite possible based upon many historical, cultural, and political factors. At present cultural and educational ties are being stressed with Indonesia playing the key part. Singapore, on the other hand, predominantly Chinese, profits from free trade in contrast to Indonesia with its basically different population and complex trade controls. Economically Singapore has long been an entrepôt for many of Indonesia's exports. An independent Indonesia has become eager to reduce this dependence, and to channel all hard currency earnings to its own coffers. In addition, Singapore is a haven for refugees from Indonesia. And at the present time it is a bastion of British power in Southeast Asia. Should it become an element of instability, both the Federation and Indonesia would be threatened.[64] The smuggling of rubber and other products from the island republic to Singapore during the revolution in the former country played an important part in helping to finance the national struggle but now the illicit trade makes for bad feeling between Singapore and Indonesia. On the other hand, consumer goods are smuggled to Indonesia, quite likely in large amounts through the Riouw Islands, sovereign Indonesian territory near Singapore, but still within the currency and customs system of the latter. With the support of local military commanders in Indonesia, the smuggling of rubber from Sumatra to Malaya and copra from Sulawesi to the Philippines, British Borneo, and Malaya has greatly increased. In long-range terms it appears that Indonesia might like to see Singapore as the twelfth member of the Federation.

As for British Borneo, where progress toward self-government is slow, Indonesia has an ethnically artificial, poorly defined boundary of around 900 miles with Sarawak and North Borneo. Relations will continue to be handled, it appears, for some time through Great Britain. The vernacular press in Kalimantan has tended to consider British Borneo as territory that should eventually go to the island republic.

American relations with Indonesia have varied considerably.

[64] The "Turk" Westerling and Bertha Hertogh cases, though different in nature, indicate the complex ramifications of Indonesian-Malayan relations.

During the struggle for the independence of the island archipelago, the United States was moved by its traditional opposition to colonialism and its desire to remain on good terms with the Netherlands in Europe. The restoration of both the Indonesian and Dutch economies was important in the American efforts to hold back Communist expansion. The United States favored the cease-fire resolutions of the Security Council of August 1, 1947, and December 24, 1948; it served on the Committee of Good Offices and its successor, the United Nations Commission for Indonesia; its representatives, Dr. Frank Graham and later H. Merle Cochran, were important figures in the emergence of Indonesia as a sovereign state in the family of nations. However, many Indonesians came to believe that the United States had not done enough for them at the right time, while the Dutch were convinced that the American republic had done too much. At the same time, it should be noted, many Indonesians were certain that the Soviet Union, for its part in championing their freedom in the United Nations, was, like the United States, more concerned in jockeying for friends in Southeast Asia as a consequence of the cold war. As for the Dutch, they resented the refusal of the United States to sell them arms for use in Indonesia after the first police action and were highly critical of what they considered to be unjustified American intervention.

The winning of independence, the intensification of the cold war, and the desire to remain outside it contributed to the decline of Indonesia's friendship for the United States. From a realistic viewpoint many Indonesians believed they were more subject to American economic and naval power than that of the Communist world, and therefore they were more sensitive to and suspicious of American policies in Asia. Indonesia has differed with the United States in policy toward the People's Republic of China, the Korean War, the recognition of Bao Dai's Vietnam, and the Manila Pact. The abstention of the United States in the voting on the West Irian question at the United Nations has displeased the leaders in Djakarta.

The question of American aid to Indonesia since independence became politically explosive in the new republic, the Sukiman government falling in February, 1952, as a result of it. Under the Mutual Security Act of 1951, an agency with a similar name (MSA) replaced the Economic Coöperation Administration (ECA). It was stipulated that states receiving military aid should pledge to contribute to "the defensive strength of the free world" (Section

511 A) but those getting economic and technical aid were not required to make this commitment (Section 511 B). Indonesia had been receiving assistance under the latter category through an agreement dated October 16, 1950. The only exception was a grant for small arms under an agreement dated August 15 to aid in equipping its constabulary pursuant to Public Law 329 of the 81st Congress of the United States. If Indonesia were expected to make a pledge for future American assistance as required under Section 511 A of the Mutual Security Act, it would be considered in Djakarta a challenge to its independent policy. As a result of negotiations between Foreign Minister Subardjo and Ambassador Cochran, a formula was worked out whereby Indonesia would receive assistance under Section 511 A with the phrase "contribute to the strength of independent and sovereign nations" replacing the phrase contribute to "the defensive strength of the free world." After the agreement was signed on January 5, 1952, a storm of protest arose in Djakarta when the terms became known. Both the party councils of the PNI and the Masjumi whose representatives were decisive in upholding the Sukiman Cabinet opposed the agreement. On February 21 Subardjo's resignation was accepted and the cabinet itself fell two days later.

In the subsequent negotiations between the Wilopo government and the United States Indonesia would not give assurances under either Section 511 A or 511 B. On December 30, 1952, the Djakarta cabinet approved a settlement with the United States involving the termination of the Subardjo-Cochran arrangement of January 5, its replacement by a new agreement administered by the Technical Coöperation Administration (TCA) and authorization for delivery as "reimbursable aid" of the undelivered amount of constabulary equipment. In the settlement it was asserted that "the Republic of Indonesia reaffirms that it will act in conformity with its obligations under the UN Charter in promoting international understanding and good will, in maintaining world peace, and in eliminating causes of international tensions."[65] President Sukarno on August 17, 1953, significantly observed relative to the changing of American aid from MSA to TCA: "In addition to that we bettered the political equilibrium by exercising our discretion in the matter of aid from outside by becoming a member of the 'Colombo Plan.' "[66]

[65] "TCA Aid to Indonesia," *Indonesian Affairs*, Vol. III (January, 1953), p. 3.

[66] "Let Us Become the Vehicle of History," *An Address Delivered by the President of the Republic of Indonesia on the Eighth Anniversary of the Proclamation of Independence, August 17, 1953*, p. 21.

In fiscal 1955 Indonesia received about $7 million from the United States largely in technical aid and in 1956 about $11 million. In 1950 the Export-Import Bank had granted it a development loan of $100 million. The need for help was truly great; in 1956 it was estimated that the nation had only about 1500 doctors, 150 qualified engineers, 400 lawyers, and 15 economists. Java, having about 68 percent of the people of the country and only 7 percent of the land area, presents a monumental problem. Transmigration to the outer islands and industrialization are answers. As of 1957 American private sources like the Ford Foundation were active in assisting Indonesia but it is clear that official aid could provide a greater amount. United States efforts to build up good will through participation, for instance, at the third annual trade fair at Djakarta could have only limited results. The Indonesian government as of early 1957 had refused to have a Fulbright program of cultural exchange with the American republic. An agreement, however, was signed between the two countries in December, 1955, for the United States to supply Indonesia with films, books, and other media. Meanwhile the United States Information Service is very active in the country, being the largest user of its mail service.

On March 2, 1956, it was announced in Washington that Indonesia had agreed to purchase in her currency $91,800,000 worth of surplus farm products. Over a two-year period the agreement called for the delivery of about 550 million pounds of rice, about 206,000 bales of cotton, 23 million pounds of leaf tobacco, and about 1,270,000 bags of wheat flour. A very large amount of the proceeds Indonesia could borrow for economic development. The next year the Export-Import Bank loaned Indonesia $15 million. Since 1952, it should be added, the United States has been paying for the work of the J. G. White Engineering and Management Consultant Services, acting as engineering consultant to the Indonesian government. Prime Minister Ali Sastroamidjojo in the outline of policy of his second government on April 9, 1956, asserted his country wanted to make use of the "capacity and readiness" to help of the United States as well as of Communist countries providing there were no strings.

American policy toward rubber and tin has directly affected relations between Indonesia and the United States. Over 70 percent of the former's exports consist of rubber, tin, and copra. In fact, it should be recalled that of the world's supply Indonesia produces close to 20 percent of the tin, 40 percent of the rubber, 33 percent of the copra, 30 percent of the pepper, 24 percent of the palm oil and 1½ percent of the petroleum. Ironically it has had to import rice, but is now moving toward self-sufficiency in food. The prices in raw materials that boomed in 1950 as a consequence of the Korean War began to decline in 1951, bringing serious financial and economic problems the next year. American efforts to lower the prices of tin, rubber, and other materials have obviously been resented in Djakarta. Indonesia at times has sought the establishment of a world scheme to stabilize rubber prices but it has met with no success in the efforts. A three-year accord was reached with the United States on March 17, 1952, on the American purchase of tin. In 1955 the island republic signed the International Tin Agreement aimed at achieving stability of price in the commodity. Indonesia has delayed in passing legislation defining the conditions of foreign investment despite a real need for this type of aid. Only limited private American capital has gone to the Republic but outstanding are the investments of Caltex and Stanvac in the Indonesian oil industry. In early September, 1955, the Harahap government announced new import regulations aimed at increasing essential imports and improving trade procedures. An increase in the price of rubber in 1954-1955 has brought some relief to Indonesia. American economic relations with the island republic, it is clear, will continue to influence the political.

In 1956 the ties between the United States and Indonesia were strengthened. This situation arose to a substantial extent from the visit of Secretary Dulles to Djakarta in March and of President Sukarno to the United States in May and June. In his call upon the President of Indonesia the American Secretary of State sought to convince the chief executive that the United States was sympathetic to the national aspirations of newly independent countries and was opposed to colonialism. Although he was not able to express support for Indonesia's claim to West Irian, he did not at the same time offer any help to the Dutch. Dulles appreciated that Indonesia did not believe it needed the protection of SEATO and he stressed that the alliance was only for those who felt the need of it. In a press conference the Secretary of State said there was no relationship between the granting of American economic aid to a country and the latter's entry into a mutual security pact with the United States. Dulles' visit to Indonesia was not well received in Dutch circles in The Hague, Washington, or Djakarta.

President Sukarno in his trip to the United States, prior to later travels to the People's Republic of China and the Soviet Union, had an opportunity to judge American leaders and the American people firsthand. It is likely that he left the United States with a deeper appreciation and fuller understanding of it. At the same time the United States gained a better insight into the real feelings of a prominent Asian leader. In his address to the joint session of Congress on May 17 he said: "Over half the world the burning words which fired the American War of Independence have been closely studied as a source of inspiration and a plan of action. Yes, this period is the period of Asian and African resurgence. . . . Nationalism may be an out-of-date doctrine for many in this world; for us of Asia and Africa, it is the mainspring of our efforts. Understand that, and you have the key to much of postwar history. Fail to understand it, and no amount of thinking, no torrent of words, and no Niagara of dollars will produce anything but bitterness and disillusionment."[67]

The Indonesian President has expressed disappointment over the inability of President Eisenhower to visit the island republic. He had hoped the American chief executive would be the first foreign distinguished visitor at the new state guest house in Bali.

American policy toward the neutrals of Asia has been less rigid since Sukarno went to Washington. President Eisenhower has recalled the long period of American neutrality and noted that political neutrality can be justified under special conditions. Although Secretary Dulles on June 9 observed that neutrality "has increasingly become an obsolete conception, and, except under very exceptional circumstances, it is an immoral and shortsighted conception,"[68] he later stated there were very few, if any, neutrals that were immoral. Vice-President Nixon on July 4 in Manila asserted that the United States felt closer to its allies but also liked nations who "share our dedication to the principles of democracy and freedom even though they have not seen fit to ally themselves with us politically and militarily."[69]

In planning a national security policy the Republic of Indonesia has to consider domestic unrest, especially if it has interna-

[67] Address to the Congress, May 17, 1956, *The Department of State Bulletin*, Vol. XXXIV (June 4, 1956), p. 929.

[68] "The Cost of Peace (Address by Secretary Dulles)," *The Department of State Bulletin*, Vol. XXXIV (June 18, 1956), pp. 999-1000.

[69] "Our Partnership in Creating a World of Peace (Address by Vice-President Nixon)," *The Department of State Bulletin*, Vol. XXXV (July 16, 1956), p. 94.

tional implications. On September 18, 1948, a Communist revolt, as previously noted, broke out in Indonesia, the insurgents under Muso, Suripno, and Sjarifuddin seizing Madiun and proclaiming a Soviet regime. Indonesian Communists had attended in the early part of the year a Southeast Asia Youth Conference at Calcutta under the auspices of the World Federation of Democratic Youth and the International Students' Union, a conference that in terms of events preceded Communist revolts not only in Indonesia but also in Malaya and Burma. President Sukarno and Premier Hatta, whom the Communists now called tools of American imperialists, hastened to put down the rebellion. Tan Malaka, a Trotskyist, was released from jail, probably in the interests of dividing the Communists. Government forces captured Madiun by the end of September and the backbone of the rebellion was broken. Sjarifuddin, Suripno, and Muso lost their lives as a consequence of the revolt.

It was some time before the PKI was able to recover from its defeat. The Indonesian government, however, allowed the members of the PKI who had not joined the revolt to function above ground. In August, 1951, the Sukiman government, later claiming it was forestalling a conspiracy supported from abroad, arrested some 15,000 people, many of them Communists or pro-Communists. But most of the individuals were released from jail within a few months. Since early 1952 the PKI favored a united front policy. The party before the elections of 1955 had 16 votes (7.6 percent) in Parliament in addition to 13 votes (6.1 percent) from associated groups and some 7 votes (3.3 percent) from individuals who belonged to no party, the theoretical total being 36 votes. The Proletarian Party or Partai Murba, once led by the late Tan Malaka, had 4 votes or 1.9 percent. The strength of the PKI is substantially based on its control of the largest labor federation in Indonesia, the SOBSI, with a possible membership of 2,500,000. In 1955 particular emphasis was placed on peasant organization. Efforts were also made, it has been reported, to gain the sympathy of business firms by providing funds from PKI sources.

Extremely well-organized and apparently well-financed, the PKI captured 6,176,914 votes or 16 percent of the total in the first Indonesian national elections from September 29 to November 30. They won 39 seats in a unicameral Parliament of 260. The Communists were bitterly opposed by the Masjumi, the Socialists, and a few other parties. In the campaign the PKI asserted that Communists were faithful Moslems and reiterated their support of

President Sukarno as a national leader and of the *Pantjasila*. Communist gains in Indonesia were approved in Moscow and Peking. In March, 1956, a second Ali Sastroamidjojo cabinet came into being based upon the Nationalist, Masjumi, and Nahdatul Ulama parties, but not the Communist. The PNI had won the largest number of popular votes or 8,434,653 with 57 seats.

In addition to the association of the PKI with the world Communist movement, other instances of outside influence have been cited or alleged. President Sukarno in his address on August 17, 1955, accused the Dutch of allowing people in the Netherlands to support the independence effort of the Republic of the South Moluccas. Organized in 1950, this Republic had not succeeded, the United Nations in September, 1955, receiving its fourth annual protest against the alleged colonialism of the Djakarta government. In West Java the revolt in early 1950 led by Captain Paul "Turk" Westerling, a former officer in the Royal Netherlands Indonesian Army (KNIL), was considered by many Indonesians to have had the tacit support of the Dutch. In the Darul Islam revolt in Central and West Java, Dutch individuals have been accused of giving assistance to the insurgents. A rebellion has broken out in southern Sulawesi and another in the Atjeh area of northern Sumatra; the leaders assert sympathy for the Darul Islam movement. Disorders have occurred in southern Kalimantan. An atmosphere of suspicion between Indonesia and the Netherlands is conducive to gossip and rumor, charges and countercharges. The Dutch are particularly sensitive to the fate of the Ambonese and Menadonese, who have been largely Christianized and from whom the Dutch recruited many of their troops in the East Indies. In fact, there is a sizable community of Ambonese living in the Netherlands.

Amid domestic unrest and political instability, the role of the Indonesian army has increased. In the "17th October Affair" of 1952, a number of army officers were involved in defiance of the Indonesian government. The first cabinet of Ali Sastroamidjojo was finally forced to resign in July, 1955, when the appointment of Major General Bambang Utojo as army chief of staff was strongly and steadily opposed by key army commanders. The Indonesian army, largely anti-Communist, coöperated with the Harahap government in trying to weed out corruption in the nation. But the Prime Minister was defied in December, 1955, by certain leaders of the air force who opposed the swearing in of a selected air force deputy chief of staff.

Political instability in Indonesia led President Sukarno to suggest on February 21, 1957, a new formula of government. His *konsepsi* or "conception," arising from his desire to "bury" political parties and to establish "guided democracy," involved the creation of a National Council, representative of all important forces including the Communists, headed by himself and giving advice to a cabinet which would represent all the important parties including the PKI. Support for the *konsepsi* came from the Nationalists and Communists but not from the major religious parties. Between December and March a succession of bloodless revolts led by army commanders in Sumatra, East Indonesia, and Kalimantan gave emphasis to the growing unrest. At issue were questions of economic improvement, of the distribution of revenues, a large part of which were earned outside Java, of the role of Communists in the state, of federal versus centralized government, of the relations between Hatta and Sukarno, the former resigning as Vice-President December 1, and of graft and corruption in high places. The second Ali Sastroamidjojo cabinet finally resigned on March 14, and President Sukarno quickly proclaimed a state of war and siege in all the archipelago. On April 8 the members of an "extraparliamentary" cabinet, one of "experts" picked for the emergency by the President, were announced. Prime Minister Djuanda found himself facing difficult times, his cabinet already criticized by Hatta, the Masjumi, and other individuals and parties on constitutional grounds. There were no Communists in it but three members were widely considered "fellow travelers." The new Prime Minister proceeded to take steps toward the establishment of a National Council including Communists; he asserted his cabinet was responsible to Parliament. In December stability further declined with the Indonesian actions against Dutch interests in the country. It was announced that President Sukarno was planning a brief vacation abroad. All these developments aroused concern in the outside world, for domestic turmoil is conducive to foreign interference.

In terms of external security, Indonesia is strongly against adherence to the Southeast Asia Collective Defense Treaty. Even before the planning of the Manila Conference began, Indonesia had indicated opposition to attending any such meeting. In fact, at the Baguio Conference, the chief Indonesian delegate stated at the opening plenary session on May 26, 1950: "It is to our interest and that of our neighbors that we refuse to take sides with this or that nation or group of nations, that we keep open the political, economic and cultural traffic lanes of the Indian and Pacific Oceans that cut across Indonesia."[70] President Quirino's visit to Djakarta in July, 1952, was followed by statements of Indonesian leaders expressing opposition to a Pacific pact. Prime Minister Ali Sastroamidjojo in a speech to Parliament on August 16, 1954, pointedly said that "the efforts to establish a collective defence in South-east Asia and [the] North-west Pacific will bring only tension."[71]

Although Indonesian leaders are reticent on the ultimate expansion of their country, apart from their claim to West Irian, certain areas may become the center of attention—Portuguese Timor, British Borneo, and eastern New Guinea. In 1950 Mohammad Yamin, an official in the Foreign Ministry, indicated in his remarks such an interest. Viewpoints of this nature, however, have been disowned by the government; officially Indonesia has a "good neighbor" attitude. This policy could bring dividends, especially in Indonesian-Philippine-Malayan relations. In the broad field of international affairs the Bandung Conference has already been an important step in raising the prestige of the island republic. Subject to favorable domestic and international conditions, Indonesia has the potential of developing into one of the leading states of the new Asia.

[70] Soebardjo speech, *Final Act and Proceedings of the Baguio Conference of 1950*, p. 36.

[71] *Times of Indonesia*, August 18, 1954.

6. Union of Burma

In her approach to foreign affairs Burma has developed a policy that in the judgment of her leading officials is best suited to the needs of the new republic. Emerging from British rule as a sovereign state on January 4, 1948, Burma was faced with serious problems on the domestic front in addition to those occasioned by the growing intensity of the cold war. It was impossible for the Union, located in a strategic part of peninsular Southeast Asia, to remain in splendid isolation from major developments in Asia and the world. Burma's officials, who were much more concerned with domestic problems, were forced to relate many of them to outside developments. As in the case of the United States in the early years of its independence, Burma was not always able to translate intentions into realities.

The constitution of the Union of Burma, adopted September 24, 1947, included provisions affirming the state's "devotion to the ideal of peace and friendly coöperation amongst nations founded on international justice and morality" (Section 212), renouncing "war as an instrument of national policy" and accepting "the generally recognized principles of international law as its rule of conduct in its relations with foreign States" (Section 211).[1] In fact, the wording of Section 212 is taken from point seven of Bogyoke Aung San's resolution of June 16 in the Constituent Assembly calling for an "Independent Sovereign Republic." This point in turn is found in almost similar words as point 14 of a resolution adopted May 23 by a convention of the Anti-Fascist People's Freedom League (AFPFL). Section 211 of the constitution relative to renouncing war and accepting international law does not appear in the seven-point resolution of June 16 or the fourteen-point resolution of May 23.

The reasons for the foreign policy of Burma as it has developed

[1] *The Constitution of the Union of Burma*, Government Printing and Stationery, Burma, p. 58.

since independence are varied, complex, and interrelated. Unlike the Philippines and Indonesia, the Union of Burma has land neighbors in peninsular Southeast Asia—Pakistan, India, China, Laos, and Thailand. Land traffic with these neighbors being severely restricted because of mountainous terrain, Burma since the arrival of the British has faced the Bay of Bengal and the Andaman Sea. Travel by sea to India, for instance, is much more practical than by land. Events associated with the Second World War stimulated the building of two roads and a railway connecting Burma with the outside. The Burma Road from Lashio into Kunming, China, completed in 1939, is still open although not in good condition. The jungle has claimed the Stilwell, formerly called Ledo, Road from Assam, India, through northern Burma to the Burma Road, built under the guidance of American engineers. The railroad linking Bangkok and Moulmein, constructed by the Japanese at terrible cost of life, has also returned to the jungle.

Despite the mountainous barriers Burma's leaders are fully aware of the fallacy of trying to isolate themselves from the world. After all, the country was settled by people of different racial composition migrating by land into the area. The course of history, moreover, has been characterized by struggles not only among the peoples of the country such as the Burmans, Mons, and Shans, but also by conflicts at times with outsiders like the Thai on the east.[2] The conquest of Burma by Great Britain in the nineteenth century and the Japanese occupation in the Second World War present further evidence of the country's involvement in world affairs. In addition to the wartime development of military routes by the various belligerents into Burma from India, China, and Thailand, it should be noted that Japan used the country as the base for her invasion in late 1944 of the Indian state of Manipur.

Since independence a number of Burma's leaders have frankly indicated their conviction that neutrals along with belligerents would suffer in another world war. Prime Minister U Nu observed in a speech on Martyrs' Day, July 19, 1954, that "once this world war breaks out, no country, whether participants or non-participants, close to the scene of war or away from it, will be spared."[3] As Burma was devastated during the last global conflict, she has no

[2] The words "Burmese" and "Burman" are not clearly distinguished in the country. The author is using "Burmese" to denote the people of Burma as a whole and "Burman" to indicate the dominant part of the population.

[3] Speech of U Nu, July 19, 1954, *Burma*, Information Bulletin of the Embassy of Burma, Washington, D.C.

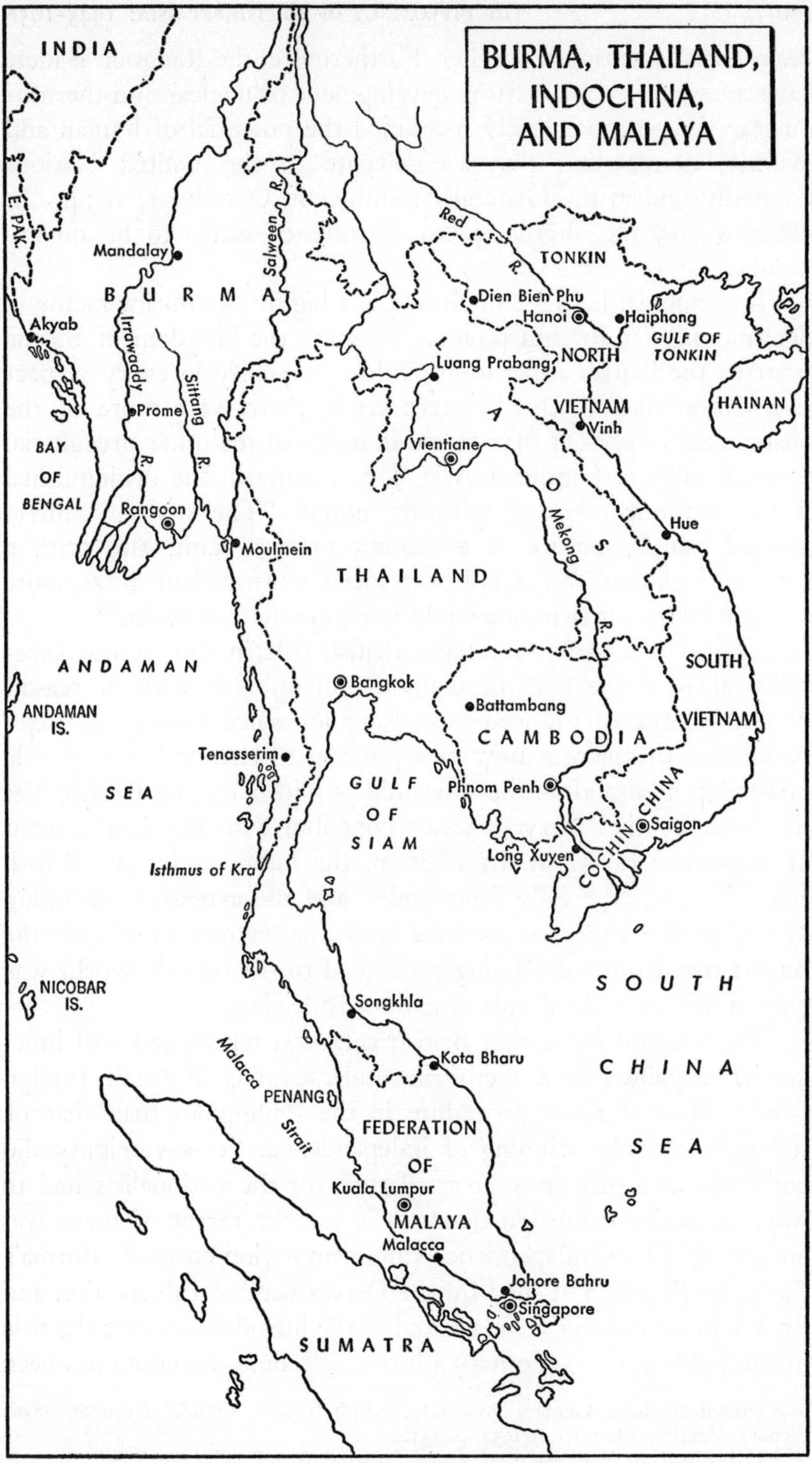
BURMA, THAILAND, INDOCHINA, AND MALAYA
INDIA
E. PAK.
Mandalay
BURMA
Salween R.
Red R.
TONKIN
Dien Bien Phu
Hanoi
Haiphong
GULF OF TONKIN
Akyab
Irrawaddy
Sittang R.
Luang Prabang
NORTH VIETNAM
HAINAN
Prome
Vinh
BAY OF BENGAL
Vientiane
LAOS
Rangoon
Mekong R.
Hue
Moulmein
THAILAND
SOUTH VIETNAM
ANDAMAN SEA
ANDAMAN IS.
Bangkok
Battambang
CAMBODIA
Tenasserim
GULF OF SIAM
Phnom Penh
COCHIN CHINA
Saigon
Long Xuyen
Isthmus of Kra
NICOBAR IS.
SOUTH CHINA SEA
Songkhla
Kota Bharu
Malacca Strait
PENANG
FEDERATION OF MALAYA
Kuala Lumpur
Malacca
Johore Bahru
Singapore
SUMATRA

desire to be a victim in another. Furthermore, the Rangoon leaders have stressed the fact that the development of nuclear and thermonuclear weapons has vastly magnified the potential of human and material destruction. Burma's delegate to the United Nations pointedly said in the General Assembly on October 1, 1954: "In other words, the alternative to coexistence seems to be no existence."[4]

The colonial heritage of Burma is a highly significant factor in determining her foreign policy. Although the kingdom of Burma prior to the British annexation could not qualify in every respect as a nation state in the Western sense, there were more of the characteristics present than found in many of the other precolonial political units in Southeast Asia. J. S. Furnivall, the distinguished British authority, has significantly noted: "The whole country, marked out by nature as a distinct political unit, and with a common religion and a uniform social culture, had a far more national character than one could find anywhere in India."[5]

Against this background the British rule in Burma was especially alien in the eyes of many Burmans. Not without reason have a number of the leaders in Rangoon since January 4, 1948, stated that Burma was now in a position to resume her own role in foreign affairs after the interlude provided by the British. Yet the latter by their very presence contributed to the development of Burman nationalism. In addition, the influx under the British rule of aliens, especially from India, and the extensive recruiting of soldiers from the Karens were influential factors. Obviously the Burma that Rudyard Kipling portrayed to the outside world was quite different in the minds of nationalist leaders.

The method by which British rule was terminated and independence gained is a factor in understanding Burma's foreign policy. More like the procedure in the Philippines than that of Indonesia was the winning of independence. Yet sovereignty did not come as a gift on a silver platter, for the nationalists had to wage an active campaign to attain it and the threat of force was not absent. In an Independence Commemoration entitled "Burma's Fight for Freedom" issued by the Department of Information and Broadcasting in 1948, it was stated in the introduction that the title of the publication "is perhaps a little misleading. Freedom has been

[4] United Nations, General Assembly, Ninth Session, *Official Records*, 485th Plenary Meeting, October 1, 1954, p. 143.

[5] J. S. Furnivall, *Colonial Policy and Practice*, p. 17.

won without a fight, a fact which testifies to Britain's wisdom and Burma's unity. . . . [Yet] Fight or no fight, one should recall the past, pay homage to the martyrs and leaders who have gone before, and re-learn whatever lessons the story of our march to independence still has for us."[6] It is interesting speculation as to what Burma's relations to the British Commonwealth and her foreign policy would have been if the United Kingdom had taken a position similar to that of the United States in the Philippines of fixing in the 1930's a date for the withdrawal of sovereignty. As it was, a Burmese crowd on the day of independence sang "Auld Lang Syne" as the last British governor, Sir Hubert E. Rance, left Rangoon.

The political and religious backgrounds of the postwar leaders of Burma have obviously contributed to the formation of foreign policy. Some of them, like U Nu, stand out as Buddhist leaders and others, like U Kyaw Nyein and U Ba Swe, as outstanding Socialist Party men. Educated largely in Burma, especially at the University of Rangoon, the nationalists who emerged after the Second World War had for the most part been looking for inspiration more to the Indians and Japanese than the Russians. Bogyoke Aung San, for instance, the strongest nationalist leader prior to his assassination on July 19, 1947, received his B.A. at the University of Rangoon in 1938, went to Japan in 1940, served as Minister for National Defense in Dr. Ba Maw's cabinet in 1943, organized the AFPFL the next year, led his Burma Defense Army against the Japanese in February, 1945, and was Deputy Chairman of the Governor's Executive Council the following year. Martyrs' Mound in Rangoon where the Bogyoke is buried is a shrine for Burmese patriots.

Domestic unrest in the Union of Burma has influenced the foreign policy of the nation. Both Aung San and U Nu were aware of the need of creating a state where the Burmans and the other peoples of the country could live and work together. The Union of Burma as set up under the constitution of 1947 consisted of Burma proper, the Shan State comprising the former Federated Shan States and the Wa States, the Kachin State making up the former Myitkyina and Bhamo Districts, and the Karenni State, later officially called Kayah State, comprising the former Karenni States, namely Bawlake, Kyebogyi, and Kantarawaddy. Mongpan

[6] *Burma's Fight for Freedom*, Department of Information and Broadcasting, p. 11.

State in the former Federated Shan States was allowed to join the Karenni State if a majority of its people so desired. A Chin Special Division was created from areas in the Chin Hills District and Arakan Hill Tracts, and provision was made for the eventual establishment under certain conditions of a Karen State. The national flag of the Union reflects this overall concept, having in the upper left-hand corner five small stars, symbolizing the Burmans, Karens, Chins, Kachins, and Shans, grouped around a large star representing Burma's Resistance Movement. All states except the Kachin State had the right to secede within ten years.

The Karens were not generally satisfied with the constitutional provisions relative to them. Some three-fourths of the Karens lived outside the Karenni State largely in the Tenasserim and Irrawaddy Delta areas where they were often mixed with the Burmans. Difficult indeed would it be to establish a Karen State, especially as the Burmans and Karens had long found it hard to coöperate. The constitution specifically provided for the establishment of a Special Region to be called *Kaw-thu-lay*, which would consist of the Salween District and adjacent Karen-occupied areas as decided upon by a special commission appointed by the president of the Union. This region along with the Karenni State could become a Karen State in the Union if the majority of the people in the areas and of the Karens living outside them desired it. After the constitution was amended Parliament passed an act in 1952 whereby the Salween District was enlarged by the addition of five townships. The act would not come into effect until the peace which had been broken was restored. Meanwhile a Karen State Government was set up with initial headquarters in the Rangoon Secretariat. In July, 1955, the Karen State came into full existence, the Kayah State previously having determined to keep its own entity.

In the Karenni State a revolt broke out in August, 1948, and the Rangoon government subsequently proclaimed martial law. Part of the trouble here concerned the methods of a newly appointed official. On September 1 a Regional Autonomy Inquiry Commission under the Chief Justice of the Supreme Court of Burma was appointed to study the ways of meeting the complaints of the Karens as well as of the Mons and Arakanese. Outside the Karenni State the Karens occupied Moulmein on September 3, one of the reasons being an effort to disarm them. The following day the head of the Karen National Union, Saw Ba U Gyi, flew to

Moulmein from Rangoon and bloodshed was temporarily averted. Nevertheless, the Karens organized provisional administrations in many parts of the Irrawaddy Delta and Tenasserim Divisions and were calling for a Karen State covering a large area where they were often in the minority. In extending its zones of control, the Karen National Defense Organization (KNDO) finally came into armed conflict with the forces of the Rangoon government. At times the Karens occupied among other places Bassein, Toungoo, Mandalay, and Insein; and on May 20, 1949, they proclaimed a Karen State with its seat at the time at Toungoo. The Burmese government despite the numerous revolts it faced managed to defeat gradually the KNDO forces. The Karen leader, Saw Ba U Gyi, was killed in August, 1950. Although handicapped by the diversion of troops to cope with the Kuomintang forces in the Shan State, the Rangoon authorities launched in late 1953 an offensive against the KNDO units in their two "commands," the hill country along the boundary with Thailand and the delta area. The important Mawchi wolfram mines were captured but Papun, the capital of *Kaw-thu-lay*, as the Karens called their state, was not taken until March 28, 1955. Significantly a prominent Karen, U Win Maung, became President of the Union of Burma on March 13, 1957.

In Arakan, a division in southwestern Burma isolated by the Arakan Yoma from the rest of the Union, another movement for a state existed but it never acquired the strength of the Karen. Since May, 1947, the separatists in Arakan, supported by the Red Flag Communists and later the White Band PVO's, had been causing serious trouble. One group of Arakanese—certain Buddhists in the south—wanted local autonomy, but a Moslem faction in the north—the Mujahids—wanted to be annexed to Pakistan. In the Burmese Chamber of Deputies there was as a consequence of the general elections in 1951 an Independent Arakanese Parliamentary Group of 17 members favoring a state for Arakan. In the 1956 elections the Arakan National United Organization won five seats in the Chamber. The Mons, mingled with the Burmans living in the Tenasserim, Pegu, and Irrawaddy Divisions, wanted local autonomy.

In addition to the unrest occasioned by constitutional problems, Communist revolts have contributed to political instability in Burma. The AFPFL, it should be noted, has remained the dominant coalition in the government of the Union with the Socialist Party based substantially on the ideology of Marx and Lenin being the main component. Communists who do not seek to overthrow the government by armed force are in effect allowed to operate in the open, but those who are in armed rebellion face the military might of the state. Thus a Communist-led group, the Burma Workers and Peasants Party (BWPP), had about 4 percent of the seats in the Chamber of Deputies elected in 1951. Operating through front organizations including students and labor, the BWPP under U Aung Than, the younger brother of the dead national hero, exerted pressure on the government. In the elections of 1956 for the Chamber of Deputies the supporters of the AFPFL captured at least 173 of the 250 seats, but the Communist-led National United Front (NUF) made substantial gains among the electorate. On June 5 U Nu resigned as premier in order to spend his time reorganizing the AFPFL, and U Ba Swe, a close associate, quickly succeeded him.

The Burma Communist Party (BCP) or White Flag Communists under Thakin Than Tun has been in armed revolt against the Rangoon government since 1948, and the Communist Party (Burma) or CP(B), the Red Flag Communists, has been fighting government forces since 1946. The BCP was once a member of the AFPFL and until the split in March, 1946, the members of the CP(B) belonged to the BCP. In addition there is another illegal Communist party—the People's Comrades Party (PCP). It is clear that the BCP constituted the most serious Communist threat, but the failure of the different Communist rebels to effect a permanent alliance among themselves or with other dissidents contributed to the growing victories of the government forces. The sincerity of Prime Minister U Nu's opposition to the Communist insurgents is clearly revealed in his play, made into a motion picture—*The People Win Through*. In October, 1955, the government offered an amnesty to those who would lay down their arms, but the response was poor. A third amnesty offer expired in March, 1956. It is obvious that U Nu is not prepared to negotiate with the rebels in armed revolt.

Other insurrections against the Rangoon regime were a rebellion of the White Band People's Volunteer Organization (PVO), and a mutiny of part of the Burma Rifles in the regular army in August, 1948. Dacoity, of course, thrived under chaotic conditions. The PVO was originally a private army of U Aung San created after the war. In 1948 the PVO split, with the minority, called the

Yellow Band PVO, remaining loyal to the government and the majority, the White Band PVO, becoming rebels. By 1955 the PVO, now often termed the "Green Communists," had been reduced to activities in a few places in the Chindwin valley.

There can be no doubt of the fact that the Union of Burma came very near to collapse as a result of the "multicolored" rebels. The "Civil War," as General Ne Win has described it, resulted in the victory of the government of Prime Minister U Nu not only because his administration was prepared to use military force to fight military force, but also because it sought to remove the grievances that gave support to many of the insurgents. Furthermore, conditions in the early years of the Union of Burma presented opportunities for foreign powers to intervene but fortunately Burma was allowed to work out her own destiny. Nevertheless, a number of outside states were involved in one way or another in the Burmese crisis.

To quite an extent, also, Burma's foreign policy has been motivated by the need to get markets for her rice, the chief export. Without these markets the country would have grave budget problems and could not forward the ambitious program of economic development it had in mind. About three-fourths of Burma's foreign exchange come from rice exports. For a period after 1953 a buyer's market developed, and the prices fell. The Communist bloc took advantage of the situation and made heavy economic inroads, barter instead of cash being the common method of trade. The United States with its own rice surplus and its efforts to export the commodity has been at a disadvantage in Burma. The latter country does not need American rice and wants to keep its own markets.

The foreign policy of the Union of Burma, as indicated from an analysis of the statements and actions of influential leaders, includes the pursuance of "neutralism" with reference to "power blocs" and of anticolonialism in world politics, the direct and indirect promotion of Asian socialism as well as of Buddhism, and efforts to improve the economic conditions of the people partly through international assistance. Rice diplomacy is important in the overall pattern. As is true in the case of the external relations of any state, Burma reacts to outside conditions, resulting in a foreign policy that is not static. Nevertheless, the fundamental outlook in Rangoon contains a large number of constant factors.

Although Indonesia tends to call its foreign policy "active and independent," Burma frequently refers to her own as "neutral." Prime Minister U Nu observed in Washington in the summer of 1955 that "we are neutrals and we must stay neutral."[7] In a Martyrs' Day address on July 19, 1954, he referred to the Burmese as "neutralists" in the world of power politics. The Prime Minister expressed a similar idea four years earlier when he said that "we do not desire alignment with a particular power bloc antagonistic to other opposing blocs."[8] On June 13, 1948, he asserted that "of the three great Western Powers, the United Kingdom, the United States and the USSR, the Communists [in Burma] wish to be in friendly relations only with [the] USSR whereas the AFPFL wish that Burma should be in friendly relations with all the three."[9]

U Kyaw Nyein, influential in Burma's foreign policy, noted in a speech on July 19, 1955, that his country was opposed to both the Imperialists and the Cominform, that it wanted to be friendly with both power blocs, and that it sought, if possible, to bring them into harmony. In a May Day address in 1953, U Ba Swe, another influential leader in foreign policy, asserted that "as we are anti-war and for lasting peace, we will not side with either of the power blocs. . . ."[10] A year later on a similar occasion he reiterated his statement, adding that "one bloc led by Soviet Russia and [an] other led by America are threatening world peace with Hydrogen Bombs which can annihilate cities and living things in wide areas."[11] James Barrington, Ambassador to the United States, in a speech at the Kobe Institute observed that his country refused to commit itself to either of the power blocs, noting "how much moral courage it requires for us to remain uncommitted."[12] At the General Assembly on October 1, 1954, he stated: "In short, we feel that our position of non-alignment serves a useful and what might become an essential purpose to the United Nations and to the cause of world peace."[13]

Burma's concept of neutrality is somewhat different from that

[7] Interview with U Nu, *U.S. News and World Report,* August 5, 1955, p. 80.

[8] Speech of Thakin Nu, July 19, 1950, *From Peace to Stability,* Government Printing and Stationery, Burma, p. 86.

[9] Speech of Thakin Nu, June 13, 1948, *Towards Peace and Democracy,* Government Printing and Stationery, Burma, p. 117.

[10] "U Ba Swe's May Day Address," *Burma,* Vol. III (July, 1953), p. 3.

[11] "U Ba Swe's May Day Speech," *Burma,* Vol. IV (July, 1954), p. 46.

[12] "The United Nations through Burmese Eyes (Speech by James Barrington)," *Burma,* Vol. IV (July, 1954), p. 41.

[13] United Nations, General Assembly, Ninth Session, *Official Records,* 485th Plenary Meeting, October 1, 1954, p. 143.

of Switzerland. The fact that the former applied for membership in the United Nations and was elected whereas the latter has not sought membership in the world organization is significant. U Nu on December 20, 1947, and on June 14, 1949, even spoke of the need of allies for his country, but obviously he had second thoughts as no defense pacts resulted. As regards United Nations membership the Prime Minister on July 19, 1950, stated: "To be candid we joined the UNO not because we are very keen to get financial or other aid but because we want [the] UN's protection in case our independence is threatened by any country."[14] And he went on to say: "To call for assistance when we want it and to look on with folded arms when others need assistance is but the way of the opportunists."[15] Burma believes that since both of the power blocs are in the United Nations she can be a nonpartisan member of the world organization without impairing her neutrality.

At the same time the Rangoon government interprets neutrality as enabling independent judgment on the merits of issues as they arise in world politics. The Burmese strongly criticize what they call bloc voting in the United Nations. Ambassador Barrington has stated: "We do not hesitate to come out openly on an issue when the facts clearly call for such an attitude," and he later added that "our actions in the United Nations are determined not by a blind neutralism, but by a close scrutiny of the merits of each issue."[16] U Nu frankly said on September 5, 1950: "If we consider that a right course of action is being taken by a country we will support that country, be it America, Britain, or Soviet Russia. . . . Although a small country, we will support what is right in the world."[17] Again in a speech on March 8, 1951, he asserted: "To be candid, we can never be the camp followers or stooge of any power. . . . The sole criteria for all our decisions is our sense of what is right and proper."[18] In other words positive neutrality is followed.

Burma's concept of neutrality, furthermore, does not envision the establishment of any third power bloc, her leaders having emphatically denied that they favor such a development. For instance, U Ba Swe asserted on May Day, 1953, that "our ideas are not in

[14] Speech of Thakin Nu, July 19, 1950, *From Peace to Stability*, p. 89.
[15] *Ibid.*
[16] "The United Nations through Burmese Eyes (Speech by James Barrington)," *Burma*, Vol. IV (July, 1954), p. 41.
[17] Speech of Thakin Nu, September 5, 1950, *From Peace to Stability*, p. 101. The Prime Minister more than once has referred to Burma as a "tender gourd among the cactus." *Ibid.*, p. 102.
[18] Speech of Thakin Nu, March 8, 1951, *From Peace to Stability*, p. 196.

terms of blocs."[19] Nevertheless, the Burmese leader believed, as he expressed it a year later, that Burma, Indonesia, and India were right in trying to enlarge the "area of peace" in their "anti-'world power-bloc' policy."[20] Consultation, to be sure, among themselves and in the Asian-African group in the United Nations takes place.

The temporary assumption by U Ba Swe of the premiership of Burma in June, 1956, obviously did not alter the policy of neutrality. In his first speech to Parliament on June 13, the new Premier asserted that the government "will continue to pursue a policy of independent neutrality," and he went on to state that "ours is an active, dynamic neutrality primarily concerned with bringing about understanding and better relations between the two opposing blocs, creating of good-will among nations and the inevitableness of co-existence."[21] At his first press conference as Premier on July 3, U Ba Swe in a government statement praised the "value and wisdom of the stand of independent neutrality."[22] On July 19 in a Martyrs' Day address the Premier observed that such a foreign policy had given Burma "prestige" in the world. At the same time he referred to "the great task of weeding out stooges, puppets and political maggots from our midst" or "the elimination of this new imperialism [occasioned by them] from our Union."[23]

Anticolonialism is a basic principle in the foreign policy of Burma. Her representatives, participating in the general debates of the United Nations General Assembly, have emphasized their opposition to colonialism. U Ohn on September 24, 1948, quoted Abraham Lincoln to the effect that "no Nation has the right to rule another."[24] The Burmese delegate hoped that the United Nations would help free from bondage such subject countries as Indonesia and Indochina. On November 11, 1952, James Barrington observed:

[19] "U Ba Swe's May Day Address," *Burma*, Vol. III (July, 1953), p. 3.

[20] "U Ba Swe's May Day Speech," *Burma*, Vol. IV (July, 1954), p. 46.

[21] Speech of U Ba Swe, June 13, 1956, *Burma Weekly Bulletin*, New Series, Vol. 5 (June 21, 1956), p. 74.

[22] Government Statement (U Ba Swe), July 3, 1956, *Burma Weekly Bulletin*, New Series, Vol. 5 (July 12, 1956), p. 99.

[23] Premier's Address, July 19, 1956, *Burma Weekly Bulletin*, New Series, Vol. 5 (July 26, 1956), p. 113. In a speech on the same occasion U Nu, President of the AFPFL, pointedly remarked: "The main problem arises from the existence of those inside the country who have no compunction to play the part of stooges, spies, fifth-columnists, and veritable sons of bitches who can sell their birthright for a mess of pottage. However keen the outside hands may be to pull distant strings, they will be helpless if traitors inside the country refuse to play the puppet." Speech of U Nu, July 19, 1956, *ibid.*, p. 119.

[24] United Nations, General Assembly, Third Session, Part I, *Official Records*, 141st Plenary Meeting, September 24, 1948, p. 73.

"Our general view is that good government is no substitute for self-government."[25] He was especially critical of French policy in Tunisia and Morocco. "Like Rip Van Winkle," he said, "the French nation has suddenly awakened to find a changed world."[26] U Myint Thein told the General Assembly on September 25, 1953, that "despite the high-sounding affirmations and the pious hopes expressed in the Charter, the Assembly itself may become the means of perpetuating colonial and imperial rule"; he went on to add that the "theory of the white man's burden is an outworn myth. But if there should be people who are yet unfit to rule themselves, it is about time that they were taken away from the not-too-gentle hands of colonial Powers and placed under United Nations trusteeship."[27] The Union of Burma, it is not surprising, has taken a decided interest in the work of the Trusteeship Council of the United Nations.

Outside the halls of the world organization, Burma has opposed colonialism at different gatherings including the Bandung Conference, meetings of the Colombo Powers, and the New Delhi Conference on Indonesia. In speeches delivered in Burma government officials have added their denunciation of colonialism, often noting that it was a fundamental cause of war. U Ba Swe in his May Day addresses in 1953 and 1954 asserted in identical words that "as imperialism in any guise leads to war, we shall give all possible help to the liberation and anti-imperialist struggles of the colonial and dependent States throughout the world."[28] In both years he specifically referred to the struggle for self-determination of Vietnam, Malaya, Tunisia, Morocco, and Kenya, adding in 1954 Puerto Rico and "Guiana in South America." Burmese leaders have tended to put considerable stress on colonialism in Africa, taking in some cases the position that the Western colonial powers were seeking by staying in Africa to make up for their losses in Asia.

The Anglo-French-Israeli aggression in Egypt in late 1956 was strongly condemned in Rangoon. On November 8 a crowd stoned the British Embassy. Burma, despite the desire of India, had not been invited to attend the first London Conference on the Suez

[25] United Nations, General Assembly, Seventh Session, *Official Records*, 394th Plenary Meeting, November 11, 1952, p. 230.

[26] *Ibid.*

[27] United Nations, General Assembly, Eighth Session, *Official Records*, 446th Plenary Meeting, September 25, 1953, p. 173.

[28] "U Ba Swe's May Day Address," *Burma*, Vol. III (July, 1953), p. 3 and "U Ba Swe's May Day Speech," *Burma*, Vol. IV (July, 1954), p. 47.

question. Nevertheless, she followed carefully developments in the Suez crisis, supported the United Nations in its efforts to restore peace, and offered a contingent for service with the emergency international police force. Burma believed Egypt had the right to nationalize the canal company but had a duty to abide by the agreements opening the canal to all countries as users of its facilities.

The Russian intervention in Hungary was not at first so bitterly received in Rangoon, but as soon as the facts of the situation were known Premier U Ba Swe did not hesitate to denounce it through his delegation at the United Nations and personally at the Second Congress of the Asian Socialist Conference in Bombay and at the New Delhi meeting of the Colombo Powers. At Bombay he referred to the Soviet action as "the most despicable form of colonialism."[29] At New Delhi he was the most outspoken in his criticism among the four prime ministers present. On November 15 the Burmese Premier asked reporters: "What is the difference between aggression [in Egypt] and intervention [in Hungary]? To my mind they are both basically the same."[30]

In condemning colonialism, Burma associates with it her abhorrence of racialism. U Thant in a statement at the United Nations on October 27, 1952, and again on November 26, observed that Burma would never support any policy tolerating or encouraging discrimination founded on color or creed. The Union of South Africa is a favorite target of criticism with its racial policies. Burma has supported United Nations efforts to solve the problem related to the treatment of persons of Indian and Pakistani origin in South Africa and to face the issues produced by racial segregation in that country. The Rangoon government has maintained that such racial questions are not domestic in nature since they violate the basic principles and human rights written into the Charter of the United Nations. "In our view," U Tun Shein even asserted in the *Ad Hoc* Political Committee on November 4, 1952, "anything which involves a challenge to the dignity of man comes within the competence of the United Nations."[31] Burma's officials point to the international ramifications of racialism in any country and in particular to the reaction in Asia and Africa to concepts of "white supremacy."

The promotion of Asian socialism is reflected in the prominent role of high officials in the Asian Socialist Conference and in the

[29] *New York Times*, November 13, 1956.
[30] *New York Times*, November 16, 1956.
[31] The Burmese government reprinted the statement of U Tun Shein made November 4, 1952, in *Burma*, Vol. III (April, 1953), p. 48.

location at Rangoon of the headquarters of the organization. As is clear, the Socialist Party of Burma is not only the most influential in the government of the country but also among any of the genuine socialist parties in Southeast Asia. The Rangoon government launched its own plans for a Welfare State at the *Pyidawtha* Conference held in August, 1952. Resolutions were passed approving ten development plans presented by the cabinet members concerned. Directed toward "radically changing the colonial system of exploitation as existed under the foreign power, to one of sincere benevolent democratic Government of the Burmese people by the Burmese people,"[32] the plans related to democratization of local administration, land nationalization, education, transport and communications, and other topics of interest. Obviously considerable time and much effort would be needed to make substantial progress toward the Welfare State. In 1957 U Nu called for a less ambitious plan of economic and social development.

Meanwhile Burma's encouragement of Asian socialism on the international level continues. Although it would be fallacious to assert that Asian socialism at present is a third force of major proportions between Communism and capitalism in Asia, if generalizations are used, the potential is present. The first Asian Socialist Conference was held in Rangoon from January 6 to January 15, 1953, under the auspices of the Burmese, Indonesian, and Indian socialist parties. Preliminary discussions had occurred among socialists of Burma, Indonesia, and India in 1947 and in 1952, between Indian socialists and representatives of the Social Democratic Party of Japan in 1951, and Indian and Lebanese socialists later the same year. The Rangoon Asian Socialist Conference brought together about 200 delegates, observers, and fraternal delegates. The socialist parties of Burma, Indonesia, India, Israel, Japan (Right and Left), Lebanon, Malaya, Pakistan, and Egypt sent 158 delegates. Observers were present from organizations in Algeria, Tunisia, Kenya, Uganda, and Nepal. The presence of the observers from Africa reflected to a large extent the concern of the Asian socialists over independence movements in that continent. Fraternal delegates came from the Socialist International including Clement Attlee, former British Prime Minister, the Communist Party of Yugoslavia, the International Union of Socialist Youth, and the Congress of Peoples against Imperialism.

In an effort to insure permanence the Asian Socialist Con-

[32] Introduction, *The Pyidawtha Conference, August 4-17, 1952, Resolutions and Speeches* (unpaged).

ference approved a resolution establishing "an organization of Asian Socialist Parties." Having as its purposes the strengthening of relations among the parties, the coördination of their political attitudes based on consent, the establishing of more intimate relations with socialist parties throughout the world, and the creating of a liaison with the Socialist International, the organization would function through three bodies—the Conference being the Supreme Body and meeting every two years, the Bureau of the Conference ordinarily convening every six months, and the Secretariat responsible to the Bureau and executing the decisions of both the Conference and the Bureau. U Ba Swe, who had been elected chairman of the Rangoon Socialist Conference, was chosen chairman of the Bureau.

A number of other resolutions were passed dealing with various topics such as "Principles and Objectives of Socialism," "Asia and World Peace," "Agrarian Policy for Asia," "Economic Development of Asia," "Common Asian Problems," and "Freedom Movements in Colonies."[33] The Conference agreed that although "democratic socialism" was against Communism as well as capitalism, it could not be neutral between totalitarianism and democracy. In no uncertain words the Conference condemned imperialism asserting that "freedom of all peoples, irrespective of race, colour and creed, is a fundamental article of faith with the Asian Socialists." Criticism was directed against both Western and Communist colonialism, and the Socialist International was urged "to take a very firm and courageous stand in relation to the question of colonialism in general." In fact, many Asian socialists were convinced that a larger number of European socialists were compromising themselves on the colonial question. Resolutions on Malaya, Uganda, Kenya, Tunisia, Algeria, and Morocco supported nationalist movements in those countries. The Union of South Africa was condemned for its racial policies. Support was given to the United Nations. The polarization of power with its rival blocs was considered a threat to world peace, but each country was left to determine its foreign policy in the cold war. "The freedom of the Asian countries," it was stated, "each to determine its own position *vis-à-vis* the problems bearing on the maintenance of world peace is an essential condition."

In Hyderabad, India, the Conference Bureau met in August, 1953, and decided to set up an Anticolonial Bureau and an Asian Economic Bureau. The Coördination Committee of the Anticolonial Bureau as well as the Asian Socialist Conference Bureau met

[33] *Report of the First Asian Socialist Conference, Rangoon, 1953, passim.*

in Kalaw, Burma, the following May. By now it was clear that the work of the Asian socialists was facing various obstacles. Although U Ba Swe stated in January, 1954, in *Socialist Asia* that the socialist policy "of creating a neutral area to arrest the polarization in world affairs has actually contributed to the lessening of tensions between the two power blocs,"[34] he stressed then and again the following May the need to make much more effective the work of the Asian Socialist Conference. Moreover, the governments of Indonesia and Pakistan had not shown a favorable attitude toward international Asian socialism, the former preventing the meeting of the Conference Bureau in Bandung as scheduled.

At Kalaw, U Kyaw Nyein chaired the meetings of the Anticolonial Bureau's Coördination Committee and was also elected chairman of the Bureau itself. He frankly asserted in an opening speech that in his judgment "the Soviet type of imperialism is, perhaps, even more degrading and even more dangerous, because it is more ruthless, more systematic and more blatantly justified in the name of world communist revolution."[35] A statement on the functions and program of the Anticolonial Bureau was subsequently approved by the Coördination Committee. U Ba Swe gave the inaugural speech at the meeting of the Asian Socialist Conference Bureau reviewing the work of the organization since the Rangoon assembly in January, 1953. The Bureau considered the applications for membership of the Vietnam Socialist Party and the Samasamaj Party of Ceylon, referring the subject to a future Asian Socialist Conference which had the power of decision. Plans were made for an Economic Experts Conference and consideration was given to a report of the Standing Committee of Economic Experts. The work of the Coördination Committee of the Anticolonial Bureau was endorsed. Other topics were considered including the revision of the United Nations Charter, youth movements, and the Indochina question. Subsequent meetings of the Asian Socialist Conference Bureau have been held.

From November 1-10, 1956, the Second Congress of the Asian Socialist Conference met in Bombay, India. As at the Rangoon meeting Burmese leaders had a key role, Premier U Ba Swe himself speaking for the Socialist Party. Among others present were Sam Sary of Cambodia, Nguyen Huu Thong of the Republic of Viet-

[34] U Ba Swe, "Tasks Ahead," *Socialist Asia*, Vol. II (Anniversary Number, 1954), p. 3.

[35] Speech of U Kyaw Nyein, May 23, 1954, *Burma*, Vol. IV (July, 1954), p. 29.

nam, Sjahrir of Indonesia, Moshe Sharett of Israel, Asoka Mehta of India, and Inajiro Asanuma of Japan. The Conference passed a number of resolutions[36] calling, *inter alia*, for the withdrawal of foreign troops from Hungary and Egypt, at the same time condemning the Soviet Union, Great Britain, France, and Israel for their recent military actions, for an end to the experiment and use of nuclear and thermonuclear weapons and for general disarmament, both under "effective and unfettered international control," for the seating of the People's Republic of China in the United Nations, for the peaceful unification of Vietnam, for a resumption of negotiations between Great Britain and Singapore relative to meeting the aspirations of the people of the latter, for the restoration of West Irian to Indonesia, for self-determination in Cyprus, and for "solidarity with the Algerian people struggling for their national independence." Egypt's right to nationalize the Suez Canal Company was recognized but the use of the waterway should be open to all nations "without exception." The Conference welcomed the coming independence of Malaya, and it opposed military bases and alliances. U Ba Swe was unanimously reëlected chairman.

The Asian Socialist Conference at Rangoon had indicated clearly the relatively close relations between Burma and Yugoslavia and Burma and Israel. The Communist Party of Yugoslavia was represented by Milovan Djilas, a member of the Belgrade cabinet, Ales Bebler, Assistant Foreign Minister, and A. Blaievic while the Socialist Party (Mapai) of Israel sent Moshe Sharett, Foreign Minister of the republic, and two others. In their speeches in Rangoon the Yugoslav and Israeli representatives went out of their way to stress the friendly relations their countries had with Burma. Moshe Sharett in his speech nominating U Ba Swe for the chairmanship of the Conference said: "I believe, comrades, that all of us know that this has not been merely a trip to a conference but also a voyage to Burma, a country which has a special place in the hearts of all of us, a country which has gone through a heroic struggle, a country in the independence of which we all rejoice."[37] Ales Bebler in a speech to the Burmese at a mass rally on January 11 noted that "my countrymen follow your endeavours with the greatest interest and admiration. Their hearts beat with your hearts."[38]

[36] The Second Congress of the Asian Socialist Conference, *Asian Socialist Conference Information Bulletin*, Vol. I (November, 1956), *passim.*

[37] Speech of Moshe Sharett, *Report of the First Asian Socialist Conference*, p. 6.

[38] Speech of Ales Bebler, *Report of the First Asian Socialist Conference*, p. 72.

Relations between Burma and Yugoslavia have been further strengthened by a visit of Marshal Tito to the Union in January, 1955, and a return visit of Prime Minister U Nu to Yugoslavia the following June. In a communiqué issued in Burma on the former occasion the Belgrade and Rangoon governments expressed agreement on the main problems of the world. The following October the Yugoslav envoy to Burma turned over to the defense minister the equipment necessary for one brigade in the Burmese army given in exchange for a certain amount of rice. On March 7, 1956, agreements on trade, technical assistance, and long-term economic coöperation were signed. U Nu also on his way to Yugoslavia paid a visit to Israel. Now Israeli technicians are active in the Union; Burmese missions have visited Israel; joint economic ventures are under way in Burma.

Against the background of the *Pyidawtha* objectives on the domestic front and the Asian socialist objectives on the international front it is not surprising that Burma's delegates in the United Nations have stressed the need for international assistance to the underdeveloped areas of the world. U Myint Thein, for instance, told the General Assembly on September 25, 1953: "We know that the under-developed areas of the world cannot be developed in five years, but we do suggest that it is important to utilize these years to build up among the peoples of the under-developed areas the prospect of a better life, if not for themselves, at least for their children; for life without hope of any kind can only result in the release of destructive forces which, once released, might easily make the present turbulent phase in the history of the world appear, by comparison, a spell of paradise."[39] As for the sources of foreign aid, Prime Minister U Nu asserted in a speech on August 4, 1952: "If any assistance is given on two conditions, which are (1) non-infringement of our sovereignty and (2) for creation of the new era, we shall accept this assistance from any source, be it Britain, United States, Soviet Russia, the People's Republic of China, Abyssinia or the Andamans."[40]

Basically, as is now clear, Burma is seeking to uproot the "colonial" economy founded upon exporting certain raw materials like rice, her mainstay in foreign trade, and minerals. The government seeks to develop industries and diversify agriculture, making

[39] United Nations, General Assembly, Eighth Session, *Official Records*, 446th Plenary Meeting, September 25, 1953, p. 174.

[40] *Toward a Welfare State, Prime Minister U Nu*, Ministry of Information, Government of the Union of Burma, p. 29.

the nation independent of imports in many items of common use. In her efforts Burma needs foreign capital and technical assistance. The need has only been partially met by help from the United Nations, under the Colombo Plan, and through bilateral agreements.

In another important aspect the Sixth Great Buddhist Council, opening outside Rangoon on May 17, 1954, symbolized the interest of Burma not only in Buddhism at home but also abroad. The fundamental ideology of the Union is Buddhism to which socialism as well as traditionalism must adjust. U Ba Swe, notable for his interest in Marxism, has significantly observed that "Marxist theory is not antagonistic to Buddhist philosophy."[41] The former, he believes, is concerned with "mundane affairs" while the latter deals with "spiritual matters." He has noted that the more he studied Marxism the more he came to believe in Buddhism. At the same time U Ba Swe did not identify Marxism with Communism, for the latter in his opinion involved acceptance of Soviet leadership. Many people, it is clear, do not agree with these interpretations.[42]

Whatever the relation between Marxism and Buddhism, the latter is the religion of the vast majority (85 percent) of the people of Burma. In fact, the Buddhist monks or *pongyis* in the country were influential in generating nationalism, especially after the Russo-Japanese War in 1904-1905. Under the national constitution freedom of religion is provided but the "State recognizes the special position of Buddhism as the faith professed by the great majority of the citizens of the Union."[43] At the same time the state recognizes Islam, Hinduism, Christianity, and Animism as some of the other existing religions. U Nu, it is significant, in an audience with Pope Pius XII assured the pontiff that Roman Catholics in Burma were being treated fairly and were suffering no discrimination.

Theravada Buddhism is a bond especially among Burma, Ceylon, Cambodia, Laos, and Thailand. On October 1, 1951, the Burmese Parliament passed a resolution expressing a conviction that measures for the moral and spiritual well-being of mankind should be devised. The Union government proceeded to establish a central fund to

[41] U Ba Swe, *The Burmese Revolution,* p. 17.

[42] See Francis Story, *Buddhism Answers the Marxist Challenge: An Analytical Comparison between the Scientific Doctrines of Buddhism and the Tenets of Dialectical Materialism, in Theory and Practical Application, passim.*

[43] *The Constitution of the Union of Burma,* p. 4. In October, 1950, the Burmese Parliament passed three measures strengthening Buddhism in the country—an act setting up two ecclesiastical courts to restore order among the monks, another establishing the Pali University, and an act creating the Buddha Sasana Council, a central organ representative of Burma's Buddhists, charged with promoting Buddhism at home and propagating it abroad.

hold the Sixth Great Buddhist Council and to erect the necessary buildings. The purpose of the Council was to reëxamine and revise the Teachings of the Buddha seeking to preserve the Buddhist Scriptures in their pristine purity and to make them more accessible through translations. In almost 2500 years since the demise of the Buddha only five previous Councils, the Burmese assert, had been held, three in India and one each in Ceylon and Burma. To be constructed next to the recently built "World Peace Pagoda," the buildings for the Sixth Great Buddhist Council including the Great Sacred Cave would subsequently be used for an International Buddhist University. It was decided in February, 1952, that the Council should be a joint undertaking of the Theravada Buddhist lands with the help of Buddhists throughout the world. Completion of the Council's work would not come until May, 1956, coinciding with the end of the 2500th year of the Buddhist Era.

The opening of the Sixth Great Buddhist Council brought together a congregation from many lands including India, Ceylon, Pakistan, Burma, Laos, Cambodia, Vietnam, Nepal, Malaya, Thailand, the Andaman Islands, and Germany. Distinguished guests included Madame Vijayalakshmi Pandit, Malcolm MacDonald and Dudley Senanayake. Good-will messages during the opening services were read from the King and Prime Minister of Thailand, the President and Prime Minister of India, the Prime Minister of Ceylon, the King and Prime Minister of Nepal, the Prime Minister of Japan, Her Majesty's Government in the United Kingdom, and others. Addresses were given by distinguished ecclesiastical and lay leaders including among the latter the President and the Prime Minister of Burma. U Win, the Union's Minister for Religious Affairs and National Planning, in an Address of Veneration on May 19 noted the international character of the Council.

The gathering of Buddhist leaders, lay and ecclesiastical, from so many different countries was per se an important cultural development. At one session or another the participants came to include the King and Prime Minister of Cambodia, the Crown Prince of Laos and the Premier of Thailand. The active role of the Rangoon government in facilitating the meeting of the Council added to the international stature of the new state. As in the case of Asian socialism Burma was taking the lead in Theravada Buddhism. The Sixth Great Buddhist Council closed on May 24, 1956.

At the Bandung Conference in April, 1955, U Nu reflected well the foreign policy of the Union. In fact, it has been stated that he was the only Prime Minister among the Prime Ministers of the Colombo Powers who remained on truly cordial relations with all his colleagues. He stressed in his final speech the educational value of a meeting of representatives from so many Asian and African countries. The idealism of the foreign policy of Burma was indicated in a resolution U Nu offered to the political committee of the Conference: "The nations assembled at the Asian-African Conference declare that their relations between themselves, and their approach to the other nations of the world, shall be governed by complete respect for the national sovereignty and integrity of other nations. They will not intervene or interfere in the territory or the internal affairs of each other or of other nations, and will totally refrain from acts or threats of aggression. They recognize the equality of races and of nations, large and small. They will be governed by the desire to promote mutual interest and coöperation, by respect for the fundamental Human Rights and the principles of the Charter of the United Nations."[44]

The appearance of the Union of Burma in 1948 was the result in the technical sense of a treaty settlement between Great Britain and Burma and of an act of the British Parliament. A consideration of the independence arrangements made between the Netherlands and Indonesia and between the United States and the Philippines indicates that the settlement between the British and Burmese, though different in some respects, was more similar to that between the Americans and Filipinos. It is significant that union concepts in the form of a superstructure like the Netherlands-Indonesian Union or the French Union in Indochina have not succeeded in Southeast Asia.

The Burma Independence Act received the Royal Assent on December 10, 1947. It provided for "the independence of Burma as a country not within His Majesty's dominions and not entitled to His Majesty's protection, and for consequential and connected matters."[45] As in the case of the Indian States under the Indian Independence Act, the Burma Independence Act provided for the lapse of the "suzerainty" of His Majesty over the Karenni States.

On the previous October 17 a treaty between Great Britain and the Provisional Government of Burma had been signed in London becoming effective January 4, 1948. The desire was stated

[44] Quoted in George McTurnan Kahin, *The Asian-African Conference*, p. 72.
[45] 11 Geo. 6, c. 3.

by the parties "to define their future relations as the Governments of independent States on the terms of complete freedom, equality and independence and to consolidate and perpetuate the cordial friendship and good understanding which subsist between them."[46] Great Britain recognized the Union of Burma "as a fully independent sovereign State" and the parties agreed to exchange diplomatic representatives. The United Kingdom agreed in the pact to cancel £15 million of the amount granted toward the Ordinary and Frontier Areas budgets, the British desiring to help Burma restore her financial standing and also to liquidate the latter's claim for the services and supplies furnished the British Military Administration. The balance beyond the £15 million would be repaid by Burma in 20 annual installments, beginning not later than April 1, 1952, each equal in amount and bearing no interest. In addition Burma would repay in full under the same conditions the balances on sums advanced by Great Britain toward projects like public utilities, balances outstanding after repayment, as already agreed upon, from proceeds of liquidation or current receipts in excess of working capital and essential outlays. The United Kingdom agreed to continue to pay Burma for expenditures relative to claims for services and supplies given the Burma Army in the campaign of 1942 and relative to release benefits payable upon demobilization to personnel in the Burma Army for services in the war. Burma reaffirmed her agreement to pay over the proceeds from the sale of Army and Civil Affairs Service (Burma) stores while the United Kingdom would make no claim on Burma for repaying the cost of the Civil Affairs Administration prior to the establishment of civil government. Unless specifically changed by this treaty and the Defense Agreement of August 29, 1947, the provisions of the Financial Agreement of April 30, 1947, providing for Britain to contribute £12 million toward the deficit in Burma's budget, 1946-1947, and £18,375,000 for rehabilitation in 1947, remained in force.

Burma and Great Britain under the pact would make as soon as possible a treaty of commerce and navigation, but until its conclusion, or for two years, the commercial relations between the two states would be conducted in such a way that the present interests of the nationals of each in the country of the other would not be

[46] Treaty between the Government of the United Kingdom and the Provisional Government of Burma regarding the Recognition of Burmese Independence and Related Matters, October 17, 1947, *Treaty Series*, No. 16 (1948), Cmd. 7360.

prejudiced. The two-year period was subject to termination after six months by either party upon a three months' notice. It was explicitly stated in a note from Clement Attlee to U Nu on October 17 that "if the Provisional Government of Burma, in the formulation of national policy, are convinced that such action [prejudicial to British business and professional interests] must be taken in any particular case they will consult with the Government of the United Kingdom in advance with a view to reaching a mutually satisfactory settlement."[47] U Nu in his reply the same day agreed, although he observed that "there may be occasional cases of emergency in which full prior consultation is impracticable and only short notice can be given to the United Kingdom Ambassador," and he called attention to the "policy of State socialism" in the constitution of Burma.[48] Nevertheless, he gave assurance of "equitable compensation" if "the expropriation or acquisition in whole or in part of existing United Kingdom interests in Burma" is involved.[49]

The treaty between the two states also included provisions relative to nationality, Burmese payment of pensions, contracts, postal, air-mail and money order services, civil aviation, war cemeteries, and/or war graves. Future agreements would be negotiated preventing double taxation and changing the interim accords on war cemeteries and/or war graves, and civil aviation. Britain's international obligations with respect to Burma in so far as applicable devolved by the treaty upon the new state; nothing in the pact prejudiced the rights and obligations of either that arose or might arise from membership in the United Nations; ways were suggested for the settlement of any differences over the application or the interpretation of the treaty. Preferential customs arrangements were continued for the time being as provided by the terms of the Burma Independence Act.

Article 4 of the treaty provided that the Defense or Let Ya-Freeman Agreement signed in Rangoon on August 29, 1947, set forth in the annex, should "have force and effect as integral parts of the present Treaty."[50] Under this Agreement the United Kingdom would evacuate British troops from Burma as quickly as possible following the transfer of power; Britain would waive certain defense charges, give "all reasonable facilities for purchase" by Burma of war material, transfer without charge to the new state a number

[47] *Ibid.*
[48] *Ibid.*
[49] *Ibid.*
[50] *Ibid.*

of small naval vessels presently loaned to her, and help financially and technically toward the maintenance in Burma of three airfields on a temporary basis. As desired by the Rangoon government, the United Kingdom would send to Burma a Service Mission of military, naval, and air force personnel to help train and strengthen the armed forces of the country and would provide facilities in British establishments for training personnel of the Burmese forces. Burma for her part would receive no Service Mission from any state outside the British Commonwealth; agreed that the military aircraft of each party during peacetime could fly over the other's respective territory and have staging facilities in designated fields, that the respective naval ships could enter each other's ports in accordance with customary peacetime practice, and "that His Majesty's forces bringing help and support to Burma by agreement with the Government of Burma or to any part of the Commonwealth by agreement with the Government of Burma and with the Government of that part of the Commonwealth shall be afforded all reasonable assistance including facilities of access and entry into Burma by air, land and sea."[51] The Defense Agreement was not to prejudice any military alliance that might later be made between the two states. The duration of the Agreement was three years in the first instance and thereafter subject to a year's notice by either party.

The majority of the political leaders of Burma was satisfied with the independence arrangement as well as the method of separation. The President of the Union of Burma, Sao Shwe Thaik, stated on January 4, 1948: "Let us rejoice . . . that the independence has come not as a result of armed conflict but as the fruit of friendly negotiations with that great nation [Great Britain] whose political bonds we replace by mutual consent today with the stronger bonds of friendship and goodwill."[52] On the same day Premier U Nu observed that "we part . . . in friendship and amity from political union with the country in whose tutelage Destiny placed us."[53] Nevertheless, the Rangoon government met with considerable criticism from the Communists who condemned the defense, financial, and nationalization aspects of the settlement. In speeches delivered on November 27, 1947, April 3 and June 13, 1948, the Prime Minister answered his critics. For instance, on April 3 he defended the obligation of Burma to provide compensa-

[51] *Ibid.*

[52] Message from the President of the Union of Burma, *Burma's Fight for Freedom*, p. 5.

[53] Message from the Prime Minister, *Burma's Fight for Freedom*, p. 6.

tion for the nationalization of foreign property, citing Communist examples in Europe. He saw "nothing extraordinary" about his country's undertaking to pay a debt for value received to Great Britain. The British defense mission, he noted, was requested by Burma, not imposed upon her; the new state, needing such a mission to build up her armed forces, turned to Great Britain who was the logical country to provide it because Burma's forces had been trained for some time on the British model; finally the Defense Agreement contained provisions for the termination of the mission.

On balance it is clear that the treaty settlement between Burma and Great Britain represented a compromise between the interests of the two governments. As U Nu said on April 3, 1948: "It is true indeed that concessions were made on both sides in order that the terms may be honourable and acceptable to either."[54] Nevertheless, an analysis of the terms, especially in the light of the time limitations, as in the case of the Defense Agreement, indicates that Britain was giving and Burma was receiving the substance as well as the appearance of independence. There was good faith on both sides providing the necessary cement for a separation with amiability.

The treaty settlement was, of course, affected by a number of subsequent accords. In an exchange of notes on October 12, 1948, it was agreed that between July 1 and December 31, 1948, Burma's expenditure in hard currency areas as listed would not exceed £2 million plus the amount she earned in such places during the period. The objective was to conserve exchange resources in the Sterling Area. In another exchange of notes on December 24, 1949, Burma and Britain, in view of the delay in the negotiation of a treaty of commerce and navigation, agreed to continue the commercial provisions of the treaty of October 17, 1947, until the conclusion and entry into force of the projected treaty or until the present arrangement was ended at the request of either on a notice of three months. On March 13, 1950, there was signed in Rangoon an agreement (with a supplementary protocol, April 4, 1951) to avoid double taxation and to prevent fiscal evasion regarding taxes on income. An air transport agreement was signed on October 25, 1952, and an exchange of notes dated August 4 and August 12, 1953, amended the schedule of routes of the United Kingdom. It was agreed in an exchange of notes, February 1 and February 19, 1954, that, as suggested by Burma, the Rangoon government would take over Britain's obligations to pay £3,300,000 sterling to the Union Bank

[54] Speech of Thakin Nu, April 3, 1948, *Towards Peace and Democracy*, p. 56.

of Burma in respect to currency redemption and Burma would make a single payment of £4 million sterling which the United Kingdom would accept in final settlement of her indebtedness. On October 1, 1953, a new tariff schedule had come into force ending the preferences Britain, India, and Pakistan had enjoyed in Burma. The previous January 3, it is significant, Burma gave the necessary notice to Great Britain for the termination of the Defense Agreement of August 29, 1947.[55]

Since the independence of Burma a number of questions have arisen to threaten the friendly relations between Great Britain and her former Asian possession. As in the case of the Dutch in Indonesia but to a far less degree, a few British nationals in Burma were found by the Rangoon government to be supporting a revolt. The Karens, like most of the Hill Peoples, had been very loyal to Great Britain. Supplying the core of the army, the Karens had helped the British put down the Burman revolt of 1931. Protestant missionaries had made substantial progress in Karen areas. Many of the Karens preferred British rule to the establishment of an independent Burma where the Burmans would constitute the dominant force. Great Britain emphatically condemned any activities of her nationals in support of the Karen revolt.

Burmese nationalization of British property aroused the concern of the United Kingdom. Prewar investments from the metropolitan power amounted to around £50 million. After independence the Rangoon government nationalized the Irrawaddy Flotilla Company and certain other British interests, effective June 1, 1948. The United Kingdom did not believe that Burma had adequately met her obligations to consult in advance, and British creditors were opposed to receiving as compensation nonnegotiable bonds of the Burmese government. Later Burma realized more clearly that nationalization presented many problems both in terms of finding money for compensation and of running the enterprises. The Rangoon government eventually bought shares in British concerns involving mining, oil production, and the tea industry, one "joint venture" being the Burma Oil Company.

[55] Although the Defense Agreement had expired, Admiral Earl Mountbatten in an address in Rangoon on March 22, 1956, observed: "We of the British Services are always delighted to help in any way we can with your Services. I am glad to think that during 1955 we were able to offer courses and training for some 250 officers and men of the Burma Navy, Army and Air Force; not to mention four women officers under training with the Royal Air Force who have shown exceptional ability and have done extremely well." Address of Admiral Earl Mountbatten, *Burma Weekly Bulletin*, New Series, Vol. 4 (March 29, 1956), p. 411.

Great Britain was quite naturally disturbed over the civil turmoil in Burma after the transfer of power. British economic interests in the country, the need in Malaya, Ceylon, and India for rice imports from Burma, and the Communist threat to the Union combined to accentuate British concern. In February, 1949, Great Britain, India, Ceylon, and Australia held informal discussions in New Delhi on the crisis in Burma. On June 28, 1950, the four countries in the Commonwealth along with another member, Pakistan, signed an agreement to loan Burma £6 million ($16,800,000), Great Britain providing 3¾ million, India 1 million, Australia and Pakistan ½ million each, and Ceylon ¼ million. Although the loan was not drawn upon, the regime of Premier U Nu remained in power partly through the encouragement of Great Britain and the Commonwealth. Visits by U Nu and other high ranking Burmese officials to the United Kingdom have further strengthened the ties between Britain and Burma. For her part the Union decorated in 1956 Admiral Earl Mountbatten, Sir Hubert Rance, and Lord Ogmore.

Relations between Burma and Japan, another foreign occupying power for a period, have become normalized. In fact, it should be stressed that Burma led the Philippines and Indonesia in making a peace settlement with Nippon. The nature of the Japanese regime in Burma did not create respect for the Nipponese and their program of Asia for the Asiatics. For instance, as Foreign Minister in a puppet government, U Nu has noted that he had only three important matters to handle: precedence at a wedding ceremony, apologizing for the action of a Burmese soldier, and negotiating to arrest the Burmese charged in a plot against Ba Maw. After the surrender of Japan in 1945 and Burma's independence from Britain in 1948, the Rangoon government was admitted to membership on the Far Eastern Commission in Washington. U So Nyun represented Burma from November 17, 1949, to October 21, 1950, and James Barrington from the latter date to the end of the Commission on April 28, 1952. Actually Burma was represented on the Commission during the period of its "twilight."

In the summer of 1951, the Union, like India, refused an invitation to attend the Japanese Peace Conference at San Francisco. She could not approve the draft treaty with Japan because she believed the latter would be able under it to evade reparations. Obviously the Rangoon government was deeply and legitimately concerned over Japanese payment of reparations. Premier U Nu discussed the peace treaty question with Prime Minister Nehru during a visit the following October. He announced on October 23 that Burma desired to make a separate peace treaty with Japan when the latter was free to do so.

In 1952 a Japanese trade mission went to Rangoon to negotiate for the purchase of more rice and for the sale of rice-polishing machines. On April 30 the state of war with Nippon was ended by the Union. In October, 1953, the Japanese Foreign Minister visited Rangoon, but Burma again asserted she would not sign a peace treaty until the reparations issue was resolved. On December 8 an arrangement was reached for the sale of 300,000 long tons of Burmese rice to Japan in 1954 and between 200,000 and 300,000 tons a year each of the following three years, for the training of technicians in Japan from Burma, for the promotion of technical coöperation between Japanese and Burmese businesses, and for favorable import treatment by both parties.

In August, 1954, a reparations mission led by U Kyaw Nyein arrived in Tokyo. After a month of negotiations an agreement was initialed on September 25 embracing a peace treaty and a reparations and economic coöperation accord. On November 5 U Kyaw Nyein and Japanese Foreign Minister, Katsuo Okazaki, signed the settlement in Rangoon, ratifications being exchanged on April 16, 1955. The treaty of peace provided for "firm and perpetual peace and amity" between the two states. Various agreements were foreshadowed. In the reparations and economic coöperation accord Japan promised to pay $200 million worth of reparations in goods and services over a ten-year period; the equivalent of $50 million would be spent during the same period in investments in joint Burmese-Japanese concerns. Not less than 60 percent of the capitalization under the original plan would be Burmese. In the appendix different projects were listed for reparations. The settlement provided for Japan's reviewing it once agreements were made with all other countries.

Considerable confusion ensued regarding the actual interpretation and implementation of the terms of the reparations provisions, and on October 18 a supplementary agreement was signed relative to operating procedures. On December 24 the schedule for the first year was settled, emphasizing the development of power and transportation. About 100 Japanese technicians would go to Burma and 40 Burmese trainees to Japan. Relations between the two countries were further strengthened by a visit of U Nu to Tokyo in the summer of 1955. Nippon has also approved a loan to Burma for the purchase of consumer goods. In May, 1957, Prime Minister Nobusuke Kishi of Japan visited Rangoon.

Among her neighbors the Union of Burma is most concerned over the policies of the People's Republic of China. Even if no other reasons existed, the Union's cordial relations with India would reflect the potentialities of Communist China's foreign policy. Burma unlike any other state in Southeast Asia has land frontiers with both India and China, the leading Asian powers to emerge after the Second World War. In analyzing the objectives of Burma's future foreign policy, Bogyoke Aung San had significantly said: "Burma must strive to attain a Union with other countries of South-East Asia. We must endeavour to establish friendly relations with the two great nations of India and China. We must also work to bring about cordial feelings between Burma and the other newly-liberated countries."[56]

China was under the Nationalist regime of Chiang Kai-shek only a short period after the independence of Burma. During that period, it will be recalled, China sponsored in the Security Council the admission of the Union to the United Nations. In the Second World War Nationalist China had sent forces to help the British in Burma against Japan. Chiang Kai-shek was represented in 1948 by a high-ranking official at the Independence Day celebrations in Rangoon.

The Chinese minority in Burma is generally said to number around 350,000, and has an important economic position in the country.[57] The Burmese have got along better with their Chinese minority than their Indian. U Myint Thein, not without reason, told the First Committee of the United Nations General Assembly on April 22, 1953, using his record, that "we have much that we admire in the Chinese and even our culture to a great extent is Chinese . . . and as a matter of fact the term in Burmese for Chinese is 'Comrade in Birth.' "[58] Boundary disputes and an influx of Chinese

[56] Quoted by U Ba Swe in Martyrs' Day speech, July 19, 1953, *Burma,* Vol. IV (October, 1953), p. 4.

[57] Tillman Durdin writing from Rangoon on June 29, 1957, in the *New York Times* notes that "students of the Chinese problem here believe the figure [for the Chinese] is now 700,000 or 800,000 if not more." *New York Times,* June 30, 1957.

[58] U Myint Thein's Speech, April 22, 1953, *Kuomintang Aggression Against Burma,* Ministry of Information, p. 76.

refugees complicated Nanking-Rangoon relations. In 1949 a local agreement between the Nationalist commander in central Yunnan and Kachin and Shan chiefs, acting for the Rangoon government, provided for coöperation in suppressing banditry and for mutual respect for the frontier. In November Liu Shao-chi, a leading figure in Communist China, condemned U Nu, Sukarno, and Nehru as puppets of imperialism and sent greetings to the Communist rebels in Burma.

The Union was the first non-Communist state to recognize the People's Republic of China. After some delay ambassadors were exchanged in August and September, 1950. A large section of the 1500-mile boundary between China and Burma being undemarcated, the potential of serious trouble existed. The Peking Convention of 1886 between China and Great Britain had provided for the definition of the boundary by a joint commission, but the agreement had not been carried out as planned and British and Chinese maps showed large variations. After Burma's independence the followers of Thakin Than Tun, the White Flag Communist leader, found it necessary to deny that he had agreed with the Chinese Communists that the disputed territory was Chinese. The Rangoon government was quite naturally concerned over the relations between the Burmese Communists in revolt and the Chinese Communists across the frontier. Rumors multiplied that the latter were encouraging a Kachin Autonomous State Movement in China under a Communist Kachin leader, Nam Seng.

Negotiations between the People's Republic of China and the Union of Burma relative to the frontier and other matters of mutual concern led to a statement by Premier U Nu in Parliament on March 8, 1951, wherein he quoted a Chinese Communist assurance to the Burmese Ambassador in Peking as follows: "There are no problems between Asian countries like China, India and Burma which cannot be solved through normal diplomatic channels. Chinese Government had no time to draw new map and had only reproduced old map. Sino-Burmese border has been shown as undemarcated boundary and we see no difficulty in sitting down together and demarcating boundary. China has no territorial ambition."[59] At the same time Nu told Parliament that there were no Chinese Communist soldiers with the underground Burmese Communists. He termed relations between Peking and Rangoon "very cordial."

[59] Assurance quoted in speech by U Nu, March 8, 1951, *From Peace to Stability*, p. 198.

After the Communist Chinese intervention in the Korean War, Burma opposed the United Nations General Assembly resolution of February 1, 1951, which called the People's Republic of China an aggressor, and abstained on the one of May 18 requesting the members of the world organization to embargo strategic items to North Korea and Communist China. Burma subsequently informed the United Nations that her exports during 1950 to the People's Republic of Mao Tse-tung were only 1.1 percent of the total value of her exports and included no items specified in the resolution.

In 1954 relations between Burma and Communist China visibly improved. Premier and Foreign Minister Chou En-lai visited New Delhi and Rangoon late in June on his return to Peking from the Geneva Conference on Indochina. On June 29 he and Premier U Nu in a communiqué, agreeing that revolution cannot be exported, asserted that the guiding principles for relations between the two countries should be: "(1) reciprocal respect for the integrity and territorial sovereignty of both states, (2) nonaggression, (3) noninterference in the internal affairs of the other state, (4) equality and reciprocity, and (5) peaceful coexistence."[60] U Nu and Chou En-lai said that "outside interference in the expressed will of the people . . . cannot be tolerated."[61] The principles, in fact, were openly based upon those established by India and the People's Republic of China as indicated in the Nehru-Chou En-lai communiqué of June 28 and previously in the Indian-Chinese agreement on Tibet of April 29. Prime Minister Nehru has stated that the "five principles of peaceful co-existence first emerged out of fairly long discussions between the Governments of India and China. No individual can be said to father them. The words 'Panch Shila' were first used by me in that connection some time after these principles had been enunciated."[62] A large number of states—Communist and uncommitted—have accepted the Five Principles, those in Southeast Asia being Burma, the Democratic Republic of Vietnam, Cambodia, Laos, and Indonesia.[63]

[60] U Nu-Chou En-lai communiqué, June 29, 1954, *Documents on American Foreign Relations, 1954*, p. 280.

[61] *Ibid.*, p. 281.

[62] Letter from Prime Minister Jawaharlal Nehru to author, June 4, 1957. See Appendix B for full text of letter.

[63] The Five Principles were incorporated in the declaration on the Promotion of World Peace and Coöperation at the Bandung Conference but the expression "peaceful coexistence" was not used. It was stated that "nations should practice tolerance and live together in peace with one another as good neighbours and develop friendly coöperation. . . ." (The Final Communiqué of the Asian-African Conference, Press Release, Permanent Mission of the Republic of Indonesia to

During the visit in June, 1954, of Chou En-lai the Burmese leaders told him about the sanctuary and training Chinese Communists were giving some of the armed rebels in the Union. Later documentation was sent to Peking on the subject. It is clear that the matter was very much in the minds of Burmese officials.

In a speech on Martyrs' Day in July, Prime Minister U Nu observed that the unity of China gratified Asians who took pride in the respect she had earned from the foreigners. He called attention to the "great strides" and "new moral climate" in Communist China. The previous April 22, Burma and the People's Republic had signed a three-year trade agreement whereby Chinese exports to the Union would include cotton goods, coal, silk, tea, and light industrial products while Burmese exports to China would include rice, raw cotton, timber, beans, and rubber. Payment would be partly in sterling, and prices and quality would be in accordance with international standards.

Late in 1954 Premier U Nu made an official visit to Communist China. In a statement issued on December 12 at the end of the visit it was agreed that Burma and China would make plans to increase their trade and better their communications; it was asserted that China would take from 1955 to the end of 1957 150,000 to 200,000 tons of Burmese rice each year and Burma would receive industrial equipment and other items; a complete delimitation of the frontier would be made through normal channels of diplomacy at an appropriate time; consuls general would be appointed in each other's appropriate cities; the nationals of one in the territory of the other would be discouraged by the mother country from engaging in political activity, the rights and interests of such nationals would be protected by the government under which they actually lived, and negotiations would begin at the earliest opportunity on the subject of dual nationality. At a farewell banquet on December 11 U Nu gave assurances that Burma would never allow bases on her soil for the enemies of China.

Subsequent negotiations led to an agreement on opening com-

---

the United Nations). The former British Ambassador to the United States, Sir Roger Makins, has pointedly observed that "though its use [peaceful coexistence] is now fully established, I am not much enamored of the expression, which has a technical meaning in the Soviet thesaurus, and which therefore has a different significance for the Western and for the Eastern mind. For the Russian it signifies a temporary detente during which they can build up Communist strength and sap the will of the free world, a state of what has been called provisional nonbelligerency." Sir Roger Makins, "The World Since the War: The Third Phase," *Foreign Affairs,* Vol. 33 (October, 1954), p. 13.

mercial air traffic along the Rangoon-Mandalay-Kunming route, and air service between Kunming and Rangoon was inaugurated on April 11, 1956. Agreements on mail and telecommunications had already been made. The Burma Road may, as envisioned in the December 12, 1954, communiqué, become an important artery of trade. A Burmese consulate general now functions in Kunming and a Chinese Communist consulate general in Lashio. Good-will missions covering many activities have been exchanged; for instance, a Buddhist, a cultural, and a military delegation went to China in September, 1955. Madame Sun Yat-sen (Soong Ching-ling) visited Burma in early 1956. The Union had previously taken a strong position in favor of inviting the People's Republic of China to the Bandung Conference and had close relations with the Chinese delegation there. On December 29, 1955, a further trade agreement involving Burmese rice and Chinese products was concluded. Burma has not complained about the price and quality of Chinese goods.

The Union has followed with interest the negotiations between Indonesia and the People's Republic of China on dual nationality, and has sought the aid of Nehru on the overall problem of the citizenship of the Chinese in Southeast Asia. It is clear that the Chinese in Burma are increasingly pro-Communist and that the Embassy of the People's Republic has a strong impact on them. Peking has two government banks and supports some of the Chinese schools in the Union. The large number of illegal immigrants from China along with the Communist agents is a matter of concern to Rangoon officials. In terms of frontier problems, a conference was held at Lweje, east of Bhamo, February 7-8, 1956, having as one of its aims the promotion of friendlier relations among the border peoples of China and Burma.

In late July, the long-standing controversy over the Burma-China frontier received considerable publicity when *The Nation* in Rangoon began to publish articles on the Chinese Communist occupation of certain disputed areas. The question was particularly delicate as the Shans, Wa, Kachins, and other ethnic communities straddle the mountainous frontier zone and both the Rangoon and Peking governments are contesting for their loyalty. Involved in the boundary dispute were four sectors: the Wa State area, technically now in the Northeastern Special District of the Shan State, between the Nam Ting and Namkha rivers; the strategic Namwan Assigned Tract in southern Kachin State, an area under perpetual lease to Burma according to an Anglo-Chinese agreement of 1897; the Irrawaddy-Salween watershed from the southeastern end of the McMahon Line of 1914 south to latitude 25°35′ north and especially the villages of Gawlum, Hpimaw, and Kangfang, commanding a number of high mountain passes leading to China; and the north boundary of Burma above Putao extending eastward and southward up to the end of the McMahon Line. In the case of the Wa State area China in 1941 accepted the findings of an earlier *ad hoc* boundary commission of the League of Nations headed by a Swiss, Colonel Iselin, but Communist China declined to approve the Iselin Line. In addition, no Chinese government ratified the convention of 1914 establishing the McMahon Line, or approved the British occupation of the watershed area to the south. In fact, the British themselves had not claimed sovereignty over Gawlum, Hpimaw, and Kangfang.

Under the circumstances the Burmese have viewed with growing concern the Chinese maps, both Nationalist and Communist, showing large areas of the Union in the present Kachin and Shan States as parts of China. When it became public in mid-1956 that Chinese Communist troops had moved to the west of the Iselin Line in the Wa State area and into the Kachin State to the north, pressure mounted for the Burmese government to get them out. Premier U Ba Swe in a press conference in September observed that Burma would oppose aggression on her soil but he indicated that the border was uncertain. India followed the frontier dispute with interest, favoring direct negotiations between Peking and Rangoon.

In late October U Nu went to Peking to discuss the matter with Chinese officials; prominent Kachin leaders, U Zanhta Sin, Sama Duwa, and Duwa Zau Lawn, came to join them. In a joint communiqué on November 10 it was stated that a "favourable basis" for settling the controversy had been found and that before the end of the year Burmese troops would leave Hpimaw, Kangfang, and Gawlum and Chinese forces the area west of the Iselin Line. U Nu in a broadcast the same day revealed that the People's Republic of China was prepared to accept the McMahon and Iselin lines as well as the watershed boundary providing Hpimaw, Gawlum, and Kangfang were considered Chinese territory and the lease on the Namwan Assigned Tract was abrogated. U Nu said that he considered the proposal for a settlement of the frontier "fair and just." The most serious opposition in Burma came from the Kachins, who would lose a small part of their territory. As their

State Council under the constitution of the Union would have to approve such a change, efforts were made by the Rangoon government to win them to acceptance. Involved was the possible moving of inhabitants who did not wish to live in China.

Chou En-lai visited Burma in December, he and Premier U Ba Swe going to Mangshih in Yunnan for a carefully staged border conference, but their joint statement on December 20 indicated no solution satisfactory to both parties. When U Nu again became premier on February 28, 1957, he addressed himself to a settlement of the controversy as "a matter of life and death." In March he went to Kunming on a good-will visit to discuss the border issue with Chou En-lai. In a while it became clear that the People's Republic of China was stalling on a final settlement.

The case of the Chinese Nationalist forces in Burma had serious international implications involving in particular the Union, Communist and Nationalist China, Thailand, the United States, and the United Nations.[64] Early in 1950 some 1700 Kuomintang troops crossed the Chinese border into Kengtung in the Shan State. They refused to leave Burma's territory or submit to disarmament and internment. Burmese forces in the latter part of 1950 drove them out of the particular area they occupied but they withdrew westward establishing a headquarters at Mong Hsat located near the Thailand-Burma frontier. Recruits were obtained from the Burma-Yunnan frontier region, and the number of Kuomintang troops rose by early 1953 to possibly 12,000. Operating east of the Salween River, the Nationalist forces in 1952 extended their efforts to areas west of the river coöperating with rebel Karen units. The overall commanding officer was General Li Mi who was known to fly from the airfield at Mong Hsat to Taiwan, the Nationalist forces in Burma being partially supplied by air from the outside. Meanwhile in the Union the Chinese troops were administering certain areas, harassing Burmese citizens, and smuggling opium to Thailand.

The domestic implications of the Kuomintang forces in Burma were widespread. The government had to divert part of its limited armed forces to fight the Nationalist Chinese, thereby substantially weakening its military operations against other rebels. The PVO's and the Communists in armed rebellion offered to join forces with

[64] The terms "Chinese Nationalist," "Kuomintang" or "KMT" to describe the outside forces or troops in Burma are controversial. The author is using these expressions although the United Nations preferred the words "foreign forces."

the government against the Chinese Nationalists but the Rangoon officials refused to enter into such an arrangement. The parliamentary opposition in Burma seized upon the Kuomintang issue to attack the government and the Burma Workers and Peasants Party offered to raise a private army to assist in eradicating the Nationalist threat.

Obviously the Union of Burma was seriously concerned over the attitude of the People's Republic of China. If the Peking regime was then looking for an excuse to move into Burma, it would find it on a silver platter in the case of the Nationalist forces in the Union. The objective of the Kuomintang troops was to assist in the overthrow of the Chinese Communist government. They had even invaded Yunnan in July, 1951, and been thrown back into Burma. One of the reasons the Rangoon government placed the question before the United Nations was to impress further upon Communist China the sincerity of its efforts to end the Nationalist threat. The Peking regime was, of course, kept informed on developments in the situation. The Chinese Communists for their part maintained what Burma considered a proper and correct attitude, blaming in their propaganda statements the United States and Thailand for the crisis.

In an address to Parliament on March 2, 1953, U Nu in a careful analysis of the Kuomintang question observed that since early 1950 his government had faced three possible courses of action. The first was to refer the matter to the United Nations, but the questions here arose as to whether the Formosa regime would deny responsibility for the forces in Burma by declaring them deserters, as to whether the Chiang Kai-shek government would claim that the soldiers in Burma were troops of Communist China wearing Nationalist uniforms, and as to whether the People's Republic of China would be antagonized by United Nations action. The second course, as defined by U Nu, was to negotiate with Nationalist China through the good offices of third powers having diplomatic relations with her in an effort to secure the withdrawal of the Kuomintang troops. The third course of action was for the armed forces of the Union to fight the Nationalists in the country. Burma, he said, had previously chosen a combination of the last two courses. The United States was asked to seek through Chiang Kai-shek the withdrawal of the Kuomintang troops; India was requested to help in all ways possible. The Prime Minister then significantly stated: "For all these efforts, the KMT aggressors, far from abandoning their aggressive activities, are now increasing their nefarious deeds, and we feel constrained to take the matter up to the United Nations Organization in spite of the possible consequences of denial by Formosa and greater complications."[65]

On January 3, 1952, A. Y. Vyshinsky of the Soviet Union had attacked the United States in the First Committee of the United Nations General Assembly on the Kuomintang question in Burma. The following February 5, Foreign Secretary Anthony Eden had suggested in the House of Commons that a mission from the United Nations be sent to Burma to get the facts. Burmese delegates in the United Nations had also on occasions criticized the Nationalist forces in the Union, but the Rangoon government had not officially brought up the question for United Nations action until March, 1953.

Burma proposed on the 25th of that month that an item entitled "Complaint by the Union of Burma regarding aggression against her by the Kuomintang Government of Formosa" be placed on the agenda of the General Assembly's seventh session. On March 31 the Assembly decided to put the Burmese complaint on the agenda, although the term "Government of the Republic of China" was used instead of "Kuomintang Government of Formosa." The First Committee considered the item from April 17 to 22, widespread discussion occurring among the delegates.

In explaining the position of his government, U Myint Thein on April 17 traced the history of the Kuomintang forces in Burma and attempted to prove that the troops were being supported and directed from Formosa. The Burmese draft resolution called upon the General Assembly to note that "the armed troops of the Kuomintang Government of Formosa have committed acts of infringement against the territorial integrity of the Union of Burma and acts of violation of its frontiers," asked the General Assembly to recommend that the Security Council "condemn the Kuomintang Government of Formosa for the said acts of aggression" and "take all necessary steps to ensure immediate cessation," and requested the General Assembly to ask all states "to respect the territorial integrity and the political independence of the Union of Burma and to be guided by the principles of the Charter in their relations with the Union of Burma."[66]

T. F. Tsiang of Nationalist China presented the reply of his

[65] Hon'ble Prime Minister's Speech, March 2, 1953, *Kuomintang Aggression Against Burma*, p. 2.

[66] Burmese draft resolution, *Kuomintang Aggression Against Burma*, p. 29.

government after the speech of U Myint Thein. He did not try to refute the Burmese case point by point but dealt more in generalities. The Chinese delegate pointed out that the charge of aggression was "monstrous"; that there was no evidence his government had ever urged any action against Burma; that the Yunnan Anti-Communist National Salvation Army, as it was called, was no longer a part of the Chinese regular army although his government still had some influence, varying from time to time, over General Li Mi and some of the officers under him; that Nationalist China had repeatedly tried to persuade the General not to enter Burma; and that his government had not sent a single man as reinforcement to the Yunnan Anti-Communist National Salvation Army. Tsiang observed that the army of General Li Mi in the eyes of the Chinese people stood as Garibaldi and his associates in the eyes of Italians when Italy was struggling for unity and independence. Nationalist China could not morally condemn the army, which received financial help from free Chinese all over the world. As a result of American appeals, Tsiang noted, his government had given assurances to try and stop the collection of money by agents of the army and not to give clearance to any plane leaving Taiwan for the border region under consideration. He criticized the Burmese draft resolution as not being helpful, just, or acceptable.

Speaking further on April 21, Tsiang stressed he was not a representative of the Yunnan Anti-Communist National Salvation Army and said Taipei would coöperate fully with the United Nations in the withdrawal of the troops from Burma. He noted that "his Government had never sent any supplies and had never allowed any of its aircraft to be used to take supplies to that army [Yunnan Anti-Communist National Salvation]. Any supplies that had been flown over had been taken in chartered and private aircraft, to which his Government would now refuse clearance for such purposes."[67]

U Myint Thein, speaking toward the conclusion of the general debate in the First Committee, reiterated the stand of Burma and pointed out weaknesses in the position of T. F. Tsiang. The Burmese delegate frankly observed, according to his official account: "The point that I have laboured is not so much the growth in manpower [of the Kuomintang forces] but the growth in equipment. Machine guns and automatic weapons cannot be locally

[67] United Nations, General Assembly, Seventh Session, *Official Records*, First Committee, 610th Meeting, April 21, 1953, p. 683.

manufactured or appropriated in the wild terrain of Monghsat, and how would Dr. Tsiang explain this continuous growth? He has indirectly admitted that these went from Formosa when he said that at last the Government at Formosa had issued orders not to give clearance to aircraft proceeding to the Monghsat area."[68]

In the debate in the First Committee widespread sympathy was expressed for Burma, although a number of delegates did not hold Nationalist China responsible for the activities of the Chinese forces in the Union. Communist and Asian speakers for the most part stood solidly behind Burma in her complaint. There was more caution expressed by Western delegates as a general rule. Among the Union's neighbors in Southeast Asia, Indonesia was convinced that Nationalist China was committing an aggression against Burma and supported the latter's resolution; Thailand thought the troops under consideration should be disarmed and interned or evacuated but the Security Council should not pronounce a condemnation of Nationalist China; the Philippines took a position much closer to that of Thailand than Indonesia. India and Pakistan, Burma's neighbors on the west, strongly supported the case of the Rangoon government. The USSR took the position that Burma's draft resolution was proper and just; the General Assembly should take steps necessary to end Kuomintang aggression against the Union and the People's Republic of China. Great Britain sympathized with Burma but was not convinced the Rangoon government had proved Nationalist China guilty of aggression. The United States believed the Burmese resolution was too strong to bring about agreement while proposing a procedure too complicated to be practicable; the best settlement was to get Nationalist China to agree to coöperate in a solution that would involve steps to disarm and evacuate the soldiers. France supported Burma in principle but not her resolution as drafted. Australia, wanting an early settlement of the controversy in the interests of security in Southeast Asia, sympathized with Burma but opposed a formula of condemning Nationalist China. Interesting to note is the fact that Burma's close friends in western Asia and eastern Europe, Israel and Yugoslavia, strongly championed the Burmese resolution.

As the debate developed, it became clear that the Union's resolution as drafted had met with considerable opposition. A Mexican draft resolution as amended was subsequently adopted by the First

[68] U Myint Thein's Speech, April 22, 1953, *Kuomintang Aggression Against Burma,* p. 77.

Committee, the vote being 58 to none with two abstentions, Burma and China. The next day, April 23, the General Assembly adopted the resolution by 59 to 0, Burma having voted in favor and China still abstaining. Under the resolution the presence of the "foreign forces" in Burma and "their hostile acts against that country" were condemned; the forces must be disarmed and either submit to internment or leave the Union of Burma forthwith; all states were urged not to give any help to the troops, and upon the request of Burma, to facilitate their peaceful evacuation; it was recommended that negotiations going on through the good offices of certain member states be continued.[69]

A Joint Military Committee, consisting of Burma, Thailand, the United States, and Nationalist China, was set up to consider the ways of implementing the General Assembly resolution. Beginning on May 22 at Bangkok the discussions resulted in an agreement on June 23, subject to the approval of the governments concerned, wherein the "foreign forces" in Burma would be evacuated through Thailand to Taiwan under the supervision of the Joint Military Committee. The Kuomintang troops in Burma showed reluctance to implement the decision and the Union on September 17 withdrew from the Committee. Negotiations among the other three members continued with an agreement reached in October for the evacuation of 2000 men with their dependents. Burma did not consider the figure at all adequate, but she agreed to suspend military activities against the Nationalist forces and grant a safety corridor to the boundary with Thailand. Although the evacuation was interrupted for a while because of the complaints of Burmese observers that some of the evacuees were nationals of the Union, the operations were completed by the end of 1953. Burma was convinced that some 10,000 Nationalist troops remained and protested that only a few arms, often unserviceable, had been surrendered.

Meanwhile on September 17 the General Assembly in its eighth session agreed to include on its agenda the "Complaint by the Union of Burma regarding aggression against it by the Government of the Republic of China: Report of the Government of the Union of Burma." The First Committee considered the subject October 31 to November 5 and November 27 to December 4. In the debate during the first period the delegates of Burma and Nationalist China reiterated their positions; countries like India, Pakistan, Indo-

[69] Resolutions Adopted by the General Assembly at Its Seventh Session during the Period from 24 February to 23 April, 1953, General Assembly, *Official Records,* Seventh Session, Supplement No. 20 A, pp. 4-5.

nesia, Israel, and Yugoslavia strongly supported Burma; the Communist speakers tended to denounce not only Nationalist China but also the United States and Thailand; and states like the United Kingdom, France, Australia, and Canada welcomed the plans to evacuate the 2000 men but hoped further progress could be made. The delegate of the United States commented on the practical arrangements for the evacuation and paid tribute to Thailand's coöperation; he indicated that President Dwight D. Eisenhower was taking a personal interest in the matter; and he asserted that Nationalist China intended to remove as many of the irregular troops as possible but exercised only limited control over them. The Thai delegate stressed the efforts of his government to implement the General Assembly resolution of April 23; noted that it had offered to spend about $160,000 on the evacuation; and observed that in view of the questioning of Thailand's good faith she might choose not to assume responsibility any longer. The First Committee decided on November 5 to adjourn further consideration to a time not earlier than November 23.

At the discussion during the meeting of the First Committee on November 27, India, Indonesia, the United Kingdom, Australia, Canada, New Zealand, Norway, and Sweden presented a draft resolution on the Kuomintang question; amendments by Thailand and the United States were offered December 1; and three days later the original sponsors with the addition of Uruguay presented a revision of their resolution which was accepted by the Committee. During the debate Burma stressed the small number of men being evacuated and the few weapons surrendered; the Chinese delegate observed that the coöperation his government was giving the Joint Military Committee had not always been appreciated; the American representative described the work of the airlift to Formosa and stated that the Joint Military Committee was dealing with the question of the arms; Thailand indicated that there was too much of a disposition to expect herself and the United States to bear the burden of the evacuation; the Soviet Union was highly critical of the part of the draft resolution expressing appreciation for the efforts of the United States and Thailand; Indonesia and India doubted the efficacy of an evacuation so limited; and the United Kingdom considered disturbing the quantity and quality of arms surrendered.

On December 8 the General Assembly adopted by a vote of 46 to 0 with Burma in the affirmative and China abstaining the resolution approved by the First Committee. It noted that "limited evacuation of personnel of these [the] foreign forces has begun as from 7 November 1953"; expressed "*concern* that few arms have been surrendered by them"; appreciated the efforts of the United States and Thailand in working for the evacuation; urged continuation of efforts by those concerned for the internment or evacuation of the "foreign forces" and for the "surrender of all arms"; reaffirmed the General Assembly resolution of April 23 and in particular urged all states not to help the forces; and requested Burma to report on the situation as appropriate to the General Assembly.[70]

In 1954 the Burma Army launched an extensive interservice campaign against the Kuomintang forces, capturing Mong Hsat airfield on March 24. Further evacuation also took place and General Li Mi on May 30 announced the end of his command. By the time the evacuation ended on September 1, 5742 troops, 881 dependents, 177 prisoners of war, and 186 refugees had been repatriated to Formosa. Possibly 3000 or more troops remained to cause trouble. Those staying have refused repatriation and Nationalist China has disclaimed all responsibility for them. In 1955, as a result of Burmese military pressure, some of the Chinese fled to Thailand.

Burma reported to the ninth session of the General Assembly on the developments in the situation. The question of the foreign forces was discussed in the *Ad Hoc* Political Committee from October 11 to October 15, 1954. Burma in the debate observed that the evacuation had substantially eased the problem but that the surrender of weapons had been disappointing; military as well as moral pressure had been used to effect the limited evacuation; she still held Nationalist China responsible for every Kuomintang soldier left in the country. China stressed that the evacuation of the irregulars had proved her good faith and the matter of the remaining men was a domestic problem of Burma. A difference of opinion was expressed between Burmese and Thai delegates about how effective had been Thailand's closing of her frontier with Burma since 1952. India raised the question about who was buying the opium in the illicit traffic in which the Kuomintang forces were engaged. In general the debate in the committee followed the previous pattern.

A draft resolution sponsored by India, Indonesia, Pakistan,

[70] Resolutions Adopted by the General Assembly at Its Eighth Session during the Period from 15 September to 9 December, 1953, General Assembly, *Official Records*, Eighth Session, Supplement No. 17, p. 4.

Australia, Canada, New Zealand, Norway, Sweden, the United Kingdom, and Uruguay was adopted as amended by the Committee on October 15. A few days later on October 27 the General Assembly approved the resolution by a vote of 56 to 0 with China not participating. The resolution noted "*with satisfaction* that nearly 7000 persons, both foreign forces and their dependents, have been evacuated from Burma and that this constitutes a substantial contribution to the solution of the problem," deplored "the fact that considerable foreign forces with a significant quantity of arms" still remained, declared that they "should submit to disarmament and internment," expressed appreciation to the United States and Thailand for their help in the evacuation done, assured Burma of "continuing sympathy," and urged all states to prevent any assistance to the foreign forces remaining.[71]

In her relations with India, Burma has in Prime Minister Nehru a loyal friend. V. K. Krishna Menon told the First Committee of the General Assembly of the United Nations on April 17, 1953, that his delegation "felt that any violation of the honour of Burma or any wrong done to that country was as significant to it as a wrong done to India,"[72] and again on November 5 that "what hurt Burma hurt India because of the links of friendship, geography and history between the two countries."[73]

Nowhere else in Southeast Asia is India's impact greater than in Burma. Obviously the foreign policy of the New Delhi government is closely watched and carefully weighed in Rangoon. To an extent much greater in India than in most other states the Prime Minister determines foreign policy. This situation arises to a substantial degree from the personality, interests, and power of Nehru, for another premier might not have the same influence in or concern about international relations. In making foreign policy Nehru is influenced particularly by two officials, V. K. Krishna Menon and K. M. Panikkar.

The foreign policy of the New Delhi government has been frequently defined by the Prime Minister.[74] It consists of "non-

[71] Resolutions Adopted by the General Assembly during Its Ninth Session from 21 September to 17 December, 1954, General Assembly, *Official Records*, Ninth Session, Supplement No. 21, p. 7.

[72] United Nations, General Assembly, Seventh Session, *Official Records*, First Committee, 605th Meeting, April 17, 1953, p. 659.

[73] United Nations, General Assembly, Eighth Session, *Official Records*, First Committee, 657th Meeting, November 5, 1953, p. 166.

[74] See especially *Jawaharlal Nehru's Speeches, 1949-1953*, Ministry of Information and Broadcasting, pp. 143-258.

alignment" with either of the power blocs. This policy is not considered "negative" but rather "positive," as India is forced to take positions on various questions. Indian officials also prefer to use the word "independent" rather than "neutral" to describe the nation's foreign policy. Nehru does not desire the creation of a third power bloc but he would like to expand the "area of peace." Although he realizes that the location of India places her in a strategic position with reference to the Middle East, South Asia, and Southeast Asia, he does not claim to be the leader of the vast area. A champion of national freedom and a foe of racial discrimination, the Prime Minister is convinced that his foreign policy is consistent with Indian history, serves the present needs of the nation, and contributes to the cause of world peace.

It is clear that the foreign outlook of New Delhi, as defined by Nehru, meets a sympathetic response in Burma. In fact, the culture of the latter country owes much to India, the Buddhist religion as well as the alphabet being examples. Although the Indians came to Burma in large numbers after the British occupation, contacts between India and Burma, it has been pointed out, long antedated the arrival of the British.

Since Burma is very sensitive to foreign influence Prime Minister Nehru has sought to allay any apprehensions in Rangoon. In an address to Parliament on March 17, 1950, Nehru significantly observed in commenting on Burma: "It is not our purpose—and it is not right for us—to interfere in any way with other countries but, wherever possible, we give such help as we can to our friends. We have ventured to do so in regard to Burma, too, without any element of interference."[75] The very first article of the Treaty of Friendship between India and Burma signed in Rangoon on July 7, 1951, obligated the two states to "recognize and respect the independence and rights of each other."[76] In India's other treaties of friendship with new states of Southeast Asia—Indonesia and the Philippines—the first article calls for "perpetual peace" and either "unalterable friendship" as in the case of Indonesia or "everlasting amity" as in the case of the Philippines. In the second article of the Burma-India treaty is found the provision relative to "everlasting peace and unalterable friendship." The two governments further agree in the pact that their representatives shall occasionally meet, as the situation demands, for the purpose of dis-

[75] *Ibid.*, p. 147.

[76] Treaty of Friendship, *The Indian Year Book of International Affairs, 1953*, Vol. II, p. 330.

cussing matters of common concern and of considering ways of coöperation. The complexity of relations between Burma and India is indicated by the provision for the negotiation of agreements on a reciprocal basis concerning customs, trade, communications, cultural relations, extradition of criminals, repatriation or immigration, and dual nationality. The consultation provision is also found in the Indian-Indonesian treaty but not in the Indian-Philippine pact.

The question of the intervention of the New Delhi government in Burma was more timely when the conflict between the Karens and the Burmans became very serious. The informal conference on Burma of certain British Commonwealth states convened in New Delhi in February, 1949, brought about discussion on mediation proposals for possible use in the Burman-Karen conflict. These proposals were dropped, for the Rangoon government looked upon them as interference in the internal affairs of the nation. India took an active part in the London Commonwealth Prime Ministers' Conference held in April, 1949, where a decision was made to help U Nu's government with loans and arms. The ambassadors in Rangoon of India, Pakistan, Ceylon, and Great Britain constituted a Burma Aid Committee resulting in the loan agreement of June 28, 1950, between five members of the Commonwealth and Burma. Indian arms at a critical time helped to keep the U Nu government in power.

Trade relations between India and Burma have been regulated by agreements, although differences over the price of Burmese rice have led at times to acrimony. In the three years between 1951 and 1953 the Union exported to various countries an average of 1¼ million tons of rice per year, receiving on occasion £70 and £80 a ton as compared with the £7 before the war. At the beginning of 1954 the State Agricultural Marketing Board had a large surplus which remained even at the price of £50 offered for sale. Obviously this situation affected the foreign exchange and revenue of the nation, intensifying an effort to find markets for rice and impairing the Welfare State program at home.

A trade agreement between the Rangoon and New Delhi governments, signed on September 29, 1951, had provided during a five-year period for the sale of Burmese rice under specified terms to India and the sale of Indian gunny bags, cotton yarn, groundnut oil, and galvanized iron sheets under given terms to Burma. It was announced in the Indian Parliament in April, 1955, that

Burma and India had reached the previous year a settlement involving rice on the former's preseparation debt to the latter. The debt amounted to £54 million including the capital and the interest. Under the Indian-Pakistani arrangement upon the partition of the Indian Empire of Great Britain, Pakistan was entitled to 17½ percent of the debt. India in her agreement with Burma wrote off half of the capital and all interest charges due from the latter. The settlement was linked with an agreement whereby India would purchase 900,000 tons of Burmese rice at £48 a ton during the current year. Burma agreed to refund for every ton purchased £13 in reduction of the debt. The amount of debt remaining would be considered as financial aid to Burma under the Colombo Plan. The Union also agreed to pay India her share of central pensionary charges, starting to pay the current dues on this amount from 1954. Arrears would be met in 20 annual installments free of interest. In the fall of 1955 a Burmese trade delegation in New Delhi was negotiating a loan; an agreement was signed on October 17 but Burma never drew upon the credits. In March, 1957, India agreed to loan Burma the equivalent of $42 million, any part at the latter's request to the Union or a Sterling Area land. On September 5, 1956, another five-year trade agreement had been concluded in an effort to increase commerce; India would purchase over the period 2 million tons of rice.

Visits between Indian and Burmese leaders including Prime Minister Nehru and U Nu have further strengthened relations. For instance, U Nu visited India and Pakistan in 1949, India and Ceylon the following January, and India and Great Britain in May, 1950. Various missions have been exchanged, and Indian scholarships of different kinds are available to Burmese. Many of the scholarships involve Indian technical assistance to the Union.

Boundary relations between India and Burma have been affected by the problem of the Nagas who live in a sector on both sides of the border, here not well defined. In India some of the 400,000 tribesmen resided in the Centrally-administered territory of Manipur, others in the Naga Hills District of Assam, and others in the Tuensang Frontier Division of the North-East Frontier Agency. In Burma the 40,000 to 50,000 Nagas inhabit areas across the frontier from India. Some of them have wanted a merger with the Indian Nagas who have better living conditions. In March and April, 1953, Prime Ministers Nehru and Nu made a tour of the border area in order to acquaint themselves with conditions on the spot. Previously in December, 1951, some Naga tribesmen had made a serious raid from Burma into India, returning with 93 heads. In early 1953 a Burmese army frontier force had fought a sizable band of rebel Nagas. In India between 2000 and 3000 Nagas have been fighting for some time for an independent Nagaland under the leadership of A. Z. Phizo. In the fall of 1956 and in 1957 the Indians took energetic "police measures" against them. India was opposed to independence, but wanted an end to the fighting. After negotiations in New Delhi, opposed by Phizo and his followers, the Indian Parliament passed a law, effective December 1, creating the Naga Hills-Tuensang Area, autonomous in nature but Centrally-administered. There was some suspicion that Burma was in favor of a greater Nagaland under her auspices. In another geographical area, far removed from the Nagas—the Burmese Coco Islands north of the Andamans in the Bay of Bengal—a Burmese leased some of the territory to Indian interests, a situation later arousing concern in Rangoon government circles.

The regulation of Indian immigration to Burma, the treatment of Indians in the Union, and the question of the Chettyar claims raise serious problems in the relations between Rangoon and New Delhi. If it were not for the Nu-Nehru ties, these subjects might gravely impair friendly relations between the two countries. Although exact figures are lacking over 1¼ million Indians live in Southeast Asia of which number about 800,000 are found in Burma. Around 20 percent of the Indians in Southeast Asia are merchants, moneylenders, and to a far lesser extent professional men while the remainder are associated with agricultural activities, often as laborers. As a general rule the Indians assimilate even less easily than the Chinese, clinging to their respective religions, languages, and customs. In Burma, the Indian minority obviously constitutes a serious problem, the large number involved and the strong economic impact being major factors.

The rise of an independent India and the personal leadership of Nehru have had a definite influence on the Indian minorities in Southeast Asia. The New Delhi government, opposed to dual citizenship, has taken the position that Indians residing abroad should either keep their Indian citizenship and therefore have the status of foreigners in the given country, or seek the citizenship of the country where they live and become identified with it. In the case of the former, India would try to secure the same treatment as that of the most favored aliens; in the event of the latter India believes that the foreign governments involved should accord the full rights of citizenship. Burmese qualifications for citizenship have excluded many Indians whose duration of living in the country is sufficiently long in the judgment of New Delhi. Protracted negotiations between the Rangoon and New Delhi governments have taken place on the subject. As for the extensive interests of the Indian Chettyars in the Union, India has indicated that she is not able to prevent the nationalization of land and industries but can only urge adequate compensation under the economic conditions prevailing. In the entry of Indian laborers in the country, New Delhi does not urge that it be unrestricted.

Anti-Indian violence occurred in Burma in 1930 and especially in 1938. As the Japanese invaded Burma, about half of the million Indians in the country fled with the British to India. Immigration restrictions since the war have contributed to prevent a great influx of Indians into the Union. The Indians who stayed in Burma during the Japanese occupation were not well treated by the Burmese, especially in the early years. Japan, generally sympathetic to the Indians for financial and military purposes, proceeded to organize the Azad Hind regime under Subhas Chandra Bose with Burma coming to be the operational base. Dr. Ba Maw's government recognized the Bose regime to whose custody in February, 1944, Japan turned over in theory the administration of the Andaman and Nicobar Islands. In Burma the land of the Indian Chettyars upon the departure of most of them had been taken over by the Burmese tenants. The Chettyars, however, had previously filed their titles in India so the land question after the war was certain to come to the forefront. The problem was serious, for it was estimated that the Chettyars who had loaned money to the Burmese and had then foreclosed on the property when the money was not repayed owned over 2½ million acres of rice land out of around 10 million acres in Lower Burma. Land nationalization measures were passed by the Rangoon Parliament but they were slow in being put into effect. Meanwhile the question of fair and reasonable compensation to the Indian owners remained a problem to be solved. As of 1954 142,747 acres had been nationalized out of a total cultivated area of 16½ million acres but since then the program has been much more rapidly implemented.

With Pakistan Burma has proper but not intimate relations. The foreign policy of the Moslem neighbor of the Union has led to adherence to the Southeast Asia Collective Defense Treaty and the

Middle East or Baghdad Treaty. Thus Pakistan has linked itself to the Western group of powers contrary to the policy of India and Burma. Although divided by India into eastern and western parts, the Islamic Republic of Pakistan has tended to be more concerned over developments in the Middle East than in Southeast Asia. At the same time it should be stressed that interest in the latter area is definitely growing.

The Karachi and Rangoon governments have not allowed the situation in Arakan to poison relations between them. In this region, it will be recalled, dwells a large Moslem minority, adjacent to East Pakistan, and some of the Moslems have expressed a desire to join their neighbor. In East Pakistan also lives a minority of Arakanese Buddhists. Banditry and rice smuggling along the frontier have raised problems for both governments; Rangoon and Karachi officials have denied that Pakistan is turning over arms to Burmese rebels. Especially in northern Arakan has the illegal immigration of Moslems from Chittagong in East Pakistan been extensive resulting in the Mujahids, as they are called, and the Rwangya or settled Chittagonians, also Moslems, outnumbering the Buddhist Arakanese living mostly in the southern part of Arakan. U Nu and the Pakistani Ambassador visited the division in early 1950; Prime Minister Husseyn S. Suhrawardy called at Rangoon in October, 1956.

Burma and Pakistan signed a treaty of friendship in 1952. Discussions the next year occurred over the sovereignty of 21 islands in the Naaf River, which forms the boundary between the two states. Prime Minister U Nu has tried to help Pakistan and India solve the Kashmir question but he has met with no success.

Differences have existed between Moslem and Hindu Indians in Burma. The former are more deeply rooted in the country although fewer in number. In 1938 some Hindus publicly supported the Burmese in their trouble with the Moslems over an alleged insult to Buddhism. In 1954 Moslems and Burmese Buddhists differed over educational policy. Prior to the partition of the Indian Empire the struggle between the Indian Hindus and Moslems was reflected on certain occasions in Burma. However, the All-Burma Muslim League and the All-Burma Indian Congress both supported the AFPFL's demand for independence.[77]

[77] It is interesting to note that Burma has the closest ties with Nepal of any state in Southeast Asia. A Nepal-Burma Friendship Association functions in Katmandu, its inspiration found in the Fourth Conference of the World Fellowship of Buddhists held in Nepal in November, 1956. The kingdom has a consulate in Rangoon.

Burma's land neighbors, south of China and to the east, Laos and Thailand, raise their own problems. The Mekong, forming the boundary between Laos and easternmost Burma for about 160 miles, gives the Union a particular interest in Indochina. In addition, it should be stressed, the Theravada Buddhism of Laos and Cambodia adds the cultural ties of religion. Although Burma is separated from Vietnam by Laos, Thailand, and Cambodia, developments in Vietnam, the most powerful of the Indochinese states, have definite ramifications in Rangoon.

Basically the government of Burma interpreted the war in Indochina as a struggle for independence against French colonialism. The growing influence of Communist China in the Vietnamese nationalist movement under Ho Chi Minh caused increased concern in Rangoon. France was considered a colonial power which should relinquish her overseas empire in the interests of indigenous nationalism, but Burma did not desire to see a satellite of Mao Tse-tung fill in the political vacuum. Although the Union declined to recognize either the regime of Ho Chi Minh or of Bao Dai, she did allow a Viet Minh information office to function in Rangoon.

Burma took part in the discussions on the Indochina question at the conference of the Colombo Powers in Ceylon and approved of the joint suggestions. At the Kalaw meeting of the Asian Socialist Conference Bureau a peace resolution on Indochina, after asserting that "only the emergence of a free and democratic government, independent of both the Power Blocs, can restore peace and stability in Indo-China and in Asia," called first for the speedy making of a military truce with the supervision of an international commission agreeable to both parties under United Nations auspices, second for the holding of "fair and free elections under international control" following the creation of a favorable climate involving the reduction of belligerent forces, the withdrawal of foreign soldiers, and economic rehabilitation under the United Nations, and third for a "joint guarantee of the independence of the free States of Indo-China by both the Power Blocs and Asian States concerned, and safeguarding these States against any military alliance with either of the Blocs."[78] In early August and again at the Bogor Conference in December, Burma joined with the other Colombo Powers in approving the Geneva settlement on Indochina concluded the previous July.

The Rangoon government recognized the Kingdom of Laos and the Kingdom of Cambodia in August, 1954, and supported

[78] Peace resolution on Indo-China, *Burma*, Vol. IV (July, 1954), p. 37.

their admission to the United Nations. Although Burma still did not recognize any regime in Vietnam, Premier U Nu visited Ho Chi Minh at Hanoi in late November en route to Peking. At a dinner given by the President of the Democratic Republic of Vietnam, U Nu commented on the colonial barriers that had existed between the people of Vietnam and Burma and hoped for future coöperation between the two. In a communiqué issued November 29, both leaders agreed on the Five Principles of coöperation previously approved by U Nu and Chou En-lai. Unlike Nehru, Premier U Nu did not stop at Saigon in connection with the trip to Communist China. Pham Van Dong, Deputy Premier and Foreign Minister of North Vietnam, visited Rangoon on his way to Bandung and a communiqué issued on April 13, 1955, called for more efforts to promote the Five Principles.

In November, 1956, U Nu, no longer Premier, paid a visit to the Republic of Vietnam as a guest of President Ngo Dinh Diem. The former indicated that he believed representatives should be exchanged between the two countries but did not specify the type, stressed that the information officer of the Viet Minh in Rangoon had no diplomatic status, invited President Ngo Dinh Diem to visit Burma, and called for closer contacts through the exchange of students and visits of different groups. The effect of the trip of U Nu to Saigon and Dalat was to strengthen diplomatically the position of Ngo Dinh Diem. In late 1957 Saigon established a consulate general in Rangoon.

King Norodom Sihanouk of Cambodia visited Burma in November, 1954, cementing ties between Rangoon and Phnom Penh. The previous August the Home Minister of the Union had gone to Cambodia as well as Laos. U Nu visited Phnom Penh in December. It was announced in January, 1955, that the two governments would have diplomatic relations at the ambassadorial level. On July 12 the first Laotian minister to Burma presented his credentials to the President of the Union. Both the President and the minister stressed that old ties were now being officially renewed. In the early part of the year some KMT soldiers sought refuge in Laos from Burma; Rangoon and Vientiane took steps to deal with the matter.

With reference to Indochina as a whole, Premiers U Nu and Chou En-lai in a statement in Peking on December 12, 1954, at the end of the former's visit observed that peace in the area must be consolidated so as to stabilize Southeast Asia. It was noted that all countries were entitled to prosperity and independence free from foreign aggression. A joint statement of Premiers U Nu and Nikolai A. Bulganin of the Soviet Union issued in Rangoon on December 6, 1955, called for a political settlement of the Indochina problem in accord with the Geneva Conference decisions of 1954.

The Union's relations with Ceylon are cordial; in fact, Ceylon exchanged envoys with Burma before it did with Thailand. The island state is a good customer of Burmese rice. Ceylon and Burma, as already noted, are both Colombo Powers, and view international relations along somewhat similar although certainly not identical lines. The defeat of Sir John Kotelawala, Prime Minister of Ceylon, in the elections of April 5, 7, and 10, 1956, and the rise to the premiership of S. W. R. D. Bandaranaike marked a further step in the evolution of Ceylon into the uncommitted camp. U Nu visited the Buddhist country in December.

In the case of the Philippines, Burma is removed from the island republic much more than she is from any other state in Southeast Asia. In 1956 Burma accredited her ambassador in Thailand as minister to the Philippines and the latter followed a similar course regarding its ambassador in Bangkok. The next step would be the establishment of actual missions in each other's capitals. Under the Japanese New Order in Greater East Asia the Laurel regime had watched with interest the winning of Burmese "independence" using it as an example for the Philippines. Contacts between the Manila and Rangoon regimes were occasionally made. When the Philippines received independence on July 4, 1946, Aung San was among the Asian leaders sending congratulations.

The Union's relations with Australia are limited despite the diplomatic ties and Australian help under the Colombo Plan, Burma becoming a member after being an observer. A factor in the relations between Australia and Burma is the fact that up to the end of May, 1956, a total of 315 fellowships under the Colombo program had been awarded to Burmese and 153 involved study and training in Australia. In 1956 the respective missions in Rangoon and Canberra were raised from legations to embassies.

Although the conflict in Indochina was geographically close to Burma, the Korean War involved the Union largely as a result of her membership in the United Nations. Here was presented a real test to the foreign policy of the new republic. It was clear that the North Koreans were guilty of aggression and that the United Nations Security Council was invoking collective measures. Yet how could Burma, following a policy called neutrality and seeking to be friends with all, carry out her obligations under the Charter of the United Nations?

On July 8, 1950, almost two weeks after the outbreak of the Korean War, the Rangoon government issued a statement that "Burma, as a member of the United Nations, and as a believer in the settlement of disputes by peaceful methods, feels bound to support the Security Council in the stand it has so far taken in regard to South Korea, which aims at stemming the aggression and restoring peaceful conditions."[79] At the same time it was asserted that the "Government of the Union of Burma desire to make it clear that their support of the Security Council's decision in regard to Korea does not in any way [a]ffect their existing foreign policy which is to maintain friendly relations with all countries."[80] A statement issued by the Executive Council of the AFPFL supported the government policy considering it "in the interest of the Union as well as in the interest of the World."[81]

Prime Minister U Nu in a speech in Parliament on September 5 carefully analyzed the reasoning behind the policy of his government. The first consideration was to protect the nation from aggression, Burma not being able to build up sufficient armament to stand by herself and needing the support of a global organization if she were attacked. "With this advantage in view," Nu observed, "we felt a reciprocal obligation to contribute our mite to the United Nations when that great organization tackles any aggressor in any place at any time."[82] The second factor in the government's decision was the policy of nonpartisanship, Burma acting on the merits of a given case and doing right as she sees it without prior commitment to the Anglo-American or the Soviet bloc. The third principle, U Nu stated, on which his country's policy was built was that of "Fair Deal," the most important of all. "It was very clear under our eyes," he said, "that the North [in Korea] was the aggressor, and we deemed it right to oppose the aggressor—North."[83]

In the General Assembly of the United Nations Burma was in

[79] Government's Statement, July 8, 1950, quoted in speech of Thakin Nu, September 5, 1950, *From Peace to Stability*, p. 95.
[80] *Ibid.*
[81] Statement of Executive Council of the AFPFL, *From Peace to Stability*, p. 97.
[82] Speech of Thakin Nu, *From Peace to Stability*, p. 99.
[83] *Ibid.*, p. 104.

favor of Resolution 376 (V), approved October 7, 1950, supporting the Security Council measures on Korea, Resolution 410 A (V), approved December 1, setting up the United Nations Korean Reconstruction Agency, and Resolution 384 (V), approved December 14, authorizing a group of three to find a basis for a cease-fire in the Korean conflict. She helped to sponsor a draft resolution submitted December 12 but not passed, calling for a committee to make recommendations to settle the issue in the Far East. On February 1, 1951, Burma offered 400 metric tons of rice as a contribution toward Korean relief, the rice subsequently arriving in the Korean theater.

The Rangoon government was well aware that the entrance of Chinese Communist soldiers into the war increased the threat that the Korean conflict might spread outside the peninsula. U Nu had informed Parliament on September 5, 1950, that the Mao Tse-tung regime should represent China in the United Nations but he said his government was neither supporting nor condoning American policy toward Formosa in connection with the Korean War. Although Burma voted against a United Nations resolution calling the People's Republic of China an aggressor and abstained on the embargo resolution, the Union for the most part upheld during the conflict the prohibition on shipping strategic goods to Chinese Communist and North Korean forces. The Rangoon government favored getting all the parties concerned into quick discussion on ending the Korean conflict and supported the principle of voluntary repatriation of prisoners of war. Pursuing a policy very similar to that of India in the Korean struggle, Burma favored the presence of India at the political conference envisioned by the Korean armistice.

Obviously the Union welcomed the end of the fighting in Korea. U Myint Thein told the General Assembly of the United Nations on September 25, 1953, that his country wanted a unified and independent Korea as soon as possible but realized the process would be slow and difficult. "If we have learned any lesson from the history of Korea over the last four years," he said, "it is that any attempt to unite Korea by force of arms is doomed to failure."[84]

The Korean War placed in sharp focus for Burma the rivalry of the United States and the Soviet Union in Asia. Although geo-

[84] United Nations, General Assembly, Eighth Session, *Official Records*, 446th Plenary Meeting, September 25, 1953, p. 172.

graphically separated from the two strongest powers of the globe, Burma could not escape their impact.

In 1857 the first Burmese diplomatic mission came to the United States. American educators and doctors have long worked in Burma, usually under missionary auspices. Technicians from the United States have served in the oil fields of the Asian country; Herbert Hoover was once a mining engineer in the lead and zinc Bawdwin mines near Lashio. The independence of the Union of Burma and the establishment of diplomatic relations between the Washington and Rangoon governments quite naturally opened a new phase in American-Burmese relations. The United States Information Agency now has an active cultural program in the Union with libraries in Rangoon and Mandalay. Between 1948 and 1955 some 300 exchanges of Americans and Burmese occurred, a Fulbright program functioning to the benefit of both countries. Ford Foundation funds are also being used in a number of projects in the Union. Commerical relations, however, between Burma and the United States are limited.

In 1950 Burma began to receive American economic and technical aid under a bilateral agreement signed September 13. A Special Technical and Economic Mission (STEM) arrived in Rangoon and a Burma Economic Aid Committee (BEAC) worked with it to handle the assistance. Projects included an economic and technical survey of the nation by Knappen, Tippets, Abbett, McCarthy, Engineers, in association with Pierce Management, Inc., and Robert R. Nathan Associates, Inc. Programs were formulated in education and audiovisual aids, agriculture and fisheries, public health and sanitation, transportation, power and other public works, maintenance of essential supplies, and general engineering advisory services. Enactment by the United States Congress of the Mutual Security Act of 1951 led to assurances found in the exchange of notes February 6 and February 9, 1952, whereby the "Government of the Union of Burma reaffirms that it will act in conformity with its obligations under the United Nations charter and in accord with the principles and purposes of the United Nations charter in promoting international understanding and good will and maintaining world peace and eliminating causes of international tension."[85] On October 24, 1952, a program agreement between Burma and the United States was concluded relative to

[85] Agreement between the United States of America and Burma, *Treaties and Other International Acts Series* 2602.

the operation of Point Four in the former country during the fiscal year of 1953.

In a note to the United States on March 17, 1953, Burma terminated the American aid program as of the last of June. The ending, however, was not abrupt, and certain projects already started were allowed to continue. A number of American technicians were even hired to work by the Burmese government. United States direct assistance to Burma under the program outlined came to total about $20 million. The Union of Burma, still needing foreign aid, continued to get assistance of different kinds such as that given under United Nations and Colombo Plan programs.

The termination by Burma of American aid was made in connection with her decision to take the case of the Kuomintang forces in the Union to the United Nations. It was widely believed in Burma that the United States should share the blame for the continued presence and armament of the Nationalist soldiers.[86] When Vice-President Richard Nixon visited Rangoon in 1953 he was informed on the spot of the Kuomintang situation. Relations between Rangoon and Washington improved with the limited evacuation of the Chinese troops.

A number of other issues have arisen to impair relations between the United States and Burma. An American medical missionary, Gordon Seagrave, was charged by the Rangoon government with aiding the rebels and sentenced in January, 1951, to six years' imprisonment. The sentence upon appeal was reduced to the 51 days Seagrave had served and in November the conviction was entirely quashed by the Supreme Court.

In the economic field the American policy of disposing of surplus rice to needy countries has caused Burmese to accuse the United States of dumping the product to the detriment of the Union's markets. A prominent Burmese official, it was reported, declared on October 18, 1954, that "dumping of American rice in Asia will force us to go to China [Communist] on our knees. We will have to depend upon China for our rice market and this will naturally tie our economy to Red China."[87] Burma wanted to sell rice to the United States in exchange for a program of technical assistance. On February 8, 1956, an agricultural commodities

[86] For an account of the American role, see extensive footnote by Frank N. Trager in Human Relations Area Files, *Burma*, Vol. III, pp. 1216-1218.

[87] *New York Times*, October 21, 1954.

agreement was signed in Rangoon wherein the Union would buy from the United States about $20.8 million worth of raw cotton, dairy products, tobacco, and fruit in Burmese currency. On June 30 the United States agreed to buy $1,100,000 worth of Burmese rice for Pakistan, the Union using the dollars to pay for American technicians and to send trainees to the United States. In the textiles agreements Burma had signed with the United Kingdom and Japan on June 18 the United States provided raw cotton for Burma's payment for the finished goods.

On March 21, 1957, agreements between the Union and the United States were signed under which the latter would loan the former $25 million for economic development and $17,300,000 in Burmese kyats from the previous sales of American farm surpluses, the American Export-Import Bank servicing the loans. In an economic coöperation agreement signed in Rangoon the American Embassy would be increased up to six people paid by the International Coöperation Administration to assist in the administering of the program.

The Union is critical of American policy toward a possible Special United Nations Fund for Economic Development (SUNFED) wherein full support would be linked to savings that would come from an international reduction in armament. At the same time Burma has approved of American policy toward the peaceful uses of atomic energy as indicated at the Geneva Conference on the subject in 1955. An American atomic library has been given the Union. Believing it was passed over by the industrial revolution, Burma does not want to be left behind by the atomic revolution.

Although visits by Vice-President Nixon and Secretary Dulles to Rangoon were appreciated, Premier U Nu's trip to the United States was more important. In remarks to the American Senate on June 30, 1955, the Burmese Premier observed that "both of our nations adopted in their early years an independent foreign policy, designed to maintain the friendship of all nations and to avoid big-power alliances."[88] He told the House of Representatives the same day that his country kept its faith in democracy despite Communist and anti-Communist revolts. A joint statement by President Dwight D. Eisenhower and Premier U Nu issued on July 2 indicated that the two executives discussed the problem of the American fliers imprisoned in Communist China, questions concerning the existing

[88] Remarks of U Nu to the United States Senate, June 30, 1955, *An Asian Speaks,* Embassy of the Union of Burma, Washington, D.C., p. 8.

rice surpluses in Burma and the United States, and matters relative to world peace and to Asian security. It was stated that the people of the two countries shared the goals of "a peaceful world and a democratic way of life." In connection with his visit U Nu gave the United States $5000 for the help of the children of members of the American armed forces who were killed or incapacitated in the Burma campaign of the Second World War.

In his speeches and interviews during his tour of the United States the Burmese Prime Minister sought to create an atmosphere that could lead to direct talks and friendly relations between the Washington and Peking governments. He noted how he had told the Chinese Communist leaders during his visit to Peking that the Americans were a brave and generous people. The Premier revealed he thought the Chinese Communists believed the United States was trying to create a ring of bases around them for aggressive purposes. He indicated he was willing to mediate on the Formosan question if both Communist China and the United States desired it. Since both countries did not want war, had nothing to gain by it, and even feared it, he believed an understanding could be reached between them. China, moreover, needed a long time to develop her economy. U Nu got the impression in Washington that the United States looked upon the seating of Communist China in the United Nations as a matter of timing.

Relations between the Soviet Union and Burma were formalized when the first Soviet ambassador to Burma presented his credentials on May 21, 1951, and the first Burmese ambassador to the Soviet Union did the same on the previous February 17. The two governments had agreed to the exchange of ambassadors in February, 1948. In 1951 a Russian cultural mission visited Burma and the next year a Burmese one went to the Soviet Union. In October, 1952, Burmese officials visited Communist China and the Soviet Union to study collective farming and agricultural methods. In September, 1954, a Burmese delegation led by the Minister of Agriculture and Forestry went to the Soviet Union and the following December another Burmese delegation led by a cabinet official arrived in Moscow to negotiate the sale of rice.

The desire of Burma for technical assistance and industrial equipment coupled with her need for markets for surplus rice created a situation that was used by the Soviet Union. The USSR thinks of technical assistance as an item that can be utilized in a trade agreement, serving as an important wedge in political and economic penetration. Using technicians as government servants and not generally critical of local proposals, the Soviet Union in the eyes of many Southeast Asians has an advantage over the United States.

On July 1, 1955, Burma and the Soviet Union concluded a three-year trade agreement on the exchange chiefly of Burmese rice and agricultural products for Soviet industrial goods, payments being in pounds sterling. Agreements have also been made between Burma and Poland, Czechoslovakia, Hungary, Bulgaria, Romania, and East Germany. In 1955 the market in Communist and non-Communist countries for Burma's rice as compared with that in 1954 indicated clearly the substantial economic inroads made by the Communists. It is also clear that technicians to train the Burmese how to use machinery from Communist countries and the supply of replacements must come from the Soviet world.

Premier U Nu visited the Soviet Union in October and November, 1955, praising his hosts for helping to save Burma from a severe crisis by purchasing rice. He indicated that his country had already requested Soviet architects to design a stadium for sports in Rangoon and a large conference hall. He proposed that in any future Bandung Conference the Soviet Union should be a participant, stressing the kinship between the republics of Soviet Central Asia and other Asian countries. In a communiqué issued on November 3 it was stated that the Burmese and Soviet Premiers "unanimously condemn the policy of knocking together blocs and consider that the policy of not entering blocs gives the peoples security and plays a positive part in consolidating peace all over the world."[89] Tribute was rendered the Bandung Conference; Communist China, it was asserted, should be seated in the United Nations and Formosa turned over to the People's Republic; effective international control was sought over the banning of atomic and hydrogen bombs and the reduction of conventional armament.

In December Premier Nikolai A. Bulganin and Nikita S. Khrushchev, Soviet Communist Party First Secretary, visited Burma in connection with their trip to India and Afghanistan. Khrushchev in his comments stressed Burma's colonial background and criticized imperialism in general, emphasized the Soviet program of importing Burmese rice and exporting industrial products and technicians, dwelt upon the role of the Kuomintang forces in Bur-

[89] Joint Statement of Premier Bulganin and Prime Minister U Nu, November 3, 1955, *Burma Weekly Bulletin*, New Series, Vol. 4 (November 10, 1955), p. 253.

ma, and severely criticized Anglo-American-French policy in Asia and the world. A joint statement by Premiers Bulganin and Nu as well as Khrushchev issued on December 6 indicated that negotiations between Burma and the Soviet Union were continuing in the economic, technical, scientific, and cultural fields in order that specific agreements might be reached. The statement closely paralleled the Moscow communiqué made by Bulganin and U Nu. In an address to the Supreme Soviet on December 29, Premier Bulganin significantly noted that "our visit to the Union of Burma once again confirmed that Burma actively advocates the maintenance of friendly relations between states, condemns the policy of setting up military blocs and champions joint collective efforts of states in the consolidation of peace."[90] He went on to assert that "the consolidation of our friendly relations with India, Burma and Afghanistan is a triumph of the Leninist principles underlying the peace-loving foreign policy of the Soviet Union, a triumph of the principles of peaceful coexistence."[91]

On December 7 Burma and the USSR concluded an economic agreement by which the latter in exchange for Burmese rice would give assistance in establishing industrial plants, developing agriculture, and building major irrigation works. The USSR would build and equip a technological institute in Rangoon as a gift, Burma donating an appropriate amount of rice and other goods to the Soviet Union. On April 1, 1956, in the presence of U Nu and Anastas I. Mikoyan, a Soviet First Deputy Premier, trade agreements were signed in Rangoon extending the 1955 agreement to five years wherein the Soviet Union would take 400,000 tons each year of Burmese rice for four years, if Burma desired, and the latter would receive an equivalent in Soviet machinery, products, and technical and other services. It was announced that the USSR would build in Burma a hospital, a theater, and a cultural and sports center.

The trade agreements with the Communist states became a real subject of criticism in Burma after the middle of 1956. Burma by then had more customers for her rice than she had supply, some of the potential buyers having hard cash. The barter arrangements with many of the Communist states, especially the USSR, had not worked out; U Nu indicated that Burma lost from 10 to 30 percent in the transactions. Communist goods were often overpriced, un-

[90] *New York Times,* December 30, 1955.
[91] *Ibid.*

certain of delivery, and sometimes of the wrong kind or poor in quality. Cement from Soviet bloc states, for example, raised problems. Some of Burma's rice to Communist countries had in turn been shipped to her cash customers, or at least the equivalent of it. At the request of Burma the Moscow government allowed her to shift part of her credit balance with the USSR to Czechoslovakia. A Burmese firm was appointed by the Soviets to handle trade with the Asian state. Other adjustments have been made with the Soviet bloc.

In her security policy Burma has opposed participation in any military alliance like the Southeast Asia Collective Defense Treaty. Nevertheless, there was not the marked hostility shown the Manila Pact in Rangoon that there was in Djakarta. In certain Burmese circles the treaty was welcomed as a counterweight to the growing power of Communist China. After attending the Bangkok Conference of the Manila Pact Powers in 1955, Secretary Dulles visited Rangoon and discussed with Premier U Nu the decisions of the recent meeting. On September 14 the Burmese Chamber of Deputies approved unanimously a resolution urging the nation to keep out of SEATO. U Hla Maung, Parliamentary Secretary to the Foreign Minister, stated that Burma would accept no economic aid under it. Nevertheless, Premier U Nu in an address on August 14 in commemoration of the eighth anniversary of Pakistan's independence observed that the two neighbors must continue their efforts to serve the cause of peace. "In serving thus," he said, "it may sometimes happen that our methods differ although our goal is the same, and we fully recognize the right of all countries to adopt their own methods which they consider best."[92]

Burma's security policy is well portrayed in a speech of U Nu on Martyrs' Day, July 19, 1954, and in an interview he gave during his visit to the United States. On the former occasion he said:

> Western blood need not be shed in countering aggression in this area. Just make the countries of South East Asia strong, because weak nations tempt aggression. When they become strong, they will take care of their own defenses in their own way and there will be no more aggression.
>
> How then are the countries of South East Asia to be strengthened? These are the processes involved:
>
> (1) Let all the countries of South East Asia be free.

[92] Speech of U Nu, August 14, 1955, *Burma Weekly Bulletin*, New Series, Vol. 4 (August 18, 1955), p. 147.

(2) Let the leaders of these countries be those whom the people trust and not those who hold office on the strength of guns.
(3) Let these leaders draw up plans for the welfare of the masses which are best suited to their respective countries.
(4) In the implementation of these plans, let there be necessary technicians and materials, on terms which are mutually advantageous to the parties giving and receiving them.

If only these four things are accomplished, then aggression will be a thing of the past in South East Asia. The absence of aggression precludes the possibility of wars breaking out.[93]

In the interview in the United States Premier U Nu asserted: "My policy is this: First, be friendly with all, whether they are friendly or not; second, fight if necessary, and build up the United Nations to prevent external aggression; third, work for the welfare of the people so they will have no cause to follow subversive leaders."[94]

It is clear that the officials of Burma have given considerable thought to the foreign policy of the new state. Idealism and realism have combined to present a foreign policy of considerable complexity. Only the future can tell whether or not Burma has made the best of the international situation.

[93] Speech of U Nu, July 19, 1954, *Burma,* Information Bulletin of the Embassy of Burma, Washington, D.C.

[94] Interview with U Nu, *U.S. News and World Report,* August 5, 1955, p. 81.

7. Kingdom of Thailand

Unique among the countries of Southeast Asia, Thailand,[1] it has been stressed, preserved her independence while all the rest of the area came under the final colonial control of the Netherlands, the United States, Great Britain, or France.[2] Thailand's independence was attributable both to the skillful diplomacy of some of her leaders in adjusting to new international situations and to the policy of Great Britain and France who preferred to keep the kingdom as a buffer state between their colonial domains. In defense of the national interest the Thai have been opportunistic in the formulation of their foreign policy. Nevertheless, an official has significantly said: "We Thai bend like the bamboo but we do not break."[3] In many respects the kingdom has often been a political barometer of the power shifts in Asia.

As a result of long independence, Thailand does not have the suspicion of the West so frequently manifested in states newly freed from European domination. Buddhism, furthermore, has contributed a moderating influence on the people. At the same time Thailand is opposed to colonialism, although the emotionalism found in Indonesia or Burma is lacking. Thai nationalism, however, is capable of being aroused, especially against the Chinese living in the kingdom or on behalf of adjacent territories once ruled by Thailand.

The general foreign policy of the country was outlined by Foreign Minister Arthakitti Banomyong on September 20, 1947,

[1] Since 1949 the kingdom has officially been called Thailand. From 1946 to 1949 it was termed Siam, from 1939 to 1946 Thailand, and before then Siam. In the Thai language it is known as Muang Thai.

[2] Portugal's possession, as previously indicated, is Portuguese Timor.

[3] Quoted by Edwin F. Stanton, *Brief Authority*, p. 171. Regarding Thai diplomats, the former United States Ambassador states: "I must say, I became increasingly impressed by their never-failing politeness and rare tact, even when the disagreeable subjects came up for discussion or negotiation. They have perfected the art of polite verbal acquiescence, but this is not necessarily followed by action if the matter is deemed not to be in their national interest." *Ibid.*, p. 184.

during Thailand's first participation in a general debate of the United Nations General Assembly. He observed that the "love of peace is a characteristic which has been instilled into the culture of the Siamese people by Buddhism, which also teaches freedom and tolerance."[4] Against this cultural background he stated that "Siam has always welcomed and promoted friendly relations with foreign countries," and he went on to assert that "the Siamese people call themselves 'Thai,' or free people; but, as true lovers of freedom, they not only like to enjoy freedom themselves, but they like to see other peoples enjoy freedom as well. . . . They therefore wholeheartedly support the principle of self-determination of peoples embodied in the Charter [of the United Nations]."[5] Noting that economic stability was as desirable as political stability, the Foreign Minister concluded by referring to his country's participation in the League of Nations and pledging fullest support to the United Nations.

Prince Wan Waithayakon further outlined the concept of Thai foreign policy in a speech he made as Minister of Foreign Affairs at the opening of the Manila Conference on September 6, 1954. He recalled that "for the preservation of peace and security Thailand has tried many policies in the past, such as those of neutrality and of non-aggression treaties but found that they did not work, nor can any reason be seen why they should work now."[6] He stated that "the only hope for peace lies in the United Nations and its Charter," for "peace is world-wide: it is one and indivisible."[7] The Foreign Minister then justified "regional arrangements for collective defense" under the auspices of the United Nations Charter; he significantly observed that "while our task at the present Conference is to unite our strength to maintain international peace and security in this area, we should have in mind that the strength we are to unite is not only military strength but also the moral strength of freedom and self-determination and the material strength of economic and social well-being."[8]

Official statements on the foreign policy of Thailand are not made so frequently as the pronouncements by some other states in

[4] United Nations, General Assembly, Second Session, *Official Records*, 87th Plenary Meeting, September 20, 1947, p. 189.

[5] *Ibid.*, pp. 189-190.

[6] Speech of Prince Wan Waithayakon, *The Signing of the Southeast Asia Collective Defense Treaty, the Protocol to the Southeast Asia Collective Defense Treaty and the Pacific Charter*, p. 36.

[7] *Ibid.*

[8] *Ibid.*, pp. 36-37.

Southeast Asia on their foreign outlook. In general the leaders of Thai foreign policy are reticent in public comments. From the constitutional side it was asserted in the constitution of 1949, Sections 56 and 57 of Chapter 5, that the state would foster friendly relations with foreign countries on the principle of reciprocity and would coöperate in preserving world peace and international justice. In the constitution of 1932, now in force as amended, it was stated in Section 38 of Chapter 111 that the "State shall preserve the national independence and coöperate with other nations in promoting world peace."[9]

In contrast to other countries of Southeast Asia who were seeking and winning independence in the years following V-J Day, Thailand as a sovereign state was forced to cope with the international problems of liquidating a situation brought about by her role in Japan's New Order in Greater East Asia. A short time thereafter, the kingdom found itself faced with the conduct of relations with newly independent neighbors—Burma to the north, northwest, and west, Laos to the north, northeast, and east, Cambodia to the southeast, and Malaya to the south. Years of experience, however, were valuable to Thai officials in dealing with the kaleidoscopic changes in world politics as it came to affect Southeast Asia.

The Thai people today are found in five countries—China, Burma, Laos, Vietnam and Thailand, a fact of considerable importance in the international relations of the area. In the Union of Burma they are called the Shans and in the Kingdom of Laos the Lao. Yunnan in south China was once the location of a powerful Thai kingdom called Nan Chao which was overthrown by the forces of Kublai Khan in the thirteenth century. Impetus was given to the further migration of many Thai southward along the valleys of the Menam, Mekong, and Salween. The first historical Thai dynasty had its capital at Sukhothai in the northern part of present-day central Thailand from about 1257 to 1349, coming to embrace the Chao Phraya River (Menam) valley and the Malay peninsula as far south as Ligor. A new dynasty, the first of three, was established at Ayuthia, capital from 1350 to its destruction by the Burmese in 1767. Bangkok was founded in 1768 with the first ruler of the present dynasty, the Chakri, assuming the Crown in 1782. For many centuries Thailand fought with varying fortunes of war Cambodia

[9] The Constitution of Thailand, B. E. 2475 (1932), *The Siam Directory*, p. 85.

on the east and Burma on the west, establishing historical precedents for territorial claims. The expansion of British power into Burma and Malaya and of French into Cambodia and Laos transferred Thailand's relations with her neighbors from Asian to European capitals. In 1896 Great Britain and France guaranteed the neutrality of the Menam basin and in 1904 the Entente Cordiale further indicated that the heart of Thailand would not be partitioned by the two European powers. With the Thai-French treaty of 1907 and the Thai-British two years later, the Kingdom of Thailand assumed its relatively permanent borders. The Bangkok government became an ally of Great Britain and France in the First World War by declaring war on Germany and Austria-Hungary on July 22, 1917, and later was a participant in the Paris Peace Conference of 1919. A signatory of the Treaty of Versailles, the Asian state upon ratification became a charter member of the League of Nations. A long diplomatic struggle for an end to extraterritoriality and other special foreign privileges was at last successfully concluded in a series of agreements signed between Thailand and the foreign states concerned.

Prior to 1932 the kingdom of Thailand had an absolute monarchy although a number of the sovereigns, especially Mongkut (Rama IV), 1851-1868, and Chulalongkorn (Rama V), 1868-1910, were outstanding in bringing Thailand into contact with the Western world and preserving its independence. On June 24, 1932, the old order of government was altered by a *coup d'état* engineered by youthful army leaders and civilian intellectuals. A limited monarchy was established under a constitution reflecting democratic, Western influence. But, as has been pointed out, "the 'revolution' of 1932 simply transferred power from a handful of princes to the only other educated group in the country—the intellectual and military bourgeoisie."[10] The ensuing struggle in Thailand has developed between the civilian liberals and the conservative army leaders with the supporters of the restoration of monarchical power backing the side which at the time appears more sympathetic. The two leading rivals for power since 1932 have been Pibul Songgram, a French-trained military officer, who led the army forces and Pridi Panomyong, a French-trained lawyer, who led the civilian liberals. From 1932 to 1938 the Pridi forces were for the most part predominant, followed until 1944 by the Pibul group; from 1944 to

[10] Virginia Thompson and Richard Adloff, "Thailand (Siam)" in Lawrence K. Rosinger and Associates, *The State of Asia*, p. 271.

1947 the Pridi forces were again in control, though by early 1946 very much divided; the Pibul group returned to power in November, 1947. Within the two large factions there were rivals involving a delicate political balance of personalities. For instance, Generals Phin Chunhaven, Sarit Thanarat, and Phao Sriyanond have been key figures in the Pibul camp. Constitutional alterations, of course, have accompanied the shifts of power, but popular participation in the coups is lacking.

Although changes of government by forceful means make headlines it should be stressed that personalities in Thailand are far more important than issues, that political parties have been really personal followings, that the people have been largely apathetic to developments in Bangkok, that the civil service continues in a routine way the day-to-day administration of the country, and that the monarchy, remaining popular, is an important consideration in the basic stability of the kingdom. Far more than usual public interest was shown in an election on February 26, 1957, for 160 seats in the first category of the National Assembly. The Seri Manangasila Party of Premier Pibul Songgram scored a moderate victory but opposition leaders raised charges of fraudulent voting. It has been asserted that the election marked a real awakening of the electorate. On September 16, Field Marshal Sarit staged a coup overthrowing the Premier. After an election in December the former made Lieutenant General Thanom Kitkhachon head of the government.

International politics has affected the political fortunes of men like Pridi and Pibul. Japan in her penetration in Thailand was able to take advantage of Thai animosity toward China and the Chinese minority in the kingdom and of the ambitions of certain Bangkok leaders to create a greater Thailand with the addition of territory inhabited by Thai peoples under foreign jurisdiction or even once under the sovereignty of the country. The Thai were not particularly fond of Japan, but some of them saw her as a possible source of strength against China and a possible means of forwarding the pan-Thai movement. Japan for her part was eager to weaken the Anglo-French position in Southeast Asia through Thai irredentism and to aggravate Thai hostility toward Chiang Kai-shek's China.

On June 12, 1940, Thailand signed nonaggression treaties with Great Britain and France in Bangkok and with Japan in Tokyo. The agreements reflected the traditional policy of Thailand in keeping peaceful relations with strong states in her area. The Franco-Thai treaty was never ratified, for the Bangkok government began to stress the need for boundary changes. For some time Thailand had wanted the deep-water channel of the Mekong as the boundary instead of the current one where all the islands in the river were French. On September 13, 1940, after the fall of France, Thailand sought from the Vichy government the retrocession of the French-held area on the west bank of the Mekong in Laos and of the Cambodian provinces of Sisophon, Siemreap, and Battambang. A few days later the Pibul government added an item to the effect that if France gave up sovereignty over Indochina she should cede Cambodia and Laos to Thailand. The Vichy regime opposed the suggested territorial cessions and sporadic hostilities between the French and the Thai broke out. The latter, however, were not strong enough to force the French to agree to the proposed boundary changes.

An ideal situation was created for the Japanese to intervene. Although they wanted to keep the French administration in Indochina as long as it coöperated with them they were also eager for strategic as well as economic reasons to bring Thailand into their orbit. Following considerable Nipponese pressure, the Vichy government indicated willingness on January 23, 1941, to accept Japanese mediation and to agree to an end of hostilities as from January 28. Negotiations between France and Thailand began in Tokyo on February 7. After an impasse developed Japan presented a compromise which Vichy accepted only under pressure exerted by both Nippon and Nazi Germany. The agreement was initialed on March 11 with the formal treaty arrangement concluded May 9. France ceded to Thailand the Laotian area on the west bank of the Mekong and about a third of Cambodia from the Mekong to Stung Treng, thence to the Tonle Sap and then southwest toward the Gulf of Siam. The boundary in the Mekong River would follow the main channel, although the islands of Khong and Khone would be under joint Thai-French administration. The ceded area would be demilitarized with equality of treatment for both the Thai and the Indochinese. France and Thailand, it should be noted, agreed in an exchange of letters with Japan to make no arrangement with a third power that might involve them in any collaboration against Japan, who guaranteed the settlement. The Nipponese occupation of southern Indochina in July greatly aroused the Bangkok government which requested arms from the United States and Great Britain. Little assistance was forthcoming, for the latter two powers had other uses for their matériel. Although it was clear that Japan planned to move into Thailand and take the Kra Isthmus in the event of a war against Great Britain, the Tokyo government was eager to let the British take the first step and be the technical aggressors. The United Kingdom in turn wanted a good defense line for the approaches to Malaya but was concerned about the reaction of the United States, which was not eager to be in the position of supporting any aggression by a colonial power in Southeast Asia. The Japanese attack on Pearl Harbor, December 7, drastically altered the situation.

The Nipponese Ambassador to Thailand was instructed to request the Foreign Minister at 10 P.M. on December 7 to open negotiations for a Tokyo-Bangkok alliance or for the peaceful passage of Japanese forces through the country. Premier Pibul Songgram was out of Bangkok at the time and the other ministers would not accept Japan's suggestions. They were told the Japanese forces would enter Thailand anyway the next morning. During the night, in fact, they began to land at Patani and Singora in the southern part of the country, meeting Thai resistance. Pibul rushed back to the capital, ordered an end to the Thai hostilities, and at 9 A.M. on December 8 made an agreement with Japan for the peaceful passage of Nipponese forces. Thailand, of course, would have preferred neutrality, but faced with overwhelming Japanese power, she bent like a reed in the wind.

A formal alliance was signed by Japan and Thailand on December 21 with a secret protocol wherein Tokyo agreed to help Bangkok get back territories lost to Britain, and Thailand undertook to assist Japan in her war against the United States and the United Kingdom. On January 25, 1942, Thailand declared war upon the two powers, an act so recognized by Great Britain but not by the United States. The Thai people in general were not sympathetic to the Japanese and were disturbed over the inhuman method of building the Thailand-Burma Railway. As economic conditions deteriorated through the effects of the war, Nippon became more and more disliked. The Japanese army in the kingdom issued Thai currency which impaired credit and encouraged inflation. Although various missions were exchanged between Tokyo and Bangkok and official relations were cordial between 1942 and 1944, Japan thought it in her best interests, as formally decided at an Imperial Conference on May 31, 1943, to turn over to Thailand the four Malay States taken by Great Britain in 1909—Kedah, Perlis, Kelantan, and Trengganu—and the two Shan States of

Kengtung and Mongpan. Thai forces, in fact, had participated in the invasion of the Shan States of Burma. A formal treaty for the transfer of the British territories in Malaya and Burma was signed on August 20, following a meeting the previous month in Bangkok of Premier Hideki Tojo of Japan and Premier Pibul. Under the terms of the pact Japanese administration would cease within 60 days from the signing of the treaty, the local boundaries of the areas concerned remaining.

The fall of Tojo on July 21, 1944, was reflected in Bangkok by the collapse three days later of the Pibul cabinet. Developments in the Pacific War were obviously adverse to the permanence of Japan's New Order in Greater East Asia. In Thailand the pro-Western group led by Pridi had been growing in strength. Pridi emerged in July as the only regent for the absent King in Switzerland, although Major Khuang Aphaiwongse headed the cabinet. Secret contacts with the United Nations were strengthened, and the Thai government with Allied aid was getting ready for a revolt to coincide with an anticipated invasion by the United Nations forces. Thus the surrender of Japan saw a pro-Allied government in power in Bangkok seeking to mitigate the effects of the previous Pibul regime.

The basic settlement Thailand as a sovereign state had to make with the victorious powers of the Second World War having special interests in her is comparable in international significance to the settlements made between the newly independent states in Southeast Asia and their former Western rulers. Thailand's role in the Second World War was not unlike that of Italy in a number of aspects. If Japan had not decided to surrender, it is even likely that a Thai government would have assisted in the expulsion of the Japanese from the kingdom and would have declared war on Nippon. A basic difference developed, however, between the British and the Americans on how to interpret the actions of the Pibul government and how to deal with the "Free Thai" movement led by Seni Pramoj, the Thai Minister to the United States. The British compared the respective positions of Denmark in Europe with reference to the Nazi occupation and of Thailand in Asia with reference to the Japanese. They observed that Thailand took the occasion to declare war and to make territorial gains. As a consequence of Thailand's declaration of war, Great Britain took the position that it would have to be legally terminated by the two powers. On the other hand, the United States ignored the declaration by the Pibul regime and recognized the "Free Thai" movement.

On August 16, 1945, the Regent of Thailand issued a proclamation, approved the same day by the National Assembly, declaring null and void the declaration of war on the United States and Great Britain. In the proclamation it was stated that Thailand has "no desire for the territories" in Burma and Malaya which Japan "entrusted" to her and "is ready to arrange for their delivery as soon as Great Britain is ready to take delivery thereof."[11] Absent from the proclamation was reference to the territory Thailand acquired from Indochina in 1941, for Thai officials were hopeful of keeping it, possibly by capitalizing on differences between the British and Americans on postwar policy in Southeast Asia. In September Thailand officially told Japan that the alliance of the two powers made in 1941 was terminated. This step was followed by the Thai denunciation of all the other political agreements made with Japan during the premiership of Pibul.

Early in September a Thai mission arrived at the South-East Asia Command headquarters under Admiral Lord Louis Mountbatten at Kandy, Ceylon, and received proposals for a military occupation with certain political provisions. Unfortunately the proposals were 21 in number leading to comparison with Japan's famous 21 Demands on China in 1915. The nature of the proposals was exaggerated in the press. Certain American officers at the South-East Asia Command supported the Thai in their apprehension over the situation and contributed to the concern indicated by the Department of State in Washington. Thailand accepted 6 points relative to military occupation but the other 15 were referred to Bangkok. Between September 7 and 13 British and Indian troops were flown into Thailand from Burma. Their chief assignment was to take responsibility for the surrendered Japanese and assist Allied prisoners of war and civilian internees.

Negotiations between Great Britain and Thailand led to the signing at Government House, Singapore, on January 1, 1946, of an "Agreement between the United Kingdom and India with Siam for the Termination of the State of War." During the negotiations the United States took a "deep interest" and informed Great Britain "in friendly communication" of its position on the proposed terms,

[11] Text in letter from Minister of Thailand to the Secretary of State, August 17, 1945, *The Department of State Bulletin*, Vol. XIII (August 19, 1945), p. 262.

being "pleased with the ready and cordial response" of the British government.[12] The Thai peace settlement also included an agreement between Australia and Thailand, signed April 3, 1946, to end the state of war between them, an agreement between France and Thailand, signed November 17, 1946, regulating their relations, notes exchanged between the Netherlands and Thailand, January 30, 1947, on diplomatic relations, and, it should be added, a treaty of amity between Nationalist China and Thailand signed on January 23, 1946.

In the peace agreement Great Britain and India signed with Thailand, a large number of the provisions amounted in effect to a restoration of the *status quo ante bellum.* Thai acquisition of territory in Malaya and Burma was declared null and void and compensation would be made for losses incurred as a consequence of the Thai occupation; British property including concessions and stocks of tin and teak would be restored with adequate compensation in case of damage or loss; trade with neighboring British areas would be reëstablished; British commercial and banking firms could resume business; payment of interest on loans and of pension arrears with interest would be made; a consular convention would be negotiated with Great Britain and new treaties of commerce and navigation with Great Britain and India. Provisions were included regarding civil aviation and war graves. The Thai application for membership in the United Nations would be supported by Great Britain and India. Thailand, recognizing as indicated by the recent war her own importance to the defense of India, Burma, Indochina, and Malaya and to the security of the Southwest Pacific and Indian Ocean, agreed to coöperate fully in all security agreements approved by the United Nations or the Security Council pertinent to her and especially in such agreements as may relate to the countries or areas mentioned.

Certain other provisions of the settlement were more controversial. Thailand agreed under Article 7 that "no canal linking the Indian Ocean and the Gulf of Siam shall be cut across Siamese territory without the prior concurrence of the Government of the United Kingdom."[13] The article indicates British concern over the possible construction of a canal across the Kra Isthmus, located in Thai territory between Burma and Malaya and only about 35 miles

[12] Resumption of Relations with Siam, *The Department of State Bulletin,* Vol. XIV (January 6 and 13, 1946), p. 5.

[13] Agreement between the United Kingdom and India with Siam, *British and Foreign State Papers, 1946,* Vol. 146, p. 457.

at its narrowest point. Such a canal had in previous years aroused German, French, Russian, and Japanese interests, for it would provide a more direct route and by-pass Singapore. Although a Kra canal would have a number of commercial disadvantages in terms of routing, it would possess strategic value. In an Anglo-Thai agreement of 1909 Thailand had been obligated not to grant any concession of strategic significance to any third power on the west coast of the Gulf of Siam. The Anglo-Thai pact of January 1, 1946, provided that former treaties between Britain and Thailand or India and Thailand were revived in so far as the British and Indian governments so desired.

The treaty provisions regarding rice were much more controversial. Thailand would prohibit the export of rice, rubber, tin, and teak until a time not later than September 1, 1947, except in accordance with the suggestions of the Combined Boards in Washington or in the case of rice a special organization to be set up; she would make available to an organization that would be British designated an amount of rice in Bangkok, free of cost, equal to the accumulated surplus in the country at the date of the treaty, the maximum being 1½ million tons, or, if agreed, its equivalent in loonzain or paddy; she would until a date not later than September 1, 1947, make available at an agreed price to the same organization all Thai-produced rice beyond that required for her own domestic needs. It was planned that the reparations in free rice, about equal to the total export from Thailand for an average year, would not become British government property but would be made available to an international organization for allocation to deficit countries. Desperate shortages in rice existed at the time in India, certain parts of Southeast Asia, and China.

Anglo-American differences over certain aspects of the rice provisions were reflected in exaggerated press accounts when the final text of the treaty became known. Events soon indicated that all the rice clauses could not be carried out. The Thai government did not own the rice and the Chinese who controlled the trade opposed the grant of 1½ million tons to the world pool. Great profits could be made by smuggling the product to Hong Kong or Malaya. In early May it was announced that a revised agreement providing for Anglo-American-Thai participation had been negotiated by Lord Killearn, British Special Commissioner in South-East Asia. Britain would buy from Thailand 1,200,000 tons of rice at a basic price of £12. 14s. per ton to be delivered within a time period of 12 months. A premium of £3 a ton would be paid on deliveries up to the end of May and of £1. 10s. a ton between that date and June 15, 1946. Thailand would make good without charge any deficiency if deliveries during the 12 months specified fell below the stated amount. The Combined Food Board in Washington would allocate the rice. Since a marked disparity in the price of rice existed when compared with that in Indochina and Burma, illegal channels continued to attract the Thai product. On December 24 another agreement was made raising the price to £24 a ton and extending the basic time aspect of the previous one to August 31, 1947.

Problems of the war affecting the relations of Great Britain and Thailand were further handled in October, 1946, when it was announced that the Bangkok government had bought for £1¼ million the part of the Thai-Burmese railroad in Thai territory. Britain planned to use the proceeds for the purpose of compensating the owners of the rails and rolling stock, taken by the Japanese from Indonesia, Burma, and Malaya, and of crediting the remainder to reparations from Japan. An exchange of notes between Great Britain and Thailand on January 6 and May 8, 1947, considered the question of settling British claims and other matters arising from the war. A British Commonwealth-Siamese Claims Committee, consisting of three members from the United Kingdom, Australia, and India and three from Thailand, would be set up. A further exchange of notes, May 4 and November 8, 1950, and January 3, 1951, provided for a settlement of the outstanding Commonwealth war claims. Thailand agreed to pay Great Britain, Australia, and India the lump sum of £5,224,220.

On January 14, 1954, an exchange of notes terminated the Agreement of January 1, 1946, as regards Great Britain and Thailand, certain provisions having already been carried out, others having lapsed, and a few being brought up to date in the current exchange. It was asserted that "the relations of peace and friendship established between the two countries by the said Agreement shall be maintained indefinitely" and "such termination shall not affect the validity of anything done under or in accordance with the said Agreement including any treaty or other international instrument revived, continued in force or to which the Government of Thailand has become a party in accordance therewith or any financial obligation of a continuing nature or which has already accrued thereunder."[14] The other two specific provisions dealt with the

[14] Exchange of Notes, Thailand and Great Britain, *Treaty Series*, No. 19 (1954), Cmd. 9090.

entering into negotiations for a consular convention and the making of an agreement on war graves.

In the years immediately after the Second World War, Britain's influence in Thailand, though reduced from the prewar period, was the strongest of any foreign power. She was the best customer and a neighbor in Malaya, although Burma's independence ended one British boundary. Pibul's return to the premiership in April, 1948, at first disturbed Great Britain, but his strong anti-Communist stand and his coöperation following the Communist rising in Malaya stood him in good stead. As American influence grew in Bangkok after Pibul Songgram's return, the British lost their leading position.

The "Final Peace Agreement" with Australia was another agreement Thailand made with a member of the British Commonwealth. Australia had declared war on the Kingdom, March 2, 1942. Prior to the Second World War the Australians had extensive tin mining interests in the country. Under the terms of the peace agreement Thailand would restore Australian interests and property with compensation in the case of damage; a consular agreement and a treaty of commerce and navigation, upon the request of the Canberra government, would be negotiated; Australian mining and commercial concerns would be allowed to resume; and arrangements would be made, acceptable to Australia, for the care of her war graves in Thailand. Provisions regarding the Kra Isthmus and reparations in rice were absent but Article 9 asserted that the "Government of Siam, recognising the importance of Siam to the defence, security and well-being of South-East Asia, the Indian Ocean area, and Australia, New Zealand and the South-West Pacific area generally, agree to participate, if requested to do so, in measures of regional political and economic coöperation consistant with the principles of the United Nations Charter and relating to the countries or areas specified."[15] Among other provisions were one relating to Australian civil air services and one to the continuance of prewar treaties. On October 30, 1947, an agreement provided for specific Thai compensation to the Australian and British tin interests in the country.

Australian relations with Thailand since the peace agreement have been cordial. Thailand has received assistance under the Colombo Plan which she joined in October, 1954. The two states have become formal allies under the Manila Pact, Australia being well

[15] Final Peace Agreement, Australia and Siam, *British and Foreign State Papers, 1946*, Vol. 146, p. 555.

aware of the strategic importance of Thailand in peninsular Southeast Asia. In June, 1955, Australian naval and air units visited the kingdom; the status of the respective missions has been raised from that of legation to embassy. The viewpoints of the Canberra and Bangkok governments have been similar in their evaluation of international Communism in their part of the world.

An exchange of notes between the Thai Foreign Minister and the Head of the Netherlands Diplomatic Mission at Bangkok provided for the resumption of diplomatic intercourse under certain terms relating, *inter alia,* to the care of war graves, civil air transportation, claims, and the continuance of certain prewar treaties. The independence of Indonesia, removing the main base of Dutch influence in Asia, has weakened the importance of the Netherlands to Thailand.

Several months ensued after the surrender of Japan before the conclusion of a basic agreement on the issues between Thailand and France. Although the Vichy government had recognized the cession of the Laotian territories west of the Mekong and the northwestern part of Cambodia, the Free French had never agreed to its validity. France was eager to restore her prestige in Indochina and in Asia and to wipe out a humiliating reminder of the Vichy regime. Thailand maintained that the agreement of May 9, 1941, had been concluded with a legal French government and that a declaration of war had not been made. Negotiations between the Bangkok and Paris governments were begun but they led to stormy discussion. By the end of April, 1946, border incidents aroused further animosity on both sides. Continuing in intensity, the incidents were often associated with the fighting between the French and Indochinese guerrillas. France, for instance, accused the Thai of allowing Indochinese rebels to use Thai bases to plunder in Laos and of helping the Lao Issarak (Free Laotian) movement in various ways.

On May 31 the Bangkok government submitted a memorandum to the Secretary-General of the United Nations describing the deterioration of relations between France and Thailand, classifying various incidents, and officially bringing the situation to the knowledge of the United Nations. The complaint, however, was not placed on the agenda of the Security Council. In early August France proposed that the territorial dispute be submitted to the International Court of Justice at The Hague, and Thailand accepted in principle the suggestion. However, a series of incidents in Cambodia contributed to further deterioration in relations. Thailand's formal application for membership in the United Nations, filed on August 3, led to a statement by the French representative in the Committee on the Admission of New Members that pending a settlement of the border question France continued to consider herself *de facto* at war with Thailand. The Soviet Union also, it should be recalled, came to oppose Thai membership, asserting that the two states had no diplomatic relations. On August 28 Thailand requested that the Security Council's consideration of her application for membership be adjourned until the territorial dispute between her and France was settled.

In view of the strong French position on the matter, of Anglo-American sympathy for France, and of failure to gain immediate admission into the United Nations, Thailand decided to give in on the boundary controversy. In October, after informal discussions between French and Thai representatives in Washington, the two governments reached agreement on a series of proposals whereby Thailand would recognize the nullity of her agreement of May 9, 1941, and would return the areas under consideration to France who would transfer them to Laos and Cambodia, the state of war would end and diplomatic relations be resumed, and a Conciliation Commission would be appointed as provided by the Franco-Siamese treaty of December 7, 1937, to examine the points of dispute and enable Thailand to present her case for a revision of the frontier on economic, geographical, and ethnic grounds. Thailand's agreement to these proposals was a serious blow to the cabinet of the Premier, Admiral Thamrong Nawasawat. The Pridi forces had already been weakened by the mysterious death of King Ananda on June 9. Pibul Songgram was able to capitalize on the political and economic discontent. Brought to trial under a War Crimes Act but discharged by the High Court in March on the basis that an act could not be used retroactively, Pibul was becoming increasingly influential as time passed.

The Franco-Thai agreement, finally signed in Washington on November 17, followed the lines of the October proposals. The disputed areas in Laos and Cambodia would be transferred to France; diplomatic relations would be resumed; Thailand would withdraw her complaint to the United Nations, and France would not oppose her admission; a Conciliation Commission would examine the claims of both parties for a frontier revision and, if the latter could not agree on the compensation for previous damage, would pass on the subject. According to the terms of the agreement, the Thai evacuation of the territory was carried out. On November 28 France and Thailand informed the Secretary-General of the United Nations that the dispute between them had been settled by negotiations, and 14 days later the Security Council unanimously recommended the admission of Thailand.

The International Commission of Conciliation met in Washington on May 5, 1947, to consider the Indochinese-Thai boundary and to make recommendations. The Commission consisted of five members, one Thai, one Frenchman, and three others, a Peruvian and an Englishman with an American as chairman. On June 27 its report supported none of the Thai claims to territory, although a number of recommendations were made to modify the existing situation. The boundary where the Mekong was the line should be redrawn to give Thailand areas of access to the deep-water channel; the work of the existing mixed commission for the Mekong River should be extended; steps should be taken to ensure a regular fish supply for the Thai market, the Tonle Sap in Cambodia being an important source of food for Thailand; and the Bangkok and Paris governments should negotiate to establish in the capital of Thailand an International Consultative Commission to consider common problems like public health, irrigation, and fisheries.

The report as a whole was not well received in Thailand. For a while it was uncertain whether or not the government would accept the recommendations. But in May, 1948, Pibul Songgram, who had become premier the previous month after the November coup of his forces, stated that Thailand accepted the French territorial claims and considered the matter closed. France, it should be noted, had been the first power to recognize the new government of Premier Pibul. Nevertheless, considerable Thai resentment has remained against France. Later the kingdom paid the equivalent of $518,000 as compensation for damages during the 1940-1941 conflict.

As provided in the 1946 agreement, the Franco-Thai treaty of friendship, commerce, and navigation of December 7, 1937, and the commercial and customs agreement concerning Indochina of December 9 were put back into force. With the war against the French in Indochina increasing in tempo, relations between France and Thailand merged into the overall question of the latter's basic policy in the global cold war. By September 8, 1954, the two states became allies under the Manila Pact.

As regards Japan, Thailand was also faced with a number of postwar problems. In an exchange of notes with Great Britain on May 8, 1947, Thailand, after observing that normal relations had been restored, would in view of her policy "to give every possible coöperation and assistance to the Allies" continue to hold Japanese and other enemy property for Allied disposal after reasonable expense deductions, and was agreeable to "the apprehension and trial of persons accused of war crimes or notable for affording active assistance to Japan."[16] Actually there was now little anti-Japanese sentiment among the Thai.

Given the wartime alliance, the restoration of diplomatic relations between Tokyo and Bangkok depended upon the Allied peace settlement with Japan. Obviously Thailand was not a participant at the Japanese Peace Conference at San Francisco. Nevertheless, trade developed between the two countries, a Thai trade representative being stationed in Tokyo and a Japanese Government Overseas Agency set up in Bangkok. In 1950, for instance, 90 percent of Japanese imports from Thailand consisted of rice with a value of $4,350,000 while Japanese exports, made up of plant equipment, textiles, and construction materials, amounted to $4,260,000. In October, 1951, an unofficial Japanese trade mission arrived in Thailand; in the following September a trade agreement was signed.

After the Japanese peace treaty approved at San Francisco came into effect Japan and Thailand restored diplomatic relations. On April 6, 1955, a cultural agreement was signed by the two powers. Three days later it was announced that they had reached an accord on Thai claims against Japan relative to the issue of yen military script to Japanese occupation forces in the country during the war. Thailand had claimed the equivalent of $375 million as compensation. In the agreement the figure was set at $41,666,666 of which Japan would pay the equivalent of $15 million in pounds sterling over a period of five years and supply Thailand services, credits and capital goods up to 9,600,000,000 yen or about $26,666,666. In April, 1956, an agreement restored trade to a normal basis from an open account. Rice would still temporarily be controlled by Thailand until her deficit to Japan was liquidated. In late May, 1957, Prime Minister Kishi arrived in Bangkok for a visit.

[16] Exchange of Notes, Siam and Great Britain, *British and Foreign State Papers, 1947*, Part 1, Vol. 147, p. 1010.

The independence of Burma, Laos, Cambodia, and the Federation of Malaya created a new framework of international relations for Thailand wherein decisions in foreign policy affecting her were no longer made in London and Paris but in Rangoon, Vientiane, Phnom Penh, and Kuala Lumpur. As the four neighbors received independence at different times, Thailand had a chance to adjust somewhat gradually to the changes.

The transition to sovereignty of Laos, Cambodia, and Burma was accompanied or followed by serious international problems affecting the future of the kingdom. Even in Malaya, the Communist uprising raised grave questions in relations with Thailand. Indeed, it is remarkable that the latter, though literally surrounded by trouble, was able to remain at peace in Southeast Asia. Having an area of a little over 200,000 square miles, each side being roughly some 400 miles, with a "tail" of some 500 miles in length extending into the Malay Peninsula, while at the same time possessing about 1200 miles of coast on the Gulf of Siam and about 300 on the Indian Ocean, the Kingdom of Thailand by its very location is open to turmoil. However, loyalty to the monarchy, prosperity based largely on rice, and faith in Buddhism whose leaders in Thailand kept out of politics have contributed to the stability of the kingdom.

The renewal of relations between Burma and Thailand as sovereign states did not lead to the close ties especially desirable where two neighbors share a long frontier of almost a thousand miles. The Thai have not forgotten the sacking of Ayuthia by the Burmese in 1767; in fact, too much stress has been placed on the incident in Thai plays and songs. Trade and travel between Burma and Thailand have always been of minor importance. Fortunately the boundary between the two countries was well established during the period of Britain's rule in Burma. The latter, of course, had not appreciated the Thai acquisition of the two Shan States during the Second World War but, as already indicated, these areas were promptly restored after the conflict. The greatest bone of contention in the postwar period has been the conviction in Rangoon that Thailand was assisting the Kuomintang forces in Burma in various ways. It was believed that if Thailand had maintained the strictest neutrality, the Kuomintang guerrillas would not have grown in strength. The Thai closing of the frontier in early 1953 worked hardship in the eastern Shan State. Debates in the forum of the United Nations indicated the animosity existing on both sides over the accusations. The activity of the guerrillas in the opium trade also raised delicate points.

In 1954 relations between the two neighboring states began to improve as a consequence of Thai coöperation along the border and assistance in the evacuation of the Chinese troops. In September plans were made to open five places along the frontier to improve trade and communications, and in November it was announced that an extradition treaty would be concluded. The Pibul government has also sought to improve relations by trying to divert attention from Ayuthia, the symbol of the past. Various good-will missions have been exchanged. U Nu himself made an official visit to Thailand in March, 1955, and discussions took place on ways of improving economic, cultural, and other relations. During the visit considerable stress was placed on the religious affinity of the peoples of Burma and Thailand. U Nu brought some banyan saplings from a famous Buddhist center in Ceylon, and although the saplings were not planted as planned at the ruins of Ayuthia by the premiers of the two Buddhist countries as a gesture of burying past hostility and cementing friendship, U Nu and Pibul did plant them in the grounds of a temple on the outskirts of Bangkok. The Premier of Burma visited Ayuthia in an unofficial capacity and gave the equivalent of $20,000 toward its rebuilding as a national monument.

Numerous incidents from 1953 to 1955 associated with Burma's military campaign against the Kuomintang forces were not allowed to destroy the possibility of developing friendship between the two neighbors. For instance, when U Nu was coming home from his visit to the United States, Pibul met him at the airport in Bangkok on July 23, 1955, and returned to him a check tendered by the Rangoon government in compensation for the accidental bombing of Thailand during operations against the Chinese Nationalist guerrillas. Upon receiving the check, U Nu handed it to the Burmese Ambassador in Bangkok to be used in performing works of merit. Mention should be made that Thailand is faced with the problem of refugee camps on her soil for Chinese Kuomintang guerrillas forced across the border.

In a significant communiqué issued on October 5 it was stated that the "Government of the Union of Burma . . . in view of the close and friendly relations so happily existing between the Union of Burma and Thailand, have now decided to waive all war claims against Thailand."[17] The claims had arisen from the latter's occupation of Kengtung and Mongpan, and Burma as an independent state had inherited the claims from Britain. The Rangoon regime had not desired to participate in the lump sum settlement agreed upon by the Thai cabinet and British Commonwealth governments concerned.

In December Premier Pibul Songgram paid a return visit to Burma. Representing as he did a country that had signed the Southeast Asia Collective Defense Treaty, Pibul would certainly present a contrast in Rangoon to Khrushchev and Bulganin who had recently visited the Union. At the same time Pibul was faced with a widespread conviction in Rangoon that he had tied himself too closely to the West and was too much under American influence. Nevertheless, the visit further strengthened the ties between the two neighbors. In fact, U Nu asserted in a speech on July 19, 1956, that "the relations between Thailand and Burma had never, in the course of our long histories, been as good as they are now."[18] In the summer Thailand showed considerable sympathy for her neighbor in its border difficulties with Communist China. On October 15 a treaty of friendship was signed in Bangkok dealing with diplomatic and consular representation, the treatment of the nationals of each in the territory of the other, and the peaceful settlement of controversies. The signatories would conclude as soon as possible treaties on extradition, consular rights and privileges, cultural relations, and commerce and navigation.

The genesis of present-day Thai relations with Laos and Cambodia as sovereign states is found in the emergence of the latter areas from French colonial rule. As a result, the Mekong diplomacy of Thailand reflects a new orientation. In general the Thai were sympathetic to the nationalist aspirations of the Cambodians, Laotians, and Vietnamese against the French. Premier Pibul asserted in July, 1948, that his country considered the Vietnamese conflict a national movement for independence and not a Communist revolt. A Viet Minh agency operated in Bangkok and asylum was given Vietnamese refugees. The Khmer Issarak (Free Cambodian) and Lao Issarak movements received considerable support, especially before the November, 1947, coup. Arms and supplies, it is clear, were finding their way to Indochina from Thailand.

[17] Text of Joint Communiqué, October 5, 1955, *Burma Weekly Bulletin*, New Series, Vol. 4 (October 13, 1955), p. 210.

[18] Speech of U Nu, July 19, 1956, *Burma Weekly Bulletin*, New Series, Vol. 5 (July 26, 1956), p. 115.

The policy of the Pibul government toward the war in Indochina was altered as a result of a number of factors. The fall of the mainland of China to the Communists, the increased strength of the Viet Minh position as a result, the threat to the security of Thailand of a hostile Vietnam allied with China, and the growing influence of the United States contributed to the change in policy. Pibul was concerned over any separatist movement in the Northeast of the kingdom, and he realized that the Vietnamese were an active and industrious people who might under favorable circumstances become the most powerful in peninsular Southeast Asia.

On February 28, 1950, Thailand recognized the Associated States of Indochina—Vietnam, Cambodia, and Laos—a step that precipitated the resignation of the foreign minister, Pote Sarasin. Also early in 1950 the Viet Minh was requested to close its agency in Bangkok. Stronger efforts were made to stop the flow of military and medical supplies to the forces fighting the French in Indochina. Nevertheless, Thailand would not coöperate at the border with France the way she did with Britain in the south. The Thai Foreign Minister in April observed that the war in Indochina was a struggle for independence.

The growing concern of Thailand over Communist inroads in Indochina was marked in 1953 and 1954. In April, 1953, Viet Minh forces of Ho Chi Minh invaded Laos and quickly approached within 12 miles of the royal capital of Luang Prabang, about 60 miles from the Thai border. A "Free Laotian Government" was established, the Pathet Lao becoming entrenched. The Peking radio meanwhile accused Pibul of sending five combat companies to help the French in the Kingdom of Laos. Thailand closed her frontier with the country and sent police and military reinforcements to the border region. In May Pibul toured the Northeast, a backward area of Thailand, the greater number of whose inhabitants are akin to the Lao. Tiang Sirikhand, an old associate of Pridi, had fled Bangkok in December, 1952, and it was feared that he might be in northern Laos with the Pathet Lao forces trying to establish a Pan-Lao Movement. In fact, the following May a number of people were arrested on the charge that they were trying to form an independent Lao state from Thai territory. With the retreat of the Viet Minh from Laos at the beginning of the heavy monsoon rains in 1953 the tension eased for a few months.

In June Thailand was faced with another problem arising from her eastern neighbors. King Norodom Sihanouk of Cambodia arrived in Bangkok as an exile of his own volition. He was seeking to put pressure on France in the Franco-Cambodian negotiations relative to the freedom of his country. Hoping that Thailand would raise the question in the United Nations, the King presented a serious diplomatic problem for the Bangkok government. The Pibul cabinet agreed on June 16 that the Cambodian monarch might stay in Bangkok as a political refugee but he was not to establish a government-in-exile or take action that would harm Thai-French relations. The return of the King to his country on June 20 ended the problem.

Toward the close of December the Viet Minh forces again invaded Laos, this time taking Thakket, a town on the central Mekong across from the Thai frontier. The Bangkok government met the situation by placing nine border provinces in a state of emergency and rushing reinforcements. In early 1954 the Viet Minh forces again approached Luang Prabang and in April they invaded Cambodia.

Although Thailand had previously considered placing the situation occasioned by Viet Minh aggression before the United Nations, she did not take the step until May 29, 1954. On that date the acting Thai permanent representative to the United Nations sent a letter to the President of the Security Council, referring to Article 34 and Article 35, Paragraph 1, of the Charter and asking for a meeting of the Security Council with Thailand as a participant. He called the attention of the Council to a situation which represented, in the eyes of his country, a threat to its security, the continuation of which was likely to endanger the preservation of international peace. He noted the extensive fighting that had repeatedly occurred near Thailand's border and the possibility of incursions in her territory. Thailand wanted the Council to provide for direct observation under the Peace Observation Commission.

The subject was discussed at a meeting of the Security Council on June 3. The Soviet Union opposed placing the topic on the agenda, for she maintained that the Indochina question was being considered at the Geneva Conference of Foreign Ministers and discussion in the Security Council might hinder a solution there. The Soviet representative intimated that the United States working through Thailand was trying to torpedo the Geneva Conference. France, who in the past had been generally opposed to any aspect of the Indochina question being considered by the United Nations, supported Thai fears as legitimate. The Paris government believed

Thailand was not seeking to put the entire Indochina question before the Security Council but was only trying to have international observation in her country. The Thai item was placed on the agenda by a vote of 10 to 1 and the representative of Bangkok took his place at the Council table. After the Thai envoy presented the case of his government, the Lebanese representative proposed that the Council adjourn to ponder the matter.

On June 16 the Security Council met again at the request of Thailand. The Bangkok representative noted that no encouraging developments had occurred in Geneva. He submitted a draft resolution which referred to General Assembly Resolution 377(V) (Uniting for Peace), Part A, Section B, establishing the Peace Observation Commission, and asked that the Council request this body to set up a subcommission of three to five members to send observers to Thailand, the members themselves visiting if necessary, and to make reports and recommendations as thought essential to the Peace Observation Commission and the Security Council. If the subcommission thought it could not carry out its task well without visiting Thailand's neighbors, it should report to the Commission or the Security Council for necessary instructions. The USSR opposed the draft resolution of Thailand, asserting that the kingdom was not threatened and that the proposal represented an American effort to aggravate the Indochina conflict and get ready for military intervention under the guise of the United Nations as was done in Korea. The majority of the members of the Security Council were in favor of the Thai proposal.

At the request of the United States the draft resolution was put to a vote on June 18. The Soviet Union opposed it, Lebanon abstained, but all the others—the United Kingdom, France, China, the United States, Colombia, Denmark, Brazil, New Zealand, and Turkey—favored it. The Soviet veto prevented its adoption.

On July 7 the Thai Minister of Foreign Affairs sent a letter to the United Nations Secretary-General. As the Security Council had rejected the Thai resolution, the kingdom now wanted the matter, "Request of Thailand for observation under the Peace Observation Commission," placed on the agenda of the General Assembly. The eighth session of the Assembly was, in fact, formally in being and could be reconvened. In view of the current developments on the Indochina problem, however, Thailand would later communicate with the Secretary-General about the matter of finding out if the majority of the United Nations members favored the reconvening of the session. In an explanatory memorandum, Thailand referred to the "hostile foreign forces" that had invaded Cambodia and Laos. "These foreign interventions," the memorandum read, "which have received and are receiving material and political support from outside of Indo-China are designed to overthrow the legal Governments of Laos and Cambodia and to establish Vietminh supremacy in those countries. At the same time, the Vietminh regime and its foreign associates have stepped up their propaganda campaign against Thailand by making serious and false charges against it, while urging within Thailand itself those elements which are subservient to them to undertake and intensify subversive activities which are directly related to the war which is being fought on Thailand's eastern and north-eastern frontiers."[19]

On August 20 the Foreign Minister of Thailand informed the Secretary-General that his government had decided not to press for a resumed session of the Assembly. Thailand was clearly waiting to see how the Geneva settlement on Indochina of July 20 and 21 worked out. In the general debate of the ninth General Assembly, the Thai delegate on September 28 traced Bangkok's efforts in the United Nations during the current year, hoped that the armistice agreements on Indochina would "function smoothly," and urged the admission of Laos and Cambodia into the world organization. He indicated his country's belief that "preparations are being made for large-scale Communist infiltrations from Yunnan through Viet-Minh into Thailand" in order to subvert the government.[20] In line with her concern over developments in Laos and Cambodia, which she believed needed constant watching, Thailand was glad to include Cambodia, Laos, and the territory under the "free Vietnamese Government" in the treaty area of the Manila Pact. Prince Wan Waithayakon stated at Manila on September 6 that "they deserve to be protected on their own merits and, as a representative of Thailand, I should also say, as neighbours to my country."[21] In June, 1957, a special mission from Bangkok arrived in Saigon to discuss common problems and a proposed friendship treaty between the two states. President Ngo Dinh Diem visited Bangkok in August.

[19] A/2665. Letter of July 7, 1954, from Foreign Minister of Thailand to Secretary-General.

[20] United Nations, General Assembly, Ninth Session, *Official Records,* 481st Plenary Meeting, September 28, 1954, p. 100.

[21] Speech of Prince Wan, *The Signing of the Southeast Asia Collective Defense Treaty, the Protocol to the Southeast Asia Collective Defense Treaty and the Pacific Charter,* p. 37.

Thailand has been especially concerned over the nearly 50,000 Vietnamese who are refugees living on her side of the Mekong across from Laos. It is estimated that 30,000 to 50,000 more Vietnamese are residing elsewhere in the kingdom. During and since the Second World War the refugees had fled from Indochina and a very large number of them were sympathizers of the Viet Minh. They were active in smuggling supplies and in giving political support to Ho Chi Minh. The Thai government was increasingly concerned about them as the forces of the Viet Minh approached at times the frontiers of the kingdom. During the first attack by Ho Chi Minh on Laos the Vietnamese were registered, and some 1500 of them were transported away from the troubled area. Later a number were arrested on charges of spying and trying to start a revolt. Although the legation of Vietnam in Bangkok offered to repatriate the Vietnamese who wanted to return home, negotiations between the Saigon and Bangkok governments dragged and the subject caused some hard feeling. Most of the refugees in Thailand did not desire to move and if they had to leave they wanted to go to the Viet Minh area. The Bangkok government did not have diplomatic relations with the Democratic Republic of Vietnam, but the subject of the refugees was discussed informally by Thai and Viet Minh representatives at the Bandung Conference. For a while it looked as though a settlement between the Thai and North Vietnamese governments could be worked out to evacuate the refugees. The Ho Chi Minh regime would like to win Thai recognition through negotiations on them. By the summer of 1957 about 200 families had been repatriated to South Vietnam.

Meanwhile Thailand had been taking active steps to develop an entente with her eastern neighbors of Cambodia and Laos. In January, 1954, a Thai diplomat in Phnom Penh had suggested as a *ballon d'essai* a Buddhist anti-Communist bloc of the three states. Cambodia and Laos did not want at the time to join any bloc without France, and the latter did not favor any steps that might weaken the French Union. Basically Thailand's Mekong diplomacy directed at such an entente had a foundation not only on religious and cultural but also on economic and political grounds. Bangkok is the center for Cambodian and Laotian Buddhists, the Indianized peoples of the three countries standing in contrast to the Sinicized Vietnamese. Thailand provides good potential outlets to the sea for Cambodian and Laotian commerce especially from western Cambodia and northern Laos. Dependency upon Vietnam as regards the outlet of the Mekong and land transportation eastward to the South China Sea could be reduced by close economic ties with Thailand. Politically the Cambodians and Laotians against this background might prefer, if a decision had to be made, to tie themselves to Thailand in the west rather than to Vietnam in the east.

With Laos Thailand had even greater advantages, for ethnical and linguistic ties can be added. Moreover, the Laotians had not resented in the way the Cambodians did the Thai occupation of a part of their territory from 1941 to 1946. Nor did the Thai find in the Laotian territory the economic assets of the Cambodian. Also in the case of Laos there are no prospects in the future of developing a sea port of her own, for the kingdom, unlike Cambodia, is landlocked.

In 1954 a number of developments gave concrete evidence of the coöperation of Thailand with Laos and Cambodia. The previous December Thailand had turned over 2000 rifles to Cambodia, and a Laotian good-will mission had been warmly received in Bangkok. In March, 1954, it was indicated that Thailand was considering the joint development of the Mekong River in terms of communication, irrigation, and hydroelectrical matters, and that, if invited, she was willing to send agricultural, forestry, and fisheries experts to Laos and Cambodia. In the same month a Thai mission to coördinate rail services between Cambodia and Thailand arrived in Phnom Penh. In March and April Thai financial concerns showed their interest in Cambodia through new banking facilities. In the latter month Thailand indicated that she was willing to allow Laotian and Cambodian imports and exports to pass through the port of Bangkok without transit charges. Cambodian and Laotian nationals could now enter Thailand without passports. Aviation service between Vientiane and Bangkok was approved in May by the Thai cabinet. Through raising late in the month at the United Nations the question of observers in Thailand under the Peace Observation Commission, the Bangkok government was showing further sympathy for its eastern neighbors. And in November, after the July settlement on Indochina, Thailand opened her frontiers with Laos and Cambodia primarily to encourage trade. In December King Norodom Sihanouk with his foreign and defense ministers paid an official visit to Bangkok.

In 1955 the entente among the three states was further developed. In February the Laotian Premier made a good-will visit to Thailand, returning a recent Thai mission of good will to Laos.

Common problems were discussed, for Communist inroads in Laos, especially in the provinces of Phong Saly and Sam Neua were a source of worry to Bangkok. It was later announced that a number of Laotian officers would go to Thailand for training in modern warfare. By the end of the year about 200 Laotian police were being trained in the neighboring country. On April 22, railroad service between Thailand and Cambodia was reopened. The Thai foreign minister indicated in Singapore April 28 after the Bandung Conference that he was not worried by the neutralist policy expressed there by Laos and Cambodia. He observed that relations with the two neighbors were "extremely cordial." On July 8 a provisional customs agreement was signed with Laos and 12 days later the Laotian Crown Prince, Premier, and foreign minister arrived in Bangkok.

Under the terms of the goods-in-transit agreement, effective November 1, between Thailand and Laos, such items could now reach Vientiane duty free through the port of Bangkok and vice versa. A later supplement was made to the agreement. It has been estimated that the cost of shipping bulk goods via Thailand was \$20 to \$25 per ton as compared with \$100 to \$150 per ton from Saigon to Vientiane. With American economic aid the Bangkok-Nakhon Ratchasima-Udon Thani railroad has been extended to Nong Khai on the Mekong across from Vientiane. Further American assistance has made possible ferry ramps on both sides of the river and the development of a short road thence to Vientiane. The expansion of transportation facilities in Thailand's Northeast not only provides an outlet for northern Laos but also strengthens the position of the Bangkok government in an area where Communists could take advantage of unfavorable economic conditions. In July, 1956, a Thai good-will mission in Vientiane discussed questions of transit and transport. It was agreed in principle to build a bridge across the Mekong River near Vientiane.

Cambodia's effort with French and American assistance to develop a port at Kompong Som on the Gulf of Siam and a highway thence to Phnom Penh is preferred by her nationalists to the Mekong route via South Vietnam or the railway to Bangkok. The Phnom Penh-Kompong Som route of about 125 miles, if fully utilized, would weaken Cambodia's interest in an outlet through Bangkok although the western provinces of the nation might still profit.

In early 1956, relations between Phnom Penh and Bangkok

were impaired by a number of factors. Cambodians were accused by Thai and vice versa of causing border incidents; a particular one at Preah Vihear aroused considerable feeling, both parties claiming the disputed area. Cambodia has been urging a boundary rectification in her favor with Thailand; the latter has been willing to establish a joint commission to take up the matter. The northern boundary, it should be noted, is not well defined. In March Thailand considered closing her frontier with Cambodia in protest against the Phnom Penh government, but in April Prime Minister Pibul Songgram offered close economic coöperation with the Cambodians in an effort to better the situation. Relations between the two neighbors improved but they did not become intimate. Agreement in general was reached in May for Cambodia to have free transit through Thailand as in the case of Laos; control patrols along the boundary would be established; and special committees would be created to decide on the possession of Preah Vihear. So far, it is fortunate, the 180,000 Cambodians in Thailand have raised no serious problems.

News of the settlement in Laos late in 1957 between the Royal Government and the Pathet Lao was received in Bangkok with some anxiety. The further orientation of Laos into the neutralist camp was deplored, but it was thought that the settlement might be hard to carry out. The economic ties between Thailand and Laos remained, although the transit arrangement was slow in being effectively implemented. Good-will missions continued to be exchanged, and practical coöperation was shown in a malaria control program. At the same time Thai officials needed to exercise care in their relations with the Laotians lest the latter become suspicious of possible intervention on the part of their influential neighbors.

With the Federation of Malaya to the south another set of problems arises for Thailand. Involved are a Malay minority of 600,000 in the southern part of the Buddhist kingdom, chiefly in the four provinces of Pattani, Narathiwart, Satun, and Yala, and the Thai interest in the Malay States of Kedah, Perlis, Trengganu, and Kelantan in the Federation. In Kedah, it might be added, dwell some 15,000 Thai Buddhists. The Communist uprising in Malaya has further complicated relations between the Bangkok and the Kuala Lumpur governments.

Thai authority had not been completely established in the four southern provinces until 1902 and differences in race as well as religion separated the Malay Moslem minority from the Thai Buddhist majority in the kingdom. Prior to his resignation as premier in 1944, Pibul had attempted to impose Thai culture on the Moslem minority by seeking to force the people to accept in one way or another the Thai language, customs, and laws. After Japan's surrender there was some hope among these Malay Moslems that the four southern provinces might be annexed to British Malaya. In 1946 unrest was pronounced in the area, partly as a result of extensive corruption by Thai government officials. In November a special commission was created to investigate the situation. The following month the previous privileges enjoyed by the Malays in matters of family and inheritance were restored. Seeking a wider use of Islamic law and a stronger position in the kingdom, the Moslem minority formed a South Siam Representative Committee to press their demands upon the Thai government.

On April 26, 1948, fighting broke out between the Malays and the Thai in the troubled area. Early the following month the government appointed a commission to investigate the situation and satisfy proper grievances, and the Bangkok regime subsequently accepted the commission's recommendations. An Adviser on Islamic Affairs would be appointed in Bangkok; honest officials, trained in Moslem customs, would be stationed in the four provinces; Malay would be taught in the primary schools; Friday instead of Sunday would be observed as a public holiday; Malays could enlist in the police and armed forces cadet schools under conditions as favorable as for the Thai; the building and maintenance of mosques would be an item in the budget; and traditional Moslem dress could be worn in government offices. After these concessions the agitation among the Moslem Malays subsided, although a number of economic, political, and cultural problems remained to be solved. Further measures, especially in the economic and cultural fields, would be considered in Bangkok.

The trouble in Thailand's southern provinces had ramifications in Malaya, for the Malays there, especially in Kedah and Kelantan, sympathized with those under the Thai. The British government was urged to protest to Thailand over the situation. Some Malays under the British were still eager to detach the four southern provinces of Thailand and add them to Malaya. Thailand, in turn, wondered if the British had designs on her territory. The Thai concessions to the Malays in the kingdom led to the betterment of relations with Malaya. And the Thai-British coöperation which developed after the Communist rising in the latter area helped to further the friendship.

With the "emergency" occasioned by the Communist revolt in June, 1948, the question of Thai-British border relations became urgent. If the Pibul government had not chosen to assist the British in their efforts to put down the revolt, the Communist menace in Malaya would have been greater and relations between Thailand and Great Britain increasingly strained. Pibul took the position that the revolt in his country's southern neighbor was in its essentials Communist-inspired terrorism conducted chiefly by Chinese and not a truly nationalistic movement to overthrow a colonial power. Britain was eager to have Thailand's coöperation in trying to check the smuggling of arms and rice to the rebels and in seeking to stop them from using jungle bases in Thailand for a training ground and refuge. Especially in the Thai areas of Sadao and Betong, sparsely populated jungle territory with big rubber plantations worked by Chinese tappers and owned by rich Chinese, have the insurgents from Malaya found favorable conditions. In Thailand's southern provinces the Communists from Malaya have organized among the Chinese "Min Yuen" cells to support the cause through supplies and intelligence.

British-Thai coöperation along the border has taken different forms. A British consul, having communications with Bangkok and Kuala Lumpur, has operated at Singora to report on border developments. Thai officials and police in the south have been ordered to prevent Communists from going to Malaya or to arrest them if they try to enter Thailand. A Thai army officer has been stationed in Kuala Lumpur for liaison purposes with the British. Joint operations along the frontier area have been allowed; Thai and Malay police have functioned across the border from 10 to 20 miles; British helicopters and reconnaissance and supply-dumping aircraft have flown across the frontier in support of joint police action. A joint intelligence center has been organized at Singora and a frontier planning staff established. Frequently visits by high British and Thai officials have furthered the coöperation.

The emergence of an independent Federation of Malaya has brought about ties between Bangkok and Kuala Lumpur on the basis of sovereign states. The problems, however, that appear in the relations between Thailand and Malaya have to a large extent already been presaged by developments, especially since the end of the Second World War. For instance, Tengku Abdul Rahman, when Chief Minister of the Federation of Malaya, indicated in a visit to Bangkok that his country did not want any present Thai territory. The Bangkok government which had wondered about the matter was very much pleased.

The People's Republic of China is a major consideration in the overall foreign policy of Thailand. The Thai apprehensions arise not only from the possible intentions of Communist China but also from the large Chinese minority living in the kingdom. The Laotian-Burmese boundary to the north separates Thailand from China but the distance, as Bangkok sees it, is not great.

Not until the treaty of amity, signed January 23, 1946, were diplomatic relations established between Thailand and China. For centuries the Middle Kingdom had looked upon Siam as a vassal state. Especially after the revolution of 1911 did China at times try to establish diplomatic relations with the Southeast Asia country, being now prepared to omit reference to vassal status. Thailand was opposed to such ties, for she feared they might strengthen the Chinese minority in the kingdom. The Thai role in the Second World War and China's position in the United Nations Security Council were important considerations in causing an alteration in policy at Bangkok.

The Chinese minority in Thailand, over 3 million in a population of over 19 million, occupies a key position in the nation. A large part of the trading and banking is in Chinese hands. With a few exceptions the export and internal trade of Thailand is handled by the Chinese and much of the import business. Thai companies sponsored by the government represent an effort to weaken the Chinese position but in one way or another, even in coöperation with Thai leaders, the Chinese hold on business remains. Chinese laborers and artisans also have a significant role in the country.

The present-day Chinese in Thailand retain for the most part their own language, customs, and culture. They think of themselves as Chinese and not as Thai. Living largely in Bangkok and other cities with also a concentration in the peninsula, having their own schools, mixing little with the Thai, and often settling their disputes among themselves and not in the Thai courts, these Chinese constitute, at least in some respects, a state within a state. Chinese remittances to the mother country have been a means of income to relatives who stayed at home and an indirect source of strength to China.

The Thai, especially under the influence of Pibul Songgram, became very conscious of the Chinese economic hold on the nation. At the same time they resented the opposition of the Chinese to assimilation, although this process was widespread before the Chinese Revolution of 1911. The policies of the Thai government, it is clear, are very important in the rate of assimilation, one that has varied, of course, depending upon the circumstances of the situation. Under the prevailing law a person born in the kingdom was a national of it unless registered at birth by his parents with the diplomatic or consular representative of his father's nationality. If there were no Chinese diplomatic or consular officials in Thailand, registration could not occur. In 1953 a Thai nationality law provided that children born in the kingdom of Chinese mothers were no longer Thai citizens by birth.

The treaty of amity governing Thai-Chinese relations has been important in the postwar period. Signed with the Nationalist government when Chiang Kai-shek controlled the greater part of the country it represented in many respects a gain for China. The treaty provided for "perpetual peace and everlasting amity" between Thailand and China, for the exchange of diplomatic and consular officials, for the making of a commerce and navigation treaty, and, in accordance with the laws and regulations concerned, for the right of residence, occupation, and travel, for security of person and property, for favorable treatment of the nationals of each in the territory of the other as regards entry and exit, for freedom of assembly and liberty to set up schools, and for freedom of religion and publication. Chinese born in Thailand could now establish Chinese nationality. Under a Thai declaration opportunity in primary schools should be given for teaching a foreign language in addition to the required Thai, and no restriction should be placed on foreign languages in the secondary schools. In an exchange of notes Thailand asserted that entrance fees on immigrants would not be prohibitive, and indicated that if a quota system were established, the size of the population of the given minority would be taken into account in admitting more immigrants. Although the immigration and education provisions of the settlement were reciprocal, they overwhelmingly favored the Chinese.

The decline of Nationalist power on the Chinese mainland accompanied by the rise of the People's Republic witnessed a cooling in the relations of Thailand with the government of Chiang Kai-shek. Four Nationalist consulates in the kingdom were closed but the embassy in Bangkok remained open. The flying of the Chinese flag at Chinese schools provoked controversy. Thailand did not want to increase the number of Chinese schools; rather she took steps to decrease them. Arrests of certain Chinese nationals evoked protests from Nationalist China. The Chinese immigration quota was reduced from 10,000 to 200 a year. Drastic measures were taken for the registration of aliens in the kingdom.

The Thai government became concerned, with the advent to national power of Mao Tse-tung, lest the Chinese minority become a fifth column for the People's Republic. Premier Pibul took a firm position against Communist China, refusing to recognize the government, arresting many Chinese in Thailand considered pro-Communist, and deporting some of them. A number of Chinese students have been leaving the kingdom to go to Communist China for higher education but they are not officially allowed to return to Thailand. Actually the Chinese Communist Party in the latter country is relatively small, possibly having 5000 active members. It operates through Chinese schools, newspapers, and labor unions as well as some commercial concerns and social and cultural organizations. The activities of the party center in the capital city of Bangkok and in the border region with Malaya. A Thai Communist Party exists, offering a front, largely of intellectuals, for the Chinese Communists and for some dissatisfied Thai. Membership in Communist organizations in the kingdom has been illegal since 1952. It is still likely that the greater part of the Chinese minority in Thailand is sitting on the fence waiting to see the final outcome in the struggle between Mao Tse-tung and Chiang Kai-shek. It may be that the Kuomintang leader has more friends in the kingdom than he has in most other areas in Southeast Asia, apart from the Philippines. Nevertheless, Chinese Nationalists in Bangkok were apprehensive in 1956 that the Thai government was moving toward normal trade and even diplomatic relations with Communist China. Five Chinese language newspapers were slanting their news in favor of the latter.

On January 31, 1953, Communist China announced the establishment of a "Thai Autonomous People's Government" in the Yunnan districts of Cheli, Nanchiao, Fuhai, and Chenyueh and parts of Liushun, Szumao, Ningkiang, and Chiangcheng. The area called Sibsongpanna by the Thai includes about 20,000 square kilometers with the Mekong flowing through it and has a population of about 200,000, the Thai being in the majority. West of Sibsongpanna is the Shan State of Burma and east is the Laotian province of Phong Saly where the Pathet Lao forces are entrenched. In their announcement the Chinese Communists stated that "at the inaugural ceremony the Chairman and council members pledged that they would learn from the Han Chinese and the example of the Han Chinese cadres to guide the Thai people to help other national minorities to implement area autonomy, make concerted efforts to smash the sabotage activities of the American imperialists and special agents of Chiang Kai-shek's bandit gang and struggle to strengthen national defense of the fatherland and construct a new Hsi-shuang-pan-na [Sibsongpanna] area under the leadership of the Chinese Communist Party, Chairman Mao Tse-tung and the Central People's Government."[22]

Former American Ambassador to Thailand, Edwin F. Stanton, has observed that "the designation of this "autonomous" government as "Thai" unquestionably indicates the existence of plans aimed at other Thai in Southeast Asia."[23] Here is another greater Thai movement, only the impetus is not from Bangkok but from Peking. At stake are the more than 15 million Thai in Thailand and the 2 million to 2½ million Thai in Burma, Laos, and North Vietnam as well as those in Sibsongpanna, China. And not without significance was the announcement in May, 1955, of the Democratic Republic of Vietnam to create a "Thai-Méo Autonomous Area" in northwest Vietnam.

The Bangkok government indicated real concern over the developments in Communist China's Yunnan province. Thai officials were afraid that Sibsongpanna would be a center where pro-Communist Thai in Southeast Asia would go and where subversive agitation could be directed against outside legitimate governments. The emergence of Pridi in Peking from political obscurity in the summer of 1954 added fuel to apprehensions in Bangkok's official circles. Pridi publicly condemned the Pibul government as a puppet of American imperialists and urged the Thai people to rise up against their oppressors. The Thai Communist Party warmly supported the Pridi position.

Thailand's continuance of diplomatic relations with Nationalist China has added to the hostility between the Peking and Bangkok governments. For instance, in April, 1953, the Peking radio ac-

[22] Quoted by Edwin F. Stanton, "Spotlight on Thailand," *Foreign Affairs*, Vol. 33 (October, 1954), p. 79.

[23] *Ibid.*

cused Thailand of letting the United States build strategic airfields and also construct military highways for supplying Nationalist Chinese troops in Burma, of sending soldiers for aggression in Korea so as to be assured of American military assistance, and of receiving American military advisers whose purpose was to control Thailand's armed forces. The Chinese Communists have vehemently criticized Pibul as persecuting the Chinese minority in Thailand and as being a puppet of the United States.

At the Bandung Conference in April, 1955, informal discussions occurred between Prince Wan Waithayakon, Thai Foreign Minister, and Chou En-lai. In fact, Prince Wan in his opening address had brought to the attention of the Conference the issues between Thailand and the People's Republic of China. The question of the citizenship of the Chinese minority in the kingdom was discussed by the two men, Chou indicating that his government wanted to settle the matter by negotiations and suggesting the Sino-Indonesian agreement as a basis. At the same time the Chinese Communist Premier did not maintain that Thai recognition of his government was a prerequisite. Prince Wan was invited to visit the People's Republic, and also a Thai delegation to tour Yunnan. Chou En-lai assured the Thai Foreign Minister that Pridi was in Peking and not in Yunnan, having only been granted political asylum. He would not be allowed to broadcast again over the Peking radio. Thai officials noted that in a public speech at the Bandung Conference Chou En-lai referred to the Thai autonomous area in Yunnan as an internal matter and not as a threat to others. Despite the discussions at Bandung Thailand decided against negotiations with Communist China on the question of citizenship and not to send officials to visit the People's Republic. Members of an informal Thai mission to Communist China were arrested in Bangkok upon their return in February, 1956. In late May Prince Wan significantly said: "The Thai Government is not blind. It realizes that the Peiping regime has *de facto* control over the majority of the Chinese people. But being a small nation, Thailand has to wait for the United Nations to admit Communist China before extending recognition."[24] In June Thailand lifted her ban on nonstrategic goods to Communist China and North Korea.

With the ally of the People's Republic, the Soviet Union, Thailand agreed in 1946 to open diplomatic relations, although the Soviet Minister did not present his credentials until May, 1948. In

[24] *New York Times*, June 3, 1956.

November, 1946, Thailand repealed her legislation proscribing Communism in order further to gain Soviet approval of admission to the United Nations. Hardly any Soviet citizens live in Thailand, and prospects of trade are very limited. Trade negotiations, however, have been considered, and the Soviet Union had an elaborate exhibition at the Bangkok International Trade Fair which opened on December 8, 1953. Comrades Khrushchev and Bulganin did not visit Thailand in their tour of South and Southeast Asia in 1955; Premier Pibul indicated that he would not have allowed them to visit the kingdom even if they had asked to do so. In February, 1956, Prince Wan observed that the USSR had made informal proposals to buy Thai rice.

Thai troops found themselves fighting North Korean and Chinese Communist forces during the Korean War. Shortly after the outbreak of the conflict in June, 1950, Thailand was among the first to offer armed forces in the name of the United Nations. Pibul directed the organizing and training of a regimental combat team in his country with a forward headquarters in South Korea. After the necessary preparation, Thailand turned over to the United Nations Command an infantry battalion, an air force transportation unit, two frigates, and a Red Cross medical unit. The kingdom also contributed 40,000 metric tons of rice valued at $4,368,000 for Korean relief.

On the diplomatic front Thailand defended the United Nations position on Korea. In March, 1950, *de jure* recognition had been given the Republic of Korea. Answering a communication of June 29 from the Secretary-General of the United Nations, Thailand approved the Security Council's resolutions of June 25 and 27. The Bangkok government supported General Assembly Resolutions 376(V), October 7, 1950, 410A(V), December 1, 1950, and 384 (V), December 14, 1950. It voted in favor of General Assembly Resolutions 498(V), February 1, 1951, and 500(V), May 18, 1951, calling Communist China an aggressor and then imposing an embargo on strategic materials. It supported General Assembly Resolutions 610(VII), December 3, 1952, involving repatriation of prisoners of war, and 711(VII), August 28, 1953, involving a Korean conference. In October, 1950, Thailand became a member of the United Nations Commission for the Unification and Rehabilitation of Korea.

As one of the 16 United Nations with military forces in Korea, Thailand was an active participant in the diplomatic negotiations leading to the July, 1953, armistice. She joined them in signing on July 27 a declaration in Washington that they would resist a renewal of the armed attack in the country. Thailand attended the Geneva Conference on Korea in 1954 and staunchly defended the principle of collective security. Prince Wan was one of the three chairmen. In looking back on the United Nations role in Korea, Prime Minister Pibul told the Senate of the United States in an address on May 4, 1955: "Thailand is proud to have stood with the United Nations and the United States in Korea against aggression, and is proud to be a partner, even though a small one, in the efforts being made by the United States to bring about a lasting period of peace."[25]

Relations between India and Thailand are nominal. Although the cultural influence has been strong, the political ties are not substantial. From 30,000 to 60,000 people make up the Indian population of Thailand with a sizable concentration in Bangkok. A large number of the Indians are merchants. Taking no part in Thai politics, they have been much more interested in developments in the mother country. During the Second World War a Thai branch of the Indian Independence League was established but it never assumed the importance of branches in Burma or Malaya. Rice has been the chief Thai export to India and textiles the main import; expansion of trade between the two states has come to be limited by the Indian purchases of Burmese rice. A number of Thai go to India for specialized training.

Prime Minister Nehru has rarely visited Thailand, an indication of the absence of close ties. He and U Nu stopped in Bangkok in December, 1954, on their way to the Bogor Conference in Indonesia. The kingdom has repaid a loan it borrowed from India in 1946. The Indian consulate in Bangkok was elevated to a legation in 1947 and to an embassy in 1951. As noted, Thailand sent an observer in 1949 to the New Delhi Conference on Indonesia. Apart from a basic difference in world outlook, there are no direct issues between Bangkok and New Delhi.

Thailand's relations with three other Colombo Powers—Pakistan, Ceylon, and Indonesia—are likewise not extensive. The kingdom is a formal ally of Pakistan under the Manila Pact, and the Karachi government, fortunately for good relations, has not shown

[25] Address to United States Senate by Prime Minister of Thailand, *The Department of State Bulletin*, Vol. XXXII (May 23, 1955), p. 842.

any sympathy for the Moslem Malays in Thailand. Although Ceylon and Thailand are united by the ties of Buddhism, an agreement to establish diplomatic relations was not made until late 1955. On November 18 Sir John Kotelawala, Prime Minister of Ceylon, arrived in Bangkok on a good-will visit to strengthen ties.

Given the foreign policies of India, Burma, Indonesia, and Ceylon, it is not surprising that Thailand was not invited to be a member of the Colombo Powers. Like the Philippines, Thailand is considered, especially in New Delhi, Djakarta, and Rangoon, to be altogether too closely tied to Western countries. Thailand for her part looks upon the Five Principles endorsed by many of the Communist and uncommitted states of Asia as weakening the chances of peace through international organization. She also questions the implications of "peaceful coexistence."

Along with Pakistan, Thailand is allied with another Asian state under the Manila Pact, the Republic of the Philippines. Nevertheless, relations between the Manila and Bangkok governments are nominal. A treaty of friendship was signed on June 14, 1949; as noted, Thailand attended the Baguio Conference in 1950; Pibul Songgram visited Manila in 1955. Before the Second World War a large number of Thai students went to the Philippines but the figure is now much smaller. Thailand has been a traditional source of rice for the island nation.

At the Bandung Conference in April, 1955, Thailand, it is clear, stood with the group of nations that were pro-Western in their outlook. The objectives there of the Bangkok government were to get the Conference to base its policy on the Charter of the United Nations and to recognize the right of collective self-defense under the Charter. In his opening speech at Bandung, Prince Wan Waithayakon assured the delegates that in being a signer of the Manila Pact "Thailand only seeks to protect itself against aggression and subversion and no one without aggressive designs need have any fear of my country."[26]

Thai foreign policy underwent a significant change in 1950 when Premier Pibul Songgram departed from the traditional policy of trying to balance the leading powers in Southeast Asia by aligning his country with the United States. British influence was largely replaced by American, but the alliance between the London and

[26] Address by Prince Wan, Press Release, Asian-African Conference, Bandung, Indonesia.

Washington governments prevented a serious rift in Anglo-American relations relative to Bangkok. The extent of Thailand's association with the United States and its allies is indicated by a comparison of Thai security policy with that of her next door neighbor, neutral Burma. Pibul became convinced that the rise to power of Communist China is a genuine threat to Thailand, and can best be met by a solid alliance with the strongest potential enemy of the People's Republic of China, namely the United States. Thailand, given her highly strategic location in Southeast Asia and her minorities, is, he thought, vulnerable to Chinese Communist pressure. Nor did Pibul in his realistic analysis of international developments see hope for lasting peace in the world.

Relations between Thailand and the United States before the Second World War had been cordial. American influence in Bangkok, however, had not been strong, partly because of the Anglo-French impact and partly because the United States did not seek to extend its power to peninsular Southeast Asia. American advisers, like those from other countries, had served at the court in Bangkok. An American, Francis Sayre, played an important part in the negotiating of Thai treaties with foreign powers presaging the end of extraterritoriality and other special foreign privileges. President Woodrow Wilson at the Paris Peace Conference had been sympathetic to Thailand's desires to end extraterritoriality, but he was not prepared then to make an effort in this direction as far as the Allied and Associated Powers were concerned. A liberal American viewpoint on extraterritoriality was clear in the subsequent treaty between the United States and Thailand signed in December, 1920.

The refusal of the United States to consider itself at war with Thailand after the Japanese occupation meant that a peace treaty between the two states was not necessary. Exerting a moderating influence on Great Britain in her peace negotiations with Thailand, the United States joined its European friend in reëstablishing diplomatic relations with the Bangkok government on January 5, 1946. On January 24 the United States announced that as a result of conversations with the Thai government "it has been recognized that the treaties and other international agreements in force between the United States and Siam prior to the outbreak of war in the Far East continue in full force and effect."[27] The Department of State reported on September 9 that Thailand had told the United States

[27] Statement by Acting Secretary Acheson, *The Department of State Bulletin*, Vol. XIV (February 3, 1946), p. 178.

she would welcome American capital in the development of her minerals. During 1947, 1948, and 1949 relations between the two countries were largely commercial. The United States was purchasing rice for southern Korea, for China, and for American troops in Japan, and rubber and tin for stockpiling. Trade was more extensive than at any past time. The United States gave certain technical help, and in August, 1949, it was announced that a mineral resources survey mission would go to Thailand. The kingdom had already agreed in August, 1947, to terms of reference for the settlement of American nationals' claims against the government arising from the recent war. In October, 1949, the United States instructed the Supreme Commander in occupied Japan to release certain earmarked gold in the country to Thailand and France. The sum of $37,300,000 had been earmarked for the Bank of Indochina and $43,700,000 for the Bank of Thailand.

Not only did 1950 mark a change in Thailand's foreign policy but also in that of the United States in Southeast Asia. The rise to power of Communist China and her alliance with the Soviet Union followed by the outbreak of the Korean War created a situation in the Far East not conducive to American interests. Southeast Asia in many respects was a power vacuum with both the Communist and Western powers eager to win support in the region and deny it to their rivals.

Obviously Thailand was a key country in the security policy of the United States in the area. American-Philippine ties had come into being as a result of many years of close association on the political as well as the economic and cultural levels, but American-Thai relations did not have such a heritage upon which to build. In February, 1950, a conference of senior American diplomats in the Far East was held in Bangkok with Philip Jessup, Ambassador-at-Large, in attendance. In April an economic survey mission visited Thailand on its trip through Southeast Asia, and in August an American military survey mission came to Bangkok, also on a trip, though less extensive, through Southeast Asia.

On September 19 an Economic and Technical Coöperation Agreement was signed between Thailand and the United States, and on October 17 a military assistance agreement. In a statement issued by the American Ambassador in Bangkok on the occasion of the signing of the latter, it was asserted that:

> This agreement is not a military alliance nor is it a defense pact. This agreement contains no provisions for military, naval, or air bases.

The Government of Thailand has not offered such bases, nor has the Government of the United States ever requested such bases or any special concession. This agreement follows the request by the Government of Thailand for arms and equipment to strengthen Thailand's forces with a view to enabling them better to defend Thailand and Thailand's people from any aggression which may threaten the peace and tranquility of this country. . . . It is in this spirit that the Government of the United States has responded to the appeal from the Government of Thailand and has decided to give army and military equipment which will replace old equipment now being used by the armed forces of Thailand and to supply a number of American officers and technicians for demonstration training purposes.[28]

On November 9, it should be added, an American consulate was opened in Chiengmai, a strategically located city in northern Thailand. On December 27 and 29, 1951, an exchange of notes between the United States and Thailand provided for the Thai assurances necessary for the kingdom to receive military aid under the Mutual Security Act of 1951.

By March 31, 1955, United States allotments for aid to the Thai amounted to $63,769,000. The first shipments of military supplies had been turned over to Thailand in January, 1951. The situation in Indochina, however, so preoccupied the United States that deliveries to Thailand were slow. The Thai armed forces were being built up with the help of the Joint United States Military Advisory Group. American economic and technical aid was being extended to the kingdom through a mission associated with the United States Embassy. On July 13, 1954, it was announced that "a new program of increased military aid and technical assistance" to Thailand had been formulated, and funds would be available for the construction of a strategic military highway of 297 miles from Saraburi in central Thailand through Korat to Ban Phai. In the Northeast the United States Information Service has been especially active; American participation has occurred in Thai international fairs; a Fulbright program has been successfully functioning between the two countries. On June 21, 1955, Thailand agreed to buy $1,900,000 worth of American tobacco.

The government of Premier Pibul continued for some time to press for an American guarantee of the nation. When in April, 1954, during the climax of the Dien Bien Phu battle in Vietnam, the United States called "for 'united action' to halt the further march of Communist aggression, Thailand was the only country

[28] Statement by Ambassador Edwin F. Stanton, *The Department of State Bulletin,* Vol. XXIII (October 30, 1950), p. 702.

that responded immediately and without reservation."[29] On June 21 Pibul asserted that his nation would welcome troops from the free world if needed to fight aggression by the Communists against Thailand, such support being similar to that of the United Nations in the Korean War. The Southeast Asia Collective Defense Treaty of September 8 was not as rigid in terms of commitment as Thailand desired. Prince Wan in a speech at Manila on September 6 asserted: "While, in the matter of wording, there is a variety of models to choose from, it is the substance that counts; and, from this point of view, my Delegation would desire to see a commitment which in substance, is as near as possible to that of NATO."[30] Better still, Thailand would have liked an automatic military guarantee of assistance. Despite the final terms of the Manila Pact, the kingdom was first to ratify it, and in an interview on February 21, 1955, Pibul asserted that if it were decided to have bases in his country under the treaty, they would be welcome.

Thailand, of course, was glad to have its capital chosen as the seat of SEATO. At the Bangkok Conference, February 23-25, held to make arrangements for implementing the provisions of the Manila Pact, Prince Wan played an important part, serving as chairman of the Council established by the treaty. Both he and Pibul in their opening addresses stressed the dangers of subversion in Southeast Asia, the Prime Minister asserting, February 23: "So far as international peace and security are concerned, the situation in our treaty area, as at no other times in its history, requires greater watchfulness and preparedness, for while the danger of armed aggression clearly exists, there also is manifest an acute threat of infiltration and subversion which forms a more insidious mode of aggression."[31] In his concluding speech at the Conference, Prince Wan significantly noted that "the countries which have urgent need of the assistance of our Organization are Laos, Cambodia, and Free Viet-Nam, and the proximity of Bangkok [the center of SEATO] to them will be helpful in this connection."[32] In March, 1956, Premier Pibul indicated Thailand would welcome

[29] Edwin F. Stanton, "Spotlight on Thailand," *Foreign Affairs*, Vol. 33 (October, 1954), p. 83.

[30] Speech of Prince Wan, *The Signing of the Southeast Asia Collective Defense Treaty, the Protocol to the Southeast Asia Collective Defense Treaty and the Pacific Charter*, p. 37.

[31] Speech of Prime Minister, *The Bangkok Conference of the Manila Pact Powers*, p. 15.

[32] Speech of Prince Wan, *The Bangkok Conference of the Manila Pact Powers*, p. 40.

South Vietnam's entrance into SEATO. The Bangkok government was pleased to have Pote Sarasin, former foreign minister and ambassador to the United States, named in July, 1957, the first Secretary General of the organization.

Thailand took the initiative in the holding of the military exercise involving land, sea, and air forces in and around Bangkok by SEATO powers in February, 1956. Subjected to pressure from Communist China and criticized at home for being committed to the West, the Thai government was eager to prove that SEATO was not a "paper tiger" as the Peking regime described it. Despite poor diplomatic preparation, forces from all SEATO powers except France and Pakistan participated. According to a Thai radio description, later played down, the planned military operation centered around a hypothetical invasion of Thailand from Burma, Laos, and Cambodia, and the subsequent role of the SEATO members in coming to her defense. The exercise did have the effect of showing that Thailand was not alone in Southeast Asia, thus contributing to the arrest of what has been called "creeping neutralism." Communist China severely criticized the maneuvers as provocations against all Asian peoples and bringing them to the brink of war.

In 1955 Pibul took an extensive trip abroad including the United States on his itinerary. Making an official visit in Washington from May 2-6, he received the Legion of Merit award from President Eisenhower, and also played a good game of golf with him. In his speeches in the United States he stressed Thailand's loyalty and commitment to the Western bloc, SEATO, and the United States in particular; he strongly supported American policy toward Nationalist and Communist China; and he discussed the threats to his country from Communist activities in its neighbors as well as at home.

Thailand followed with considerable interest the international developments associated with the Geneva meeting at the "summit" of the American, British, French, and Russian heads of government in the summer of 1955; she also watched the American-Chinese Communist direct talks in Geneva. She did not want to find herself alone or almost alone in Southeast Asia if the "summit" atmosphere proved permanent. At stake was the future of Thai-Chinese Communist relations. Already cheap but serviceable Chinese Communist goods via Hong Kong or Singapore were in the stores of Bangkok as well as "literature" from the People's

Republic. Indeed, there were some in the capital who believed that Burma's foreign policy of noncommitment, of not being a member of SEATO, and of accepting aid from both camps in the cold war was in the end more wise and statesmanlike. It was thought in some circles that the United States took Thailand for granted. As an important rice exporter, the kingdom resented what it considered the dumping of American surplus rice in its export markets. Thailand did not have the great difficulties of Burma for a while in marketing her rice partly because of the high quality of the product, but the situation favorable to her might not remain. There was also the suspicion that the United States was forcing down the prices not only of Thai rice but also of tin and rubber. American economic and military assistance to Thailand led to the criticism that the kingdom was losing its independence and was becoming a puppet of the United States. Frequent press attacks occurred. There was pressure for more American economic assistance during Dulles' visit in 1956. Communist propaganda, of course, took advantage of any criticism of the United States, and contributed substantially to it.

One thing could be certain about the future of Thai foreign policy. It would have its roots in Thailand's years of experience as a sovereign state in an important part of the world and would reflect to a substantial extent the shifts in global power and the changes in world politics.

8. *Vietnam, Laos, Cambodia*

Although the question of Indochina was kept by France as long as possible a domestic problem, the controversy in the end assumed the proportions of major international importance. As early as January and February, 1950, the Communist powers had recognized the Democratic Republic of Vietnam under President Ho Chi Minh and the Western allies in numerous cases had recognized the State of Vietnam under Bao Dai along with the kingdoms of Cambodia and Laos.[1] In 1953 and 1954 outright invasions of Laos by regular Viet Minh[2] troops, and in 1954 similar action by Ho Chi Minh in Cambodia, accompanied in the case of the former by the establishment of a Pathet Lao resistance government in opposition to the constitutional royal one of Laos and in the case of the latter of a Khmer resistance government taking a similar position in Cambodia, clearly indicated that the war in Indochina officially as well as unofficially was no longer restricted to Vietnam. In the climactic battle of Dien Bien Phu French and Vietnamese soldiers were fighting Viet Minh forces in a great test of physical and psychological strength, the former being materially aided by the United States and the latter by the People's Republic of China. At the height of the battle in April, 1954, the real possibility existed that the war in Indochina might become global in scope. In Washington, London, Paris, Peking, Moscow, and New Delhi

[1] Vietnam refers to a country that has been subjected to a number of changes in political terminology. The French employed the words Tonkin, Annam, and Cochin China; later North, Central, and South Vietnam were used; now Bac-Phan, Trung-Phan, and Nam-Phan can be considered official. North Vietnam, north of the seventeenth parallel, is under the Democratic Republic of Vietnam and South Vietnam, south of the parallel, is under the Republic of Vietnam. The State of Vietnam under Bao Dai as Chief of State preceded the Republic of Vietnam with Ngo Dinh Diem as President.

[2] Technically the Viet Minh refers to the League for the Independence of Vietnam. Although the organization as such was abolished in 1951, Viet Minh as an expression is still commonly used to describe the dominant political organization in the Democratic Republic of Vietnam. The Republic of Vietnam prefers the expression Vietcong.

government officials at the "summit" labored with the problem. Now involved in the Indochina conflict were questions of power position and international prestige affecting the world. It is significant that the Geneva Conference on Korea and Indochina, opening in April, held at the suggestion of the Berlin Conference of American, Russian, British, and French foreign ministers in January and February, was the first occasion when the five strongest powers emerging from the Second World War—the United States, the Soviet Union, the United Kingdom, France, and the People's Republic of China—sat in effect in such a capacity around the conference table. And it is also significant that India was unofficially present.

GENEVA SETTLEMENT

The negotiations at Geneva on Indochina were protracted, complicated, and acrimonious. Basic was the fact that the military situation was not favorable to the Western powers and that the Communist states were eager to take every advantage of it. Likewise the United States, Great Britain, and France were not closely agreed on how to deal with the Indochina problem, dissension of any kind naturally working to the advantage of the Communists. Although there is evidence that the Democratic Republic of Vietnam was not always in harmony with the policies of the People's Republic of China and the Soviet Union, the monolithic approach of the Communist powers toward Indochina was not impaired. Finally most of the Asian states outside the Communist bloc were opposed to French and American policy in Indochina, thus creating an atmosphere in a large part of Asia upon which the Communists capitalized.

A comparison of the original positions of the Viet Minh, supported by Communist China and the Soviet Union, and of France and the State of Vietnam at Geneva with the final settlement reveals the extent of compromise. Of course, it is obvious that the original desiderata of each participant represented the maximum under the circumstances, and the final agreement the minimum under the prevailing conditions. Unlike many postwar conferences, there was real negotiating at Geneva, accompanied by important diplomatic activity far beyond the place of meeting.

Pham Van Dong of the Democratic Republic of Vietnam after his delegation was seated proposed on May 10 that France recognize the independence of Vietnam and of Pathet Lao and Khmer (the first, of course, referring to the Ho Chi Minh regime and the second and third to the pro-Communist Pathet Lao and Khmer resistance governments in Laos and Cambodia); that all foreign troops be withdrawn from the three states with French forces temporarily in only a minimum of assembly areas; that the Viet Minh would make a declaration of willingness to consider the question of entrance into the French Union along with similar statements by the Pathet Lao and Khmer governments; that the cultural and economic interests of France in the three states would be recognized; that free elections would be held in the three countries to set up a unified government in each instance, both sides in the three states participating in advisory conferences before the elections which would be held under conditions providing for "freedom of activity for the patriotic social parties, groups and organizations";[3] that collaborators would not be prosecuted and prisoners of war would be exchanged; and that hostilities would end before the previously cited measures were carried out, the parties concerned agreeing to a cease-fire, to the termination of entry of arms and military units from the outside, and to the establishment of mixed commissions of the belligerents to supervise the settlement. Chou En-lai of Communist China and V. M. Molotov of the USSR subsequently supported the Viet Minh proposals although the latter suggested that a neutral nations commission should supervise the armistice.

Foreign Minister Georges Bidault of France, two days before Pham Van Dong gave his proposals, presented the French position. He proposed with respect only to Vietnam that regular units of the armed forces be grouped in assembly areas established by the Geneva Conference; that elements neither concerned with keeping order nor serving in the military be disarmed; that civil internees and prisoners be at once freed; that international commissions supervise the proposed actions; and that a cease-fire come into effect as soon as an agreement for the foregoing provisions had been signed. As regards Cambodia and Laos Bidault proposed that all Viet Minh units, whether regular or irregular, be withdrawn with a subsequent procedure like that of Vietnam. France wanted the participants of the Geneva Conference to guarantee the decisions relative to the three states of Indochina. The representatives of Cambodia and Laos subsequently expressed themselves as being

[3] Proposals by the North Viet Nam Delegation, *Documents on International Affairs, 1954*, p. 127.

broadly in support of the French proposals. The envoys of both states denied the validity of the Pathet Lao and Khmer resistance governments and wanted the complete withdrawal of the Viet Minh forces from their countries.

On May 12 Nguyen Quoc Dinh, after discussing the French-Vietnamese agreement of April 28, presented the proposals of the State of Vietnam, proposals based upon opposition to any partition of the country, upon the sole recognition of the State of Vietnam under Bao Dai as Chief of State, upon free elections under United Nations auspices when the Security Council was convinced they could really be free, and upon an international guarantee of the State of Vietnam in terms of political and territorial integrity. The United States supported the position of Nguyen Quoc Dinh and welcomed the efforts of Great Britain to reach a solution.

After a number of restricted sessions with various leaks to the press and of open meetings, Anthony Eden in a speech at a plenary session on June 10 summarized the state of the negotiations. As far as the cessation of hostilities was concerned, it was agreed that a cease-fire should be simultaneous in all the three states with the Vietnamese problem being examined first. With reference to armistice supervision, it was agreed that some kind of international supervision was necessary but wide differences existed on the composition, procedures, and powers of the international armistice commission. As far as the future of Laos and Cambodia was concerned, the Conference was still deadlocked on the question of the role of Pathet Lao and Khmer. Eden significantly observed that Cambodia and Laos were different from Vietnam in culture, religion, language, and race and that the Viet Minh invaders had crossed a frontier that separated the two great Asian cultures—the Chinese and the Indian. Eden, Molotov, and Bedell Smith of the United States left Geneva June 20 and Chou departed from Switzerland a little later after talks in Bern with Pierre Mendès-France, the new French Premier. The Conference continued at lower echelons. Later the five men met in Geneva, the negotiations being finally concluded with the settlement of July 20 and 21.

Meanwhile a number of important developments were occurring outside the Geneva Conference affecting the final agreement. Eden on April 29 had sent a telegram to the three Commonwealth prime ministers of the Colombo Powers who were meeting in Ceylon, asking the Asian leaders what they were prepared to do to support a settlement on Indochina if they approved of it. In a communiqué on May 2 the Colombo Powers presented their proposals for a solution of the Indochina problem but they made no promise of a specific guarantee. On May 15 Australia suggested that military staff talks by the United States, Great Britain, France, New Zealand, and herself should begin to review the situation in Indochina. Prime Minister Nehru in a speech the same day publicly asserted that India would accept an invitation to participate in a settlement of the controversy, and V. K. Krishna Menon arrived in Geneva on May 22 for informal talks. On May 29 Thailand requested the United Nations Security Council to provide for international observation in her country under the Peace Observation Commission. On June 3, the military staff talks, previously suggested by Australia, began in Washington. Five days later Eden suggested that the Colombo Powers, acting by a majority vote, should make up the international control commission in Vietnam. On June 17 Pierre Mendès-France became Premier of France; he stated that by July 20, if he failed to bring about a satisfactory settlement on Indochina, he would offer his resignation. On June 25 Chou En-lai arrived in New Delhi from Geneva where he discussed the Indochina problem with Nehru. Three days later he arrived in Rangoon for similar talks with U Nu. Later he discussed the situation with Ho Chi Minh, leaving afterwards for Peking. On June 28 a communiqué in Washington after talks among Eisenhower, Churchill, Dulles, and Eden indicated that Indochina and a Southeast Asia security pact were discussed. Two days later an ANZUS meeting was held. On July 14 it was announced after conversations in Paris among Dulles, Eden, and Mendès-France that General Bedell Smith would return to Switzerland for discussions on Indochina so that the United States would be represented by a high-ranking official. During the negotiations at Geneva there was in the background, as indicated in the Washington communiqué of June 28, the problem of the establishment of collective security in Southeast Asia if the Conference failed or after a settlement was reached. In fact, an Anglo-American study group began to function at the beginning of July.

The Geneva settlement on Indochina included in its documentary form three cease-fire agreements: one for Vietnam signed by Brigadier-General Delteil for the French Union Forces in Indochina and Ta-Quang-Buu for the People's Army of Vietnam, another for Cambodia signed by General Nhiek Tioulong for the Khmer National Armed Forces and Ta-Quang-Buu for the Khmer Resistance

Forces and the Vietnamese Military Units, and a third for Laos signed by Brigadier-General Delteil for the French Union Forces in Indochina and Ta-Quang-Buu for the fighting units of Pathet Lao and the People's Army of Vietnam; six unilateral declarations, two each by Cambodia, Laos, and France; and a Final Declaration of the Conference taking note, *inter alia*, of certain agreements and declarations, being adopted in the words of Mendès-France "by the ensemble of the Conference,"[4] without being signed by the participants, although observations were added by different ones.

The cease-fire agreement for Vietnam included provisions for the Democratic Republic of Vietnam to get full control over northern Vietnam south to a specific line drawn roughly along the seventeeth parallel, with a demilitarized zone on either side;[5] for the French evacuation of the Hanoi perimeter within 80 days, of the Haiduong perimeter within 100 days, and of the Haiphong perimeter within 300 days of the armistice coming into effect and for the Viet Minh evacuation of areas south of the seventeenth parallel in periods varying from 80 to 300 days; for the repatriation of interned civilians and prisoners of war; for the right, until the movement of troops north or south of the seventeenth parallel was ended, of any civilian to migrate north or south of the dividing line; for the prevention of reprisals against people and the guarantee of their "democratic liberties"; for the entrance of troops and equipment in Vietnam only on a specified rotation and replacement basis at points of entry internationally supervised; for the establishment of a Joint Commission with joint groups of Viet Minh and Franco-Vietnamese representatives to supervise the technical carrying out of the cease-fire and for the setting up of an International Commission with mobile and fixed inspection teams of India, Canada, and Poland with India as chairman to supervise the points of entry and the "proper execution" of the cease-fire, decisions being generally made by a majority vote but in case of failure to agree on specific subjects involving a threat to the peace to report to the Conference powers. National elections to unify Vietnam were foreseen in Article 14(a) of the accord.

[4] *Journal Officiel de la République Française, Débats Parlementaires, Assemblée Nationale*, vendredi 23 juillet 1954, p. 3534.

[5] "The provisional military demarcation line is fixed as follows, reading from east to west: the mouth of the Song Ben Hat (Cua Tung River) and the course of that river (known as the Rao Thanh in the mountains) to the village of Bo Ho Su, then the parallel of Bo Ho Su to the Laos-Viet-Nam frontier." Article I, annex to the agreement on the cessation of hostilities in Viet-Nam, External Affairs (Canada), Supplementary Papers, No. 54/22.

In the cease-fire agreement on Laos provision was made for the withdrawal of the regular Viet Minh and French forces within 120 days of the armistice coming into effect, but the fighting units of Pathet Lao were allowed to concentrate in a regroupment area involving two northeast provinces, Phong Saly and Sam Neua, with a corridor connecting them, "pending a political settlement." A French military mission not to exceed 1500 men to train the Laotian National Army could remain and France could have two military establishments, one at Seno and the other in the Mekong Valley either in the province of Vientiane or downstream, not exceeding in number of effectives 3500. Provision was made for the exchange of civilian internees and prisoners of war. Under Article 9 the "introduction into Laos of armaments, munitions and military equipment of all kinds is prohibited, with the exception of a specified quantity of armaments in categories specified as necessary for the defense of Laos."[6] A Joint Commission with joint groups was established to implement the cease-fire and an International Commission with inspection teams of India, Canada, and Poland with India as chairman was set up to supervise the execution by the parties of the armistice.

The cease-fire agreement in Cambodia provided for the withdrawal of the French and Viet Minh forces from the kingdom within 90 days from the coming into effect of the armistice. Significantly no regroupment area was established for the use of Cambodian dissidents; it was stated that the "Khmer Resistance Forces shall be demobilized on the spot."[7] Prisoners of war and civilian internees would be freed and repatriated. A Joint Commission which might establish joint groups was set up to carry out the cease-fire and an International Commission, consisting of Canada, Poland, and India as chairman, was established to supervise through its inspection teams the armistice.

Among the six declarations one of the two Laotian asserted that the Royal Government would "take the necessary measures to integrate all citizens, without discrimination, into the national community," affirmed that "all Laotian citizens may freely participate as electors or candidates in general elections by secret ballot," and announced that before the elections "special representation in the Royal Administration of the provinces of Phong Saly

[6] Article 9, agreement on the cessation of hostilities in Laos, External Affairs (Canada), Supplementary Papers, No. 54/22.

[7] Article 5, agreement on the cessation of hostilities in Cambodia, External Affairs (Canada), Supplementary Papers, No. 54/22.

and Sam Neua" would be given the interests of the Laotian nationals who failed to support the Royal Government during the hostilities.[8] The Cambodian declaration relative to domestic politics, inserted into the cease-fire agreement unlike the Laotian, pledged the government to integrate without discrimination all citizens into the national community and allow them "freely [to] participate as electors or candidates in general elections by secret ballot."[9] It should be recalled that France for her part in one declaration agreed to withdraw her troops from Vietnam, Laos, and Cambodia upon the request of the parties concerned except where agreement between two governments called for "a certain number of French troops" remaining "at specified points and for a specified time";[10] and in another declaration asserted that "for the settlement of all the problems connected with the reëstablishment and consolidation of peace in Cambodia, Laos and Viet Nam" she would "proceed from the principle of respect for the independence and sovereignty, the unity and territorial integrity of Cambodia, Laos and Viet Nam."[11]

The Final Declaration of the Conference, July 21, 1954, began by simply listing the nine participants.[12] The Conference took "note" of the three armistice agreements and expressed "satisfaction" at the termination of hostilities. "Note" was also taken of the Cambodian and Laotian declarations on national elections "which, in conformity with the constitution of each of these countries, shall take place in the course of the year 1955, by secret ballot and in conditions of respect for fundamental freedoms." As regards Vietnam, the Conference recognized that the "military demarcation line is provisional and should not in any way be interpreted as constituting a political or territorial boundary." Especially significant is paragraph 7 where the Conference declared that

So far as Viet Nam is concerned, the settlement of political problems, effected on the basis of respect for the principles of independence, unity and territorial integrity, shall permit the Vietnamese people to

[8] Laotian Declaration (on domestic policy), Great Britain, Foreign Office, *Further Documents relating to the discussion of Indo-China at the Geneva Conference, June 16-July 21, 1954*, Cmd. 9239.

[9] Cambodian Declaration (on domestic policy), *Further Documents relating to the discussion of Indo-China at the Geneva Conference*, Cmd. 9239.

[10] French Declaration (on withdrawal of forces), Cmd. 9239.

[11] French Declaration (on independence of Vietnam, Cambodia and Laos), Cmd. 9239.

[12] Final Declaration, *Further Documents relating to the discussion of Indo-China at the Geneva Conference*, Cmd. 9239, *passim.*

enjoy the fundamental freedoms, guaranteed by democratic institutions established as a result of free general elections by secret ballot. In order to ensure that sufficient progress in the restoration of peace has been made, and that all the necessary conditions obtain for free expression of the national will, general elections shall be held in July 1956, under the supervision of an international commission composed of representatives of the Member States of the International Supervisory Commission, referred to in the agreement on the cessation of hostilities. Consultations will be held on this subject between the competent representative authorities of the two zones from July 20, 1955, onwards.

The Conference stressed again the cease-fire provisions against reprisals in North and South Vietnam and in Cambodia and Laos; it also reiterated in its own words the armistice provision to "allow everyone in Viet Nam to decide freely in which zone he wishes to live." "Note" was taken of the two French declarations on Cambodia, Laos, and Vietnam, of the clauses in the cease-fire in Vietnam relative to the introduction of foreign troops, arms, and munitions and relative to military bases and alliances, and of the Cambodian and Laotian declarations concerning these subjects. Each participant of the Geneva Conference in its relations with Cambodia, Laos, and Vietnam undertook "to respect the sovereignty, the independence, the unity and the territorial integrity of the above-mentioned States, and to refrain from any interference in their internal affairs." Finally under paragraph 13 the members agreed "to consult one another on any question which may be referred to them by the International Supervisory Commission, in order to study such measures as may prove necessary to insure that the agreements on the cessation of hostilities in Cambodia, Laos, and Viet Nam are respected."

At the final meeting of the Conference the United States, in the words of General Bedell Smith, asserted that it could not, as already indicated on July 18, "join" in such a declaration as submitted.[13] However, it made a unilateral declaration wherein it took "note" of the three cease-fire agreements and of all the paragraphs except paragraph 13 of the Final Declaration, and declared with reference to the aforesaid agreements as well as paragraphs that it would "refrain from the threat or the use of force to disturb them" in accordance with the United Nations Charter, Article 2(4), and would "view any renewal of the aggression in violation of the aforesaid agreements with grave concern and as seriously threatening international peace and security." As for the reference in the Final

[13] United States Declaration, External Affairs (Canada), Supplementary Papers, No. 54/22, *passim*.

Declaration to free elections in Vietnam, the United States recalled its statement made with Great Britain in Washington on June 29, 1954, which read: "In the case of nations now divided against their will, we shall continue to seek to achieve unity through free elections, supervised by the United Nations to insure that they are conducted fairly."[14] The United States, General Smith indicated, would not join in any arrangements that would hinder the right of peoples to decide their own future.

General Smith's statement as well as that of President Eisenhower on July 21 and Secretary Dulles on July 23 indicated that the Geneva settlement contained provisions that the United States did not like, and that it did not consider itself a party to or bound by them. There was a general conviction in Washington that the facts of the military situation in Indochina could not be erased in a diplomatic settlement at Geneva. American prestige, it appeared, suffered a severe setback as a consequence of many of the decisions reached at the Indochina Conference.

France formulated, in the words of Prime Minister Mendès-France at the final meeting of the Conference on July 21, observations concerning the future of the Roman Catholics in Tonkin, in particular those living in the bishoprics of Phat-Diem and Bui-Chou. She hoped they would continue to have freedom of religion, reference being made to a recent declaration of President Ho Chi Minh approving this policy. Tran Van Do of the State of Vietnam even called in his declaration for the demilitarization and neutralization of the bishoprics in the Delta of North Vietnam. Pham Van Dong of the Democratic Republic of Vietnam in his closing speech definitely promised freedom of religion, mentioning specifically the bishoprics of Bui-Chou and Phat-Diem.

For France the Geneva agreement was a severe blow although the termination of the war was almost universally hailed. Pierre Mendès-France informed the National Assembly on July 22 that he had no doubts about the harsh contents of the agreement because it "consecrates cruel facts." At the same time he noted concessions made by the Communists, believed that France could keep "her presence in the Far East," offered the possibility that the end of the "nightmare" in Indochina might strengthen French policy in Europe and Africa, and paid tribute to the roles of the United States and Great Britain at Geneva.

In the Communist world the Indochina settlement was greeted

[14] For original Eisenhower-Churchill statement, see *The Department of State Bulletin*, Vol. XXXI (July 12, 1954), p. 49.

with widespread jubilation. Chou En-lai of Communist China stated it was a tremendous victory for peace in Asia and the world. In his final speech at the Conference on July 21 he also indicated his belief that "after the armistice the three states of Indo-China will refrain from joining any military alliance, and that the establishment of military bases on their respective territories by any foreign country will not be allowed."[15] Mao Tse-tung sent a message to Ho Chi Minh, calling the agreement a significant victory for the Vietnamese.

V. M. Molotov noted in a conference speech on July 21 that the Geneva settlement was an important step in lessening tension in the world. He stressed that the agreement marked a triumph for the national liberation forces in Vietnam. *Pravda,* the organ of the Communist Party of the Soviet Union, asserted in an editorial on July 22 that "the world prestige of the U.S.S.R. is today at an unprecedented high and the U.S.S.R. is considered the standard bearer of peace."[16]

The British attitude toward the Indochina agreement was different from that of the American. Foreign Secretary Anthony Eden in a speech in the House of Commons on July 22 expressed qualified optimism although nothing in his remarks indicated the confidence Neville Chamberlain revealed after returning from the Munich Conference in 1938. Prime Minister Winston Churchill as well as the British public in general praised Eden for his work at Geneva. Great Britain took the position that the Indochina settlement was the best that could be made under the circumstances. Not only was the war ended in Indochina but also the risk of its developing into a global conflict. The British recognized that the agreement included many unsatisfactory provisions but the final test in their opinion would be the way the Communists implemented it.

Comment favorable to the settlement came from India, Nehru asserting in New Delhi on July 21 that it was "one of the outstanding achievements of the post-war era."[17] Although he did not believe that Asia was well represented at Geneva, he thought the meeting of the prime ministers of India, Pakistan, Ceylon, Burma, and Indonesia at Colombo had exerted a strong influence on the discussion.

[15] Speech of Chou En-lai, *U.S. News and World Report,* July 30, 1954, p. 87.
[16] *Pravda* editorial, *U.S. News and World Report,* July 30, 1954, p. 92.
[17] Statement by Nehru, *U.S. News and World Report,* July 30, 1954, pp. 87-88.

IMPLICATIONS FOR FRANCE AND CHINA

The Geneva agreement on Indochina marked a drastic decline in French power in Southeast Asia and the rise to considerable influence of the People's Republic of China in the area. In 1939 at the outbreak of the Second World War France had an impressive position in Southeast Asia, based substantially upon her "balcony on the Pacific," Indochina. To the Federation of Indochina—Cochin China, Annam, Tonkin, Cambodia, and Laos—was added in 1898 the territory leased from the Middle Kingdom, Kwangchowwan, located on the southeastern coast of China. In addition the French claimed the Paracel and Spratly islands in the South China Sea.

In parts of southern China France had a special position. The large island of Hainan under Chinese sovereignty, south of the mainland of China, controlling the eastern approaches to the Gulf of Tonkin, could not be alienated to any foreign power under an agreement with France in 1897. Hainan is only about 125 miles from Haiphong, some 50 miles from Kwangchowwan and some 300 miles from Cam Ranh Bay where the French in 1938 began to construct a naval base taking advantage of the natural harbor. In 1898 France received a nonalienation pledge from China relative to the provinces bordering Indochina, namely, Kwangtung, Kwangsi, and Yunnan. In another agreement in 1898 France or a French company received the exclusive right to construct a railway from the border of Tonkin to Kunming in Yunnan, the railway linking Kunming and Haiphong being completed in 1910. As regards the development of mines in Yunnan, Kwangsi, and Kwangtung, China agreed in 1895 that she would turn first to the engineers and manufacturers of France, and later she agreed to give priority to French capital if needed for mining and railway enterprises in Kwangsi. In April, 1938, a Sino-French contract was signed for the building of a railroad to link Tonkin with Nanning.

Particularly important was the stress on French culture in Indochina. The University of Hanoi and the École Française d'Extrême-Orient stand out. French became a language of the local élite; Roman Catholicism flourished, especially in Tonkin. The *présence française* and the *mission civilisatrice* in Indochina were important aspects in the basic outlook of the mother country toward her large Far Eastern possession. Moreover, France came to look upon Indochina as having a certain tutelage over her possessions in the Pacific. Many Indochinese migrated to New Caledonia, Tahiti, and the New Hebrides.

Apart from North Africa, Indochina was considered the most valuable possession in the French empire. About a third larger than France and having almost half her population, Indochina before the Second World War exported more than it imported, being the third greatest rice exporter in the world. Nor should exports of rubber and corn be ignored. The mines of Indochina contained anthracite coal, wolfram, tin, iron, zinc, manganese, and phosphates. Some 40,000 Europeans, the far greater number being Frenchmen, lived in Indochina. The French controlled the police, army, and administration of the area; they owned more than 95 percent of the foreign investments, the overall figure in 1938 being estimated at $384,200,000; mining and the production of rubber were almost exclusively in their hands. Influential in the economy was the Bank of Indochina.

The Second World War created the conditions that altered the foundations of French power in Indochina and Southeast Asia. French prestige was greatly lowered as a result of the fall of the mother country to Hitler and of the Japanese inroads in Indochina. War conditions led to the drastic dislocation of trade, affecting the economy of the area. Nationalism grew to the extent that France at the conclusion of the Second World War was faced with a new political climate. Communism under Ho Chi Minh, capitalizing on nationalism, constituted a challenge to the restoration of French power. Consequently France after the surrender of Japan was forced to adjust to a new situation in Asia—especially to developments in China, Indochina, and India.

One of the first French objectives was to bring about the withdrawal of the Chinese Nationalist occupation troops north of the sixteenth parallel in Indochina. Even before the occupation began, France in a convention with China on August 18, 1945, had returned the leased territory of Kwangchowwan. On the previous July 16 Japan had handed over the area to its puppet Nanking government. France, of course, had been very apprehensive about the Potsdam decision calling for the Chinese and British occupation of Indochina, fearful that the former might come to stay. Chiang Kai-shek on August 24 pointedly observed that China had no territorial ambitions in the area. He took the position he would like to see Indochina independent, but he indicated he would not encourage an independence movement nor would he help the French suppress it. The Chinese came in the middle of September, and their occupation was not unsympathetic to Ho Chi Minh's regime. After intermittent negotiations, France and China reached a number of agreements signed on February 28, 1946, leading to the evacuation. The price, however, was at the expense of French interests.

Under an agreement regarding Sino-Indochinese relations France would deliver to China by "advanced repurchase" from French funds the property and equipment of the portion of the Haiphong-Kunming Railway in Chinese territory; goods shipped to or from China over the Tonkin railways were guaranteed exemption from transit and customs duties, a free zone for merchandise from or to China being established in Haiphong; Chinese nationals in Indochina were given the legal rights of French nationals, were not to pay taxes heavier than those the Indochinese nationals paid, and were to "continue to enjoy the rights, privileges and exemptions which they have traditionally held in Indochina";[18] a commercial agreement would regulate commerce between China and Indochina on the basis of the most-favored nation. On the same day a treaty was signed between China and France whereby the latter relinquished the former extraterritorial and related rights, thus following the American and British precedents of 1943. In an exchange of letters the same day China agreed to withdraw her troops stationed in Indochina by the end of March. Actually the greater number, it should be stressed, did not leave until the summer.

With the conquest of China by the forces of Mao Tse-tung the French position further declined. Like the United States, France did not recognize the Communist government in Peking. A number of Chinese Nationalist troops, fleeing to Indochina, were disarmed and interned by French authorities. Some time later the soldiers were allowed to go to Formosa, a situation not conducive to good relations between the Peking and Paris governments. The role of France in the Korean War and of Communist China in the Indochinese conflict indicated the hostility between the two countries.

After the Geneva settlement in the summer of 1954 France in effect lost her empire in Southeast Asia. The political links from the overall viewpoint were drastically reduced; the economic bonds were greatly weakened; and even the cultural ties were threatened. After great sacrifice in casualties as well as money France faced

[18] Agreement respecting Sino-Indochinese relations, *United Nations Treaty Series,* Vol. 14, No. 216, p. 143.

a dismal situation. Gone was her prewar position also in China and India, her agreement with the latter in late 1954 providing for the relinquishment of all her remaining historic enclaves in the subcontinent.

As for the People's Republic of China, a contrasting situation developed in respect to power and influence. At Geneva in 1954 and at Bandung in 1955 the impact of the Chinese Communists in Southeast Asia was clearly revealed although in the case of the former conference Chou En-lai was more adamant in his approach to the situation and in the case of the latter more conciliatory. "The relative power of Communist China," it has been pointed out, "in an Asia weak from the ravages of war and in the throes of a major political revolution and economic readjustment in itself represented a basic alteration in the balance of Asian power as it had existed prior to the war. With this Communist regime linked directly to the Soviet world, the shift in power acquired drastic dimensions."[19]

As a result of the victory of Mao Tse-tung the Chinese Communist Party has acquired an "overwhelmingly dominant position in the Asian Communist scene," China providing a powerful base in support of Communist parties in Southeast Asia.[20] The latter in the past, alone, divided, and far from the Soviet Union, were under the circumstances limited in influence. But Communist China, being herself an Asian state, occupying a key position in the Far East, is able to give a definite kind of unity and a real degree of direction to the Communist parties of the area. "Asia's Communists," it has been stated, "now see a Chinese Communist Party, claiming a membership of about 7 million, in control of Asia's largest army, with vast territories populated by more than 500 million people and with a party leadership unrivaled in experience and prestige in the Asian Communist world."[21]

Through various channels the government of Mao Tse-tung has been developing organization links with the Communist parties of the Far East. An Asian and Australasian Trade Union Conference was held in Peking from November 16 to December 3, 1949, only a few weeks after the formal establishment of the Central People's Government of the People's Republic of China on October 1. From Southeast Asia "delegates" came from Vietnam, Thailand,

[19] John M. H. Lindbeck, "Communist China and American Far Eastern Policy," *The Bulletin of the Department of State*, Vol. XXXIII (November 7, 1955), p. 752.
[20] *Ibid.*, p. 754.
[21] *Ibid.*

Burma, Malaya, the Philippines, and Indonesia. A World Federation of Trade Unions liaison bureau for Asia and Australasia was established at Peking, serving as an important channel in coördinating the Asian Communist movement. Liu Shao-chi, honorary president of the All-China Federation of Labor, at a rally on November 23 frankly told the delegates that "the Chinese working class has to shoulder the grave responsibility of rendering assistance to the working class and working people of capitalist countries in the world, especially colonial and semi-colonial countries in Asia and Australasia."[22] An Asian and Pacific Region Peace Conference was held in Peking from October 2 to 13, 1952, with many delegates from Southeast Asia. In an "appeal," the Conference noted, *inter alia*, that "armed intervention in Viet Nam, Malaya and other countries" sought "to crush the people's desire for freedom," and called for "an end to the wars in Viet Nam, Malaya and other regions, and the withdrawal of all foreign troops from these regions."[23] A peace liaison committee was established in Peking with Madame Sun Yat-sen at its head. Other international agencies of the world Communist movement with branches in Asia are the Women's International Democratic Federation, which, for instance, held a regional conference in Peking in December, 1949, and the World Federation of Democratic Youth.

The Chinese Communist, Soviet, and North Korean radios broadcast Communist propaganda in their programs directed toward Southeast Asia, and the North Vietnamese radio operates within the area itself. In the countries where the governments recognize the Mao Tse-tung regime, Chinese Communist diplomatic and consular representatives are active. In some places the Communist Bank of China is a significant vehicle of Peking's influence. Friendship and cultural organizations on a bilateral basis with the People's Republic of China are utilized. Overseas branches of the Chinese Communist Party prove helpful. The Peking government provides agents, funds, and propaganda to further the Communist effort in Southeast Asia; it is known to harbor Southeast Asian leaders who might return to positions of leadership in their countries and to train and equip military personnel from a part of the region. "Through organizational ties, ideological guidance, the development of operational methods, and central direction," it can

[22] Quoted by Milton Sacks in "The Strategy of Communism in Southeast Asia," *Pacific Affairs,* Vol. XXIII (September, 1950), p. 236.

[23] Appeal from Asian and Pacific Peace Conference, *Documents on International Affairs, 1952,* pp. 467-468.

be summarized, "Peiping is converting local Communist parties into a regional force."[24]

The Chinese Communist government like that of the Nationalist has given attention to the Chinese overseas in its governmental structure. An Overseas Chinese Affairs Commission was set up in November, 1949, having a number of functions including the channeling of remittances from overseas, helping Chinese students from abroad continue their studies in the People's Republic, promoting the welfare of the overseas Chinese in their respective lands of domicile, facilitating close ties between the Chinese abroad and the home government, and promoting investments from the Chinese overseas in the mainland. A few weeks before on September 29, the Chinese People's Political Consultative Conference had adopted a Common Program wherein it was stated that the government "shall do its utmost to protect the legitimate rights and interests of overseas Chinese."[25] In the electoral law for the All-China People's Congress, promulgated on March 1, 1953, provision was made for the overseas Chinese to elect 30 deputies.[26] In a report on February 11 by Teng Hsiao-ping, Vice-Premier and a member of the Committee for Drafting the Electoral Law, it was stated that the provision for the overseas Chinese, totaling "some eleven million," reflected "the special concern" of the government for them. In November a large overseas Chinese conference was held in Peking. Under the constitution of Communist China, adopted September 20, 1954, the "People's Republic of China protects the proper rights and interests of Chinese resident[s] abroad."[27]

The functions of the Overseas Chinese Affairs Commission in Peking are an indication of the interest of the People's Republic in the Chinese living outside the homeland. Remittances at first voluntary and later subject to pressure have influenced the attitude of the Chinese in Southeast Asia. Dual citizenship has raised many problems that have not been solved. Communist China's support of the overseas Chinese has antagonized newly established nationalist governments in Southeast Asia. In competition is Nationalist China with its own overseas Chinese commission and its own program. In

[24] Lindbeck, *op. cit.*, p. 754.

[25] Article 58, *The Common Programme*, Foreign Languages Press, Peking, p. 21.

[26] At the first All-China People's Congress in 1954 overseas Chinese from Southeast Asia came from Burma (1), Thailand (4), Vietnam, Laos and Cambodia (2), Malaya (5), North Borneo and Sarawak (1), Indonesia (4) and the Philippines (1).

[27] Article 98, Constitution of the People's Republic of China, S. B. Thomas, *Government and Administration in Communist China*, rev. ed., p. 196.

late 1952 a large meeting of more than 200 delegates of overseas Chinese was held in Taipei where support was pledged to Chiang Kai-shek in his efforts to return to the mainland. Rivalry among the Chinese has been indicated in Southeast Asia in the observance of the Communist national holiday on October 1 and the Nationalist or Double Tenth on October 10.

At the Geneva Conference on Korea and Indochina in 1954 Chou En-lai emerged as one of the strongest voices in Asia. His attitude and activity at the Conference implied that Communist China was not merely carrying out orders from Moscow. In his comments on May 12 relative to Indochina he developed the idea that China was forced to watch carefully a war in a neighboring country, capable of spreading farther. He denied the intervention of his government in the conflict and accused the United States of meddling in Indochina with the goal of seizing the area and using it as a base of aggression against all Southeast Asia. Chou noted that the Viet Minh Declaration of Independence in September, 1945, contained much of the substance of the American Declaration of Independence in 1776 and the French Declaration of the Rights of Man in 1791 but that the countries where these declarations had been made were now not prepared to give to others the freedom they once claimed for themselves.

In his final address at Geneva, Chou En-lai stressed the importance of Asian solidarity. He called attention to the Sino-Indian and Sino-Burmese statements recently made by him with Nehru in New Delhi and with U Nu in Rangoon and to the expression of support from Ho Chi Minh; he noted the approval expected from the Colombo Powers for the Geneva settlement; and he expressed his conviction that collective peace in Asia could be preserved through consultation and coöperation on the basis of the Five Principles.

At Bandung in 1955 Chou En-lai came to be specific in outlining China's overt policy in Southeast Asia. Not only did he express his views in personal conversations with other delegates but also in formal speeches at the Conference. In a mimeographed speech for distribution to the delegates, Chou on April 19 presented the world outlook of Communist China, thereby setting the stage for later specific comments.[28] He noted that "most of the countries of Asia and Africa in varying degrees have been subjected to the plunder

[28] Speech by Premier Chou En-lai, April 19, 1955, Press Release, Asian-African Conference, Bandung, Indonesia, *passim*.

and oppression of colonialism" which had not ended since "new colonialists are attempting to take the place of the old ones." He pointedly stated: "The people of Asia shall never forget that the first atomic bomb exploded on Asian soil and that the first man to die from [an] experimental explosion of [the] hydrogen bomb was an Asian." He carefully dwelt upon other points that would arouse sympathy among his fellow Asians and Africans—the evils of racial discrimination, the need for universal human rights, the consequences of economic backwardness, and the justice of self-determination. Chou praised the Geneva settlement on Indochina but called for its full implementation. He stressed the Five Principles as the basis for international relations not only between China and the Indochinese states but also between her and all the nations of Asia and Africa. In a supplementary speech on April 19 Chou observed that his delegation had come to Bandung "to seek unity and not to quarrel."[29] Opposition to colonialism should provide the common ground of understanding; toleration for one another's ideological and social systems should make for harmony; and non-interference in the internal affairs of one another should destroy suspicion. "It is China," he observed, "that is suffering from the subversive activities which are openly carried out without any disguise by the United States of America."[30]

In a key statement to the political committee of the Bandung Conference on April 23, Chou indicated his opposition to "antagonistic military alliances" like the North Atlantic and Manila treaties.[31] He listed seven points, pledging China would use them as a basis for peaceful coöperation, and he cited in some cases illustrations from Southeast Asia. As regards respect for national sovereignty and territorial integrity, he mentioned China's relations with Burma and denied his country had any claims to the territory of its neighbors, saying only peaceful methods would be used to settle boundary differences. With reference to abstention from aggression and threats of it, he said he had assured Prince Wan and General Romulo that China would not commit aggression or make threats against Thailand and the Philippines. As for noninterference in the internal affairs of other countries, Chou noted, for example, he had given assurances to Cambodia and Laos. Concerning the

[29] Supplementary Speech by Premier Chou En-lai, April 19, 1955, Press Release, Asian-African Conference.

[30] *Ibid.*

[31] Speech by Premier Chou En-lai, April 23, 1955, George McTurnan Kahin, *The Asian-African Conference, passim.*

recognition of racial equality, he observed that the "new China has not practiced any discrimination"; and regarding the recognition of the equality of all nations, he asked any country represented if it felt slighted by him to let him know. In commenting on the right of each state to select its own political and economic system, Chou noted that his country respected the choice of the American as well as the Japanese people in this matter. On the last or seventh point, abstention from doing damage to another country, he called for trade on equal and mutually beneficial terms.

Reporting to the Standing Committee of the People's Congress in Peking on May 13, 1955, on the Bandung Conference, Chou En-lai asserted that the "principles underlying the foreign policy of the People's Republic of China are the defence of its national independence, freedom, sovereign rights and territorial integrity, supporting a lasting international peace and friendly coöperation among the peoples of all countries, and opposition to the imperialist policy of aggression and war. These principles are at one with the common desires and demands of the peoples of the Asian and African countries."[32] On July 30 in a report to the closing session of the People's Congress he observed that "at present a concrete solution of the question of general disarmament is not yet achieved, the threat of an atomic war is not yet eliminated, the chain of military bases and military blocs encircling our country is not yet removed. We cannot but take into account the possibility of being suddenly attacked. In these circumstances we must remain vigilant and must strengthen our necessary national defenses."[33] It is significant that in late 1956 in a tour of a number of countries in South and Southeast Asia the Chinese Premier stressed the opposition of his country to "great-nation chauvinism."

VIETNAM

The "Land of the South" or Vietnam has the potential of becoming very influential in Southeast Asian politics. Having an area of around 127,000 square miles, the country extends for over 1000 miles from southern China to the Gulf of Siam. It dominates the west coast of the South China Sea. Vietnam has good harbor facilities developed by the French and possesses the potential of an excellent naval base at Cam Ranh Bay. Eastward by water is

[32] "Chou En-lai on the Asian-African Conference at Bandung," *United Asia,* Vol. 7 (December, 1955), p. 308.

[33] *New York Times,* July 31, 1955.

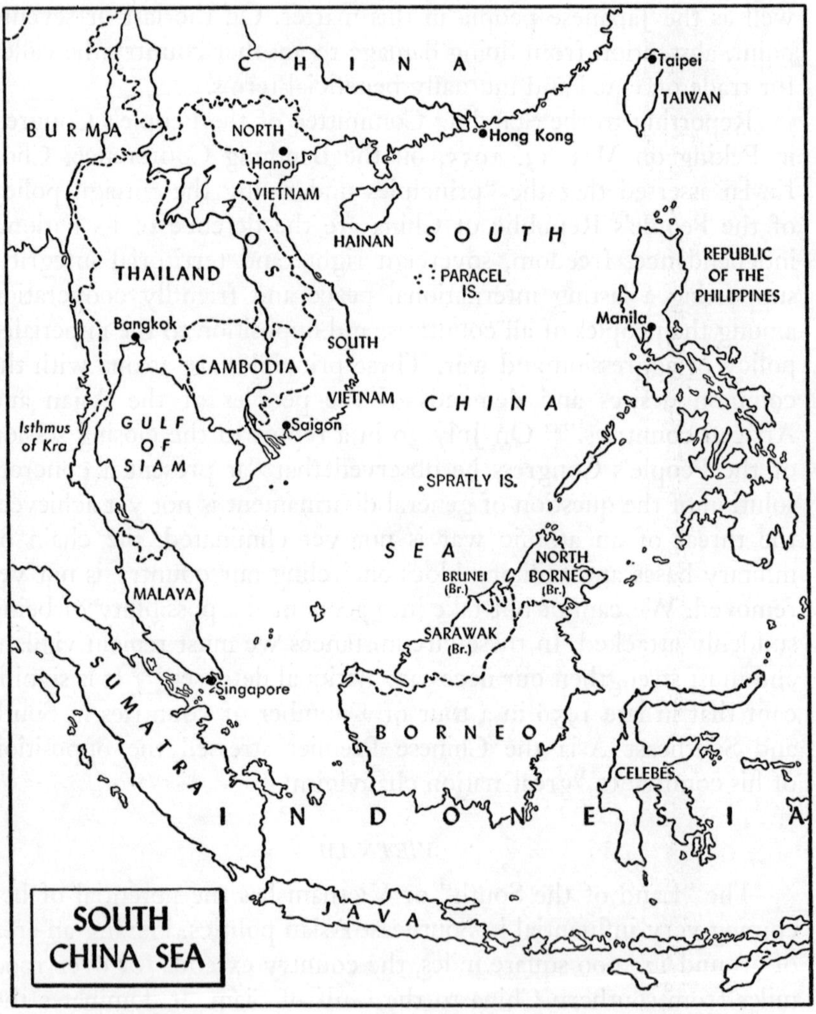
C H I N A
Taipei
TAIWAN
B U R M A
NORTH
Hanoi
VIETNAM
L A O S
Hong Kong
HAINAN
S O U T H
REPUBLIC OF THE PHILIPPINES
THAILAND
PARACEL IS.
Bangkok
SOUTH
CAMBODIA
Manila
VIETNAM
C H I N A
Isthmus of Kra
G U L F O F S I A M
Saigon
SPRATLY IS.
S E A
NORTH BORNEO (Br.)
BRUNEI (Br.)
MALAYA
SARAWAK (Br.)
S U M A T R A
Singapore
B O R N E O
CELEBES
I N D O N E S I A
J A V A
SOUTH CHINA SEA

the Republic of the Philippines, southeastward British Borneo, and southward Indonesia. Significant in the future politics of Southeast Asia may be the relations between Vietnam and the Philippines lying opposite each other in the South China Sea. In terms of land neighbors, Vietnam is bounded on the north by the People's Republic of China with its strategic island of Hainan east of the Gulf of Tonkin. The proximity of Vietnam to China, regardless of the government in power in that vast country, is a fact of major significance in the future of the Vietnamese. Westward the neighbors of Vietnam are Laos to the north and Cambodia to the south. Given the basic weakness of Laos and Cambodia, the location of Thailand and Burma further to the west and of Malaya further to the southwest is significant in the politics of peninsular Southeast Asia. Vietnam's location, it is clear, both with reference to the South China Sea and mainland Southeast Asia gives her decided advantages.

The inhabitants of Vietnam number over 24 million, making the country the most populous of all Southeast Asia, apart from Indonesia. The overwhelming proportion of the people, about 22 million, is racially Vietnamese or Annamite, often considered the most energetic of the people living in Southeast Asia. The ancestors of the Vietnamese lived partly in the area eventually called Tonkin; by the end of the 1400's they had conquered the greater part of Champa located substantially in territory later called Annam; and by 300 more years they had moved into an area subsequently termed Cochin China, once territory of Cambodia. In fact, Vietnamese sometimes refer to their acquisition of South Vietnam as a process like the westward expansion of the United States. Conquered by China in 111 B.C. Vietnam broke away in A.D. 938 although a shadowy status of vassalage remained at different periods. The Vietnamese are the only Sinicized people of Southeast Asia, reflecting the Chinese impact in religion and culture, though remaining distinctive. They are concentrated in the Red River delta of the north and the Mekong delta of the south and along the narrow lowlands on the west coast of the South China Sea, east of the Annamite Chain. In the extensive highlands of Vietnam live more than 1,500,000 people divided into different racial tribes like the Thai, Méo, and Cham.

Before the Second World War Vietnam was the third largest exporter of rice in the world. Other agricultural products were rubber, corn, tea, coffee, sugar cane, and tobacco. Minerals included coal in particular and iron, zinc, tin, tungsten, and manganese. Vietnam possesses an economic potential of considerable import.

The partition of the country at the Geneva Conference in the general area of the seventeenth parallel focused attention on the two divisions. The State of Vietnam south of the parallel had at the time an estimated population of between 10 and 11 million and in general an underpopulated area of around 65,000 square miles. By July 20, 1955, it is estimated that almost 900,000 people, a large number Roman Catholics, had crossed from the north to live in the south. The Democratic Republic of Vietnam had an estimated population at the time of partition numbering between 12 and 13 million and in general an overpopulated area of around 62,000 square miles. Some 4000 refugees are estimated to have moved from south to north of the parallel. At the present time the Democratic Republic is believed to have something more than half the people living in Vietnam.

The State of Vietnam has been more than self-sufficient in rice, the area being in the past the rice bowl of Indochina. In contrast the territory of the Democratic Republic has had a deficiency in rice, having traditionally to import it from the south. As for mining, the north has the advantage, anthracite coal being an important item. Here the French built, in particular, cement plants and textile mills. In terms of wartime destruction the north, being the chief battlefield of the conflict, suffered far greater damage than the south. As for major ports, the north had the advantages of Haiphong upon transfer and the south of Saigon. Hanoi once again came to be the seat of Ho's regime but the south retained the city of Tourane.

The State of Vietnam under Premier Ngo Dinh Diem took the position that the Saigon government was not technically bound by the cease-fire agreement; it is stressed that the armistice was signed by a French officer of the French High Command. Nor did the State of Vietnam approve the "Final Declaration" of the Geneva Conference. Nevertheless, Foreign Minister Tran Van Do asserted at the Conference on July 21 that the State of Vietnam would not use force to oppose the carrying out of the cease-fire agreement.[34]

[34] The Saigon delegation at the last meeting of the Geneva Conference failed to have inserted in the Final Declaration the following:

"The Conference takes note of the Declaration of the Government of the State of Viet Nam undertaking:

The objections of the Saigon government were well formulated in its protest of July 21 to the Conference. Here it solemnly protested against the "hasty conclusion of the armistice agreement" between France and the Viet Minh despite the control of Vietnamese troops by the French High Command "only through a delegation of authority by the Chief of State of Viet-Nam," against the abandoning of territory to the Viet Minh, part of which was still in the possession of the State of Vietnam, and against "the fact that the French High Command has arrogated to itself without preliminary agreement with the delegation of the State of Viet-Nam the right to fix the date of future elections, notwithstanding that a matter of a clearly political character is concerned."[35] Opposed to the partition of his country, Tran Van Do subsequently resigned his post as Foreign Minister. In Saigon Premier Diem in a broadcast on July 22 denounced the Geneva settlement and ordered flags at half-mast for three days.

Vietnamese nationalists in Saigon were also opposed to Article 19 of the armistice whereby "no military base under the control of a foreign State may be established in the re-grouping zone of either party; the two parties shall ensure that the zones assigned to them do not adhere to any military alliance and are not used for the resumption of hostilities or to further an aggressive policy."[36] Under Article 18 "the establishment of new military bases" in all Vietnam was also prohibited.[37] In the "Final Declaration" the conference in addition to taking "note of the clauses in the agreement on the cessation of hostilities in Viet Nam prohibiting the introduction into Viet Nam of foreign troops and military personnel as well as of all kinds of arms and munitions," noted in its words the clauses "to the effect that no military base at the disposal of a foreign state may be established in the regrouping zones of the two parties, the latter having the obligation to see that the zones allotted to them shall not constitute part of any military alliance, and shall

---

"to make and support every effort to reëstablish a real and lasting peace in Viet Nam;

"not to use force to resist the procedures for carrying the cease-fire into effect, in spite of the objections and reservations that the State of Viet Nam has expressed, especially in its final statement."

Great Britain, Foreign Office, Cmd. 9239.

[35] Protest by the Vietnamese Delegation, *Documents on American Foreign Relations, 1954*, p. 315.

[36] Article 19, agreement on the cessation of hostilities in Viet-Nam, External Affairs, Supplementary Papers, No. 54/22.

[37] Article 18, agreement on the cessation of hostilities in Viet-Nam, External Affairs, Supplementary Papers, No. 54/22.

not be utilized for the resumption of hostilities or in the service of an aggressive policy."[38] Vietnamese nationalists in Saigon believed that the Geneva Conference had no right to prevent the Vietnamese from organizing their own defense as they saw fit and from choosing military allies if they desired.

The work of the International Commission of India, Poland, and Canada to supervise the proper execution of the cease-fire agreement for Vietnam was obviously affected by the attitude of the State of Vietnam. At the same time the Democratic Republic of Ho Chi Minh raised obstacles of its own. Canada in accepting membership on the Commission regretted that the supervision of the settlement was not directly under United Nations aegis but noted that membership did not involve guaranteeing or enforcing the cease-fire. A conference of the parties concerned met in New Delhi from August 1 to August 6, 1954, Nehru inaugurating it, to plan the administrative work of the Commission.

In its first interim report dated December 25, 1954, covering August 11 to December 10, the International Commission asserted that "despite difficulties of communication, frayed tempers due to eight years of strife and differences in the degrees of effectiveness of administration in various parts of Viet-Nam, the provisions of the Agreement which are of a military or semimilitary nature have on the whole been carried out according to the time-schedules and directions given in the Agreement."[39] The Commission criticized both sides in their ways of implementing the democratic freedoms aspect of the cease-fire agreement, especially in the case of failure to establish in certain areas a stable administration in South Vietnam and failure to insure freedom of movement in North Vietnam. Both sides also preferred a "narrow legalistic interpretation" of the cease-fire agreement relative to the "tasks and the spheres of movement" of the fixed and mobile inspection teams of the International Commission.

In its second interim report for the period December 11, 1954, to February 10, 1955, the Commission noted that "each party is more keen to get the Commission to denounce the other than to take reasonable measures to get the [cease-fire] Agreement implemented."[40] However, there was so far no case where either of the High Commands had refused to carry out a recommendation of the Commission but there were "cases of intransigence on the part of

[38] Final Declaration, Cmd. 9239.

[39] First Interim Report of the International Commission for Supervision and Control in Viet-Nam, External Affairs, Supplementary Paper, No. 55/1.

[40] Second Interim Report, *ibid.*, No. 55/4.

local civil or military authorities."[41] In an appendix was a letter from the Indian Chairman of the International Commission to General Vo Nguyen Giap, Commander-in-Chief of the People's Army of Vietnam, relative to the latter's memorandum, December 5, 1954, regarding violations of the Geneva Agreement in South Vietnam, particularly the "activities of the special American Mission headed by General Collins."[42] The International Commission in effect sought more detailed information of the charges from General Giap.

The third interim report dated April 25, 1955, covered the period from February 11 to April 10. It was noted that the "delay" in implementing the cease-fire provision relative to freedom of movement in the Democratic Republic of Vietnam was "a matter of serious concern to the Commission."[43] On the other hand, it was indicated that the State of Vietnam was impairing the work of the Commission in the south, reference being made to "demonstrations involving violence against the Commission's Teams and the personnel working with them."[44] In a "note" by the Canadian delegation, submitted with the interim report, the attention of the cochairmen of the Geneva Conference (Foreign Ministers Eden and Molotov being the original ones) was directed to the Commission's observations on freedom of movement in North Vietnam. Concerned with the early end of the 300-day period for the implementation of the provision and the record up to the present time, the Canadian delegation requested that the question of implementing the freedom of movement clause be referred to the members of the Geneva Conference. In a statement to Parliament on May 3, the Canadian Secretary of State for External Affairs, L. B. Pearson, frankly observed: "If one of the parties to the agreement is evading its clear obligations and responsibilities with respect to the freedom of movement for civilians, it is not going unnoticed by our representative on the Commission or by the Government."[45]

The International Commission in its fourth interim report, dated October 1, 1955, covering the period April 11 to August 10, analyzed the work done as a result of the completion of the regroupment process and noted the tasks that remained.[46] The parties directly concerned, it was made clear, had indicated satisfaction

[41] *Ibid.*
[42] Appendix VI, *ibid.*
[43] Third Interim Report, *ibid.*, No. 55/6.
[44] *Ibid.*
[45] Statement on Vietnam of L. B. Pearson, *External Affairs*, Vol. 7 (May, 1955), p. 164.
[46] Fourth Interim Report of the International Commission for Supervision and Control in Viet-Nam, External Affairs, Supplementary Paper, No. 55/12, *passim.*

with the way in which the withdrawals as well as the transfers had been carried out. Provision for the freedom of movement had been extended from May 18 to July 20 at the suggestion of the Commission but the Polish and Indian members on the one hand and the Canadian representative on the other differed in their analysis of its general implementation. The former members, although noting the "narrow and complicated administrative procedures" in North Vietnam, were not so critical of the Ho Chi Minh regime in the matter of the refugees as the Canadian representative. The entire Commission agreed that "in the case of the zone of the French Union High Command . . . the independent attitude of the Government of the State of Vietnam, which controlled the civil administration and which had not signed the Geneva Agreement, made . . . obstructions and difficulties progressively more serious and the French High Command could not take adequate remedial action." The Indian and Polish members were more critical of the State of Vietnam than the Canadian representative. The former wanted the cochairmen and the Geneva Powers "at a very early date" to settle satisfactorily the difficulties and the latter favored the "parties directly concerned" working out "a more durable and dependable arrangement." The Indian, Polish, and Canadian representatives agreed that the chief remaining tasks of the Commission dealt with the supervision of the demarcation line and the demilitarized zones, the "proper execution" of the provision opposing reprisals against people and guaranteeing their "democratic liberties," supervision and control of the carrying out of the provisions on freedom of movement and liberation of prisoners of war and civilian internees as regards "pending cases," and supervision at airfields, ports, and along all the frontiers of Vietnam in connection with executing the provisions in the cease-fire agreement relative to the entry of war material and military personnel and the obligations on military bases and alliances.

The fifth interim report dated January 8, 1956, covered the period of August 11 to December 10, 1955. It stressed the difficulties occasioned by the attitude of the Saigon government toward the Geneva settlement and once more showed the cleavage between India and Poland on the one hand and Canada on the other. A sixth interim report, September 9, 1956, described developments from December 11, 1955, to July 31, 1956.

The question of elections in all Vietnam became increasingly important with the approach of July 20, 1955, the date set in the Final Declaration of the Geneva Conference for the beginning of discussions on the subject between the authorities in North and South Vietnam. On June 6 the Democratic Republic of Vietnam publicly warned that the provisions relative to the elections must be carried out. It indicated readiness to start the discussions with the Saigon government. On April 10 Nehru and Pham Van Dong in a communiqué in New Delhi had "agreed on the importance of free elections and the achievement of [the] unity of Viet Nam as provided for by the Geneva Agreements."[47] In June and July Ho Chi Minh in visits to Communist China and the Soviet Union received the support of those countries. Ngo Dinh Diem on July 16 indicated that his government did not reject the principle of elections but insisted that they be "absolutely free." Three days later the Viet Minh regime sent a note to the Saigon government requesting the establishment of the consultative conference on the elections. On August 9 the latter indicated in a declaration no change in its policy of not holding the consultations. Meanwhile, President Eisenhower, Prime Minister Eden, and Premier Edgar Faure considered the Vietnam situation at the "summit" conference in Geneva.

Diplomatic activity in early 1956 relative to the proposed elections in July was marked. India wanted the foreign ministers of Great Britain and the Soviet Union, as cochairmen of the Geneva Conference, to meet on the subject. The Soviet Union desired a conference of all the Geneva participants of 1954 as well as the three countries on the International Commission, but Great Britain was opposed to this procedure. The Democratic Republic of Vietnam continued to exert pressure on the USSR and the People's Republic of China relative to the necessity of the elections. On March 30 the Soviet Union sent a note to the United Kingdom suggesting discussions by the cochairmen and referring to a note from the Democratic Republic of Vietnam on February 14 charging numerous violations by South Vietnam of the Geneva settlement. The situation in the area became more urgent when the French High Commissioner in Saigon on April 3 wrote a letter to the International Commission giving notice that the French Union High Command would completely withdraw from South Vietnam

[47] Joint Communiqué of Nehru and Pham Van Dong, Allan B. Cole, ed., *Conflict in Indo-China and International Repercussions, A Documentary History, 1945-1955*, p. 236.

on April 28. The Commission proceeded to ask the cochairmen for directions as to its future.

On April 5 the United Kingdom in a reply to the Soviet note of March 30 agreed in principle on the proposed discussions relative to Vietnam, and suggested they begin on April 11 between Lord Reading and A. A. Gromyko whom the USSR had designated. In another note dated April 9 the United Kingdom replied in detail to the Soviet position on developments in Vietnam. As regards the holding of elections, the British government reiterated that it wanted them held, and suggested consultations between the North and South Vietnamese authorities "in order to ensure that all the necessary conditions obtain for a free expression of the national will as a preliminary to holding free general elections by secret ballot."[48] Yet the British government, the note asserted, "do not agree that the Government of the Republic of Viet-Nam were legally obliged to follow this course."[49] It was indicated that Great Britain's first objective was to keep the peace between North and South Vietnam.

The position of the United States on the proposed elections was well expressed by Assistant Secretary of State Walter S. Robertson on June 1 when he asserted that "we believe in free elections, and we support President Diem fully in his position that if elections are to be held, there first must be conditions which preclude intimidation or coercion of the electorate."[50] Australia took a smilar position. France indicated in the words of Foreign Minister Christian Pineau on February 23 that she did not have the "practical means" to oblige the parties concerned to carry out elections within the time limit laid down at Geneva and that "consequently she cannot settle this problem by herself."[51]

On April 6 the government of President Ngo Dinh Diem issued a statement of considerable importance relative to the role of the International Control Commission after the withdrawal of the French Expeditionary Corps. Reiterating that "it will aim at the reunification of the country which is dear to its heart, by all peaceful means, in particular through really free and democratic elections, when all the conditions for freedom of vote have really been

[48] Note from the United Kingdom to the Soviet Union, *Vietnam in World Affairs*, Secretariat of State for Foreign Affairs (Saigon), Vol. I (June, 1956), p. 127.

[49] *Ibid.*

[50] Address of Walter S. Robertson, *Vietnam in World Affairs*, p. 116.

[51] *Journal Officiel de la République Française, Débats Parlementaires, Conseil de la République*, vendredi 24 février 1956, p. 198.

secured," the government asserted that it considered the International Control Commission an "organisation working for peace" and will "continue to give it effective coöperation, will ensure the safety of its members and will, as far as possible, facilitate the accomplishment of its peaceful mission."[52] On April 19 the International Commission was informed by the cochairmen of the Geneva Conference that they were considering the situation in Vietnam and wanted the international body to continue its normal activities pending a final decision. Actually discussions in London on the subject between Lord Reading and A. A. Gromyko had begun on April 11 and came to an end on May 8. On May 2 the International Commission informed the cochairmen that it would remain in being as requested but wanted them to take steps to solve the problems hindering its effective work. The Canadian delegation sent a separate note on May 3 placing less emphasis on the importance of the work of the Joint Commission of the two parties to the cease-fire agreement.

The cochairmen on May 8 sent messages to the International Commission and to France and a joint message to the governments of North and South Vietnam. The Saigon and Hanoi governments were asked to keep the peace, coöperate with the International Commission, and transmit "their views about the time required for the opening of consultations on the organisation of nation-wide elections in Viet-Nam and the time required for the holding of elections as a means of achieving the unification of Viet-Nam."[53] France was asked to discuss with the Saigon government the problems arising from the dissolution of the French Union High Command in order to reach a satisfactory arrangement to all concerned, and in the meantime to preserve the *status quo*. The International Commission was requested to keep up its efforts toward maintaining and strengthening peace in Vietnam on the basis of carrying out the Geneva settlement. On May 27 the Commission indicated its approval of the request by the cochairmen. The Republic of Vietnam in its reply on May 22 stressed its position of April 6 and noted that preëlectoral and electoral arrangements could not be made at the moment because of the absence of freedom in North Vietnam. The Hanoi government agreed with the cochairmen that the peace should be preserved and the work of the International Com-

[52] Statement by the Government of the Republic of Viet-Nam, *Vietnam in World Affairs*, p. 107.

[53] The Co-Chairmen of the Geneva Conference to the Republic of Viet-Nam and the Democratic Republic of Viet-Nam, *Vietnam in World Affairs*, p. 129.

mission continued. France indicated that she was prepared to discuss with the Saigon government all existing problems. Under the circumstances it is obvious that no nation-wide elections were held in Vietnam in July, 1956. The country remained partitioned at the seventeenth parallel. The efforts of the Democratic Republic of Vietnam for early elections continued but higher considerations prevailed in Moscow and Peking. Two Germanys, two Koreas, two Chinas, and two Vietnams reflected the vicissitudes of the cold war.

Meanwhile the State of Vietnam could certainly not be considered a puppet of France; the Diem regime became a going concern and gained momentum. On July 7, 1954 (a Double Seventh), Ngo Dinh Diem had formed a government, the Chief of State Bao Dai making him Premier and at his request giving him full powers. The obstacles facing the new Premier appeared almost unsurmountable in any direction he turned. Sincere, honest, and persevering, Diem, a Roman Catholic, was a genuine Vietnamese nationalist, opposed to Communism, and determined to establish a strong government in South Vietnam even if he had to use force to do it. It is quite likely that only the support of the United States enabled him at times to stay in power. The Washington government came to look upon him as the last real alternative to Ho Chi Minh.

A succession of events tested the mettle of the Premier who at the beginning lacked administrative "know-how." General Nguyen Van Hinh, National Army Chief of Staff, defied Diem's order of September 11, 1954, to go to France for a six months' leave. The General was finally dismissed by Bao Dai, himself in France, on November 29. Diem later had to cope with a "United Front" of Binh Xuyen, Hoa Hao, and Caodaist forces. In late March, 1955, the Binh Xuyen, a group of gangsters who controlled the police as well as the vice of Saigon, rose in revolt. In general the National Army remained loyal, and at the end of April when fighting broke out again, the Binh Xuyen forces were driven from Saigon-Cholon after extensive bloodshed.[54] Having allied themselves with powerful dissidents of the Hoa Hao, a Buddhist religious sect, the Binh Xuyen continued for some time to give the government trouble. It was necessary for Diem to mount an offensive against Hoa Hao forces who had concentrated at Can Tho and Vinh Long and also

[54] Not without reason, President Eisenhower observed on April 27, 1955, regarding developments in South Vietnam, that "it is a strange and it is almost an inexplicable situation." *New York Times*, April 28, 1955.

in the Seven Mountains redoubt near the Cambodian border. Leading generals of the Caodaists, the largest religious sect in terms of number, had previously made their peace with Diem without resorting to armed rebellion. By the spring of 1956 Diem had broken the military threat of the sects. Obviously the existence of states within a state, as the Binh Xuyen, Hoa Hao, and Caodaist forces came to represent in many respects, was not in line with Diem's concept of a national Vietnam. There was no place in his thinking for armed forces outside those truly incorporated in those of the nation.

In his struggle with Bao Dai, Premier Diem finally triumphed. A "revolutionary committee" proclaimed the removal of the absentee leader as Chief of State; the Council of the Imperial Family, Nguyen Phuoc, called for similar action.[55] After a census a referendum held on October 23, 1955, favored the deposition of Bao Dai as Chief of State and his replacement by Diem, the majority being 98.2 percent. Three days later the Republic of Vietnam was proclaimed with Ngo Dinh Diem as President. The United States, France, and Great Britain quickly recognized it. Diem then pushed forward his plans for the drafting of a constitution and the establishment of an elected national assembly. On March 4, 1956, a constituent assembly was elected to draw up a constitution. On October 26 President Diem, having suggested certain changes in the draft and having received it back with alterations, promulgated it as the constitution of the Republic of Vietnam.

While involved in the grave problems relating to the consolidation of his position, Diem had to cope with the question of the "French presence" and the threat of Ho Chi Minh north of the seventeenth parallel. The French had in the past helped to support the Binh Xuyen, Hoa Hao, and Caodaist forces, and it was widely believed in political circles around Diem that the French were generally in sympathy with Bao Dai and opposed to the Premier on the grounds that he was too nationalist as a leader. Ho Chi Minh for his part looked with concern at the growing strength of Diem, the Viet Minh opposing the referendum on deposing Bao Dai and urging Vietnamese in the south to make void their ballots. Ho and Diem were clearly struggling for the loyalties of southern Vietnamese, especially those living in areas recently evacuated by the

[55] In the spring of 1955 the Crown Domain of Bao Dai in South Vietnam, a mountain region of backward peoples, was ended, the territory being placed on an administrative footing similar to that of the lowland areas and the tribesmen receiving a status like the Vietnamese.

Viet Minh whose agents undoubtedly remained in the country.

The Diem government did not favor the earlier Franco-Vietnamese Declaration of April 28, 1954, referring to the Heads of Agreement on Vietnamese Independence and on Association in the French Union. Initialed June 4, the treaties were never signed or, of course, ratified. In effect, however, the Heads of Agreement on Vietnamese Independence came into force although the Heads of Agreement on Vietnamese Association in the French Union awaited future developments involving a new definition of the French Union. Under the Vietnam independence treaty, France in addition to recognizing Vietnam as "a fully independent and sovereign State" agreed to transfer to her "all jurisdictions and public services" retained in the country.[56] Vietnam for her part would assume the obligations as related to her of the international treaties and conventions France had made. In the Vietnamese association treaty, the two contracting governments, in addition to affirming "their will to associate freely within the French Union" and to make the necessary relevant conventions, proceeded to define the role of the President of the French Republic as President of the Union, of the High Council, and of a court of arbitration.[57] Significantly, under Article 3 France and Vietnam in the High Council "shall . . . jointly assure, with respect for the principle of the sovereign equality of States, the coördination of their efforts and the harmonization of their respective policies in matters of common interest."[58]

The Geneva settlement on Indochina, concluded a few weeks later, so altered the situation in Vietnam that the basic relations between France and Vietnam remained to be defined. France was bitter when she compared the results with the cost of the war—almost 90,000 killed, died, and missing of the French Union forces including some 20,000 Frenchmen; and the equivalent of well over $8 billion spent including over $1.2 billion in American aid that actually arrived (some later withdrawn). The quadripartite arrangements established among France, Vietnam, Cambodia, and Laos as a result of the Pau agreements of November, 1950, as well as the related policy of France toward the two Vietnams, Cambodia, and Laos clearly needed to be reconsidered.

[56] Heads of Agreement on Vietnamese Independence, *Documents on American Foreign Relations, 1954,* p. 270.

[57] Heads of Agreement on Vietnamese Association in the French Union, *Documents on American Foreign Relations, 1954,* p. 271.

[58] *Ibid.*

The agreements reached at Pau, embodied in a number of conventions in December, regulated matters in which France and the Associated States were jointly concerned. Vietnam, Cambodia, and Laos were to establish a customs union, for a while 71 percent of the receipts going to Vietnam, 7 percent to Laos and 22 percent to Cambodia; approval was also given the principle of having free trade within the French Union. A joint technical board and an intergovernmental conference were to direct the customs services, France having a definite voice. Laos and Cambodia would have transit rights and free zones in the port of Saigon, recognized as Vietnamese. The port would be open to the shipping of states not at war with any unit of the French Union as well as, of course, to Union shipping. The Mekong as far as Phnom Penh would be free to the shipping of the French Union and its three Associated States. Quadripartite organs would handle navigation on the Mekong and the port of Saigon. Although Vietnam, Cambodia, and Laos would manage their own finances, an interstate organization (Institut d'Emission) would replace the Bank of Issue and the Foreign Exchange Office which were controlled by France. Each Associated State would be responsible for immigration with consultation in the interests of coördination. Likewise each would control its foreign trade and make commercial agreements, but a study group would coördinate policies and submit recommendations to an intergovernmental conference. Telegraph, telephone, and postal systems in Indochina would be under the control of the respective Associated States though linked by a study committee and conferences. The participation of France in the "interstate structure" insured a strong position for the Paris government.

The Pau agreements obviously restricted the independence of Vietnam, Cambodia, and Laos while clearly giving France a voice not generally appreciated in Indochina. After the Geneva Conference Vietnam, Cambodia, Laos, and France met on August 26 in Paris to alter the Pau accords. In a settlement reached December 29 and December 30 the four parties ended the customs and economic union. Vietnam, Cambodia, and Laos would each have its own customs duties. Vietnam was to pay retroactively customs due Cambodia and Laos. As of January 1, 1955, three central banks and three exchange control boards came into being. Each country would issue its own currency, though agreement was reached to maintain parity among the three currencies and to keep a common rate of exchange with reference to the French franc for a while.

Distribution was planned for the assets and liabilities of the Institut d'Emission. The three Indochinese states approved the right of freedom of navigation on the Mekong River; a Mekong Commission would be organized to consider the way the right would be exercised. Cambodia and Laos in bilateral conventions with Vietnam would get privileges in the port of Saigon. Thus France, Vietnam, Cambodia, and Laos would govern their relations with one another chiefly on a bilateral rather than a quadripartite basis.

It is clear from the Pau and Paris discussions that the Mekong River presents geographical problems that require a common policy. When France ruled Indochina the Mekong was a subject of bilateral negotiations with Thailand to the west. But with the emergence of independent Laos, Cambodia, and Vietnam, the Mekong becomes the primary concern of four sovereign states. The real test of coöperation in the future among them will be the way the problems relevant to the river are handled. Rising in Tibet and flowing through the gorges of Yunnan, the Mekong forms the boundary of Laos and Burma, later of Laos and Thailand, and flows through Cambodia and South Vietnam to the South China Sea. Under the partition arrangements at Geneva, the Democratic Republic of Vietnam has no territory through which the Mekong flows. Steamers can travel on the river at all seasons from Kratie in Cambodia to the sea, a distance of 270 miles; junks and sampans can travel to above Vientiane in Laos although rapids at intervals interfere. The delta of the river begins at Phnom Penh, the key city of Cambodia. Obviously the Mekong is important to Laos which is landlocked, to Cambodia which only recently has begun to develop its own short seacoast, and to Vietnam, the outlet of the water artery. In addition to problems of navigation and transportation, there arise those relating to irrigation and hydroelectric development. Significantly, representatives of Vietnam, Laos, and Thailand met with American engineering experts in Saigon in February, 1956, to discuss matters of common concern. With the help of Cambodia, a preliminary survey of the lower Mekong has been made by the American Bureau of Reclamation. At the tenth annual meeting of ECAFE in Bangkok, March 18 to March 28, 1957, Cambodia, Laos, Vietnam, and Thailand agreed in a joint statement on coöperation in developing the water resources of the lower Mekong. In November Lieutenant General Raymond A. Wheeler was appointed by United Nations' authorities to visit the lower Mekong basin and evaluate draft projects for developing the region. It has been claimed that part of President Eisenhower's special Asian fund for regional economic development might be profitably spent in the river area. Thailand has suggested that work might be done under SEATO.[59]

The duality of French policy toward South and North Vietnam since the Geneva settlement has been pronounced, especially in the beginning period. Although France continued to recognize the State of Vietnam as the legal government of the country, the armistice providing a temporary partition, the stationing of a mission in the north under Jean Sainteny, "Delegate General in North Vietnam," caused apprehension in the State of Vietnam under the premiership of Ngo Dinh Diem. The Saigon government took the position that France was compromising it by the negotiations with Ho Chi Minh.

A basic communiqué,[60] it is important to note, issued after Franco-American conversations, September 27 to September 29, 1954, asserted that France and the United States would "continue to assist Cambodia, Laos, and Viet-Nam in their efforts to safeguard their freedom and independence and to advance the welfare of their peoples." It was stated that "pending the further development of national forces for this purpose [security of the area]," France was prepared "to retain forces of its Expeditionary Corps, in agreement with the government concerned, within the limits permitted under the Geneva agreements and to an extent to be determined." The United States would consider financial assistance to the Expeditionary Corps in addition to helping the forces of the three Associated States. "The channel," it was indicated, "for French and United States economic aid, budgetary support, and other assistance to each of the Associated States will be direct to that state." Efforts would be made to coördinate the French and American aid programs to Vietnam, Cambodia, and Laos.

In summarizing accomplishments on the first anniversary of his government, Premier Diem on July 7, 1955, significantly asserted with reference to France:

> Its [his government's] first task was in recovering complete sovereignty and the right of the people to self determination. After long negotiation, France restored to us all civil authority. We resumed

[59] In the latter part of 1956 arrangements were made under the auspices of the United States to make a survey relative to a possible regional telecommunications network for South Vietnam, Laos, and Thailand.

[60] Franco-American Communiqué, *The Department of State Bulletin*, Vol. XXXI (October 11, 1954), p. 534.

charge of broadcasting stations, the office of exchange, the port of Saigon, civil air service, meteorological services, light houses, beacons, the Chamber of Commerce and the University. Mixed jurisdiction and the security forces maintained by the French were discontinued. Independence Palace was also returned to us. In the field of national defense we resumed command of all military regions. Discussions concerning the commander-in-chief are now taking place.[61]

With the departure of General Paul Ely, still holding the titles of Commissioner General and Commander-in-Chief, in the spring of 1955, the question of the rank and title of his successor had been raised. The State of Vietnam wanted to receive a French representative in the capacity of an ambassador and desired to conduct relations with France through the Ministry of Foreign Affairs rather than the Ministry for the Associated States. Henri Hoppenot came to be accredited to the Saigon government with the rank of "Ambassadeur de France en mission extraordinaire" and "Haut Commissaire de la République Française au Viet-Nam." Later only the rank of ambassador remained for a French representative. And no longer is there Vietnamese representation in the High Council of the French Union.

The question of keeping the French Expeditionary Corps in South Vietnam was also considered by the French and Vietnamese governments. The troops involved were progressively reduced and France was obligated, as already indicated, to withdraw all of them at the request of the Saigon regime. The presence of the French soldiers was a reminder to nationalistic Vietnamese of their former colonial status. By early 1955 the United States was playing a major part in the training and reorganizing of the National Army of Vietnam although the French were participating in the work. On March 30, 1956, France and the Republic of Vietnam reached an agreement on the timetable for the complete withdrawal of the French Expeditionary Corps as requested by Saigon on January 19. The Republic of Vietnam did not want foreign troops or foreign bases on its territory. The Expeditionary Corps quickly left the country, and the French Military Mission itself came to an end on May 31, 1957.

As for cultural affairs, where France has put considerable emphasis, an agreement with South Vietnam in the latter part of 1955 dealt with relations between Vietnamese and French universities, the Institute of Oceanography at Nha Trang, the French Cultural Institute, and French educational establishments in Viet-

[61] Address of Premier Ngo Dinh Diem, July 7, 1955, *Embassy of Viet-Nam [Washington], Press and Information Service*, Vol. 1 (No. 17).

nam. Also discussed at a conference were the École Française d'Extrême-Orient, the use of the Vietnamese and French languages in curriculums and technical exchanges. Among the good number of Vietnamese in France are many students. There is in Saigon a large French cultural mission and a Vietnamese-French friendship association has been formed.

In the economic field relations between the Paris and Saigon governments were stormy. On December 30, 1954, a monetary and commercial convention was signed for one year, providing for free monetary transfers and preferential tariffs between France and the State of Vietnam. It is significant that the French share in the imports of Vietnam has been dropping; the reduction and final withdrawal of the Expeditionary Corps, moreover, has meant a great decline in the supply of francs. With American aid no longer channeled in any category through France, Vietnam is taking advantage of the situation by buying in competitive world markets. On December 21, 1955, it was announced in Saigon that the Vietnamese piastre would from then on belong to the dollar bloc. On October 29 the Vietnamese government had denounced the monetary and commercial agreement of the previous December. Although the expiration date was later extended to the end of the following February, negotiations were difficult. France was finally given a minimum customs tariff. The United States is accused by many Frenchmen of seeking to get an economic foothold in Vietnam at their expense. Meanwhile many Frenchmen, in addition to the armed forces, have been leaving South Vietnam. In October, 1955, it was estimated that only some 7000 natural-born and about 25,000 naturalized French citizens were left; the total figure in early 1957 was about 20,000.

During 1955 French economic aid to South Vietnam came to the value of $9 million, and $33 million were spent for refugee evacuation. A French mission for economic and technical coöperation is active in Saigon. France has been earmarking money to enable South Vietnam to buy lands owned by the French and distribute them to the Vietnamese. In 1956 France agreed to buy $30 million worth of American surplus agricultural goods and the United States would put the proceeds into an account in francs to help Vietnam buy French imports. Despite many changes the French still have strong economic interests in the area.

Relations between the United States and the State of Vietnam have existed on the diplomatic level since the former's recognition of the latter on February 7, 1950. Actually during the Second World War President Franklin D. Roosevelt had given thought to the postwar situation in Indochina. He was opposed to the restoration of the area to France and favored an international trusteeship over it.[62] Roosevelt believed that his approach to the problem was supported by Stalin and Chiang Kai-shek. On the other hand, Secretary of State Cordell Hull favored the restoration of Indochina to France providing independence would eventually be given. President Harry Truman wanted at some suitable time to ask France to give a real indication of her plans to establish liberties and increasing self-government in the area.

From the surrender of Japan to the Communist victory in China the United States showed relatively little interest in developments in Indochina. The implications of the successful rise to power of Mao Tse-tung, however, were realized in Washington. Economic and military survey missions in 1950 included Indochina in their travels in Southeast Asia. After the outbreak of the Korean War President Truman on June 27 announced the acceleration of "military assistance to the forces of France and the Associated States in Indochina and the dispatch of a military mission to provide close working relations with those forces."[63] On December 23 an agreement for "mutual defense assistance in Indochina" was signed at Saigon between the United States and France, Vietnam, Cambodia, and Laos. It provided for American military aid in terms of equipment, material, and service. On September 7, 1951, an economic coöperation agreement was signed between Vietnam

[62] An interesting conversation between Stalin and Roosevelt on Indochina occurred at Yalta on February 8, 1945:

"THE PRESIDENT then said he also had in mind a trusteeship for Indochina. He added that the British did not approve of this idea as they wished to give it back to the French since they feared the implications of a trusteeship as it might affect Burma.

"MARSHAL STALIN remarked that the British had lost Burma once through reliance on Indochina, and it was not his opinion that Britain was a sure country to protect this area. He added that he thought Indochina was a very important area.

"THE PRESIDENT said that the Indochinese were people of small stature, like the Javanese and Burmese, and were not warlike. He added that France had done nothing to improve the natives since she had the colony. He said that General de Gaulle had asked for ships to transport French forces to Indochina.

"MARSHAL STALIN inquired where de Gaulle was going to get the troops.

"THE PRESIDENT replied that de Gaulle said he was going to find the troops when the President could find the ships, but the President added that up to the present he had been unable to find the ships."

Roosevelt-Stalin Meeting, February 8, 1945, 3:30 P.M., *Foreign Relations of the United States, Diplomatic Papers, The Conferences at Malta and Yalta, 1945*, p. 770.

[63] Statement by President Truman, *The Department of State Bulletin*, Vol. XXIII (July 3, 1950), p. 5.

and the United States, authorizing American economic and technical help to Vietnam. Assurances required by the Mutual Security Act of 1951 were later given by the Asian state.

Apprehension over the possible intentions of Communist China in Indochina, Thailand, or Burma was indicated when on January 28, 1952, John Sherman Cooper at the United Nations General Assembly's First Committee asserted that "his government had instructed him to state that any such communist aggression in south-east Asia, would, in its view, be a matter of direct and grave concern requiring the most urgent and earnest consideration by the United Nations."[64] The place of the war in Indochina as a part of the global struggle was indicated in a communiqué issued on June 18 after a conference between French and American officials: "The principle which governed this frank and detailed exchange of views and information was the common recognition that the struggle in which the forces of the French Union and the Associated States are engaged against the forces of Communist aggression in Indochina is an integral part of the world-wide resistance by the Free Nations to Communist attempts at conquest and subversion."[65] It was noted that the United States had a large portion of the task in Korea, and France the primary assignment in Indochina. On December 17 the North Atlantic Council, meeting in Paris, adopted a resolution acknowledging that the "resistance of the free nations in South-East Asia or in Korea is in fullest harmony with the aims and ideals of the Atlantic Community" and agreeing that "the campaign waged by the French Union forces in Indo-China deserves continuing support from the NATO governments."[66]

It is not surprising, therefore, that prior to the Geneva settlement American help to France and the Associated States grew to great proportions. Senator Mike Mansfield asserted on October 15, 1954, that "as a result largely of American assistance . . . the non-Communist forces possessed great superiority—estimated as high as 10 to 1—in armaments, and the flow of American aid was constant and increasingly heavy."[67] In September, 1953, France had

[64] United Nations, General Assembly, Sixth Session, *Official Records*, First Committee, 503rd Meeting, January 28, 1952, p. 267.

[65] Text of Communiqué, *The Department of State Bulletin*, Vol. XXVI (June 30, 1952), p. 1010.

[66] Resolution on Indochina of North Atlantic Council, *Documents on International Affairs, 1952*, p. 502.

[67] *Report on Indochina*, Report of Senator Mike Mansfield on a Study Mission to Vietnam, Cambodia, Laos, October 15, 1954, Committee Print, Senate Committee on Foreign Relations, 82d Congress, 2d Session, p. 3.

adopted the Navarre Plan which included a quick building of indigenous forces. In the words of Secretary Dulles, the "United States . . . agreed to underwrite the costs of this Plan."[68] By the time of the Geneva Conference the United States was bearing 78 percent of the cost of the war. Washington had turned over to the French, bombers, transport planes, tanks, guns, and warships. Around 250 Air Force technicians were in Vietnam servicing planes supplied France. Announcement came from Washington on April 21, 1954, that the United States Air Force was assigned to fly "certain French Union personnel" from France and North Africa to Indochina. Early the preceding March General Claire Chennault's Civil Air Transport Company had signed a contract with France to operate a number of "Flying Boxcars" supplied France by the United States, in Indochina, involving the services of a number of American civilian pilots. It is obvious that the American contribution in military and economic assistance was so extensive that a settlement not favorable to France and the Associated States would impair the standing of the United States.

At the same time, the Washington government hesitated to take the step that might mean open intervention. In April during the climax of the battle of Dien Bien Phu the French were solicitous, and the United States pondered its course of action. Congress, however, was not willing to see Indochina become another Korea, and Great Britain was determined to wait the results of the Geneva Conference. Misunderstanding arose, nevertheless, between the London and Washington governments over the question of security in Southeast Asia. Secretary Dulles in a speech on June 11 asserted that conditions that might justify American intervention were "an invitation from the present lawful authorities; clear assurance of complete independence of Laos, Cambodia, and Viet-Nam; evidence of concern by the United Nations; a joining in the collective effort of some of the other nations of the area, and assurance that France will not itself withdraw from the battle until it is won."[69] He significantly noted that "overt military Chinese Communist aggression" would threaten the United States and raise another issue.

After the Geneva settlement American policy toward Vietnam, south of the seventeenth parallel, centered around aid programs associated in effect with Ngo Dinh Diem. Senator Mansfield asserted

[68] Address of Secretary of State Dulles, June 11, 1954, *Documents on American Foreign Relations, 1954*, p. 276.

[69] *Ibid.*, p. 277.

in October, 1955: "The consistent support of the United States has done much to uphold Diem. . . . It has also contributed to raising the international stature of his government. Through the aid program, moreover, our policy is helping to resettle the refugees from the north, to revitalize the national army, to sustain the Vietnamese economy and to improve the civilian administration."[70] A member of the Senate Committee on Foreign Relations, Senator Mansfield had frankly asserted on October 15, 1954, after a study mission to Indochina that if the Diem government fell "the United States should consider an immediate suspension of all aid to Vietnam and the French Union forces there, except that of a humanitarian nature, preliminary to a complete reappraisal of our present policies in Free Vietnam."[71]

As already indicated, the American and French governments had agreed on September 29, 1954, a few weeks after the Geneva settlement, on a basic approach to Vietnam, Cambodia, and Laos. On October 23 the American Ambassador to the State of Vietnam, Donald R. Heath, delivered a message to Premier Diem from President Eisenhower wherein the American chief executive referred to the granting of the requests of the Vietnamese leader for help in the moving of refugees from the north to the south and suggested to him that he and the American Ambassador in Saigon examine "how an intelligent program of American aid given directly to your Government can serve to assist Viet-Nam in its present trial, provided that your Government is prepared to give assurances as to the standards of performance it would be able to maintain in the event such aid were supplied."[72] The President, moreover, expected that "this aid will be met by performance on the part of the Government of Viet-Nam in undertaking needed reforms."[73] It should be noted that in the Mutual Security Act of 1954 Congress provided that assistance should, as far as possible, go directly to Vietnam, Cambodia, and Laos.

On November 3 the President designated General J. Lawton Collins as Special United States Representative in Vietnam for the purpose of coördinating and furthering the work of all American agencies in the country. It was announced in Washington on

[70] *Viet Nam, Cambodia, and Laos,* Report by Senator Mike Mansfield, October 6, 1955, Committee Print, Senate Committee on Foreign Relations, 84th Congress, 1st Session, p. 3.

[71] *Report on Indochina,* October 15, 1954, p. 14.

[72] President Eisenhower to Ngo Dinh Diem, *The Department of State Bulletin,* Vol. XXXI (November 15, 1954), p. 735.

[73] *Ibid.*

December 31 that on the following day the United States would begin to give financial aid directly to the governments of Vietnam, Laos, and Cambodia to strengthen their defense "against the threat of Communist subversion and aggression," thus reaffirming "the independent status these Governments now possess."[74] Economic aid since 1950, it was pointed out, had been granted directly to the three states.

Especially in the evacuation of almost 900,000 people including 40,000 Nung tribesmen from North to South Vietnam has the United States played an important part. "Operation Exodus" involved the coöperation of France, the United States, Vietnam, and various foreign voluntary assistance groups. American navy transport and cargo ships participated in the evacuation; Americans assisted in the staging centers in the north and in the reception centers in the south. The United States also made great efforts to help resettle the refugees and integrate them into the Vietnamese economy as quickly as possible. An American expert in land problems, Wolf Ladejinsky, arrived in Saigon to expedite the work. The location of the new settlements as well as the loyalty of the settlers could be of major significance in the political stability of the Diem administration. South Vietnam is fortunate in having rich undeveloped land available for the refugees.

In its information program the United States Information Service is active in the country. Vietnam is also benefiting from the Smith-Mundt Act for cultural exchange. A Viet Nam-American Association has been formed in Saigon and an American Friends of Viet Nam organization in the United States.

In another important field of activity the work of equipping, training, and reorganizing the armed forces of Vietnam is progressing under American auspices. France concentrated on the navy and air forces of Vietnam. General John W. O'Daniel was in charge for some time of the American training mission as well as of the United States Military Assistance Advisory Group. The Vietnamese National Army which has been absorbing men from the sects is being prepared to hold its own, at least for a while, in the event of an attack from the north. There are about 150,000 men in the regular army and some 45,000 in the mobile civil guard. United States officers point out that their training methods have proved effective in Greece, Korea, Turkey, and other countries.

[74] Direct Defense Support for Laos, Cambodia, and Viet-Nam, *The Department of State Bulletin,* Vol. XXXII (January 10, 1955), p. 51.

Americans are also helping to train and equip the police forces.

On the international level the Southeast Asia Collective Defense Treaty, extended to Free Vietnam, Cambodia, and Laos by a protocol, is an important aspect in the protection of South Vietnam in the event of overt aggression on the part of Ho Chi Minh. Here the support of the United States would be crucial. Saigon officials have definitely expressed their satisfaction with the Manila protocol. They have sought on occasion a meeting of the foreign ministers of the United States, Great Britain, and France in Saigon to consider the international problems facing Vietnam. They have been especially sensitive to discussions of their country without their participation.

In May, 1957, President Ngo Dinh Diem visited the United States as a guest of the government. In an address to a joint meeting of Congress on May 9 he expressed "profound gratitude" for the aid given. Critical of both Communism and colonialism, Diem was sympathetically received. A joint statement of the American and Vietnamese chief executives on May 11 "confirmed the determination of the two governments to work together to seek suitable means to bring about the peaceful unification of Viet Nam in freedom in accordance with the purposes and principles of the United Nations Charter."[75] Both expressed "concern over continuing Communist subversive capabilities in this area [Southeast Asia] and elsewhere."[76] Reference was made to SEATO and its protection of the Republic of Vietnam. The visit of President Diem was an important factor in American understanding of the problems of the new Asian state.

The policy of Great Britain in Vietnam has been conditioned by her alliance with the United States and France, her consideration of the views of the Commonwealth, especially India and Australia, and by the impact of developments in Indochina on Malaya. As is known, British forces occupied Indochina south of the sixteenth parallel after the Second World War and their presence worked to the advantage of the French. But Britain's policy toward granting independence within or outside the Commonwealth to India, Pakistan, Burma, and Ceylon was bound to encourage nationalism in Indochina. Although Great Britain recognized the State of Vietnam on February 7, 1950, she delayed raising her consulate general

[75] Joint Statement, *News from Viet-Nam* (Washington Embassy), Vol. 3 (May 31, 1957), p. 8.
[76] *Ibid.*, p. 9.

in Saigon to a legation. Visits between British and French civilian and military officials increased in Indochina and Malaya. Malcolm MacDonald, British Commissioner-General for South-East Asia, was a frequent visitor in Saigon.

On January 11, 1952, Foreign Secretary Eden in a speech at Columbia University in New York pointedly observed: "It should be understood that the intervention by force by China Communists in South-East Asia—even if they were called volunteers—would create a situation no less menacing than that which the United Nations met and faced in Korea. In any such event the United Nations should be equally solid to resist it."[77] John Sherman Cooper, as already indicated, made a similar statement 17 days later in the United Nations General Assembly's First Committee. Discussions among British, French, and American high-ranking military officers considered the question of security in Southeast Asia.

After the Geneva settlement, British policy toward the State of Vietnam once more paralleled American in many respects. The United Kingdom, however, with its Communist insurrection in Malaya, its different commitments, and its limited resources, was not in a position like the United States to assist extensively in the rehabilitation of Vietnam. Under the protocol to the Manila Pact Great Britain is pledged to defend South Vietnam under certain contingencies.

Six other members of the Commonwealth of Nations have special interests in the Vietnamese—Australia, New Zealand, Canada, India, Pakistan, and the Federation of Malaya. Australia is aware of the strategic importance of Indochina to the security of Southeast Asia and the Southwest Pacific. She established a legation in Saigon and the Australian Red Cross has helped the refugees. Australia as well as New Zealand indicated support of the Geneva settlement, and both as signatories of the Manila Pact with its protocol have assumed obligations for the defense of South Vietnam. High-ranking Australian and New Zealand officials come to Saigon; President Ngo Dinh Diem has paid a visit to Canberra. The Republic of Vietnam is receiving aid under the Colombo Plan and is a member of its Consultative Committee.

Canada's direct interests in Vietnam arise from her membership on the International Commission. As she indicated when she accepted the responsibility, "Canada is geographically remote from Indochina and her collective security responsibilities in Southeast

[77] Speech of Eden, *Documents on International Affairs, 1952,* p. 45.

Asia are limited to those that arise from membership in the United Nations."[78] On the International Commission for Vietnam Canada has reflected to an extent the pro-Western approach to Indochina in contrast to Poland which has sympathized with the pro-Communist.

India as chairman of the International Commission has a very great responsibility in Vietnam. The New Delhi government was sympathetic to the cause of Vietnamese nationalism but had refused to recognize either the Ho Chi Minh or Bao Dai regimes. In October, 1949, India had favored the admission of representatives of both governments to the conference at Singapore of the Economic Commission for Asia and the Far East. The Indians living in Vietnam are small in number but some of them are Chettyars of considerable means. After the Geneva Conference the Indian impact on the Saigon and Hanoi governments of the two Vietnams was more noted. Prime Minister Nehru arrived in Saigon on October 30, 1954, on his return to New Delhi from Peking. Although well received by Premier Diem, Nehru was the object of both friendly and critical demonstrations. He reportedly discussed, *inter alia*, the Five Principles with Diem. A South Vietnamese trade delegation visited New Delhi in August, 1956, and was received by Nehru. Later in the year it was indicated that Vietnam would open a consulate general in New Delhi. A trade agreement was signed in 1956. In November of the following year President Diem visited the Indian capital. In December, 1954, Pakistan, India's fellow Commonwealth member in the subcontinent, granted *de facto* recognition to both the northern and southern governments in Vietnam. A signer of the protocol to the Manila Pact, Pakistan has certain defense obligations to South Vietnam.

The Federation of Malaya as an independent state in Southeast Asia is naturally interested in developments in a country as close as Vietnam. Even before Merdeka Day missions of different kinds were exchanged between Saigon and Kuala Lumpur, and plans were made for the future stationing of diplomatic representatives. Tengku Abdul Rahman agreed to visit Saigon in the future.

The Republic of Vietnam in its foreign policy toward Nationalist China has been influenced by the entente existing between Mao

[78] Statement on Canadian Membership in the International Commissions for Vietnam, Laos, and Cambodia, July 28, 1954, External Affairs, Supplementary Papers, No. 54/22.

Tse-tung and Ho Chi Minh. Nationalist China once maintained consular offices in the entire country, closing these in the north after the Geneva settlement. As indicated, the People's Republic of China for its part entered into diplomatic relations with the Democratic Republic of Vietnam. In December, 1955, the Saigon government under President Diem agreed to establish diplomatic relations with Nationalist China at the legation level. Saigon in its appeal to the Vietnamese has made it a point to stress the alleged degree of Chinese Communist influence north of the parallel. The Vietnamese Ambassador in Washington, Tran Van Chuong, for instance, asserted in March, 1955, "The Vietnamese in the North are now realizing with horror that the Viet Minh have imposed and are imposing on them incredible hardships and sacrifices only to replace French colonialism by a much harsher one: Communist Chinese Colonialism, which is the worst of all."[79]

Within South Vietnam live about 950,000 Chinese, possibly close to one-tenth of the population, as compared with around 60,000 in the North. Cholon, the "twin" of Saigon, is overwhelmingly a Chinese city. Obviously the role of the Chinese minority in South Vietnam is a subject of considerable importance to the future of the area. Although very prominent in economic activities, the Chinese under the Republic of Vietnam have generally taken a passive attitude toward politics. The Vietnamese for their part are resentful of the economic hold of the Chinese.

In August and September, 1956, President Diem took strong measures relative to the Chinese minority in the country. Persons born in Vietnam of one or two Chinese parents before or after an ordinance of August 21 were made Vietnamese citizens without any option in the matter. It is reported that about 500,000 people were affected. Chinese in Vietnam born in China were considered aliens but they could be naturalized. Noncitizens, subject to certain qualifications, could not legally own in the near future businesses of 11 different types including many retail trades. All private Chinese secondary schools could not reopen until the director was a Vietnamese national and the regular Vietnamese secondary school curriculum was followed. Chinese could be taught only as an additional language to Vietnamese. Infants of Vietnamese nationality could be given only Vietnamese names.

The Chinese community was aroused over the measures; some

[79] Ambassador Tran Van Chuong, The Vietnamese Problem, March, 1955 (mimeographed).

individuals withdrew money from the banks and others went to Cambodia. The Republic of Vietnam rejected a suggestion from the legation of Nationalist China that the citizenship ordinance be suspended pending an agreement between the Taipei and Saigon governments. President Diem took the position that the matter was one of domestic jurisdiction; Chinese born in Vietnam could go to Formosa if they desired. In December the first Chinese Minister to the Republic of Vietnam arrived in Saigon. On May 6, 1957, Chinese nationals demonstrated before the legation against the Diem policies, some even entering the building. The Taipei government was willing to repatriate the Chinese who wanted to leave Vietnam. Relations between Nationalist China and the Republic of Vietnam were obviously strained over the issue of "forced" versus "free choice" citizenship.

With Japan South Vietnam has inherited issues arising from the Nipponese role during the Second World War. The State of Vietnam participated in the Japanese Peace Conference at San Francisco and signed the treaty of peace. In his speech[80] at a plenary session on September 7, 1951, Prime Minister Tran Van Huu, after referring to the human and material losses inflicted upon his country by the Japanese, welcomed the reconciliation aspects of the treaty and pointedly asserted, "We shall neglect no effort toward contributing to the rebuilding of a sober, industrious Asian nation like Japan, convinced that the Asiatics should be the main artisans of their common prosperity, that they should count on themselves to banish all imperialism, and that, in the establishment of a new world order, Asian solidarity is as necessary as European solidarity." The Vietnamese delegate, however, was critical of the reparations clauses of the treaty, asking that "other more effective formulas for payment be studied" and seeking in addition to the methods provided a "normal indemnification" when Japan had restored her economy. Furthermore, he significantly affirmed "our right to the Spratly and Paracel Islands, which have always belonged to Vietnam." Under the peace treaty, it should be indicated, Japan renounced "all right, title and claim to the Spratly Islands and to the Paracel Islands" but no reference was included as to whom the renunciation was made.[81] The Vietnamese Prime Minister also wanted a "collective security system" in his part of the world.

[80] Speech of Tran Van Huu, *Conference for the Conclusion and Signature of the Treaty of Peace with Japan, passim.*

[81] Treaty of Peace with Japan, *Conference for the Conclusion and Signature of the Treaty of Peace with Japan,* p. 314.

Under the framework of the Japanese peace treaty Saigon was aware that bilateral and multilateral agreements between Japan and the other signatories could be negotiated relative to mutual problems like reparations, claims, and trade. On September 16, 1953, Japan and the State of Vietnam signed an agreement wherein the former would pay partial reparations estimated in cost at $2,250,000 in the form of ship salvaging. A determination had to be made as to the jurisdiction of the waters where the sunken ships were located. Ratification of the agreement was dependent upon political developments in Vietnam. Japan was eager to settle the overall question of reparations with the new state. Some progress was made during the visit of Prime Minister Kishi to Saigon in November, 1957.

Trade between Japan and South Vietnam has greatly expanded since the latter was actually in a position to buy in the world market. The French in South Vietnam have complained that Japan has been "dumping" goods to reduce the purchase of their products. A number of Vietnamese students are studying in Nippon, which is very much interested in the question of technical assistance to the Republic of Vietnam. A private commercial fishing agreement was made in 1956 providing for Japanese technical aid.

On the diplomatic level, Japan in February, 1955, raised her mission in Saigon from legation to embassy status. The legation from Tokyo had been set up on October 15, 1954. Vietnam has likewise raised her legation in Japan to the rank of an embassy. In presenting his credentials to President Diem, the Japanese Ambassador in early 1956 expressed the faith of his country in the future of Vietnam and its present leadership.

The Republic of Korea under President Syngman Rhee recognized the State of Vietnam in 1950. It was announced in late 1955 that the republics of Vietnam and Korea had decided to exchange diplomatic missions at the legation level. During the Korean War the State of Vietnam had contributed the equivalent of $10,000 toward relief in South Korea and had offered on November 22, 1952, ten tons of rice. In response to a question from the United Nations headquarters on measures taken as a result of the General Assembly resolution of May 18, 1951, applying an embargo on strategic materials to Communist China and North Korea, Vietnam replied that she supported the resolution and would take necessary steps to prevent the export of rubber, and even rice, to the areas mentioned. After the Geneva Conference officials in Saigon could not but compare the partition of Korea and its subsequent developments with the partition of Vietnam and its uncertain future. President Diem visited President Rhee in September, 1957.

Within Southeast Asia the Republic of Vietnam, bounded on the west by Cambodia and southern Laos and on the north by the Democratic Republic of Vietnam, has had to adjust both to the partition of the country and to the end of Indochina as a political unity under the French. With the Philippines the Diem administration cultivated increasingly friendly relations and with Thailand it sought close ties. Indonesia accorded *de facto* recognition after the Geneva settlement and consuls general were exchanged. As for Burma, Premier U Nu, it should be recalled, has visited both Ho Chi Minh in Hanoi and Ngo Dinh Diem in Saigon. South Vietnamese consulates have been set up in Hong Kong and Singapore; in 1957 a consulate general in Rangoon and a legation in Kuala Lumpur were added.

The general world outlook of the Republic of Vietnam is clearly emerging from a highly confused background. It is not surprising under the circumstances that the partition of the country and the exodus of many refugees from the north to the south, each having international implications, are stressed in speeches of Saigon officials dealing with foreign affairs. At the Bandung Conference of Asian-African powers, the delegation from South Vietnam put considerable emphasis on these topics.

The constitution of the Republic of Vietnam, promulgated October 26, 1956, asserted in Article 8: "The Republic of Viet Nam shall adhere to the principles of international law which are not contrary to the exercise of national sovereignty and the realisation of equality of nations. The Republic shall endeavour to contribute to the maintenance of world peace and security as well as to strengthen the bonds of friendship which unite it with other peoples on a basis of freedom and equality."[82] President Diem had previously suggested to the Constituent Assembly a clause reading: "The Republic of Viet Nam recognizes and respects the principles of International Law. The State will do all in its power to build up and protect international peace and security and to maintain and develop friendly relations with all people on a foundation of liberty and equality."[83]

[82] The Constitution of the Republic of Viet Nam, *News from Viet-Nam*, Vol. 3 (November 17, 1956), p. 2.

[83] *News from Viet-Nam*, Vol. 3 (October 27, 1956), p. 3.

Strong opposition to colonialism in any form, whether French or Communist, is a major aspect of foreign policy in Saigon. Ambassador Tran Van Chuong in a statement in March, 1955, for instance, frankly asserted: "We must understand that most of the Asiatic peoples are inclined to be neutral because they are afraid of Colonialism and because they are poor. Nevertheless they must be saved from Communism if the Free World is to be saved and they cannot be saved from Communism if they are not first liberated from Colonialism and from poverty."[84] He went on to observe that in the recent war in Indochina "most of the Asiatic nations of South-East Asia openly favored the Viet-Minh and put the blame on France" and later "most of the Asiatic nations applauded the Geneva Armistice which is a grave defeat for the West and abandoned to the Communists half of Viet Nam: inspired by dislike of Colonialism, they applauded a Communist victory which may lead to their own enslavement."[85] Again, the head of the South Vietnamese delegation at Bandung, Nguyen Van Thoai, in his opening speech noted: "Deeply aware of all the sufferings of an oppressed people such as in our case, we are naturally the most ardent supporters of all undertakings which may help small nations gain quickly their independence. . . ."[86] He asked for the complete application of the "self-determination of peoples." During the Conference, Nguyen Van Thoai opposed an Indian resolution calling for the full execution of the Geneva agreement but he sought an extension of the time limit for the movement of people north and south of the parallel.

It is not surprising that the Republic of Vietnam expressed deep sympathy for the Hungarians who fought in late 1956 the efforts of the Russians to conquer them. Saigon favored "the intervention of international forces" in Hungary "in order to defend liberty and the right of people to govern themselves."[87]

Toward the question of foreign aid the South Vietnamese government is well aware of its importance in the development of the nation. Vu Van Mau, for instance, told the Consultative Committee of the Colombo Plan in Singapore, 1955: "The Government of Viet Nam and the Vietnamese people are very grateful not

[84] Ambassador Tran Van Chuong, The Vietnamese Problem, March, 1955 (mimeographed).

[85] *Ibid.*

[86] Speech of Nguyen Van Thoai, Press Release, Asian-African Conference, Bandung, Indonesia.

[87] Government Statement, November 6, 1956, *News for Viet-Nam,* Vol. 3 (November 10, 1956), p. 1.

only for the generous help given by the United States and France, but also for the aid given within the framework of the Colombo Plan, by Britain, Australia, Canada and New Zealand. We appreciate this aid fully in that it is making it possible for us to conquer Communism by combatting poverty."[88] Saigon was pleased to be the host of the meeting of the Consultative Committee in 1957. Vietnamese officials also have expressed appreciation for help granted by the United Nations through various agencies of the world organization. An economic survey mission has visited the country under the joint auspices of the United Nations, FAO and ILO.

In its commercial policy the Republic of Vietnam, having been freed from the tight French-dominated economy of the past, is seeking to trade with the United States, Japan, and other states like Italy and West Germany along with France. The Vietnamese claimed in April, 1955, that for the first time a commercial agreement with a foreign power—Italy—was signed on their soil. The agreement was a protocol to the commercial pact made by the two countries on November 14, 1953. Discussions between West German and South Vietnamese officials have included not only the question of further trade but have led to an agreement to exchange diplomatic missions.

In another aspect concerning foreign policy, the presence of some 2 million Catholics in all of Vietnam, large numbers of whom have moved to south of the seventeenth parallel since the Geneva settlement, is a tie of the Republic of Vietnam to the Catholic states of the West and to the Philippines across the South China Sea. The Vatican recognized the State of Vietnam and later the Republic of Vietnam. It has been estimated that of the 1035 priests who represented ten apostolic vicarates in North Vietnam, 603 went to the south with the refugees, 374 stayed in the north and 58 left Vietnam. Diem in 1955 had difficulties with the Vatican over the appointment of a bishop of Saigon. Significantly two chiefs of state in Southeast Asia are Roman Catholic—Garcia of the Philippines and Diem of Vietnam.

As for territorial claims, the Republic of Vietnam, as indicated, is concerned over the status of the Paracel and Spratly Islands in the South China Sea. Located about 250 miles east of central Vietnam and lying southeast of Chinese Communist Hainan, the Para-

[88] Address of Vu Van Mau, *Embassy of Viet Nam* [*Washington*], *Press and Information Service*, Vol. 2 (No. 1).

cels are divided into the Amphitrite and Crescent groups. Coral like the Spratlys in origin, the Paracels too have deposits of phosphates. Their importance today arises largely from their strategic location in the South China Sea.

Emperor Gia-Long, founder of the Nguyen dynasty, annexed the Paracels to the Empire of Annam in 1816. France on June 15, 1932, made the islands an administrative district attached to the province of Thua Thien. In 1939 Japan claimed the Paracels and occupied them. As already pointed out, she formally relinquished them in the peace treaty signed at San Francisco in 1951, and the State of Vietnam at the conference on September 7 declared its rights over them. In a treaty of peace with Nationalist China on April 28, 1952, Japan renounced claims over the islands. A similar postwar attitude was taken by Japan with reference to the Spratlys. Nationalist China has continued to claim the Paracels, and on May 29, 1956, Communist China took a similar position. In fact, the Chinese term the Paracels along with the Spratlys the Nansha Islands or Islands of the South. One of the northern Paracels is actually occupied by the Chinese Communists. On June 1 the Republic of Vietnam formally reaffirmed its historic rights over the islands. A unit of its armed forces has landed on the archipelago. France for her part has taken the position that the Paracels are now subject to Vietnamese jurisdiction.

The controversy over the Spratly or Tempest Islands is even more complex. Strategically located south and southeast of the Paracels, about 280 miles southeast of Cam Ranh Bay and 775 miles northeast of Singapore, the Spratlys comprise 11 island groups, one of which is itself called Spratly. Although France placed the tricolor on one of the islands in 1930 she formally took possession of all of them in 1933. They were attached to the province of Baria in Cochin China. Japan protested the French action, and on March 30, 1939, announced her decision to place the Spratlys under her jurisdiction, occupation following the next year. At the San Francisco Peace Conference the State of Vietnam, it should be stressed, took the same position on the Spratlys that it did on the Paracels.

On March 17, 1956, Tomas Cloma, director of a Philippine maritime institute, announced his discovery of some islands in the South China Sea which he called "Freedomland." The Philippine government, though very much interested in them for strategic reasons, hesitated to support the claims of Cloma. Nationalist China quickly asserted that the Spratlys were Chinese, and later sent an armed unit to the area. On May 29 the People's Republic of China claimed the territory. France took the position that the islands were still under French sovereignty. On June 1 the Republic of Vietnam thought it necessary "to reaffirm its traditional rights to sovereignty" over the area. On June 6 the Foreign Minister asserted that "the transfer to Viet-Nam of sovereignty over the whole territory of Viet-Nam . . . automatically entails the transfer of French sovereignty over the Spratly Islands which were attached to Cochin-China."[89] Later in August an armed detachment from the Republic of Vietnam landed on the Spratlys. Both Communist and Nationalist China were concerned over the Vietnamese action.

In early 1957 the Department of Foreign Affairs in Saigon issued a significant declaration, asserting that the "Government of the Republic of Viet Nam wants to recall that its position [relative to the Paracel and Spratly Islands] remains unchanged and to reaffirm its rights. The sovereignty of Viet Nam on the islands in question cannot be denied either *de jure* or *de facto*. Furthermore, the forces of the Republic of Viet Nam have never ceased to exert their control on these two archipelagos."[90]

In the future of the United Nations Vietnam, although not a member, has a real interest. Premier Diem in an address[91] on United Nations Day, 1955, asserted that his "faith in the United Nations has not wavered and continues to grow." He stressed the value of the world organization especially for the "small nations." The Premier noted the military role of the United Nations in the Korean War and the efforts of its various organs to raise the standard of living of Asian peoples. He observed that "the noble and humanitarian aim of the United Nations is in accord with the legitimate aspirations of the Vietnamese people." Pursuing a policy of taking an active part in the specialized agencies of the world organization, Vietnam was admitted in 1956 to the World Bank and Monetary Fund.

In terms of national security the Republic of Vietnam realizes the important role of the United States and other Western powers, and is well aware of its own strategic location within Southeast Asia. Ambassador Tran Van Chuong, for instance, observed in March, 1955, that "Viet Nam is strategically at least as important

[89] Foreign Secretary's Interview, *Vietnam in World Affairs*, p. 108.

[90] Declaration on Paracel and Spratly Islands, *News from Viet-Nam*, Vol. 3 (March 8, 1957), p. 6.

[91] Address of Premier Ngo Dinh Diem, *Embassy of Viet Nam, Press and Information Service*, Vol. 1 (No. 16), *passim*.

as Formosa for, after losing the Chinese mainland, the Free World cannot afford to lose Indo-China which is the gateway to India."[92] He asserted on October 17 that "we want to open our country wide to friendly relations with the whole Free World, particularly with our Asian neighbors, with France and with the United States who is helping us to freedom."[93]

In connection with the proclamation of the Republic of Vietnam on October 26, 1955, President Ngo Dinh Diem received ranking officials of the diplomatic and consular corps in Saigon. Ambassadors from Great Britain, France (High Commissioner), the United States, and Japan, Ministers from Thailand, the Philippines, Australia, and Italy and consular officials from Nationalist China, India, Indonesia, the Netherlands, Belgium, and Sweden were present. Significant is the fact in the international relations of the Republic of Vietnam that all of the representatives listed as present except for those from India, Indonesia, and Sweden came from states allied with the United States through various agreements, multilateral like the North Atlantic Treaty and the Manila Pact or bilateral like the Japanese-American security treaty. Diplomatic representation in Saigon after the arrival of ministers from the Republic of Korea and the Republic of China would reflect even more this political alignment. On the occasion of the promulgation of the constitution on October 26, 1956, military units were pointedly present from the United States, Australia, France, Great Britain, Thailand, and the Philippines.[94]

In the Democratic Republic of Vietnam under President Ho Chi Minh a very contrasting pattern of international relations has de-

[92] Ambassador Tran Van Chuong, The Vietnamese Problem, March, 1955 (mimeographed).

[93] Speech of Ambassador Tran Van Chuong to the *New York Herald Tribune* Forum, March 17, 1955 (mimeographed).

[94] A conference of Vietnamese diplomats was held in Saigon in early October. The individuals present indicate the extent of Vietnamese representation abroad as of that time—ambassadors to France, the United States, Thailand, Great Britain, and Japan, ministers to Italy and Spain, the Philippines, Korea, Laos, and Nationalist China, a consul general to Indonesia and consuls to Singapore and Hong Kong. The ambassador to the United States arrived late; the representative to Cambodia was not present; a consul general to India would soon be sent. On the other hand, the foreign representation in Saigon as of June included embassies from Great Britain, the United States, Japan, Thailand, and France (Office of High Commissioner), legations from Australia, the Philippines, Belgium, Italy, Korea, Spain, and Nationalist China, consulates general from the Netherlands, Indonesia, and India and consulates from Denmark, Greece, Norway, Sweden, and Switzerland. The Vatican and West Germany were also represented, the latter by a commercial mission.

veloped since Geneva. At the end of the Conference the chief Viet Minh delegate, Pham Van Dong, praised the settlement, terming it a "great victory for peace." He called for the unity of Vietnam, for coöperation with the peoples of Southeast Asia and Asia on the basis of the Five Principles, and for ties with France along economic and cultural lines based on equality. Ho Chi Minh for his part in a radio broadcast on July 25 appealed to all patriots without distinction to work for peace, unity, and democracy in the country.

It had been a long and difficult road for the Viet Minh from the Declaration of Independence on September 2, 1945, to the signing of the cease-fire. In the former document, written partly under the influence of the American Declaration of Independence and the French Declaration of the Rights of Man, the leaders of the Democratic Republic of Vietnam under Ho Chi Minh had denounced the colonial rule of the "French imperialists" in scathing words and declared "that we shall henceforth have no relations with imperialist France, that we cancel all treaties which France has signed on the subject of Viet Nam, that we abolish all the privileges which the French have arrogated to themselves on our territory."[95] Absent from the declaration was the frequent use of Communist terminology later found in Viet Minh official statements. Nor does the constitution of the Democratic Republic of Vietnam, adopted on November 8, 1946, proclaimed the following day, and quickly suspended because of war, employ very much Communist verbiage.

In these years it appears that Ho Chi Minh was appealing for the support of both the Communist and Western worlds in his struggle for Vietnamese independence. In fact, the Indochinese Communist Party was officially ended in November, 1945, and did not emerge as the Vietnam Workers' Party (Lao Dong) until February, 1951. The Viet Minh or League for the Independence of Vietnam, founded in 1941, was finally merged in March, 1951, with the Lien Viet or League for the National Union of Viet Nam, set up in 1946, thus forming the Viet Nam Front of National Union or Lien Viet Front. In September, 1955, the Lien Viet Front announced its incorporation into a "Fatherland Front" for the unification of Vietnam. Throughout these developments a hard core of leaders remained—men like Ho Chi Minh, Pham Van Dong, and Vo Nguyen Giap, all of whom had signed the Declaration of Independence.

The Lao Dong Party is the dominating force in the Democratic

[95] Declaration of Independence, Harold R. Isaacs, ed., *New Cycle in Asia*, p. 165.

Republic of Vietnam. In its manifesto[96] in early 1951, replete with Communist terminology, the party recommended in the field of foreign affairs: "The Viet Nam people must unite closely with and help the peoples of Cambodia and Laos in their struggle for independence and, with them, liberate jointly the whole of Indo-China; actively support the national liberation movements of oppressed peoples; unite closely with the Soviet Union, China and other people's democracies; form close alliances with the peoples of France and the French colonies so as to contribute to the anti-imperialist struggle to defend world peace and democracy." The manifesto also asserted that "overseas Vietnamese in foreign countries must be protected" and "Chinese nationals [in Vietnam] in particular, if they so desire, will be allowed to enjoy the same rights and perform the same duties as Vietnamese citizens." A guide to foreign policy was revealed when the manifesto frankly stated: "The theory of the party is Marxism-Leninism. The principle of organization of the party is democratic centralism. The discipline of the party is strict self-discipline." The announced program of the Lao Dong Party paralleled the manifesto.[97]

The French position in the Democratic Republic of Vietnam after the Geneva settlement was difficult. On July 21, 1954, Premier Pierre Mendès-France received a letter from Pham Van Dong on the economic and cultural aspects of France in North Vietnam. As regards economic matters, the Democratic Republic would not hinder the departure of Frenchmen who wished to leave, the ownership of enterprises and assets would be protected, public service facilities maintained, businesses could continue without hindrance and without discrimination, and the legitimate interests of the French would be considered in the case of expropriation or requisition. As regards cultural matters, the Ho regime would al-

[96] Manifesto of Lao Dong Party, *Documents on International Affairs, 1951*, *passim.*

[97] In considering the political evolution of the Ho regime Bernard B. Fall asserted in 1954:

"After a hopeful beginning of constitutional democratic government, a single party gained control of the state apparatus, the armed forces and the bulk of the local administrative machinery. This party—a direct successor of the Indochinese Communist Party—has successfully consolidated its grip upon the State so that today the acts and policies of the Democratic Republic closely resemble those of any other state of the Soviet orbit." Bernard B. Fall, *The Viet-Minh Regime*, p. 116. Milton Sacks stated in September, 1950: "Today the 'Vietnam Democratic Republic' is a full-fledged partner in the camp of the Soviet Union and Communist China. It has moved in this direction gradually, and the success of the Communist leadership in Vietnam was greatly aided by the Chinese Communist victories." Sacks, *op. cit.*, p. 237.

low the French establishments to function and would participate in any conversations that might be needed. Pham Van Dong in a statement published on July 24 by *Tass*, after stressing the need to cultivate economic and cultural relations with the Soviet Union, the People's Republic of China, and the countries located in Southeast Asia, called for "normal relations" with France, especially in the economic field. The following November Ho Chi Minh in an interview mentioned that "the possibility and eventual conditions for Vietnam's participation in the French Union may be discussed between the Governments of the two countries if both wish it."[98]

The French selection of Jean Sainteny on August 7 as Delegate General in North Vietnam to preserve, if possible, the extensive French cultural and economic interests was significant. Sainteny had been the first French commissioner in Tonkin after the Second World War, had negotiated the agreement of March, 1946, with Ho Chi Minh and, although having been seriously wounded the following December, remained a strong believer in a peaceful settlement with the Viet Minh. Despite the fact that France considered the government of the State of Vietnam as the only legal one in the country, it appeared that the Paris authorities were seeking to reach a *modus vivendi* with Ho Chi Minh. Sainteny was in a difficult position, for France could not be immune to American opposition to negotiations with the Viet Minh, and the Democratic Republic of Vietnam was in a position to do what it wanted in the north. Nevertheless, the latter needed foreign technicians, industrial equipment, and capital.

In the cultural field Sainteny was more successful than in the economic. The University of Hanoi and the Lycée Albert Sarraut opened with French faculty members, the former under a French chancellor who at the same time was Dean of the Hanoi Medical School. French personnel remained with the École Française d'Extrême-Orient, the Radium Institute, and the Pasteur Institute of Hanoi. As time went on, however, there were fewer Frenchmen involved. Later the Pasteur Institute closed.

On December 10, 1954, the French and Viet Minh concluded at Hanoi a preliminary economic agreement providing for the free movement of French businessmen in the north, the remittance of profits, and the continuation of French business. The agreement, however, was in general terms and there were many loopholes. Specific accords were to be negotiated by individual businessmen.

[98] Quoted in *The Annual Register of World Events, 1954*, p. 318.

On April 9, 1955, the Société Française des Charbonnages du Tonkin with its extensive anthracite coal mines representing in all an investment of around $57 million reached agreement with the Viet Minh whereby the latter would purchase the property of the company, paying over a period of 15 years annual installments of coal totaling in the end 1 million tons. Although the Democratic Republic of Vietnam acquired the ownership of the northern coal mines, American-supplied industrial equipment had been removed at the urging of the United States, a development strongly resented by the Viet Minh. A few weeks later on June 2 the Hanoi municipal authorities bought from the French company concerned the transport facilities the latter owned in Hanoi.

In the end neither the French nor the Viet Minh in North Vietnam had sufficient confidence in each other to enable French business to retain a real position. By October, 1955, only 150 French nationals remained, and a great many of these people were government officials. Even the Indian and Pakistani merchants have been leaving the north. Nevertheless, a trade agreement was signed between France and the Viet Minh on October 14. The next year the French consulate in Haiphong was closed, reflecting the state of business. In the early part of 1957 the Ho Chi Minh government held for a while a French freighter on charges of having sunk on February 24 a Chinese Communist fishing boat. It is significant that President Ho did not visit France in his tour in Europe later the same year.

In many respects the role of the People's Republic of China with reference to the Democratic Republic of Vietnam is similar to that of the United States with the Republic of Vietnam. Communist China is the most influential power in the future of the Hanoi government of Ho Chi Minh as the United States is in the hopes of the Saigon regime of Ngo Dinh Diem. Yet the parallel should not be exaggerated, for different conditions exist. China has a long border with North Vietnam, Laos lying to the west of the latter and the Republic of Vietnam south of the seventeenth parallel. The Vietnamese have been aware of the Chinese for centuries. In fact, there has grown up a traditional dislike of them, this attitude being reinforced after the Second World War by the Chinese Nationalist occupation of Indochina north of the sixteenth parallel. As for Americans, they are newcomers in Vietnam and, although subject to vehement Communist propaganda, have not been there long enough to become the possible object of traditional dislike. Moreover, there is no American minority in Vietnam, the large number of Chinese in the "Land of the South" presenting a marked contrast.

The political alignment of the Mao and Ho governments in Peking and Hanoi reduces the barrier that might otherwise exist along the Sino-Vietnamese frontier. In terms of topography the terrain is generally rugged and does not provide easy access from either side. Under present plans a few roads and two railroads will cross the border. One railway, upon restoration, will link Kunming with Hanoi and Haiphong, and the other, recently built, links Nanning with Hanoi and Haiphong. In the past the Kokiu tin mines in Yunnan were developed as a consequence of the Indochina-Yunnan railway which obviously had an important role in the economy of Yunnan. In 1938 it is indicated that 378,626 tons of freight were carried on the railroad, of which 4 percent represented Yunnan-Tonkin traffic and 21 percent traffic between Yunnan and abroad. In the same year, 4,462,000 passengers traveled on some part of the railway. Although both northern Vietnam and southern China are underdeveloped areas and have similar economic needs, the expansion of railways in China linked with those in northern Vietnam coupled with the entente between the governments of the People's Republic of China and the Democratic Republic of Vietnam can have important consequences in Vietnam, Indochina, and Southeast Asia.

Using the occasion of the establishment of the People's Republic of China in 1949, Ho Chi Minh telegraphed Mao Tse-tung: "The fraternal relations between China and Vietnam which have a history of centuries will grow closer so as to develop freedom and happiness for our nations and defend world democracy and lasting peace in common."[99] Mao replied on November 26: "China and Vietnam are meeting on the front line of an imperialist struggle. With the victorious development of our struggles for liberation of the two peoples, the friendship between our two peoples will surely become closer day by day. . . ."[100] The Vietnamese and Chinese Communists joined in warning the French not to utilize fleeing Kuomintang troops in the war in Indochina.

Ho Chi Minh in a public appeal on January 14, 1950, asked recognition from the governments of the world, asserting that the

[99] Quoted in Sacks, *op. cit.*, p. 240.
[100] *Ibid.*

Democratic Republic of Vietnam was prepared "to establish diplomatic relations with any government which would be willing to treat her on a basis of equality and mutual respect, of national sovereignty and territory."[101] The next day the Ho Chi Minh regime formally recognized the Mao Tse-tung government. On January 18 Chou En-lai informed the Viet Minh of the willingness of Communist China to establish diplomatic relations at the ambassadorial level. The action of the Mao Tse-tung government was important in preventing France from recognizing Communist China. A Viet Minh embassy with a large information staff has beeen set up in Peking, the day, April 28, 1951, being the official date of opening. In 1954 after the Geneva settlement the Mao Tse-tung government established an embassy in Hanoi. Viet Minh consulates have been opened in Kunming and Nanning.

Chinese Communist assistance to Ho Chi Minh, it is obvious, was made possible after the loss of the mainland by Chiang Kai-shek, but the help was greatly facilitated by the armistice in the Korean War reached in July, 1953. There can be no doubt that events in Korea and Indochina had a direct relationship in the planning of the Peking government. Nevertheless, Communist China did not openly invade Indochina as she did Korea. She helped the Ho regime by giving it training facilities in China and by providing supplies. This assistance grew in proportions until at the battle of Dien Bien Phu Chinese technicians, arms, and advice proved a major factor in Ho's victory.

Efforts were made in the Democratic Republic of Vietnam to counteract the apprehension of many Vietnamese about the Chinese. The relatively small number of Chinese living in the north was a factor working to the advantage of the Democratic Republic. A Vietnam-Chinese Friendship Association has been formed as well as a Vietnam-Soviet Friendship Association. In January, 1954, a Vietnam-China-U.S.S.R. Friendship Month was launched. Radio Peking as well as Radio Moscow has been contributing to the cause by broadcasting in Vietnamese. Ho Chi Minh, by cultivating friendly relations with Mao Tse-tung on the official level and by trying to work with the Chinese minority on the local level, is adjusting to the fact that he and Mao are fellow Communists. At the same time the Chinese Communist Party has its own organization in Vietnam.

The partition of Vietnam at the seventeenth parallel found the

[101] *Ibid.*, p. 242.

Ho Chi Minh government facing more serious economic problems than those confronting the Diem administration. The economic policy of the Ho regime toward France was partly motivated by this situation. It is possible that keeping the door open with France would also serve to balance even in a small degree the impact of Communist China. Yet the agreements reached between the Hanoi and Peking governments on December 24, 1954, were an index to the ties between the two Communist regimes. A joint railroad and highway construction program would be undertaken, the building of the Hanoi-Dong Dang railway in Vietnam leading to Nanning in China being a specific objective; civil air traffic would be established between the two countries and the necessary airports and meteorological facilities built; telecommunications and postal services would be formally set up; and equipment would be shipped from China to restore five agricultural hydraulic facilities in North Vietnam. The Peking government assumed the role of providing the necessary technicians and equipment for carrying out the provisions of the accord. In April, 1956, the Chinese People's Republic Airline began service on the Canton-Nanning-Hanoi route. By spring of 1958 it was planned to reopen the Hanoi-Kunming railroad.

On July 7, 1955, it was announced in Peking that another agreement between the Democratic Republic of Vietnam and the People's Republic of China, a treaty of friendship and aid, had been concluded. The former would receive from the latter as a gift the equivalent of about $325 million for factory, road, and railway construction, for supplying textiles and textile machinery, and for electrical, agricultural, and medical equipment. In addition China agreed to furnish technical help to her Communist neighbor. Educational and health experts would go to North Vietnam; the latter would send workers as apprentices to certain Chinese enterprises in the People's Republic. Trade would be expanded and students exchanged. Ho, who had arrived in Peking on June 25, issued a communiqué with Chou En-lai accusing the United States of sabotaging the Geneva settlement by putting Laos, Cambodia, and South Vietnam in the "designated area" guarded by the Southeast Asia Collective Defense Treaty and by seeking to turn South Vietnam into an American military base and colony. The joint communiqué called for national elections to reunite Vietnam and accused the United States of obstructing the consultations on holding them.

Premier Chou En-lai paid a visit to Hanoi in November, 1956.

He observed that the People's Republic of China and the Democratic Republic of Vietnam were members of a family headed by the Soviet Union. Chou called for the peaceful unification of Vietnam and criticized the policy of the United States in supporting South Vietnam. Obviously his words on unification were welcomed by Ho Chi Minh. At the same time the Chinese leader's visit came during a period when the Hanoi regime was trying to cope with domestic unrest. Among other developments, a number of Vietnamese, especially intellectuals, had taken at face value a speech of Mao Tse-tung the previous February where he said, "Let the hundred flowers bloom, let the hundred schools [of thought] contend." Ho visited Peking in the summer of 1957.

Communist China has played a significant part in the building up of the armed strength of the Democratic Republic of Vietnam. Foreign Minister Eden told the House of Commons as early as November 8, 1954:

> . . . agreements reached in Geneva have in no way diminished the formidable military power of [the] Vietminh, to say nothing of that of their Chinese allies. On the contrary, since the Geneva settlement there has been considerable reorganisation and rapid expansion of the Vietminh regular army. By the end of this year this will probably mean that the Vietminh will have twice as many regular field formations as at the time of the Geneva settlements. From the relatively small population which they control—some 14 million in all—the Vietminh have already raised more regular troops than either Pakistan or Indonesia, each with a population of over 70 million.[102]

In a note to the Soviet Union on April 9, 1956, Great Britain asserted that "the Viet-Minh army has been so greatly strengthened by the embodiment and reequipment of irregular forces that, instead of the seven Viet-Minh divisions in existence in July, 1954, there are now no less than twenty."[103] United States Assistant Secretary of State Walter S. Robertson told a meeting of the American Friends of Vietnam in Washington on June 1 that "our reports reveal that in complete disregard of its obligations, the Viet Minh have imported voluminous quantities of arms across the Sino-Viet Minh border and have imported a constant stream of Chinese Communist military personnel to work on railroads, to rebuild roads, to establish airports and to work on other projects contributing to

[102] *Parliamentary Debates (Hansard)*, 5th Series, Vol. 532, *House of Commons Official Report*, November 1-12, 1954, col. 929.

[103] Note from the United Kingdom to the Soviet Union, *Vietnam in World Affairs*, p. 127.

the growth of the military potential of the zone under Communist occupation."[104] It is clearly obvious that the International Supervisory Commission for Vietnam is not physically capable of observing at all points of the Chinese-Vietnamese boundary whether or not the cease-fire restrictions relative to military supplies are being executed.

The Soviet Union in its relations with the Democratic Republic of Vietnam has occupied a secondary place to the People's Republic of China. The Soviet recognition of the Ho Chi Minh government on January 30, 1950, revealed the faith of the Moscow Communists in the future of Ho. They had by contrast refused in the end to recognize the Greek rebels under General Markos. Although Ho had studied in Russia and was a Marxist, the Soviet Union was far removed from the Democratic Republic of Vietnam, and Soviet aid would have to come largely through the People's Republic of China. Nevertheless, Moscow gave propaganda support to the Viet Minh, and when it became possible, military aid. On April 23, 1952, the latter established an embassy in the USSR. At the Geneva Conference Molotov provided diplomatic support to Pham Van Dong.

Ho Chi Minh in the summer of 1955 included Moscow on his visit abroad. Leaving Peking, Ho stopped briefly at Ulan Bator, the capital of the Mongolian People's Republic, and arrived in Moscow on July 12. He was enthusiastically received, and on July 18 a joint communiqué of the USSR and the Democratic Republic of Vietnam revealed that the former had agreed to allocate to the latter as a gift the equivalent of $100 million to build 25 "enterprises," to train technicians, and to assist in restoring Vietnamese economy. Assistance would also be given in organizing medical facilities and making geological surveys. The communiqué criticized efforts to make South Vietnam, Laos, and Cambodia subject to the Manila Pact, called for consultations between North and South Vietnam in preparation for the July, 1956, elections, and praised the work of the International Supervisory Commission. It was noted that a trade agreement had been concluded, and that economic, cultural, and political ties would be strengthened. Later the Soviet Union sent the Democratic Republic via Polish ships 150,000 tons of rice purchased from Burma. In April, 1956, Anastas I. Mikoyan visited Hanoi and in the next year President Kliment Y. Voroshilov. Ho went to Moscow in the summer of 1957, and

[104] Address of Walter S. Robertson, *Vietnam in World Affairs*, p. 115.

again in November in connection with the celebration of the fortieth anniversary of the Bolshevik Revolution. Trade and/or aid agreements have been made with Czechoslovakia, Hungary, and Bulgaria; Poland is granting considerable assistance.

It is clear that Ho's visits to Peking and Moscow were directed not only toward getting economic aid for his country but also toward securing diplomatic assistance in implementing the Geneva provisions relative to the unification of Vietnam. At the same time the relative prestige of the Soviet Union and the People's Republic of China in Hanoi is difficult to assess. The Chinese Communists are far more in evidence, and possibly Hanoi wants the presence of Russians partly to balance the situation. It is reported that in the Viet Minh there are pro-Soviet, pro-Chinese, and even pro-Tito factions. At any rate the coöperation of the Moscow and Peking governments is certain to work for greater harmony in North Vietnam.

With India the Democratic Republic of Vietnam has a number of contacts, partly as a result of the position India holds on the International Commission. Although Nehru has discussed problems with Ho Chi Minh and Pham Van Dong, India has only given *de facto* recognition, this being accorded on December 15, 1954. Each has a consul general in the capital of the other. On October 17, Nehru en route to Peking visited Ho Chi Minh in Hanoi. A joint communiqué the next day indicated that both leaders were interested in completely implementing the Geneva settlement. Ho pledged himself to coöperate fully with the International Commission in carrying out the agreement; he desired to settle all problems peacefully and envisioned an Indochina living without outside interference. Ho supported the Five Principles and wanted to apply them in the relations of his government with Laos, Cambodia, and other states. Later in Saigon Nehru indicated that he considered Ho Chi Minh a man of integrity who wanted peace.

Pham Van Dong visited New Delhi in April, 1955, en route to the Bandung Conference. A joint communiqué issued on April 10 by the two powers "reaffirmed their belief that good neighbourly relations and respect and tolerance for one another between Viet Nam, Cambodia and Laos in accordance with the principles of the Geneva Agreement and the Panch Shila would serve to promote the political settlement in Indo-China and further the cause of peace in South East Asia."[105] A three-year trade agreement was signed in

[105] Joint Communiqué of Nehru and Pham Van Dong, Cole, *op. cit.*, p. 236.

September, 1956, by India and North Vietnam; Hanoi has established a commercial office in the former. Ho Chi Minh accepted an invitation to visit New Delhi in 1958.

Relations between the Democratic Republic of Vietnam and Japan have been unofficial and at times tense. In May, 1956, the North Vietnamese and a number of Japanese businessmen signed in Hanoi an agreement for trade amounting to $8,400,000. Although Japan does not recognize the Democratic Republic, the agreement had the tacit approval of the Tokyo government. For a while the trade would be carried on through Hong Kong, but North Vietnam would later open Hon Gai and two other ports to the ships of Japan. Twice in August the Democratic Republic put forth a claim for reparations from Nippon as a consequence of the Second World War. Hanoi has flatly rejected the position taken by Japan that negotiations on reparations would only be held with the Saigon government.

Toward the United States the Viet Minh maintains a hostile attitude, blaming Washington, as already indicated, for many of its international difficulties. On January 1, 1955, a large New Year celebration provided the occasion for demonstrations against the United States. In a message Ho Chi Minh asserted that "we must be vigilant and be on our guard against the plans of the imperialistic Americans who are seeking to intervene in Indochina, to incite their lackeys, to sabotage the armistice accords and to cause war."[106] General Vo Nguyen Giap accused the "American imperialists" along with "elements of the French colonialists" and "their lackeys, the clique of Ngo Dinh Diem" of plotting "to transform South Vietnam into a military base and an American colony."[107]

Despite the acquisition by Ho Chi Minh of all North Vietnam under the Geneva settlement, the United States maintained for some time its consulate in Hanoi, insisting that it was still accredited to the State of Vietnam as the legal government of the country. On October 27, 1954, the Viet Minh regime asserted that it did not "recognize" the American consulate, for northern Vietnam under the Geneva agreements "is temporarily placed under the administration of the Democratic Republic of Vietnam."[108] In December, 1955, the United States finally closed its office in Hanoi. The United Kingdom for its part raised its consulate in the city to a

[106] *New York Times*, January 3, 1955.
[107] *Ibid.*
[108] *New York Times*, October 29, 1954.

consulate general, and was not challenged by the Viet Minh government.

Toward Southeast Asia the Viet Minh has shown an interest in acquiring a strong position in the local Communist movements. Cambodia and Laos, of course, presented special opportunities for Ho Chi Minh. On March 11, 1951, a Vietnam-Khmer-Pathet Lao alliance under Ho's influence was established. Tran Van Giau, a Moscow-trained Vietnamese, led the Southeast Asia League which ended in 1948; Nguyen Van Long, another Vietnamese trained in Moscow, led the now defunct Ku Sap Be or Liberation Party of Vietnam, Laos, Cambodia, Burma, and Thailand for the Salvation of the Fatherland; later Nguyen Van Long headed the Communist Coördination Committee for Southeast Asia. Despite its efforts the Democratic Republic of Vietnam has been unable to win *de jure* recognition from the Southeast Asian states. But, as indicated, it has been able to operate a Vietnam news service in Rangoon, transferred there from Bangkok. Consuls general have been exchanged with Indonesia. More recently a news service has been set up in Cambodia.

In its world outlook the Democratic Republic of Vietnam has been greatly motivated by domestic considerations. Since the Geneva settlement Ho has stressed that he wants "peace, unification, independence and democracy" for all Vietnam. As already indicated, great efforts were made in Hanoi, especially in 1955 and 1956, to bring about unification through the elections called for under the Geneva agreements. The Communist world has united in condemning the Republic of Vietnam for holding elections on March 4, 1956, for a constituent assembly, claiming they were a step toward making the seventeenth parallel a permanent line. Ho has asserted that Vietnam must not become another Korea split by an arbitrary boundary.

Meanwhile the Democratic Republic has urged the establishment of "normal relations" with the South as a preliminary step toward unification. It has publicly favored the granting of facilities for people to cross to either side of the parallel for business activities and has come out in support of coöperation in cultural, scientific, and sporting matters.

In 1956 developments inside North Vietnam worked to the advantage of the South. Unrest in the former, largely as a consequence of the rigid implementation of the agrarian reform program, led to the removal in the latter part of the year of Truong Chinh as Secretary General of the Lao Dong Party and the assumption of the post by Ho Chi Minh. A revolt of Vietnamese intellectuals was evident in the newspaper called Nhân-Van or "The Humanities." It was announced on November 2 that elections would be held the next year. Bloodshed occurred during the middle of the month in a part of North Vietnam, inhabited largely by Roman Catholics, when government forces and peasants clashed. On November 29 the Republic of Vietnam sent a message to the Secretary-General of the United Nations noting that the world organization should take an interest in the fate of the people in North Vietnam and initiate steps to stop further massacres. On the same day President Ngo Dinh Diem issued a declaration on the subject of the uprisings in North Vietnam, comparing the reprisals of the Ho regime with those of the Soviet Union in Hungary.

In terms of its international stature, there can be no doubt of the concern of the Hanoi government about the large exodus of Catholics to the South after the Geneva agreements. Pham Van Dong at Bandung explained the situation as being the result of coercion on the part of the southern regime and deceit in telling the people that "God has gone to the South, those who stay behind in North Viet-Nam not only will lose their souls but will even die from atom [bombs] which the Americans will drop on North Viet-Nam."[109] The Viet Minh policy toward the Catholics has, in fact, varied from time to time. Until 1950 there was a sympathetic attitude, for many Catholics were active in the nationalist movement. On September 23, 1945, four Vietnamese bishops had appealed to Pope Pius XII to support the independence of Vietnam. From 1950 on relations were increasingly strained until the Viet Minh attacked the bishopric of Phat-Diem in the fall of 1951. In 1955 there appeared to be a softening of Hanoi's policy toward the Catholics, about 600,000 of whom remained in the North.

In dealing with the tribesmen, numbering more than a million in North Vietnam, the Ho regime, aware of the strategic areas involved, has called attention to the provisions found in the constitution for the equality of all the people. "Besides enjoying full and equal rights," it is stated, "ethnic minorities are to receive every help and encouragement to enable them to reach the common level of advancement as speedily as possible."[110] It is not surprising, however, that the Vietnamese dominate the scene. In May, 1955, the

[109] Statement by Pham Van Dong, Press Release, Asian-African Conference, Bandung, Indonesia.

[110] The Constitution of the Democratic Republic of Vietnam, Fall, *op. cit.*, p. 123.

Democratic Republic's decision, as announced, to establish a "Thai-Méo Autonomous Area" in the northwest part of the country involved a territory of 19,300 square miles and about 330,000 people. The autonomous area was bounded on the north by the People's Republic of China, on the south and west by the Kingdom of Laos, on the southeast by Hoa Binh province, and on the east by the Fan Si Pan Mountains. Later the autonomous area of Viet Bac was set up, and one for the Lao Cai area was planned.

The Democratic Republic of Vietnam is also concerned over the Vietnamese living outside of the country. Viet Minh cells, for instance, exist among the Vietnamese in New Caledonia and the New Hebrides in the Pacific. Relations between Hanoi and Paris have been strained over French measures against Communism in the areas. Among the more than 40,000 Vietnamese living in France, many of them students, the Viet Minh has made inroads. North Vietnamese students are studying in the Soviet Union and its satellites in eastern Europe as well as in Communist China.

On the world stage the Democratic Republic of Vietnam conducts its international relations as a genuine Communist state. The government or the dominant party has sent delegations to numerous international conferences under the auspices of the Communists—youth festivals in Bucharest and East Berlin, peace conferences at Vienna, and gatherings of Communist labor, women's and other organizations. As of early 1957, 11 Communist states had diplomatic missions in Hanoi—the Soviet Union, the People's Republic of China, Poland, North Korea, Hungary, Albania, Romania, Czechoslovakia, Bulgaria, East Germany, and the Mongolian People's Republic. India, Indonesia, and the United Kingdom each maintained a consulate general in Hanoi although the British consul general has no exequatur from the Viet Minh government. Communist China had a consular office in Haiphong. In addition Canada along with Poland and India was represented in Hanoi on the International Commission. As already indicated, France had a delegate general in the Democratic Republic. The Hanoi government had diplomatic missions in all the Communist countries which sent them to the Democratic Republic except Albania. Consuls general were sent to India and Indonesia, consuls to Nanning and Kunming, and representatives of an official news service to Rangoon and Phnom Penh without consular or diplomatic status.

In two major international conferences, at Geneva in 1954 and Bandung in 1955, the Democratic Republic has been ably represented by Pham Van Dong. In both gatherings he has clearly expressed the foreign policy of his government. Perhaps in his statement[111] to the Bandung Conference on April 20, 1955, is found the best expression of Viet Minh foreign policy. After describing the evils of the colonial system in some detail, he asserted that "the essential task of this assembly is to manifest in an unmistakable and energetic manner the Asian-African peoples' will to coexist peacefully among themselves and with the other peoples in the world. . . . For the Asian-African peoples as well as for the peoples of the world, peaceful life is inseparable from national independence and equality among the peoples. . . . The Asian-African peoples demand a lasting and stable peace, the right to national independence and equality among the peoples, because they want to build a happy and prosperous life." The Foreign Minister specifically opposed "all aggressive military pacts" and called for the "complete withdrawal of all foreign troops from Asia and Africa"; he wanted the destruction of stocks of atomic and hydrogen bombs and no more production of these weapons; he supported Communist China's struggle to regain her "territorial integrity" and Communist Korea's efforts for the unity of the peninsula. Pham Van Dong recommended the solution of problems like Goa, West Irian, Malaya, and Kenya on the "basis of respect of territorial integrity and the right to independence and equality among the peoples"; he called for economic and cultural coöperation and "the expanding and strengthening of relationships in every field between the Asian and African countries [particularly between his government and Communist China, India, Burma, and Indonesia] upon the basis of the 5 principles of peaceful coexistence." The North Vietnamese went out of his way to deny that his country had increased its military power by several divisions and called the struggle "by free general elections" for the unity of his nation "a holy struggle of the entire Vietnamese people." He noted that the "aggressive imperialists" have "tried their best to increase their intervention in the internal affairs of the South, to set up new military bases and send new weapons and military personnel to South Viet-Nam." Pham Van Dong summed up the foreign policy of the Ho Chi Minh regime in these words: "Today, the Vietnamese people and the Government of the Democratic Republic of Viet-Nam are fighting for peace, unity, independence and democracy in Viet-Nam, are

[111] Statement by Pham Van Dong, Press Release, Asian-African Conference, *passim.*

making a contribution to the struggle for the independence of oppressed countries and equality among all nations, for peace and security in Asia, Africa and the whole world, for peaceful coexistence and coöperation between various countries."

LAOS

The Kingdom of Laos, the most remote and underdeveloped of the countries of Indochina, is new in terms of Western statehood but old in terms of Asian history. Occupying today an area of 88,780 square miles, a little more than the size of Kansas, and extending some 800 miles from north to south, the landlocked kingdom is bordered by the People's Republic of China on the north, Burma and Thailand on the west, Cambodia on the south, the Democratic Republic of Vietnam for about two-thirds of the frontier on the east, and the Republic of Vietnam for the remainder. It is obvious that Laos is located in a critical area of Southeast Asia, subjected along its northern and the greater part of its eastern boundaries to Communist pressure from Peking and Hanoi, along the greater part of its western as well as its southeastern borders to influence from Bangkok, Saigon, and Washington, and along its short boundaries with Burma and Cambodia to neutralist sentiment from Rangoon and Phnom Penh. Within the Kingdom of Laos itself the Communist pressure is manifested especially in the province of Phong Saly along the Chinese and Viet Minh frontier and in the province of Sam Neua a little to the south along the Viet Minh border. Not without significance to Laos is the establishment of the Thai autonomous area north of the kingdom by Communist China and the Thai-Méo autonomous area northeast of Laos by the Democratic Republic of Vietnam.

The 1½ million to 3 million people living in sparsely-populated Laos are dominated by the Lao, about a half of the population, their ancestors being a part of the migration of Thai southward.[112] At the same time there are numerous non-Lao tribes living in different remote parts of the kingdom. The state religion of the country is Buddhism, constituting a force in the social stability of the people. The cultural impact of India is still evident in the country.

Unified in the middle 1300's, Laos or Lan Xang was a powerful kingdom for a long period in Southeast Asia. Wars were waged at times with the Cambodians, Burmese, Annamites, and Siamese. In

[112] Lao is here used to indicate the dominant people of Laos and Laotians the nationals of the kingdom.

1707 the Kingdom of Lan Xang was divided into the Kingdom of Luang Prabang (now largely Upper Laos) and the Kingdom of Vientiane (now Middle and Lower Laos). By the time the French came, Vientiane was a province of Siam, Luang Prabang a vassal, and Bassac in Lower Laos a fief.

It was France who gave the Kingdom of Laos its present frontiers, establishing a protectorate in 1893 over the Kingdom of Luang Prabang and later extending Laotian territory at the expense of Siam. The Paris government in 1893 may not have been aware of the historic role of the kings of Luang Prabang, for it tended to look upon Laos largely in terms of rival principalities. In fact, France, outside the protectorate of the Kingdom of Luang Prabang, ruled in effect the rest of Laos directly. Japan encouraged King Sisavang Vong of Luang Prabang to proclaim independence from France which he did in April, 1945. With the collapse of Japan, Prince Pethsarath on September 15, 1945, declared the unity of all Laos under the Crown of Luang Prabang. In the *modus vivendi* of August 27, 1946, between France and the King of Luang Prabang, the former recognized the latter as King of Laos including the territory of Luang Prabang and that formerly ruled directly by France. Prince Boun Oum renounced his rights over Champassak (Bassac) in the south. Thus the territorial unification of the country was accomplished although separatist sentiment still exists, especially in Lower Laos.

The Indochinese Federation under the French had to make a substantial contribution toward the maintenance of the Laotian area. Well over 90 percent of the people are peasants, the economy resting upon subsistence agriculture. It is estimated that 1,976,000 acres of rice were cultivated in the year 1953-1954. Laos has copper, antimony, tungsten, coal, lead, zinc, gold, and bauxite, producing in 1953 about 500 metric tons of tin as compared with 2000 in 1940. The two chief cities in the country are Luang Prabang, the royal capital, and Vientiane, the administrative capital, the former with a population of about 15,000 and the latter with around 20,000. Since Laos is mountainous, the transportation problems are serious. There are no railroads, but the Mekong River offers limited navigation facilities. A number of key roads, now often in disrepair, were constructed by France linking Laos with Vietnam. One of the outstanding examples is the highway from Quang Tri now in the Republic of Vietnam to Savannakhet in Laos on the Thai border. Another very important road runs from Cambodia northward, roughly paralleling the Mekong, to Vientiane and then to Luang Prabang. A few highways also run from Laos to Thailand. In terms of ports for Laotian exports and imports, Saigon in South Vietnam is 745 miles from Vientiane and Bangkok in Thailand 310 miles. The chief exports of the kingdom are teak, tin, coffee, cattle, lamé cloth, and benzoin, and the chief imports are manufactured goods. There is a traffic of opium grown in the northern mountains.

On May 11, 1947, King Sisavang Vong formally gave the Laotians a constitution. He had previously convoked an assembly to act on the territorial unity of Laos and to draw up the constitution. The preamble to the document, as of 1947, refers to the unity of the country, to its membership in the French Union, and to the rights and duties of Laotians. The king is the head of state, commander-in-chief, and high protector of Buddhism. There is provision for a prime minister and a cabinet, responsible to a national assembly, elected every four years by universal suffrage. In view of the age of the king, Crown Prince Savang Vathana has assumed many of his duties. It has proved much easier in the Kingdom of Laos to draft a document providing for a democratic, constitutional monarchy than to make it truly work.

The Geneva settlement on Laos placed certain limitations on the foreign policy of the kingdom. Under the cease-fire agreement new military bases could not be established, and the International Commission of India, Canada, and Poland would supervise "at ports and airfields and along all the frontiers of Laos" the execution of the provisions on the introduction into the kingdom of military personnel and war materials and the rotation of personnel and supplies for the French Union forces allowed in the country.[113] In a declaration Laos also asserted:

> The Royal Government of Laos is resolved never to pursue a policy of aggression and will never permit the territory of Laos to be used in furtherance of such a policy.
>
> The Royal Government of Laos will never join in any agreement with other States if this agreement includes the obligation for the Royal Government of Laos to participate in a military alliance not in conformity with the principles of the Charter of the United Nations or with the principles of the agreement on the cessation of hostilities

[113] Agreement on the cessation of hostilities in Laos, External Affairs, Supplementary Papers, No. 54/22.

or, unless its security is threatened, the obligation to establish bases on Laotian territory for military forces of foreign powers.

The Royal Government of Laos is resolved to settle its international disputes by peaceful means so that international peace and security and justice are not endangered.

During the period between the cessation of hostilities in Viet-Nam and the final settlement of that country's political problems, the Royal Government of Laos will not request foreign aid, whether in war material, in personnel or in instructors, except for the purpose of its effective territorial defence and to the extent defined by the agreement on the cessation of hostilities.[114]

In the "Final Declaration" the Conference took "note" in paragraphs 4 and 5 of the Laotian declaration.

In a final speech at the Geneva Conference Phoui Sananikone of Laos asserted that the forces of peace had been successful and he hoped for the future implementation of the settlement. The Laotian government also issued a statement approving the agreement.

The International Commission for Laos in its first interim report issued January 15, 1955, covered developments from August 11, 1954, to the end of the year.[115] The Commission reported that transport, weather, and language difficulties, especially at the beginning, hindered progress and that the "vagueness of some of the provisions of the Geneva Agreement" caused more difficulties. In regard to interpretation, the Joint Commission, made up of representatives from the Vietnamese People's Volunteers/Pathet Lao side and the Franco-Laotian side, was often divided. As far as military withdrawals under the cease-fire agreement, the International Commission reported that despite early delays they "were carried out in time, and almost without incident." A very difficult problem, still unsettled, related to the provinces of Phong Saly and Sam Neua. With the withdrawal of the French Union Forces, apart from the 5000 men authorized under the cease-fire to stay in Laos, and the Vietnamese People's Volunteers, only in the two northern provinces were soldiers of both the Laotian National Army and the "fighting units of 'Pathet Lao' " left. The Commission, never-

[114] Laotian Declaration (on foreign policy), Great Britain, Foreign Office, Cmd. 9239.

[115] First Interim Report of the Activities of the International Commission for Supervision and Control in Laos, External Affairs, Supplementary Paper, No. 55/2, *passim.* In terms of communication the Commission reported: "There are no organized normal press and publicity facilities in Laos. The Government of Laos publish a daily French bulletin (500 copies) and a bi-weekly Laotian language bulletin (350 copies), both mimeographed. There is also the Lao National Radio with about 3,000 listeners." In April, 1957, the first newspaper began to publish.

theless, pointed out that in the withdrawal of the Vietnamese People's Volunteers from Laos and the Pathet Lao units to Phong Saly and Sam Neua, identification was "not possible," for "no details" as to their identity were given and "they wore no badges or distinguishing signs by which personnel could be identified." It is specifically reported that "owing to last minute non-availability of helicopters, the withdrawals of the Vietnamese People's Volunteer troops in the province[s] of Phong Saly and Sam Neua and of the 'Pathet Lao' troops in the province of Luang Prabang could not be satisfactorily checked by the International Teams." Other items were considered in the first report of the International Commission.

On August 26, 1955, the Commission issued its second interim report covering the period from January 1 to June 30. A number of items taken up in the first report were further considered. The Joint Commission, following the final withdrawal of the foreign troops on November 19, 1954, ceased to function on February 15, 1955. The Vietnamese People's Volunteers/Pathet Lao delegation had opposed the end of the Joint Commission but the Franco-Laotian delegation had insisted that the Commission had performed its duties. A Pathet Lao Liaison Mission with the International Commission was to be set up. After February 12 the International Commission received no letters relative to prisoners of war and civilian internees; and "it is stated that neither Party admits having any Prisoners of War or Civilian Internees of the other Party in its custody."[116] Nevertheless, each claims the other has a large number of detained persons although most of the French nationals were released. An impasse remained on the charges of the Franco-Laotian delegation that the opposite side was engaging in forced recruitment after the cease-fire, the latter strongly denying the accusations. The International Commission continued its efforts, subject to the cease-fire terms, to prevent the introduction of fresh military personnel and war material into the kingdom.

The most controversial issue relative to the political settlement in Laos related to the provinces of Phong Saly and Sam Neua. The Commission had pointed out in its first report that the Pathet Lao and the Vietnamese People's Volunteers had insisted that under the cease-fire agreement, pending a political settlement, the Pathet Lao had received the right to have all the two northern provinces as a concentration or final assembly area with a corridor between them for travel purposes. The Pathet Lao claimed both military

[116] Second Interim Report, External Affairs, Supplementary Paper, No. 55/9.

and administrative control. The Franco-Laotian side had asserted that Phong Saly and Sam Neua were a part of the Kingdom of Laos and that the Pathet Lao could regroup only in certain areas of the two provinces. The Pathet Lao wanted a political settlement in Laos before the establishment of a Royal Administration in the disputed provinces while the Royal Government, being the sovereign authority, insisted on establishing an administration in Phong Saly and Sam Neua. Moreover, the Pathet Lao maintained there had been no Franco-Laotian troops in the two provinces since March, 1953, while the Royal Government asserted that there were areas under the control of their own "Special Commandos" on or before August 6, 1954, the cease-fire date. The Pathet Lao looked upon the Commandos as "pirates," not regular Franco-Laotian troops, and asserted that the Franco-Laotian side had paradropped regular Laotian National Army units after the cease-fire.

On November 4, 1954, the Pathet Lao delegate at a meeting of the International Commission and the Joint Commission made a statement by authorization of Prince Souphanou Vong, the Pathet Lao leader, that his forces "recognise the Royal Government and that in principle the administration of 'Pathet Lao' in the two provinces of Sam Neua and Phong Saly is classified under the Supreme Authority of the Royal Government."[117] Prince Souvanna Phouma, Prime Minister of Laos and half brother of Prince Souphanou Vong, welcomed on November 4 the statement of the Pathet Lao delegate, the former asserting, "The unity of government implies of necessity the unity of administration and unity of the Armed Forces."[118] On November 23 Katay D. Sasorith, while presenting to the National Assembly his government, asserted he would offer his resignation as Prime Minister after the "integration of all partisans of the 'Pathet Lao' into the national community" so as "to give to the National Assembly the possibility of associating with the task of national restoration the most competent and most capable children of the land without distinction of origin or of blood."[119]

On January 18, 1955, a Joint Declaration signed by representatives of the Royal Government and the Pathet Lao at a Consultative Political Conference noted that they would try to negotiate all the questions involving the independence of Laos. A Political Con-

[117] Appendix I, First Interim Report, External Affairs, Supplementary Paper, No. 55/2.

[118] Appendix J, *ibid.*

[119] Appendix K, *ibid.*

ference met from late January to early March. On April 8 the Royal Government told the International Commission that the political discussions were hindered because the Pathet Lao "consider themselves still under the authority of the Vietminh High Command, and as having conquered the provinces of Phong Saly and Sam Neua."[120] The Pathet Lao in a communication received by the Commission on April 22 accused, *inter alia*, the Royal Government of coöperating with the United States. It called for a Joint Political Council of the two parties to establish a national coalition government of the Pathet Lao and Royal Government factions. A Draft Interpretative Resolution introduced by the Canadian delegation on the International Commission on May 3 to help the two parties in reaching a political settlement was opposed by the Polish delegation on the grounds that it was outside the competence of the Commission. The National Assembly of Laos on June 10 decided to postpone the election date from August 28 to December 25.

The position of the Royal Government on Phong Saly and Sam Neua came to be supported by the Canadian delegation and that of the Pathet Lao by the Polish. In October, 1954, the International Commission had decided to investigate the position and strength of the units of the Laotian National Army in the two provinces as of the cease-fire. The Indian and Canadian delegations agreed that some Royal troops were in the two provinces before and at that time. The Polish delegation disagreed. The Pathet Lao flatly asserted Royal troops had no right to be there and should leave. An incident in January, 1955, at Nong Khang in Sam Neua was considered by the Indians and Canadians to be caused by a violation by the Pathet Lao forces but the Poles supported the latter. The International Commission reported that "the Polish Delegation was emphatic that no attempt should be made either to give legal recognition to the presence of Laotian National Army troops or

[120] Second Interim Report, External Affairs, Supplementary Paper, No. 55/9.

In May, 1955, the Royal Government of Laos published a white paper on its interpretation of developments relative to the application of the Geneva agreements in the kingdom. The documentation included a memorandum reviewing the situation, sent to the International Commission, April 13, 1955, a supplement on illegal and forced recruitment, and another on the situation in Sam Neua and Phong Saly, a reply from the International Commission, April 29, two letters from the Royal Government of Laos to the International Commission, each dated May 14, a memorandum presented to Prime Minister Nehru during his visit to Laos, October 17, 1954, and an addendum consisting of a letter from the International Commission to the Royal Government, June 15, 1955, and a reply of the latter to the former, June 24. The Kingdom of Laos, *Application of the Geneva Agreements in Laos,* Presidency of the Council of the Royal Government of Laos, May, 1955.

to divide the provinces between the opposing forces."[121] On May 24 the Canadians submitted a resolution on reëstablishing the Royal Administration in the two provinces but the Polish delegation believed the parties themselves should decide the matter.

In October Pathet Lao and Royal Laotian representatives met in Rangoon for a conference. They agreed on the principles of a cease-fire in Phong Saly and Sam Neua and to meet in Vientiane for discussions on the general elections for the National Assembly as well as other matters. The Vientiane conference proving abortive, the Royal Government decided to go ahead with the holding of the elections on December 25 without the participation of the Pathet Lao. The latter wanted a number of changes in election practices—reducing the voting age, allowing women to vote, and establishing mixed control committees to supervise the elections. The Royal Laotian government gave increased consideration to asking the two cochairmen of the Geneva Conference to "interpret" the Geneva agreement. Despite the urging of the Pathet Lao to boycott the national elections, the Laotians, outside the two troubled provinces, went to the polls with little hindrance. And even here, the Royal Government dropped ballots by parachutes to its enclaves located in the two areas. All the candidates of the four main parties in the kingdom were anti-Communist and urged the full restoration of Sam Neua and Phong Saly. As a result of the elections, a pro-Western coalition of the National Progressive and Independent parties continued in power.

L. B. Pearson, Canadian Secretary of State for External Affairs, frankly analyzed conditions in Laos when he told the House of Commons on January 31, 1956, that the "situation is not so good. Elections have . . . been held there, but the Communist Pathet Lao forces . . . have refused to accept the Laotian Government or the authority of that government and to take part in the election. Hence no reduction there has been found possible either in the numbers of the commission or in its activities up to the present time."[122] The elections in effect tended to confirm at least for a while the *de facto* partition of Laos into the ten provinces under the Royal Government and the two under the Pathet Lao.

On January 7 the International Commission in Vientiane called

[121] Second Interim Report of the Activities of the International Commission for Supervision and Control in Laos, External Affairs, Supplementary Paper, No. 55/9.

[122] Foreign Policy Statement of L. B. Pearson, Statements and Speeches, Information Division, Department of External Affairs, Canada.

for the reëstablishment of the control of the Royal Government over Phong Saly and Sam Neua without delay and for the Royal Government to take at once the steps necessary to integrate the Pathet Lao into the national community. India and Canada voted in favor of the measure and Poland abstained. The Pathet Lao did not accept the proposal but the Royal Government did. The International Commission informed the cochairmen of the Geneva Conference of the situation. On April 5 Great Britain indicated in a note to the Soviet Union that in connection with the forthcoming discussion on Vietnam by the two powers she would raise the problem of Laos. Despite conversations in London during a part of May between Soviet and British representatives, acting for the cochairmen, no solution was reached on the Laotian question.

Meanwhile on March 21 Prince Souvanna Phouma presented a new cabinet with himself as Prime Minister to the National Assembly. He indicated clearly that the settlement of the Pathet Lao problem was his first major concern. In July a delegation went to Bangkok to urge Prince Pethsarath to return to Laos. As head of the family to which the Prime Minister and the Pathet Lao leader belonged, his return might facilitate a settlement. The Prince agreed to the suggestion although he did not go to Laos until the following March.

On August 1 Prince Souvanna Phouma and Prince Souphanou Vong met in Vientiane. The half brothers negotiated a settlement, announced August 5 and August 10, on behalf of the Royal Government and Pathet Lao with the good offices of the International Commission. The provisions included the ending of hostilities between the two sides; Sam Neua and Phong Saly would be placed under Royal administration; the Pathet Lao forces would be brought into the Royal Army; the national government would allow political organizations of the Pathet Lao to operate legally and would respect without discrimination the democratic liberties and rights of all citizens in the country; supplementary general elections would be held on the basis of the secret ballot and adult suffrage to increase the number of deputies from 39 to 60; the Pathet Lao would be represented in a Government of National Union; and joint political and military commissions would make detailed arrangements for the integration of the Pathet Lao into the civilian and military life of the nation and for the transfer of Sam Neua and Phong Saly to Royal control. In the field of foreign affairs, the Laotian government would follow a policy of neutrality and peace, maintain friendly relations with all states, especially neighbors, support the Five Principles, make no military alliances, and allow no foreign bases on Laotian soil apart from the provisions of the Geneva settlement.

Implementation of the August agreement was slow, a fact not surprising in view of the heritage of hostility and suspicion, the complexity of the arrangements, and the international ramifications. On December 28 a joint statement by Prince Souvanna Phouma and Prince Souphanou Vong indicated they had agreed on the early forming of a Government of National Union, the return of Phong Saly and Sam Neua to Royal administration, and the integration of the Pathet Lao into the national community. The new government would be formed before the supplementary elections to the National Assembly. The Pathet Lao would operate as a political party called "Neo Lao Haksat" (Patriotic Party of Laos).

Prince Pethsarath, after his return to Vientiane in March, became active in the country. He received the title of "Viceroy," visited the Pathet Lao area, and was praised by the Hanoi radio. The Prince attacked American aid and called for diplomatic relations with Communist states. When the Pathet Lao early in 1957 urged the acceptance of economic and technical aid from the People's Republic of China and the establishment of formal diplomatic ties with Communist countries, the negotiations between the Royal Government and the Pathet Lao reached a further crisis. Meanwhile it was reported that Communist forces in the Pathet Lao area were being strengthened by aid from outside. On May 29 the National Assembly voted against continuing negotiations under the circumstances with the Pathet Lao, and Premier Souvanna Phouma subsequently resigned. After a long cabinet crisis he formed a new government approved by the National Assembly on August 9, Katay D. Sasorith being Interior Minister and Phoui Sananikone Foreign Minister.

In November the National Assembly finally approved a "Union Cabinet" with Prince Souvanna Phouma as Premier and Prince Souphanou Vong as well as Katay D. Sasorith and Phoui Sananikone holding portfolios. The Pathet Lao forces were formally transferred to the King, and Phong Saly and Sam Neua officially integrated into the kingdom. Nevertheless, the future of the coalition effort was uncertain and the reality of integration a question.

The Pathet Lao problem, as the evidence indicates, is directly associated with the Vietnam of Ho Chi Minh and the China of Mao Tse-tung. If it were not for the attitude of Communist Vietnam and Communist China, the Royal Government of Laos would probably have handled the Pathet Lao easily. Under the Chinese Nationalist occupation of most of Laos after the surrender of Japan encouragement had been given the Lao Issarak movement directed at independence from France. Lao Issarak leaders—Prince Pethsarath and Prince Souphanou Vong—had established a government in Vientiane. With the Chinese withdrawal and the return of the French, the supporters of the Lao Issarak effort fled in great numbers to Thailand. After the treaty signed between France and Laos on July 19, 1949, making the latter an independent state in the French Union, the Lao Issarak movement with its headquarters in Bangkok announced its support of the terms and the Laotian Government facilitated the return of many of the exiles. Some of its leaders, however, remained in opposition, especially Prince Souphanou Vong who has a Vietnamese wife known to favor Communism. He and his followers came to form the nucleus around which the Viet Minh could develop the Pathet Lao.

When the forces of the Democratic Republic of Vietnam invaded Laos in the spring of 1953, Prince Souphanou Vong was set up in Sam Neua as the head of a "Free Laotian Government." Behind the Prince were the National United Front of the Pathet Lao or the Neo Lao-Issala Front and the Laotian Liberation Army. "When the Viet Minh withdrew," it has been later pointed out, "they left behind them several thousand political and military agents. These have not been idle. They are training and organizing Laos peasants into guerilla units which operate nominally under the so-called 'Free Laos Government.' . . ."[123] Senator Mike Mansfield in October, 1955, noted: "Available estimates indicate that the strength of the Pathet Lao armed forces has increased from about 1,000 at the time of the truce to 4,000 to 6,000 at present. There is also evidence that Vietminh officers and cadres hold key positions in these forces."[124] Laotian cadres are reportedly being trained in the Democratic Republic of Vietnam and the People's Republic of China. War material probably came from North Vietnam, and China sent in supplies of rice. The Pathet Lao has asserted that aid from Ho Chi Minh stopped with the Geneva armistice.

As for the Royal Government of Laos, relations with the Democratic Republic of Vietnam have obviously been stormy. In

[123] Edwin F. Stanton, "Spotlight on Thailand," *Foreign Affairs*, Vol. 33 (October, 1954), p. 75.

[124] *Viet Nam, Cambodia, and Laos*, Report by Senator Mike Mansfield, October 6, 1955, p. 18.

the invasion of April, 1953, the Vientiane government appealed to the free world to condemn the Viet Minh aggression. Although the United States favored taking the matter to the United Nations, France was opposed to "internationalizing" the war. United States cargo aircraft with American civilian pilots were placed at French disposal. Laos again appealed to the world in December after another Viet Minh invasion. Following the Geneva Conference, Ho Chi Minh, it should be recalled, told Nehru during the latter's visit to Hanoi in October, 1954, that he wanted to apply the Five Principles in the relations of his government with Laos and Cambodia. The Viet Minh government in the negotiations on implementing the truce in Laos eventually took the position that in the withdrawal of the Vietnamese People's Volunteers even Vietnamese who had lived in Laos before joining the Volunteers would leave. The Royal Government continued to be disturbed over Viet Minh activities on behalf of the Pathet Lao.

At the Bandung Conference in April, 1955, Nehru, Chou En-lai, Pham Van Dong, and Katay Sasorith, Prime Minister of Laos, held an informal meeting, the result of which was an agreement between the North Vietnamese and Laotian leaders wherein the Democratic Republic of Vietnam asserted that the settlement to be made between the Royal Government and the Pathet Lao as a consequence of the Geneva agreements "is a question of internal order which the Royal Government of Laos and 'Pathet Lao' are entirely free to solve in the best way possible in the higher interests of the country and people of Laos."[125] Secondly the Hanoi and Vientiane governments would "develop and harmonize the good neighborly relations which tie and should tie these countries to each other, within the framework of the Five Principles defined in the Sino-Indian Agreement of April 29, 1954."[126] Chou En-lai in commenting later observed that "this statement will contribute to the thorough implementation of the agreements of the Geneva Conference and in the consolidation of peace in Indo-China.[127]

In a speech delivered during his visit to Peking in the summer of 1955 Ho Chi Minh asserted that his government wanted to set up relations on the basis of "peaceful coexistence" with any country, especially with the Royal Government of Laos, Cambodia, and other Southeast Asian states. In November, however, Foreign Min-

[125] Quoted in Kahin, *op. cit.*, p. 27.
[126] *Ibid.*
[127] "Chou En-lai on the Asian-African Conference at Bandung," *United Asia*, Vol. 7 (December, 1955), p. 314.

ister Phoui Sananikone of the Royal Government charged the Hanoi regime with breaking its promise at Bandung not to interfere in Laotian affairs. "We know that Pathet Lao is a creation of the Communists," he said, and went on to observe that the Manila Pact "assures us our territory will be defended against subversion."[128] It is clear that the Royal Laotian Government was apprehensive about the role of the Viet Minh army in the event the Pathet Lao forces were militarily weakened by Royal troops in Phong Saly and Sam Neua. Later charges against the Viet Minh have been made by the Royal Laotian leaders.

Other issues complicated relations between the Hanoi and Vientiane governments. The Laotians are aware of the fact that the Vietnamese once ruled a large part of present Laotian territory and they fear that the Viet Minh have specific designs on not only Phong Saly and Sam Neua but also Luang Prabang and Huei Sai as well as Tranninh. A territorial dispute actually exists, as indicated by the International Commission, over the Ban Ken Dou area. And others are present.

The Vietnamese still living in Laos, possibly 15,000 to 30,000 of them, also present a problem, some continuing to be sympathetic to the Viet Minh. Many of them have lived in Laos a long time; the French employed a good number in the administration of the country.

After the settlement between the Royal Government and the Pathet Lao in August, 1956, the Prime Minister, Prince Souvanna Phouma, made a visit to Peking and Hanoi, later going to Saigon. In an agreement with the Democratic Republic of Vietnam on August 29, Laos affirmed her policy of peace and neutrality, promised to make no military alliances as long as her security was not threatened, and stated she would not allow foreign military bases in the kingdom apart from those existing. At the same time Laos was not ready to establish economic or diplomatic relations with the Ho Chi Minh regime. In March, 1957, a postal convention was signed, and in September an agreement made for both to withdraw armed forces from border areas.

The relations of the Royal Government with the Democratic Republic of Vietnam obviously overshadow those with the Republic of Vietnam. Not until 1956 were diplomatic ties at the legation level established by Vientiane and Saigon. With the end of quadripartism, agreements on the port of Saigon and preferential

[128] *New York Times*, November 13, 1955.

tariffs were made on December 29, 1954; a payments agreement was signed on January 21, 1956. Minimum tariffs now apply in the trade relations between the two states. The Laotian Prime Minister received a friendly reception during his visit to Saigon in September. In May, 1957, an economic mission from Vientiane under the sponsorship of the Chamber of Commerce of Laos arrived in Saigon to discuss the possibility of using Tourane (Da Nang) for transit goods, especially in southern Laos.

In considering relations with the People's Republic of China, the Kingdom of Laos is aware of the common boundary, rugged and cragged as it is, of the some 10,000 Chinese who live in Laos and who have a grasp of the retail and wholesale trade, of the links between the Pathet Lao, the Democratic Republic of Vietnam and the People's Republic of China, and of the growing power of the colossus to the north. During the Korean War Laos had adhered to the resolution of the United Nations General Assembly, May 18, 1951, calling for an embargo on strategic materials to Communist China as well as North Korea. At the Bandung Conference Chou En-lai made it a point to assure Laos and Cambodia that his government did not intend to interfere in the domestic affairs of the two kingdoms. He noted that the People's Republic had previously assured Laos and Cambodia on the matter at the Geneva Conference on Indochina, that Eden and Molotov had been told about it, and later Nehru and U Nu.

As a result of the visit of Prince Souvanna Phouma to Peking in August, 1956, a communiqué on August 25 issued by the Prime Minister and Premier Chou En-lai pledged Laos to a "policy of peace and neutrality." The statement was similar to the one made four days later in Hanoi by Laos and the Democratic Republic of Vietnam. At the same time Laos was not ready to accept at once economic aid offered by Communist China or to enter into economic or diplomatic relations. In June, 1956, the Soviet Union decided to recognize Laos and wanted an exchange of diplomatic, cultural, and economic representatives.

India under Prime Minister Nehru has shown a special interest in developments in the Kingdom of Laos. Nehru visited Vientiane briefly on October 17, 1954, en route to Hanoi and Peking, and discussed the work of the International Commission with the Prime Minister, Prince Souvanna Phouma. The Indian leader was given a carefully written memorandum on the position of Laos in Indochina.[129] High-ranking Laotian officials, including the Crown Prince, have also visited New Delhi. India granted the Kingdom of Laos *de facto* recognition on December 15, 1954, and in 1956 established a legation in Vientiane. She has indicated a desire to give technical and financial help to Laos. It is clear that India is aware of the cultural impact she once had in the country and would like to have close ties today.

The Kingdom of Laos attended the Japanese Peace Conference at San Francisco and was one of the signers of the treaty. The Laotian delegation included the Crown Prince, Prime Minister, and Foreign Minister. Japan, it should be noted, after she had overthrown the formal French rule in Laos, had let the Laotians practically run their own affairs. In speaking at a plenary session at San Francisco on September 6, 1951, the Laotian Crown Prince observed that his delegation had "studied with the greatest of interest" the draft peace treaty, that it was not "perfect" but that it received the "full approval" of the kingdom.[130] The Crown Prince made it a point to explain the presence of Laos in San Francisco "as a victim of the war, and as a free and democratic country."[131] Japanese businessmen since the Second World War have become active in the kingdom, but a diplomatic mission from Tokyo was late in being set up in Vientiane. In December, 1956, it was indicated that Laos had waived all reparations claims against Nippon and welcomed Japanese investments. A Laos-Japan Association has been established in Tokyo. Prime Minister Kishi visited Vientiane in November, 1957, and made a specific offer of economic and technical help.

The Kingdom of Laos by and large was the most pro-French of any of the Associated States of Indochina. Earlier, when the Japanese took over in March, 1945, the King of Luang Prabang assisted French forces in their retreat toward China or the southern jungles. After the fall of Japan France reasserted her authority in Laos south of the sixteenth parallel but Chinese forces arriving in the north disarmed the French there. Although France returned to

[129] Memorandum delivered to Nehru, The Kingdom of Laos, *Application of the Geneva Agreements in Laos*, pp. 35-38. It is here interesting to note the detachment of Laos regarding Vietnam. The memorandum asserted, *inter alia*: "In fact, events which have taken place since 1946 in Vietnam have borne the characteristics of a civil war, towards which the Kingdom of Laos has always tried to conserve an attitude of strict neutrality, limiting itself to taking certain measures necessary for the safeguard of its territorial integrity."

[130] Speech of Crown Prince Savang, *Conference for the Conclusion and Signature of the Treaty of Peace with Japan*, pp. 146-147.

[131] *Ibid.*, p. 146.

power after the Chinese withdrew, it was only following the defeat of the Free Laotians.

A series of agreements between the Royal Government and France between August 27, 1946, and October 22, 1953, established the legal basis of Franco-Laotian relations. These included the *modus vivendi* of August 27, 1946, an exchange of letters between the French President and the King of Laos, November 25, 1947, and January 14, 1948, a treaty of July 19, 1949, a supplementary agreement of February 6, 1950, implementation conventions of June 13, and the Franco-Laotian Treaty of Amity and Association of October 22, 1953.

The Treaty of Amity and Association was the first of its kind to be signed between France and an Associated State.[132] In the first article France recognized that Laos was "a fully independent and sovereign State," thereby assuming prior international obligations contracted by France for Laos or Indochina, and in the second article the kingdom reaffirmed its membership in the French Union defined as "an association of independent and sovereign peoples, with freedom and equality of rights and duties, in which all the associates place in common their resources in order to guarantee the defence of the Union as a whole." Laos also reaffirmed her decision to sit in the High Council which, it is significantly pointed out, "under the chairmanship of the President of the French Union, ensures the coördination of these resources and the general conduct of the affairs of the Union." France promised "to support and uphold the sovereignty and independence of Laos before all international bodies"; each pledged "to guarantee [on its own territory] to the nationals of the other the same treatment as reserved to its own nationals." The two contracting parties would jointly participate in any negotiation that would modify the present settlement. If the agreements governing economic relations were changed, Laos and France would "mutually pledge themselves to grant to each other certain privileges, especially in the form of preferential tariffs." It was provided that special conventions would define the "modalities of the association" between the two countries.

Annexed to the Treaty of Amity and Association were three conventions—diplomatic, settlement, and judicial. Under the diplomatic convention France and Laos would exchange high representatives with all diplomatic privileges, and if necessary, represen-

[132] Treaty of Amity and Association, *Ambassade de France* [Washington], *Service de Presse et d'Information*, Indochinese Affairs, No. 1, *passim*.

tatives with consular privileges; the diplomatic and consular officials of France in countries where Laos was not directly represented were placed at the disposal of Laos; the King of Laos would appoint the delegates of the kingdom to the High Council of the French Union; Laos promised to seek nationals of the French Union as experts and technicians in preference to others providing within six months of the request Paris could offer them, and France promised in so far as she could to provide the requested personnel and pay their salaries and expenses.

In the settlement convention, "absolute reciprocity" would govern the rights and privileges of the nationals of each in the territory of the other. Among the numerous provisions was one whereby the nationals of each "shall, in all cases, have the right to transfer, into the currency of the State of which they are the subjects, all business profits and proceeds from the voluntary assignment of investments made on the territory of the other State."[133] A joint Advisory and Arbitration Commission would be set up to "ensure the regular application" of the various provisions of the convention. If the Commission disagreed on a matter, it should go at the request of one of the parties to the High Council of the French Union.

The judicial convention provided for the end of the courts in Laos of the French Union. Five French "judicial experts" at the expense of France would serve the Laotian government, which pledged "to ensure to French citizens all the guarantees of full rights and complete impartiality desirable in judicial matters."[134] The convention would go into effect November 15, 1953.

On the occasion of the signing of the treaty with its conventions in Paris, Vincent Auriol, President of France and of the French Union, addressed King Sisavang Vong of Laos, observing that the monarch had understood that "there is neither freedom nor tranquillity for a people in isolation, and that the only solution lies in a union of nations and free peoples, which must succeed in ensuring not only peace but also security and prosperity for the Laotian people."[135] President Auriol went out of his way to say that the French Union is "no obstacle to national independence" and that "its aim is to guarantee and defend it."[136] He hoped the other Associated States would make agreements as Laos had done.

[133] Annex II, Settlement Convention, Treaty of Amity and Association.
[134] Annex III, Judicial Convention, Treaty of Amity and Association.
[135] Address of Vincent Auriol, Treaty of Amity and Association.
[136] *Ibid.*

King Sisavang Vong in reply spoke most warmly of the role of France in his kingdom. "It is a great pleasure for me," he said, "to pay tribute to France for having kept her promises by defending the kingdom against external dangers and for restoring on this day, by the Treaty we have just signed, complete and full sovereignty to the Kingdom of Laos."[137] On November 16, 1956, a number of Franco-Laotian conventions were signed in Paris relating to taxation, commercial, monetary, judicial, and French personnel matters.

The Geneva settlement greatly compromised the French position in Laos although the kingdom remained in the French Union and France was allowed to keep, as noted, 5000 officers and men in the country. The Paris agreements of December, 1954, among France, Laos, Cambodia, and the State of Vietnam further reduced the French position. France has continued to give economic and technical assistance to Laos and is responsible for the training of the National Army. There is no significant agitation among the Royal Government officials to end the French military role. As a signatory of the Manila Pact and of its protocol relative to Laos, Cambodia, and South Vietnam, France has added responsibilities toward Laos. The French have continued to have favorable treatment in trade. Although the Kingdom of Laos has amended its constitution to omit the reference in the preamble to membership in the French Union, Laotian officials have indicated that the alteration does not mean withdrawal from the organization. The number of Laotian representatives in the French Union Assembly has been actually increased to five. The high representatives have also been raised to ambassadors.

American assistance to Indochina before the Geneva settlement included the Kingdom of Laos. The Mutual Defense Assistance Agreement of December 23, 1950, involving the United States and Laos, Cambodia, the State of Vietnam, and France, was followed by the Economic Coöperation Agreement of September 9, 1951, between Laos and the United States and the Laotian assurances under the Mutual Security Act of 1951 through an exchange of notes between the two countries on December 18 and 31, 1951. After the Geneva settlement the United States continued to give help, subject, of course, to the new restrictions. Senator Mansfield observed in October, 1955, that the Laotian government in view of the prevailing tension is maintaining an army "far greater in size than the country can begin to afford. As it is now, the financial

[137] Address by Sisavang Vong, Treaty of Amity and Association.

burden of the armed forces rests almost exclusively on the United States. . . ."[138] In addition, Washington is assisting road construction, public health, and agriculture. Planes flown by Civil Air Transport have dropped American food and supplies to the government-held enclaves in Phong Saly and Sam Neua.

On the diplomatic level the United States, it should be recalled, recognized the Kingdom of Laos on February 7, 1950, the American representative in Saigon being accredited also to Laos. At his press conference on July 21, 1954, President Eisenhower stated that the United States was asking Laos to agree to the appointment of an envoy resident in the kingdom. On August 10, 1955, it was officially announced that Washington and Vientiane had agreed to raise their respective legations to embassies as "a symbol of the ever-closer ties" between them. The United States Information Service is active in the kingdom. Crown Prince Savang Vathana visited Washington in September, 1956.

The United States, having assumed obligations to Laos under the protocol to the Manila Pact, is closely watching developments in the kingdom. Secretary Dulles paid a memorable visit to Vientiane on February 27, 1955, and later reported that the Laotian government was worried lest "if it suppresses the Communists within, it will be struck by the Communists from without."[139] Dulles said he hoped that that "worry is now allayed" with a "better understanding of the protective nature of the Manila Pact."[140] In response to a request from the Royal Government regarding American policy, the United States in a note,[141] dated April 16, 1957, confirmed "its interest in the peace, sovereignty, independence, unity, and territorial integrity of the Kingdom of Laos." Full support was given the "principle of the complete authority of the Royal Government of Laos over all its territory"; reunification should be effected according to the principles of the Geneva settlement of July, 1954, and the International Control Commission's resolution of January 7, 1956. The Pathet Lao was criticized for imposing "extraneous conditions." The American government in the note welcomed "the firmness with which the Kingdom of Laos has resisted this maneuver and is confident that the Royal

[138] *Viet Nam, Cambodia, and Laos*, Report by Senator Mike Mansfield, October 6, 1955, p. 18.

[139] Address by Secretary Dulles, March 8, 1955, *The Department of State Bulletin*, Vol. XXXII (March 21, 1955), p. 460.

[140] *Ibid.*

[141] Note from the United States to Laos, *The Department of State Bulletin*, Vol. XXXVI (May 13, 1957), *passim*.

Government will continue in its determination that the political future of the Kingdom of Laos shall not be dictated by dissident groups enjoying no constitutional status." As for the "extraneous conditions" of the Pathet Lao, a Department of State spokesman specifically listed on April 24 the requests for the exchange of diplomats with Communist states, for acceptance of technical and economic aid, especially from Communist China, and for the establishment of a coalition government including the Communists. Similar notes were given the Royal Government by Great Britain and France.

The United Kingdom, it is obvious, is interested in Laotian developments. The British are aware that events in the landlocked kingdom could greatly influence the rest of Southeast Asia and in particular Malaya. Laos is a member of the Consultative Committee of the Colombo Plan and is receiving help under it. Great Britain, having recognized the kingdom on February 7, 1950, accredited first her representative in Saigon to Laos as well as Cambodia; on September 21, 1954, she indicated she would open a legation in Laos and on August 9, 1955, she raised it to the status of an embassy. Foreign Secretary Eden indicated clearly Britain's interest in the kingdom when he told the House of Commons on November 8, 1954, that his government was "closely watchful" of developments in northern Laos.

In its world outlook the Kingdom of Laos belongs to the uncommitted group of states. Prince Souvanna Phouma has declared: "We have a neutral, but not a neutralist, position. Ours is a position of complete neutrality like Switzerland's, but not that of [neutralism] as have [has] been adopted by certain countries. There is no question of neutrality between two philosophies, but neutrality between two military blocs. Neutrality is for us a vital necessity."[142] He has indicated that this policy permits no military alliances or bloc alignments. At the same time Laos would reconsider its neutrality if threatened by aggression or subversion from within. Prince Souvanna Phouma has asserted that the foreign policy of Laos is inspired by the Five Principles, having their origin in Buddhist teaching and conforming to the democratic principles of the United Nations Charter, and by the Laotian declaration at Geneva in July, 1954, under which the kingdom would not enter into any military alliance as long as its security was not threatened. It should

[142] *The Times of Viet Nam,* September 8, 1956.

be stressed that Laos is eager to have good relations with its neighbors as well as with all countries. A policy of live and let live is evident.

Katay D. Sasorith, another prominent Laotian, has asserted that the foreign policy of his country, at least while he was Prime Minister, was aimed at good relations with neighboring countries regardless of their type of government, friendship with all nations that aid Laos without conditions, coöperation with all peoples wanting peace and justice, observance of the Five Principles of Peaceful Coexistence and recognition of the economic interdependence of peoples.

Under the circumstances it is not surprising that Laos at one and the same time is a member of the French Union, cultivates ties with the Theravada Buddhist nations, supports the Five Principles, is not opposed to the extension of the Manila Pact to her territory, and participates in the Colombo Plan.

The admission of Laos to the United Nations was a source of great gratification to the Vientiane government. At the ninth session of the General Assembly Australia, stressing the new status of Laos and Cambodia as a result of the Geneva settlement on Indochina in the summer of 1954, had tried to secure general approval for their admission to the world organization. Australia was strongly supported by Thailand. The United States for its part sought to include the admission of the State of Vietnam. The Australian and American efforts failed in breaking the impasse over membership.

Cambodia and Laos were finally admitted to the United Nations on December 14, 1955, in a "package deal" of 16 nations amid an atmosphere of dramatic climax. On December 1 a draft resolution finally sponsored by 28 powers was submitted to the *Ad Hoc* Political Committee of the General Assembly calling for the Security Council to consider the pending applications of all states with no unification problem and to report during the present tenth Assembly. The resolution was later revised to insert the number "18" but not to name the individual countries. Nationalist China wanted the admission of South Vietnam and South Korea and opposed the five people's republics, especially the Mongolian People's Republic. The *Ad Hoc* Political Committee approved the revised draft resolution of the 28 powers by 52 to 2 with 5 abstentions.

On December 10 the Security Council considered the question of membership in the light of the new developments. The proposal for the admission of 18 states and Chinese resolutions calling for the entry of 11 of them plus the Republics of Vietnam and Korea were discussed. On December 13 China indicated further opposition to the package deal of 18, being supported by the United States, France, and Great Britain in her efforts to have the Republics of Korea and Vietnam admitted. In the voting in the Security Council the two received 9 votes but New Zealand abstained and the Soviet Union exercised the veto. In voting on the 18 applicants China vetoed the Mongolian People's Republic and the Soviet Union then vetoed the non-Communist applicants including Cambodia and Laos. On December 14 the Security Council met at the suggestion of the Soviet Union which called for a package deal of 16 with Japan and the Mongolian People's Republic omitted. The proposal was successful and the 16 were approved, Laos and Cambodia unanimously. The General Assembly quickly met and 41 states submitted a joint draft resolution in favor of the package. On the same day, December 14, the 16 were approved by the General Assembly, Laos and Cambodia each receiving 57 votes to 0 with no abstentions. Subsequent efforts were vainly made to secure the entrance of the Republic of Vietnam into the United Nations, the Soviet Union taking the position in the eleventh General Assembly that both North and South Vietnam should be admitted.[143]

In her first speech during a general debate of the regular General Assembly, Laos at the eleventh session faced squarely the issues of the day. Katay D. Sasorith welcomed the creation of the United Nations Emergency Force in the Suez crisis and indicated Laos was willing to contribute a company to it. The kingdom also, according to the delegate, showed its sympathy for the Hungarians by deciding to offer 1 million French francs for their relief. The former Prime Minister observed that the United Nations for a small state like his own was the best guarantee that "might shall not prevail over right." He paid tribute to the help France, the United States, the partners of the Colombo Plan, and the United Nations was giving his country in its five-year plan.

The diplomatic ties of the Kingdom of Laos as of late 1956 in terms of missions were still largely with the West or pro-West

[143] On February 28, 1957, the General Assembly called for the admission of South Vietnam as well as South Korea by a vote of 40 to 8 with 18 abstentions in the case of the former and 40 to 8 with 16 abstentions in the case of the latter. Members from Southeast Asia were divided, some favoring and some abstaining. The negative votes came from the Soviet bloc. The Special Political Committee of the General Assembly had recommended the action on January 30; in the case of South Vietnam the vote was 44 to 8 with 23 abstentions and of South Korea 45 to 8 with 22 abstentions. As regards both countries, Thailand and the Philippines were in favor, and Indonesia, Burma, Laos, and Cambodia abstained. On September 9 the Soviet Union again vetoed the entrance of the Republics of Vietnam and Korea into the United Nations.

states—high representatives (later ambassadors) exchanged with France, ambassadors with Great Britain, the United States, and Thailand, and ministers with the Republic of Vietnam. Although India had a minister in Vientiane, Laos did not have one in New Delhi. In contrast, Laos had an ambassador in Japan but the latter had none resident in Vientiane. It is significant that all the countries as of late 1956 with missions located in Vientiane except India were signatories of the Manila Pact or sympathetic to it. Australia and the Philippines had envoys in Saigon, also accredited to Laos. Only New Zealand and Pakistan, among the Manila Pact powers, had no diplomats stationed in Indochina. India, Canada, and Poland as members of the International Commission, of course, had representatives in Vientiane. It was becoming more common for foreign governments to accredit their envoys in Bangkok or Saigon to Laos. In 1957 the Laotian minister in Saigon was also accredited to the Philippines.

CAMBODIA

The Kingdom of Cambodia has been developing a foreign policy that is frankly directed at preserving the independence of the nation on the possibility that the rest of Indochina may go Communist. A great effort is being made to establish the status of Cambodia as a sovereign state not associated with the vicissitudes of Vietnam and Laos. Weak in power but strategically located, Cambodia is attempting to balance off the various countries interested in Southeast Asia.

The kingdom of the Khmers has an area of around 66,800 square miles, being smaller than Laos or Vietnam. The nation is bounded on the west and part of the north by Thailand, on the rest of the north by Laos and on the east and southeast by the Republic of Vietnam. It has a relatively short, unfavorable coastline on the Gulf of Siam with the small harbors of Ream and Kep. Cambodia, unlike Laos and South Vietnam, has no frontier with a Communist area.

The population of the nation is about 4½ million, over 85 percent being the descendants of the illustrious Khmers. The rest of the population consists mostly of Chinese, Vietnamese, Cham-Malays[144] and backward tribal peoples. Buddhism is the state re-

[144] The Cham-Malays number about 85,000. They represent a fusion of people coming from the former kingdom of Champa in southern Vietnam and from Malaya. Although they are Moslems, they constitute no serious minority problem in Cambodia.

ligion, the king being the head of the two orders, the Thommayut and the Mohanikay.[145] Unifying factors in the kingdom include devotion to Buddhism and to the king, a homogeneous language, widespread peasant ownership of the soil, self-sufficiency in fish and rice, and rising nationalism.

Agriculture dominates the economy of the underdeveloped and underpopulated state with the Mekong River complex being the chief benefactor. Rice, maize, pepper, and rubber are important products. Rice itself occupies 85 percent of the tilled land with Battambang the richest area. An average of 200,000 metric tons of rice is exported each year unless there is a failure of the crop. The French own large plantations where rubber is cultivated. One of the most important fishing reservoirs in Asia is the Tonle Sap or Great Lake where shallow floods cover a large area from early in June creating favorable conditions in about 3000 square miles for fresh-water fish to spawn and grow. Chinese, Malay, and Vietnamese migrant fishermen have joined the Khmers during the best fishing season extending from October to January. At the high-water season, it should be noted, water from the Mekong flows into the Tonle Sap, reducing the flood danger in the long delta of the river. As for known mineral resources in Cambodia, they are limited, although phosphates, iron, and others are present.

A railway links Phnom Penh with Bangkok but not with Saigon. A number of roads have been built connecting Cambodia and South Vietnam, one also running to Laos and another to Thailand. The Mekong is an artery of trade and Phnom Penh a good river port; transshipments are important at Saigon, Singapore, and Hong Kong. Cambodian exports include rice, rubber, pepper, maize, salted fish, palm-sugar, and cattle, and imports include textiles, salt, chemicals, and cigarettes. The only large city of the kingdom is Phnom Penh, its population of 350,000 being about 40 percent Cambodian, 30 percent Vietnamese and 30 percent Chinese.

The history of Cambodia has centered around the empire built by the Khmers who, making up the kingdom of Chenla, took over about the middle of the 500's the kingdom of Funan. The Indian cultural, religious, and administrative impact on Funan was strongly reflected in its successor. The Khmer rulers constructed the famous edifices at Angkor, among the most monumental and impressive in the world, during the Angkor period extending from 802 to 1432. Weakened by wars with the Thai and the Vietnamese, the power

[145] The Roman Catholic population is about 120,000.

of the old Khmer empire declined. Angkor was captured by the Thai in 1431 and the capital in 1432 was moved finally to the southeast part of the nation. The French protectorate in 1863 prevented the complete destruction of the kingdom, France coming to be a champion of it. With the independence of Cambodia in late 1953 the leaders of the country put great stress on the glories of the Angkor period. Distinguished guests were given tours of Angkor Wat and Angkor Thom.

The Cambodian constitution was promulgated by King Norodom Sihanouk on May 6, 1947. It provided for a monarchy with a Council of the Kingdom, prime minister, cabinet, and National Assembly elected every four years by direct suffrage. Despite the promulgation of the constitution the political development of Cambodia has been characterized by instability. Norodom Sihanouk who became king April 23, 1941, and who abdicated on March 2, 1955, is the most powerful political figure in the country.[146] His greatest rival has been Son Ngoc Thanh of Khmer-Vietnamese descent, who came to be leader after the Japanese overthrew French rule and who later was very active in the Khmer Issarak. He was strongly anti-French and believed in Asia for the Asiatics. The constitution has been a source of controversy, Norodom Sihanouk becoming a critic of many of its provisions. Political loyalties in Cambodia have been fluid, and parties little more than personal followings.

In September, 1949, the king dissolved the National Assembly. In an election two years later another National Assembly was chosen, but the king soon had difficulties with it. In June, 1952, the cabinet ruled by the Democratic Party was dismissed by the monarch who dissolved the National Assembly the following January. Son Ngoc Thanh had returned to Phnom Penh in October, 1951, had conducted a campaign against Cambodia's being in the French Union, but had fled the capital in March, 1952. In June, 1952, when the king dismissed the cabinet he sought and received from the National Assembly full powers to run the country for three years. He promised at the end of that time to submit his actions to a "people's court."

On February 7, 1955, Norodom Sihanouk held a referendum in Cambodia on the subject as to whether he had accomplished his

[146] Born on October 31, 1922, the grandson of King Sisowath Monivong, Norodom Sihanouk was educated in French schools in Saigon and Paris. The French placed him on the throne instead of Prince Monireth who was the elder son of King Sisowath Monivong.

"Royal Mission" of strengthening the nation undertaken in June, 1952. The results were favorable to him, 925,812 to 1834 (99.8 percent) although some irregular procedures were reportedly used. On February 10 the monarch lifted the emergency measures of 1952 to facilitate elections to the National Assembly projected for April 17. On February 19 the king announced to the International Commission and the Diplomatic Corps plans for a referendum on his proposals to revise substantially the 1947 constitution, therefore not holding elections for the National Assembly as constituted, providing the people approved his proposals. In effect the suggested changes through the residential qualifications of the voters and candidates would exclude former members of the Khmer Resistance Forces from voting. The members of the International Commission were concerned with the proposals in terms of their being compatible with the Geneva provisions against discrimination. On March 2 King Norodom Sihanouk abdicated in favor of his father and mother, the former ascending the throne as King Norodom Suramarit and the latter as Queen Monivong Kossamak.

On March 15 the Cambodian government announced that the general elections planned for April 17 would be held September 11 under the electoral system provided by the 1947 constitution and not proposed by the former king on February 19. Prince Norodom Sihanouk stated on April 6 that he would form a People's Social Community (Sangkum Reastr Niyum) for the elections based on a program of support for his constitutional reforms. Held as planned on September 11, the elections resulted in a complete victory for the People's Social Community or Sangkum, the prince's followers capturing all 91 seats in the National Assembly. Almost 762,000 people or 75 percent of the registered electors voted; the Sangkum received 83 percent of the votes while 12 percent of the rest were in favor of the Democratic Party, a nationalist party with right and left wings at times interested in a republic and opposed to American aid. There was very little support (4 percent) for the Communist-inspired People's Party (Pracheachun) favored by the Hanoi radio. The elections were peaceful although during the campaign some of the members of the opposition to the government were arrested. It should be noted that Son Ngoc Thanh had surrendered in October, 1954, but he later fled to Thailand. At a press conference on September 13 the prince said he was "slightly embarrassed" at the "too complete victory." He wanted constitutional changes to end the "dictatorship by Parliament" and he promised a general amnesty to the political opposition. Prince Norodom Sihanouk either as prime minister or as a private citizen remained the dominant figure in Cambodia.

The cease-fire agreement made at the Geneva Conference on Cambodia reflects the influence of the kingdom's officials not only in the terms but also in the actual drafting. Cambodian diplomats at Geneva under Foreign Minister Tep Phan and Nong Kimny, Ambassador to the United States, did not take a back seat to France in the negotiations. The Cambodians delayed the night of July 20 the completion of the Geneva settlement until modifications were made in their favor. They were insistent that the kingdom should have no regroupment area for the Viet Minh-led Cambodian dissidents and that it should have the right as a sovereign state to make alliances and get foreign aid if it considered that the situation so demanded. The Viet Minh, supported by the Chinese and Russian Communist delegations, after failing to secure conference recognition for the Khmer Resistance Government under Son Ngoc Minh, sought to establish a regroupment area for their Cambodian allies in the kingdom and to neutralize the state in world affairs. Successful in getting a regroupment area in Phong Saly and Sam Neua in Laos and in effect in establishing that kingdom as a neutral state, the Viet Minh thought the same pressure would be successful in the case of Cambodia. After various meetings the final crisis for the Cambodians began at Anthony Eden's villa close to midnight, July 20. There in a long discussion including Eden, Molotov, Mendès-France, and Pham Van Dong, Molotov finally broke the deadlock in the early hours of July 21 and gave in to Cambodian desires. Laos, although forced to retain the regroupment area, received similar benefits as a sovereign state in the international field.

The Cambodian declaration of July 21 follows (with the escape clauses insisted upon by the Cambodian delegates in italics):

> The Royal Government of Cambodia is resolved never to take part in an aggressive policy and never to permit the territory of Cambodia to be utilised in the service of such a policy.
>
> The Royal Government of Cambodia will not join in any agreement with other states, if this agreement carries for Cambodia the obligation to enter into a military alliance *not in conformity with the principles of the Charter of the United Nations*, or, *as long as its security is not threatened*, the obligation to establish bases on Cambodian territory for the military forces of foreign powers.
>
> The Royal Government of Cambodia is resolved to settle its inter-

national disputes by peaceful means, in such a manner as not to endanger peace, international security and justice.

During the period which will elapse between the date of the cessation of hostilities in Viet-Nam and that of the final settlement of political problems in this country, the Royal Government of Cambodia will not solicit foreign aid in war material, personnel or instructors *except for the purpose of the effective defence of the territory.*[147]

The second and fourth paragraphs were actually inserted into the cease-fire agreement. A comparison of the Cambodian declaration with the Laotian shows the similar escape clauses that Laos also gained. In the "Final Declaration" of the Geneva Conference "note" was taken in paragraphs 4 and 5 of the Cambodian declaration. Under the cease-fire agreement, it should also be noted, the International Commission would "supervise, at ports and airfields and along all the frontiers of Cambodia, the application of the Cambodian declaration concerning the introduction into Cambodia of military personnel and war materials on grounds of foreign assistance."[148]

At the final plenary meeting of the Geneva Conference on July 21, the Cambodian Foreign Minister made a statement relative to the claims of his country on certain parts of South Vietnam, and there was given to members of the Conference a note on the subject. The representative of the Democratic Republic of Vietnam made "the most express reservations" on the Cambodian statement.[149] Anthony Eden, chairman at the time, asserted that the Conference could take "note" of the two positions just presented. He observed a little earlier: "I do not think it is any part of the task of this Conference to deal with any past controversies in respect of the frontiers between Cambodia and Viet Nam."[150]

Cambodia on the whole was pleased with the Geneva settlement as it related to herself. Foreign Minister Tep Phan in a closing speech at Geneva on July 21 defended the position taken by his government in the negotiations because the Cambodian cause was right and therefore could not be bypassed. He was conciliatory to the delegates and hoped for the real application of the Geneva agreement. In a government communiqué issued July 25 Cambodia expressed satisfaction over the "appreciable results" at Geneva,

[147] Cambodian Declaration (on foreign policy), Great Britain, Foreign Office, Cmd. 9239. The italics are the author's.

[148] Agreement on the cessation of hostilities in Cambodia, External Affairs, Supplementary Papers, No. 54/22.

[149] Statement of Pham Van Dong, Great Britain, Foreign Office, Cmd. 9239.

[150] Statement of Anthony Eden, Great Britain, Foreign Office, Cmd. 9239.

especially regarding the withdrawal of the Viet Minh soldiers and the recognition of the Royal Government as the only legitimate one.

The International Commission for Supervision and Control in Cambodia in its first progress report issued January 1, 1955, covering the period ending December 31, 1954, observed that the cease-fire had been put into effect by August 7 and that the Royal Government of Cambodia and the Khmer Resistance Forces (KRF) with the Vietnamese Military Units had implemented by October 20 the military clauses of the settlement. By August 22, the Khmer Resistance Forces had been unilaterally demobilized, and by October 18 the Vietnamese Military Units had left the kingdom. The only French military personnel remaining consisted of a number of instructors and the French Military Mission. On October 20 the Joint Commission of the two sides was dissolved. It was indicated that the Royal Government, however, was not convinced that all the Khmer Resistance Forces had been demobilized and that all their arms had, as alleged, been destroyed on the spot. The government also believed that some former Vietnamese military units stayed in the kingdom, merging with the Vietnamese minority. The International Commission in its first report stated that a solution to the mutual release of prisoners of war and civilian internes had been found. Under an amnesty not fully satisfactory, it was noted, the Royal Government had been and was releasing prisoners of the Khmer Resistance Forces. The Commission carried out the Geneva provisions relative to the entry of military personnel and war material, military alliances, and establishment of foreign bases. Fixed and mobile teams were set up in the country, serving "as the eyes and ears of the Commission" in Phnom Penh. It also came to find that the "complete reintegration of demobilized persons into the National Community in such a way that they will be guaranteed immunity from reprisals and the enjoyment of all the rights of citizenship" presented difficult problems which remained to be solved.[151] Significantly the Indian, Polish, and Canadian delegations "worked in close harmony" during the period under review.

In its second progress report[152] issued at Phnom Penh on April 11, 1955, for the first three months of the year the International Commission analyzed its activities with particular reference to "major developments in the internal political situation which had

[151] International Commission for Supervision and Control in Cambodia, Progress Report on the Implementation of the Geneva Agreement for the Period Ending December 31, 1954, External Affairs, Supplementary Paper, No. 55/3.

[152] *Ibid.*, for the Period January 1 to March 31, 1955, No. 55/5, *passim.*

their repercussions on the work of the Commission." As regards the reintegration problem, the Royal Government on January 14 at the suggestion of the Commission issued a statement defining again the procedure for getting reintegration cards and clarifying policy concerning the right of people who had been reintegrated to engage in constitutional political activity. The International Commission discussed with the government the amnesty of October 12, 1954, especially as regards the principles involved in handling "mixed cases," i.e., prisoners charged with crimes, political and criminal. The government set up a "Commission de Grace" to adjudicate such cases. Significantly the International Commission stated that "investigations by our teams do not bear out the charge of the Government that bands of former KRF are moving round the country." As regards the referendum held on February 7, the Commission considered the matter outside "its competence since it was not envisaged at Geneva and was also extra-constitutional." Its teams, however, observed the referendum and reported on the basis of a questionnaire the Commission sent them. Concerning the monarch's reform proposals of February 19, the Commission asserted that it "did not take an official stand . . . till the time of the abdication of King Norodom Sihanouk," for it had not received an official text and the members wanted time to consult their governments on the information they had. On February 26 the international body asked the prime minister for an audience with the king to get "clarifications on certain aspects" of the proposals. When the prime minister two days later confirmed that the elections would take place on the basis of the present constitution, the Commission withdrew its request for an audience. It reported that "for a variety of reasons, most of them concerned with developments in the internal political situation in Cambodia, King Norodom Sihanouk decided to abdicate. . . ." On March 14 the International Commission issued a communiqué asserting that "at no time has any complaint regarding its activities been received . . . from the Royal Government."[153]

In its fourth interim report issued October 3, 1955, for the period April 1 to September 30 the International Commission focused on the national elections of September 11. In instructions to its inspection teams, the international body had noted that it "has no direct responsibility for the running of the elections, nor is the Commission concerned with their supervision in any executive ca-

[153] *Ibid.*, text of Communiqué.

pacity. Elections will be conducted by the Royal Government according to the Cambodian Constitution. The Commission has, however, a responsibility to see that former members of the KRF are allowed to participate fully as electors or candidates."[154] It was reported that the International Commission intervened "decisively" with the Phnom Penh government for the registration of the People's Party, a new political party set up by some former members of the Khmer Resistance Forces. The Commission asserted that "with the completion of general elections in Cambodia, a general political settlement may be said to have been achieved."[155] In fact, the Canadian delegate, A. C. Smith, stated at a Commission meeting on October 3 that the "history of Cambodia and of this International Commission during the past thirteen months has been the success story of the Geneva settlement."[156] As the major part of the task of the international body was over, its personnel has been substantially reduced. The Royal Government of Cambodia, nevertheless, has wanted the International Commission to stay as it could help guard the neutrality of the kingdom. Canada has favored the termination of the Commission. A fifth interim report covered the period October 1, 1955, to December 31, 1956.

In its relations with the governments of North and South Vietnam the Kingdom of Cambodia faces a number of problems. Vietnam as a whole with its tradition of expansion at the expense of its neighbors and its rapidly growing and energetic population is certain under the best of circumstances to cause apprehension in Phnom Penh. In fact, the Cambodians are more concerned over the Vietnamese than the Thai. Moreover, there live in Cambodia 300,000 Vietnamese, and in South Vietnam including the island of Phu Quoc about 400,000 Cambodians.

The Viet Minh under Ho Chi Minh had shown for some time an interest in making Cambodia a Communist satellite. After much difficulty it infiltrated and seized control of a substantial part of the Khmer Issarak movement. The latter, operating in different parts of Cambodia and at times in South Vietnam and, as noted, in Thailand, was factional but opposed to French rule. The Viet Minh found in Son Ngoc Minh, a Khmer Marxist, a leader who would coöperate with international Communism in Indochina. A Khmer

[154] International Commission for Supervision and Control in Cambodia, Fourth Interim Report, External Affairs, Supplementary Paper, No. 55/13, Appendix C.
[155] *Ibid.* (body of report).
[156] *Ibid.*, Appendix H.

People's Congress met in April, 1950, recognized officially the Khmer National United Front, and elected a Provisional National Liberation Committee. The large Vietnamese minority in Cambodia obviously provided fertile ground for Viet Minh agents. Especially in the "Southwestern Zone" of the kingdom did the Viet Minh gain an organized foothold. After the Lao Dong Party was created in the Democratic Republic in 1951, a Revolutionary Cambodian People's Party came into being in the Buddhist country. This provided a nucleus for the Cambodian Resistance Government led by Son Ngoc Minh.

Taking advantage of their strength already in the kingdom and getting ready for the Geneva Conference, the Viet Minh with the aid of the Khmer People's Liberation Army launched an invasion of northeast Cambodia from southern Laos on April 2, 1954. Other invaders came from Cochin China. The Cambodians rallied behind the king in fighting the aggressors. On April 15 the Royal Government issued a "solemn appeal" through its ambassador in Washington to the United Nations protesting against the "open aggression" by Viet Minh troops on Cambodian soil. It noted that Viet Minh irregulars had been in the kingdom since 1946 and that the open aggression was accompanied by intensification of Viet Minh infiltration. Son Ngoc Minh whom the forces of Ho Chi Minh were supporting was condemned as a nonentity. The Secretary-General of the United Nations was only asked to circulate the note to all members of the organization but the Cambodian government reserved the right to request what it called "specific action."

After the Geneva Conference, Ho Chi Minh stressed that he wanted to apply the Five Principles in the relations of the Democratic Republic of Vietnam with Cambodia. This attitude was reflected in Viet Minh statements to Nehru in October, 1954, and April, 1955. At the Bandung Conference Pham Van Dong in an opening statement reiterated the readiness of his government to establish relations with Cambodia on the basis of the "five principles of peaceful coexistence." A little later at an informal meeting including Nehru and Chou En-lai, Pham Van Dong assured the Cambodian representative that his government did not want to interfere in the kingdom's domestic affairs.

On August 20 Cambodia informed the International Commission that Viet Minh elements had attacked "legal forces" in the area of Voeunsai in the province of Stung Treng on August 5, 14, and 16. An extraordinary meeting of the Commission was held on Sunday, August 21, and an inquiry was ordered. The International Commission in Laos was requested to investigate the validity of charges by the Cambodian government that five battalions of regular Viet Minh troops were stationed at Siempoy in southern Laos. The international body in Cambodia reported to the Royal Government on September 8 that "the identity of the attacking elements cannot be established" and "there is no evidence to show that the armed bands in the region, or the attackers of Voeunsai, were regular units of the Viet Minh forces."[157] Aerial reconnaissance over the Siempoy area of Laos failed to indicate any troop concentrations but ground investigation was not possible because of transportation difficulties.

Another problem in Cambodian-Viet Minh relations arose on August 25 when the prime minister of the kingdom informed the International Commission that the Hanoi radio was broadcasting items in Cambodian that constituted a campaign of interference in the domestic affairs of the country. After the International Commission reported the matter to the Democratic Republic of Vietnam, the latter not only protested on September 8 the Cambodian charges relative to Viet Minh attacks at Voeunsai but also justified the broadcasting of newspaper extracts from the Cambodian press. The International Commission on September 30 addressed letters to the governments of both Cambodia and the Democratic Republic of Vietnam. In the letter to the former it was indicated the Hanoi government had suggested that questions that might lead to misunderstanding should be settled by direct diplomatic negotiations between the two parties. The International Commission requested Cambodia and the Democratic Republic of Vietnam to find ways of ending hostile propaganda. Both governments took steps to improve the situation.

On September 13 Prince Norodom Sihanouk asserted that Cambodian diplomatic recognition should be given Vietnam as soon as the country was united. In the meantime political missions could be exchanged with both the Hanoi and Saigon governments. In the case of the former the Viet Minh would have to cease its provocations against Cambodia. The Hanoi radio has called for the establishment of diplomatic relations between Cambodia and the Democratic Republic but not even "representatives" have been exchanged as in the case of Cambodia and the Republic of Vietnam.

[157] *Ibid.* (body of report).

In July, 1956, a delegation of Cambodian journalists visited Hanoi, pointing the way to subsequent exchanges along similar lines.

As regards the Republic of Vietnam, boundary and minority questions are creating difficulties. It has been pointed out that the southward expansion of the Vietnamese into what was later called Cochin China was at the expense of Cambodia. For instance, in the provinces of Tra Vinh, Soctrang, and Rachgia, the majority of the inhabitants are still Cambodians. At the signing of the Franco-Khmer treaty of November 8, 1949, Cambodia made reservations regarding her interests and again when a French law was enacted adding Cochin China to the rest of Vietnam. At the closing meeting of the Geneva Conference on July 21, 1954, Foreign Minister Tep Phan asserted:

> Paragraphs 7, 11 and 12 of the final Declaration stipulate respect for the territorial integrity of Viet Nam. The Cambodian Delegation asks the Conference to consider that this provision does not imply the abandonment of such legitimate rights and interests as Cambodia might assert with regard to certain regions of South Viet Nam. . . . Faithful to the ideal of peace, and to the international principle of non-interference, Cambodia has no intention of interfering in the internal affairs of the State of Viet Nam and associates herself fully with the principle of respect for its integrity, provided certain adjustments and regularisations be arrived at with regard to the borders between this State and Cambodia, borders which so far have been fixed by a mere unilateral act of France.[158]

Pham Van Dong in making the "most express reservations" showed the awareness of the Democratic Republic of the Cambodian claims.

The 400,000 Cambodians in South Vietnam and the 300,000 Vietnamese in Cambodia raise numerous minority problems. The Cambodians have accused the Vietnamese of persecuting their compatriots. In Cambodia the Vietnamese, almost completely unassimilated, occupied under the French important positions as civil servants, administrators, doctors, and engineers. They still provide labor on French rubber plantations and are active as rice growers and fishermen. Some are engaged in professional activities and others are merchants and artisans. In the negotiations after the cease-fire in Cambodia, it should be stressed that agreement was reached that the Vietnamese domiciled in the kingdom who became soldiers in the fighting against the government or who with similar objectives held "supervisory or directive positions in the war" would be evacuated but "lesser offenders" could stay in Cambodia.

[158] Statement of Tep Phan, Great Britain, Foreign Office, Cmd. 9239.

Difficulties arose over evacuation modalities. Vietnamese in the kingdom have accused the Cambodians of discrimination against them in many respects. Phnom Penh's implementation of a recent law banning 18 professions to foreigners has hurt numerous Vietnamese. The Saigon government is giving them relief and has offered to repatriate those wishing to leave Cambodia. In January, 1957, around 2500 arrived in South Vietnam.

Border raids involving irregular forces from southern Vietnam have concerned the International Commission in the Khmer kingdom. Basically Cambodia has had serious doubts about the future of the Republic of Vietnam in view of the strength of Ho Chi Minh. Saigon for its part has been somewhat scornful of its neighbor to the west. It was believed that in time of trouble the Khmer kingdom would turn to the Republic of Vietnam but otherwise intrigue against it. Ties between Cambodia and the People's Republic of China would work to the advantage not of the Khmers but of the Chinese in the kingdom. Cambodia's efforts on the world stage without having any power herself were looked upon in Saigon with considerable doubt.

In early 1956 relations between South Vietnam and Cambodia reached a serious stage. A dispute arose over some islands in the Gulf of Siam. Cambodia for some time has been concerned over Phu Quoc strategically located near Kompong Som, a Khmer seaport being developed on the coast. South Vietnam was apprehensive over the activities of political opponents of Ngo Dinh Diem in Cambodia. Prince Norodom claimed that the refugees, though allowed to enter the kingdom, had to keep out of the affairs of the Saigon regime. He asserted that Cambodia was willing to establish a consulate general in South Vietnam without exequatur and to allow the latter to do the same in the former. The Saigon government wanted at least an exchange of political representatives. It had, in fact, been pressing since 1952 for full diplomatic relations. When the Republic of Vietnam was carrying on operations in the west near Cambodia against subversive elements, it exercised close control of the frontier to end clandestine traffic. The Saigon government claimed the frontier was not closed although Cambodians put this interpretation upon it. At the same time the Republic asserted it was not involved in Cambodian domestic politics. In the middle of May Cambodia announced that normal trade would be renewed with South Vietnam. The exchange of representatives by the two governments resolved a controversial question between Saigon and Phnom Penh authorities.

Obviously the economic relations between Cambodia and South Vietnam cannot be divorced from the political. Agreements relative to customs and to the port of Saigon were signed on December 29, 1954. The principle of preferential margins in customs duties was approved for the respective national goods. Navigation on the Mekong between Phnom Penh and the sea was considered maritime. Delay in applying the settlement led to the establishment of a commission of experts. After a number of meetings in April, 1955, a joint final note was issued on April 29 covering economic and commercial questions, customs and payments. After negotiations in July in Phnom Penh, an exchange of letters on August 31 further defined economic relations. On September 24 a payments agreement was signed by the two neighbors. The following December 30 the Republic of Vietnam decided to apply its minimum customs tariff on the basis of reciprocity to Cambodian goods as from January 1, 1956. In 1955, it might be noted, Cambodia bought 13.9 percent of Vietnam's exports and the latter took 2 percent of its imports from the former. Cambodia is eager to decrease her economic dependence upon South Vietnam. The construction of Kompong Som as a seaport on the Gulf of Siam is obviously a significant step in this direction. In a security move a number of Cambodian peasants have been resettled in Kampot province on the seacoast. At the same time the Khmer kingdom is concerned over any developments affecting navigation on the Mekong and the port of Saigon.

Cambodian relations with Laos, despite the geographical proximity of the two kingdoms and their religious and cultural ties, are limited. There are no boundary or minority questions of consequence to create trouble. Only a few Cambodians live in Laos and around 20,000 Laotians reside in the Khmer kingdom. Despite the artery of the Mekong, trade between the two Buddhist nations is limited. With the end of quadripartism an agreement between Cambodia and Laos was made on December 29, 1954, on transit trade and preferential tariffs. In the summer of 1956 a payments agreement was signed, following negotiations that began the previous December. A Cambodia-Laotian military transit accord has also been made. Cambodia agreed in June to the establishment of diplomatic relations with Laos at the request of the latter, but implementation has been slow.

The development of Cambodian-French relations for a period after the Second World War was characterized by considerable acrimony. At the suggestion of the Japanese, it will be recalled, King Norodom Sihanouk on March 13, 1945, had declared the protectorate established by France null and void, and had proclaimed the independence of the kingdom. After a force of British, Indian, and French troops occupied Phnom Penh in early October, French power was restored. On January 7, 1946, it has been pointed out, an agreement in the form of a *modus vivendi* was made between the French and Cambodian governments; the protectorate was terminated in name and Cambodia became an autonomous unit in the Indochinese Federation as then projected. A factor working to the advantage of France was her efforts and final success in getting Thailand to restore to Cambodia territory taken from her under Japanese auspices. A series of agreements defining relations between France and Cambodia followed the *modus vivendi.* They included an exchange of letters between the King of Cambodia and the President of France on November 27, 1947, and January 14, 1948, another letter from the latter to the former, November 25, the Franco-Khmer treaty of November 8, 1949, a supplementary agreement of June 15, 1950, protocols announced May 9, 1953, and further agreements in August, September, and October. A basic treaty defining the relationship of France and Cambodia in the light of developments in the kingdom and the French Union still awaits negotiation.

The key figure in Franco-Cambodian relations is, of course, Norodom Sihanouk. Despite his selection by the French and his training he has become a Cambodian nationalist. Undoubtedly the pressure of the Khmer Issarak in his kingdom had forced him at times into stronger anti-French positions than otherwise might have been expected. The king frankly asserted as regards France in February, 1947: "No one is more desirous of complete independence than I, but we must look facts in the face. We are too poor to support or defend ourselves. We are dependent upon some major power to give us technicians and troops. If not France it would be some other great nation. We are a small power of 3,000,000 people, sandwiched between 20,000,000 Annamese and 12,000,000 Siamese."[159]

By early 1953 King Norodom Sihanouk was fearful that he was losing the leadership of the nationalist movement; he believed

[159] *New York Times,* February 13, 1947.

that France was not moving rapidly enough in meeting Cambodia's legitimate demands. He went to Paris in February and stayed there until April. Not satisfied with the results he visited the United States in an effort to get support. In an interview[160] in New York the king frankly developed his position, indicating that if France did not grant more independence in the "next few months" the people might revolt against the government and unite with the Communist-led Viet Minh; his people, he said, "do not want to die for the French and help them stay [in Cambodia]"; he noted that "Paris does not like my coming to America because it says I am applying pressure here. I cannot be doing that because I represent a very small nation that cannot very well apply pressure on anyone." Returning home via Japan where he received a good reception, the young monarch suddenly left his kingdom for Bangkok in June. Imposing upon himself an exile, he sought to dramatize to France and the world the plight of his nation. The king asserted he would not return until Cambodia had won her independence, although he subsequently left Bangkok for Siemreap in the western part of his country. Many in the Khmer Issarak came to support the monarch and his popularity grew among his people.

The offer of the new Premier of France, Joseph Laniel, on July 3 to "perfect" the independence of the Associated States led to further negotiations between Cambodia and France. Subsequent agreements in the defense, internal security, and legal fields had the real effect of giving Cambodia her independence toward the end of 1953. Norodom Sihanouk returned to his capital in triumph on November 8. The transfer of services proceeded rapidly in 1954.

The question of the use of Cambodian troops outside the kingdom had been a serious matter. In September, 1953, Prime Minister Penn Nouth had asserted that his country would not oppose Viet Minh military operations outside Cambodia and therefore aroused France and the United States which wanted a common war effort in Indochina against the Viet Minh. The premier then let it be known that independence for Cambodia would result in a different policy. Upon his return to Phnom Penh the king asserted that the Viet Minh was the chief threat to the nation. Cambodian forces were withdrawn from southern Viet Nam and were restricted to the Buddhist kingdom.

Although Cambodia did not believe that France gave her sufficient support at the Geneva Conference, relations between the

[160] *New York Times*, April 19, 1953.

two states have definitely improved as a result of independence. The French role in the projected assistance to the kingdom was well shown, it will be recalled, in the Franco-American communiqué of September 29, 1954. The economic and technical aid from the French has been forthcoming and they have been training the Cambodian army. France has been constructing the seaport at Kompong Som and is active in other projects. Senator Mansfield reported in October, 1955, that "at present, French prestige in Cambodia is probably at its highest level in the postwar years. This change is attributable, in my opinion, primarily to the achievement of independence, to the principle of national equality which now governs relationships between the two countries, and to the prompt adjustment of French policy to the change. There is no more exodus of French nationals from Cambodia; on the contrary, some French firms are transferring operations from Viet Nam to that country."[161] The French military, economic, and cultural missions remain active; in Pierre Gorce France has had a distinguished high commissioner in Phnom Penh. The continued presence of many Cambodian students in France is indicative of the strong cultural ties between the two governments, and the importance of trade should not be ignored. In 1956 Royal Air Cambodge came into being with the assistance of Air France.

On September 25, 1955, the National Assembly of Cambodia unanimously adopted an amendment to the constitution substituting "Cambodia, an independent and sovereign State" for "Cambodia, self governing State belonging to the French Union as an Associated State"; Norodom Sihanouk had previously indicated this step would be taken because Cambodia no longer wanted to participate in the High Council and Assembly of the French Union "whose powers and existence are incompatible with her conception of independence" and she does not have to mention in her constitution "alliances which it [she] might freely form or dissolve with other countries."[162] He noted that the final decision on the relationship between Cambodia and France would be determined by the people who would consider membership in the French Union only if it were altered along the lines of the British Commonwealth. On September 26 the National Assembly called for the limitation of the French language to diplomatic, technical, and administrative necessity.

[161] *Viet Nam, Cambodia and Laos*, Report by Senator Mike Mansfield, October 6, 1955, p. 16.

[162] *Keesing's Contemporary Archives*, 14484 A.

In her relations with Asian states outside Indochina, Cambodia has had to cope with different sets of problems. Obviously India, Japan, and China have been centers of interest though each for different reasons. Within Southeast Asia Cambodian relations with Thailand and Burma are more extensive than with the Philippines and Indonesia. Norodom Sihanouk had done considerable traveling in Asia to promote good will for his nation. Included in his visits have been Tokyo, Peking, Manila, Bandung, Bangkok, Rangoon, New Delhi, and Colombo.

India has shown special interest in Cambodian developments since the Geneva Conference. Prime Minister Nehru visited Phnom Penh in the fall of 1954 on his return from Peking. He was very much impressed by the cultural impact of India on the Buddhist kingdom. The Cambodians, moreover, have been influenced by Indian nationalism. On December 13 India extended modified diplomatic recognition to Cambodia and appointed a "political representative" with the personal rank of minister to the kingdom. In March, 1955, Prince Norodom visited Prime Minister Nehru in New Delhi. A joint communiqué[163] issued on March 18 referred to the "historical connections and close cultural affinity" between the two countries and indicated that they "provide a guarantee for the continuance of friendly relations in the future." Cambodia and India agreed in effect that the Five Principles offer "the best guarantee for peace in the world and for friendship between countries." The Geneva settlement should be "fully implemented" and "every effort should be made to preserve and strengthen the independence of Cambodia and improve the condition of its people." Significant is the fact that the Government of India "assured the Cambodian Delegation of their desire to give such assistance to Cambodia as lay in their power." Cultural coöperation would be developed "to the maximum extent possible" and diplomatic missions at the legation level exchanged. Prince Norodom Sihanouk is greatly impressed by Prime Minister Nehru and is definitely influenced by Indian foreign policy.

As regards Japan, Cambodia did not suffer during the occupation like Burma or the Philippines. After the Japanese urged the kingdom to declare its independence in March, 1945, the Cambodian who came to be the first Minister of Foreign Affairs was none other than Son Ngoc Thanh. At the San Francisco Peace Conference, Cambodia was one of the powers signing the peace treaty

[163] International Commission for Supervision and Control in Cambodia (Progress Report, January 1 to March 31, 1955), Appendix I, *passim.*

with Japan. On September 6, 1951, Foreign Minister Neal Phleng told a plenary session that Cambodia believed "the imposition of severe conditions upon the Japanese people as regards reparations would be an illusion and would only serve to keep alive in Japan the spirit of revenge" but she hoped to "receive from Japan as appropriate and quick reparation of . . . damages as possible."[164] Diplomatic relations were later established at the legation level and in February, 1955, raised to embassy status.

Cambodia in late November waived any reparations from Nippon and gave to the Japanese Red Cross the indemnity of 1 million yen that Japan was obligated to pay Cambodians made prisoners by her during the war. The Red Cross in turn gave Cambodia the equivalent value in terms of drugs and vitamin pills. When Prince Norodom Sihanouk arrived in Tokyo in December he was warmly received. He wanted 10,000 Japanese immigrants for Cambodia, increased trade, and technical assistance in rice production. On December 9 a treaty of friendship was signed calling for "eternal peace." It provided for strengthening cultural and economic ties and for exchanging technical assistance. Later a Japanese team arrived in Cambodia to plan a proposed tourist resort. Some of the possibilities of Cambodian-Japanese coöperation have not proved practical, and progress has been slow. Prime Minister Kishi visited the kingdom in November, 1957, making a specific offer of assistance in the economic development of the nation.

In considering China, Cambodia is well aware of the impact of the People's Republic on Indochina and Southeast Asia. Within the kingdom dwell some 250,000 Chinese, most of whom are unassimilated. Some, however, have married Cambodians and their descendants have occasionally become distinguished citizens. Trade in the country is largely in the hands of the Chinese; they are the entrepreneurs and the middlemen; some are fishermen, others artisans. The pepper plantations are almost completely operated and owned by them. The Cambodian government after the Second World War firmly opposed granting to the Chinese the same juridical rights enjoyed by French citizens for a period of time. It is making a definite effort to break the Chinese monopoly on the rice trade. The denial in May, 1956, of certain professions to foreign residents has aroused the Chinese as well as the Vietnamese minority. On March 1 a decree was issued forbidding political ac-

[164] Speech of Neal Phleng, *Conference for the Conclusion and Signature of the Treaty of Peace with Japan*, p. 163.

tivities among the Chinese residents of the kingdom. It is believed that they are more favorably disposed to the China of Mao Tse-tung than to that of Chiang Kai-shek.

In Phnom Penh a Chinese Nationalist consulate functions, although its precise status has not been determined. At the invitation of Prince Norodom Sihanouk, Foreign Minister George Yeh of Nationalist China visited Cambodia in the summer of 1956. He was well received by Cambodian officials; the prince himself was in Europe. The Nationalist leader declined to comment on the foreign policy of Cambodia but he urged the Chinese in the kingdom to work for its prosperity. In July a Cambodian delegation largely of journalists was received by Chiang Kai-shek in Taiwan.

At the Bandung Conference in April, 1955, Chou En-lai of the People's Republic had gone out of his way to assure Cambodia of Communist China's good intentions. He invited Norodom Sihanouk to his house for lunch and in the words of the latter "personally assured me that China will always faithfully adhere to the Five Principles [of Co-Existence] in its relations with Cambodia and have a friendly feeling toward my country."[165] This assurance was also given in the presence of Nehru and again to the political committee of the Conference on April 23. On April 26 the prince told newsmen in Singapore that "as far as Cambodia is concerned China and North Vietnam have assured me that they would respect [the] independence, political ideology and sovereignty of my country."[166]

On September 13 Prince Norodom told a news conference that he favored diplomatic recognition of China after it was united. Following a trip to the Philippines beginning late in January, 1956, the prince a few days later went to Peking. His visit in the People's Republic was widely publicized in the Chinese Communist press, hailed as another indication of "peaceful coexistence." A joint communiqué issued by Norodom Sihanouk and Chou En-lai called for the steady cultivation of direct contacts and stressed the importance of economic and cultural relations. The prince's stress on neutrality and his opposition to protection under the Manila Pact were well received in Communist China. After his return from Peking, Norodom Sihanouk indicated that Cambodia would send a delegation to the People's Republic to make a commercial agreement. Involved in the negotiations would also be the questions of Chinese economic aid and of cultural coöperation.

[165] Quoted in Kahin, *op. cit.*, p. 15.
[166] *Indonesian Observer*, April 27, 1955.

In April a trade and payments pact was signed, calling for up to $14 million worth of business each way for a year. On June 21 an economic aid agreement was concluded under which Communist China would give Cambodia in goods and services over a period of two years the equivalent of $22.4 million. Textile, paper, plywood, and cement factories would be built as part of the program. The Cambodians asserted that the aid was unconditional and that they would not have accepted it if there had been strings attached. Nevertheless, the presence of technicians in Cambodia from the mainland of China is certain to create opportunities for liaison with the local Chinese minority. Mixed commissions in connection with the administration of the program have been established in Peking and Phnom Penh. Basic in an understanding of contemporary relations between Cambodia and the People's Republic of China is the conviction of Prince Norodom Sihanouk that the latter is sincere in basing its policy toward the Khmer kingdom on the Five Principles, that Mao Tse-tung would restrain Ho Chi Minh if he sought to invade Cambodia, and that the Chinese minority in the latter state now constitutes no real menace to the security of the nation.

In late November Chou En-lai paid a formal visit to Phnom Penh; he also journeyed with Norodom Sihanouk to see the Khmer ruins at Angkor. Careful security provisions were taken by the Royal Government. Chou En-lai made it a point in Cambodia to oppose "great-nation chauvinism," thus seeking to destroy fears of China as an aggressive power. A joint Chinese-Cambodian communiqué called for the observance of the Five Principles. The visiting premier urged the Chinese in Cambodia to respect the laws of the kingdom and to keep out of politics.

Relations between Cambodia and the Soviet Union also underwent a drastic change in 1956. After the latter had recognized the former, plans were made for the eventual exchange of ambassadors. In September the first Cambodian ambassador to the Soviet Union presented his credentials and the Royal Government approved the nomination of the first Soviet ambassador to Cambodia. It was planned in Phnom Penh to accredit the Cambodian ambassador in Moscow to a number of Eastern European states.

During the summer of 1956 Prince Norodom Sihanouk visited numerous countries in Europe—Spain, Austria, Poland, Czechoslovakia, Yugoslavia, and the Soviet Union. The most important in terms of the foreign policy of Cambodia was the Soviet Union. Warmly received in Moscow and other Russian cities, the prince stressed the neutrality of his country and praised the Five Principles. In a joint communiqué of July 7 by Premier Nikolai A. Bulganin and Norodom Sihanouk it was stated that the Soviet Union would grant economic and technical assistance without conditions to Cambodia and that Soviet experts would go to the Khmer kingdom to consider questions of help in setting up industrial and other enterprises and in training necessary technicians. The USSR proposed to build and equip a hospital at Phnom Penh as a gift. Tribute was paid to the Five Principles as the basis of relations between the two states. The plan for the exchange of ambassadors was formally announced. It was indicated that Bulganin and Nikita S. Khrushchev had accepted an invitation to visit Cambodia. By the end of November the Soviet Union had 16 men in the Khmer kingdom in connection with the implementation of the aid program. In 1957 subsequent agreements on trade and coöperation were made.

As a result of the visit of Norodom Sihanouk to Poland, the latter promised to send aid to Cambodia. In fact, it was indicated that a surgical room would be given for the projected hospital. Czechoslovakia, through the prince's visit, agreed to send an economic, technical, and scientific mission to Phnom Penh to negotiate a trade agreement as well as one on scientific and technical aid. It is significant that in the joint Khmer-Czech declaration the seating of the People's Republic of China in the United Nations was requested. Diplomatic relations through the prince's negotiations during his trip would be established between Cambodia on the one hand and Poland, Czechoslovakia, and Yugoslavia on the other. Czech-Cambodian trade and technical aid agreements were signed on October 6, 1956; Premier Joseph Cyrankiewicz of Poland visited Cambodia in March, 1957.

As for North and South Korea the government in Phnom Penh has considered itself far removed from the Korean problem. In response to an inquiry from the United Nations on measures taken under the General Assembly resolution of May 18, 1951, relative to an embargo on strategic materials to North Korea and Communist China, Cambodia replied that she had no commercial relations with the countries concerned as to the items mentioned in the resolution. During the Korean War the kingdom donated salted fish and rice to South Korea.

Relations between the United States and Cambodia have reflected developments both in Indochina and in the world at large. The United States, it will be recalled, recognized the kingdom on February 7, 1950, and Cambodia was a participant in the Agreement for Mutual Defense Assistance in Indochina signed December 23. An Economic Coöperation Agreement providing for American economic and technical help was signed by Cambodia and the United States on September 8, 1951.[167] Cambodia gave assurances as required under the Mutual Security Act of 1951 in an exchange of notes December 18 and 28. After the Geneva settlement the United States and France in a communiqué on September 29, 1954, agreed on assistance to Cambodia.

On the previous July 21 President Eisenhower had announced that the United States wanted to appoint a resident envoy at Phnom Penh. The chief of the mission in Saigon had also been accredited to Cambodia first as minister and later as ambassador with a chargé d'affaires in Phnom Penh. On October 2 the first resident American ambassador to Cambodia presented his credentials. At the same time he delivered a message from President Eisenhower to King Norodom Sihanouk. The President noted: "At this time when Cambodia has so convincingly demonstrated its independence and its stern determination to maintain that independence, I desire Your Majesty to know that my Government will be pleased to consider ways in which our two countries can more effectively coöperate in the joint task of stemming the threats facing your territories and maintaining peace and prosperity in your Kingdom."[168] It was later announced that American aid in all categories to Cambodia as of January 1, 1955, would be direct and not through France.

On May 16, 1955, the United States and Cambodia reached an agreement for direct American military aid to the Buddhist kingdom. A United States Military Assistance Advisory Group limited to about 30 officers and men would be sent to Cambodia. They would judge the needs of the Royal Khmer Army and insure the right use of the aid. In a communiqué on May 29 Cambodia asserted that "there is no question of the granting of military bases nor of a military alliance of any sort nor of the sending of American military instructors to Cambodia."[169]

[167] For an interesting account of the proposed gift of an elephant by the King of Cambodia to the President of the United States, see the *New York Times*, October 14, 1951.

[168] President's Message, *The Department of State Bulletin*, Vol. XXXI (October 25, 1954), p. 615.

The International Commission was informed of the agreement by the Cambodian government on May 23. As a result of objections raised in the Commission about certain parts of the agreement not being strictly in conformity with the Geneva settlement, the Cambodian government was asked for certain clarifications. On May 30 the prime minister in discussion with the Commission gave the understanding and interpretation of his government. On June 17 the Royal Government requested the Commission to examine the military aid agreement against the Geneva settlement. Three days later General Vo Nguyen Giap, writing for the Democratic Republic of Vietnam, protested to the International Commission that the agreement violated the Geneva terms. He said that it took "the character of a military alliance with the USA, the leaders of the SEATO aggressive bloc."[170] In order to have a formal record of how the Cambodian government interpreted the military aid accord the Commission on July 5 sent a letter to the Royal Government setting forth the understanding as hitherto indicated. Eight days later Cambodia confirmed that her understanding and position were accurately expressed in the Commission's letter of July 5. The International Commission in a unanimous resolution[171] on July 23 welcomed Cambodia's clarifications and "its assurance that it will scrupulously and always respect the terms of the Geneva Agreement." It took "note of the assurance of the Royal Government that it will follow a policy of neutrality." The Commission concluded that "although it may still be argued that some of the clauses of the new military aid agreement in terms go beyond the limitations imposed by the Geneva Agreement, the Commission accepts the assurances given by the Cambodian Government and is confident that in practice the receiving of aid under the new military aid agreement will be in conformity with the terms of the Geneva Accord."

In the election of September 11 the opponents of Prince Norodom Sihanouk accused him of impairing Cambodian independence by the military accord with the United States although he was technically not responsible for it. The victory of the ex-king at the polls meant that the military agreement would stand. American aid to the kingdom, it should be stressed, has extended far beyond the strict military field: assistance in road construction between the new port of Kompong Som and Phnom Penh, in furnishing rice

[169] International Commission for Supervision and Control in Cambodia, Third Interim Report, External Affairs, Supplementary Paper, No. 55/8, Appendix B.

[170] *Ibid.*, Appendix C.

[171] *Ibid.* (body of report), *passim.*

when the Cambodian crop failed, and in irrigation, health, education, and other projects. Interesting is the fact that the North American republic is helping to restore part of the old irrigation facilities at Angkor. The United States now maintains in the kingdom not only an embassy and a military mission but also an economic aid mission and an information staff. It participated in a fair in Phnom Penh.

Before the Geneva settlement Cambodia was especially eager to receive a military guarantee from the United States. Under-Secretary of State Walter Bedell Smith was sympathetic to Cambodia at the Geneva Conference but the United States was hesitant to make an ironclad promise. At the Manila Conference in September, 1954, Washington strongly favored extending the treaty area in the proposed pact to include Cambodia. In the Southeast Asia Collective Defense Treaty under the protocol, the United States as well as Great Britain, France, Australia, New Zealand, the Philippines, Thailand, and Pakistan assumed defense obligations to the Khmer kingdom. It should be added, however, that under Article IV, Section 3, "no action on the territory of any State designated by unanimous agreement . . . or on any territory so designated shall be taken except at the invitation or with the consent of the government concerned."[172]

Cambodian support for the assurances under the Manila Pact has greatly declined since September, 1954. Secretary of State Dulles in his conversation with Norodom Sihanouk on February 28, 1955, told the king that SEATO afforded his nation real protection against Communist aggression. The monarch reportedly expressed satisfaction over the results of the recent Bangkok meeting of the Manila Pact powers. The change in Cambodian attitude toward SEATO was well indicated by Norodom Sihanouk when he asserted on February 18, 1956, in Peking: "Cambodia is neutral. The people themselves request me to maintain neutrality whatever may happen. The Southeast Asian treaty powers have told us that we would be automatically protected. We reject such protection because it can only bring us dishonor."[173]

Although Prince Norodom Sihanouk was well received in the Philippines in early 1956 he opposed any idea that Cambodia might orientate her foreign policy to parallel that of the island republic.

[172] The Southeast Asia Collective Defense Treaty, *The Signing of the Southeast Asia Collective Defense Treaty, the Protocol to the Southeast Asia Collective Defense Treaty and the Pacific Charter*, p. 77.
[173] *New York Times*, March 2, 1956.

He later observed that he thought the Filipino hospitality was an American effort to influence him. He criticized the kind of American aid to his nation and opposed what he suspected was an effort on the part of the United States to buy the loyalty of the kingdom. The closing of the frontier by South Vietnam and later by Thailand, as Cambodia interpreted the situation, was considered a further American attempt to bring pressure. The Chinese Communists have contributed to arousing Cambodian apprehensions. Toward the end of March Prince Norodom Sihanouk resigned as prime minister after he had broadcast a statement attacking the American press for alleged insults.

On April 19 the American ambassador to the Khmer kingdom delivered a letter from Secretary Dulles to Foreign Minister Nong Kimny in which the United States denied that it was trying to force Cambodia to enter SEATO under the penalty of holding back economic aid and that it had forced Thailand and Vietnam to employ economic measures against Cambodia to accomplish the same objective. It was noted that the American ambassador on April 2 had officially told the king and queen that the United States had not made any "official public observation" on the foreign policy of the kingdom. Cambodia, the letter stated, had officially requested military aid on May 20, 1954, and military and economic help on September 1; only on this basis was the aid extended. It was asserted that "United States policy in Cambodia is based on a single precept: That is, the United States through its military and economic aid programs seeks to assist the Cambodian Government in its endeavor to maintain the sovereign independence of the Kingdom."[174] Stress was placed on the fact that although Washington believed collective defense was the best way to face the threat of Communist aggression, it did not seek mutual defense ties with countries that did not want them. The United States "considers it to be in its national interest to help in the economic and social advancement of all free nations."[175] Later relations between Cambodia and the United States improved, Prince Norodom Sihanouk making it a point to praise American aid.

As already indicated, British and Indian troops along with French forces occupied Cambodia after the Second World War and the policy of the United Kingdom worked to the advantage

[174] Secretary Dulles to Foreign Minister Nong Kimny, *The Department of State Bulletin*, Vol. XXXIV (April 30, 1956), p. 727.
[175] *Ibid.*

of the French restoration. On January 28, 1946, the Control Commission of General Douglas D. Gracey in Saigon was dissolved and the British officer left Indochina. Great Britain's role in the Khmer kingdom was in the course of events drastically reduced. The London government having recognized on February 7, 1950, the Kingdom of Cambodia, a legation was eventually established in Phnom Penh. It was raised to an embassy on September 21, 1954. Foreign Secretary Anthony Eden took an active part at the Geneva Conference in the negotiations on Cambodia although he did not give the kingdom the support it desired. On November 8, 1954, he told the House of Commons that the "independence and integrity" of Cambodia and Laos are "matters of the first importance to us all. They are indeed the test by which these agreements [made at Geneva] will be judged by public opinion in many countries, and not least in those three countries [in Indochina] of South-East Asia."[176] In the controversy in early 1955 over the constitutional changes proposed by King Norodom Sihanouk, the British ambassador in Phnom Penh conveyed to the Cambodian government the concern of Anthony Eden, Cochairman of the Geneva Conference. On the economic level Cambodia as a member of the Colombo Plan has been receiving assistance under it.

In its basic outlook toward world affairs, the Khmer kingdom, although anti-Communist on the domestic front, is neutral in foreign policy. At the same time, Phnom Penh does not consider military neutrality and moral neutrality synonymous. Cambodia, recently a colonial territory, is very nationalistic and is thinking in definite terms of her own interests. Norodom Sihanouk was once asked: "What is your choice between Mr. Nehru and the SEATO?" He replied, "I choose Cambodia!"[177]

Sovereignty, independence, and neutrality are closely linked in the Cambodian outlook. Neutrality is one of the expressions of nationalism and is applied even with reference to the uncommitted states of Asia. Cambodia, in fact, does not desire to be considered in any bloc of states. She would like to be a bridge between the powers of the East and the West. The kingdom has a heritage of trying to balance the Thai and Vietnamese and is now playing a similar role in the opposing forces of the cold war. In 1956 it was

176 *Parliamentary Debates (Hansard)*, 5th Series, Vol. 532, *House of Commons Official Report*, November 1-12, 1954, col. 928.

177 Zoltan M. Szaz, "Cambodia's Foreign Policy," *Far Eastern Survey*, Vol. XXIV (October, 1955), p. 157.

planned that aid from the Western powers, especially the United States and France, would be countered by that from the Communist states, particularly the People's Republic of China and the Soviet Union. Obviously this policy involved considerable diplomatic skill if it were to be successfully implemented. In September Prince Norodom Sihanouk suggested to the National Assembly that a law should be passed proclaiming the neutrality of the kingdom and imposing respect for such a policy on Cambodian citizens and foreigners alike in the nation. Thus neutrality came to be a law of the state.

In two statements on foreign policy the prince has well explained the basic orientation of his country—at a plenary meeting of the Bandung Conference in April, 1955, and to the Philippine Congress on February 3, 1956. He noted at Bandung that:

> I am proud of having had the privilege of leading my people in their struggle for independence and to have, after the Geneva Conference, determinedly steered our national policy towards the Pancha Shila, towards the community of neutral nations—among them: India and Burma.
>
> Independent and neutral Cambodia now finds herself on the separating line of two civilizations, of two races, of two political worlds—and, as such, she has the dangerous privilege of standing the test and the application of the principles of the Pancha Shila.
>
> My country has adopted these principles and wishes to apply them to the fullest extent. In so doing, she only requests an absolute reciprocity. She requests that her independence, her integrity, her security, her traditions and political ideology be not threatened.
>
> It will be the task of more powerful nations to set the example, to give proofs and guarantees to smaller nations, and thereby to take the only course of action that is necessary to overthrow those barriers of suspicion and mistrust I have mentioned.[178]

Later Prince Norodom proposed a resolution whereby "the Asian-African Conference . . . recommends that each participating country should scrupulously respect the independence of all other countries, particularly of those which, like Cambodia, are either by their situation or by agreements, neutral and determined: (a) to remain neutral so long as their security is not threatened; (b) not to be used as a base of aggression."[179]

In his Manila speech[180] the prince told the Philippine Congress that Cambodian "neutrality is not only the result of Geneva. It

[178] Statement by Prince Norodom Sihanouk, Press Release, Asian-African Conference, Bandung, Indonesia.

[179] Quoted in Kahin, *op. cit.*, p. 22.

[180] Text, *Manila Daily Bulletin*, February 4, 1956.

is not occasional. For it likewise answers the feelings and deep convictions of the Khmer people, who has learned in the course of the last four years to mistrust the quarrels of the great and rely mainly upon his [its] own self. But the fact that we are neutral does not mean that we are simple-minded to the extent of being lured by the amiabilities of Communist governments towards us. . . . For we do not wish that Communist powers (and also non-Communist, for that matter) could threaten us with impunity." He noted that "the neutral policy we practice deprives the Communists of any subject of complaint against us, or of any pretext at intervention." The prince went on to say, however, that even if Cambodia is neutral, "she does not conceal that she intends to closely coöperate with countries who have the same democratic and social ideals, the same aspiration for justice, liberty and well-being of the masses." And "this ideal," he said, "is precisely that of the Philippines."

As of early 1957, the representation pattern of Cambodia abroad reflected the kingdom's ties more to the Western than the Eastern grouping of states. A high commissioner was stationed in France, ambassadors in the United States, Great Britain, Japan, Thailand, and the Soviet Union, a minister in India, and a representative in the Republic of Vietnam. Corresponding foreign representation was found in Phnom Penh, including a Nationalist Chinese consul. Among others, the Australian and Philippine ministers to Cambodia were resident in Saigon and the Burmese ambassador in Bangkok. Australia at the time had a chargé in the Khmer capital. In January it was announced in Karachi that the Pakistani ambassador in Bangkok would also become minister in Phnom Penh; Cambodia would take comparable action. In August the Cambodian ambassador in Thailand was also accredited minister to the Philippines. Of course, the International Commission of India, Canada, and Poland had representatives in the Khmer kingdom.

Cambodia was obviously gratified by her election to membership in the United Nations. In his first speech during the general debate of a regular General Assembly, Nong Kimny at the eleventh session, called for a stricter adherence to the principles of the United Nations and for greater economic aid under its auspices. He proposed, as suggested by Prince Norodom Sihanouk, the creation of a special commission of inquiry under the United Nations to visit the scene of conflict in the Middle East and decide the legitimacy or illegitimacy of the action taken by the parties concerned. Prime Minister Nehru should preside over the commission; the other representatives should come from two neutral countries in Europe (selected among Switzerland, Austria, Sweden, and Yugoslavia), one other neutral state in Asia (Cambodia was willing to serve), and one country from the American continent. Nong Kimny recommended the enlargement of the Security Council and the Economic and Social Council in view of the recent admission of a number of states and the need for the greater representation of Asia. He observed that countries with different types of government and ideology had to live together, for the only alternative was general destruction in an atomic era. Strict neutrality in the national interest was essential for a small state like Cambodia whose role must be moral based on psychological and political rather than military or economic strength.

9. *Malaya*

Malaya with its great city of Singapore and its mainland across the Johore Strait is in some respects a microcosm of Southeast Asia. Located at the juncture of the Strait of Malacca and the South China Sea linking the Indian and Pacific Oceans, Malaya[1] has reflected the vicissitudes of sea power. Forming for the most part a land bridge from peninsular Southeast Asia to the islands of Indonesia, Malaya is important in the defense of Australia to the southeast or of the rest of mainland Southeast Asia to the north. Singapore, it is not surprising, is a significant sea and air base in the region.

Basic Asian influences on Malaya come from China to the northeast, India to the northwest, and Indonesia to the south and southeast. The large numbers of Chinese and Indians as well as the Indonesians who have moved into Malaya not only have ties in varying degrees to the lands of their birth but also raise political, economic, and social problems for the indigenous Malays. These considerations are least applicable to the kindred Indonesians, for they are similar in culture to the Malays. The rise of the People's Republic of China to a position of great influence in Asia, the appearance of an independent India led by a powerful prime minister, Jawaharlal Nehru, and the emergence of a highly nationalistic Republic of Indonesia cannot but provide certain centrifugal forces for Malaya.

After the Second World War Malaya became in course of time the last colonial area of major importance in Southeast Asia to receive independence from a Western power. Indeed, the United Kingdom in a number of respects moved ahead of many of the inhabitants in facing up to the problem of self-government. In addition to Britain's impact, Malaya has been influenced by other Western powers, especially the United States. Exports have made the Asian area the greatest dollar earner in the sterling group of

[1] Malaya is here used to include the State of Singapore and the Federation of Malaya. Malayan denotes an inhabitant of Malaya and Malay a person of the Malay race. Malaysia refers to Malaya plus Indonesia. The Malay world, following the usage of Charles Robequain, embraces Malaya, the Philippines, and the East Indies including British Borneo, and Portuguese Timor but excluding New Guinea. After the independence of the Federation of Malaya in 1957 it became increasingly common to refer to it as Malaya.

countries. And finally Malaya has faced an emergency at home, an armed revolt led by local Chinese Communists on the peninsula, indicative of the Communist conflict in Asia and the world.

Having an area of 50,690 square miles, less than that of Florida, Malaya constitutes, apart from the island of Singapore, a peninsula that stretches almost to the equator. The only land boundary is with Thailand to the north but some of the islands of Indonesia across the Singapore Strait are very close. Sumatra on the opposite shore of the Strait of Malacca, extending northward almost to the same extent as Malaya, is not far distant from the latter. East of Malaya in the South China Sea are island groups belonging to Indonesia, in particular Kepulauan Anambas, Kepulauan Bunguran Utara, and Kepulauan Bunguran Selatan. Further east is Borneo divided among Indonesia, Sarawak, Brunei, and North Borneo. In fact, the northward extension of North Borneo is comparable to that of Malaya. From Kota Bharu in the Federation across the Gulf of Siam is the Republic of Vietnam. Thus Malaya in the family of nations has as immediate neighbors, Thailand, Indonesia, and Vietnam. If a federal government were established for the areas the British organized as the Crown Colony of Singapore and the Federation of Malaya on the west coast of the South China Sea and the Crown Colony of Sarawak, the Protected State of Brunei, and the Crown Colony of North Borneo on the east coast, the South China Sea would be the geographical element of unity, quite in contrast to the Republic of India that separates East and West Pakistan.

The population of Malaya in 1952 was over 6.5 million of which 44 percent was Chinese, 43 percent Malay, and the rest chiefly Indian and Pakistani. High birth rates and low death rates prevailed. As of mid-year in 1952 the following estimated figures may be cited:[2]

	MALAYSIANS	CHINESE	INDIANS AND PAKISTANI	OTHERS	TOTAL
Singapore	131,664	830,079	80,096	35,316	1,077,155
Federation of Malaya	2,716,899	2,092,218	617,257	80,073	5,506,447
	2,848,563	2,922,297	697,353	115,389	6,583,602

These statistics indicate that if Malaya were under one govern-

[2] Colony of Singapore, *Annual Report, 1952*, p. 30; Federation of Malaya, *Annual Report, 1952*, p. 21. "Malaysians," as here used, include the indigenous Malays and the immigrant, kindred Indonesians in Malaya. Subsequent statistics indicate broadly relative population increases. It was estimated in 1956 that the total population of the Federation had risen to 6,252,000 and that of Singapore to 1,264,000.

ment the Chinese would have the largest single population. But the separation of Singapore and the mainland gives the former an overwhelmingly Chinese population and the latter a Malay lead over the Chinese.

The Malay, Indian, and Chinese population groups differ in many respects. The Malays are Moslems, the Indians are predominantly Hindus, the Chinese are largely Confucianists, Taoists, and Buddhists. The Europeans and Eurasians, it might be added, are chiefly Christians. Religion is one of the important reasons for limited contact among the Malays, Chinese, and Indians. There is little intermarriage. Economic considerations also help to solidify the situation. The cultures of the three population groups are each linked to a nearby heavily populated state—China, India, and Indonesia. It does not seem likely that the mainland of Malaya can become a "melting pot" as occurred in the United States. Obviously under the circumstances, the creation of an independent Federation of Malaya presents great problems from the viewpoint of national unity. A. D. C. Peterson, a British observer of developments, has noted that on the mainland "a new form of State" is necessary. This must be "a secular State in which racially distinct communities, whose cultural and social life is still separate, develop a common political loyalty."[3]

Although 80 percent of Malaya is jungle, the area is one of the greatest sources of tin and rubber in the world. In 1953, 56,252 long tons of tin concentrates were produced, and in the same year 572,792 tons of rubber. Penang and Singapore have important smelters for tin. Copra, palm oil, and iron are included among the products. At the same time Malaya has had to import large supplies of rice to meet the needs of the rapidly growing population. The Malays themselves, living in kampongs, are chiefly peasants and fishermen; they have, in fact, shown little interest in commerce although some have gone into government service. On the mainland of Malaya the Public Works Department maintains over 6000 miles of public highways and the railway system of over 1000 miles links Singapore with Thailand. The city of Singapore is a great entrepôt in Asia located on an island by the same name, the latter having an area of 224 square miles with its adjacent islets. Singapore is linked to the mainland by the Johore Causeway with its road and railway. In 1956 nine overseas airlines operated in and out of the island. The

[3] A. D. C. Peterson, "The Birth of the Malayan Nation," *International Affairs*, Vol. XXXI (July, 1955), p. 314.

per capita level of national income in Malaya is the highest of all the Far East. British investments in business enterprises in the area were worth around $260 million before the last war.

After the Second World War the British reorganized their territories formerly classed as the Straits Settlements, the Federated Malay States, and the Unfederated Malay States. On April 1, 1946, the Malayan Union was set up consisting of the former Federated Malay States of Perak, Selangor, Negri Sembilan, and Pahang, the former Unfederated Malay States of Johore, Kedah, Perlis, Kelantan, and Trengganu, and the British Settlements of Penang and Malacca. Singapore became a separate colony; Labuan went to British North Borneo and later the Cocos or Keeling Islands to Australia.[4] Christmas Island in the Indian Ocean stayed with Singapore for a longer period.[5] The change from the Malayan Union to the Federation of Malaya on February 1, 1948, did not alter the territorial base. The king and the Malay rulers, however, possessed the power to admit by mutual agreement other territory into the Federation.

Constitutional developments in Malaya prepared the way for self-government. After the collapse of Japan a British Military Administration governed the area until April 1, 1946. Prewar legislation was restored but plans for change were intensified. With the Malayan Union, sovereignty had been formally transferred to the British Crown from the Malay rulers and a Malayan Union citizenship was to be brought into being. A storm of protest arose over many of the aspects of the Union leading to Malay political organizations. The United Malays National Organization (UMNO) under Dato Onn bin Ja'afar became the most important. The British treaties with the sultans negotiated by Sir Harold MacMichael were severely criticized because the rulers did not like to lose their sovereignty and they claimed pressure methods were used in getting them to accept the agreements. The Malays were concerned that the citizenship definition would weaken their position in favor of

[4] The Cocos Islands are located in the Indian Ocean about 1160 miles from Singapore. They had been incorporated in the Settlement of Singapore in 1903. The islands now form a link in the air route from Australia to South Africa.

[5] It was officially announced in London, June 6, 1957, that arrangements were being made to transfer to Australia the administration of Christmas Island, a step resulting from plans to establish the State of Singapore. The island, about 225 miles south of the western end of Java, has a population of around 2000, the Chinese being almost three-fourths of the total. Some objection was expressed to the transfer in the Singapore Assembly by opposition leaders but the government was in favor of the action.

the "aliens" or Chinese and Indians. Chinese merchants were apprehensive of the economic effect of separating Singapore from the mainland. The opposition led to a reconsideration of the various aspects of the Malayan Union, and its subsequent end.

With the Federation of Malaya as successor, sovereignty had been restored to the sultans, and the requirements for citizenship by non-Malays were more rigidly defined. The king and the Malay rulers jointly delegated power to the high commissioner who for the king had control over external relations and defense. The Malay rulers agreed to accept the advice of the high commissioner in governmental matters except those concerning Malay custom and the Moslem religion. He was responsible for guarding "the special position of the Malays" and "the legitimate interests of other communities." On the federal level there was in addition to an executive council a legislative council, consisting of the high commissioner, replaced in August, 1953, by a speaker, of 3 ex officio, 11 official and 50 unofficial members and a representative of each settlement council and state, which had defined legislative powers concerning the Federation as a whole. Each Malay State had its ruler, a council of state, and an executive council, and each settlement a resident commissioner, a settlement council, and a nominated council. In the matters of each state a British adviser had the power of advice except on subjects relative to Malay custom and the Moslem religion.

A "member" system was introduced in April, 1951, whereby nine of the official members in the Federal Legislative Council became responsible for certain government departments and functions. This system, pointing toward later ministerial responsibility, was an important step in the development of the Federation.

In a directive to General Sir Gerald Templer, High Commissioner for Malaya, the Secretary of State for the Colonies publicly indicated on February 7, 1952, the British attitude at the time toward the future of the area when he said: "The policy of H.M. Government in the United Kingdom is that Malaya should in due course become a fully self-governing nation. H.M. Government confidently hope that that nation will be within the British Commonwealth. . . . To achieve a united Malayan nation there must be a common form of citizenship for all who regard the Federation or any part of it as their real home and the object of their loyalty. . . . H.M. Government will not lay aside their responsibilities in Malaya until they are satisfied that Communist terrorism has been defeated and that the partnership of all communities, which alone can lead to true and stable self-government, has been firmly established."[6]

In November the high commissioner in a speech to the Federal Legislative Council outlined the progress made toward electing local, town and municipal councils and observed that the "next phase in the building program will be the erection of the uprights, that is to say, the creation of elected State and Settlement Councils."[7] In the summer of 1953 a Federal Elections Committee of 46 members was brought into being by the high commissioner for the basic purpose of reporting to the Federal Legislative Council on the subject of elections to that body and of constitutional changes arising from them.

The Federal Elections Committee issued its report on February 1, 1954, a working body representative of Malays, Chinese, Indians, Ceylonese, Eurasians, and Europeans doing most of the actual labor. Although the Elections Committee opposed the election of all members to the Federal Legislative Council under present conditions, a majority recommended that in an interim period a slight numerical superiority be given the nominated members and a minority favored setting the number of elected members at 60 as compared with 40 nominated ones. The Committee was not in favor of a communal basis of elections, calling for direct elections on the basis of territorial constituencies.

The report in part was strongly opposed by a number of organizations in the Federation, the UMNO-MCA Alliance, a combination of the United Malays National Organization, and the Malayan Chinese Association, taking an active part in the opposition. Although the colonial secretary in London refused for some time to receive a delegation from the Alliance, the British government came to reject the majority report of the Elections Committee on the elected minority. A White Paper was issued in Kuala Lumpur, the capital of the Federation, on April 27 wherein the Legislative Council would have 52 elected members and 46 selected from direct categories, the elections to be held in 1955. A Delineation Commission divided the Federation into 52 single member constituencies.

The elections set for July, 1955, occasioned great political activity in the Federation. The UMNO-MCA Alliance led by Tengku Abdul Rahman, brother of the Sultan of Kedah, who took

[6] Directive to General Sir Gerald Templer, *Documents on International Affairs, 1951*, pp. 675-676.

[7] Speech of General Sir Gerald Templer, *British Information Service*, Washington, December 11, 1952.

over leadership of the UMNO from Dato Onn, and by Sir Cheng-lock Tan of the Malayan Chinese Association had demonstrated in certain municipal and state elections that a winning formula existed in the collaboration of the two largest communities. In 1953 the foundations of the Alliance had been strengthened by a common approach to the question of federal elections. It is significant that the UMNO party has set the pace. Later the Malayan Indian Congress (MIC) joined the Alliance. A rival group, the Malayan National Conference (MNC), dominated by Dato Onn, came into being. Conservative in outlook, it included seven Mentris Besar (each the chief executive officer in a Malay State), a number of the leaders in the Independence of Malaya Party (IMP) ruled by Dato Onn, and a few Chinese, Indians, Ceylonese, and Eurasians. On February 28, 1954, the MNC changed its name to Party Negara. The small Pan-Malayan Labour Party (PMLP) had its own outlook though it often tended to work with the Alliance. Three parties were associated with Perak provincialism, but a Pan-Malayan Islamic Party (PMIP) stressing Islam gave greater promise. The Federal Elections Committee, it might be noted, had felt in particular the influence of MNC and Alliance leaders.

In commenting on the political scene in the Federation of Malaya in July, 1954, Francis G. Carnell, University Lecturer in Colonial Government at Oxford University, wrote: "The Alliance looks like the first political organization with a genuine claim to the title of a Malayan national movement. In addition to enjoying the prestige of having wrested the new constitution from the Malay Rulers and the British, it has Chinese money and organizing skill behind it and a proved technique for winning elections on the basis of communal voting."[8] He observed that "their leaders are, for the most part, well disposed toward the British, conservative in outlook, and with a definite economic stake in the country."[9] As regards the Party Negara, Carnell believed that its "driving force" was fear by the Malays of the Chinese.

The election in July, 1955, resulted in an overwhelming victory for the Alliance; its candidates won 51 of the 52 seats and 818,013 votes or 79.6 percent. Successful under the Alliance were 34 Malays, 15 Chinese, 1 Indian, and 1 Ceylonese. The Party Negara won no seats but polled 78,909 votes. The Pan-Malayan Is-

[8] Francis G. Carnell, "Constitutional Reform and Elections in Malaya," *Pacific Affairs*, Vol. XXVII (September, 1954), pp. 233-234.
[9] *Ibid.*, p. 235.

lamic Party acquired the only seat not taken by the Alliance. The three Perak parties, the Labour Party, and the independents gathered 6 percent of the vote. Carnell has pointed out, however, that "the fact is, the Alliance walk-over was a Malay rather than a Malayan victory. It cannot be regarded as a real test of Chinese opinion. Out of an estimated eligible electorate of about 1,600,000, no less than 1,280,000 voluntarily registered themselves and 85 percent of these voted. But of the registered electorate, 84 percent were Malays, 11 percent were Chinese . . . and rather less than 5 percent were Indians."[10]

In terms of issues the key one of the Alliance was *merdeka* or freedom. The Tengku, aware of the nationalist tides in Asia and in Malaya against colonialism, took advantage of the opportunities offered him. As for timing, the Alliance wanted self-government in four years, the Party Negara in five. But the voters were suspicious of the Party Negara in view of its associations with the Malay sultans. Moreover, the Party in effect was anti-Chinese and favored a communal approach in politics. All but one of its 30 candidates were Malays. As a result of the elections, the Federal Executive Council became a quasi cabinet with Tengku Abdul Rahman the Chief Minister. He had the support of at least 71 of the 98 members of the Federal Legislative Council.

In the building of an independent Federation of Malaya there were many outstanding problems, some of them relating to citizenship, the armed services, police, civil service, and education. "Malayanisation" is not an easy process. A common citizenship to unite with a common loyalty those who regard the Federation as their true home has been established.[11] The citizenship qualifications have been subsequently amended so as to widen the base. It has been estimated that by September 15, 1952, around 72 percent of the population were citizens by operation of the law—about 98 percent of the Malays, 50 to 60 percent of the Chinese, and 30 percent of the Indians. With immigration severely restricted and children of the older generation becoming citizens, the Federation is truly moving in the direction of giving reality to the ideal of a general Malayan citizenship. In terms of the armed services, the Malay Regiment with seven battalions as of the end of 1955 has been

[10] Francis G. Carnell, "The Malayan Elections," *Pacific Affairs*, Vol. XXVIII (December, 1955), p. 316.

[11] General Sir Gerald Templer in his inaugural address and in a report to the Federal Legislative Council the following November stressed the subject of common citizenship.

supplemented by the Federation Regiment with one battalion authorized in 1952 to provide a fighting force cutting across the racial communities. Training of officers at home and in Great Britain and Australia is progressing. Efforts have also been made to establish a police force not exclusively composed of Malays. In the civil service the Malays have likewise seen the admission of Chinese and Indians though at a theoretical ratio of four Malays to one non-Malay Asian. As regards the education of the youth, problems of curriculum especially language, religion, recruiting of teachers, mixing of students, organization of schools, and finances are complex. The Federation has an objective of providing free, primary, compulsory education in National Schools in Malay and English with Chinese or Tamil also if desired. The illiteracy of the adult population was estimated to be 60 percent in 1947.

As a result of the London Conference between representatives of Great Britain and the Federation of Malaya held from January 18 to February 6, 1956, an agreement in the form of a report was signed on February 8 calling for "every effort" to achieve the independence of the Federation in the British Commonwealth of Nations by August, 1957. During the transition period the chief minister would have greater power, and in the immediate future Malayan ministers would take over the control of internal defense and security, finance, and commerce and industry. An Emergency Operations Council and a Federation Armed Forces Council would be created. During the time before independence, Britain would remain responsible for external defense and foreign affairs; an External Defense Committee would be established. A commission would be appointed to draft as soon as possible a constitution for the new state. The Federation indicated its desire to stay in the sterling area and to attract overseas capital. The settlement also provided for the withdrawal of the British advisers to the Malay rulers within about a year. A Public Service Commission, a Judicial Service Commission and a Police Service Commission would be set up. A "compensation scheme for loss of career" with respect to British personnel would be worked out. The United Kingdom would continue to grant economic and military aid against the Communist insurgents. After the independence of the Federation, a defense and mutual assistance treaty with Great Britain would deal with military matters.[12] The agreement of February 8, of course,

[12] In view of the importance of the provision in the future foreign policy of the Federation, Article 26 is cited:

"The Government of the Federation of Malaya will afford to Her Majesty's Government in the United Kingdom the right to maintain in the Federation

required the formal approval of all concerned but acceptance was a foregone conclusion. Tengku Abdul Rahman who led the Malayan delegation observed that the agreement heralded "the birth of a new nation."[13] He called the London Constitutional Conference a "complete success."

In a speech to the Federal Legislative Council on March 14, the chief minister analyzed the report of the London Conference and commented on the plans for a defense and mutual assistance treaty with the United Kingdom. He presented in detail the arguments behind the attitude taken by his government when he said:

> There has been some adverse comment against this proposed Treaty. It is said that with the Commonwealth troops being stationed in Malaya this country would invite attack by the enemy and that Malaya would be used as a battlefield in the event of this attack. It is also said that the presence of Commonwealth troops would compromise the sovereignty of independent Malaya. In my opinion this is a very short-sighted view to take. It must be appreciated that with the geographical and strategic position of this country Malaya offers herself an easy target and will always be opened to aggression if she is not properly guarded. Therefore she must need have at her command a very powerful army, air force and navy. To build up these forces to the required strength the people of this country must be forced to shoulder a very heavy burden of taxation. The expenditure in this direction would also impose a very heavy restriction on our social and economic advancement. Some countries have to spend 80% of their revenue on defence with the result that social progress in those countries is so severely retarded that the people die in the streets. I would not wish this to happen to this country, and so if we are able to get help from the U.K. and other Commonwealth countries in maintaining the strength of our defence, we should welcome it. Our revenue can then be directed in maintaining the high standard of administration, social and other services. I am taking a realistic view of the situation in Malaya and I am certain that a majority of the people will accept my view particularly because of the Communists and other enemy activities even from within our own territory which in itself require a very large force constantly occupied.[14]

---

the forces necessary for the fulfilment of Commonwealth and international obligations; and Her Majesty's Government in the United Kingdom will undertake to assist the Government of the Federation in the external defence of its territory. Her Majesty's Government in the United Kingdom will continue to be afforded facilities needed in the Federation for the maintenance and support of these forces; they will include the Commonwealth Strategic Reserve, which would remain in the Federation. Provision will be made for consultation by Her Majesty's Government with the Federation Government in regard to the exercise of their rights under the Treaty." Great Britain, Colonial Office, *Report by the Federation of Malaya Constitutional Conference Held in London in January and February, 1956*, Cmd. 9714.

[13] Speech of Tengku Abdul Rahman to Federal Legislative Council, March 14, 1956, Federation Government Press Statement.

[14] *Ibid.*

On March 21 the complete terms of reference of the commission to draw up a draft constitution for the independent Federation of Malaya were published in Kuala Lumpur. The Constitutional Commission would have a United Kingdom chairman, one other member from that state, and a member each from Canada, Australia, India, and Pakistan. The terms of reference called for a "federal form of constitution" with a "strong central government" and "Parliamentary democracy with a bicameral legislature," the preserving of the "position and prestige" of the Malay rulers but a "constitutional Yang di-Pertuan Besar [head of state] for the Federation" chosen from among them, the "safeguarding of the special position of the Malays and the legitimate interests of other communities" and a common nationality for the Federation.[15] The British chairman of the commission was Lord Reid and the other members were Sir Ivor Jennings of the United Kingdom, Sir William McKell of Australia, Mr. B. Malik of India, and Mr. Justice Abdul Hamid of Pakistan, Canada not having a member.

On February 20, 1957, the draft constitution was published, clearly reflecting the terms of reference. The independent Federation of Malaya would consist of the nine Malay States and the Settlements of Malacca and Penang which would become States with the lapse of the Queen's sovereignty. It was evident from the Reid Report that the Federation would be a member of the Commonwealth of Nations with the Queen recognized as Head of the world-wide association but not sovereign of Malaya at the time of independence, therefore establishing a precedent. The House of Representatives would consist, after a transitional provision, of 100 members elected on a territorial basis from single-member constituencies; the Senate would have 33 members, two-thirds elected by the legislative assemblies of the 11 States and one-third nominated by the head of state. Detailed provisions of citizenship were suggested based to a large extent upon proposals agreed upon by the Alliance Party. It would be possible under certain conditions to have both Federation and Commonwealth citizenship but undivided loyalty to the former was required. Malay would become the national language, no state religion was provided, and the Malays would continue to enjoy their present preferences although these preferences would gradually come to an end.[16] Elections would not

[15] *The Constitutional Commission, Terms of Reference*, Kuala Lumpur, March 21, 1956.

[16] The Constitutional Commission significantly stated: ". . . it seemed to us that a common nationality was the basis upon which a unified Malayan nation was to

be held before early in 1959 but the target date of Merdeka Day was set for August 31, 1957.

After careful consideration of the Reid Report in the Federation as well as constitutional talks in London, agreement was reached by the United Kingdom, the Conference of Rulers of the Malay States, and the elected government of the Federation on a revised constitution. The title of the head of state was changed to Yang di-Pertuan Agong, the number of nominated senators was raised from 11 to 16, a Conference of Rulers was given additional functions, the provisions for citizenship were altered in a number of respects, Islam was made the state religion but the state was considered secular, the privileges of the Malays were in general strengthened, and elections might be delayed until later in 1959. The final draft constitution was officially approved by the necessary authorities in the Federation and Great Britain. Although it had previously been suggested by some Malayan leaders that "Malaysia" be the name of the new state, the term "Federation of Malaya" was retained.

In January, 1957, the chief minister reached a settlement in London with British officials on a number of financial and security matters. It was agreed that the United Kingdom would contribute £3 million each year from 1957 to 1959 for the campaign against the terrorists, and more in the next two years as a grant or interest-free loan up to a possible total of £11 million. The unpaid balance on a grant already promised for the expansion of the Federation army (£6.5 million on January 1, 1956) would be contributed. Another £5.5 million would be given to buy British equipment and £1.3 million for local purchases of army supplies and for developing the Federation navy. The amount of £4.5 million would be handed over to cover all uncompleted schemes begun under Co-

be created and that under a democratic form of Government it was inherent that all the citizens of Malaya, irrespective of race, creed or culture, should enjoy certain fundamental rights including equality before the law. We found it difficult, therefore, to reconcile the terms of reference if the protection of the special position of the Malays signified the granting of special privileges, permanently, to one community only and not to the others. The difficulty of giving one community a permanent advantage over the others was realised by the Alliance Party, representatives of which, led by the Chief Minister, submitted that—'in an independent Malaya all nationals should be accorded equal rights, privileges and opportunities and there must not be discrimination on grounds of race and creed. . . .' The same view was expressed by their Highnesses in their memorandum, in which they said that they 'look forward to a time not too remote when it will become possible to eliminate Communalism as a force in the political and economic life of the country.'" Great Britain, Colonial Office, *Report of the Federation of Malaya Constitutional Commission, 1957*, Colonial No. 330.

lonial Development and Welfare. The Federation, it might be added, would receive the facilities to raise a loan in London in the ordinary way. Britain would take steps to help the Asian state become a member of the World Bank and Fund.

Under the broad terms of the proposed defense agreement, the United Kingdom would help in the external defense of the Federation and in training its armed forces; the Federation would permit Great Britain to keep forces in Malaya, including the Commonwealth Strategic Reserve, essential for carrying out Commonwealth and international obligations. Coöperation under the treaty was clearly related to armed attack on Singapore, North Borneo, Brunei, Sarawak, Hong Kong, or, of course, the Federation of Malaya; in any other area the United Kingdom would have to secure the approval of the Federation before committing forces in active measures which involved using the bases in the latter's territory. Provisions were made relative to the status of the British forces in the Federation and jurisdiction over them. Australia and New Zealand, it is obvious, became associated with the pact. A working party had previously been organized to consider different aspects of the proposed treaty, consisting of representatives from Great Britain and the Federation of Malaya with the Commissioner-General for the United Kingdom in South-East Asia as chairman and observers from Australia and New Zealand.

On July 31 Queen Elizabeth gave the royal assent to a bill passed by Parliament establishing the Federation of Malaya as a sovereign state within the Commonwealth of Nations. The Commonwealth Prime Ministers in a communiqué on July 5 at the end of a ten-day conference in London had extended "to the Federation their warm good wishes for its future and they looked forward to being able to welcome an independent Malaya as a member of the Commonwealth on the completion of the necessary constitutional processes."[17] On August 5 an agreement was signed in Kuala Lumpur wherein Great Britain renounced her position as protector of the Malay States and ceded the Settlements of Penang and Malacca to the Federation of Malaya as of the date of independence. Merdeka Day, August 31, 1957, marked the culmination of the Anglo-Malayan efforts.

In the Crown Colony of Singapore events likewise moved at a rapid pace. A separate colony by an Order-in-Council in 1946,

[17] *New York Times,* July 6, 1957.

Singapore was administered until 1948 by a governor with an Advisory Council consisting of seven official and ten nominated unofficial members. In 1948 Executive and Legislative Councils were established. In the former at the beginning were the governor as chairman, four ex-officio, two official, and four unofficial members, in all cases appointed by him. The Legislative Council had the governor as president, four ex-officio, five nominated official, four nominated unofficial, and nine elected members. Among the nine people elected, three were chosen by the three Chambers of Commerce (Chinese, Indian, and European) and six by popular vote. The latter number was raised to nine by the end of 1950, six people representing single-member constituencies in the municipal part of the Crown Colony and three in the rural area. The unofficial members elected two from themselves to the Executive Council.

In 1952 the governor of the colony appointed a committee of all the unofficial members of the Legislative Council to consider the problem of increasing further the number of elected members. Following the report of the committee, a commission was appointed in July, 1953, for the purpose of making a thorough review of the constitution and of the relationship between the city of Singapore and the government of the colony. The Rendel Report was published in February, 1954, and became the basis for a revised constitution, effective in February, 1955.

Under the new constitution the Legislative Assembly consisted of 32 members—3 were ex-officio holding ministerial positions, 4 were nominated unofficial members, and 25 elected unofficial members. A speaker presided over the body. All those elected came from single-member constituencies, the seats for the three Chambers of Commerce having been abolished. Voters' registration was automatic. A Council of Ministers with a chief minister replaced the Executive Council, having responsibility in all matters but defense, external affairs, and internal security. Although the principle of ministerial responsibility was well developed, the governor retained reserve power for use under certain conditions.

Political development in the Crown Colony paralleled constitutional changes. In the first elections in 1948 for six seats in the Legislative Council, the people generally qualified to vote were British subjects resident in Singapore. Less than 23,000 registered, almost half being Indians, and only 63 percent went to the polls. Three Indians, one Chinese, one Malay, and one European were elected. In the 1951 elections the franchise had been extended to residents in Singapore born in Brunei, North Borneo, Sarawak, or the Federation. A little over 48,000 registered but only 51 percent went to the polls. Among the nine members elected, three were Indians, three were Chinese, one Ceylonese, one Eurasian and one European. In terms of parties six were Progressive, two Labour, and one independent. It was obvious that the Indians were taking an active part in the elections and the Chinese a passive role.

The first elections for the Legislative Assembly, held on April 2, 1955, were a better index of politics in the colony. Automatic registration had increased the electorate to a little over 300,000, more than 60 percent being Chinese. There were five chief political parties contesting for the 25 elected seats. The Labour Front led by David Marshall and the People's Action Party led by Lee Kuan Yew and Lim Chin Siong made up the left wing and the Progressives, the UMNO-MCA-SMU (Singapore Malay Union) Alliance, and the Democrats made up the right. With 53 percent voting, the Labour Front secured ten seats, the People's Action Party three, the Progressives four, the Alliance three, the Democrats two, and Independents three. The defeat of the Progressives who had been influential in the old Legislative Council was substantially the result of close identification with the British. The Progressives also opposed a multilingual Legislative Assembly while the Democrats favored it, thus helping to divide the right-wing vote. The Labour Front, formed to fight in the elections, was not well organized or united, made excessive promises, and ridiculed the Progressives as defenders of colonialism and capitalism. The People's Action Party was created in late 1954 having as an objective the arousing to political consciousness of the Chinese who were Chinese-educated. Lee Kuan Yew assisted by Lim Chin Siong won great popularity from the Chinese students. The Party was strongly anticolonial and advocated quick independence with withdrawal from the Commonwealth. Many of its opponents considered it pro-Communist; it had, in fact, a left as well as a right wing. David Marshall formed a cabinet depending upon the support of the Labour Front, of the UMNO-MCA-SMU Alliance and the three ex-officio and two of the four nominated members. Later the Progressive and Democratic Parties formed the Liberal Socialist Party.

In August, 1955, a constitutional dispute involving the powers of the British governor and the chief minister of Singapore reached a climax. The latter wanted a liberal interpretation of the constitution and was supported by the Legislative Assembly. Great

Britain proved coöperative in this respect; the governor would act strictly on the advice of the chief minister in a wide field of operation. Moreover, the constitution itself would be reviewed a year after its working and Marshall would visit London in December for preliminary discussion.

In April, 1956, following Merdeka Week in March, a delegation from Singapore went to the British capital to work out the future relationship of the Asian area with Great Britain. Prior to departure, the Legislative Assembly on April 5 approved by a vote of 27 to 0 with 4 abstentions and 1 absentee a resolution that the delegation be instructed "to seek forthwith for Singapore the status of an independent territory within the Commonwealth, and to offer an agreement . . . whereby the Government of the United Kingdom would in respect of Singapore exercise control over external defence and give guidance in foreign relations other than trade and commerce."[18]

In a memorandum prepared for submission to the Singapore constitutional conference, the delegation from the Crown Colony included arguments to show that Singapore had the prerequisites for independence.[19] In terms of population it had more people than 7 independent countries at that time in the United Nations. Its revenue was greater than that of 16 members of the world organization. Conditions were calm in Singapore in contrast to the warfare on the mainland of Malaya. The Crown Colony was in good economic standing and was seeking no financial aid from the United Kingdom. Singapore could contribute as much to the sterling area as the latter to it. In terms of Asia its standard of living was high and its educational system good.

On April 23 the negotiations began between the Singapore delegation and the British government. Chief Minister Marshall led the former with progovernment and opposition members in the group. Alan Lennox-Boyd, Colonial Secretary, negotiated for the British. On the agenda were a "definition of internal self-government," a date for effecting it, the future of the public services, foreign affairs and external defense, citizenship, and a reconstitution of the Legislative Assembly. On May 15 the negotiations collapsed, for Great Britain was determined to keep ultimate control

[18] Quoted in Memorandum Submitted at the Singapore's Constitutional Conference, London, April, 1956, *Singapore News Summary*, Public Relations, Singapore, Vol. III (May 31, 1956), p. 25.

[19] This memorandum, as cited above, is especially valuable in giving the reader a new orientation on Singapore.

over internal security as it affected external defense and foreign affairs while the delegation from the Crown Colony was opposed to such a stand. Singapore, as noted, was prepared to accept membership in the British Commonwealth and allow Great Britain to have responsibility for foreign relations except trade and commerce. She could also be in charge of external defense, keeping her bases on the island. Great Britain was willing to give the colony internal self-government with a fully elected and enlarged Legislative Assembly as well as a fully elected Council of Ministers and to grant a separate citizenship for Singapore equivalent to that found in self-governing members of the Commonwealth. The Crown Colony was willing, for a transitional period of six years, to have Britain suspend the constitution, if necessary, as an emergency measure.

On May 16 Chief Minister Marshall made an effort at agreement on his own responsibility, for the Singapore delegation was divided on his proposals. Britain was not prepared to accept them *in toto*; and later on June 7 Marshall resigned, being quickly replaced by a Chinese, Lim Yew Hock, another member of the Labour Front.

It is obvious from the negotiations that Great Britain, though sympathetic to the cause of self-government, did not believe that Singapore was ready for it in all respects. Moreover, Lennox-Boyd significantly noted that "we do not intend that Singapore should become an outpost of Communist China. . . ."[20] Australia and New Zealand were in sympathy with Great Britain. David Marshall for his part believed that the best way to fight Communism in Singapore was through the achievement by April, 1957, of full self-government.

On December 9, 1956, Chief Minister Lim Yew Hock left for London to make preparations for another constitutional conference. An announcement was made on December 21 that such a meeting would begin the following March 11. Upon his return to the Crown Colony he stressed the need for party unity on the constitutional question. Meanwhile the Singapore government was pushing forward a program of Malayanisation of the civil service and police force. On February 9, 1956, the Legislative Assembly decided that English, Malay, Chinese, and Tamil might be used in its debates. Singapore has a plan for free, universal, primary education; children are being taught English and their native language in the primary

[20] Speech of Alan Lennox-Boyd, April 23, 1956, *Singapore News Summary*, Vol. III (April 30, 1956), p. 8.

schools with a third language optional in the secondary. With one infant being born every ten minutes, the school population, if given opportunity, will greatly increase. David Marshall significantly asserted on April 23 that "we seek to build a nation composed of many races of radically different ethnic groups fused by a unity of purpose and created . . . by the stimulus of a common geographical and human environment."[21]

The second Singapore constitutional conference met in London from March 11 to April 11, 1957, with Chief Minister Lim Yew Hock leading the Singapore delegation and Colonial Secretary Alan Lennox-Boyd the British. On April 11 agreement between the two parties was announced. Under the suggested constitutional arrangements, internal self-government would come into effect sometime after January 1, 1958. The Crown Colony of Singapore would become the State of Singapore; the head of state would be a person born in Malaya, having the title of Yang di-Pertuan Negara, and appointed by the Queen on the advice of the government of the United Kingdom after consulting that of Singapore; the chief minister would become prime minister responsible with his cabinet to a Legislative Assembly having 51 elected members; the government of the United Kingdom would be represented by a commissioner. Great Britain would continue to have responsibility for external defense and external relations while Singapore would have charge of all other matters. With respect to external defense, the United Kingdom would have bases and installations in the State, but as regards commercial and cultural relations, the latter with the approval of the former would handle such matters with third countries.[22] As consultation would obviously be necessary, provision was

[21] Speech of David Marshall, April 23, 1956, *Singapore News Summary*, Vol. III (April 30, 1956), p. 4.

[22] The complexity of the provision relative to commercial and cultural relations was realized in the report of the Conference. It was stated: "The Singapore Delegation were anxious that the authority in the field delegated to the Singapore Government should be as clear and specific as possible. We recognised, however, in our discussions on this subject that international law made it impossible to create an 'international person' responsible only for certain specific fields of external affairs of any one territory, with the result that so long as the United Kingdom Government remained responsible in international law for the external affairs of Singapore, they could be held ultimately responsible for any agreements made by the Singapore Government. We also recognised that it would be difficult to formulate once and for all, or to define in precise terms in the constitutional instruments, the extent of the field to be delegated to the Singapore Government." Great Britain, Colonial Office, *Report of the Singapore Constitutional Conference Held in London in March and April, 1957*, Cmd. 147. See Appendix B to the report for detailed consideration to the division of responsibilities between Singapore and Great Britain on trade and cultural matters.

made for an intergovernmental committee, meeting regularly, under the chairmanship of the British commissioner.

On the controversial subject of internal security a formula was found whereby the Singapore government would assume responsibility, with the United Kingdom keeping a vital interest. An Internal Security Council would be established with three members from Singapore (the prime minister and two of his colleagues in the cabinet), three from the United Kingdom (the commissioner and two others) and the seventh, a minister from the government of the Federation of Malaya (subject to its agreement which could be ended on a notice of six months). The United Kingdom commissioner would be chairman of the group. If the government of Singapore failed to carry out a decision within the Council's competence, the latter's chairman would advise the Yang di-Pertuan Negara of what steps to take, the measure having the force of law.

The government of Singapore would also bear in mind the "special position" of the indigenous Malays in the State and foster their interests including the Malay language. A separate citizenship for Singapore would be established by its own legislation; Great Britain would amend her Nationality Act of 1948 so that Singapore citizens would be recognized under it as Commonwealth citizens and British subjects. The constitution of the State could be amended by the Singapore legislature in purely internal affairs; the United Kingdom could also amend it but would take such action only in agreement with the Singapore government unless the constitution had been suspended by the British. The latter step could be taken if they believed there was a deterioration in the internal situation where the United Kingdom was threatened with not being able to carry out its obligations regarding defense or external relations, or if the Singapore government had taken action in contravention of the constitution. Safeguards involving members of the British Overseas Civil Service were included and the constitution would provide for a Public Service Commission. Under an extended franchise as a consequence of the carrying out of the citizenship proposals, elections would be held before the new constitution came into force.

At the final plenary session of the conference the British introduced a provision that individuals known to have been active in subversion should not be allowed to qualify for election to the first legislative assembly under the new arrangements. The Singapore delegation strongly resisted the suggestion but the British made it an integral part of their overall proposal. In the end the Singapore group "took note with regret" of the provision.[23] Lim Yew Hock indicated in a press statement on April 11 that he believed there were about ten individuals in the category of detainees. It might be noted that the outstanding detainee under the Preservation of Public Security Ordinance was Lim Chin Siong, secretary-general of the People's Action Party; others included leaders of the Factory and Shop Workers Union that had been dissolved.

On April 30 the Singapore Legislative Assembly accepted a motion of Lim Yew Hock expressing approval of the constitutional proposals but opposing the ban relative to the subversives. The vote was 23 to 2 with 5 abstentions. David Marshall criticized certain aspects of the constitutional settlement, resigning on April 12 from the Labour Front, and giving up on April 30 his seat in the Assembly. Later he formed a Workers' Party.

The separation of Singapore from the mainland of Malaya in 1946 created a number of problems in addition to solving others. The United Kingdom in a statement in January, 1946, asserted that "it is no part of the policy of His Majesty's Government to preclude or prejudice in any way the fusion of Singapore and the Malayan Union in a wider union at a later date should it be considered that such a course were desirable."[24] The Under-Secretary of State for the Colonies recalled to the House of Lords on March 10, 1954, that "the policy of Her Majesty's Government is to favour a closer association or union between the two territories, but . . . the form and timing of such association are matters which the Governments and the peoples of the two territories should work out for themselves."[25]

As it is, there has been considerable coöperation between the Federation and Singapore. A Joint Coördination Committee established in 1953 with Malcolm MacDonald as chairman listed in an interim report on January 31, 1955, 55 subjects, some of them with subdivisions, concerning which "there must be consultation and coördination," and 10 subjects, some with subdivisions, concerning which "there must be consultation and, if possible, coördination," in both categories, "on policy and, where appropriate, administration between the Governments of Singapore and the Fed-

[23] *Report of the Singapore Constitutional Conference*, Cmd. 147.

[24] Great Britain, *Malayan Union and Singapore, Statement of Policy on Future Constitution*, Cmd. 6724.

[25] *Parliamentary Debates (Hansard)*, 5th Series, Vol. 186, *House of Lords Official Report*, March 2-April 15, 1954, col. 261.

eration of Malaya."[26] Listed were the "existing means of achieving consultation and coördination"—the Secretary of State for the Colonies, the Commissioner-General, direct consultation between the Governor of Singapore and the High Commissioner of the Federation, meetings between individuals or groups of the two Executive Councils, joint select committees of the two Legislative Councils, committees, boards, or councils, administrative or statutory, "some of which are joint and serve both Territories, others of which are separate for each Territory but have an element of common membership, and yet others of which are separate but have representatives from the other Territory in each case," the War Damage Commission, Pan-Malayan departments as well as organizations, departments with the same officer as the head in both Territories, and the large category of "correspondence and/or *ad hoc* departmental meetings."[27]

The Joint Coördination Committee frankly expressed the reasons for consultation and coördination on policy when it listed with examples:

(a) The geographical propinquity of the two Territories:—
- (i) The Malayan Railway could not operate satisfactorily without consultation and coördination between the two Territories.
- (ii) It would not be practicable to organise effectively a census of the inhabitants of the two Territories without previous consultation and coördination between the two Administrations.
- (iii) The control of the Johore Causeway must depend on consultation and coördination between the two Territories.

(b) The historical ties between the two Territories:—
- (i) It has already been seen that the territories now included in the Federation of Malaya and the Colony of Singapore were closely connected administratively before the last war. Residents of one Territory have not in the past and do not now regard the other Territory as a foreign country or themselves as strangers to it.
- (ii) The associations which have existed between the Territories in the past and the unity of administration in which they found expression, have created in the minds of many an instinctive feeling that in certain matters the Territories should meet their problems in the same way and act in unison. There is little doubt that this feeling and the previously existing

[26] *Interim Report of the Joint Coördination Committee*, Government Printing Office, Singapore, *passim.*
[27] *Ibid., passim.*

arrangements have played their part in producing common services such as those provided by the Pan-Malayan departments.

(c) Racial affinities:—
  (i) The racial composition of the two Territories is similar.
  (ii) Many of the residents in each Territory have family and personal ties with those living in the other Territory.

(d) Financial and economic bonds:—
  (i) The currency in use in both Territories is the same.
  (ii) The policies of banking and insurance companies have a common origin and are based on similar principles.
  (iii) Economically the two Territories are very largely dependent on each other. Many firms have branches in both Territories.

(e) Inter-dependence of two Territories on matters of defence, both internal and external:—
  (i) The maintenance of internal law and order in either of the Territories is a matter of supreme concern to the other; as witness to this, similar Emergency Regulations have been introduced in both Territories.
  (ii) In war the two Territories must, for their own sakes, organise their defence on a joint basis.

(f) The need to act together in international relations:—
  (i) The immigration policy of the two Territories must be the same in view of the ease of travel between them.
  (ii) The common element in international problems facing the two Territories has been so apparent that it has been the general practice for the Colony of Singapore and the Federation of Malaya to be represented at international conferences by joint teams made up of representatives from both Territories.[28]

In the field of defense the British have followed a policy based upon the protection of Malaya as a whole. The Federation has raised military forces necessary for land defense and Singapore has been contributing funds and personnel for the Royal Malayan Navy that protects the entire coastline. The Crown Colony as of 1956 had strong police units and the part-time trained Singapore Military Forces, but in 1957 a small full-time regular army was established. Many Singapore leaders believed that the defense arrangement between the Federation and the Crown Colony worked to the advantage of the former since its armed forces operated on the mainland while the naval units of Singapore protected the entire coast. It was announced in Kuala Lumpur in September, 1957, that the Royal Malayan Navy would be transferred to the Federation and be based there as soon as suitable facilities

[28] *Ibid.*, pp. 9-10.

were constructed. In the riots of October, 1956, in the Crown Colony, it should be noted, the Federation sent police reserves and was willing to rush troops. Previously in 1950 a number of Singapore police served in Johore during Anti-Bandit Month. The stationing of British forces in Singapore as well as the Federation has been a stabilizing factor. From an economic viewpoint one-sixth of the labor force of Singapore has been employed by the British armed forces who at the same time occupy valuable real estate.

In another field, the economic ties between the Federation and Singapore have been particularly close despite the revenue tariff of the former. In 1952 Singapore handled 74 percent of the direct imports of Malaya and 67 percent of the total exports. The chief banking center is Singapore: 28 of the 31 banks in Malaya in 1956 were represented there in contrast to 15 represented on the mainland. The Federation is now developing Port Swettenham in addition to the free port at Penang, and the airport at Kuala Lumpur has been improved to serve international traffic.

Involved in a union of the Federation and Singapore are many basic issues such as the maintenance of the latter as a free port and, as already stressed, the relative numerical strength of the Chinese and Malays. The dominant Chinese of Singapore would not like to have Malay the national language, Islam the official religion, and the role of the Malay rulers upheld. The UMNO of the island has already called for a Malay as the highest ranking official, Malay the national language in ten years, and Islam the state religion. Nevertheless, both the Labour Front and the People's Action Party have sought political union with the Federation. Since 1950 Singapore has extended to the latter economic credit worth $10 million. David Marshall asserted on April 4, 1956, that "only unity between the Federation and Singapore can make a truly great Malayan nation and that without such unity there is grave danger to the very survival of both entities."[29] Tengku Abdul Rahman, on

[29] Speech of David Marshall, *Chief Minister and His Merdeka Mission*, Public Relations, Singapore. He stated later: "What can Singapore do? I believe that since April 1955, the Singapore Government has done all it can. The point has been reached where having found the woman who will give meaning to your life you plead with her to marry you, and she says 'No, definitely. Your father was a drunkard and I am afraid you will take to drink and beat me. I will wait a few years and see how you act.' What should you do? I believe you should learn to live alone, keeping and creating contacts for better understanding and pray that the young lady will have faith and fulfill both your lives before it is too late. I fear the longer Singapore and the Federation remain apart, the greater will be the antagonism of growing vested interests, and the more difficult the ultimate union." Speech of David Marshall, "What I Believe," January 24, 1957 (mimeographed).

the other hand, has come to oppose a merger, believing that the problems of the Federation would be immensely increased by such an act. He prefers, as he sees it, a less prosperous but more peaceful Federation without Singapore to a more prosperous but less peaceful Federation with Singapore.

Among the Asian states the impact of the People's Republic of China upon Malaya both the Federation and Singapore is the greatest. The attitude of Communist China toward Malaya and of the Chinese living in the area toward the People's Republic is certain to remain highly significant in international politics. As British control over foreign affairs is withdrawn, the Kuala Lumpur government has to cope with grave long-range problems in the field of Malayan-Chinese relations. And Singapore, of course, is an important consideration in the complex situation.

Relations between Great Britain and China relative to Malaya since 1945 have centered around the Chinese minority, the Emergency, the recognition of the People's Republic of China, and the United Nations embargo on strategic materials. The Peking government has condemned what it has considered the British persecution of Chinese in Malaya. For instance, on March 8, 1951, the chairman of the Relief Committee for Overseas Chinese Refugees from Malaya sent a telegram to Prime Minister Attlee announcing that an investigation team had been organized to go to Malaya for the purpose of looking into the plight of the overseas Chinese. Entry permits were requested. The Secretary of State for the Colonies told the House of Commons on April 6[30] that "we have nothing to hide but equally we have no intention whatsoever of permitting such a mission now or at a later date to enter Malaya." He went on to state that the press in the area was "free and independent" so that "the facts of the situation there are known to all." He noted that the "great majoriy of Chinese in Malaya are peaceful, contented, and law-abiding citizens." The Colonial Secretary observed that 11,000 Chinese were in detention camps but they were mainly aliens who had been actively assisting the terrorists and whom China had refused to take back.

Although individual Chinese from the People's Republic have probably assisted the rebels in Malaya, no general help from Communist China has gone to them. Unlike the boundary with Vietnam

[30] *Parliamentary Debates (Hansard)*, 5th Series, Vol. 486, *House of Commons Official Report*, April 3-20, 1951, re. 31.

the People's Republic has no common border with Malaya. And, moreover, the Communist rebels, despite their propaganda, do not lead a nationalist movement. Peking, however, accused Britain in July, 1957, of suppressing an independence struggle and the United States of seeking to replace the British.

The United Kingdom's recognition of the People's Republic of China in place of the Republic of China on January 6, 1950, caused misgivings in Malaya. Malcolm MacDonald in his capacity as Commissioner-General gave a speech over the radio the same day[31] in which he pointedly said: "The Chinese Government is a Communist Government. Some people in Malaya ask whether Britain's recognition of it implies that the British authorities are growing sympathetic to Communism. Does it, for example, mean that we shall adopt a more lenient attitude towards the Communist terrorists in Malaya? I can tell you at once that the answer to that question is an emphatic 'No.'" He went on to assert that diplomatic recognition did not "signify approval of the politics of the recognized government. It merely means that we recognize that the government concerned is in effective control of its country." MacDonald stressed that Communist rebels in Malaya did not represent the people; he stated that Peking "must not interfere in the national affairs of peoples outside China"; and he declared "afresh our faith in our own, different political conceptions." As of 1957 the People's Republic of China had no consular offices in Singapore or the Federation.

The United Nations embargo on strategic goods to Communist China clearly affected Malaya. After the outbreak of the Korean War rubber exports to the Chinese mainland had greatly increased. The embargo on rubber served to point out clearly in Singapore and Kuala Lumpur that foreign policy was in the hands of Great Britain. It was noted that Ceylon was able to ship the product to the People's Republic. Britain lifted the rubber embargo in June, 1956.

As for the Chinese in Malaya, immigration has dated chiefly from early in the 1800's, reaching a peak around 1900, and continuing on a large scale until the early 1930's when the depression struck. Although the Chinese went to Malaya chiefly to make money and return home, many of them, taking advantage of conditions created by Great Britain, stayed. In fact, the "Straits Chi-

[31] Broadcast Talk by Malcolm MacDonald, *Documents on International Affairs, 1949-1950, passim.*

nese" have long lived in Malaya and are often more British than Chinese in their outlook. In 1931 less than 33 percent of the Chinese living in the area had been born there but in 1947 the proportion of Malayan-born was almost doubled. The Chinese are becoming a settled community, living to a great extent in urban areas. It has, moreover, been estimated that the Chinese population is increasing each year at a rate of over 3 percent in comparison with the rough 2 percent rate of the Malay. The emergency beginning in June, 1948, with the possibility of Chinese being drafted for military service contributed to an exodus on a small scale from Malaya. Immigration restrictions for entry or reëntry are rigid. The economic hold of the Chinese on the area is great, for much of commerce, mining to a certain extent, some of the rubber growing and much of industry are in their hands. Often beginning as laborers, cultivators, and artisans, some have become wealthy and influential. The Chinese have clearly made a major contribution to the economic development of Malaya.

The Emergency has produced great effects on the Chinese of the area. After the surrender of Japan the Malayan Communist Party (MCP), whose membership was almost entirely Chinese, was technically illegal, but the implementation of the pertinent regulations was held in abeyance. Banishment also was in effect suspended. The British government sought the coöperation of the Communists in the maintenance of order in Malaya. During the Japanese occupation the Communists had gone underground, had fought the enemy and had worked with the United Nations. Coöperation between the Japanese and Malays had contributed to the hostility between the Chinese and Malays in the country. After liberation the Communists hoped to establish a Republic of Malaya, taking advantage of the serious economic conditions such as the shortage of rice and housing and the inflation in the cost of living and of the grave security problems brought about by the demoralization of the police force and the general postwar climate. Especially in the trade unions did the MCP gain a powerful position, being organized first under the General Labour Union and in 1946 under the Singapore Federation of Trade Unions and the Pan-Malayan Federation of Trade Unions, the respective headquarters located in Singapore and Kuala Lumpur. Contacts were maintained with Communists in Australia, India, China, and elsewhere.

After failing through infiltration and coercion to produce chaos on the mainland, the MCP decided to concentrate on Singapore in the hope of causing paralysis in the great port. Working through the Singapore Harbour Labourers' Union (SHLU) and the Singapore Workers' Protection Corps, the MCP attempted in the spring of 1948 by strike and demonstration to create the desired situation. Firm action by the British authorities thwarted the attempt of the Communists, who then went underground. A meeting of a youth conference at Calcutta early in the year had served as a front for an international gathering of Communists who, analyzing the situation as favorable to them in the Far East, had agreed upon subsequent courses of action.

In June an effort began to overthrow the government of the Federation of Malaya through armed force. By trying to conquer piecemeal different areas in the country in the hope of eventual consolidation, the Communists sought to establish their own republic. Also by attempts to paralyze the work in mines and on plantations they would deny tin and rubber to the United States from Malaya and destroy the dollar earning capacity of the country for Great Britain. On June 18 the government reacted by declaring a state of emergency for all the Federation, extending the area from Johore and Perak, proclaimed in a similar state two days earlier.

The Chinese Communist rebels were orthodox Marxists, looking for inspiration to the Communists of China as well as the Soviet Union. They were very young in age and naïve in their outlook on Malayan and world affairs. Chin Peng, the leader, served as secretary-general of the party which had its Politburo and Central Executive Committee. Regional committees have been organized in southern, central, and northern Malaya as well as State committees. As of February, 1949, the armed forces were called the Malayan Racial Liberation Army (MRLA). The number of armed rebels has been between 1800 and 5000, about 95 percent Chinese, the rest Malays and Indians. Most of the Chinese were immigrants, and in addition to a hard core of Communists there were plain adventurers. The Min Yuen or People's Movement, organized in undercover groups to help the MRLA with supplies, money, intelligence, and recruits, had possibly at one time 60,000 members, largely Chinese. Most Min Yuen members did not belong to the MCP. Many Chinese squatters along the jungles from Johore to Kedah voluntarily or involuntarily gave food and other help to the rebels. And the Sakai or aborigines within the jungle itself could also provide food if necessary.

In meeting the revolt of the "Communist terrorists (CT's)" or "bandits" the British not only mobilized various armed units within Malaya but also poured forces in from outside. There eventually came into being an effective welding of the civil, police, and military powers of the government in ground activities against the CT's. Real efforts were made to adapt to the necessities of jungle warfare. Food control measures were extensive, even involving efforts to win the Sakai in the jungle. The Malays in the Federation rallied to the defense of the government but the Chinese assumed in general a passive role. In an effort to cut off the CT's from their source of supply, well over 500,000 Chinese squatters were resettled in New Villages. These people, who had become squatters as a result of the great depression and of the Japanese occupation, were largely not under effective administrative rule. Begun as the Briggs Plan in 1950, the resettlement of between a fourth and a fifth of the Chinese in the Federation or more than a tenth of the total population is bound to have great economic, social, and political effects.

Gradually the British were able to declare more areas "white" or cleared of terrorists and free from the restrictions under the Emergency Regulations Ordinance of July, 1948. By the end of April, 1956, it was estimated that 2,500,000 people lived in "white" areas. Many wealthy Chinese became more willing to oppose the paying of protection money to the Communists although by far the greater number of victims were Chinese. General Sir Gerald Templer as High Commissioner and Director of Operations from February, 1952, to May, 1954, pursued an energetic policy in Malaya. Steps toward self-government and independence further weakened the hold of the rebels. The CT's were not able to wreck the economy of the country but they occasioned a severe drain upon it. At the same time the British were not able to stamp out the revolt although psychologically the initiative passed to them.

On September 9, 1955, the government of Chief Minister Tengku Abdul Rahman in conjunction with that of Chief Minister David Marshall and with the British put into effect an amnesty. Among the provisions, CT's who surrendered would be "investigated." If they truly intended to be loyal to the government, they would be given aid in rehabilitating themselves. Others would have their liberty restricted. If they desired to go to China, careful consideration would be given their request. The response of the Communists was not encouraging; in fact, the government claimed they were operating in "safe areas" set aside for surrender purposes.

In June the MCP under Chin Peng had offered to negotiate at a round-table conference an end to the bloodshed, but the British and chief Malayan leaders in Kuala Lumpur rejected the idea of negotiation with it. The elections of July and the consequent changes in the government undoubtedly stole much of the Communist fire of fighting British imperialism. After preliminary discussions at lower levels on the conditions of peace talks a conference began on December 28 at Baling near the Thai border among Tengku Abdul Rahman, David Marshall, Sir Cheng-lock Tan, and Chin Peng. The talks were suspended the next day, for agreement could not be reached at the time. The Communists, while opposing surrender as such, insisted that if they put down their arms there should be no investigation and detention; they should have complete freedom of movement and the MCP should be recognized. Tengku Abdul Rahman asserted that certain investigations and detentions were necessary and the Communist Party would have to be dissolved. Communists wishing to go to China would not be investigated. However, if many of the leaders and followers went to China, the few who stayed might not be investigated but would have to report where they were. He did not want to see Malaya divided like Korea and Vietnam. Chief Minister Marshall asserted that Singapore would not at present recognize the MCP. Later Tengku Abdul Rahman and David Marshall indicated the amnesty offer would be withdrawn February 8, 1956, and the war intensified. During the Baling discussions the Communists said: "As soon as the Federation obtains control of internal security and local armed forces, we will end hostilities, lay down our arms and disband our forces"; yet this "does not amount to accepting the present amnesty terms."[32] On March 15 the chief minister of the Federation made a new surrender offer, but on April 2 he rejected Communist proposals. The approach of Merdeka Day in 1957 saw a definite lull in Communist activity; another amnesty offer was announced September 3.

In Singapore the Emergency Regulations became a subject of political controversy. David Marshall in a preëlection pledge had promised to raise them, but the later responsibility of office tempered his attitude. The Emergency in the Crown Colony had caused occasional and sporadic violence but not of the sustained nature of that on the mainland. Singapore for its part has con-

[32] *Report by the Chief Minister of the Federation of Malaya on the Baling Talks*, Government Press, Kuala Lumpur, p. 12.

tributed somewhat to the Emergency costs of the Federation.

After assuming office in the spring of 1955, Chief Minister Marshall was faced with two serious problems—strikes and the agitation of Chinese students—both aided by the Communists. Indeed, it has been asserted that the "ferment" was "even greater than that of the years 1945-48."[33] On the eve of May Day the Harbour Board clerical workers began the strike wave; riots occurred on May 12 from the dispute of the Hock Lee bus workers; for a month about 5000 Middle School (private secondary) Chinese students engaged in strikes; on June 12 a general strike, though not truly general in effect, was called in protest against the arrest of a few suspected Communist agents and lasted five days. The coöperation between the left-wing unions and the Chinese Middle School students was marked. In fact, the government had previously refused to register the Chinese Middle School Students' Union occasioning the agitation of almost 10,000 students shortly before the April elections. On May 12 the Chinese students took an important part in the riots. Although the situation remained explosive, the government was able to get control of it, partly because of the support of the more conservative labor unions.

In September, 1956, Chief Minister Lim Yew Hock began energetic measures to stamp out Communist influence in Singapore. By late October his policies had led to riots instigated by the Communists. A number of trade union officials and others, sympathetic to the People's Action Party and considered subversive by the government, were arrested; several were ordered banished to China. Communist front organizations were dissolved; the Chinese Middle School Students' Union was banned. Two Chinese Middle Schools were closed after over 140 students were dismissed and a large number refused to leave the school properties. Bold action was taken almost two weeks later to force the students from the buildings. The government raided the branch headquarters of the leftist Factory and Shop Workers Union and the Singapore Bus Workers Union. Later Lim Chin Siong of the People's Action Party was placed under two-year detention. The government with outside aid was able to cope with Communist-inspired strikes and to put down the serious riots. On November 6 the Legislative Assembly gave the chief minister a vote of confidence. For its part the Federation banned the entry of parties of more than five Chinese students

[33] Francis G. Carnell, "Political Ferment in Singapore," *Far Eastern Survey*, Vol. XXIV (July, 1955), p. 97.

from Singapore. The Kuala Lumpur government did not want to see subversion develop in the Chinese schools on the mainland. Nevertheless, it had to take strong action in November in a sit-down strike of 600 students in a Chinese Middle School in Penang; further school trouble occurred the following April. In early January, 1957, serious disturbances broke out between Chinese and Malays at George Town in connection with the centenary celebrations of the Penang city. In August a White Paper in Singapore indicated the present strength of the Communist movement, arrests were made, and efforts to cope with developments in the People's Action Party were intensified. In the Singapore municipal election of December the latter party won 13 of the 14 seats it contested.

In the case of the Chinese students in the island metropolis, the Communist inroads have especially great potentialities. Since around 1950 the Communists have been actively working to organize the Middle School students, many of whom are overage. As over half the population of Singapore is under 21 years old and the franchise has been favorable to younger people, the implications of the Communist effort are clear. And the Communists can take advantage of many educational grievances: if the students go to the People's Republic for a university education, they will probably never get back to Malaya; if they remain in Singapore, they face the premium on English at the noncommunal University of Malaya. The new Nanyang University with Chinese as a medium of instruction provides a limited outlet. It is perhaps not surprising that the Chinese Middle Schools have become centers of Communist infiltration, and that the schism of the Singapore Chinese, long existing between the very small English-speaking minority and the large Chinese-speaking majority, has been accentuated. It will be recalled that among the important issues that have affected the Chinese are those relating to a multilingual Assembly, a distinctive Singapore citizenship, the Emergency Regulations, and discrimination in and out of government.

Chief Minister Marshall in assessing the future of Singapore, if it should fall as a result of Communist inroads, asserted on November 3, 1955: "We do not grow anything here and we could not live on the things we have. We live on the things we import. To import we must buy; to buy we must pay; to pay we must have money, and in order to have the money the only thing we can sell is our services to the free world. If we go Communist we will have no buyers for those services. Once we are behind the Iron Curtain, that is the end of Singapore and that is the beginning of starvation in Singapore."[34]

In August, 1956, a large trade delegation from the Crown Colony and the Federation arrived in Peking. David Marshall, who was making a study tour of a number of Asian states, served as an adviser. The delegation was interested in encouraging trade between Malaya and the People's Republic of China, especially with the end of the embargo on rubber. Premier Chou En-lai indicated in a reception to the delegates that if the different peoples in Singapore and the Federation worked together each of the two could get independence like that of India, but if the racial groups failed to coöperate the British would continue to divide and rule.

In the first half of 1956 Malaya's trade with the Communist bloc had registered notable gains, the Soviet Union making substantial purchases of rubber and Communist China shipping rice. The People's Republic, moreover, has given credit to some Malayan business firms. In August an informal agreement was made for the export of 10,000 tons of rubber from Malaya to mainland China and the import of 20,000 tons of rice. Neither Communist nor Nationalist China nor any Communist state, for that matter, was invited to send representatives to Merdeka Day celebrations at Kuala Lumpur in August, 1957. Nevertheless, the Federation was eager to expand trade with the People's Republic of China. Events would prove whether David Marshall was correct in his conviction that the "present Chinese Government is firmly convinced that the welfare of the overseas Chinese as well as China's own need for friendly nations, requires that the overseas Chinese give genuinely of their loyalty to the land of their domicile."[35] At any rate Peking recognized the newly independent Federation of Malaya although critical of the latter's ties with Great Britain.

The relations of India with Malaya are influenced by the Indian minority in the Federation and in Singapore, by the rise of an independent India and the personal influence of Nehru, and by the economic relations between Malaya and India.

In June, 1941, before the outbreak of the Pacific War, somewhat over 700,000 Indians lived in Malaya, possibly a quarter having been born there; by 1952 the figure was less, around 618,000 in the Federation and about 80,000 in Singapore. There was a much

[34] *New York Times*, November 5, 1955.
[35] Speech of David Marshall, "What I Believe," January 24, 1957 (mimeographed).

larger number of local-born, about 50 percent in 1947. The Indian population suffered severely during the Japanese occupation. Even before then, since 1938, unskilled laborers had not been allowed by India to migrate to Malaya. Furthermore, postwar developments have not been conducive to extensive immigration. The Indians who came to Malaya were largely Tamils from Madras, were encouraged by conditions created by the British, and were brought under intergovernmental auspices. The Indians supplied labor to the rubber plantations and government branches, some were merchants, others became shopkeepers, and a few entered the professional classes. The Chettyars became wealthy as a result of their financial transactions, but their operations were controlled by law. Sikhs have also been active as moneylenders. Indians formed a very important part of the membership in labor unions; the leadership of the Malayan Trade Union Council in Kuala Lumpur was largely Indian. It is estimated that by the end of 1952 about 200,000 Indians had acquired citizenship in the Federation.

On the political level the Japanese had sought to utilize the Indian population of Malaya in the Indian Independence League, Indian National Army, and Provisional Government of Azad Hind. The Azad Hind movement undoubtedly contributed to an arousing of political consciousness. The postwar struggle of India for independence was reflected in the concern shown among Malayan Indians. Conflicts between the Hindus and Moslems in India resulted in riots between the two groups in Malaya. Chinese Communist penetration into labor unions further weakened the Indian community. In August, 1946, the Malayan Indian Congress was formed partly to counteract the Communist influence. Its orientation indicated a dualism of attitude toward India and Malaya. In Singapore, as already noted, Indians took an active part in elections to the Legislative Council, taking advantage of the noncommunal nature of politics. With the Emergency the Malayan Indians assumed a somewhat passive role, only a few supporting the rebels. In general the Indian community in Malaya has been more attached to the mother country than the Chinese.

Nehru made a visit to Malaya in 1937 before the Second World War. He returned in March, 1946, well over a year before the independence of India. The Indians were frankly told they must choose between being nationals of Malaya or India, for he was opposed to dual nationality. He looked to Singapore as the scene of Asian unity with its Chinese, Indian, and Malay populations, and he saw India upon her independence being a champion of subject peoples. In June, 1950, Nehru again visited Malaya, stopping at Singapore and Kuala Lumpur.

Although India since independence has occasionally intervened in specific Malayan matters and often to no avail, Nehru has recognized the nature of the Emergency and the problems of creating a Malayan nation or two independent states. In contrast, the Indian Communist Party has called the revolt in Malaya nationalist, and Nehru has been accused of supporting British colonialism.

In connection with his trip to London in December, 1955, Chief Minister David Marshall visited Ceylon, India, and Pakistan. He was a guest of Sir John Kotelawala, Prime Minister of Ceylon, who indicated sympathy for the constitutional aspirations of Singapore and offered technical assistance in a number of fields. In New Delhi Marshall met Prime Minister Nehru who had recently wished "all success to the people of Singapore and the Federation of Malaya in their march to freedom."[36] India was willing to grant technical assistance whenever required and whenever she could do it. The prime minister of Pakistan indicated that Singapore's aspirations were perfectly natural. Marshall hoped Ceylon, India, and Pakistan would champion Singapore's cause for independence at the meeting of the Commonwealth prime ministers in June.

After the failure of his mission in April, 1956, the chief minister stopped in New Delhi on his way home. He emphasized that he was not seeking advice or promises from Nehru but rather trying to present "the true picture." At the Commonwealth Prime Ministers' Conference in late June and early July, Nehru did not strongly champion the cause of Singapore. He believed the colony was possibly moving too fast under the circumstances in its efforts to get independence.

It may be surprising that despite the Moslem ties uniting the Malays and Pakistani, there is little interest between the two peoples. The Indian Moslems in Malaya have not been successful in organizing effective Moslem Leagues. A Pan-Malayan Muslim Indian League orientated toward Pakistan went into eclipse, and later a weak Malayan Pakistani League came into being. Its president called upon the Pakistani in the Federation to consider themselves Malayans and Malaya their home. Mr. Justice Abdul Hamid of Pakistan had an active part on the Reid Commission in the

[36] Quoted by David Marshall in speech of February 8, 1956, *Chief Minister Reports*, Public Relations, Singapore.

drafting of the Federation of Malaya constitution, submitting a "note of dissent" on a number of items. A commissioner for the Federation assumed office in Pakistan even before Merdeka Day.

If the Chinese influence should grow to the extent that the Malays on the mainland are convinced they are about to be submerged, a strong movement on their part for a kind of association, possibly a political union, with the kindred Moslem Indonesians in the Republic of Indonesia is possible. On the other hand, Dato Onn observed after the July, 1955, election that only Indonesian immigration to Malaya could prevent the submergence of the indigenous Malays. As already indicated, there has been considerable movement of people from certain parts of Indonesia to Malaya. The ties between many inhabitants of Negri Sembilan and the Sumatran Minangkabau are close; Bugis went to Selangor from the Celebes; a large number of immigrants came from Java. It has been reported that some of the Malayan Communists have been active in Sumatra across the Strait of Malacca from the Federation.

A few political organizations in Malaya have stressed the need for close links with Indonesia. The Malay Nationalist Party (MNP), a left-wing group, later banned, might be mentioned. A youth movement, called *Angkatan Permuda Insaf* (API), also was interested in Indonesian ties. The colors of the Indonesian flag, red and white, appeal to many Malay nationalists. The development of a strong Indonesia is certain to exert a great influence on Malaya. Mention has even been made of a federation of the Malays in Southeast Asia involving Malaya, Indonesia, and the Philippines.

One Asian state has gone from the Malayan scene in terms of external political pressure—Japan. During the New Order in Greater East Asia, Japan conquered all the areas subject to the jurisdiction of British Malaya or Borneo except the Cocos Islands in the Indian Ocean. She even occupied on April 10, 1942, Christmas Island in the same body of water. Favoring the Malays and discriminating against the Chinese, Japan contributed to communal tension. Using extensive Indian labor from Malaya in helping to build the Thailand-Burma Railway, Japan caused the deaths of possibly some 20,000 Indians. The quick defeat of the British forces in Malaya by the Japanese dealt a serious blow to the prestige of the United Kingdom. But no Malayan nationalism arose to the extent that it could challenge the return of the British.

As Malaya had reverted to its status of a British dependency, peace with Japan came with the ratification of the San Francisco peace treaty by Great Britain and other sovereign powers as provided in the pact. A Japanese consulate general was established in Singapore in October, 1952, but by 1956 no similar step had been taken in Kuala Lumpur. Considerable dislike of the Japanese lingered in Malaya. Nevertheless, the questions of war damages and reparations have been all but settled from confiscated Japanese property; advance reparations payments had been made before the peace treaty. The British have relaxed regulations relative to quantities and kinds of Japanese imports, and trade is flourishing between Malaya and Japan. The Japanese are interested in the iron ore and coal of the Federation. Nevertheless, in 1956, only a few Japanese businessmen were allowed in Singapore and their operations were limited. In the Federation the situation was even much more dismal from the Japanese viewpoint. Relations were improved by a visit of Prime Minister Kishi of Japan to Kuala Lumpur and Singapore in late 1957.

In the foreign policy of an independent Federation of Malaya, the key Western power is Great Britain. The decision of the Federation to stay in the Commonwealth of Nations and to allow Commonwealth forces to be stationed on Malayan territory speaks for itself. In this connection the ties of the Federation with Australia and New Zealand are also important. The Federation receives aid under the Colombo Plan and participates in its meetings. In addition to assistance in training Federation military officers in Australia, the Canberra government is helping to prepare some of the future officers of the diplomatic service of the new Malayan state. Britain has a similar role. The Federation even before independence sent a commissioner and an assistant commissioner to Australia. There was also a commissioner for Singapore and the Federation in London with an information officer and a trade commissioner.

The influence of the United States continues to be important, although not conspicuous, in Kuala Lumpur. As a key purchaser of Malaya's rubber and tin, the United States through its economic policy has a great impact on the Federation's economy and politics. The Federation does not require American military or economic aid but would like private investment. During the Emergency the United States allowed the shipment of arms to help defeat the rebels. An American information service and a Fulbright program are functioning. A loan would eventually come.

With its only land neighbor, Thailand, the Federation has inherited a number of problems, many arising from the Emergency. Tengku Abdul Rahman, the son of a Shan princess, in a visit to Bangkok in March, 1956, observed that "we cannot go one way and Thailand another."[37] He asserted that the "task of holding a friendly relationship between the two countries will be very easy."[38] In November, 1955, the Tengku had visited Indonesia, a country whose relations with an independent Federation are very important. Trade has fluctuated with Thailand and Indonesia as well as Burma. The ties between the Philippines and the Federation are being strengthened by a growing realization of similar racial backgrounds, by the common problems of newly won independence, and by a basic similarity in outlook toward the former mother countries.

Obviously the large Chinese and Indian populations in the Federation have a great influence on the relations between India and the Federation and China and the Federation. In the case of China, the question of citizenship is especially important. It will be interesting to note if the People's Republic of China will seek to negotiate with the Federation a citizenship treaty like that made with Indonesia. Many of the Malayan Chinese are more loyal to China as a strong power in Asia than to Chinese Communism. The Federation's relations with Japan largely center around commercial and business matters.

As a country with a large number of Moslems, the role of the Federation in the Moslem world could be significant. Indonesia and Pakistan in Southeast and South Asia, it should be recalled, are also Moslem states. In the elections of July, 1955, the Pan-Malayan Islamic Party took an active part. It put up 11 candidates, won one seat, and polled 40,667 votes or 3.9 percent of the total. The PMIP, greatly influenced by the Muslim College of Malaya, could not agree on supporting an Islamic State for Malaya but it may signify an Islamic revival. Tengku Abdul Rahman made plans in 1957 to make a pilgrimage to Mecca the next year.

Upon independence the Federation as a sovereign state established high commissions in the United Kingdom, Australia, India, and Pakistan, embassies in Thailand, Indonesia, and the United States and planned to set up the following year embassies in Japan and France, a legation in Egypt, and a consulate in Saudi Arabia. The United Kingdom, Australia, India, and New Zealand sent high commissioners to the new state, Ceylon a commissioner, Thailand,

[37] *New York Times*, March 28, 1956.
[38] *New York Times*, March 27, 1956.

Indonesia, the United States, Japan, the Federal Republic of Germany, and France ambassadors, the Netherlands and the Republic of Vietnam ministers, and Belgium, Denmark, Norway, and Sweden consuls.

Great Britain had controlled the invitational list in connection with the ceremonies marking Merdeka Day. Invited were Canada, Australia, New Zealand, India, Pakistan, Ceylon, Ghana, the Central African Federation, South Africa, Burma, Cambodia, Indonesia, Laos, Nepal, the Philippines, Thailand, the Republic of Vietnam, Belgium, France, the Federal Republic of Germany, Italy, Japan, the Netherlands, the United States, Iraq, Iran, Jordan, Lebanon, Libya, Morocco, the Sudan, Tunisia, Turkey, Yemen, Afghanistan, Ireland, and Singapore, Hong Kong, Sarawak, Brunei, North Borneo, and Fiji. All accepted but Libya and Yemen.

The Federation of Malaya was obviously pleased with election in September, 1957, as the eighty-second member of the United Nations, the vote being unanimous in both the Security Council and the General Assembly. A few days later it was admitted to the International Bank for Reconstruction and Development and the International Monetary Fund. Next would be membership in WHO, FAO, UNESCO, ILO, ITU, ICAO, UPU, and WMO. The new state quickly became a contracting party to the General Agreement on Tariffs and Trade (GATT). Along with Singapore, Brunei, North Borneo, and Sarawak, the Federation had previously contributed to UNICEF, and the Malaya-British Borneo Group had membership in WMO and associate membership in ITU and ECAFE. With independence for the Federation of Malaya the British ceased to transmit information on it to the United Nations under Article 73e of the Charter. SEATO had a far less appeal to the Federation than the United Nations. It was believed that membership would arouse opposition from many of the Chinese and from the uncommitted states of Asia. Moreover, the new state was protected by its defense agreement with Great Britain. Despite urging from Thailand, the Kuala Lumpur government hesitated to adhere to the Manila Pact. The Federation like Indonesia approves of the International Tin Agreement and is a member of the International Tin Council.

For the State of Singapore, the pattern of international relations is somewhat different. Economically as a free port and an entrepôt, the island area is tied largely to the West, racially as a large Chinese city chiefly to China, and politically to Great Britain and the Commonwealth. Under the circumstances pressures for a neutral attitude are present. Relations with Thailand do not have the importance of those between the Federation and its neighbor to the north. On the other hand, Singapore's relations with Indonesia, though not based substantially on racial or religious ties, are important for geographic and economic reasons. Chief Minister Marshall called attention to the situation by his visit to Indonesia in September, 1955. Japan in her economic diplomacy in Southeast Asia seeks close ties with Singapore. India's minority and trade interests also figure in the latter's international relations. The island area received aid under the Colombo Plan and participates in its meetings, David Marshall being chairman at the Singapore gathering of the Consultative Committee. Australia has an obvious interest in the State.

In 1956 a large Commonwealth and consular representation was found in Singapore. Australia, Ceylon, and India had commissioners for Malaya; Pakistan, Canada, the United Kingdom, and the Union of South Africa had trade commissioners for various areas; the United Kingdom had a commissioner-general for South-East Asia and New Zealand a commissioner for South-East Asia. Consular officials of different categories represented Belgium, Burma, Denmark, France, West Germany, Greece, Indonesia, Iraq, Italy, Japan, the Netherlands, Norway, Panama, the Philippines, Portugal, Spain, Sweden, Switzerland, Thailand, the United States, and South Vietnam. Within Southeast Asia only North Vietnam, Cambodia, and Laos were not represented.

Along a sector of the eastern shores of the South China Sea are the British territories of North Borneo, Brunei, and Sarawak whose future could be linked to that of Malaya. British Colonial Secretary Alan Lennox-Boyd has even suggested a federation of North Borneo, Brunei, Sarawak, the Federation of Malaya, and Singapore. The initiative should come from the peoples concerned. Chief Minister Tengku Abdul Rahman has said the Federation would welcome as members the three units in British Borneo with Singapore. The Liberal Socialist Party in the latter area has called for a confederation of the territories mentioned. Already a degree of relationship has developed though subject to change; for instance, the Malayan dollar has been legal tender in British Borneo and Malaya. Singapore is the focus of many economic activities of British Borneo. Among the recommendations of a survey mission in Malaya by the International Bank for Reconstruction and Development in 1954 was the establishment of a Central Bank of Malaya that "would serve both the Federation and Singapore and, possibly, the three British Borneo territories now in the Malayan currency area, unless they elected to have their own currency."[39] The latter possibility, however, is to become a reality. In another field of activity Malayan Airways operates in effect on a domestic basis between British Borneo and Malaya. The Commissioner-General for the United Kingdom in South-East Asia and the Malaya-Borneo Defence Council have coördinating functions in the areas under consideration.

North Borneo, which became a Crown Colony on July 15, 1946, was a British protectorate from 1888 administered under a royal charter granted in effect to the British North Borneo Company formed in 1882. North Borneo, having a present area of 29,387 square miles, has a land frontier with Sarawak and Indonesia, and the Philippines as a sea neighbor. It borders the South China Sea, Sulu Sea, and Celebes Sea. On July 15, 1946, the island of Labuan, 6 miles off the southwest coast of North Borneo and important in sea and air communications, was made a part of the latter colony. It became a free port in 1956. With a stress on the production of rubber, North Borneo trade is largely through Singapore and Hong Kong. Only some 100 miles of railway and some 200 miles of metaled roads exist in the colony.

The population of North Borneo, according to the census of 1951, was 334,141 of which 241,831 were indigenous inhabitants, 74,374 were Chinese and 1213 Europeans and Eurasians. Significant is the fact that in the 20 years between 1931 and 1951 the indigenous population increased by 18.4 percent and the Chinese by 48.6 percent.[40] The most important community among the 241,831 is the Dusuns, other peoples including the Muruts, the Bruneis, the Kedayans, and the Bajaus, some of them possibly coming from the Philippines. Many are Moslems, others pagans; the *lingua franca* of the country is Malay. Indigenous inhabitants coming to North Borneo from Sarawak, Malaya, or Indonesia have no trouble in quickly assimilating with the people in the majority. In fact, some of the Indonesians brought in by the Japanese during the recent war have not chosen to be repatriated. There are also some post-

[39] International Bank for Reconstruction and Development, *The Economic Development of Malaya*, p. 228.

[40] In the given dates figures for Labuan are included although the island was not a part of North Borneo in 1931.

war immigrants from Indonesian Borneo, and some 1500 immigrants have come from the Cocos Islands. As regards the large number of Chinese in 1951, 48,862 of them were born in North Borneo. The Chinese are active in commerce, agriculture, and local industries. In the Sandakan area many of them have connections with mainland China and Hong Kong but on the west coast others have more ties with Singapore. Since the advent of Communist China the United Kingdom has prohibited direct immigration into British Borneo from the People's Republic.

Japan occupied North Borneo from January, 1942, to September 10, 1945, with heavy damage a consequence of the war. Jesselton became the postwar capital in place of Sandakan. After the establishment of the Crown Colony in 1946, the British made efforts to widen the governmental base. Progress has been made in local government, and a constitution for the colony was granted in 1950. A governor, executive council, and legislative council govern the colony with its three residencies. None of the members is yet elected but an effort is made to include Borneans, Chinese, and Europeans. Since December, 1951, all British Borneo has had a common judiciary at the top. The police in the three areas work very closely.

Brunei, under British control since 1888, remains a Protected State but it is under the supervision of the governor of Sarawak, who in 1948 became the high commissioner for Brunei. The State is bounded by Sarawak which, in fact, divides it into two parts. Its coastline on the South China Sea is only about 100 miles but it is developing port and airfield facilities. According to the census of 1947, 40,657 people lived in Brunei with its area of 2226 square miles; 31,161 people were considered indigenous, Malays and Borneans, 8300 were Chinese and the rest chiefly Indians and Europeans.[41] Islam and paganism are the main religions of the indigenous people, some of whom move between Brunei and North Borneo and Brunei and Sarawak. The State depends largely on the oil industry, the Seria oilfields being very important, with processing in Sarawak. In 1955 a new source of oil was found at Jerudong. There are over 160 miles of roads in the country. Brunei has been able to make a loan to the Federation of Malaya and offer one to Sarawak.

Japan occupied the sultanate from the middle of December, 1941, to June 10, 1945; British military administration ceased on July 6, 1946. The highest authority in the State is the Sultan in

[41] The population in 1957 was estimated to have risen to around 60,000.

Council. In July, 1957, draft constitutional proposals were published for Brunei providing for a Privy Council, Executive Council, and Legislative Council. The sultanate with its capital Brunei Town is divided into four districts. It may be significant that a Brunei political leader, Azahari, is organizing a party calling for a federation of British Borneo and eventual Merdeka. The State is far removed from its status in the sixteenth century when its ruler controlled all Borneo and neighboring Philippine areas including the Sulu Archipelago and Palawan. In fact, the present boundaries of the three units of British Borneo do not have an ethnic basis; they are the result of external rather than internal forces. To a large extent Brunei remains the religious and cultural and to a degree the political center of all the Moslem Malays in British Borneo.

The origins of the English in Sarawak present a classic example of how an adventurer was able to secure for himself an area that later came under the Union Jack. James Brooke, by helping the viceroy of the Sultan of Brunei put down a revolt at Kuching, was ceded Sarawak proper in 1841 and became rajah. The territory was enlarged between 1861 and 1905, and in 1888 became a protectorate of Great Britain. Having a present area of around 47,000 square miles and a coastline of 450 miles along the South China Sea, Sarawak has a long mountainous border with Indonesia and a much shorter one with North Borneo. As already noted, Brunei is divided by the territory of Sarawak.

The estimated population of the country in December, 1954, was 605,000. Included in the number were 167,700 Chinese, 213,200 Sea Dayaks or Iban, 47,500 Land Dayaks, 137,700 Malays and Melanaus, and 32,300 Kayans, Kenyahs, Muruts, and other similar peoples. The indigenous population of Sarawak includes over 70 percent of the total inhabitants. In the census of 1947 the indigenous people were defined as "those persons who recognise no allegiance to any foreign territory, who regard Sarawak as their homeland, who believe themselves to be a part of the territory, and who are now regarded as natives by their fellow men."[42] There is some movement between Sarawak and Indonesia, especially of the Land Dayaks who have a kinship to the people across the border. Other movement takes place with North Borneo and Brunei. Many of the people are Moslems. The Chinese economically have the first place in the colony; numerically they come after the Sea Dayaks; culturally their influence is next to that of the Europeans.

[42] *Annual Report on Sarawak, 1952*, p. 13.

The trade of Sarawak is largely with Singapore. Important oilfields have been developed at Miri; the country also produces rubber, its main industry, with other products including sago, pepper, and timber. Almost three-fourths of its imports in 1952 came from Brunei and North Borneo, mostly oil from the former. There are only some 150 miles of metaled roads in the colony. Sarawak since 1950 has extended to North Borneo economic credit worth $2.2 million.

Japan occupied Sarawak in December, 1941, and Australian forces entered Kuching, the capital, on September 11, 1945. Sir Charles Vyner Brooke, the third rajah, resumed the administration of the protectorate on April 15, 1946. The rajah having proposed cession to the British Crown, the Council Negri of Sarawak on May 17 by a vote of 19 to 16 on the third reading favored the step. On July 1 by an Order-in-Council Sarawak became a Crown Colony. Under a constitution effective April 1, 1957, the colony has a governor, a Supreme Council, half elected, and a Council Negri with an elected unofficial majority. Sarawak is divided for administrative purposes into five divisions. Local government authorities, representative of all races, with their own treasuries are being established.

It is clear that nationalism has not yet become a force of importance in British Borneo. Until it does, the British will have certain difficulties arising from the situation in trying to hand over authority in North Borneo, Brunei, and Sarawak. As of the present most of the peoples are not really aware of themselves as making up three political units. It is possible that only the Malays of Sarawak and North Borneo would favor unification with Brunei. In 1953 the Sarawak, North Borneo, and Brunei Conference was established as a standing body to promote coöperation among the three units. Whenever these areas, each by itself, united together, or a part of a large Malayan federation, acquire independence, foreign policy will move out of British hands. In the case of North Borneo relations with the Philippines will be particularly important; all three, North Borneo, Brunei, and Sarawak, will be concerned with relations with Indonesia occupying by far the larger part of Borneo. The historic role of Great Britain and the numerically large and economically important Chinese population, coupled with the impact of a strong China, will be factors of importance. British Borneo, it might be added, is already associated with the Colombo Plan. Some American aid has been given.

Great Britain's interests in Southeast Asia are obviously not restricted to Malaya and Borneo. They were defined in 1946 with respect to the Pacific as:

(I) The maintenance of the political association with the Dominions;
(II) a general responsibility towards all the Pacific territories which are associated with her;
(III) good relations with China;
(IV) commercial interests, including her investments in Pacific countries, trade and exchange of products;
(V) communications, in which oceanic shipping and air routes are of prime importance;
(VI) the defence of individual territories; and
(VII) on a different plane, general support in the Pacific as elsewhere for "liberal" tendencies and regimes.[43]

As for the policy of Great Britain toward the nations of Southeast Asia, Foreign Secretary Eden told the House of Commons on November 8, 1954, that in this part of the world "we have an opportunity to help these countries to develop their own way of life in freedom and in peace. This is all that we seek to do—nothing else at all. The best, indeed the only way, to do this is by economic help and by treaties which make these countries feel protected and secure."[44] Malcolm MacDonald told the National Press Club in Washington on October 8 that "the two great Asian causes of political freedom and economic progress are, of course, right causes. They should receive our unqualified and consistent support."[45]

British policy in Southeast Asia has been coördinated by a commissioner-general in the area. Before the Second World War when the Empire was more extensive in the region, the governor of the Straits Settlements who was also high commissioner for Malaya reported to the Colonial Office, the governor of Burma to the Burma Office, and the diplomatic or consular representatives in Thailand, Indochina, the Philippines, and the Netherlands East Indies to the Foreign Office. After the Second World War a Special Commissioner with ambassadorial rank, Lord Killearn, was appointed on February 18, 1946, and sent to Singapore to advise the British government on Southeast Asia and Hong Kong. The organization of the distribution of rice through a Liaison Conference was one

[43] Royal Institute of International Affairs, *British Security*, p. 129.

[44] *Parliamentary Debates (Hansard)*, 5th Series, Vol. 532, *House of Commons Official Report*, November 1-12, 1954, col. 936.

[45] Speech of Malcolm MacDonald, *British Information Services*, New York, October 18, 1954.

of his most important tasks, and valuable experience was gained in regional economic coöperation. After his retirement Malcolm MacDonald who had been appointed Governor-General of Malaya and British Borneo on January 29, 1946, took over on May 1, 1948, with the title of Commissioner-General for the United Kingdom in South-East Asia, combining the functions of the two positions. From Phoenix Park he reported to the Colonial Office on the British dependencies and to the Foreign Office relative to the independent countries. In his relations with foreign states he had the personal rank of ambassador. A large part of his responsibilities was to advise on coördinating British regional policy in Southeast Asia. He was active in promoting coöperation among all the British territories in the area. His functions as Commissioner-General were not executive or administrative; he was not to detract from the obligations of the British colonial and diplomatic officials in the region.

In October, 1955, MacDonald was succeeded by Sir Robert Scott. Instead of representing the colonial and foreign secretaries, Sir Robert was appointed as a representative of the prime minister. In addition, the Commissioner-General now serves as the United Kingdom delegate on the SEATO Council in Bangkok. When *all* its activities are included Phoenix Park, in the words of Sir Robert, has come to be "the little Whitehall of the Far East."[46]

In another aspect the Emergency in Malaya has indicated how far-flung still are Britain's military resources. The response to the revolt was not limited to the United Kingdom and Malaya. Australia and New Zealand sent air and later naval and ground support. Gurkhas from Nepal were used by the British, although some criticism arose in India.[47] Dayak trackers were brought in from Sarawak. Some men of the King's African Rifles saw action, and others fought from the Fiji Infantry. When trouble arose in Sarawak in August, 1952, as a result of Communist-inspired banditry the RAF flew in military equipment from Singapore and the Federation of Malaya. North Borneo loaned two platoons of police, also transported by the RAF.

Malaya has come to be a forward base in the defense of the Commonwealth of Australia and the Dominion of New Zealand.

[46] Speech of Sir Robert Scott, February 20, 1956, *Phoenix Park, Singapore*, The Regional Information Office, Singapore, 1956.

[47] The Gurkhas, known for their qualities as fighters, form important battalions in the British and Indian armies. The recruits for the British forces, no longer allowed training facilities in India, are sent to Malaya for instruction.

From the cultural, racial, and political viewpoint, Australia's ties are with the West but from the geographic with the East. The Minister for External Affairs, R. G. Casey, significantly stated on August 10, 1954, in the House of Representatives: "170 million Asian people live within a radius of 2,000 miles from Darwin. It is in these Asian countries to the north-west of Australia that the largest share of the world's supplies of tin, rubber, rice and other important commodities are produced. This area also provides the most obvious route for potential aggression against Australia."[48] The Japanese invasion of the Southwest Pacific and of Southeast Asia clearly brought home to Australians their geographical relationship to Asia.

After the Second World War the marked decline of Great Britain's power in the Pacific raised in Canberra the question of the future security of the Commonwealth "down under." The rise of nationalism and the emergence of new states in Southeast Asia, Australia's "Near North," especially the appearance of the Republic of Indonesia, her closest neighbor, have changed the control of foreign policy in nearby areas from friendly Western powers, the Netherlands, Great Britain, France, and the United States, to unpredictable Asian states. Moreover, the substitution of Communist imperialism under the Chinese and Russian regimes for Japanese imperialism has presented a challenge to the Australians.

The policy of the Canberra government toward Southeast Asia was well defined by R. G. Casey in his closing remarks at the Bangkok Conference of the SEATO powers on February 25, 1955:

> Australia . . . is the nearest non-Asian country to the threatened area and so perhaps in particular we're most interested and concerned in this Southeast Asian area, an interest and concern that we've tried to show through the placing of Australian diplomatic posts in every country of this area and, [for] what it's worth, by frequent visits myself to . . . practically every part of this area. . . . we don't attempt in any way, or at any time, to try to tell the countries of this area how to run their own affairs but it does mean to us . . . that we take the greatest interest in the area; we are going to do everything possible to see, if possible, that it survives as a free area. We are going to devote to it, as we have tried in the past, all the resources that we can spare in Australia in aid of the economies and the defensive arrangements of these countries.[49]

[48] Statement by R. G. Casey, *Current Notes on International Affairs,* Vol. 25 (August, 1954), p. 580.

[49] Statement by R. G. Casey, *The Bangkok Conference of the Manila Pact Powers,* p. 29.

At the same time the Commonwealth has not altered its so-called "White Australia" policy, based upon the Immigration Restriction Act, and closely related to the "Australian standard of living." It is maintained that the immigration policy preserves the nation from racial controversy and guards its living standard. Nevertheless, toward the end of 1955 Australia had received her one-thousandth Asian student under the Colombo Plan. In all there were at the time about 3500 Asians studying in the Commonwealth. Yet the "White Australia" policy has caused considerable resentment in Southeast Asia, being an important factor in the development of relations between Australia and the region in general.

The three pillars of Australia's security policy in Southeast Asia are the Colombo Plan, the Manila Pact, and close coöperation with the democracies having interests in the area. Australia had a very important part in the origin and development of the Colombo Plan which arose from the Spender Plan. At a conference of the foreign ministers of the British Commonwealth of Nations in January, 1950, at Colombo, Ceylon, Percy C. Spender, then Australian Minister for External Affairs, made a proposal for economic and technical assistance to Southeast Asia, broadly interpreted in terms of area. The proposal, although previously considered in Canberra, was largely drafted on the plane trip to Colombo. It was realized that through economic aid Communism would be challenged and Australia's security strengthened. The proposal was adopted in principle at the Colombo Conference and a Consultative Committee came into existence. At its meeting in Sydney in May, the Consultative Committee recommended the preparation of a six-year plan for the area with each government making by September 1 a frank statement of its economic conditions and of its development program. This was done by India, Pakistan, Ceylon, Singapore, the Federation of Malaya, North Borneo, and Sarawak. A London meeting of the Consultative Committee was held in September and October to prepare from the statements submitted a comprehensive report on the resources and the needs of the countries in the area with the objective of a development program of six years founded upon resources available in the countries concerned and from other states and sources interested. Political leaders from Singapore and the Federation of Malaya were present at the London meeting.

The Consultative Committee issued its first report in November on the "Colombo Plan for Coöperative Economic Development in South and South-East Asia." A six-year plan was presented; a

Council for Technical Coöperation had already come into being. The total required capital was set at about \$5.2 billion with at least \$3 billion needed from outside the area. The Plan would get under way in mid-1951. The report clearly stressed that non-Commonwealth members in the area would be welcome to participate and the coöperation of outside powers would be sought. By the end of the Ottawa meeting of the Consultative Committee in October, 1954, all the non-Communist countries from Pakistan to Japan except Formosa and South Korea were members. The Colombo Plan group came to include within Asia Pakistan, India, Ceylon, Nepal, Burma, Thailand, Laos, Cambodia, the Republic of Vietnam, the Federation of Malaya, Singapore, British Borneo, Indonesia, the Philippines, and Japan. Outside the area mentioned, the contributing or donor countries came to be Great Britain, Australia, Canada, New Zealand, and the United States. Japan also became known as a contributor. At the Consultative Council meetings observers are present from the International Bank for Reconstruction and Development, the United Nations Technical Assistance Board, and the Economic Commission for Asia and the Far East. Aid, it should be noted, is bilaterally given.

In the Economic Development Programme under the Colombo Plan Sir Percy Spender estimated in May, 1955, that 82 percent of the finance for development projects had originated within Asia and only 18 percent from the outside. Stress was placed on agriculture, communications and transport, and electric power. The Technical Coöperation Scheme with its Council for Technical Coöperation and executive Bureau in Colombo has been very successful in work related to training Asian students, recruiting foreign experts, and getting necessary equipment for institutions. At the Singapore meeting of the Consultative Committee in October, 1955, it was decided to extend the life of the Committee with the Plan and the Scheme to June 30, 1961, further consideration to be given at the 1959 meeting.

In terms of military security pacts Australia has come to look to the United States, although this policy has weakened her position in the eyes of many Asians. On January 21, 1944, during the Pacific War, Australia signed with New Zealand the Canberra pact providing, *inter alia,* that "within the framework of a general system of world security a regional zone of defense comprising the Southwest and South Pacific areas shall be established and that this zone should be based on Australia and New Zealand, stretching through the arc of islands north and northeast of Australia to Western Samoa and the Cook Islands."[50] Close and continuous coöperation in a wide field was envisioned by the Australian-New Zealand Agreement.

In fulfillment of one of the purposes of the pact a South Seas Conference was held in Canberra from January 28 to February 6, 1947. An agreement was signed on the latter date by Australia, New Zealand, Great Britain, France, the Netherlands, and the United States to promote through a South Pacific Commission the social and economic welfare and progress of the people administered by them in the non-self-governing territories of the South Pacific area. The agreement was obviously not a military security pact. In 1949, however, Australia, New Zealand, and the United Kingdom agreed to coördinate their planning for defense in the ANZAM region which included the homelands of Australia and New Zealand and British Borneo and Malaya with adjacent sea areas.

With the approach of a peace treaty with Japan the United States, which had opposed a Pacific security pact, was increasingly urged by Australia and New Zealand to enter into a formal alliance with them. American approval in the end was based partly upon the desire to secure the acceptance by Australia and New Zealand of the Japanese peace treaty. It was clear that the two powers were still apprehensive about future Japanese militarism and that they looked to the United States for help in a new emergency. On September 1, 1951, a few days before the signing of the Japanese peace treaty at San Francisco, Australia, New Zealand, and the United States signed a tripartite security treaty providing that an armed attack on any one of the parties in the Pacific area would be dangerous to the others, and in such an event all would take action to meet the common danger under their constitutional processes. The area of armed attack included the metropolitan territory of the parties, the Pacific islands under their jurisdiction and their aircraft, armed forces, and public vessels in the Pacific. Indefinite in duration, the ANZUS Treaty, as it came to be called, provided for a Pacific Council of foreign ministers or their deputies which would be so organized that it could convene at any time. After the first meeting of the ANZUS Council in Hawaii, it was announced on August 7, 1952, that the necessary organization to im-

[50] Agreement between Australia and New Zealand, *Documents on American Foreign Relations, 1943-1944*, p. 629.

plement the treaty had been established, including provision for an annual meeting of the Council. In January, 1953, a Five-Power Staff Agency of Australia, New Zealand, Great Britain, the United States, and France came into existence for military staff discussions covering Southeast Asia. It lasted until the Manila Pact.

The crisis in Indochina and the Geneva settlement on Vietnam, Cambodia, and Laos, it has been pointed out, provided the impetus for the Southeast Asia Collective Defense Treaty of September 8, 1954, uniting the ANZUS powers with Great Britain, France, Pakistan, Thailand, and the Philippines. Under SEATO, Australia further defined her military commitments in Southeast Asia and the Southwest Pacific, although she did not approve of the looseness of the treaty terms. Since the Manila Conference Australia has sought to strengthen the pact in various ways. The Commonwealth has refused to recognize the People's Republic of China, and it has sought to prevent a war between Communist China and the United States over the offshore islands.

A major departure in Australian foreign policy was announced on April 1, 1955, when the government officially stated it was planning to station peacetime troops in Malaya. Although the decision produced one of the sharpest disputes on foreign policy in the House of Representatives, the House approved the policy by a vote of 55 to 41. From the strategic viewpoint Australia was shifting her pivot of defense from the Middle East where her forces had fought in the last two world wars to Malaya.[51] After the outbreak of the Emergency in June, 1948, Australia had not at first sent arms, apart, of course, from those owned by the British government. The embargo on Australian weapons was not lifted until August 2. The Australian Seamen's Union threatened to boycott the ships that took arms to Malaya. Sympathy in the emergency swung to the British side, especially when it was learned that Australian planters were becoming victims of the guerrillas. Airmen and aircraft were sent by the Canberra government to Malaya. Criticism in the Labour Party of stationing troops in the strategic area was based upon opposition to military service outside Australia in time of peace and upon the charge of maintaining "colonialism" in Malaya by their use.[52] The Australian soldiers were, in fact, shifted from Singapore

[51] It is significant that in the Suez crisis late in 1956 Australia and New Zealand were among the few powers sympathetic to the policy of Great Britain.

[52] The Labour Party, constituting the opposition to the Menzies government, has continued to urge the withdrawal of Australian forces from Malaya, has advocated the recognition of the People's Republic of China and its seating in the

to Penang, and Prime Minister R. G. Menzies asserted that they were helping self-government by checking the terrorists.

As for the American position on the stationing of Australian units in Malaya, the subject was discussed by Prime Minister R. G. Menzies and President Eisenhower in Washington in March, 1955. The former reported an "agreed statement" to the House of Representatives in Canberra on April 20; it was asserted that "in the general task of preventing further Communist aggression, the United States considered the defense of South-East Asia, of which Malaya is an integral part, to be of very great importance. . . . I was informed that though the tactical employment of forces was a matter which would have to be worked out in detail on the Services level, the United States considered that such effective coöperation was implicit in the Manila Pact."[53] At the Commonwealth Prime Ministers' Conference in London, January 31-February 8, Great Britain, Australia, New Zealand, and Pakistan had discussed the importance of Malaya in the defense of Southeast Asia.

Australia was also pleased by the British decision announced January 19 to prepare three airfields in the Federation of Malaya—Alor Star, Kuantan and Gong Kedak—for the possible use of jet aircraft. Other bases capable of such use have been built. In another area the Labour Party of Australia had suggested a regional security pact among Indonesia, the Netherlands, and Australia for the protection of Indonesia and New Guinea. Coöperation in a number of fields has occurred between Australian and Netherlands New Guinea. A significant statement was issued in Canberra and The Hague on November 6, 1957, indicating that more extensive coöperation could be expected in the interests of the advancement of the indigenous people on the island.

New Zealand in her foreign policy has traditionally been influenced by membership in the British Commonwealth, loyalty to Great Britain, geographical isolation, and an agricultural and pastoral economy. Moreover, New Zealand's Ambassador to the United States, L. K. Munro, has noted: "Weighty considerations

United Nations, and has called for a reshaping of policy toward SEATO. At a conference at Brisbane in March, 1957, the Party observed that "S.E.A.T.O. has failed to perform its basic functions, that it is fast becoming an instrument for bolstering reactionary regimes as in Thailand, and that the Liberal-Country Party Coalition Government [in Canberra] has contributed to S.E.A.T.O. ineffectiveness." Labour Policy on International Affairs, Brisbane Conference, March, 1957 (mimeographed).

[53] Statement by Prime Minister R. G. Menzies, *Current Notes on International Affairs,* Vol. 26 (April, 1955), pp. 289-290.

of geography and mutual interest have naturally brought Australia and New Zealand into the closest relations."[54] In fact, the latter tends to follow the former in many aspects of foreign policy. Japanese expansion in the Second World War proved to New Zealand the weakness of Great Britain in the Pacific and raised the question of basing the Dominion's forces in the Middle East. As in the case of Australia, New Zealand came to turn to the United States for security, the ANZUS Treaty and SEATO being examples.

The revolution in the Dominion's foreign policy became clear in February, 1955, after the Commonwealth Prime Ministers' Conference in London. New Zealand would provide ground forces, small as they were, for peacetime service in Malaya. In the event of a major war the Dominion's main Expeditionary Force would not go to the Middle East as in the last two global conflicts but to the Pacific. As a New Zealand scholar, Frederick L. W. Wood, has pointed out: "By a decision within the Commonwealth fraternity, the Southern Dominions became, for military purposes, Pacific and not European countries."[55]

In defining New Zealand's policy toward Southeast Asia, Minister of External Affairs T. L. Macdonald told the SEATO Conference at Bangkok on February 23, 1955: "By her adherence to the Manila Treaty and by her participation in the work of this Organization, New Zealand wishes to make clear her concern for the security and well-being of the peoples and the states of the Southeast Asian area. As a Pacific country, New Zealand cannot fail to take a vital interest in the future of Southeast Asia. Together with other countries, New Zealand is a member of the Colombo Plan which seeks, through capital aid and technical assistance, to promote the economic development of countries in this area. We believe that the Colombo Plan has proved both rewarding and fruitful."[56]

Indicative of New Zealand's interests in the "Near North" was the establishment in July, 1955, of the Office of the Commissioner for New Zealand in South-East Asia. Singapore was chosen as its location, for the city is conveniently situated and New Zealand has a special interest in the economic, political, and constitutional development of Singapore and of the Federation. The first Commis-

[54] L. K. Munro, "New Zealand and the New Pacific," *Foreign Affairs*, Vol. 31 (July, 1953), p. 642.

[55] Frederick L. W. Wood, "New Zealand and Southeast Asia," *Far Eastern Survey*, Vol. XXV (February, 1956), p. 25.

[56] Statement by T. L. Macdonald, *The Bangkok Conference of the Manila Pact Powers*, p. 21.

sioner, Foss Shanahan, was named New Zealand representative on the SEATO Council, formally accredited to the governments of Singapore, the Federation of Malaya, North Borneo, Brunei, and Sarawak, and in July, 1956, made Ambassador to Thailand with the establishment of a New Zealand embassy in Bangkok. Through an exchange of letters between the New Zealand Minister of External Affairs and corresponding officials in Cambodia, Laos, the Republic of Vietnam, and the Philippines, the Commissioner is received by those Asian governments for discussion on matters of mutual concern. The New Zealand Commission in South-East Asia, in addition to functions relating to a diplomatic and consular post and the promotion of trade, is concerned with negotiations under the Colombo Plan and to some extent the activities of SEATO.

The revolution in weapons has caused New Zealand as well as Australia to reconsider the question of armament. The White Paper of the United Kingdom on April 5, 1957, was related to a statement of Prime Minister R. G. Menzies in the House of Representatives on April 4 and a New Zealand White Paper on June 12. Although Great Britain was planning to maintain striking power that would be flexible and substantial in the region of primary interest to Australia and New Zealand it was clear that in the event of a general war she would not be able to preserve supply lines to Southeast Asia whereas the United States could. In the White Paper Britain planned to stress the development of nuclear weapons, delivered by planes, guided missiles, and rockets, and the maintenance of a central reserve in the United Kingdom capable of a high degree of mobility as the situation demanded. A mixed British-Gurkha force would be kept in Southeast Asia, a small navy based on Singapore, a garrison in Hong Kong and some air units. Australia, New Zealand, and Great Britain would continue to contribute to the Commonwealth Strategic Reserve in Malaya. Australia announced she would stress equipment and mobility rather than numbers in her military policy, and seek arms standardization in planes, artillery, and small weapons with the United States. New Zealand asserted she wanted to create a highly mobile unit for immediate overseas duty in the event of war and to send in the near future an infantry battalion and a squadron of Canberra jet bombers to Malaya as part of the Commonwealth Strategic Reserve.

10. *Regionalism in Southeast Asia*

The Asian Relations Conference, meeting in New Delhi from March 23 to April 2, 1947, was in many respects the predecessor of the Bandung Conference held a little over eight years later. Unofficial in nature, the Asian Relations Conference convened at a time when many of its participants did not come from sovereign states but were engaged in the process of achieving independence. Significant on the program, for instance, was a reception by the Viceroy of India and Lady Mountbatten at the Viceroy's House in New Delhi followed by a reception by Pandit Jawaharlal Nehru at 17, York Road. As far as Southeast Asia was concerned, only the Philippines along with Thailand was independent. In South Asia, India, Pakistan, and Ceylon had not yet emerged as sovereign states, and the Muslim League even boycotted the meeting. Obviously the ties uniting the Burmese, Indonesians, and many others at the Conference were those of a common determination to win freedom. Nationalist China for her part had only recently succeeded in ending the "unequal treaties." It may be, in retrospect, that in an atmosphere, technically unofficial, where many of the Conference delegates were united in a common goal of independence, the highest feasible degree of regional solidarity was reached.

In his opening speech Pandit Jawaharlal Nehru attempted to portray the sentiment of the delegates. He said:

> We live in a tremendous age of transition and already the next stage takes shape when Asia takes her rightful place with the other continents. It is at this great moment that we meet here and it is the pride and privilege of the people of India to welcome their fellow Asians from other countries, to confer with them about the present and the future, and lay the foundation of our mutual progress, well-being and friendship. . . . The old imperialisms are fading away. The land routes have revived and air travel suddenly brings us very near to each other. This Conference itself is significant as an expression of that deeper urge of the mind and spirit of Asia which has persisted in spite

of the isolationism which grew up during the years of European domination. As the domination goes, the walls that surrounded us fall down and we look at each other again and meet as old friends long parted. . . . There is a new vitality and powerful creative impulse in all the peoples of Asia. The masses are awake and demand their heritage. . . . Let us have faith in these great new forces and the things which are taking shape. Above all let us have faith in the human spirit which Asia has symbolised for these long ages past.[1]

The widespread participation at the Asian Relations Conference was indicative of deep interest. From Southeast Asia came representatives from Indonesia, the Philippines, Malaya, Burma, Thailand, the Democratic Republic of Vietnam, and the Cochin China, Laos, and Cambodia grouping. Even the Prime Minister of Indonesia, Sutan Sjahrir, eventually arrived. Messages were read from such leaders as Aung San of Burma and Ho Chi Minh of Vietnam. In addition to Nehru, Mahatma Gandhi addressed the Conference.

But it was clear that Asia did not speak with one voice, even though a great effort was made to keep controversial topics off the program. The unofficial Indian Council of World Affairs had organized the Conference and no resolutions were to be passed.[2] The Round Table Groups considered economic, cultural, racial, and labor topics along with "national movements for freedom" and the "status of women and women's movements." Neither India nor Nationalist China wanted to see the other emerge from the Conference as the leader of Asia. The Egyptians did not agree with the Palestine Jewish delegates. The representatives of Ho Chi Minh were aloof from those of Cochin China, Cambodia, and Laos. The Chinese at the Conference criticized the treatment of Chinese living in parts of Southeast Asia. The delegates from the Republic of Indonesia and the Democratic Republic of Vietnam, of course, were seeking the support of their fellow Asians but did not gain all that they wanted. Malaya's delegates, it should be noted, were largely radical labor leaders, anti-British, and not representative of the country. The Filipinos spoke warmly of the United States but the Thai took a generally passive role. None of the Southeast Asians wanted to be dominated by India or China.

[1] Speech of Pandit Jawaharlal Nehru, March 23, 1947, *Asian Relations, Being Report of the Proceedings and Documentation of the First Asian Relations Conference, New Delhi, March-April, 1947, passim.*

[2] The Indian Council of World Affairs in its new building at Sapru House in New Delhi has developed the most extensive research program in international relations in Asia. The work of the Council has received the sympathetic interest of Prime Minister Nehru.

Nevertheless, there was basic agreement on the need for freedom and for raising living standards. The Japanese slogan of "Asia for the Asiatics" was not adopted in any way. Coöperation among the nations of Asia and with the world was stressed. The meeting of the Asians at a conference of 28 participants including Egypt was in itself significant.

Only India, however, was truly interested in establishing a permanent organization. The Conference agreed in a resolution, an exception to the policy of no resolutions, to set up an Asian Relations Organization to foster study and understanding among the peoples and to further their well-being and progress. The Organization would consist of nongovernmental National Units, one for each country. A Provisional General Council was appointed with Nehru later elected President. Plans were made for a meeting of the Conference in China in 1949 but this event never took place. Also from the Conference arose an Institute of Asian Studies. But neither the Organization nor the Institute lived up to its expectations, especially in the eyes of the Indians.

In many respects Southeast Asia after the emergence of independent states with the end of Western empires in the area resembles the Balkans with the waning of Ottoman power. Viewing the situation in pessimistic terms, Charles A. Fisher, Senior Research Officer, Institute of Colonial Studies, University of Oxford, had warned in 1949:

> Basically the cause of this instability [in Southeast Asia] is the demographic immaturity of the area in which, since geographical position has made it a zone of passage, no lasting adjustment has yet been reached between land and state. To the political geographer the parallel with the Balkans is depressingly obvious. And both the historian who remembers that the Second Balkan War followed swiftly on the heels of the First, and the psychologist who recognizes the violence with which temporarily transferred hatreds may return to their original objects, will surely join the geographer in suggesting that the present phase of comparative friendliness among the peoples of Southeast Asia may be merely the prelude to a renewal of strife, should the Europeans finally withdraw from the area.[3]

Events will provide the answer.

It is true that Southeast Asia, as already indicated, does not possess many of the aspects necessary for regional unity. Racial and

[3] Charles A. Fisher, "Southeast Asia" in W. Gordon East and O. H. K. Spate, *The Changing Map of Asia*, p. 235.

religious, linguistic and cultural diversity characterizes the people. Geographic barriers add to the problems of communication and transportation. Old animosities have lingered among the peoples of the area. Since independence the countries of Southeast Asia have sought their security by alliance with the Western group or the Communist bloc of nations or by pursuing an uncommitted policy associated with India. Every state is clearly jealous of its newly won sovereignty. From the economic viewpoint the countries of Southeast Asia have largely competitive economies. Before the Second World War they tended to turn their backs to their neighbors in the area. Even the limited railway networks in different countries on the mainland led to ports which linked the metropolitan state and its tropical possession. Interchange of goods within the area was largely restricted to the movement of rice and such items as petroleum and coal. Guy Wint of the *Manchester Guardian* has frankly observed that "the domestic instability and disunity of the individual countries is probably . . . a graver threat to tranquillity than the international discords and confusion."[4] And Nathaniel Peffer of Columbia University has written that there is not "such a thing as Southeast Asia except for cartographic purposes. . . . It is a place on the globe where certain groups of people, holding little in common, live contiguous to one another."[5]

But there is another side of the problem of regionalism in Southeast Asia worthy of consideration. A common colonial background with the winning of independence in almost all of the areas concerned has produced within a relatively few years a certain identity of viewpoint. The defeat of the Western powers accompanied by the Japanese occupation created a somewhat common reaction in the various countries. Later the new states inherited many similar problems. In addition, modern means of transportation, especially the airplane, are breaking down geographic barriers. And the peacetime uses of atomic energy offer the hope of reducing some of the rivalry characteristic in the spread of the Industrial Revolution. The frequent meeting of Asian leaders at conferences for different purposes is creating personal relations conducive in many cases to understanding and tolerance. Indeed, as William Henderson of the Council on Foreign Relations has pointed out, "political power in the countries of Southeast Asia is now largely in the hands of

[4] Guy Wint, "South Asia, Unity and Disunity," *International Conciliation,* No. 500 (November, 1954), p. 189.

[5] Nathaniel Peffer, "Regional Security in Southeast Asia," *International Organization,* Vol. VIII (August, 1954), pp. 311, 312.

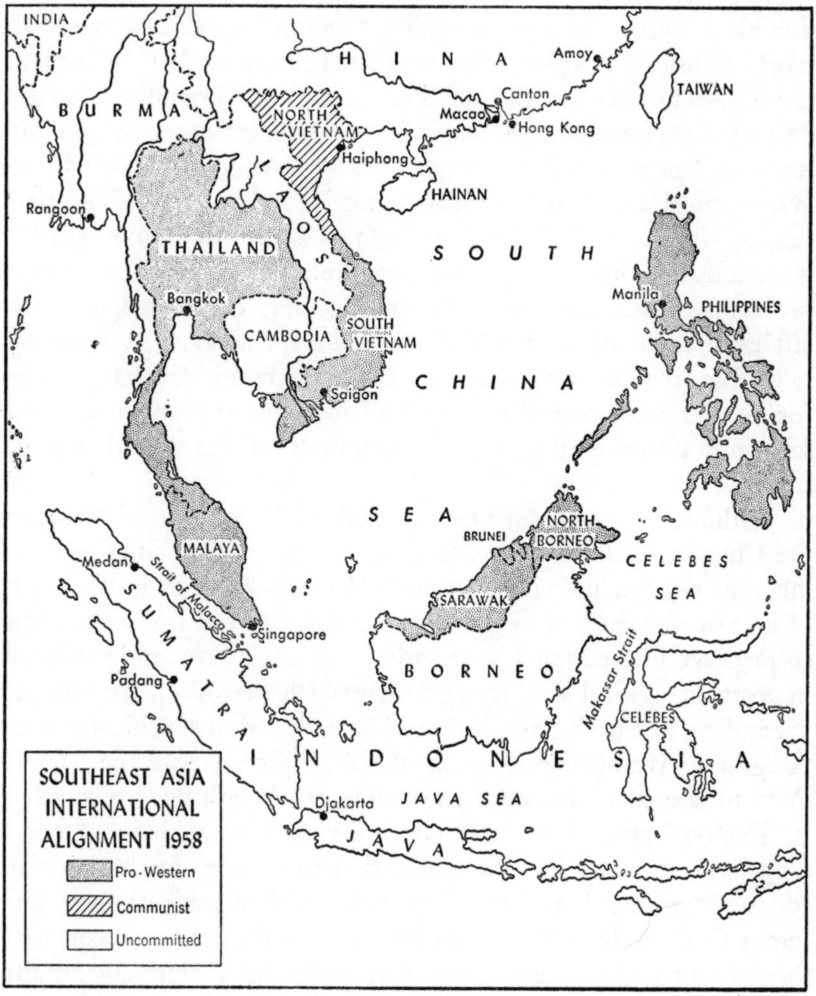
INDIA
C H I N A
Amoy
TAIWAN
B U R M A
Canton
Macao
Hong Kong
NORTH VIETNAM
Haiphong
HAINAN
L A O S
Rangoon
THAILAND
S O U T H
Manila
PHILIPPINES
Bangkok
CAMBODIA
SOUTH VIETNAM
C H I N A
Saigon
S E A
NORTH BORNEO
BRUNEI
CELEBES SEA
MALAYA
Medan
Strait of Malacca
SARAWAK
S U M A T R A
Singapore
B O R N E O
Padang
Makassar Strait
CELEBES
I N D O N E S I A
SOUTHEAST ASIA INTERNATIONAL ALIGNMENT 1958
Pro-Western
Communist
Uncommitted
Djakarta
JAVA SEA
J A V A

modernized élite groups that are themselves the product of the western impact. There exists among them a unity of outlook which transcends in large measure their undoubted racial, linguistic and cultural diversity."[6]

Regionalism, despite the absence as a general rule of precise geographical boundaries for a so-called "region," is well expressed in world politics by regional arrangements. Norman J. Padelford of the Massachusetts Institute of Technology has broadly defined a "regional arrangement in the sphere of international politics" in terms of "an association of states, based upon location in a given geographical area, for the safeguarding or promotion of the participants."[7] K. M. Panikkar, a prominent Indian, has observed: "It is obvious that States in the same geographical region have common problems, have similar interests and are more concerned with the affairs of each other than States situated far away. . . . Properly looked at, regional organizations should be considered as agencies for dealing with special problems of local interest and not as institutions usurping the security functions of the world organization."[8]

Although regionalism was not defined in exact legal terms in the Charter of the United Nations, Article 51, referring to "the inherent right of individual or collective self-defense" in the event of an armed attack until the Security Council has taken the steps to preserve international peace and security, is frequently utilized in postwar regional security agreements. Chapter VIII, Articles 52, 53, and 54, of the Charter, it should be added, deal specifically with "Regional Arrangements." The ANZUS Treaty and the Manila Pact, to cite examples, refer to Article 51, though not by name.

Regional agreements may cover a variety of subjects of common interest. They include in addition to security matters, social, economic, cultural, and political subjects. A combination of different fields of interest is frequent. It is significant, however, that there is no regional agreement that embraces exclusively all the states of Southeast Asia. At the same time they have widely participated in different meetings affecting their part of the world.

For purposes of classification, the role of Southeast Asia in re-

[6] William Henderson, "The Development of Regionalism in Southeast Asia," *International Organization*, Vol. IX (November, 1955), p. 464.

[7] Norman J. Padelford, "Regional Organization and the United Nations," *International Organization*, Vol. VIII (May, 1954), p. 204.

[8] K. M. Panikkar and Others, *Regionalism and Security*, pp. 2, 6.

gionalism may be analyzed with respect to security, political, and economic, social and cultural matters. With the approaching fall of China to the Communists President Quirino of the Philippines was especially interested in the establishment of a Pacific security pact. In July, 1949, he and Chiang Kai-shek met in Baguio and called for a union of states to meet the common danger. President Syngman Rhee of the Republic of Korea strongly supported the idea. With Chiang's visit to Rhee in August, both leaders urged Quirino to convene a conference to consider an anti-Communist pact. In an address to the American Senate on August 9 President Quirino called for a union of the free countries of Asia. Returning to Manila, he still hoped to get Burma, Thailand, Indochina, Indonesia, Nationalist China, the Republic of Korea, India, Pakistan, Ceylon, Australia, and New Zealand to attend a conference. Although Premier Pibul Songgram suggested a much smaller gathering of his own, Thailand came to support Quirino.

It became clear to the Philippine President that a large number of Asian states did not want to attend a conference with Nationalist China and South Korea. Moreover, the United States and India at the time did not favor a security pact, although Australia supported the idea. When Quirino agreed that his projected conference at Baguio would not include Nationalist China and South Korea and would not be anti-Communist in nature, a number of states accepted invitations. Opening on May 26, 1950, the Baguio Conference was attended by Indonesia, Thailand, and the Philippines from Southeast Asia and India, Pakistan, Ceylon, and Australia from outside the area. Social, economic, and cultural questions were discussed, but not military matters. Resolutions on the former question were passed but no organization for implementation was established.

The mutual defense pact between the Philippines and the United States signed August 30, 1951, the ANZUS Treaty among Australia, New Zealand, and the United States of September 1, and the security pact between Japan and the United States seven days later provided links in the defense chain in the western and southwestern Pacific. However, only the Philippines in Southeast Asia was involved, and both the Philippine-American and ANZUS treaties used the expression in the preamble "pending the development of a more comprehensive system of regional security in the Pacific Area."[9] There was some discussion in Manila of the Philip-

[9] Tripartite Security Treaty, *Documents on International Affairs, 1951*, p. 677.

pines' becoming a partner in the ANZUS pact, but the United States for one was opposed to increasing the membership of the tripartite treaty. President Quirino continued to press for the creation of a broad security pact, even in effect during his visit to Indonesia in July, 1952. Once more he found Indonesia, Burma, and India opposed.

Under the impetus of the Indochina crisis as it developed in the spring of 1954, followed by the Geneva settlement, the United States strongly supported the idea of a Southeast Asian security alliance. As is known with reference to the Asians, only the Philippines and Thailand within Southeast Asia and Pakistan in South Asia became signatories to the Manila Pact. Burma and Indonesia in addition to India and Ceylon, despite sincere efforts on the part of some powers, were not prepared to go to Manila and sign the projected treaty. However, the covering of Malaya and British Borneo through Great Britain's adherence and the including of Laos, Cambodia, and South Vietnam in the treaty area gave the Manila Pact wider territorial extent than might appear on the surface. In another direction Tengku Abdul Rahman of the Federation of Malaya has talked in terms of some kind of a Southeast Asia defense union, and Prime Minister S. W. R. D. Bandaranaike of Ceylon in June, 1956, suggested some form of regional defense organization, possibly among Burma, Indonesia, Malaya, Ceylon, Pakistan, and India.

The Asian Relations Conference in 1947, the New Delhi Conference on Indonesia in 1949, and the Bandung Conference of 1955 represent large meetings not primarily concerned with security. As already noted, the Asian Relations Conference was unofficial, and possibly marked the high tide of Asian solidarity. All the meetings focused world attention on the peoples of Asia and to a lesser extent of Africa who would play an increasingly greater role in global affairs. The New Delhi and Bandung conferences, however, did not lead to significant permanent organizations.

The second Dutch "police action" against the Republic of Indonesia in December, 1948, had prompted Nehru to call an emergency conference on the official level in New Delhi to marshal opinion from Africa to New Zealand against the Netherlands. From Southeast Asia came representatives of the Philippines and Burma with an observer from Thailand. The Indonesian Republic was represented and a Vietnamese was unofficially present. Thailand was apprehensive, as were some of the Western states, lest the Conference result in a third bloc of powers. Prime Minister Nehru in an opening speech on January 20 told the delegates and observers that the meeting was a regional conference under the United Nations framework to help the Security Council in its handling of the Indonesian question. It is certain that the Conference had a good influence in the final settlement of the problem.

In addition to making recommendations to the Security Council in the Indonesian-Netherlands conflict, the Conference urged the nations participating at New Delhi to keep in contact with one another through diplomatic channels or at the United Nations in order to preserve coöperation in the dispute. It was also agreed that the "participating Governments should explore ways and means of establishing suitable machinery, having regard to the areas concerned, for promoting coöperation within the framework of the United Nations."[10]

The Asian-African Conference at Bandung, April 18-24, 1955, was by far the most impressive of the so-called "regional" gatherings, especially in terms of its official participants. Yet despite a large measure of agreement, it should be recalled that the 29 countries did not agree among themselves on matters relating to the cold war. Southeast Asia's participation was the most extensive in history—all but Malaya and British Borneo. From Burma came Prime Minister U Nu, from Thailand Foreign Minister Prince Wan Waithayakon, from Cambodia Prince Norodom Sihanouk, from Laos Prime Minister Katay D. Sasorith, from the State of Vietnam Minister of Planning Nguyen Van Thoai, from the Democratic Republic of Vietnam Foreign Minister Pham Van Dong, from the Philippines General Carlos Romulo, and from Indonesia Prime Minister Ali Sastroamidjojo. In retrospect William Henderson has pointed out: "From the point of view of establishing once and for all the new status of the Asian and African nations in international politics and their claim to a place in the counsels of the nations, Bandung must be put down as a resounding success. . . . With respect to the concrete problems of contemporary international relations, the conference would appear to have been less fruitful."[11]

The Colombo Powers, it has been noted, consisting of Burma, Indonesia, Ceylon, Pakistan, and India, sponsored the Bandung Conference. The prime ministers of the five states had met twice

[10] Quoted in *Chronology of International Events and Documents*, Vol. V (21 January-3 February, 1949), p. 81.
[11] Henderson, *op. cit.*, p. 467.

in 1954 prior to attending the Bandung gathering. But even in a much smaller geographical area and with only five governments concerned, differences in foreign policy could not be removed. Basically all opposed the polarization of power and believed in co-existence with the People's Republic of China. But many issues divide them, examples being the Kashmir dispute between India and Pakistan and the latter's adherence to the Manila and Baghdad pacts. Pakistan did not even attend the New Delhi meeting in November, 1956.

In the United Nations the development of the so-called "Asian-Arab" or "Asian-African" bloc might be considered an example of regional coöperation within the global organization. Werner Levi of the University of Minnesota has pointed out that "there is very little collective political action among any large number of Asian nations outside the international agencies [especially the United Nations]."[12] It is not surprising that most of the viewpoints expressed at the Asian conferences are also voiced in the discussions of United Nations bodies. This observation is especially valid with the application of the principle of universality of membership to the world organization.

A number of other efforts in the field of political regionalism have occurred but the results have not been impressive. Aung San of Burma, before his assassination in July, 1947, gave consideration to a possible regional federation, and a number of delegates returning from the Asian Relations Conference in 1947 stopped in Rangoon to take up the matter. France suggested in the summer at a meeting of a Franco-Thai conciliation commission in Washington that a Pan-Southeast Asia Union of Thailand and Indochina be established with subsequent enlargement to other countries in the area. Thailand wanted an independent Cambodia and Laos to be members and France was not prepared at the time to accept the suggestion. In September unofficial representatives from Vietnam, Laos, Cambodia, Malaya, Indonesia, Burma, and Thailand set up in Bangkok a Southeast Asia League but it soon became clear that the League was in reality a Communist front to help Ho Chi Minh in Indochina. In August, 1954, Thailand expressed interest in some kind of a union of the Buddhist Mekong countries of Laos, Cambodia, and herself. Sjahrir of Indonesia has talked of Pan-Asian unity and Quirino of the Philippines of a Southeast Asia Union. As noted, a Pan-Malay Union stretching from Thailand to New

[12] Werner Levi, *Free India in Asia*, p. 61.

Guinea and including Malaya, Indonesia, the Philippines, and Borneo has been at times suggested.

In the field of economic, social, and cultural regional coöperation in Southeast Asia the record has been more impressive. The creation of the South-East Asia Command (SEAC) under Admiral Lord Louis Mountbatten at the Quebec Conference of President Franklin D. Roosevelt and Prime Minister Winston Churchill in August, 1943, was a wartime predecessor to many peacetime developments. At first the Command only included Ceylon, Burma, Thailand, Malaya, and Sumatra with Indochina an "additional area in which guerrilla forces operated" and northeastern India "under temporary operational control." On August 15, 1945, the boundaries of SEAC were extended to include Indochina south of the sixteenth parallel, all Borneo, and all Indonesia. The island of Timor, however, was excluded; the Philippines was under General Douglas MacArthur's Southwest Pacific Command; and northern Indochina was under the command of Generalissimo Chiang Kai-shek.

The occupation problems facing SEAC were extremely grave. Fighting the war was one consideration, administering the occupied areas another. In the latter situation economic and political matters came to the forefront. Writing later, Vice-Admiral the Earl Mountbatten of Burma said: "I had suggested that soon after the war either a Governor-General, or perhaps a Special Commissioner, should be appointed for the whole area of South-East Asia; but I admit that I had not thought out clearly, or in detail, what his functions would be."[13] Malcolm MacDonald arrived in Singapore on May 21, 1946, as Governor-General of Malaya and British Borneo, and Lord Killearn the previous March 16 as Special Commissioner. A British Defence Committee in South-East Asia was set up composed of the Supreme Commander, Governor-General and Special Commissioner.

It was in the economic field that Lord Killearn played a key role. Under him an Economic Organization came into being with an Economic Department, with monthly Liaison Meetings at first of representatives of British areas and then, in addition, of outside countries, and with special regional conferences on topics like nutrition, social welfare, fisheries, and statistics.

[13] Vice-Admiral the Earl Mountbatten of Burma, *Report to the Combined Chiefs of Staff by the Supreme Allied Commander, South-East Asia, 1943-1945*, p. 217.

In 1947 the United Nations Economic Commission for Asia and the Far East (ECAFE) came into existence. It has strengthened the regional approach to meeting common economic problems. By February, 1955, as far as Southeast Asia is concerned, Burma, Thailand, the State of Vietnam, Cambodia, Laos, the Philippines, and Indonesia were full members of ECAFE and Malaya and British Borneo an associate member. The Democratic Republic of Vietnam was not a participant. Other United Nations organizations are active in Southeast Asia.

In the Colombo Plan, another example of the regional approach in the broad sense to economic problems, the membership has expanded to include all Southeast Asia except the Ho Chi Minh republic. Meetings of the Consultative Committee of the Colombo Plan for Coöperative Economic Development in South and South-East Asia provide the facilities for the development of attitudes that are not restricted to national boundaries. The Colombo Plan Technical Coöperation Scheme with its Council and Bureau also promotes regional knowledge by its technical assistance programs.

Efforts of the United States through its aid program to produce a truly regional approach have not been very successful. In early 1955 it was known that the United States was planning to establish a regional fund for economic development in Asia. It was hoped the Asians would formulate projects for the use of the money. India called a conference in May at Simla to consider the matter as well as the subject of foreign aid. From Southeast Asia came delegates representing Cambodia, Laos, South Vietnam, Indonesia, Thailand and through Great Britain North Borneo, Sarawak, and Malaya. Burma refused to attend and the Philippines sent an observer. The Simla Conference failed to recommend a regional approach, for in the words of its conclusion: "The general view was that in the present stage of economic development of the Asian region and, having regard to the order of additional funds likely to be available, there would be no advantage in having an intermediate regional organization."[14] It stated that "country programs may continue to be bilateral as at present and strengthened so far as possible."[15] Nevertheless, the United States was hoping progress could be made in a few instances as in the case of the Mekong region. It had not been anticipated anyway that American assistance would not be largely bilateral. In fact, the contribution of the United States to

[14] *New York Times*, May 14, 1955.
[15] *Ibid.*

the Colombo Plan is the sum of its help for economic development to the member countries.

Southeast Asians have participated in a number of international activities that embrace subjects far apart in scope. In May, 1954, the Second Asian Games were held in Manila, bringing together athletes from a large number of countries, including Burma, Thailand, Cambodia, the State of Vietnam, the Federation of Malaya, Singapore, North Borneo, the Philippines, and Indonesia. Communists from Southeast Asia have attended Asian conferences under different guises in Calcutta and Peking. For instance, a famous Calcutta youth conference opening in early 1948 brought "youth" delegates from the Philippines, Indonesia, Vietnam, Burma, and Malaya in addition to other areas. In January, 1953, it will be recalled, the Asian Socialist Conference was held in Rangoon including Socialists from Burma, Indonesia, and Malaya. On May 31, 1947, an All-Asia Buddhist Convention met in New Delhi with Buddhists from Burma, Ceylon, Nepal, Tibet, China, and India present. On May 17, 1954, the Sixth Great Buddhist Council met just outside Rangoon including, as previously noted, Buddhists from Burma, Cambodia, Laos, Thailand, Vietnam, and Malaya within Southeast Asia. Moslem conferences were held in Karachi, for instance, in 1949 and 1951. Within Southeast Asia Pakistan and Indonesia joined the International Islamic Economic Organization founded in Karachi in November, 1949.

Trade union organizations in the Federation of Malaya, Singapore, Thailand, and the Philippines are included in the membership of the Asian Regional Organization, founded in 1951 with headquarters in Calcutta, of the International Confederation of Free Trade Unions. The ICFTU, organized in 1949 from the World Federation of Trade Unions (WFTU) which became Communist-dominated, maintains a branch office in Singapore. At the third conference of the WFTU in Vienna in 1953 labor representatives came from Burma, Indonesia, and the Democratic Republic of Vietnam. In November, 1949, the WFTU had staged an Asian Conference in Peking. The International Chamber of Commerce set up in 1952 a Commission on Asian and Far Eastern Affairs at New Delhi, and coöperation has come from groups in Burma, Indonesia, the Philippines, Thailand, and Indochina. National Parliamentary Groups belonging to the Inter-Parliamentary Union from Southeast Asia are found in Thailand, Indonesia, Burma, the

Republic of Vietnam, and the Philippines. An Asian Legal Consultative Committee met for the first time on April 18, 1957, in New Delhi, Indonesia and Burma among those being represented. The International Rubber Study group has a membership that includes among others Burma, Cambodia, Indonesia, Thailand, the Republic of Vietnam, the United Kingdom, and the United States. The International Tin Study group includes with others Thailand, Indonesia, the United States, and the United Kingdom. Other organizations are the Pan Pacific Women's Association, the Pacific Area Travel Association, and the Pacific Science Association. The Institute of Pacific Relations, with its national councils in different countries, promotes research and holds conferences. Despite the diversity of the many activities, participants from Southeast Asia often find a common denominator of interest, a factor that can become important under favorable circumstances in the development of regionalism.

II. *Southeast Asia in the United Nations*

The work of the United Nations has a direct impact in Southeast Asia and most of the countries of the area by their membership in the world organization have a voice through their own right in it. In a region where the new states are very conscious of their sovereignty, the machinery of the United Nations in New York as well as in Southeast Asia provides a way of meeting the challenge of national sensitivities. It is clear that in many cases the new states of the region would rather receive economic and technical aid on a multilateral than a bilateral basis. And it is easier for a sovereign state to accept the decision of an international body like a council or a commission of the United Nations than the verdict of a single government. The United Nations has also served to center world attention on a number of problems directly concerning a particular country in Southeast Asia. Discussion in the General Assembly on West New Guinea as well as on the Kuomintang forces in Burma are cases in point. The United Nations played an important part in the birth of Indonesia. Thailand in 1954 brought about discussion in the Security Council on the war in Indochina. It should be noted that the role of the Security Council of the United Nations in Korea caused the member states in Southeast Asia to take a stand they might not in all cases have otherwise chosen. The United Nations tends to "globalize" international problems.

Within Southeast Asia Bangkok has become a center of United Nations activity. In fact, the government of Thailand has donated a building, Sala Santitham, for the use of the world organization. The headquarters of the United Nations Economic Commission for Asia and the Far East is in Bangkok; here also are FAO's regional office for Asia and the Far East, ICAO's Far East and Pacific office and UNICEF's Asia regional office. The TAB (Technical Assistance Board) has a regional representative, and WHO a Thailand representative in Bangkok. Also present is an information officer of the United Nations covering the areas of Cambodia, Laos, and Thailand. It is clear that the Bangkok government is encouraging the world organization to look to Thailand as a regional center of activities in Southeast Asia. Prince Wan Waithayakon told the General Assembly during the general debate in 1955 that the Bangkok radio began its daily programs by broadcasting articles from the Thai constitution, the United Nations Charter, and the Universal Declaration of Human Rights.

Apart from Thailand, the Technical Assistance Board has resident representatives in Southeast Asia in Indonesia, Burma, and the Philippines. In some instances the personnel is large and the office very important; Burma is a case in point. Information officers of the United Nations are found in Djakarta and Manila in addition to Bangkok. WHO has a regional office for the Western Pacific in Manila and an Epidemiological Intelligence Station in Singapore and UNESCO has a Science Coöperation Office in Djakarta. Various conferences under United Nations auspices covering diverse topics and involving different Asian states have been held.

ECAFE is one of the most important United Nations bodies functioning in Southeast Asia. Although in existence only since March 28, 1947, when the Economic and Social Council of the United Nations created it, the Commission has been called "the economic parliament of Asia." The original members were the United States, Great Britain, France, the Soviet Union, Nationalist China, Australia, the Netherlands, India, and two states in Southeast Asia, Thailand and the Philippines. The change in membership is a good index of political development in Asia and of the expansion of ECAFE activities. By the end of 1953 the full membership had grown to 15 with the addition of Burma, Indonesia, Pakistan, New Zealand, and Afghanistan. There were now 9 associate members who fully participated in the discussions of the Commission but who did not vote in plenary sessions—Ceylon, Cambodia, Malaya and British Borneo, Nepal, Hong Kong, Laos, the Republic of Korea, the State of Vietnam, and Japan. By the middle of 1955 the associate members had become full members with the exception of Malaya and British Borneo and Hong Kong. Burma and Indonesia had, it might be pointed out, earlier passed through the stage of associate membership.

Dr. P. S. Lokanathan, when Executive Secretary of ECAFE, observed that "the evolution of the rights and responsibilities of the associate members, especially of countries which were non-self-governing, is one of the most interesting chapters in the history of the Commission."[1] Here some of the associate members gained their initial experience in international relations. Election to associate and full membership involved in a number of cases international controversy. The Economic and Social Council has the power of electing the full members and ECAFE the associate ones. The Netherlands at the time opposed on technical grounds the admission of the Republic of Indonesia to associate membership. France sponsored the State of Vietnam, and the Soviet Union the Democratic Republic of Vietnam as associate members. The USSR has also favored the seating of the People's Republic of China in place of the Republic of China and has received support from some other members of ECAFE including India. The election of Japan to associate membership was not unanimous, and the Korean question was reflected in ECAFE's discussions. The Economic and Social Council on April 22, 1954, favored Cambodia, Laos, and the State of Vietnam for full ECAFE membership, after the completion of certain formalities, by a vote of 13 to 2 with 3 abstentions in each case. The general resolution including Ceylon, Japan, the Republic of Korea, Nepal, and the three states in Indochina with respect to full membership was passed by 14 to 2 with 2 abstentions. The actual geographical scope of ECAFE, determined by the Economic and Social Council, embraces an area from the People's Republic of Mongolia to Australia and from Iran to Papua but not including the four areas mentioned.

Significant are the growth and role of the regional members as compared with the nonregional ones. In March, 1947, the latter outnumbered the former by 6 to 4; at the end of 1953 the figures were 8 to 7 respectively; by the middle of 1955 the regional members had 15 and the nonregional 7. It is clear that the regional members of ECAFE believed that they should have a stronger voice in problems affecting their area. In 1951 the Commission concluded that "the member countries of the Commission not in the region would be willing, as a general rule, to refrain from using their votes in opposition to economic proposals predominantly concerning the region which had the support of a majority of the countries of the region."[2]

[1] Dr. P. S. Lokanathan, "ECAFE—The Economic Parliament of Asia," *The Indian Year Book of International Affairs, 1953,* Vol. II, p. 9. Dr. Lokanathan asserts that the Prime Minister of Indonesia in an opening address at the previous session of the Commission used the expression "economic parliament of Asia."

[2] Report of the Economic Commission for Asia and the Far East (seventh session) to the Economic and Social Council, United Nations, Economic and Social Council, *Official Records,* Thirteenth Session, Supplement No. 7, p. 41.

The first headquarters of ECAFE was located in Shanghai but later it was moved to Bangkok. Sessions of the Commission are now held on an annual basis at different cities in Asia and the Southwest Pacific. The secretariat is basically a part of the Department of Economic Affairs of the United Nations with the professional members UN officers. It has an executive secretary, six divisions, and a Bureau of Flood Control and Water Resources Development. The Commission established a Committee on Industry and Trade with standing subcommittees on iron and steel, mineral resources development, trade, and electric power; and an Inland Transport Committee with inland waterway, highway, and railway subcommittees. There are, of course, a number of *ad hoc* working parties. In 1957 it was agreed to end the Committee on Industry and Trade, creating a Committee on Industry and National Resources and raising the subcommittee on trade to committee level.

The tasks of the Economic Commission for Asia and the Far East are officially stated in the following terms:

> To initiate and participate in measures for facilitating concerted action; to make or sponsor investigations and studies of economic and technological problems and development; to undertake or sponsor the collection, evaluation and dissemination of economic, technological and statistical information; to perform such advisory services as countries of the region may desire, provided that these do not overlap with the United Nations technical assistance programs; to assist the Economic and Social Council, at its request, in discharging its functions within the region in connection with any economic problems including problems in the field of technical assistance.[3]

ECAFE is in no position to give orders or to enforce decisions; it can take no action regarding any country without the approval of its government. But within the mandate of the "economic reconstruction and development of the region" and "the maintenance and strengthening of . . . economic relations" among the countries and with the world, ECAFE can be as fully utilized as its members may desire.

Major activities of the Commission and its secretariat relate to agriculture, industrial development, flood control and water resources, trade and finance, technical training and assistance, research and statistics, and inland transport. At first the greater part of the Commission's work was devoted to research and statistics. Economic planning by the respective governments required reliable data and

[3] *Helping Economic Development in Asia and the Far East, The Work of ECAFE,* United Nations Department of Public Information, p. 6.

here ECAFE could provide assistance. The Commission's *Economic Survey of Asia and the Far East*, published each year, the monographs and other items have furnished valuable information on the area. As of late 1953 ECAFE through its Inland Transport Committee had convened two regional conferences on statistics and one on flood control, and through its Committee on Industry and Trade one mineral resources conference and two trade promotion conferences. Working parties had been established, including one on small-scale and cottage industries and handicraft marketing, one on the mobilization of domestic capital, and one on the financing of economic development.

Dr. C. Hart Schaaf, while Deputy Executive Secretary of ECAFE, in an analysis of its contributions has stated that the Commission "(a) has furthered economic development, (b) has strengthened the United Nations, (c) has both assisted and tempered the rise of nationalism, (d) has helped elucidate some of the issues of the cold war, (e) has been worth its cost, and (f) can perhaps expect to increase its impact and usefulness partly in proportion to its willingness to make its recommendations increasingly specific."[4]

In the field of technical assistance the impact of the United Nations is significant. The Economic and Social Council adopted in August, 1949, a resolution, supported in November by the General Assembly, calling for an Expanded Program of Technical Assistance for Economic Development of Under-Developed Countries. The financing would come from voluntary contributions each year by governments of countries members of the United Nations or one of its specialized agencies. The United Nations was already giving technical aid under its regular budget in public administration, social welfare, and economic development. In 1950 the Technical Assistance Administration (TAA) was set up with operational responsibility for the aid under the regular budget and under the Expanded Program. Participation in the latter case is by the United Nations and seven specialized agencies—FAO, ILO, WHO, UNESCO, ICAO, WMO, and ITU. The International Bank for Reconstruction and Development and the International Monetary Fund coöperate. A Technical Assistance Board with an executive chairman and the executive heads of the eight participating units or their representatives coördinates the work carried out by the organ-

[4] C. Hart Schaaf, "The United Nations Economic Commission for Asia and the Far East," *International Organization*, Vol. VII (November, 1953), p. 470.

izations under the Expanded Program and reports to a Technical Assistance Committee (TAC). The latter is a standing committee of the Economic and Social Council and reports to the Council itself. The resident representative in a given country is responsible to the Technical Assistance Board.

In 1955 the United Nations Expanded Program provided technical assistance worth $706,950 to Burma, $180,776 to Cambodia, $778,542 to Indonesia, $73,592 to Laos, $53,465 to Malaya, $35,325 to North Borneo, $357,057 to the Philippines, $24,798 to Sarawak, $50,378 to Singapore, $563,394 to Thailand, and $104,100 to the Republic of Vietnam. In the same year Burma pledged to the Expanded Program the equivalent of $18,000, Cambodia $2000, Indonesia $65,790, Laos $1429, the Philippines $55,000, and Thailand $40,000. The State of Vietnam pledged $7500 in 1954. It should be stressed that substantial local contributions, apart from payment into the central account, have been made.

Some states in Southeast Asia not only receive experts in certain fields or get scholarships for individuals to study abroad, but have been sending specialists of their own for services elsewhere. Included here are Burma, Indonesia, Thailand, the Philippines, and the Federation of Malaya. In 1952 scholars and fellows appointed by the United Nations or its specialized agencies for study abroad numbered among the new states of Southeast Asia 35 from Burma, 6 from Cambodia, 51 from Indonesia, 10 from Laos, 64 from the Philippines, and 5 from the State of Vietnam. In the same year Burma received 62 experts, Cambodia 4, Indonesia 64, Laos 3, the Philippines 27, and the State of Vietnam 5.

Guy Wint, in summarizing the contributions of technical assistance under the United Nations, has noted: "The sum of its efforts had been very much like those of the Colombo Plan. The individual governments have been aided. The number of technicians in the area has been increased. Ideas have been popularized. New concepts have been introduced. The Board has helped in creating a new climate of opinion in which all the countries of the region urgently desire to employ up-to-date knowledge in the solution of their problems."[5] The twelfth General Assembly adopted a resolution to establish a fund of $100 million increasing the scope of the assistance.

FAO, it should be stressed, has an important part in Southeast

[5] Guy Wint, "South Asia, Unity and Disunity," *International Conciliation*, No. 500 (November, 1954), p. 183.

Asia, often in coöperation with other United Nations activities. It has regional organizations—the Indo-Pacific Fisheries Council, the International Rice Commission, and the Asian-Pacific Forestry Commission.[6] FAO sponsors regional meetings and seminars on specific problems. For instance, a land reform seminar was held in Bangkok in November and December, 1954, with widespread participation from Southeast Asia. The organization has a research and publication program. UNESCO is active in Southeast Asia with National Commissions, programs, and experts. To cite an example, a pilot project in primary education was carried out, largely under UNESCO technical supervision, at Bayambang in the Philippines, and another in Chachoengsao, Thailand. In August, 1955, a regional International Music Council was held in the Philippines. ILO holds regional and technical conferences in Asia. As an example of its work, ILO in 1954 provided assistance in occupational safety to Burma and Thailand and in occupational health to Indonesia. WHO has regional committees and conferences. In 1954 malaria-control projects in Southeast Asia, having the help of WHO personnel, were operating in Cambodia, Sarawak, the Philippines, Indonesia, and Burma. An interregional conference on malaria for Southeast Asia and the Western Pacific was held in the Philippines.

ICAO has its own regional air navigation meetings. In 1953 a South East Asia and Limited South Pacific Regional Air Navigation Meeting was held in Melbourne, Australia. As of the end of 1955, ICAO had technical assistance program missions in Indonesia, the Philippines, and Thailand. WMO has six regional associations with conferences and representatives. One of the associations is for Asia and another for the Southwest Pacific. ITU also has direct interests in Southeast Asia, for telecommunications obviously are not restricted to any part of the world. The International Bank for Reconstruction and Development had made loans before the end of 1957 to Thailand, the Philippines, and Burma; a general survey mission was sent to Malaya in 1954 and later another went to Thailand. UNICEF or the United Nations Children's Fund, a special body of the Economic and Social Council, has been active in Southeast Asia. In 1954 Burma, Thailand, Cambodia, the Federation of Malaya, Singapore, Brunei, North Borneo, Sarawak, the Philippines, and In-

[6] The Indo-Pacific Fisheries Council was established in February, 1948, and came to include within Southeast Asia Burma, Cambodia, Indonesia, the Philippines, Thailand, and the Republic of Vietnam. The International Rice Commission established in November has similar membership within the area with the addition of Laos.

donesia contributed to the Fund, and the area profited in return. On a per capita basis the ten biggest government contributors in the world included Brunei, Thailand, and Sarawak.

There are numerous joint efforts, it is clear, among the United Nations agencies functioning in Southeast Asia. ECAFE, for instance, works in close coöperation with FAO. The Commission has sent observers to regional meetings of FAO in Asia and the Far East and the latter is represented at meetings of ECAFE. A joint agricultural unit has been set up in the ECAFE secretariat. In certain activities ILO, UNESCO, and the International Monetary Fund have also worked with ECAFE. Dr. P. S. Lokanathan has pointed out: "The nature of these relations covers a wide field: preparation of joint studies, inter-secretariat working parties, exchange of documentation, working out of joint programmes, submission of reports for the special consideration of the Commission, mutual representation at meetings of the Commission and of the specialized agencies, and so on."[7] The work of the United Nations resident representative is in itself an indication of the numerous activities of the world organization in a country where he may be serving.[8]

The governments of Southeast Asia have been glad to receive the individuals sent by the United Nations. In the Philippines the government once sought the transfer of ECAFE headquarters to Manila. In Indonesia and Burma the United Nations personnel has got along well with the Indonesians and Burmese. Different countries have their United Nations Associations or equivalents to promote the world organization. In the Philippines, for instance, the association stages an elaborate United Nations Day observance.

Although the impact of the United Nations in Southeast Asia has been significant, Indonesia, Burma, the Philippines, Thailand, Cambodia, Laos, and the Federation of Malaya are having their influence in the world organization. As of the spring of 1957 all those then members had "permanent missions" to the United Nations although Cambodia and Laos had the same "permanent representative" as ambassador to the United States. At the commemoration in San Francisco, June 20-26, 1955, of the tenth anniversary of the signing of the Charter, statesmen from Southeast Asia expressed their viewpoints on the world organization. General Carlos P.

[7] Lokanathan, *op. cit.*, p. 13.

[8] For a detailed account, for instance, of United Nations activities in Burma, see the entire issue of *Burma Weekly Bulletin*, November 1, 1956, or in the Philippines, the description in the *Manila Chronicle*, April 28, 1956.

Romulo of the Philippines stated on June 22: "Asia and Africa take the United Nations seriously—very seriously indeed. Asia and Africa are looking to the principles enshrined in our Charter to underwrite their newly-won independence. Asia and Africa know that there can be no real security against aggression or colonialism or imperialism, old and new, unless the cause of independence and inter-dependence among nations is tied together. And if the United Nations is going to safeguard the rights of the smaller nations, proper responsible authority will have to be provided."[9] U Pe Kin of Burma asserted on the same day: "In spite of the unhappy cleavage between the East and the West which all lovers of peace deplore, it [the United Nations] forms the only platform in the world on which representatives with clashing ideologies can meet and attempt to reconcile what appeared to be irreconcilable viewpoints."[10]

On June 23 Prince Wan Waithayakon of Thailand stressed that the United Nations "has not only come to Thailand but has come to work among the Thai people. . . . I think the splendid work of the United Nations in the field of technical assistance deserves to be better known. It is appreciated by all the nations concerned; and, in my opinion, it constitutes a true form of coöperation, characteristic of the United Nations and calculated to bring home to the people of each country the determination of the United Nations 'to promote social progress and better standards of life in larger freedom.' "[11] On the next day Dr. Sudjarwo Tjondronegoro of Indonesia asserted: "The painful truth is that this Organization, or rather part of its membership, seems to shun colonial issues whose solution is so imperative for the promotion of freedom and peace among nations. Sometimes it seems as if we were afraid of freedom, afraid of equality among nations, afraid of the true meaning of our Charter. It seems that man's mind has lagged behind the revolutionary changes prompted by the wars and revolutions of the past decades, events that no one can reverse. I indeed sometimes wonder what is really needed: a revision of the Charter or a revision in the minds of men."[12]

Up to the opening of the tenth session of the General Assembly

[9] Speech of General Carlos P. Romulo, *Tenth Anniversary of the Signing of the United Nations Charter, Proceedings of the Commemorative Meetings*, p. 102.

[10] Speech of U Pe Kin, *Tenth Anniversary of the Signing of the United Nations Charter*, p. 145.

[11] Speech of Prince Wan Waithayakon, *Tenth Anniversary of the Signing of the United Nations Charter*, p. 183.

[12] Speech of Dr. Sudjarwo Tjondronegoro, *Tenth Anniversary of the Signing of the United Nations Charter*, p. 232.

in 1955, only the Philippines had been elected to two of the councils of the United Nations. The Republic had served on the Economic and Social Council and on the Trusteeship Council. Thailand had served on the latter body. General Romulo had been chosen president of the fourth General Assembly. At the tenth session of that body Yugoslavia was elected to the Security Council for two years but there was a "gentleman's agreement," by no means unanimous, that the Philippines would be selected for the second year of the term upon the resignation of the original member. Indonesia was elected to the Economic and Social Council, and Burma to the Trusteeship Council upon the admission of Italy to membership in the United Nations. After the eleventh General Assembly met, the Philippines, over strong Russian objections arising largely from geographical considerations, was elected to finish the term begun by Yugoslavia on the Security Council. Prince Wan Waithayakon was chosen president of the General Assembly.

The present selection of the nonpermanent members of the Security Council by the General Assembly with regard to "equitable geographical distribution" has met with protests from Asians and Africans. This opposition was well expressed at the Bandung Conference. Although not written into the Charter, practice, beginning with a "gentleman's agreement" in London in 1946, led to the election of an Arab or Middle Eastern member, a British Commonwealth state, a Central or Eastern European member, a Western European state, and two Latin American countries.[13] Efforts are also made in elections to the Economic and Social Council and Trusteeship Council to afford geographical distribution. Obviously the growth in United Nations membership, especially in Asia and Africa, is creating pressure for a change in the present geographical approach of representation.

A revision of the United Nations Charter might, *inter alia*, give Asian-African members greater representation in the councils of the United Nations. Article 109 of the Charter provides that if a general conference to review it has not been held before the General Assembly's tenth session, the proposal to call one should be put on the agenda. The conference would then be held if the meeting was favored by any seven of the Security Council and a majority

[13] Under the Statute of the International Atomic Energy Agency, as approved, subject to ratification, in the fall of 1956, it is interesting to note that provision was made for representation from North America, Latin America, Western Europe, Eastern Europe, Africa and the Middle East, South Asia, Southeast Asia and the Pacific, and the Far East.

of the General Assembly. In Southeast Asia the Philippines, Indonesia, Thailand, and Burma have indicated that they favor a review of the Charter. Thailand believed a conference should be held to determine whether a revision was necessary. Burma thought the General Assembly in its tenth session should provide for a conference to review the Charter leaving the date open for future determination. The General Assembly on November 21, 1955, finally decided by a vote of 43 including the four Southeast Asian members to 6 with 9 abstentions to call a conference to review the Charter but at an "appropriate" time. Subsequent discussions occurred on the topic.

Within the United Nations an Asian-African bloc has come to function.[14] Although the exact number has varied, the membership before December, 1955, included Egypt, Syria, Lebanon, Iraq, Saudi Arabia, and Yemen from the Arab League, Indonesia, the Philippines, Burma, and Thailand from Southeast Asia, and Iran, Afghanistan, Turkey, Pakistan, India, Ethiopia, and Liberia. Turkey has not been a consistent participant, and Ethiopia and Liberia have not always been very active. From the new members of the United Nations elected in December, 1955, are a number of recruits—Jordan and Libya of the Arab League and Ceylon, Nepal, Cambodia, and Laos. Certain other states who later entered the United Nations—the Sudan of the Arab League, Morocco, Tunisia, Ghana, Japan, and the Federation of Malaya—are also participants. In fact, the Asian-African bloc may become too large for action; Ghana has been interested in an African grouping.

In December, 1950, the bloc assumed definite being as a result of events arising from the outbreak of the Korean War the previous June. Both the Soviet Union and the United States were looking for support among Asian-African nations and the latter realized their advantages in the situation. India has long been active in the work of the bloc although certainly does not dominate it. Some of the members, however, look to her for leadership. Informal in nature,

[14] For a valuable article on bloc voting, see M. Margaret Ball, "Bloc Voting in the General Assembly," *International Organization*, Vol. V (February, 1951), pp. 3-31. Benjamin Akzin notes: "One might say that the blocs are largely a response of individual States to the public and quasi-parliamentary procedures current in international organizations, procedures which have replaced to some extent the proceedings typical of the classical diplomatic conference meeting behind closed doors, and that the blocs serve *mutatis mutandis* those functions which rudimentary and loosely-organized clubs and factions have played at an early stage of the development of parliaments." Benjamin Akzin, *New States and International Organizations*, p. 155.

the Asian-African bloc has no real organization through which to operate; the chairmanship actually rotates on a monthly basis; in 1956 a subcommittee of Egypt, Ethiopia, India, Indonesia, and Pakistan was created on Algeria. The bloc is not united by any political alliances; the participants tend to be individualistic. At the same time the members of the Asian-African group see certain advantages of maneuver, especially in voting in the General Assembly on some matters, as a result of their coalition. A case in point is the use of the caucus and the effort to elect afterwards certain Asians and Africans.

The strongest unifying force in the coalition is opposition to imperialism and racialism; another common denominator is interest in economic development. The bloc has also sought to mediate in the cold war between the East and the West. It has coöperated in problems relating to such countries as Algeria, Morocco, Tunisia, and the Union of South Africa. It was active in the Suez crisis of late 1956 and early 1957. The members have been far less united on cold war issues such as the Korean conflict and the seating in the United Nations of the People's Republic of China. In general, the bloc exerted a moderating influence conducive to the Korean armistice of July, 1953. At the same time it has been noted that "there is real reason to fear that a multi-national grouping such as the Arab-Asian bloc may end in generating more passion than wisdom, and more aggravations than solutions."[15]

In the eleventh General Assembly the members from Asia and Africa actually tended to divide into three voting groups: the participants of the Baghdad and/or Manila pacts—Pakistan, Iran, Iraq, Turkey, the Philippines, and Thailand—plus Ethiopia and Liberia—often coöperating with the United States; India and Egypt with Afghanistan, Indonesia, Syria, Yemen, Saudi Arabia, and the Sudan less often coöperating; and a floating group of 11—Burma, Cambodia, Laos, Japan, Libya, Ceylon, Jordan, Tunisia, Morocco, Lebanon, and Nepal.[16] It should be pointed out that with the admission of Ghana and the Federation of Malaya the total number comes to 29; recommendations on important questions in the General Assembly are made by a vote of two-thirds of the members (82 in all) present and voting. Thus the Asian-African states have a collective veto if they agree.

[15] Sherman S. Hayden, "The Arab-Asian Bloc," *Middle Eastern Affairs*, Vol. 5 (May, 1954), p. 153.

[16] Ghana was not admitted until March 8, 1957. Japan was admitted on December 18, 1956.

In the finances of the United Nations, Indonesia, Burma, Thailand, the Philippines, Cambodia, Laos, and the Federation of Malaya pay their portion of the expenses of the organization and its specialized agencies. The scale of assessments for the 1956-1958 period of the United Nations itself, as approved by the General Assembly on December 15, 1955, but later altered, was 0.56 percent for Indonesia, 0.45 for the Philippines, 0.18 for Thailand, and 0.11 for Burma. These figures may be compared, for instance, with Sweden, Denmark, and Norway—1.59, 0.72 and 0.54 respectively. States from Southeast Asia contribute at different percentages for various specialized agencies. For instance, during 1956 for ILO the percentage for Indonesia was 0.43, the Philippines 0.37, Thailand 0.22, and Burma 0.16; and for FAO, Indonesia 0.71, the Philippines 0.57, Thailand 0.23, and Burma 0.14. Provision was made in 1955 by the General Assembly for states not then members of the United Nations but participating in some of its activities to make a financial contribution at a certain percent toward the respective expenses. The percent for Laos was 0.04, Cambodia, 0.04, and Vietnam 0.17. New memberships, of course, altered the general scale of assessments.

Difficult as it is to classify the many items on the agenda of the General Assembly, reference to its six main committees and the *ad hoc* or special political committee (made a main one in 1956) adding some help, subjects may be considered under political and security, colonial, and economic and social headings. Even here the topics should be selective, for the discussion each year is voluminous. Nevertheless, the members of the United Nations from Southeast Asia have greater interest in certain aspects of the work of the United Nations, and geographically they have tended to show great concern for Africa as well as for Asia. A definite pattern has developed in their attitudes toward many of the items that come before the United Nations. At the same time it should be noted that a number of important subjects like the war in Indochina did not reach as such the agenda of the General Assembly.

In terms of political and security issues the cold war between the East and the West has predominated. The United Nations role in the Korean War including the resolutions of the General Assembly on the People's Republic of China as an aggressor and the embargo on strategic materials to her and North Korea marked the greatest effort to date of the world organization in the Far East.

Laos and Cambodia joined Thailand and the Philippines with Burma and Indonesia abstaining in a vote of the eleventh General Assembly on January 11, 1957, supporting a resolution of the United States reaffirming the objectives of the United Nations in Korea. With the 1953 armistice in the peninsula the question of the seating of the People's Republic of China in the United Nations became increasingly urgent. On September 20, 1955, for instance, the General Assembly decided during the tenth regular session not to consider proposals to exclude the representatives of the Republic of China or to seat representatives of the People's Republic of China. The vote was 42 in favor of the resolution, 12 opposed, and 6 abstaining. Among the 12 were Burma and Indonesia in Southeast Asia and among the 42 the Philippines and Thailand. In the general debate of the General Assembly Burma had frankly stated she did not believe that Communist China would be seated during the present session but she wondered how long the United Nations could continue its policy without doing itself serious and possibly irreparable harm. The Bandung Conference, she believed, had clearly revealed Communist China's respect for the United Nations. On November 16, 1956, the eleventh General Assembly by a vote of 47 to 24 with 8 abstentions took a stand similar to that of the tenth on the Chinese representation issue; the final vote in the twelfth General Assembly, September 24, 1957, was 48 to 27 with 6 abstentions.

On the burning question of admitting new members into the world organization during the tenth General Assembly, Thailand, Indonesia, Burma, and the Philippines had very decided views. When the final votes were taken in the General Assembly on December 14, 1955, relative to the admission of 16—Cambodia, Laos, Ceylon, Nepal, Jordan, Libya, Italy, Finland, Ireland, Austria, Spain, Portugal, Romania, Bulgaria, Hungary, and Albania—Thailand, Burma, and Indonesia favored the admission of all and the Philippines abstained on Albania, Bulgaria, Hungary, and Romania. In the general debate of the General Assembly Thailand had favored the admission of Cambodia, Ceylon, Japan, Jordan, Laos, Libya, Nepal, a unified Vietnam, Austria, Finland, Ireland, Italy, Portugal, and Spain. Indonesia had indicated she believed every state should be given the chance to live and work in the framework of the United Nations. Burma had asserted she favored the admission of all applicants under any generally accepted formula except the divided states. She made the exception in the latter cases because she believed their admission would add to the difficulties of unification. The Philippines along with Burma, Indonesia, and Thailand had supported a draft resolution of the *Ad Hoc* Political Committee calling for the admission of 18 states, those subsequently admitted on December 14 plus Japan and the Mongolian People's Republic. All of the countries of Southeast Asia belonging to the United Nations, including Cambodia and Laos, voted in favor of the admission of Japan in December, 1956, and of the Federation of Malaya in September, 1957.

In the field of disarmament United Nations members from Southeast Asia as well as all the states of Indochina had a basic outlook that they expressed well at Bandung. There can be no doubt of their concern over the subject. At the tenth session of the General Assembly a resolution on disarmament was passed on December 16, 1955, by a vote of 56 to 7. Burma, Indonesia, Thailand, and the Philippines voted with the majority; Cambodia and Laos did not take part. The Disarmament Commission's Subcommittee of Canada, France, the United Kingdom, the United States, and the Soviet Union was urged to continue to try and reach accord on a comprehensive disarmament plan, priority being given to early agreement on and carrying out of President Eisenhower's proposals for "mutual aerial inspection" and exchange of military blueprints and Premier Bulganin's plan for setting up "control posts at strategic centres." The Soviet bloc voted against the resolution, although its final draft incorporated amendments proposed by the USSR, India and jointly by Pakistan, Mexico, and Costa Rica.

In the Palestine issue in the United Nations the states of Southeast Asia have not been so active as they have been on questions involving their own part of Asia. Moreover, the Asian-African bloc as a whole has been more effective on colonial issues like Tunisia, Morocco, and Algeria. Indonesia, the Federation of Malaya, and Pakistan as Moslem states in Southeast and South Asia are more sympathetic to the Arabs than Burma, Thailand, Cambodia, and Laos which as Buddhist countries do not have religious ties to the Middle East. All of them, however, want a peaceful solution to the controversy between Israel and the Arab states, for a conflagration in the Middle East might spread to the entire world. The Bandung Conference, it should be recalled, supported "the rights of the Arab people of Palestine, and called for the implementation of the United Nations resolutions on Palestine and of the peaceful settlement of the Palestine question."[17]

Earlier in a General Assembly of the United Nations the Philip-

[17] The Final Communiqué of the Asian-African Conference, Press Release, Permanent Mission of the Republic of Indonesia to the United Nations.

pines had in the end favored the partition of Palestine; Thailand had opposed it in committee but did not vote in the plenary session. Burma voted against the admission of Israel to the United Nations, the Philippines supported the measure, and Thailand abstained. Burma and the Philippines favored the internationalization of Jerusalem but Thailand again abstained. Indonesia, not to mention Cambodia, Laos, and the Federation of Malaya, were not yet members of the United Nations when these votes were taken.

The "Uniting for Peace" resolution, a highly significant measure of the General Assembly, was supported by all four members from Southeast Asia at the time. Planned as a means for effective action by the General Assembly if the Security Council were paralyzed by the veto in the event of a threat to or breach of the peace or an act of aggression, the Uniting for Peace measure won support on November 3, 1950, by a vote of 52 to 5 with 2 abstentions. Among the provisions a Peace Observation Commission was established which could report on areas of international tension, and a Collective Measures Committee was set up to advise United Nations members on steps that could be used to strengthen peace and security. The members of the Peace Observation Commission for 1951 and 1952, named in the resolution, did not include any state from Southeast Asia, but Burma and the Philippines were named to the Collective Measures Committee. The Committee was extended for another year by the General Assembly on January 12, 1952, Indonesia abstaining, and Burma, Thailand, and the Philippines being with the majority; subsequent extensions were voted. The Peace Observation Commission, of course, has continued in existence.

In both the Suez and Hungarian crises of late 1956 and 1957 the Uniting for Peace resolution, following the use of the veto in the Security Council, was invoked. At the time, the six members of the United Nations from Southeast Asia did not favor the Anglo-French-Israeli invasion of Egypt and all of them eventually were critical of Soviet intervention in Hungary. On December 12, 1956, Thailand, the Philippines, Burma, and Laos with Cambodia and Indonesia abstaining condemned Soviet military intervention in Hungary and asked for the withdrawal "under United Nations observation" of Russian troops. The vote on the General Assembly resolution was 55 to 8 with 13 abstentions. In an important decision on January 10, 1957, all the members from Southeast Asia were found on the majority side—59 to 8 with 10 abstentions—of a resolution calling for the establishment of a five-nation committee to investigate the Hungarian situation, to hear the testimony of refugees, and to enter Hungary. All the Southeast Asian members favored the cease-fire in the Suez crisis, were sympathetic to the creation of a United Nations Emergency Force, and wanted the withdrawal of Anglo-French-Israeli forces from Egypt. They were pleased when France and Britain completed their evacuation of the Suez area on December 22, 1956, and Israel later withdrew from Egyptian territory.

The states of Southeast Asia in the United Nations have been especially interested in the colonial questions that have come before the world organization. During the tenth session of the General Assembly the topic of colonialism played an extremely important role, the admission of 16 new members in December, 1955, followed by others adding strength to the so-called "anticolonial" powers. The questions of the Middle East and Hungary stood out in the eleventh General Assembly but colonialism was associated with each.

The case of Morocco had been discussed in the General Committee of the General Assembly in November, 1951, after Egypt requested that the topic "Violation of the Principles of the Charter and of the Declaration of Human Rights by France in Morocco" be placed on the agenda. The Committee decided to recommend to the Assembly that consideration of placing the item on the agenda be postponed "for the time being." On December 13 the General Assembly adopted the Committee's recommendation by a vote of 28 to 23 with 7 abstentions. It is significant that the 23 votes came from Burma, Indonesia, and the Philippines in Southeast Asia, the six members of the Arab League in the United Nations, the five members of the Soviet bloc and Yugoslavia, three Latin American states (Ecuador, Mexico, and Guatemala), and the Asian and African members, outside Southeast Asia, Afghanistan, Ethiopia, India, Iran, and Pakistan. Thailand and Liberia as well as China were among those who abstained. The 28 members supporting the resolution included France, the United States, Great Britain, the Netherlands, Belgium, Australia, and New Zealand as well as Israel and Turkey. In many respects the pattern of voting was indicative of things to come when North African problems—Morocco, Tunisia, and Algeria—and certain other colonial issues came before the United Nations.

On September 3, 1952, Afghanistan, Burma, Egypt, India, Indonesia, Iran, Iraq, Lebanon, Pakistan, the Philippines, Saudi Arabia,

Syria, and Yemen requested that the question of Morocco be placed on the agenda of the seventh session of the General Assembly. The latter body adopted a resolution on December 19 by a vote of 45 to 3 with 11 abstentions urging France and Morocco to "continue negotiations on an urgent basis." Burma, the Philippines, Indonesia, and Thailand voted with the majority. On July 9, 1953, the same 13 states with the addition of Thailand and Liberia requested a consideration of the Moroccan issue at the eighth General Assembly; and on August 21, the 15 states asked the president of the Security Council to call an urgent meeting of the Council to investigate the trouble in Morocco. At meetings of the latter body to consider placing the item on the agenda, France denied the competence of the United Nations on the subject, and on September 3 it was decided not to put the topic on the agenda. On November 3 the General Assembly failed to approve by a two-thirds vote a draft resolution on Morocco adopted by the First Committee. The vote on the operative part was 32 in favor and 22 against with 5 abstentions. Among the 32 were the four members from Southeast Asia.

On July 28, 1954, 14 members, Liberia being the missing one, requested that the Moroccan question be placed on the agenda of the ninth General Assembly. On December 17 the Assembly adopted a resolution, 55 to 0 with 4 abstentions, postponing further consideration for the time being as it was reported that negotiations between France and Morocco would be initiated. On July 20, 1955, 15 members asked the Secretary-General to employ his good offices to end the bloodshed in Morocco. Six days later they requested that the question appear on the agenda of the tenth General Assembly. A resolution generally like the one of the previous year was passed on December 3. Independence for Morocco removed the controversy from the United Nations.

The Tunisian question before the world body has had a somewhat similar experience. On April 2, 1952, Afghanistan, Burma, Egypt, India, Indonesia, Iran, Iraq, Pakistan, the Philippines, Saudi Arabia, and Yemen called the attention of the situation in Tunisia to the Security Council. After discussion the Council on April 14 decided not to place the item on the agenda. On June 20 the 11 Asian-African states with Lebanon and Syria requested a special session of the General Assembly to take up the Tunisian question, but the required majority of members approving the meeting could not be obtained. Although Indonesia, Burma, and the Philippines favored it, Thailand abstained on the question. The 13 states on

July 30 asked that the Tunisian matter be placed on the agenda of the seventh General Assembly. On December 17 the Assembly after long debate in the First Committee adopted a resolution, 44 to 3 with 8 abstentions, hoping "the parties will continue negotiations on an urgent basis."

On March 16, 1953, the 13 members plus Liberia drew the attention of the president of the General Assembly to the situation in Tunisia. On July 9 the 14 plus Thailand requested that the matter be placed on the agenda of the eighth General Assembly. On November 11, the Assembly failed to adopt a resolution on Tunisia by a two-thirds majority, the vote being 31 in favor and 18 against with 10 abstentions. All four members from Southeast Asia voted with the 31. On July 28, 1954, the 14 members, Liberia the missing one, asked that the Tunisian question be placed on the agenda of the ninth General Assembly. The Assembly adopted a resolution on December 17 by 56 to 0 with 3 abstentions whereby it noted "with satisfaction" that negotiations by the parties concerned had begun and were still in progress. The resolution postponed "for the time being further consideration" of the item. The Tunisia question did not appear on the agenda of the following General Assembly, for home rule was given the country.

The case of Algeria brought about the temporary withdrawal of France on September 30, 1955, from the tenth General Assembly. In the past when Tunisia and Morocco had been discussed in the First Committee France had refused to participate, but when Algeria was placed on the agenda she took more drastic action. The Paris government considered Algeria a part of metropolitan France. Fourteen Asian-African states had requested that the question of the North African area be placed on the agenda of the tenth General Assembly. The General Committee on September 22 voted not to inscribe the topic but the General Assembly eight days later reversed the decision by a vote of 28 to 27 with 5 members abstaining. In such a crucial vote the attitude of the powers is especially important. The 28 were Afghanistan, Burma, Egypt, India, Indonesia, Iran, Iraq, Lebanon, Liberia, Pakistan, the Philippines, Saudi Arabia, Syria, Thailand, and Yemen from Asia and Africa, the five members of the Soviet bloc and Yugoslavia, the Latin American states of Argentina, Bolivia, Costa Rica, Guatemala, Mexico, and Uruguay, and Greece. Opposed were Australia, Belgium, Brazil, Canada, Chile, Colombia, Cuba, Denmark, the Dominican Republic, Ecuador, France, Haiti, Honduras, Israel, Luxembourg, the Netherlands, New Zealand, Nicaragua, Norway, Panama, Peru, Sweden, Turkey, South Africa, the United Kingdom, the United States, and Venezuela. Abstaining were China, El Salvador, Ethiopia, Iceland, and Paraguay. It is significant that all Asian members except China, Israel and Turkey voted with the majority. After the vote France announced she would consider "null and void" any recommendations in connection with Algeria, and the French delegation left the Assembly Hall.

The seriousness of the French step was realized in the United Nations and ardent efforts were made at conciliation behind the scenes. The General Assembly adopted unanimously on November 25 a procedural motion made by V. K. Krishna Menon of India "not to consider further the item entitled 'The Question of Algeria,'" therefore being "no longer seized of this item" on the agenda of the present session. France subsequently returned to participation in the Assembly's work.

As the Algerian situation deteriorated in 1956, the conflict between the French and the Front of National Liberation in Algeria mounting, 16 Asian-African states including Burma, Indonesia, and the Philippines sent a letter on April 16 to the Security Council deploring the conditions in the North African area but not requesting action. On June 18, 13 Asian-African states appealed to the Security Council to take up the Algerian matter without delay. Thailand and Indonesia were among the 13 but Burma and the Philippines did not support the request. On June 26 the Security Council at a meeting decided by a vote of 7 to 2 with 2 abstentions not to place the item on its agenda. Fifteen members of the Asian-African bloc later requested that the Algerian question be placed on the agenda of the eleventh General Assembly. From Southeast Asia were Burma, Indonesia, and the Philippines. Eighteen Asian-African states including Burma and Indonesia sponsored a resolution calling upon France to recognize the right of the Algerian people to self-determination and urging her and the people of Algeria to enter into negotiations at once for a cease-fire and a general settlement with the assistance of the Secretary-General of the world organization. Thailand, the Philippines, and Japan sponsored a milder resolution. On February 15, 1957, the General Assembly unanimously adopted, France not participating in the vote, a resolution hoping "in a spirit of coöperation, a peaceful, democratic and just solution" would be reached "through appropriate means" conforming to the principles of the Charter. The twelfth General

Assembly after long committee debate adopted on December 10, by a vote of 80 to 0 with France not participating, a mild resolution on Algeria seeking talks on the issue.

In another part of Africa, the areas of the former Italian Empire, the states of Southeast Asia, members of the United Nations, have shown an interest. Under the Treaty of Peace with Italy, signed February 10, 1947, if the United States, the Soviet Union, France, and Great Britain could not agree on a disposal of the Italian colonies in Africa—Libya, Eritrea, and Italian Somaliland—within a year from the coming into force of the peace treaty, the General Assembly could decide the issue with the four powers accepting the decision. On September 15, 1948, the latter informed the United Nations that they could not agree on a settlement.

A complex pattern of voting resulted in the General Assembly, reflecting the diverse interests of different members and groups of states. Burma wanted the independence of a united Libya—Cyrenaica, Fezzan, and Tripolitania—after a period of United Nations trusteeship with France and Italy excluded from any administrative authority. The Philippines favored the same with the United Kingdom as the Administering Authority until the United Nations could find a better answer. Burma believed part of Eritrea should be annexed to Ethiopia and the rest placed under a United Nations trusteeship without Italy or France having any administrative role. The third General Assembly was not able to agree on a solution and the matter was postponed to the fourth. In her actual voting in the General Assembly, Burma had opposed putting Cyrenaica, Fezzan, and Tripolitania under the temporary trusteeship respectively of Britain, France, and Italy until the establishment of an independent Libya in ten years, giving Italy a trusteeship over Somaliland with a view toward independence, and making Eritrea a part of Ethiopia except for the Western Province. The Philippines abstained on the Cyrenaica clause, opposed the Fezzan, Tripolitania, and Somaliland sections and favored the Eritrean part. Thailand supported the Cyrenaica clause, abstained on the Fezzan and Tripolitania sections, and favored the Somaliland and Eritrean parts.

The fourth session of the General Assembly on November 21, 1949, reached a solution to the Italian colonial problem. Burma, Thailand, and the Philippines agreed on the Libyan and Somaliland aspects, but the Philippines abstained on the Eritrean while Burma and Thailand voted in favor. Under the settlement a unified Libya would be independent not later than January 1, 1952; Italy would have a trusteeship over Somaliland, but the area would have its independence at the end of ten years from the approval of the trusteeship agreement by the General Assembly; and a commission of Burma, Guatemala, Norway, Pakistan, and the Union of South Africa would make proposals for a solution to the Eritrean question after travel in the area. The Philippines was named to an Advisory Council to the Administering Authority for Somaliland. On December 2, 1950, the General Assembly adopted a resolution recommending that Eritrea become an autonomous unit within Ethiopia under the sovereignty of the latter's Crown. The United Nations Commission for Eritrea had disagreed, Burma believing that the area should be a self-governing unit in a federation with Ethiopia.

The states of Southeast Asia who belong to the United Nations have been interested in all the trust territories of Africa—Togoland, the Cameroons, and Tanganyika, each under Great Britain as the Administering Authority, Togoland and the Cameroons, each under France, and Ruanda-Urundi under Belgium.[18] Togoland in particular has been a subject of consideration. In June, 1954, the United Kingdom submitted a memorandum to the Secretary-General observing that the Gold Coast was in the final stage of constitutional evolution to independence. When it became sovereign, the United Kingdom would no longer be able from the constitutional viewpoint to administer the trust territory of Togoland as an integral part of the Gold Coast. The British government suggested that the General Assembly request the Trusteeship Council to make recommendations for the consideration of the Assembly at its tenth session under which the viewpoints of the inhabitants of the British trust territory could be ascertained, especially as regards unification with the Gold Coast.

The question of Togoland, once a German colony, has, in fact, been discussed in the United Nations for a number of years. The Ewe tribes living in British and French Togoland and the Gold Coast have sought one government. Later there was stress on the unification and independence of Togoland.

On December 14, 1954, the General Assembly decided that steps should be taken to find out the desires of the Africans regarding their future, and requested the Trusteeship Council to

[18] The trust territories outside Africa, also of interest, are those of the Pacific Islands under the United States, Western Samoa under New Zealand, New Guinea under Australia, and Nauru under the United Kingdom, New Zealand, and Australia.

send a special mission to both British and French Togoland to make a study of the situation. During the debate in the Fourth Committee the Philippines opposed the integration of British Togoland and the Gold Coast, Indonesia favored an independent, united Togoland, and Burma wanted the people in both Togolands to be consulted. A regular visiting mission left for West Africa in August, 1955, studied conditions in British and French Togoland, and reported to the Trusteeship Council. On October 30 the mission called, *inter alia*, for a plebiscite at an early date in British Togoland to decide its political future. The Trusteeship Council considered the report and made recommendations to the tenth General Assembly.

On December 15 the world body by a vote of 42 to 7 with 11 abstentions called for a plebiscite without delay in British Togoland to decide whether it should join the Gold Coast upon the latter's independence or be separated under British administration from the Gold Coast with the maintenance of the trusteeship "pending the ultimate determination of its political future." The British government would organize the plebiscite in consultation with a United Nations Plebiscite Commissioner and it would be held under the supervision of the world organization. By a vote of 45 to 6 with 9 abstentions the Assembly also supported the visiting mission in its views that the carrying out of the political reforms planned by France in French Togoland would help in enabling the inhabitants to determine their future status at an early time. It recommended that the consultation of the population be made under the supervision of the United Nations and asked the Trusteeship Council to make a special study on the matter, working with France as Administering Authority and reporting, if possible, to the eleventh General Assembly. In both votes Burma, Thailand, and the Philippines were with the majority and Indonesia abstained.

The plebiscite in British Togoland was the first of its kind in a trust territory. It was held on May 9, 1956, and 58 percent of the registered voters favored union with an independent Gold Coast. The eleventh General Assembly by a vote of 64 to 0 with 9 abstentions approved the union, thus ending one of the trusteeships. Burma was among the sponsors of the measure. All the states of Southeast Asia, members of the United Nations, favored it although Laos was absent at the time of the voting. The Assembly also voted 53 to 16 with 7 abstentions to send a commission of six members to French Togoland to examine the situation there resulting from the application of a new French statute. Laos, Cambodia, Thailand, and the Philippines voted with the majority while Burma and Indonesia abstained. A majority of the Togolese who voted in October, 1956, had favored independence in the French Union to maintenance of the trusteeship. The referendum was not held under the auspices of the United Nations, despite a French request for observers, and the trusteeship committee of the eleventh General Assembly withheld recognition of the change. The twelfth General Assembly appointed a commissioner to supervise elections in 1958 in the area. The developments in Togoland, it might be pointed out, provide a precedent for the British and French Cameroons, once a German colony. The former is administered as a part of Nigeria, which is soon to receive independence.

The Southeast Asian members of the United Nations find agreement in opposing many of the policies of the Union of South Africa. They agree that the latter should place within the trusteeship system of the world organization South West Africa which is a mandated territory of the Union of South Africa granted by the League of Nations. On December 3, 1955, the General Assembly for the ninth time urged South Africa to place the area under trusteeship. The vote was 43 to 2 with 9 abstentions. The tenth General Assembly also passed nine other proposals regarding South West Africa. Thailand has long served on the Assembly's committee on this area. On December 6 the world body adopted a resolution against the policies of *apartheid* in the Union, the resolution being the third passed in recent years. Significantly the General Assembly decided to end the Commission on the Racial Situation in South Africa established in 1952, the provision not receiving the necessary two-thirds vote (33 to 17 with 9 abstentions). A draft resolution to continue the Commission had been introduced by Afghanistan, Bolivia, Burma, Egypt, Ethiopia, Haiti, India, Indonesia, Iran, Iraq, Lebanon, Liberia, Pakistan, the Philippines, Saudi Arabia, Syria, and Yemen, and in the final vote had also been supported by Thailand, the Soviet bloc, Greece, Yugoslavia, and eight Latin American states. South Africa had walked out of the tenth General Assembly on November 9 in protest against what she considered United Nations interference in her internal affairs. On December 14 the General Assembly adopted 46 to 0 with 8 abstentions a resolution urging Pakistan, India, and the Union of South Africa to pursue negotiations directed at effecting a settlement of the question of the treatment of individuals of Indian origin in the Union. Indonesia, Burma, Thailand, and the Philippines were with the majority. Once again this was a problem about which the General Assembly had for some time been passing similar resolutions.

In the case of Cyprus the states of Southeast Asia were not inclined to survey the problem entirely from the colonial viewpoint. On August 16, 1954, Greece had requested that the issue of self-determination for the people of Cyprus be put on the agenda of the ninth session of the General Assembly. As about 80 percent of the population of the island, a Crown Colony of Great Britain, was Greek in origin as well as language, the Athens government believed self-determination would mean union with Greece (*enosis*). On December 14 and 15 the First Committee discussed the issue. Great Britain, Australia, New Zealand, and the Union of South Africa stressed that the subject was a matter of domestic jurisdiction. It was asserted that one member of the United Nations was in effect trying to get sovereignty over the territory of another. Greece was aided in the debate by Indonesia and the Philippines from Southeast Asia; Turkey supported the British position. The Committee approved a resolution, later adopted by the Assembly, deciding "not to consider further the item" as it did not appear appropriate "for the time being" to adopt a resolution on the subject. In the committee stage the Philippines and Indonesia voted in favor of the key part of the resolution and Burma and Thailand abstained.

On July 23, 1955, Greece requested that the Cyprus issue be placed on the agenda of the tenth General Assembly. The General Committee rejected the inscription of the item, the Assembly on September 23 accepting the decision despite a full debate. The vote was 28 to 22 with 10 abstentions. Burma, Indonesia, and the Philippines abstained and Thailand voted with the majority. Both Greece and Great Britain requested that the Cyprus controversy be placed on the agenda of the eleventh General Assembly. On February 26, 1957, it adopted 57 to 0 with Afghanistan abstaining a resolution calling for a "peaceful, democratic and just solution" and expressing a "hope" for a resumption of negotiations on the subject. The controversy would again appear in the United Nations.

In the Trusteeship Council the Philippines, Thailand, and Burma have had an opportunity to influence policy. Indonesia as of 1956, not to mention Cambodia and Laos, had not yet served on the body. All members, however, have had an impact in the work of the General Assembly as it relates to dependent peoples. Indonesia, the Philippines, and Burma, for instance, have served on the Assembly's Committee on Information from Non-Self-Governing Territories. In the trust territories the United Nations has recognized responsibilities founded upon agreements made between the Administering Authorities and the world organization. Chapters XII and XIII of the Charter deal with the international trusteeship system and the Trusteeship Council. One of the basic objectives of the trusteeship system is to promote in the trust territories "the political, economic, social, and educational advancement of the inhabitants" and "their progressive development towards self-government or independence as may be appropriate to the particular circumstances of each territory and its peoples and the freely expressed wishes of the peoples concerned, and as may be provided by the terms of each trusteeship agreement."[19] Under Chapter XI, dealing with non-self-governing territories, members having such responsibilities are obligated "to develop self-government" and under Article 73 (e) to send regularly to the Secretary-General "for information purposes, subject to such limitation as security and constitutional considerations may require, statistical and other information of a technical nature relating to economic, social, and educational conditions in the territories" other than those to which Chapters XII and XIII apply.[20]

In the General Assembly the colonial powers and Administering Authorities have as a rule found themselves in opposition to most Asian and African states on matters relating to Chapter XI. The latter have generally wanted political information included with that required by Article 73 (e); they have favored keeping the Assembly's Committee on Information from Non-Self-Governing Territories and have wanted it to mention areas by name in its recommendations; they have urged the General Assembly to decide the point at which a metropolitan power no longer has an obligation to report on a former non-self-governing territory and they have suggested that indigenous inhabitants of the areas concerned be attached to the delegations of the administering powers. It is obvious that efforts to increase the control of the United Nations over non-self-governing territories are considered by the

[19] Charter of the United Nations, *The Department of State Bulletin*, Vol. XII (June 24, 1945), pp. 1129-1130.

[20] *Ibid.*, p. 1129.

colonial powers as attempts to interfere in their domestic jurisdiction. Belgium, for instance, has boycotted the Committee on Information from Non-Self-Governing Territories since 1952.

In the trust territories most of the Asian and African states want to speed the evolution to self-government or independence; they have urged the Administering Authorities to set terminal dates for the achievement of the desired goal. Likewise they have wanted qualified indigenous inhabitants from the trust territories to participate in the work of the Trusteeship Council.

As the Asian-African members have real voting power in the General Assembly, they have urged resolutions that have been passed directed at the meeting of their desiderata as regards the trust territories and the non-self-governing territories. From Southeast Asia, Burma, Indonesia, the Philippines, Thailand, Cambodia, and Laos have generally supported this policy. The colonial powers and Administering Authorities, however, being in control of the areas concerned, have in effect decided what to do about the resolutions of the General Assembly.

In a closely related aspect of United Nations activity, most of the Asian and African powers have sought to have the Commission on Human Rights of the Economic and Social Council incorporate in the draft covenants on human rights the theory of self-determination. The United Nations in various of its organs has considered the right of self-determination since 1950, and the General Assembly on February 5, 1952, specifically decided that the Commission on Human Rights should incorporate the theory in the draft covenant or covenants. The United States and a number of other powers have taken the position that the question of self-determination should be given a thorough study to determine its precise meaning, but most of the Asian and African states believe that self-determination is so important that it needs to be immediately implemented without waiting for a precise definition. The tenth General Assembly on December 14, 1955, decided to continue consideration of the two draft covenants on political and civil rights and on economic, social, and cultural rights at the eleventh session and also to postpone to the same time recommendations regarding "international respect for the right of peoples and nations to self-determination." Further delaying action was taken by the eleventh General Assembly. Meanwhile the Universal Declaration of Human Rights, adopted by the Assembly in December, 1948, remains as a landmark.

Economic and social matters have greatly interested the states of Southeast Asia who belong to the United Nations. Once more it is difficult to classify the items that might be considered in this broad category. United Nations activities relative to the peaceful uses of atomic energy certainly have great economic and social implications. On December 8, 1953, President Eisenhower suggested to the General Assembly that an International Atomic Energy Agency be organized associated with the United Nations to devise ways for using fissionable material for "peaceful pursuits." On December 4, 1954, the General Assembly adopted unanimously in the end a resolution hoping "the International Atomic Energy Agency will be established without delay" and calling for "an international technical conference of Governments" under the aegis of the United Nations on the peaceful uses of atomic energy through the means of international coöperation. The motion had been submitted by Australia, Belgium, Canada, France, the Union of South Africa, the United Kingdom, and the United States but was modified by amendments. Portugal, not yet a member of the United Nations, had participated in prior discussions. These eight states constituted in the non-Communist world the ones which either had atomic energy programs well advanced or raw material resources definitely available.

From August 8 to 20, 1955, the international conference requested by the General Assembly met in Geneva. Over a thousand papers were submitted by the scientists and experts; 84 countries had been invited—the 60 members at the time of the United Nations and the 24 nonmembers who participated in the specialized agencies—and 73 nations attended. On December 3 the General Assembly unanimously passed a resolution expressing satisfaction over the Geneva International Conference on the Peaceful Uses of Atomic Energy and recommending that another one be held in two or three years. At the same time the General Assembly noted with satisfaction the progress made toward negotiation on the draft statute for an International Atomic Energy Agency. Burma, Indonesia, and the Philippines took an active part in the discussion.

The actual creation of the Agency was quite naturally a matter of considerable interest in Southeast Asia. Although the states of the region were not participants in the drafting of the preliminary statute, the Philippines, Indonesia, the Republic of Vietnam, Cambodia, Thailand, and Burma attended the world conference at United Nations headquarters from September 20 to October 26,

1956, where a revised statute was approved. Laos declined an invitation to be present. On October 26 Cambodia, the Republic of Vietnam, Thailand, the Philippines, and Indonesia signed the statute; later Burma and Laos followed. Indonesia was chosen to be a member of the Preparatory Commission to make the necessary plans for setting up the new agency, Vienna becoming the chosen site.

Meanwhile international coöperation on the peaceful uses of atomic energy involving the states of Southeast Asia was progressing along other lines. By July 11, 1955, the United States had signed agreements with 24 states permitting them to get from the former fuel necessary to operate research reactors. Section 123 of the Atomic Energy Act of 1954 enabled the United States to make such agreements. In Southeast Asia, Burma, Thailand, the Philippines, and Indonesia had been contacted about the possibility of their signing. The Philippines made a bilateral agreement on June 14 and Thailand on July 7. The United States also has a program for installing research reactors abroad.

At a meeting of the Consultative Committee of the Colombo Plan in Singapore on October 20 the American representative, John P. Hollister, discussed the use of the atom "for economic and social progress in Asia." He proposed the establishment in the area under the auspices of the Colombo Plan of a center devoted to nuclear research and training, and stated the United States was prepared "to contribute substantially toward it," possibly a small power reactor. He stressed that the "burden of setting up the center and carrying it forward, and the obligation of staffing it, would rest with the Asian members of the Colombo Plan. The fruits of the effort would also belong to Asia."[21] As already indicated, the United States in March, 1956, selected the Philippines as the location of the center.

In a related field, the United Nations has been concerned over the effects of atomic radiation on human beings. India on April 8, 1954, proposed to the Disarmament Commission a standstill agreement on further hydrogen bomb explosions. Eleven members of the Marshallese Congress Hold-Over Committee along with 100 citizens in the Trust Territory of the Pacific Islands petitioned in May to the Trusteeship Council concerning the effects of nuclear

[21] Statement of John B. Hollister, "Using the Atom for Economic and Social Progress in Asia," *The Department of State Bulletin*, Vol. XXXIII (November 7, 1955), p. 749.

weapon experimentation in the area. On December 3, 1955, the General Assembly adopted without objection a resolution setting up a scientific committee to collect, judge, and disseminate information on the effects of radiation on human beings and their environment. The states of Southeast Asia are clearly interested in the topic; the Philippines and Indonesia took an active part in the United Nations debate. They are aware of the first dropping of atomic bombs on human beings in Japan, an Asian country, and of the experiments in atomic and hydrogen warfare on the part of the United States and Great Britain in the Pacific.

The countries of Southeast Asia have shown particular interest in financing economic development in various ways through United Nations facilities like the International Bank for Reconstruction and Development. Numbering among the underdeveloped states of the world, the Southeast Asian members of the United Nations need and want foreign aid but their newly won sovereignty, as indicated, causes them in many cases to prefer the multilateral to the bilateral approach. The Expanded Program of Technical Assistance has proved its worth. In an effort to quicken the flow of foreign capital necessary for economic development the Southeast Asian states have called for an International Finance Corporation (IFC) and a Special United Nations Fund for Economic Development (SUNFED).

In April, 1955, the International Bank for Reconstruction and Development submitted the charter of the IFC to its members for ratification. In essence the IFC would make direct loans without government guarantees to private enterprises in underdeveloped countries. At the ninth session of the General Assembly the United States and Great Britain had reversed their positions and indicated they were willing to support the IFC. The corporation was established and Indonesia, Thailand, the Philippines, and Burma were members by the end of August, 1957.

In 1953 a proposal for a SUNFED was submitted by a group of experts who had been appointed by the Secretary-General. Since then the proposal has been altered and modified as a result of further study. In essence SUNFED would make grants-in-aid and long-term, low-interest loans in underdeveloped nations for development projects like hospitals, schools, and roads, projects which though essential have no direct financial return. The United States and the United Kingdom have opposed the immediate establishment of SUNFED, stressing their financial commitments that already exist. They have indicated willingness, however, to favor it if substantial armament reduction could be achieved, thus releasing funds for SUNFED. The states of Southeast Asia believe that the elimination of the great differences between the standards of living in the developed and underdeveloped parts of the world is essential to world peace and security.

Economic development, of course, cannot be separated from numerous other aspects that enter into the overall pattern. The states of Southeast Asia in the United Nations are concerned over the widespread absence of regulatory machinery that is in a position to stabilize world markets in primary goods produced in their countries. In 1954 a Commission on International Commodity Trade was set up to advise the Economic and Social Council on how to avoid excessive fluctuations in the prices and in the volume of trade as regards primary commodities. The Commission so far has proved ineffective. In another aspect Burma and Indonesia became early Contracting Parties to the General Agreement on Tariffs and Trade (GATT) to lower tariffs in world commerce. GATT was planned to be a stopgap measure prior to the establishment of the International Trade Organization (ITO), a would-be specialized agency of the United Nations that failed to materialize.

The work of the United Nations in the field of relief and rehabilitation has met with sympathetic response in Southeast Asia. Since the Second World War the centers of activity in relief and rehabilitation have shifted, especially to the Near East and Korea. The reports of the Agent-General of the United Nations Korean Reconstruction Agency, of the Director of the United Nations Relief and Works Agency for Palestine Refugees in the Near East, and of the High Commissioner for Refugees reflect the problems in these respects before the United Nations.

Although the voices of the states of Southeast Asia in the councils of the United Nations do not carry the weight of those of the Great Powers, it is clear that Burma, Indonesia, Thailand, the Philippines, Cambodia, Laos, and the Federation of Malaya cannot be ignored. It can be expected that no bloc will develop among the seven members on cold war issues but the entente on colonial and economic questions will hold. Without the United Nations, the states of Southeast Asia would clearly have a more restricted role in world affairs.

12. *Conclusion*

The emergence of the states of Southeast Asia, creating a new pattern in the international relations of the area, is one of the most significant developments in Asia since the end of the Second World War. Europe, weakened by two global conflicts in the twentieth century, has ceased to guide the destinies of most of Southeast Asia. The making of foreign policy has been transferred from London, Paris, and The Hague as well as Washington to Rangoon, Kuala Lumpur, Saigon, Hanoi, Phnom Penh, Vientiane, Djakarta, and Manila.

Yet it is obvious that the new governments of Southeast Asia in formulating foreign policy are not operating in a vacuum. Action and reaction are normal processes in any foreign office although the time sequence varies with the government and the situation. Many of the states of emergent Southeast Asia look back to the period before the advent of Western colonialism when they existed as kingdoms and principalities having their own friends and enemies in changing combinations of power. Indeed, there is a real tendency, not surprising under the circumstances of newly won independence, to exaggerate the importance of the precolonial past and all it represented.

Despite the history of Southeast Asia before European colonialism, the Western powers are responsible to a large degree for the present political geography of the region. The new states have inherited the boundaries often constituted by the Western powers in agreements among themselves. Independence has meant in effect the confirmation of the territorial base when the metropolitan power relinquished sovereignty. West New Guinea, of course, constitutes an exception. But Burma, the Philippines, the Federation of Malaya, Cambodia, Laos, Vietnam, and most of Indonesia substantiate the assumption. The disintegration of the present pattern of political geography in the region is possible but does not appear likely on any extensive scale. The European concepts of international law and relations will continue to function in the new Southeast Asia.

International developments on the world scene have had a direct impact on the foreign policies of all the states of the area. The governments of the countries are forced to adjust their policies to world events. Even a kingdom as isolated from the leading capitals as Laos is not able to pursue a policy of splendid isolation. It is clear that Asia, which for a long time was dormant, has now awakened. And the world of the twentieth century that confronts her is far different from that existing before the period of European expansion.

The separation of domestic and international politics is increasingly difficult for all states including those of Southeast Asia. The foreign offices of the new governments are generally small but they are increasing in size and scope; the minister of foreign affairs often occupies a key position. At the same time the orthodox approach to international relations in terms of official channels is somewhat limited. The Chinese Communists, for instance, operate not only through official missions when possible but also behind constituted authorities through local minority groups. Thus the governments of Southeast Asia are confronted with both a domestic and an international problem. The stress since the Second World War on open diplomacy, as indicated in the functioning of the organs of the United Nations, further ties together domestic and international politics. Once a government publicly presents its case on an issue of burning importance, the vicissitudes of success or failure in accomplishing desired objectives affect domestic politics. The Burmese followed with great interest the presentation of their government's case in the United Nations on the subject of Kuomintang forces in the Union.

Since the foreign policies of the states of Southeast Asia are influenced in most cases by the precolonial and colonial past as well as by contemporary world events, they have a certain originality in many respects. In interpreting the main controversy in world politics as being between nationalism and colonialism instead of between democracy and Communism many of the states of the region find themselves at odds with the major Western powers. This situation alone often results in foreign policies that differ from those originating not only in Washington but also in Moscow.

As a result of developments, the traditional role of Southeast Asia as a passive region into which outside forces pour is changing. The time is coming when the area will generate definite strength of its own and have a real impact on the outside world. At present no state is sufficiently strong or respected to be followed in foreign policy by another, and any country in or outside the region that deliberately pursued an open policy of leadership toward it would fail in the attempt. Even acclaim for visiting leaders in a given Southeast Asian state is often associated with the presence of a popular local figure. The search for national security will continue for some time to cause basic differences in the foreign policies of the states of the area.

For want of a better word, "forces" may be used to identify certain dynamic "isms" in Southeast Asia. The forces, it should be stressed, are not isolated but interrelated, and their relative strength may vary from time to time. They include nationalism, imperialism, Westernism, Communism, neutralism, pacifism, racialism, regionalism, and internationalism. The isms, of course, represent generalizations, and have all the dangers inherent in broad terminology.

The consistently strongest force in Southeast Asia is nationalism. Emotional and dynamic, it has fired the revolt against foreign rule and has helped to make possible the birth of new states. It is reflected in pride in national sovereignty, in the demand for the equality of nations, in rabid opposition to any foreign interference in domestic affairs. Nationalism is basically responsible for the widespread genuine suspicion of the former colonial powers; it subordinates to a degree, hard to understand in the West, the real threat of Communist imperialism; it has distinct racial overtones that could become more important in the years to come. To many people in Southeast Asia, nationalism is almost synonymous with anticolonialism. Under the circumstances great interest is shown in developments in Africa. The Asians are eager to hasten the end of the Dark Continent in terms of its being to a large extent a political extension of Europe.

Imperialism is still a force in Southeast Asia, for many nationalist leaders do not confine it to the termination of direct foreign rule. They are inclined to look upon certain remaining Western activities as vestiges of imperialism. These include military bases, security pacts, and economic interests like banking, shipping, and investments. The foreign flags have been lowered but the alleged vestiges afford convenient whipping posts. Especially important is the fact that imperialism in the eyes of many leaders in Southeast Asia is only associated with the Western powers and not with the Soviet Union and the People's Republic of China. West New

Guinea, it should be stressed, is largely considered a colonial problem in the region.

In terms of Westernism the newly independent countries of the area have generally adopted constitutional representative government. Universal suffrage, secret elections, a judiciary that is independent, a legislature that is responsible, an executive who is accountable, bills of civil and political rights, and written constitutions are the usual elements. In most cases the parliamentary rather than the presidential system has been utilized. The holding of popular elections under difficult conditions is evidence of the widespread faith in constitutional representative government in Southeast Asia. Nevertheless, it cannot be expected that Western political processes can be transplanted in Asian soil without significant adjustments. Traditionalism, unrest, poverty, illiteracy, inexperience, and Communist subversion are factors influencing the success of the experiment.

Communism is a force in Southeast Asia subject to a number of varying interpretations and evaluations. If it promises the peasant what he wants, it may be good in his judgment. If Communism succeeds in convincing the local nationalist that Western imperialism is still the great menace to independence, it is not necessarily a threat in his eyes. If Communism is successful in converting the Asian intellectual to the Lenin thesis that imperialism is the last step of monopoly capitalism, it may be sound ideology as he sees it. Moreover, the urge in Southeast Asia to effect major changes rapidly is conducive to state planning and socialist approaches. And the heritage of colonialism has created suspicion of Western capitalism. At the same time nationalization proceedings have been encouraged, for the Europeans and Chinese widely dominate industry and commerce and there is practically no middle class to offer effective resistance. The tactics of the Communists vary from place to place in Southeast Asia; examples, as is clear, have been the encouragement of nationalism in Indochina and the exploitation of agrarian unrest in central Luzon. The Communists offer quick and dazzling solutions to the ills of the region although a situation exists that calls for evolutionary reform.

Despite the Communist activity of indigenous groups and of the resident Chinese, many governments in the area think it is possible to divorce policy toward the Communists at home from policy toward those abroad. Within this frame of reference military operations may be conducted against Communism on the domestic front while every effort is made to oppose collective action on the international level.

Neutralism is a force of growing importance in Southeast Asia. Although it certainly has different shades of meaning in Indonesia, Burma, Cambodia, and Laos, the effect is basically the same. Even in Thailand and the Philippines neutralism should not be ignored. SEATO may have tended to push the uncommitted states into greater independence of attitude; they interpret the Manila alliance in terms of dividing, not uniting, the countries of Southeast Asia. The powers favoring neutralism generally look upon the Five Principles as a better basis for international relations in the area and in the world. At the same time it should be stressed that neutralism is not isolationism, for no state in Southeast Asia wants to be a hermit.

Pacifism is important to some extent in the region. The new states are busily engaged in putting their houses in order and want no war to interfere with their efforts. Moreover, the memories of the Japanese occupation have not yet faded, and recovery from the devastation of war has been in some instances slow. A number of the states oppose SEATO in the conviction that it brings them closer to war; others, it is clear, believe the alliance is the best guarantee against aggression. The testing of nuclear and thermonuclear weapons is a matter of concern. Some of the governments are apprehensive lest President Chiang Kai-shek or President Syngman Rhee precipitate a major conflict.

Although certain elements of racialism are present, it has not yet become a major force in Southeast Asia. Part of the prestige of Communist China is based upon racial considerations. Definite in their desire for racial equality among the nations of the world, the states of the region are very sensitive to any discrimination. The treatment of the Negroes in the United States is a topic of considerable interest. At the same time many of the leaders of the area are eager to prevent the development of racialism in any form, whether toward groups of people at home or abroad.

Regionalism is not presently a powerful force although it may be in the years to come. The Bandung Conference represented a certain regional spirit despite the elements of vagueness and diffusion. The existence in Southeast Asia of a common bond of colonial experience and newly won independence apart from Thailand cannot be ignored. Yet Western colonialism divided the area into segments, and the people as a general rule are just beginning to rediscover their neighbors. Little basis presently exists for effective regional coöperation on any truly extensive scale; the forces separating the countries are much stronger than those uniting them. There is in reality no voice of Southeast Asia.

Internationalism is also not a strong force in the region, but membership in the United Nations, its specialized agencies, and related bodies is an indication of interest in and concern for the outside world. Further evidence is found in widespread participation in the Colombo Plan and certain other international activities. Indeed, membership in the United Nations often forces the states to take positions on many questions that ordinarily would not concern them. The world organization for its part, as has been pointed out, affords the states of Southeast Asia the means of getting technical and other aid without infringing upon national sensitivities.

Past experience and present aspirations have combined to create a system of values influencing behavior in Southeast Asia. It has been aptly stated that these values include:

1. The equality of all men before the law.
2. The inalienable rights of men which governments must neither deny nor abridge.
3. The greatest good of the greatest number.
4. A government of laws responsive to the consent and needs of the people.[1]

Obviously these values are locally expressed in different forms, representing the diversity of the Asian context. And it is possible that alterations will occur.

Associated with the values are economic uplift, freedom both on the individual and national levels, and peace. In efforts to improve the welfare of the people through the use of technology and industrialization the governments of Southeast Asia face an uphill battle. As is known, the people are generally lacking in modern skills; there is very little surplus domestic capital for investment; and incomes on a per capita basis are low. It is difficult to change an agricultural economy into an industrial economy in the short time desired by many Asian leaders. Poverty cannot be eradicated overnight. And the increase in population can easily wipe out progress in economic development. It is easier to establish the forms of constitutional representative government although its successful func-

[1] Kenneth T. Young, Jr., "The Challenge of Asia to United States Policy," *The Department of State Bulletin*, Vol. XXXV (August 27, 1956), p. 342.

tioning is tied in a large measure to the improvement of the living conditions of the people. As for the preservation of national independence in the world of today, the states of Southeast Asia can contribute to peace but they are in no position to prevent the outbreak of a global war. In the ultimate analysis, it should be noted, peace is probably essential to the independence of the states of the area.

In the effort to make progress the leaders of the region, mainly trained by the West and relatively small in number, have great responsibility. As they have generally led the independence movements, their thinking tends to be conditioned by memories of the recent past. A key person or a handful of leaders with a dominant revolutionary group still holds the reins in a number of states in Southeast Asia. The implementation of national programs, of course, depends upon competent administration, and here a great burden is placed upon the small but growing body of trained public servants. The coming élite, it is clear, will not be educated for the most part in the old Western mold.

The future of Southeast Asia will be closely related to political stability in the countries of the area. Revolution whether peaceful or by force always creates conditions of instability. In some cases independence came too soon, especially in countries where the leaders were not adequately prepared and/or where areas were devastated during the Second World War. Against this background the difficulties of setting up the government machinery of a new state as well as the complexities of making it a going concern are even more real. It is still a question whether the governments of Southeast Asia will follow the pattern widely found in Latin America or that in Western Europe. The lessening of the gap between political promise and realistic performance will be essential to the stability of the region.

APPENDIXES

A. *List of Interviews, Discussions, Correspondence*[1]

PHILIPPINES

Ramon Magsaysay, President of the Philippines
Elpidio Quirino, President of the Philippines, and later as former President
Sergio Osmeña, former President of the Philippines
Carlos P. Garcia, Vice-President of the Philippines and Secretary of Foreign Affairs
Fernando Lopez, Vice-President of the Philippines
Carlos P. Romulo, Secretary of Foreign Affairs, and later as Ambassador to the United States
Emilio Aguinaldo, former revolutionary leader
José P. Laurel, Senator
Claro M. Recto, Senator
Emmanuel Pelaez, Senator
Tomas Cabili, Senator
Arsenio Lacson, Mayor of Manila
Felino Neri, Undersecretary, Department of Foreign Affairs, and later as presidential adviser
Leon Ma. Guerrero, Undersecretary, Department of Foreign Affairs
Raul S. Manglapus, Undersecretary, Department of Foreign Affairs
Proceso E. Sabastian, Ambassador to Indonesia
Manuel V. Gallego, former Ambassador to Indonesia
Bernabe Africa, former Minister to Thailand
Manuel A. Adeva, Minister to the Republic of China
Jose F. Imperial, Chief, Mission in Japan
Rafaelita Soriano, Department of Foreign Affairs
Carlos P. Abrera, Department of Foreign Affairs
Maximino G. Bueno, Alternate Representative, United Nations Commission on Korea
Enrique Fernando, presidential adviser
Alfredo Morales, United States Educational Foundation
Pedro L. Baldoria, University of the Philippines
Vidal Tan, President, University of the Philippines
Albino Sy Cip, China Banking Corporation, Manila

[1] Titles at time of contact are listed. Indication is given in each case where the contact was by correspondence.

Simeon Sy, China Banking Corporation, Cebu
Tirso Uy Tengsu, Chinese Chamber of Commerce, Cebu
Uy Sieng, Chinese Chamber of Commerce, Iloilo
Myron M. Cowen, United States Ambassador
Raymond A. Spruance, United States Ambassador
Daniel W. Bell, Chief, United States Economic Survey Mission to the Philippines
William S. B. Lacy, United States Embassy
Evett D. Hester, United States Embassy
Edward E. Rice, United States Embassy
Eileen R. Donovan, United States Embassy
James J. Dalton, Asia Foundation
Charles O. Houston, Jr., University of Manila
H. Otley Beyer, University of the Philippines
Clyde Heflin, Silliman University
David Sternberg, correspondent, *Christian Science Monitor*
A. V. H. Hartendorp, *The American Chamber of Commerce Journal*
Carson Taylor, *Manila Daily Bulletin*
Ford Wilkins, *Manila Daily Bulletin*
Theo Rogers, *Philippines Free Press*
Alvin H. Scaff, Fulbright Professor
George A. Malcolm, former Justice, Supreme Court of the Philippines
Edward W. Mill, Visiting Ford Foundation Fellow
Friedrich Leopold von Fuerstenberg, Minister from the Federal Republic of Germany
J. P. B. Ross, Acting United Nations Resident Representative
M. R. A. Baig, Minister from India
G. Mapara, International Confederation of Free Trade Unions
Harold Bullock, Australian Legation
Toru Nakagawa, Chief, Japanese Mission

INDONESIA

Sukarno, President of Indonesia
Mohammad Hatta, Vice-President of Indonesia
Ali Sastroamidjojo, Prime Minister of Indonesia
Sutan Sjahrir, former Prime Minister
Wilopo, former Prime Minister
Sukiman Wirjosandjojo, former Prime Minister
Hadji Agus Salim, Elder Statesman
Soenarjo, Minister of Foreign Affairs
Supomo, President, University of Indonesia
Bahder Djohan, President, University of Indonesia
Soepeni Poedjoboentoro, prominent woman leader
Djaidin Purba, Member of Parliament
Abdul Muis, Member of Parliament
D. N. Aidit, General Secretary, Communist Party of Indonesia (letter)
Moekarto Notowidigdo, Ambassador to the United States
Tjokroadisumarto, Chargé, Indonesian Embassy, Manila

Ibnu Suwongso Hamimzar, Indonesian Embassy, United States
H. Merle Cochran, United States Ambassador
Hugh S. Cumming, Jr., United States Ambassador
R. W. Furlonger, Australian Embassy
Jacob D. Beam, United States Embassy
Willard A. Hanna, United States Information Agency
Edward R. Johnson, United States Information Agency
William Palmer, American businessman

<div align="center">BURMA</div>

U Nu, Prime Minister of the Union of Burma
U Kyaw Nyein, Acting Foreign Minister, Minister for Industry
U Tun Win, Minister of Information
U Win, Ambassador to the United States
James Barrington, Ambassador to the United States
Dr. Ba Maw, former Head of State
U Thant, Secretary to the Prime Minister
U Cho, Fulbright officer
Dr. Htin Aung, Rector, University of Rangoon
Dr. Ma Thin Kyi, University of Rangoon
Colonel Thin Kyi, General Staff ✗ WRONG
Dr. Tha Hla, University of Rangoon
Richard Tin, Attorney General's Office
Daw Mya Sein, President, National Council of Women in Burma
K. K. Chettur, Indian Ambassador
William J. Sebald, United States Ambassador
H. D. White, Chargé, Australian Legation
Abdul Ghayur, Pakistan Embassy
A. J. Wakefield, United Nations Resident Representative
Joseph Satterthwaite, United States Ambassador (letter)
J. S. Furnivall, Economic Adviser, Government of Burma
Albert B. Franklin, United States Embassy
Lionel Landry, United States Information Agency
Dr. Antonio Lozano, WHO, Rangoon
Cecil Hobbs, Library of Congress
Dr. Richard A. Musgrave, University of Michigan
Robert Emery, Fulbright student
Janet Welsh, Fulbright student

<div align="center">THAILAND</div>

Field Marshal Pibul Songgram, Prime Minister of Thailand
Prince Wan Waithayakon, Minister of Foreign Affairs
Pote Sarasin, Ambassador to the United States
Prince Dhani Nivat, President, Privy Council
Chitti Sucharitakul, Minister to the Philippines
Luang Ratanadib, Minister to Indonesia
Dr. Malai Huvanandana, Ministry of the Interior
Dean Kasem Udyanin, Chulalongkorn University

Y. Huntrakoon, Chulalongkorn University
Edwin F. Stanton, United States Ambassador
Howard L. Parsons, United States Embassy
Albert D. Moscotti, United States Embassy
Kenneth P. Landon, United States Department of State
Dr. C. Hart Schaaf, Deputy Executive Secretary, ECAFE
Dr. H. D. Fong, Chief, Research and Statistics Division, ECAFE
William Tanzer, Information Officer, ECAFE
M. L. Qureshi, ECAFE official
Professor Lucien M. Hanks, Jr., Cornell Research Center
Kenneth Wells, Presbyterian Mission, Bangkok

VIETNAM

Ngo Dinh Diem, President, Republic of Vietnam
Tran Van Chuong, Ambassador to the United States
Nguyen Khoa Toan, Minister to Thailand
Do Hung, Acting Foreign Minister
Pham Dang Lam, Ministry of Foreign Affairs
Le Van Loi, Department of Foreign Affairs
Hoang Quoc Cang, Viet-Nam News Service, Rangoon (letter)
Henri Froment-Meurice, Office of French Commissioner General
Mike Mansfield, United States Senator
Donald R. Heath, United States Ambassador
G. Frederick Reinhardt, United States Ambassador
Edmund A. Gullion, United States Embassy
John I. Getz, United States Embassy
Randolph A. Kidder, United States Embassy
Herbert Reiner, Jr., United States Embassy
Thomas W. Ainsworth, United States Embassy
Wesley Fishel, Michigan State University
Tillman Durdin, *New York Times*
René de Berval, Editor, *France-Asie*
Arthur Menzies, Department of External Affairs, Canada
F. G. Ballachey, Department of External Affairs, Canada
Paul Martin, Minister of National Health and Welfare, Canada (letter)

LAOS

Prince Souvanna Phouma, Prime Minister (letter)
Souphanou Vong, Pathet Lao leader (letter)
Katay D. Sasorith, former Prime Minister (letter)
Bouasy, Secretary of State for Foreign Affairs
Ourot R. Souvannavong, Ambassador to the United States
Khamtan Pradith, Ministry of Foreign Affairs
Tay Keoluangkhot, Director General, Ministry of Education
Samar Sen, Chief, International Commission for Supervision and Control in Laos, and Indian Commissioner
Jan Balicki, Polish Commissioner, International Commission
James Langley, Political Adviser, Canadian Delegation to International Commission

M. Bitard, First Secretary, French High Representation
Philip Ziegler, First Secretary, British Embassy
John Pedler, Chief of Information, British Embassy
W. Wendell Blancke, Chargé, United States Embassy
Seymour M. Finger, United States Embassy

CAMBODIA

Prince Norodom Sihanouk, former King and Prime Minister (letter)
Sam Sary, Member, Royal Council
Nong Kimny, Ambassador to the United States
Huot Sam Ath, Minister of Public Works
Huot Sambath, Secretary of State for Education
Mau Say, Minister of Finance
Chuop Samloth, Minister of Foreign Affairs
Robert McClintock, United States Ambassador
Martin Herz, United States Embassy
General George O. N. Lodoen, United States Military Assistance Advisory Group
L. H. La Vigne, Acting Canadian Commissioner, International Commission for Supervision and Control in Cambodia
Ajai K. Mitra, Indian Chargé
David Anderson, Australian Chargé
Leonard Overton, Asia Foundation

MALAYA

Tengku Abdul Rahman, Chief Minister, Federation of Malaya
David Marshall, former Chief Minister, Singapore (letter)
Sir Cheng-lock Tan, Malayan Chinese Association (letter)
L. K. Lawrence, Secretary to Lim Yew Hock, Chief Minister, Singapore (letter)
Inche Othman bin Mohamed, Ministry of External Affairs, Federation of Malaya (letter authorized)
A. D. C. Peterson, Director General, Department of Information, Federation of Malaya
G. S. Thomson, Public Relations Officer, Singapore
Professor E. H. G. Dobby, University of Malaya
Sir Sydney Caine, Vice-Chancellor, University of Malaya
Malcolm MacDonald, Commissioner-General for the United Kingdom in South-East Asia
A. A. Dudley, Foreign Service Deputy, Office of the Commissioner-General
John Rayner, Office of the Commissioner-General
J. I. McGhie, Office of the Commissioner-General (letter)
Sir George Maxwell, former Chief Secretary, Government, Federated Malay States (letter)
Foss Shanahan, Commissioner for New Zealand in South-East Asia (letter)
R. L. Jermyn, Office of the Commissioner
R. G. Casey, Minister for External Affairs, Australia (letter)

Sir Percy Spender, Australian Ambassador to the United States (letter authorized)
Eric Kocher, United States Consul, Kuala Lumpur
Thomas K. Wright, United States Consul General, Kuala Lumpur
Elbridge Durbrow, United States Consul General, Singapore
Charles T. Cross, United States Consulate General, Kuala Lumpur
Oscar V. Armstrong, United States Consulate, Kuala Lumpur
William K. Braun, United States Information Agency, Kuala Lumpur
James J. Halsema, United States Information Agency, Singapore
L. A. Peter Gosling, University of Michigan

REPUBLIC OF CHINA

Chiang Kai-shek, President of Republic of China
Chen Cheng, Premier of Republic of China
K. C. Wu, Governor of Taiwan
Chang Tao-fan, President, Legislative Yuan
Lo Chia-luen, former Ambassador to India
Cheng Yin-fun, Chairman, Overseas Chinese Affairs Commission
Chu Chia-hua, President, Academia Sinica
Shu Shiao-yen, Vice-Minister of Foreign Affairs
Hollington K. Tong, Chinese journalist
Shen Chang-huan, Office of Government Spokesman
Dapen Liang, Chinese Association for the United Nations
Karl L. Rankin, United States Ambassador

HONG KONG

Ralph N. Clough, United States Consulate General
Howard L. Boorman, United States Consulate General
David Collier, United States Consulate General
Arthur H. Rosen, United States Consulate General
Arthur Hummel, United States Information Agency
Brian Harrison, University of Hong Kong
Delmer M. Brown, Asia Foundation
Edward S. Yanne, journalist

INDIA

Jawaharlal Nehru, Prime Minister of India (letter)
K. Vithal Babu, Congress Party
Harish Chandra, Ministry of Education
S. L. Poplai, Indian Council of World Affairs
George V. Allen, United States Ambassador
Robert Trumbull, *New York Times*

PAKISTAN

Mohammed Ali, Ambassador to the United States
Ahmed Ali, Ministry of Foreign Affairs and Commonwealth Relations
L. A. Sherwani, Pakistan Institute of International Affairs
Mohammed Azhar Ali Khan, journalist
Samuel H. Rickard, Asia Foundation

JAPAN

Shinsuke Hori, Private Secretary to Prime Minister Nobusuke Kishi (letter)
Taisaku Kojima, Ministry of Foreign Affairs
Eiji Wajima, Ministry of Foreign Affairs
N. Sugawara, Ministry of Foreign Affairs
B. Hoshi, Ministry of Foreign Affairs
Miss Moto Uwano, Ministry of Foreign Affairs
Seiichi Katsumata, Socialist leader
Fusao Yamaguchi, Socialist leader
Samuel D. Berger, United States Embassy

OTHERS

Ralph Bunche, Under-Secretary, United Nations
Francis O. Wilcox, Assistant Secretary of State, United States (letter)
James W. Barco, United States Mission to the United Nations (letter)
Jack W. Lydman, South East Asia Branch, Division of Research for Far East, Department of State, United States
Professor Eric Stein, University of Michigan
William Henderson, Council on Foreign Relations
Syngman Rhee, President, Republic of Korea

B. *Letter from Jawaharlal Nehru*

No. 1038-PMH/57.

New Delhi,
June 4, 1957.

Dear Professor Fifield,

Thank you for your letter of May 28 in which you enquire about the origin and development of the idea of the Panch Shila.

I might mention that we prefer the spelling "Panchasheel" as this spelling represents the pronunciation more correctly. But it is true that the prevalent way of spelling this is "Panch Shila" even in India.

These words "Panch Shila" are from Sanskrit and mean the five foundations. They have been used from ancient times to describe the five moral precepts of Buddhism relating to personal behaviour. Even now Buddhists repeat these words in their prayers.

After the Indonesian revolution 8 or 9 years ago, the Government of Indonesia adopted these words to describe their five basic policies. This, of course, had nothing to do with Buddhism. In Indonesia, a large number of Sanskrit words have been incorporated in their language. Most of the names of individuals there are also from Sanskrit, such as President Sukarno's name. I do not quite remember the five Indonesian principles, but the first one laid down faith in God and the others dealt with independence, economic freedom, etc.

In India's agreement with the People's Republic of China relating to Tibet, five principles were mentioned to regulate our relations with each other. The words "Panch Shila" were not used or mentioned in that connection at that time. That agreement was the result of long correspondence between the Government of India and the People's Government of China. Premier Chou En-lai was not personally concerned with this matter, though no doubt he must have been consulted, as I was in India.

Later, in June 1954, Premier Chou En-lai visited India and a joint statement was issued by him and me in which reference was made to those five principles. They were:

1) mutual respect for each other's territorial integrity and sovereignty;
2) non-aggression;
3) non-interference in each other's internal affairs;

4) equality and mutual benefit;

and

5) peaceful co-existence.

Even at that time the words "Panch Shila" were not used. Subsequently, these five principles were mentioned in the course of joint statements with leaders of many other countries. In the joint statement which I signed with Mr. N. A. Bulganin, Prime Minister of the USSR, in June 1955, there was a slight amendment and extension of these principles. No. (3) became "non-interference in each other's internal affairs for any reasons of economic, political or ideological character." Thus far the words "Panch Shila" were not mentioned anywhere.

When I was in Indonesia about two years ago and I heard the words "Panch Shila" mentioned there in an entirely different context, that is, in their Indonesian meaning, it struck me immediately that this was a suitable description of the five principles of international behaviour to which we had subscribed. I said so there and repeated it on my return to India. The words caught on, especially in India, where they were easily understood, being derived from Sanskrit.

You will thus see that the five principles of peaceful co-existence first emerged out of fairly long discussions between the Governments of India and China. No individual can be said to father them. The words "Panch Shila" were first used by me in that connection some time after these principles had been enunciated.

Yours sincerely,
[signed] JAWAHARLAL NEHRU

Professor Russell H. Fifield,
Professor of Political Science,
University of Michigan,
Ann Arbor,
USA.

C. *The Final Communiqué of the Asian-African Conference*[1]

The Asian-African Conference, convened by the Governments of Burma, Ceylon, India, Indonesia and Pakistan, met in Bandung from the 18th to 24th of April, 1955.

In addition to the sponsoring countries, the following twenty-four countries participated in the conference:

Afghanistan, Cambodia, People's Republic of China, Egypt, Ethiopia, Gold Coast, Iran, Iraq, Japan, Jordan, Laos, Lebanon, Liberia, Libya, Nepal, the Philippines, Saudi Arabia, Sudan, Syria, Thailand, Turkey, Democratic Republic of (North) Vietnam, State of Vietnam and Yemen.

The Asian-African Conference considered the position of Asia and Africa and discussed ways and means by which their peoples could achieve the fullest economic, cultural and political coöperation.

A. ECONOMIC COÖPERATION:

1. The Asian-African Conference recognized the urgency of promoting economic development in the Asian-African region. There was general desire for economic coöperation among the participating countries on the basis of mutual interest and respect for national sovereignty.

The proposals with regard to economic coöperation within the participating countries do not preclude either the desirability or the need for coöperation with countries outside the region, including the investment of foreign capital.

It was further recognized that assistance being received by certain participating countries from outside the region through international or under bilateral arrangements had made a valuable contribution to the implementation of their development programs.

2. The participating countries agreed to provide technical assistance to one another in the form of:

Experts, trainees, pilot projects and equipment for demonstration purposes, exchange of know-how, and establishment of national and, where possible, regional training and research institutes for imparting technical knowledge and skills in coöperation with the existing international agencies.

[1] Press Release, Permanent Mission of the Republic of Indonesia to the United Nations.

3. The Asian-African Conference recommended:

The early establishment of a special United Nations fund for economic development;

The allocation by the International Bank for Reconstruction and Development of a greater part of its resources to Asian-African countries;

The early establishment of an international finance corporation, which should include in its activities the undertaking of equity investment; and

Encouragement of the promotion of joint ventures among Asian-African countries in so far as this will promote their common interest.

4. The Asian-African Conference recognized the vital need for stabilizing commodity trade in the region.

The principle of enlarging the scope of multilateral trade and payments was accepted. However, it was recognized that some countries would have to take recourse to bilateral trade arrangements in view of their prevailing economic conditions.

5. The Asian-African Conference recommended that collective action be taken by participating countries for stabilizing international prices of and demand for primary commodities through bilateral and multilateral arrangements, and that as far as practicable and desirable they should adopt a unified approach on the subject in the United Nations Permanent Advisory Commission on International Commodity Trade and other international forums.

6. The Asian-African Conference further recommended:

Asian-African countries should diversify their export trade by processing their raw materials whenever economically feasible before export; intra-regional trade fairs should be promoted and encouragement be given to the exchange of trade delegations and groups of businessmen; exchange of information and of samples should be encouraged with a view to promoting intra-regional trade; and normal facilities should be provided for the transit trade of landlocked countries.

7. The Asian-African Conference attached considerable importance to shipping and expressed concern that shipping lines reviewed from time to time their freight rates, which are often to the detriment of participating countries. It recommended a study of this problem and collective action thereafter to induce the shipping lines to adopt a more reasonable attitude. It was further suggested that a study of railway freight of transit trade may be made.

8. The Asian-African Conference agreed that encouragement should be given to the establishment of national and regional banks and insurance companies.

9. The Asian-African Conference felt that exchange of information on matters relating to oil, such as remittance of profits and taxation, might eventually lead to the formulation of a common policy.

10. The Asian-African Conference emphasized the particular significance of the development of nuclear energy for peaceful purposes for Asian-African countries.

The Conference welcomed the initiative of the powers principally concerned in offering to make available information regarding the use of atomic energy for peaceful purposes; urged the speedy establishment of an international atomic energy agency which should provide for adequate representation of the Asian-African countries on the executive authority of the agency; and recommended that Asian and African governments take full advantage of the training and other facilities in the peaceful uses of atomic energy offered by the countries sponsoring such programs.

11. The Asian-African Conference agreed to the appointment of liaison officers in participating countries, to be nominated by their respective national governments, for the exchange of information and ideas on matters of mutual interest.

It recommended that fuller use should be made of the existing international organizations, and participating countries who were not members of such international organizations, but were eligible, should secure membership.

12. The Asian-African Conference recommended that there should be prior consultation of participating countries in international forums with a view, as far as possible, to furthering their mutual economic interest. It is, however, not intended to form a regional bloc.

B. CULTURAL COÖPERATION:

1. The Asian-African Conference was convinced that among the most powerful means of promoting understanding among nations is the development of cultural coöperation. Asia and Africa have been the cradle of great religions, which have enriched other cultures and civilizations while themselves being enriched in the process.

Thus the cultures of Asia and Africa are based on spiritual and universal foundations. Unfortunately, cultural contacts among Asian and African countries were interrupted during the past centuries.

The peoples of Asia and Africa are now animated by a keen and sincere desire to renew their old cultural contacts and develop new ones in the context of the modern world. All participating governments at the Asian-African Conference reiterated their determination to work for closer cultural coöperation.

2. The Asian-African Conference took note of the fact that the existence of colonialism in many parts of Asia and Africa, in whatever form it may be, not only prevents cultural coöperation but also suppresses the national cultures of the peoples.

Some colonial powers have denied their dependent peoples basic rights in the sphere of education and culture, which hampers the development of their personality and also prevents cultural intercourse with other Asian and African peoples.

This is particularly true in the case of Tunisia, Algeria and Morocco, where the basic right of the people to study their own language and culture has been suppressed.

Similar discrimination has been practiced against Asian and Colored people in some parts of the Continent of Africa.

The Conference felt that these policies amount to a denial of the fundamental rights of man, impede cultural advancement in this region and also hamper cultural coöperation on the wide international plane. The Conference condemned such a denial of fundamental rights in the sphere of education and culture in some parts of Asia and Africa by this and other forms of cultural suppression. In particular, the Conference condemned racialism as a means of cultural suppression.

3. It was not from any sense of exclusiveness or rivalry with other groups of nations and other civilizations and cultures that the Conference viewed the development of cultural coöperation among Asian and African countries.

True to the age-old tradition of tolerance and universality, the Conference believed that Asian and African cultural coöperation should be developed in the larger context of world coöperation. Side by side with the development of Asian-African cultural coöperation, the countries of Asia and Africa desire to develop cultural contacts with others. This would enrich their own culture and would also help in the promotion of world peace and understanding.

4. There are many countries in Asia and Africa which have not yet been able to develop their educational, scientific and technical institutions. The Conference recommended that countries in Asia and Africa which are more fortunately placed in this respect should give facilities for the admission of students and trainees from such countries to their institutions. Such facilities should also be made available to the Asian and African people in Africa, to whom opportunities for acquiring higher education are at present denied.

5. The Asian-African Conference felt that the promotion of cultural coöperation among countries of Asia and Africa should be directed towards:

First, the acquisition of knowledge of each other's country;

Second, mutual cultural exchange; and

Third, exchange of information.

6. The Asian-African Conference was of the opinion that at this stage the best results in cultural coöperation would be achieved by pursuing bilateral arrangements to implement its recommendations and by each country taking action on its own wherever possible and feasible.

C. HUMAN RIGHTS AND SELF-DETERMINATION:

1. The Asian-African Conference declared its full support of the fundamental principles of human rights as a common standard of achievement for all peoples and all nations. The Conference declared its full support of the principle of self-determination of peoples and nations as set forth in the Charter of the United Nations and took note of the United Nations resolutions on the right of peoples and nations to self-determination, which is a prerequisite of the full enjoyment of all fundamental human rights.

2. The Asian-African Conference deplored the policies and practices of racial segregation and discrimination which form the basis of government and human relations in large regions of Africa and in other parts

of the world. Such conduct is not only a gross violation of human rights, but also a denial of the fundamental values of civilization and the dignity of man.

The Conference extended its warm sympathy and support for the courageous stand taken by the victims of racial discrimination and especially by the peoples of African and Indian and Pakistani origin in South Africa; applauded all those who sustained their cause; reaffirmed the determination of Asian-African peoples to eradicate every trace of racialism that might exist in their own countries; and pledged to use its full moral influence to guard against the danger of falling victims of the same evil in their struggle to eradicate it.

D. PROBLEMS OF DEPENDENT PEOPLE:

1. The Asian-African Conference discussed the problems of dependent peoples and colonialism and the evils arising from subjection of peoples to alien subjugation, domination and exploitation. The Conference agreed:

First, in declaring that colonialism in all its manifestations is an evil which should speedily be brought to an end;

Second, in affirming that the subjection of peoples to alien subjugation, domination and exploitation constitutes a denial of fundamental human rights, is contrary to the Charter of the United Nations and is an impediment to the promotion of world peace and coöperation;

Third, in declaring its support of the cause of freedom and independence for all such peoples; and

Fourth, in calling upon the powers concerned to grant freedom and independence to such peoples.

2. In view of the unsettled situation in North Africa and of the persisting denial to the peoples of North Africa of their right to self-determination, the Asian-African Conference declared its support of the rights of the people of Algeria, Morocco and Tunisia to self-determination and independence and urged the French Government to bring about a peaceful settlement of the issue without delay.

E. OTHER PROBLEMS:

1. In view of the existing tension in the Middle East caused by the situation in Palestine and of the danger of that tension to world peace, the Asian-African Conference declared its support of the rights of the Arab people of Palestine, and called for the implementation of the United Nations resolutions on Palestine and of the peaceful settlement of the Palestine question.

2. The Asian-African Conference, in the context of its expressed attitude on the abolition of colonialism, supported the position of Indonesia in the case of West Irian, based on the relevant agreements between Indonesia and the Netherlands. The Asian-African Conference urged the Netherlands Government to reopen negotiations as soon as possible to implement their obligations under the above-mentioned agreements and expressed the earnest hope that the United Nations

could assist the parties concerned in finding a peaceful solution to the dispute.

3. The Asian-African Conference supported the position of Yemen in the case of Aden and the southern parts of Yemen known as the protectorates, and urged the parties concerned to arrive at a peaceful settlement of the dispute.

F. PROMOTION OF WORLD PEACE AND COÖPERATION:

1. The Asian-African Conference, taking note of the fact that several states have still not been admitted to the United Nations, considered that for effective coöperation for world peace membership in the United Nations should be universal, called on the Security Council to support the admission of all those states which are qualified for membership in terms of the Charter.

In the opinion of the Asian-African Conference the following among the participating countries which were represented in it—Cambodia, Ceylon, Japan, Jordan, Laos, Libya, Nepal and a unified Vietnam—were so qualified.

The Conference considered that the representation of the countries of the Asian-African region on the Security Council in relation to the principle of equitable geographical distribution was inadequate. It expressed the view that as regards the distribution of the non-permanent seats, the Asian-African countries which, under the arrangement arrived at in London in 1946, are precluded from being elected, should be enabled to serve on the Security Council so that they might make a more effective contribution to the maintenance of international peace and security.

2. The Asian-African Conference having considered the dangerous situation of international tension existing and the risks confronting the whole human race from the outbreak of global war in which the destructive power of all types of armaments, including nuclear and thermonuclear weapons, would be employed, invited the attention of all nations to the terrible consequences that would follow if such a war were to break out.

The Conference considered that disarmament and the prohibition of production, experimentation and use of nuclear and thermonuclear weapons of war are imperative to save mankind and civilization from the fear and prospect of wholesale destruction. It considered that the nations of Asia and Africa assembled here have a duty toward humanity and civilization to proclaim their support for the prohibition of these weapons and to appeal to nations principally concerned and to world opinion to bring about such disarmament and prohibition.

The Conference considered that effective international control should be established and maintained to implement such prohibition and that speedy and determined efforts should be made to this end. Pending the total prohibition of the manufacture of nuclear and thermonuclear weapons, this Conference appealed to all the powers concerned to reach agreement to suspend experiments with such weapons.

The Conference declared that universal disarmament is an absolute necessity for the preservation of peace and requested the United Nations to continue its efforts and appealed to all concerned speedily to bring about the regulation, limitation, control and reduction of all armed forces and armaments, including the prohibition of the production, experimentation and use of all weapons of mass destruction, and to establish effective international control to this end.

3. The Asian-African Conference gave anxious thought to the question of world peace and coöperation. It viewed with deep concern the present state of international tension with its danger of an atomic world war.

The problem of peace is correlative with the problem of international security. In this connection all states should coöperate especially through the United Nations in bringing about the reduction of armaments and the elimination of nuclear weapons under effective international control. In this way international peace can be promoted and nuclear energy may be used exclusively for peaceful purposes. This would help answer the needs, particularly of Asia and Africa, for what they urgently require are social progress and better standards of life in larger freedom.

Freedom and peace are interdependent. The right of self-determination must be enjoyed by all peoples in freedom, and independence must be granted with the least possible delay to those who are still dependent peoples. Indeed all nations should have the right freely to choose their own political and economic systems and their own way of life in conformity with the purposes and principles of the Charter of the United Nations.

Free from distrust and fear and with confidence and goodwill toward each other, nations should practice tolerance and live together in peace with one another as good neighbours and develop friendly coöperation on the basis of the following principles:

1. Respect for fundamental human rights and for the purposes and principles of the Charter of the United Nations.

2. Respect for the sovereignty and territorial integrity of all nations.

3. Recognition of the equality of all races and of the equality of all nations, large and small.

4. Abstention from intervention or interference in the internal affairs of another country.

5. Respect for the right of each nation to defend itself singly or collectively in conformity with the Charter of the United Nations.

6. A. Abstention from the use of arrangements of collective defense to serve the particular interests of any of the big powers.

6. B. Abstention by any country from exerting pressures on other countries.

7. Refraining from acts or threats of aggression or the use of force against the territorial integrity or political independence of any country.

8. Settlement of all international disputes by peaceful means such as negotiation, conciliation, arbitration or judicial settlement, as well as other peaceful means of the parties' own choice in conformity with the Charter of the United Nations.

9. Promotion of mutual interest and coöperation.

10. Respect for justice and international obligations.

The Asian-African Conference declares its conviction that friendly coöperation in accordance with these principles would effectively contribute to the maintenance and promotion of international peace and security, while coöperation in the economic, social and cultural field would help bring about the common prosperity and well-being of all.

The Asian-African Conference recommended that the five sponsoring countries consider the convening of the next meeting of the Conference in consultation with the participating countries.

Bandung, April 24, 1955

D. *Bibliography*

I. BIBLIOGRAPHIES

U.S. Library of Congress, Orientalia Division. *Southeast Asia: An Annotated Bibliography of Selected Reference Sources*, compiled by Cecil Hobbs, Washington, D.C., 1952.

Embree, John F. *A Selected Bibliography on Southeast Asia*, 2d ed., revised and expanded by Bruno Lasker, New York, 1952. (Subsequent revisions)

Hobbs, Cecil. *Southeast Asia, 1935-1945: A Selected List of Reference Books*, Washington, D.C., 1946.

Far Eastern Bibliography, 1946, *The Far Eastern Quarterly*, May, 1947.

Far Eastern Bibliography, 1947, *The Far Eastern Quarterly*, June, 1948.

Far Eastern Bibliography, 1948, 1949, 1950, 1951, 1952, 1953, *The Far Eastern Quarterly*, August, 1949, 1950, 1951, 1952, 1953, 1954.

Far Eastern Bibliography, 1954, 1955, *The Far Eastern Quarterly*, September, 1955, 1956.

Bibliography of Asian Studies, 1956, *The Journal of Asian Studies*, September, 1957.

Pelzer, Karl J. *Selected Bibliography on the Geography of Southeast Asia*; Part I, *Southeast Asia—General*; Part II, *The Philippines*; Part III, *Malaya*; New Haven, 1949, 1950, 1956.

Embree, John F., and Dotson, Lillian O. *Bibliography of the Peoples and Cultures of Mainland Southeast Asia*, New Haven, 1950.

Philippine Studies Program (University of Chicago). *Selected Bibliography of the Philippines*, directed by Fred Eggan, New Haven, 1956.

Abrera, Carlos P. "Bibliography on Foreign Relations and Foreign Policy of the Republic of the Philippines since 1945," *Journal of East Asiatic Studies, 1* (April, 1952), 131-138.

British Borneo Research Project (University of Chicago). *Bibliography of British Borneo*, New Haven, 1956.

Kennedy, Raymond. *Bibliography of Indonesian Peoples and Cultures*, rev. ed., Thomas W. Maretzki and H. Th. Fischer, eds., 2 vols., New Haven, 1955.

Galis, K. W. *Bibliography of West New Guinea*, New Haven, 1956.

Burma Research Project (New York University). *Annotated Bibliography of Burma*, Frank N. Trager, ed., New Haven, 1956.

Southeast Asia Program (Cornell University). *Bibliography of Thailand*, directed by Lauriston Sharp, Ithaca, N.Y., 1956.

U.S. Library of Congress, Reference Department. *Indochina: A Bibliography of the Land and People*, compiled by Cecil Hobbs and others, Washington, D.C., 1950.

Laos Research Project (University of Chicago). *Bibliography of Laos*, New Haven, 1956.

Cambodia Research Project (University of Chicago). *Bibliography of Cambodia*, New Haven, 1956.

Irikura, James K. *Southeast Asia: Selected Annotated Bibliography of Japanese Publications*, New Haven, 1956.

Oey, Giok Po. *Survey of Chinese Language Materials on Southeast Asia in the Hoover Institute and Library*, Ithaca, N.Y., 1953.

Rubinstein, Alvin Z. "Selected Bibliography of Soviet Works on Southern Asia, 1954-56," *The Journal of Asian Studies*, *17* (November, 1957), 43-54.

Langer, William L., and Armstrong, Hamilton Fish, eds. *Foreign Affairs Bibliography, 1919-1932*, New York, 1933.

Woolbert, Robert G., ed. *Foreign Affairs Bibliography, 1932-1942*, New York, 1945.

Roberts, Henry L., ed. *Foreign Affairs Bibliography, 1942-1952*, New York, 1955.

U.S. Library of Congress, Orientalia Division. *Southern Asia: Publications in Western Languages, A Quarterly Accessions List*, Washington, D.C., 1952-1956; *Southern Asia Accessions List*, Washington, D.C., 1956–.

U.S. Department of State, Office of Intelligence Research, External Research Staff. *External Research, A Listing of Recently Completed Studies, Southeast Asia*, Washington, D.C. (Occasionally issued)

II. GENERAL SOURCES AND AIDS

Current Notes on International Affairs, Department of External Affairs, Australia.

External Affairs Review, Department of External Affairs, New Zealand.

External Affairs, Department of External Affairs, Canada.

Foreign Affairs Record, Ministry of External Affairs, India.

India News Bulletin, Embassy of India, Washington, D.C.

Japan Report, Embassy of Japan, Washington, D.C.

People's China, and *Supplements*, Peking.

Chinese News Service, Republic of China, New York.

China Handbook, Taipei.

Treaties and Other International Acts Series (United States).

United States Treaties and Other International Agreements.

The Department of State Bulletin (United States).

Congressional Record; Senate Committee on Foreign Relations, House of Representatives Committee on Foreign Affairs: miscellaneous hearings, reports, and studies relative to the Philippines and Southeast Asia.

Treaty Series, Great Britain, Foreign Office.

British and Foreign State Papers.

Hansard; *Parliamentary Papers* relative to Southeast Asia, especially Malaya, British Borneo, and Burma.

Commonwealth Survey, A Record of United Kingdom and Commonwealth Affairs.
Journal Officiel de la République Française.
Direction de la Documentation. Notes et Études Documentaires, especially relative to Indochina.
Netherlands Information Service, diverse items relative to Indonesia and Netherlands New Guinea.
League of Nations Treaty Series.
Documents on International Affairs, Royal Institute of International Affairs.
Documents on American Foreign Relations, World Peace Foundation, later Council on Foreign Relations.

United Nations, *Official Records* (General Assembly, especially the general debates, Security Council, Trusteeship Council, Economic and Social Council).
Permanent Missions to the United Nations.
United Nations Treaty Series.
Yearbook of the United Nations.
Demographic Yearbook.
Statistical Yearbook.
World Economic Survey.
United Nations Review.
Economic Commission for Asia and the Far East, *Economic Survey of Asia and the Far East*, and the *Economic Bulletin for Asia and the Far East.*
The Chronicle of United Nations Activities.

Asian Annual.
The United States in World Affairs, annual.
Survey of International Affairs, annual.
The Annual Register of World Events, A Review of the Year.
Political Handbook of the World; Parliaments, Parties and Press, annual.
The Statesman's Year-Book; Statistical and Historical Annual of the States of the World.
Current Digest of the Soviet Press.
Indian Press Digests.
Survey of China Mainland Press.
Chronique de Politique Étrangère.
Keesing's Contemporary Archives.
Asian Recorder.
Europa-Archiv.
Letters and Reports, American Universities Field Staff.
The New York Times.
New York Herald Tribune.
Christian Science Monitor.
Manchester Guardian.
Times (London).

The Economist.
Le Monde.
New Times (Moscow).

III. WORKS PRIMARILY CONCERNED WITH OR SOMEWHAT RELATED TO SOUTHEAST ASIA

Anderson, Wilhelm. "The Political Significance of the Rice Bowl of Asia," *Foreign Agriculture, 17* (July-August, 1953), 127-130.

Andrus, J. Russell. *Basic Problems of Relief, Rehabilitation and Reconstruction of Southeast Asia*, New York, 1945.

Armstrong, Hamilton Fish. "Neutrality: Varying Tunes," *Foreign Affairs, 35* (October, 1956), 57-71.

Aron, R. "La Situation dans le Sud-Est Asiatique: de Bangkok à Bandoeng," *Politique Étrangère, 20* (July, 1955), 283-298.

Benda, Harry J. "Communism in Southeast Asia," *Yale Review, 45* (Spring, 1956), 417-429.

Birdwood, Lord. "The Defence of South-East Asia," *International Affairs, 31* (January, 1955), 17-25.

Braibanti, Ralph. "The Southeast Asia Collective Defense Treaty," *Pacific Affairs, 30* (December, 1957), 321-341.

Broek, Jan O. M. "Diversity and Unity in Southeast Asia," *The Geographical Review, 34* (April, 1944), 175-195.

Butwell, Richard. "Communist Liaison in Southeast Asia," *United Asia, 6* (June, 1954), 146-151.

Callis, Helmut G. *Foreign Capital in Southeast Asia*, New York, 1942.

Carnell, Francis G. "Southeast Asia and the Modern World," *India Quarterly, 13* (April-June, 1957), 101-120.

Chatham House Study Group. *Collective Defence in South East Asia: The Manila Treaty and Its Implications*, London, 1956.

Chatterji, B. R. "Southeast Asia in Transition," *India Quarterly, 12* (October-December, 1956), 388-399.

Christian, John L. "Anglo-French Rivalry in Southeast Asia; Its Historical Geography and Diplomatic Climate," *The Geographical Review, 31* (April, 1941), 272-282.

Crosby, Sir Josiah. "Observations on a Post-War Settlement in South-East Asia," *International Affairs, 20* (April, 1944), 357-368.

"Das Ende des Kolonialismus und der Aufstieg Neuer Nationen in Südostasien," *Europa-Archiv, 10* (August 5, 1955), 8037-8052.

Dobby, E. H. G. *Southeast Asia*, London, 1954.

Du Bois, Cora. *Social Forces in Southeast Asia*, Minneapolis, 1949.

Eighty-fifth Congress, Second Session. Subcommittee on Disarmament, Senate Committee on Foreign Relations, Staff Study No. 9, *Control and Reduction of Armaments, Disarmament and Security in Eastern and Southern Asia*, Washington, D.C., 1957.

Eighty-third Congress, Second Session. Senate Committee on Foreign Relations, *The Southeast Asia Collective Defense Treaty*, Hearings on Executive K, 2 parts, Washington, 1954, 1955; Eighty-fourth Congress, First Session. Senate Committee on Foreign Relations, Report on Executive K, Executive Report No. 1, Washington, D.C., 1955.

Emerson, Rupert. *Representative Government in Southeast Asia*, Cambridge, Mass., 1955.

Emerson, Rupert. "Problems of Representative Government in Southeast Asia," *Pacific Affairs, 26* (December, 1953), 291-302.

Emerson, Rupert, Mills, Lennox A., and Thompson, Virginia. *Government and Nationalism in Southeast Asia*, New York, 1942.

Firth, Raymond. "The Peasantry in South East Asia," *International Affairs, 26* (October, 1950), 503-514.

Fisher, Charles A. "The Concept of South-East Asia," *Eastern World, 7* (March, 1953), 12-14.

Fisher, Charles A. "Crisis in Southeast Asia," *Queen's Quarterly, 63* (Spring, 1956), 104-118.

Furnivall, J. S. *Progress and Welfare in Southeast Asia*, New York, 1941.

Furnivall, J. S. *Educational Progress in Southeast Asia*, New York, 1943.

Gard, Richard A. "Ideological Problems in Southeast Asia," *Philosophy East and West, 2* (January, 1953), 292-307.

Hadow, R. H. "Military, Naval, and Strategic Aspects in the Struggle for Southeast Asia," *World Affairs Interpreter, 24* (Spring, 1953), 36-41.

Hall, D. G. E. *A History of South-East Asia*, New York, 1955.

Hall, D. G. E. "Thoughts on the Chinese Question in South-East Asia," *Asian Review, 50* (April, 1954), 138-148.

Harrison, Brian. *South-East Asia: A Short History*, New York, 1954.

Heine-Geldern, Robert. "Conceptions of State and Kingship in Southeast Asia," *Far Eastern Quarterly, 2* (November, 1942), 15-30.

Henderson, William. "The Development of Regionalism in Southeast Asia," *International Organization, 9* (November, 1955), 463-476.

Henderson, William. "Communist Movements in Southeast Asia," *Journal of International Affairs, 8*, No. 1 (1954), 32-42.

Henderson, William. *New Nations of Southeast Asia*, New York, 1955.

Hobbs, Cecil. *An Account of an Acquisition Trip in the Countries of Southeast Asia*, Ithaca, N.Y., 1952.

Hobbs, Cecil. *Account of a Trip to the Countries of Southeast Asia for the Library of Congress, 1952-1953*, Ithaca, N.Y., 1953.

Jacoby, Erich H. *Agrarian Unrest in Southeast Asia*, New York, 1949.

Jones, Francis Clifford, Borton, Hugh, and Pearns, B. R. *The Far East, 1942-1946*, London, 1955.

King, John Kerry. *Southeast Asia in Perspective*, New York, 1956.

King, John Kerry. "Rice Politics," *Foreign Affairs, 31* (April, 1953), 453-460.

Kusano, Fumio. "Communist Activities in Southeast Asia," *Contemporary Japan, 19* (April-June, 1950), 162-179.

Landon, Kenneth P. *Southeast Asia: Crossroad of Religions*, Chicago, 1949.

Landon, Kenneth P. "Nationalism in Southeastern Asia," *Far Eastern Quarterly, 2* (February, 1943), 139-152.

Lasker, Bruno. *Human Bondage in Southeast Asia*, Chapel Hill, N.C., 1950.

Lasker, Bruno. *Peoples of Southeast Asia*, New York, 1944.

Le May, Reginald. *The Culture of South-East Asia: The Heritage of India*, London, 1954.

Levi, Werner. "Power Conflicts in South-East Asia," *Fortnightly, 171* (June, 1949), 361-369.

MacDonald, Malcolm. "There's a Chance to Hold Southeast Asia," *U.S. News and World Report*, December 3, 1954, 76-82.

MacDonald, Malcolm. *The Asian Revolution*, Regional Information Office, Singapore, 1953.

British Information Services, Speech of Malcolm MacDonald to the National Press Club, Washington, D.C., October 8, 1954, New York, October 18, 1954.

McDonald, A. H. "Political Development in Southeast Asia," *Australian Outlook, 2* (March, 1948), 27-41.

Mallory, Walter H. "Chinese Minorities in Southeast Asia," *Foreign Affairs, 34* (January, 1956), 258-270.

Mendé, Tibor. *South-East Asia Between Two Worlds*, London, 1955.

Meyer, Milton W. "Regional Coöperation in Southeast Asia," *Columbia Journal of International Affairs, 3* (Spring, 1949), 68-77.

Mills, Lennox A., and Associates. *The New World of Southeast Asia*, Minneapolis, 1949.

Mills, Lennox A. "The Cold War in Southeast Asia," *Virginia Quarterly Review, 26* (Summer, 1950), 366-378.

Mook, H. J. Van. *The Stakes of Democracy in Southeast Asia*, New York, 1950.

Müller, W. D. "Zur Innenpolitischen Garantieklausel des Südostasienpaktes," *Aussenpolitik, 6* (February, 1955), 117-122.

Okita, Saburo. "South and Southeast Asia and the Japanese Economy," *Japan Quarterly, 1* (October-December, 1954), 8-18.

Okita, Saburo, and other Japanese. "Problems of Economic Development in South-East Asia," articles, *Asian Affairs, 1* (March, 1956).

Panikkar, K. M. *The Future of South-East Asia, and Indian View*, New York, 1943.

Parkinson, F. "From Berlin to Bangkok," *The Year Book of World Affairs, 1955*.

Peffer, Nathaniel. "Regional Security in Southeast Asia," *International Organization, 8* (August, 1954), 311-315.

Pelzer, Karl J. *Pioneer Settlement in the Asiatic Tropics: Studies in Land Utilization and Agricultural Colonization in Southeastern Asia*, New York, 1945.

Peyronnet, Marcel. "Chronique Économique du Sud-Est Asiatique," *France-Asie, 6* (March, 1951), 1056-1060.

Pillai, P. P., ed. *Labour in South-East Asia*, New Delhi, 1947.

Purcell, Victor. *The Chinese in Southeast Asia*, London, 1951.

Purcell, Victor. *The Colonial Period in Southeast Asia, An Historical Sketch*, New York, 1953.

Report to the Combined Chiefs of Staff by the Supreme Allied Commander, South-East Asia 1943-1945, Vice-Admiral the Earl Mountbatten of Burma, London, 1951.

Sacks, Milton. "The Strategy of Communism in Southeast Asia," *Pacific Affairs, 23* (September, 1950), 227-247.

Scalapino, Robert A. " 'Neutralism' in Asia," *American Political Science Review, 48* (March, 1954), 49-62.

Seabridge, G. W. "Some Problems of the White Man's Return to South-East Asia," *International Affairs, 21* (April, 1945), 196-205.

Shepherd, Jack. *Industry in Southeast Asia*, New York, 1941.

Shvedkov, Y. "American 'Aid' and the South-East Asian Countries," *International Affairs* (Moscow), June, 1956, 83-93.

Skinner, G. William. *Report on the Chinese in Southeast Asia*, Ithaca, N.Y., 1950.

Southeast Asia and the Economy of the Free World. A Report by the Foreign Commerce Department Committee of the Chamber of Commerce of the United States, Washington, D.C., 1952.

Sudjatmoko, S. "Point Four and Southeast Asia," *Indonesië, 4* (July, 1950), 1-11.

Talbot, Phillips, ed. *South Asia in the World Today*, Chicago, 1950.

Thayer, Philip W., ed. *Southeast Asia in the Coming World*, Baltimore, 1953.

Thayer, Philip W., ed. *Nationalism and Progress in Free Asia*, Baltimore, 1956.

The Signing of the Southeast Asia Collective Defense Treaty, the Protocol to the Southeast Asia Collective Defense Treaty and the Pacific Charter: Proceedings, Manila, 1954.

Thomas, Winburn T., and Manikran, Rajah B. *The Church in Southeast Asia*, New York, 1956.

Thompson, Virginia. "Labor in Southeast Asia," *Far Eastern Survey, 20* (June 27, 1951), 129-135.

Thompson, Virginia. *Labor Problems in Southeast Asia*, New Haven, 1947.

Thompson, Virginia, and Adloff, Richard. *Cultural Institutions and Educational Policy in Southeast Asia*, New York, 1948.

Thompson, Virginia, and Adloff, Richard. *The Left Wing in Southeast Asia*, New York, 1950.

Thompson, Virginia, and Adloff, Richard. *Minority Problems in Southeast Asia*, Stanford, Calif., 1955.

Thompson, Virginia, and Adloff, Richard. "Southeast Asia Follows the Leader," *Far Eastern Survey, 18* (November 2, 1949), 253-257.

Unger, Leonard. "The Chinese in Southeast Asia," *The Geographical Review, 34* (April, 1944), 196-217.

U.S. Department of State. *The Bangkok Conference of the Manila Pact Powers*, Washington, D.C., 1955. (Subsequent Annual Reports of the Council Representatives and Final Communiqués of the yearly

SEATO Council meetings are found in the *Department of State Bulletin.*)
U.S. Department of State. *Human Values in Social Change in South and Southeast Asia and in the United States,* Washington, D.C., 1956.
U.S. Department of State. *Southeast Asia: Critical Area in a Divided World,* Washington, D.C., 1955.
Vandenbosch, Amry, and Butwell, Richard A. *Southeast Asia among the World Powers,* Lexington, Ky., 1957.
Vlekke, B. H. M. "Communism and Nationalism in South East Asia," *International Affairs, 25* (April, 1949), 149-157.
Wales, H. G. Quaritch. *The Making of Greater India; A Study of South-East Asian Culture Change,* London, 1951.
Wales, H. G. Quaritch. "A Cultural Approach to the Postwar Problems of Southeast Asia," *Far Eastern Quarterly, 4* (May, 1945), 217-223.
Whittingham-Jones, Barbara. "Southeast Asia and the Western Powers," *Quarterly Review, 287* (April, 1949), 257-268.
Wint, Guy. "South Asia: Unity and Disunity," *International Conciliation,* No. 500 (November, 1954).
Wolf, Charles, Jr. "Economic Development and Reform in South and Southeast Asia," *Far Eastern Quarterly, 12* (November, 1952), 27-42.
Wyatt, Woodrow. *Southwards from China,* London, 1952.
Young, Kenneth T., Jr. "The Challenge of Asia to United States Policy," *The Department of State Bulletin, 35* (August 27, 1956), 340-352.
"Southeast Asia in Transition," *Journal of International Affairs, 10,* No. 1 (1956).
"Southeast Asia," *Current History, 23* (August, 1952).
Issue on Southeast Asia, *Far Eastern Quarterly, 2* (November, 1942).
Issue on Southeastern Asia and the Philippines, *Annals of the American Academy of Political and Social Science, 226* (March, 1943).

Ahmad, M. "Die Stellung Pakistans in der Weltpolitik," *Europa-Archiv, 10* (January, 1955), 7195-7198.
Angus, H. F. *Canada and the Far East, 1940-1953,* Toronto, 1953.
"Australian Foreign Policy in a Changing World," *Australian Outlook, 2* (March, 1957), 5-22.
Australian Institute of International Affairs. *Australian Policies Toward Asia,* Australian papers, Institute of Pacific Relations Conference, 7 parts (1 vol.), Melbourne, 1954.
Ball, W. Macmahon. "An Australian View of Southeast Asian Security," *Far Eastern Survey, 23* (November, 1954), 165-168.
Beloff, Max. *The Foreign Policy of Soviet Russia, 1929-1941,* 2 vols., New York, 1947 and 1949.
Beloff, Max. *Soviet Policy in the Far East, 1944-1951,* New York, 1953.
Borrie, W. W. "Australian Population Policy and Its Relation to Asia," *Australian Outlook, 4* (September, 1950), 162-169.

Burns, Sir Alan. *In Defence of Colonies*, London, 1957.
Cady, John F. *The Roots of French Imperialism in Eastern Asia*, Ithaca, N.Y., 1954.
Campbell-Johnson, Alan. *Mission with Mountbatten*, New York, 1953.
"Canadian Policy in the Far East," *External Affairs*, *2* (September, 1950), 326-330.
Carter, Gwendolen M. "New Zealand, Dependable Ally," *Far Eastern Survey*, *21* (February 13, 1952), 28-32.
Casey, R. G. *Friends and Neighbors*, East Lansing, Mich., 1955.
Chiang Kai-shek. *China's Destiny*, New York, 1947.
"Communist China in World Politics," *Journal of International Affairs*, *11*, No. 2 (1957).
Dai, Shen-yu. *Peking, Moscow and the Communist Parties of Colonial Asia*, Cambridge, Mass., 1954.
DeConde, Alexander. "Is China a Great Power?" *United States Naval Institute Proceedings*, *79* (January, 1953), 29-37.
Donnison, F. S. V. *British Military Administration in the Far East, 1943-46*, London, 1956.
Dulles, John Foster. "Security in the Pacific," *Foreign Affairs*, *30* (January, 1952), 175-187.
Dutt, Vidya Prakash. "India's Foreign Policy—With Special Reference to Asia and the Pacific," Indian Paper, 11th Conference of the Institute of Pacific Relations, Lucknow, October, 1950, New Delhi, 1950.
"East Pakistan," *Swiss Review of World Affairs*, *2* (July, 1952), 13-15.
Elsbree, Willard H. *Japan's Role in Southeast Asian Nationalist Movements, 1940 to 1945*, Cambridge, Mass., 1953.
Evatt, Herbert V. *Foreign Policy of Australia*, Sydney, 1945.
Evatt, Herbert V. *Australia in World Affairs*, Sydney, 1946.
Farley, Miriam S. *United States Relations with Southeast Asia, 1950-55*, rev. ed., New York, 1955.
Finkelstein, Lawrence S. *American Policy in Southeast Asia*, rev. ed., New York, 1951.
Ganguli, Birendranath. *India's Economic Relations with the Far Eastern and Pacific Countries in the Present Century*, New York, 1956.
Ghosal, A. K. "Panch Shila," *The Indian Journal of Political Science*, *17* (January-March, 1956), 59-63.
Gillan, Sir Angus. "Australia's Mission in South-East Asia," *Journal of the Royal Central Asian Society*, *39* (July-October, 1952), 209-217.
Gilmore, Robert J., and Warner, Denis, eds. *Near North: Australia and a Thousand Million Neighbours*, Sydney, 1948.
Greenwood, Gordon. "Australia's Triangular Foreign Policy," *Foreign Affairs*, *35* (July, 1957), 689-703.
Greenwood, Gordon. "Australian Attitudes Towards Pacific Problems," *Pacific Affairs*, *23* (June, 1950), 153-168.
Greenwood, Gordon, and Harper, Norman D., eds. *Australia in World Affairs, 1950-1955*, New York, 1957.

Haines, C. Grove, ed. *The Threat of Soviet Imperialism*, Baltimore, 1954.

Harper, Norman D. "Pacific Security as Seen from Australia," *International Organization, 8* (May, 1953), 213-228.

Harper, Norman D. "Australia and Southeast Asia," *Pacific Affairs, 28* (September, 1955), 203-220.

Holland, William L. "Japan and the New Balance of Power in the Far East," *International Affairs, 28* (July, 1952), 292-297.

Hudson, G. F. "Will Britain and America Split in Asia?" *Foreign Affairs, 31* (July, 1953), 536-547.

Huszar, George B. de, and Associates. *Soviet Power and Policy*, New York, 1955.

Hyma, Albert. *A History of the Dutch in the Far East*, rev., Ann Arbor, Mich., 1953.

"Interview with Ceylon's New Prime Minister S. W. R. D. Bandaranaike," *U.S. News and World Report*, April 20, 1956, 60-62, 64, 66.

Jones, Francis Clifford. *Japan's New Order in East Asia; Its Rise and Fall, 1937-45*, London, 1954.

Karunakaran, K. P. *India in World Affairs, August 1947-January 1950*, New York, 1952.

Kase, Toshikazu. "Japan's New Role in East Asia," *Foreign Affairs, 34* (October, 1955), 40-49.

Kirkpatrick, E. M., ed. *Target: The World*, New York, 1956.

Knorr, Klaus E. *Ruble Diplomacy, Challenge to American Foreign Aid*, Princeton, N.J., 1956.

Kondapi, E. *Indians Overseas, 1838-1949*, New Delhi, 1951.

Kotelawala, Sir John Lionel. *An Asian Prime Minister's Story*, London, 1956.

Kundra, J. C. *Indian Foreign Policy, 1947-1954*, New York, 1957.

Latourette, Kenneth Scott. *The American Record in the Far East, 1945-1951*, New York, 1952.

Levi, Werner. "Australia and the New Asia," *Far Eastern Survey, 19* (April 19, 1950), 73-78.

Levi, Werner. *Free India in Asia*, Minneapolis, 1952.

Levi, Werner. *Modern China's Foreign Policy*, Minneapolis, 1953.

Lévy, Roger. *Regards sur l'Asie: Chine, Japon, Corée, Viet Nam, Haute-Asie*, Paris, 1952.

Lévy, Roger, Lacam, Guy, and Roth, Andrew. *French Interests and Policies in the Far East*, New York, 1941.

Lindbeck, John M. H. "Communist China and American Far Eastern Policy," *The Department of State Bulletin, 33* (November 7, 1955), 751-759.

Lindsay, Michael. "Chinese Foreign Policy," *International Journal, 10* (Spring, 1955), 79-89.

Lindsay, Michael. *China and the Cold War: A Study in International Politics*, Melbourne, 1955.

Malenbaum, Wilfred. "U.S. Economic Policy in South and Southeast Asia," *India Quarterly, 12* (April-June, 1956), 107-116.

McAuley, James. "Australia's Future in New Guinea," *Pacific Affairs, 26* (March, 1953), 59-69.

McDonald, A. H. "Japanese Occupation Policy and Propaganda in South-East Asia," *Australian Outlook, 4* (March, 1950), 18-28.

Menzies, Robert Gordon. "The Pacific Settlement Seen from Australia," *Foreign Affairs, 30* (January, 1952), 188-196.

Miller, Agnes Roman. "American Investments in the Far East," *Far Eastern Survey, 19* (May 3, 1950), 81-89.

Milner, Jan F. G. *New Zealand's Interests and Policies in the Far East*, New York, 1940.

Monk, W. F. "New Zealand Faces North," *Pacific Affairs, 26* (September, 1953), 220-229.

Mosely, Philip E. "Soviet Policy and the Revolutions in Asia," *Annals of the American Academy of Political and Social Science, 276* (July, 1951), 91-98.

Munro, L. K. "New Zealand and the New Pacific," *Foreign Affairs, 31* (July, 1953), 634-647.

Olver, A. S. B. "Outline of British Policy in East and Southeastern Asia, 1945—May 1950," United Kingdom Paper, 11th Conference of the Institute of Pacific Relations, Lucknow, October, 1950, London, 1950.

Olver, A. S. B. "The Special Commission in South-East Asia," *Pacific Affairs, 21* (September, 1948), 285-291.

"Pakistan and Her Neighbours," *Round Table, 46* (June, 1956), 236-245.

Pauker, G. J. "Panikkarism, the Highest Stage of Opportunism," *World Politics*, 7 (October, 1954), 157-177.

Pearson, L. B. "Basis of Canadian Far Eastern Policy," *External Affairs, 3* (February, 1951), 38-46.

"Présence de la France en Asie," *France-Asie, 12* (October-December, 1956).

Price, M. Philips. "Russia and the Neutral World in Asia," *Contemporary Review, 183* (February, 1953), 65-69.

Rigby, T. H. "Soviet Comment on Southeast Asia," *Australian Outlook, 5* (December, 1951), 203-212.

Robertson, Walter S. "The United States Looks at South and Southeast Asia," *The Department of State Bulletin, 33* (August 22, 1955), 295-302.

Rostow, W. W. *The Prospects for Communist China*, Cambridge, Mass., 1954.

Royal Institute of International Affairs. *The Pattern of Pacific Security*, London, 1946.

Royal Institute of International Affairs. *British Security*, London, 1946.

Rubinstein, Alvin Z. "Russia, Southeast Asia and Point Four," *Current History, 28* (February, 1955), 103-108.

Schwartz, Benjamin I. *Chinese Communism and the Rise of Mao*, Cambridge, 1951.

Scott, Sir Robert. *Phoenix Park, Singapore*, Regional Information Office, Singapore, 1956.

Shepherd, Jack. *Australia's Interests and Policies in the Far East*, New York, 1940.

Sovani, N. V. *Economic Relations of India with South-East Asia and the Far East*, New York, 1951.

"Soviet Political Strategy in Asia," *The World Today*, *12* (May, 1956), 192-201.

"Soviet Radio Propaganda in the Far East," *The World Today*, *6* (October, 1950), 434-441.

Spender, P. C. "Partnership with Asia," *Foreign Affairs*, *29* (January, 1951), 205-218.

Srinivasamurthy, A. K. "A Nehru Doctrine for Asia," *The Indian Year Book of International Affairs, 1953*.

Steiner, H. Arthur. "The United States and China: The Prospect Before Us," *The Yale Review*, *44* (December, 1954), 161-179.

Steiner, H. Arthur. "Mainsprings of Chinese Communist Foreign Policy," *American Journal of International Law*, *44* (January, 1950), 69-99.

Sun, E-tu Zen. "The Pattern of Railway Development in China," *Far Eastern Quarterly*, *14* (February, 1955), 179-199.

"The Foreign Policy of the Chinese People's Republic," *The World Today*, *13* (April, 1957), 162-173.

"The Fundamentals of Pakistan's Foreign Policy," *Pakistan Horizon*, *9* (March, 1956), 37-50.

Thomas, S. B. *Communist China and Her Neighbours*, Toronto, 1955.

Trovini, Leo. "Development of Economic Relations between Italy and the Countries of South and Southeast Asia," *East and West*, *2* (October, 1951), 141-146.

Vinacke, Harold M. *The United States and the Far East, 1945-1951*, Stanford, Calif., 1952.

Walker, Richard L. *China under Communism; The First Five Years*, New Haven, 1955.

Wiens, Herold J. *China's March toward the Tropics: A Discussion of the Southward Penetration of China's Culture, Peoples, and Political Control in Relation to the Non Han-Chinese Peoples of South China and in the Perspective of Historical and Cultural Geography*, Hamden, 1954.

Wint, Guy. *The British in Asia*, rev. ed., New York, 1954.

Wolf, Charles, Jr. "Soviet Economic Aid in Southeast Asia: Threat or Windfall?" *World Politics*, *10* (October, 1957), 91-101.

Wood, Frederick L. W. "Anzac Dilemma," *International Affairs*, *29* (April, 1953), 184-192.

Wood, Frederick L. W. "New Zealand and Southeast Asia," *Far Eastern Survey*, *25* (February, 1956), 23-27.

Yeh Chi-chuang. "China's Economic Relations with Asian and African

Countries: Progress and Prospects," *People's China*, No. 6, March 16, 1956, 12-15.

Yoshida, Shigeru, "Japan and the Crisis in Asia," *Foreign Affairs, 29* (January, 1951), 171-181.

Younger, Kenneth. "A British View of the Far East," *Pacific Affairs, 27* (June, 1954), 99-111.

Younger, Kenneth. "Western Policy in Asia," *Pacific Affairs, 25* (June, 1952), 115-129.

A Guide to New China, Peking, 2d ed., rev., 1952.

Alexander, C. H. "Foreign Investment Laws and Regulations of the Countries of Asia and the Far East," *International and Comparative Law Quarterly, 1* (January, 1952), 29-39.

Appadorai, A. *The Bandung Conference*, New Delhi, 1955.

Asian Relations, Being Report of the Proceedings and Documents of the First Asian Relations Conference, New Delhi, March-April, 1947, New Delhi, 1948.

Bailey, Sydney D. *Parliamentary Government in Southern Asia*, London, 1953.

Ball, W. Macmahon. *Nationalism and Communism in East Asia*, rev. ed., New York, 1956.

Balogh, Thomas. "The Challenge of Totalitarian Planning in Asia," *International Affairs, 31* (July, 1955), 300-310.

Bandung Conference, Selected Documents, issued by Institute of Pacific Relations, 1955.

Basch, Antonin. "The Colombo Plan: A Case of Regional Economic Coöperation," *International Organization, 9* (February, 1955), 1-18.

Bauer, Pèter Tamàs. *The Rubber Industry: A Study in Competition and Monopoly*, Cambridge, Mass., 1948.

Beer, Max. "Another Problem for the UN: The Asiatic-Arab Alignment," *Swiss Review of World Affairs, 2* (July, 1952), 16-18.

Benham, Frederic. *The Colombo Plan and Other Essays*, New York, 1956.

Bhargava, G. S. "Positive Aspects of Asian Socialism," *Pacific Affairs, 26* (September, 1953), 236-244.

Blakeslee, George H. *The Far Eastern Commission, A Study in International Coöperation, 1945 to 1952*, Washington, D.C., 1953.

Boorman, Howard L., Eckstein, Alexander, Mosely, Philip E., and Schwartz, Benjamin. *Moscow-Peking Axis, Strengths and Strains*, New York, 1957.

Bowles, Chester. *Ambassador's Report*, New York, 1954.

Bowles, Chester. "A Fresh Look at Free Asia," *Foreign Affairs, 33* (October, 1954), 54-71.

Braisted, William R. "Nationalism in Eastern Asia," *The Journal of Modern History, 26* (December, 1954), 356-363.

Brenchley, T. F. "The Work of the Economic Commission for Asia and the Far East of the United Nations," *Journal of the Royal Central Asian Society, 40* (January, 1953), 59-69.

Buss, Claude A. *The Far East*, New York, 1955.

Carr-Gregg, John R. E. "The Colombo Plan; A Commonwealth Program for Southeast Asia," *International Conciliation*, No. 467 (January, 1951).

Chaudhri, M. H. "The Afro-Asian Conference," *Pakistan Horizon, 8* (March, 1955), 306-311, *8* (June, 1955), 382-390.

Chou En-lai. "On the Asian-African Conference at Bandung," *United Asia*, 7 (December, 1955), 308-315.

Clyde, Paul H. *The Far East*, 2d ed., New York, 1952.

Commonwealth Consultative Committee on South and South-East Asia, *New Horizons in the East*, London, 1950.

Conference for the Conclusion and Signature of the Treaty of Peace with Japan, Record of Proceedings, Supplement, 2 vols., Washington, D.C., 1951.

Cousins, Norman. "Report from Bandung," *The Saturday Review, 38* (May 21, 1955), 7-9, 54-56.

Cressey, George B. *Asia's Lands and Peoples*, 2d ed., New York, 1951.

Dalisay, Amando M. *Economic Aspects of the Baguio Conference of 1950*, Manila, 1950.

East, W. Gordon, and Moodie, A. E., eds. *The Changing World*, New York, 1956.

East, W. Gordon, and Spate, O. H. K., eds. *The Changing Map of Asia: A Political Geography*, 2d ed., rev., London, 1953.

Eickstedt, Egon von. "Der Motor der Ostasiatischen Völkerdynamik," *Zeitschrift für Geopolitik, 24* (February, 1953), 69-78.

Eldridge, F. B. *Background of Eastern Sea Power*, London, 1948.

Emerson, Rupert. "Paradoxes of Asian Nationalism," *Far Eastern Quarterly, 13* (February, 1954), 131-142.

Final Act and Proceedings of the Baguio Conference of 1950, Manila, 1950.

FitzGerald, C. P. "East Asia after Bandung," *Far Eastern Survey, 24* (August, 1955), 113-119.

Greene, Fred. *The Far East*, New York, 1957.

Hailey, Foster B. *Half of One World*, New York, 1950.

Hayden, S. S. "The Arab-Asian Bloc," *Middle Eastern Affairs, 5* (May, 1954), 149-153.

Holland, William L., ed. *Asian Nationalism and the West*, New York, 1953.

Howard, Harry N. "The Arab-Asian States in the United Nations," *The Middle East Journal*, 7 (Summer, 1953), 279-292.

Hudson, G. F. "Balance Sheet on Bandung," *Commentary, 19* (June, 1955), 562-567.

Institute of Pacific Relations. *The Development of Upland Areas in the Far East*, 2 vols., New York, 1949-1951.

Isaacs, Harold R., ed. *New Cycle in Asia: Selected Documents on Major International Developments in the Far East*, New York, 1947.

Isaacs, Harold R. *No Peace for Asia*, New York, 1947.

James, C. W. "The Colombo Plan Passes Halfway," *Australian Outlook, 9* (March, 1955), 29-42.

Kahin, George McTurnan. *The Asian-African Conference; Bandung, Indonesia, April 1955*, Ithaca, N.Y., 1956.

Keynes, Mary K. "The Arab-Asian Bloc," *International Relations, 1* (October, 1956), 238-250.

Keynes, Mary K. "The Bandung Conference," *International Relations, 1* (October, 1957), 362-376.

Knorr, Klaus E. *Tin Under Control*, Stanford, Calif., 1945.

Knorr, Klaus E. *World Rubber and Its Regulation*, Stanford, Calif., 1945.

Lasker, Bruno. *Asia on the Move*, New York, 1945.

Latourette, Kenneth Scott. *A Short History of the Far East*, rev. ed., New York, 1951.

Linton, Ralph, ed. *Most of the World: The Peoples of Africa, Latin America and the East Today*, New York, 1949.

Lokanathan, P. S. "ECAFE—The Economic Parliament of Asia," *The Indian Year Book of International Affairs, 1953*.

Low, Sir Francis. *The Struggle for Asia*, New York, 1955.

MacNair, Harley F., and Lach, Donald F. *Modern Far Eastern International Relations*, 2d ed., New York, 1955.

Madan, B. K., ed. *Economic Problems of Underdeveloped Countries in Asia*, New Delhi, 1953.

Mansergh, Nicholas. "The Asian Conference," *International Affairs, 23* (July, 1947), 295-306.

Mao Tse-tung. *Selected Works*, Vol. I, 1926-1936, Vol. II, 1937-1938, Vol. III, 1939-1941, Vol. IV, 1941-1945, New York, 1954, 1955, 1956.

Michael, Franz H., and Taylor, George E. *The Far East in the Modern World*, New York, 1956.

Mitchell, Kate L. *Industrialization of the Western Pacific*, New York, 1942.

Montagne, Robert. "Modern Nations and Islam," *Foreign Affairs, 30* (July, 1952), 580-592.

Mookerjee, Girija. "Peace Settlements in the Far East since 1945," *India Quarterly, 6* (July-September, 1950), 262-276.

Natsir, Mohammad. *Some Observations Concerning the Role of Islam in National and International Affairs*, Ithaca, N.Y., 1954.

Nehru, Jawaharlal. *The Discovery of India*, New York, 1946.

Nehru, Jawaharlal. *An Autobiography, with Musings on Recent Events in India*, new ed., London, 1949.

Nehru, Jawaharlal. *Independence and After, A Collection of the More Important Speeches, from September 1946 to May 1949*, New Delhi, 1949.

Jawaharlal Nehru's Speeches, 1949-1953, New Delhi, 1954.

Palmer, Norman D. "Organizing for Peace in Asia," *Western Political Quarterly, 8* (March, 1955), 1-43.

Panikkar, K. M. *Asia and Western Dominance; A Survey of the Vasco da Gama Epoch of Asian History, 1498-1945*, London, 1953.

Panikkar, K. M. "Regional Organization for the Indian Ocean Area," *Pacific Affairs, 18* (September, 1945), 246-251.

Parkinson, F. "Bandung and the Underdeveloped Countries," *The Year Book of World Affairs, 1956.*

Payne, Robert. *Red Storm Over Asia,* New York, 1951.

Payne, Robert. *The Revolt of Asia,* New York, 1947.

Pearcy, G. Etzel, and Associates. *World Political Geography,* 2d ed., New York, 1957.

Peterson, A. D. C. *The Far East; A Social Geography,* 2d ed., rev., London, 1951.

Poplai, S. L., ed. *Asia and Africa in the Modern World,* New York, 1955.

Poplai, S. L. "The Colombo Conference of South-East Asian Prime Ministers," *Foreign Affairs Reports,* July, 1954.

Roerich, G. N. "The Cultural Unity of Asia," *India Quarterly, 6* (January-March, 1950), 38-44.

Romulo, Carlos P. *The Meaning of Bandung,* Chapel Hill, N.C., 1956.

Romulo, Carlos P. "The United Nations and the New States of Asia," *Yale Review, 40* (December, 1950), 193-200.

Rosinger, Lawrence K., and Associates. *The State of Asia: A Contemporary Survey,* New York, 1951.

Rowan, Carl T. *The Pitiful and the Proud,* New York, 1956.

Roy, M. N. "The Communist Problem in East Asia: An Asian View," *Pacific Affairs, 24* (September, 1951), 227-240.

Roy, M. N. "Democracy and Nationalism in Asia," *Pacific Affairs, 25* (June, 1952), 140-146.

Roy, M. N. "Asian Nationalism," *Yale Review, 42* (September, 1952), 96-102.

Roy, M. N. "The State of Socialism in Asia: Rangoon and After," *Pacific Affairs, 26* (June, 1953), 135-139.

Rubinstein, Alvin Z. "The State of Socialism in Asia: The Rangoon Conference," *Pacific Affairs, 26* (June, 1953), 131-134.

Russell, Sir E. John. "Asia's Food Problems and Their Impact on the Western Countries," *International Affairs, 26* (July, 1950), 316-328.

Saposs, David J. "The Split Between Asian and Western Socialism," *Foreign Affairs, 32* (July, 1954), 588-594.

Sastri, K. A. Nilakanta. "Inter-State Relations in Asia," *The Indian Year Book of International Affairs, 1953.*

Schaaf, C. Hart. "Economic Coöperation in Asia," *International Conciliation,* No. 460 (April, 1950).

Schaaf, C. Hart. "The United Nations Economic Commission for Asia and the Far East," *International Organization,* 7 (November, 1953), 463-481.

Secretariat, Economic Commission for Asia and the Far East. *Foreign Investment Laws and Regulations of the Countries of Asia and the Far East,* New York, 1951.

Spencer, Joseph E. *Asia: East by South,* New York, 1954.

Stamp, L. Dudley. *Asia, A Regional and Economic Geography*, 8th ed., rev., New York, 1950.

Starke, J. G. "Security in the Pacific," *The Year Book of World Affairs, 1956*.

Strausz-Hupé, Robert, Cottrell, Alvin J., and Dougherty, James E., eds. *American-Asian Tensions*, New York, 1956.

Taylor, George E. "The Intellectual Climate of Asia," *Yale Review, 42* (Winter, 1953), 184-197.

Taylor, George E. "Power in Asia," *Virginia Quarterly Review, 30* (September, 1954), 342-354.

"Ten Years of Effort for Asia and the Far East," *United Nations Review, 3* (March, 1957), 45-47.

The Colombo Plan for Coöperative Economic Development in South and South-East Asia. Report by the Commonwealth Consultative Committee, London, September-October 1950, Cmd. 8080.

The Common Programme and Other Documents of the First Plenary Session of the Chinese People's Political Consultative Conference, Peking, 1952.

The Chinese People's Liberation Army, Peking, 1950.

The Electoral Law of the People's Republic of China, Peking, 1953.

"The Inter-Asian Relations Conference," *Round Table, 37* (June, 1947), 237-243.

Thomas, S. B. *Government and Administration in Communist China*, 2d ed., rev., New York, 1955.

Thompson, Warren S. *Population and Peace in the Pacific*, Chicago, 1946.

Ueyama, Shoji. "Afro-Asian Conference," *Japan Quarterly, 2* (July-September, 1955), 291-294.

United Nations, Department of Public Information. *Helping Economic Development in Asia and the Far East, The Work of ECAFE*, New York, 1953.

United Nations, Department of Social Affairs, Population Division. "International Migrations in the Far East During Recent Times," *Population Bulletin*, No. 1 (December, 1951), 13-30; No. 2 (October, 1952), 27-58.

United Nations, Economic and Social Council. *Official Records*, 3d Year, 6th Session, Supplement No. 8, Report of the Economic Commission for Asia and the Far East on Its First and Second Sessions. (Subsequent reports on the sessions.)

U.S. Department of State. *Report of the Consultative Committee on Economic Development in South and Southeast Asia—Fourth Meeting at Karachi, Pakistan, March, 1952*, Washington, D.C., 1952. (Subsequent Annual Reports of the Consultative Committee and communiqués at end of its annual meetings.)

Vinacke, Harold M. *Far Eastern Politics in the Postwar Period*, New York, 1956.

Wales, H. G. Quaritch. *Years of Blindness*, New York, 1943.

Wickizer, V. D., and Bennett, M. K. *The Rice Economy of Monsoon Asia*, Stanford, Calif., 1941.

Wint, Guy. *Spotlight on Asia*, London, 1955.

Zhukov, E. "The Bandung Conference of African and Asian Countries and Its Historic Significance," *International Affairs* (Moscow), May, 1955, 18-32.

Zhukov, E. "The Eastern Peoples and the World's Destiny," *International Affairs* (Moscow), April, 1956, 45-51.

Zinkin, Maurice. *Asia and the West*, rev. ed., New York, 1953.

Zinkin, Maurice. *Development for Free Asia*, Fair Lawn, N.J., 1956.

Akzin, Benjamin. *New States and International Organizations*, Paris, 1955.

Ball, M. Margaret. "Bloc Voting in the General Assembly," *International Organization, 5* (February, 1951), 3-31.

Bowie, Robert R. "Tasks Ahead for the Free World," *The Department of State Bulletin, 36* (May 27, 1957), 835-839.

Brzezinski, Z. "The Politics of Underdevelopment," *World Politics, 9* (October, 1956), 55-75.

Churchill, Winston S. *The Second World War*, Vol. VI, *Triumph and Tragedy*, Boston, 1953.

Dulles, John Foster. *War or Peace*, New York, 1950.

Eagleton, Clyde. "Excesses of Self-Determination," *Foreign Affairs, 31* (July, 1953), 592-604.

Eighty-fifth Congress, First Session. Senate Document No. 52, *Foreign Aid Program, Compilation of Studies and Surveys*, Washington, D.C., 1957.

Eighty-fifth Congress, First Session. Senate Report No. 139, *Technical Assistance, Final Report of the Committee on Foreign Relations*, March 12, 1957, Washington, D.C., 1957.

Eighty-third Congress, Second Session. Special Subcommittee on Security Affairs, Senate Committee on Foreign Relations, *Strength of the International Communist Movement*, Washington, D.C., 1954.

Furniss, Edgar S., Jr. "A Reëxamination of Regional Arrangements," *Journal of International Affairs, 9*, No. 2 (1955), 79-89.

Grégoire, Roger. *National Administration and International Organizations*, Paris, 195-.

Gross, Leo. "Progress Towards Universality of Membership in the United Nations," *American Journal of International Law, 50* (October, 1956), 791-827.

Haas, Ernst P. "Regionalism, Functionalism, and Universal International Organization," *World Politics, 8* (January, 1956), 238-263.

Higgins, Benjamin, and Malenbaum, Wilfred. "Financing Economic Development," *International Conciliation*, No. 502 (March, 1955).

Hull, Cordell. *The Memoirs of Cordell Hull*, 2 vols., New York, 1948.

Jessup, Philip C. "Self-Determination Today in Principle and in Practice," *Virginia Quarterly Review, 33* (Spring, 1957), 174-188.

King, Ernest J., and Whitehill, Walter Muir. *Fleet Admiral King: A Naval Record*, New York, 1952.

Leahy, William D. *I Was There: The Personal Story of the Chief of Staff to Presidents Roosevelt and Truman Based on His Notes and Diaries Made at the Time*, New York, 1950.

Lie, Trygve. *In the Cause of Peace*, New York, 1954.

Makins, Sir Roger. "The World Since the War: The Third Phase," *Foreign Affairs, 33* (October, 1954), 1-16.

Millis, Walter, ed. *The Forrestal Diaries*, New York, 1951.

Padelford, Norman J. "Regional Organization and the United Nations," *International Organization, 8* (May, 1954), 203-216.

Panikkar, K. M. "The Twentieth Century in Asian and World History," *India Quarterly, 12* (July-September, 1956), 217-249.

Panikkar, K. M., and Others. *Regionalism and Security*, Bombay, 1948.

Peaslee, Amos J. *International Governmental Organizations, Constitutional Documents*, 2 vols., The Hague, 1956.

Peaslee, Amos J. *Constitutions of Nations*, 2d ed., 3 vols., The Hague, 1956.

Pickard, Bertram. *The Greater United Nations*, New York, 1956.

Reitzel, William, Kaplan, Morton A., and Coblenz, Constance G. *United States Foreign Policy, 1945-1955*, Washington, D.C., 1956.

Report to Congress on the Mutual Security Program for the Six Months Ended December 31, 1956, Washington, D.C., 1957. (Also prior and subsequent reports.)

Ridgway, General Matthew B. (as told to Harold H. Martin). *Soldier; The Memoirs of Matthew B. Ridgway*, New York, 1956.

Rivlin, Benjamin. "Self-Determination and Dependent Areas," *International Conciliation*, No. 501 (January, 1955).

Sorensen, Max. "The Quest for Equality," *International Conciliation*, No. 507 (March, 1956).

Staley, Eugene. *The Future of Underdeveloped Countries*, New York, 1954.

Stein, Eric. *Some Implications of Expanding United Nations Membership*, New York, 1956.

Truman, Harry S. *Memoirs*, Vol. 1, *Year of Decision*, Garden City, 1955; Vol. 2, *Years of Trial and Hope, 1946-1952*, Garden City, 1956.

United Nations. *Tenth Anniversary of the Signing of the United Nations Charter: Proceedings of the Commemorative Meetings*, New York, 1955.

United Nations, Department of Public Information. *Pooling Skills for Human Progress*, New York, 1956.

U.S. Department of State. *Foreign Relations of the United States: The Conferences of Malta and Yalta 1945*, Washington, D.C., 1955.

U.S. Department of State, Department of Defense, and International Coöperation Administration. *The Mutual Security Program, Fiscal Year 1958, A Summary Presentation, June 1957*, Washington, D.C., 1957.

Wickizer, V. D. *Coffee, Tea and Cocoa: An Economic and Political Analysis*, Stanford, Calif., 1951.

Wickizer, V. D. *Tea Under International Regulation*, rev. ed., Stanford, Calif., 1951.

Wolf, Charles, Jr. "Political Effects of Economic Development," *Far Eastern Survey, 20* (May 2, 1951), 81-87.

IV. PHILIPPINES

Official Gazette, Republic of the Philippines.
Department of Foreign Affairs Review (formerly *The Department of Foreign Affairs Quarterly*).
Department of Foreign Affairs, Treaty Series.
Official texts of speeches, Division of International Information, Department of Foreign Affairs.
Diplomatic and Consular List, Department of Foreign Affairs.
Ministry of Foreign Affairs *Bulletin*, Vol. 1, No. 1 (October 14, 1943-February 15, 1944), No. 2 (February 16, 1944-March 31, 1944), No. 3 (April, 1944).
H. Otley Beyer Collection, Manila.
The Philippines Free Press.
Manila Daily Bulletin, especially the Annual Editions.
The Fookien Times Yearbook.
Abaya, Hernando. *Betrayal in the Philippines*, New York, 1946.
Aberlarde, Pedro E. *American Tariff Policy Toward the Philippines, 1898-1946*, New York, 1947.
Araneta, Salvador. "Basic Problems of Philippine Economic Developments," *Pacific Affairs, 21* (September, 1948), 280-285.
Aruego, Jose M. *Philippine Government in Action*, Manila, 1953.
Aruego, Jose M. *The Framing of the Philippine Constitution*, 2 vols., Manila, 1936.
Baldoria, Pedro L. "Political Geography of the Philippines," *Philippine Geographical Journal, 1*, No. 1 (1953), 15-23.
Bernstein, David. *The Philippine Story*, New York, 1947.
Beyer, H. Otley. "Early History of Philippine Relations with Foreign Countries, Especially China," in E. Arsenio Manuel, *Chinese Elements in the Tagalog Language*, Manila, 1948.
Blair, Emma Helen, and Robertson, James Alexander, eds. *The Philippine Islands, 1493-1898*, 55 vols., Cleveland, 1903-1909.
Buss, Claude A. "The Philippines in World Politics," *World Affairs, 5* (January, 1951), 37-47.
Bustos, Felixberto G. *And Now Comes Roxas, The Story of the First President of the Republic of the Philippines and the Occupation*, Manila, 1946.
Cannon, M. Hamlin. *Leyte, The Return to the Philippines*, Washington, D.C., 1954.
Cuaderno, M. "The Bell Trade Act and the Philippine Economy," *Pacific Affairs, 25* (December, 1952), 323-333.
Curry, Roy W. "Woodrow Wilson and Philippine Policy," *The Mississippi Valley Historical Review, 41* (December, 1954), 435-452.
Dalton, James J. "Honest Elections in the Philippines," *Foreign Policy Bulletin, 33* (February, 1954), 1-2.

Dalton, James J. "Ins and Outs in the Philippines," *Far Eastern Survey, 21* (July 30, 1952), 117-123.

Eggan, Fred, and Associates. *The Philippines*, 4 vols., New Haven, 1956.

Eyre, James K., Jr. "Russia and the American Acquisition of the Philippines," *The Mississippi Valley Historical Review, 28* (March, 1942), 539-562.

Fabella, Gabriel, Jr. "The Contemporary Indian Community in the Philippines," *Philippine Social Sciences and Humanities Review, 19* (March, 1954), 15-24.

Fifield, Russell H. "The Challenge to Magsaysay," *Foreign Affairs, 33* (October, 1954), 149-154.

Fifield, Russell H. "Philippine Foreign Policy," *Far Eastern Survey, 20* (February 21, 1951), 33-38.

Fifield, Russell H. "The United States and the Philippines," *South Atlantic Quarterly, 50* (October, 1951), 459-469.

Fifield, Russell H. "The Hukbalahap Today," *Far Eastern Survey, 20* (January 24, 1951), 13-18.

Fonacier, Tomas S. "The Chinese Exclusion Policy in the Philippines," *Philippine Social Sciences and Humanities Review, 14* (March, 1949), 3-28.

Forbes, W. Cameron. *The Philippine Islands*, 2 vols., Boston, 1928.

Gayet, Georges. "Le Rôle des Philippines dans le Sud-Est Asiatique," *Politique Étrangère, 15* (April-May, 1950), 201-212.

Golay, Frank H. "The Philippine Monetary Policy Debate," *Pacific Affairs, 29* (September, 1956), 253-264.

Golay, Frank H. "Economic Consequences of the Philippine Trade Act," *Pacific Affairs, 28* (March, 1955), 53-70.

Golay, Frank H. *The Revised United States-Philippine Trade Agreement of 1955*, Ithaca, N.Y., 1956.

Gosnell, Harold F. "An Interpretation of the Philippine Election of 1953," *American Political Science Review, 48* (December, 1954), 1128-1138.

Grunder, Garel A., and Livezey, William E. *The Philippines and the United States*, Norman, Okla., 1951.

Harrison, Francis Burton. *The Cornerstone of Philippine Independence*, New York, 1922.

Hartendorp, A. V. H. *Short History of Industry and Trade of the Philippines*, Manila, 1953.

Hartendorp, A. V. H. "Short History of Industry and Trade of the Philippines: The Quirino Administration; Foreign Affairs," *The American Chamber of Commerce Journal, 31* (December, 1955), 530-536, *32* (January, 1956), 14-19.

Hassel, Elizabeth L. "The Sri-Vijayan and Majapahit Empires and the Theory of Their Political Association with the Philippines," *Philippine Social Sciences and Humanities Review, 18* (March, 1953), 3-86.

Hayden, Joseph Ralston. *The Philippines: A Study in National Development*, New York, 1942.

Hayden, Ralston. "What Next for the Moro?" *Foreign Affairs, 6* (July 1928), 633-644.

Hayden, Ralston. "Higher Officials in the Philippine Civil Service," *American Political Science Review*, *27* (April, 1933), 204-221.

Hunt, Chester L. "Cotabato: Melting Pot of the Philippines," *Philippine Social Sciences and Humanities Review*, *19* (March, 1954), 40-72.

Hunt, Chester L. "The 'Americanization' Process in the Philippines," *India Quarterly*, *12* (April-June, 1956), 117-130.

Hunt, Chester L. "Moslem and Christian in the Philippines," *Pacific Affairs*, *28* (December, 1955), 331-349.

Issue on the Philippines, *Far Eastern Quarterly*, *4* (February, 1945).

Jenkins, Shirley. *American Economic Policy Toward the Philippines*, Stanford, Calif., 1954.

Kirk, Grayson L. *Philippine Independence: Motives, Problems and Prospects*, New York, 1936.

Kolb, Albert. *Die Philippinen*, Stuttgart, 1950.

Krieger, Herbert W. *Peoples of the Philippines*, Washington, D.C., 1942.

Kroeber, Alfred L. *Peoples of the Philippines*, New York, 1928.

Kurihara, Kenneth K. *Labor in the Philippine Economy*, Stanford, Calif., 1945.

Lansang, Jose A. "The Philippine-American Experiment: A Filipino View," *Pacific Affairs*, *25* (September, 1952), 226-234.

Laurel, José P. *Forces That Make a Nation Great*, Manila, 1944.

Laurel, José P. *Bread and Freedom*, Manila, 1953.

Lava, Jose. "Basic National Problems and an Outline of Viable Solutions," January 14, 1954 (memorandum).

Liang, Dapen. *The Development of Philippine Political Parties*, Hong Kong, 1939.

Magsaysay, Ramon. "Roots of Philippine Policy," *Foreign Affairs*, *35* (October, 1956), 29-36.

Malcolm, George A. *The Commonwealth of the Philippines*, New York, 1936.

Malcolm, George A. *First Malayan Republic*, Boston, 1951.

McHale, Thomas R. "Problems of Economic Development in the Philippines," *Pacific Affairs*, *25* (June, 1952), 160-169.

McMillan, Robert T. "Local Government in the Philippines," *Philippine Sociological Review*, *2* (July, 1954), 18-27.

Mill, Edward W. "The Philippines in the World Setting," *Philippine Social Sciences and Humanities Review*, *20* (March, 1955), 3-37.

Mill, Edward W. "First Philippine Foreign Affairs Training Group," *The American Foreign Service Journal*, *23* (April, 1946), 15-16, 49-50.

Mill, Edward W. "Philippine Foreign Affairs Training Program," *The Department of State Bulletin*, *14* (February 3, 1946), 148-149.

Morton, Louis. *The Fall of the Philippines*, Washington, D.C., 1953.

Orosa, Sixto Y. *The Sulu Archipelago and Its People*, Yonkers, N.Y., 1931.

Osias, Camilo. *The Filipino Way of Life: The Pluralized Philosophy*, New York, 1940.

Osmeña, Sergio. *The New Philippine Ideology*, Manila, 1945.

Pascual, Ricardo R. *Partyless Democracy; A Blue-Print for Political Reconstruction of Post-War Philippines*, Quezon, 1952.

Pier, Arthur S. *American Apostles to the Philippines*, Boston, 1950.

Pink, Louis H. "Unfinished Business in the Philippines," *Foreign Affairs*, *25* (January, 1947), 263-274.

Porter, Catherine. "New Light on the Fall of the Philippines," *Pacific Affairs*, *27* (December, 1954), 370-377.

"Presidential Policy in the Philippines," *The World Today*, *12* (December, 1956), 512-523.

Quezon, Manuel Luis (posthumous). *The Good Fight*, New York, 1946.

Quirino, Elpidio. *The New Philippine Ideology* (speeches and other public pronouncements), Manila, 1949.

Quirino, Elpidio. *Philippines: The Quirino Way; Collection of Speeches and Addresses*, Manila, 1955.

Ravenholt, Albert, "The Philippines: Where Did We Fail?" *Foreign Affairs*, *29* (April, 1951), 406-416.

Recto, Claro M. *Three Years of Enemy Occupation*, Manila, 1946.

Recto, Claro M. *My Crusade*, Manila, 1955.

Renne, Roland R. "Agrarian Problems and Foreign Aid in the Philippines," *Far Eastern Survey*, *22* (December, 1953), 179-183.

Report of the President [of the Commonwealth] of the Philippines to the President of the United States, 4 vols., Washington, D.C., 1937 to 1940.

Report to the President of the United States by the Economic Survey Mission to the Philippines, Washington, D.C., 1950.

Report of the United States High Commissioner to the Philippine Islands to the President and Congress of the United States, 7 vols., Washington, D.C., 1937 to 1947.

Rivera, Generoso F., and McMillan, Robert T. *The Rural Philippines*, Manila, 1952.

Rizal, José. *Noli Me Tangere*, Manila, 1899.

Rizal, José. *El Filibusterismo*, Manila, 1900.

Romani, John H. *The Philippine Presidency*, Manila, 1956.

Romani, John H., and Thomas, M. Ladd. *A Survey of Local Government in the Philippines*, Manila, 1954.

Romulo, Carlos P. *I Saw the Fall of the Philippines*, New York, 1942.

Romulo, Carlos P. *I See the Philippines Rise*, New York, 1946.

Romulo, Carlos P. *Crusade in Asia: Philippine Victory*, New York, 1955.

Romulo, Carlos P., and Gray, Marvin M. *The Magsaysay Story*, New York, 1956.

Rosinger, Lawrence K. "The Philippines—Problems of Independence," *Foreign Policy Reports*, *24* (September 1, 1948), 82-95.

Roxas, Manuel. *The Problems of Philippine Rehabilitation and Trade Relations* (speeches), Manila, 1947.

Salazar, Meliton. "Philippine Labour Unions: An Appraisal," *Pacific Affairs*, *26* (June, 1953), 146-155.

Santos, Vicente Abad, and Lennhoff, Charles D. T. "The Taganak

Island Lighthouse Dispute," *American Journal of International Law*, *45* (October, 1951), 680-688.

Scaff, Alvin H. "Class Stratification in the EDCOR Communities," *Philippine Sociological Review*, *2* (July, 1954), 4-11.

Scaff, Alvin H. "Democracy vs. Communism in the Philippines," *Problems of Communism*, *4* (September-October, 1955), 27-36.

Scaff, Alvin H. *The Philippine Answer to Communism*, Stanford, Calif., 1955.

Seeman, Bernard, and Salisbury, Lawrence. *Cross-Currents in the Philippines*, New York, 1946.

Special Committee on Un-Filipino Activities, House of Representatives, Congress of the Philippines. *Report on I. The Illegality of the Communist Party of the Philippines; II. The Functions of the Special Committee on Un-Filipino Activities*, Manila, 1951.

Special Committee to Reëxamine Philippine-American Relations and Agreements, House of Representatives, Congress of the Philippines. *Report on the Military Bases Agreement of 1947 Between the Philippines and the United States*, Manila, 1956.

Spencer, J. E. *Land and People in the Philippines; Geographic Problems in Rural Economy*, Berkeley, Calif., 1952.

Statistical Handbook of the Philippines 1903-1953, Manila, 1954.

Taruc, Luis. *Born of the People*, New York, 1953.

The First National City Bank of New York. *The Philippines, A Report on Business and Trade*, New York, 1956.

Tillah, Santanina C. "On Sulu's Claim to British North Borneo," *Philippine Law Journal*, *26* (October, 1951), 199-210.

Transcript of Stenographic Notes Taken at the Joint Meeting of the Committee on Foreign Affairs and Committee on National Defense, Held on March 3, 1950, at the Conference Room, Office of the Speaker, Manila, 1950.

U.S. Department of Commerce. *Investment in the Philippines*, Washington, D.C., 1955.

U.S. Department of State. *The Philippines: Early Years of the Republic; Background*, Washington, D.C., 1951.

U.S. Department of State. *The Philippines, 1954; Background*, Washington, D.C., 1954.

Ututalum, Salik. "The Beginnings of Islam in the Philippines," *Islamic Review*, *40* (December, 1952), 29-31.

Wickberg, Edgar. "Spanish Records in the Philippine National Archives," *Hispanic American Historical Review*, *35* (February 1955), 77-89.

Wickberg, Edgar. "The Philippine National Archives," *Journal of East Asiatic Studies*, *3* (April, 1954), 345-349.

Worcester, Dean C. *The Philippines Past and Present*, 2 vols., New York, 1914.

Wurfel, David, "The Philippine Rice Share Tenancy Act," *Pacific Affairs*, *27* (March, 1954), 41-50.

Zaide, Gregorio F. *Philippine Political and Cultural History*, 2 vols., Manila, 1949.

V. INDONESIA

Indonesian Affairs, Ministry of Information, Djakarta.

Indonesian Review, June-December, 1950, Ministry of Information, Djakarta.

Report on Indonesia, Embassy of Indonesia, Washington, D.C.

Indonesian News Roundup, Indonesian Embassy, Manila.

Diplomatic and Consular List, Ministry of Foreign Affairs.

Speeches of President Sukarno, issued on occasion by the Ministry of Information, Djakarta.

Indonesian Observer.

Times of Indonesia.

Almanak Nasional, "Gapura," Djakarta.

"A Short Review of the Indonesian Struggle for Independence," Ministry of Information, Djakarta (mimeographed).

Aidit, D. N. *General Report* (delivered to Fifth Plenum of Central Committee of the Communist Party of Indonesia), Djakarta, 1957.

Allen, G. C., and Donnithorne, Audrey. *Western Enterprise in Indonesia and Malaya*, New York, 1957.

Asbeck, F. M. Van. "The Birth and Decline of the Netherlands Indonesian Union," *The Year Book of World Affairs, 1953*.

Aziz, Muhammed A. *Japan's Colonialism and Indonesia*, The Hague, 1955.

Aziz, Qutubuddin. "Indonesia's First General Elections," *Pakistan Horizon, 8* (September, 1955), 400-405.

Basic Information on Indonesia, Ministry of Information, Djakarta, 1953.

Benda, Harry T. "Indonesia," *Australian Outlook, 4* (March-June, 1950), 41-50, 86-97.

Bhatnagar, A. K. "West New Guinea," *India Quarterly, 7* (April-June, 1951), 162-174.

Boeke, J. H. *Economics and Economic Policy of Dual Societies, as Exemplified by Indonesia*, New York, 1953.

Bone, Robert C., Jr. "Organization of the Indonesian Elections," *American Political Science Review, 49* (December, 1955), 1067-1084.

Bousquet, Georges H. *A French View of the Netherlands Indies*, New York, 1941.

Brockway, J. T. "The Dutch and Indonesia," *Fortnightly, 175* (June, 1951), 364-371.

Cator, Writser J. *The Economic Position of the Chinese in the Netherlands Indies*, Chicago, 1936.

Coast, John. *Recruit to Revolution; Adventure and Politics in Indonesia*, London, 1952.

Collins, J. Foster. "The United Nations and Indonesia," *International Conciliation*, No. 459 (March, 1950).

Donnithorne, Audrey G. "Western Business in Indonesia," *Pacific Affairs, 27* (March, 1954), 27-40.

Emerson, Rupert. "Reflections on the Indonesian Case," *World Politics*, ✓
1 (October, 1948), 59-81.

Feith, Herbert. "Toward Elections in Indonesia," *Pacific Affairs*, *27*
(September, 1954), 236-254.

Finkelstein, Lawrence S. "Indonesia's Record in the United Nations," ✓
International Conciliation, No. 475 (November, 1951).

Finkelstein, Lawrence S. "Irian in Indonesian Politics," *Far Eastern* ✓
Survey, *20* (April 13, 1951), 76-80.

Finkelstein, Lawrence S. "The Indonesian Federal Problem," *Pacific* ✓
Affairs, *24* (September, 1951), 284-295.

Fisher, Charles A. "West New Guinea in Its Regional Setting," *The*
Year Book of World Affairs, *1952*.

Fisher, Charles A. "The Eurasian Question in Indonesia," *International*
Affairs, *23* (October, 1947), 522-530.

Fisher, Charles A. "Les Hollandais et l'Indonésie," *Politique Étrangère*,
19 (March, 1954), 45-58.

Furnivall, J. S. *Netherlands India: A Study of Plural Economy*, New
York, 1944.

Gemengde Commissie Nieuw-Guinea (Irian). *Rapport van de Com-*
missie Nieuw-Guinea (Irian) 1950, 4 vols., The Hague, 1950.

Gerbrandy, P. S. *Indonesia*, London, 1950.

Hatta, Mohammad. "Indonesia's Foreign Policy," *Foreign Affairs*, *31*
(April, 1953), 441-452.

Hawkins, Everett H. D. "Prospects for Economic Development in Indonesia," *World Politics*, *8* (October, 1955), 91-111.

Henderson, William. *Pacific Settlement of Disputes; The Indonesian*
Question, 1946-1949, New York, 1954.

Higgins, Benjamin. "Indonesia's Development Plans and Problems,"
Pacific Affairs, *29* (June, 1956), 107-125.

Hornbeck, Stanley K. "The United States and the Netherlands East
Indies," *Annals of the American Academy of Political and Social*
Science, *225* (January, 1948), 124-135.

"Indonesia, Political and Economic Realities," *The World Today*, *5*
(February, 1949), 52-63.

International Recognition of Sovereignty, Ministry of Information,
Djakarta, 1952.

Issue on the Netherlands Indies, *Far Eastern Quarterly*, *5* (February,
1946).

Kahin, George McT. *Nationalism and Revolution in Indonesia*, Ithaca,
N.Y., 1952.

Kahin, George McT. "Indonesia's Strengths and Weaknesses," *Far*
Eastern Survey, *20* (September 26, 1951), 157-162.

Kahin, George McT. "Communist Leadership in Indonesia," *Far*
Eastern Survey, *18* (August 10, 1949), 188-189.

Kat Angelino, A. D. A. de. *Colonial Policy*, 2 vols., Chicago, 1931.

Kennedy, Raymond. *The Ageless Indies*, New York, 1942.

Kennedy, Raymond. *Islands and Peoples of the Indies*, Washington,
D.C., 1943.

Kleffens, Eelco N. Van. "The Democratic Future of the Netherlands Indies," *Foreign Affairs*, 21 (October, 1942), 87-102.

Kroef, Justus M. Van Der. *Indonesia in the Modern World*, 2 vols., New York, 1954, 1956.

Kroef, Justus M. Van Der. "Pantjasila: The National Ideology of the New Indonesia," *Philosophy East and West*, *4* (1954), 225-231.

Kroef, Justus M. Van Der. "The Term Indonesia: Its Origin and Usage," *Journal of the American Oriental Society*, *71* (July-September, 1951), 166-171.

Kroef, Justus M. Van Der. "The South-Moluccan Insurrection in Indonesia: A Preliminary Analysis," *Journal of East Asiatic Studies*, *1* (July, 1952), 1-20.

Kroef, Justus M. Van Der. "The Indonesian Revolution in Retrospect," *World Politics*, *3* (April, 1951), 369-398.

Kroef, Justus M. Van Der. "Indonesia: Independent in the Cold War," *International Journal*, 7 (Autumn, 1952), 283-292.

Kroef, Justus M. Van Der. "The Arabs in Indonesia," *Middle East Journal*, 7 (Summer, 1953), 300-323.

Kroef, Justus M. Van Der. "The Eurasian Minority in Indonesia," *American Sociological Review*, *18* (October, 1953), 484-493.

Lahirnja Pantjasila (*The Birth of Pantjasila*), Ministry of Information, Djakarta, 1952.

Lasker, Bruno. "Western New Guinea, Past and Future," *Far Eastern Survey*, *21* (April 16, 1952), 53-59.

Logemann, J. H. A. "The Indonesian Parliament," *Parliamentary Affairs*, *6* (Autumn, 1953), 346-353.

Lubis, Mochtar. "The Indonesian Communist Movement Today," *Far Eastern Survey*, *23* (November, 1954), 161-164.

Lubis, Mochtar, "The Press in Indonesia," *Far Eastern Survey*, *21* (June 4, 1952), 90-94.

Mallory, Walter H. "Making a Friend of Indonesia," *Foreign Affairs*, *32* (January, 1954), 282-295.

McVey, Ruth Thomas. *The Development of the Indonesian Communist Party and Its Relations with the Soviet Union and the Chinese People's Republic*, Cambridge, Mass., 1954.

Metzemaekers, L. "The Western New Guinea Problem," *Pacific Affairs*, *24* (June, 1951), 131-142.

Ministry of Overseas Territories, Ministry of Foreign Affairs. *Report on Netherlands New Guinea for the Year 1954* [presented by the Netherlands to the Secretary-General of the United Nations pursuant to Article 73 (e) of the Charter].

Mook, H. J. Van. "Indonesia," *International Affairs*, *25* (July, 1949), 274-285.

Mook, H. J. Van. "Indonesia and the Problem of Southeast Asia," *Foreign Affairs*, *27* (July, 1949), 561-575.

"Nationalism in Indonesia," *The World Today*, *4* (February, 1948), 52-61.

Nieuwenhuijze, C. A. O. Van. "The Dar ul-Islam Movement in Western Java," *Pacific Affairs*, *23* (June, 1950), 169-183.

Palmier, Leslie H. "Sukarno, the Nationalist," *Pacific Affairs, 30* (June, 1957) 101-119.

Palmier, Leslie H. "Modern Islam in Indonesia: The Muhammadiyah After Independence," *Pacific Affairs, 27* (September, 1954), 255-262.

Permanent Mission of the Republic of Indonesia to the United Nations, *Press Releases*, Asian-African Conference at Bandung, Indonesia.

"Perspective of Indonesia," supplement, *The Atlantic Monthly, 197* (June, 1956).

Provisional Constitution of the Republic of Indonesia, Ministry of Information, Djakarta, 1953.

Reed, Stephen W., ed. *Indonesia*, 3 vols., New Haven, 1956.

Ritter, C. W. "Dutch New Guinea," *Contemporary Review, 179* (April, 1951), 222-226.

Sastroamidjojo, Ali, and Delson, Robert. "The Status of the Republic of Indonesia in International Law," *Columbia Law Review, 49* (March, 1949), 344-361.

Schiller, A. Arthur. *The Formation of Federal Indonesia, 1945-1949*, The Hague, 1955.

Shuck, L. E., Jr., "Indonesia Loosens the Bonds," *World Affairs Interpreter, 24* (Autumn, 1953), 260-272.

Sjahrir, Soetan. *Out of Exile*, New York, 1949.

Stanvac in Indonesia, 1957.

The Case of West Irian (West New Guinea), Indonesian Embassy, Cairo.

The Future of West Irian, Embassy of the Republic of Indonesia, London.

"The Indonesian Settlement," *Round Table, 40* (March, 1950), 114-120.

The Question of West Irian, Ministry of Foreign Affairs, Djakarta, 1955.

Thomas, M. L. "Sources of Indonesian Foreign Policy," *South Atlantic Quarterly, 54* (October, 1955), 453-460.

United Nations, Department of Public Information. *Peaceful Settlement in Indonesia*, New York, 1950.

U.S. Department of Commerce. *Investment in Indonesia*, Washington, D.C., 1956.

Vandenbosch, Amry. *The Dutch East Indies*, 3d. ed., Berkeley, Calif., 1942.

Vandenbosch, Amry. "Nationalism and Religion in Indonesia," *Far Eastern Survey, 21* (December 17, 1952), 181-185.

Vandenbosch, Amry. "The Netherlands-Indonesian Union," *Far Eastern Survey, 19* (January 11, 1950), 1-7.

Van Der Veur, Paul W. "The Eurasians of Indonesia: Castaways of Colonialism," *Pacific Affairs, 27* (June, 1954), 124-137.

Vlekke, B. H. M. *Nusantara. A History of the East Indian Archipelago*, Cambridge, Mass., 1943.

Vlekke, B. H. M. *Indonesia in 1956: Political and Economic Aspects*, New York, 1957.

Wang En-yuan. "President Sukarno in Peking," *People's China*, No. 21, November 1, 1956, 8-12.

Wehl, David. *The Birth of Indonesia*, London, 1948.
Wertheim, W. F. *Indonesian Society in Transition*, The Hague, 1956.
Western New Guinea and the Netherlands, The Hague, 1954.
Willmott, Donald E. *The National Status of the Chinese in Indonesia*, Ithaca, N.Y., 1956.
Wolf, Charles, Jr. *The Indonesian Story*, New York, 1948.
Wolf, Charles, Jr. "Problems of Indonesian Constitutionalism," *Pacific Affairs, 23* (September, 1950), 314-318.
Wolf, Charles, Jr. "The Men Who Made Merdeka," *Far Eastern Survey 16* (September 3, 1947), 181-184.
Woodman, Dorothy. *The Republic of Indonesia*, New York, 1955.
Yershov, T. "The Indonesian People's Fight for Peace and National Independence," *International Affairs* (Moscow), September, 1956, 21-27.

VI. BURMA

Burma Weekly Bulletin, Ministry of Information.
Burma (quarterly), Ministry of Information, especially the independence anniversary issues beginning in January, 1951.
Burma's Fight for Freedom, Ministry of Information, 1948.
Burma's Freedom, The First Anniversary, Ministry of Information, 1949.
Burma's Freedom, The Second Anniversary, Ministry of Information, 1950.
List of Representatives of Foreign States and International Organizations in the Union of Burma, Foreign Office, Rangoon.
Speeches of Prime Minister U Nu, separately published, Ministry of Information.
New Times of Burma.
Burma Trade Directory.
Ady, Peter. "Economic Bases of Unrest in Burma," *Foreign Affairs, 29* (April, 1951), 475-481.
"American Aid to Burma, 1950-53," *Burma* (Embassy of the Union of Burma, Washington), February 1, 1954.
An Asian Speaks, A Collection of Speeches Made by U Nu, Prime Minister of Burma, During a Visit to the United States of America, June 29-July 16, 1955, Embassy of the Union of Burma, Washington, D.C., 1955.
Andrus, J. Russell. *Burmese Economic Life*, Stanford, Calif., 1947.
Appleton, G. "Burma Two Years after Liberation," *International Affairs, 23* (October, 1947), 510-521.
Appleton, G. "The Burmese Viewpoint," *Asiatic Review, 44* (July, 1948), 233-251.
Baldwin, J. W. "The Karens in Burma," *Journal of the Royal Central Asian Society, 36* (April, 1949), 102-113.
Ba Swe, U. *The Burmese Revolution*, Rangoon, 1952.
Ba Swe, U. "Party Organization," *Socialist Asia, 3* (July, 1954), 4-9.
Baxter, James. *Report on Indian Immigration*, Rangoon, 1941.

Bower, Ursula Graham. *Drums Behind the Hill*, New York, 1953.
Burma and the Insurrections, Rangoon, 1949.
Burma During the Japanese Occupation, 2 vols., Simla, 1943-44.
Burma Speaks: A Collection of Broadcast Talks from the Burma Broadcasting Station, Rangoon, 1950.
Cady, John F. *Political Institutions of Old Burma*, Ithaca, N.Y., 1954.
Cady, John F. "Religion and Politics in Modern Burma," *Far Eastern Quarterly*, *12* (February, 1953), 149-162.
Cady, John F. "The Situation in Burma," *Far Eastern Survey*, *22* (April 22, 1953), 49-54.
Cady, John F., Barnett, Patricia B., and Jenkins, Shirley. *The Development of Self-Rule and Independence in Burma, Malaya and the Philippines*, New York, 1948.
Christian, John L. *Modern Burma, A Survey of Political and Economic Development*, Berkeley, Calif., 1942.
Christian, John L. *Burma and the Japanese Invader*, Bombay, 1945.
Christian, John L. "Burma: Where India and China Meet," *The National Geographic Magazine*, *84* (October, 1943), 489-512.
Collis, Maurice. *Last and First in Burma (1941-1948)*, London, 1956.
Collis, Maurice. *Lords of the Sunset, A Tour of the Shan States*, London, 1938.
Collis, Maurice. *Trials in Burma*, London, 1938.
"Communism in Burma; The Policies of Thakin Nu," *Round Table*, *38* (September, 1948), 768-773.
Deignan, H. G. *Burma—Gateway to China*, Washington, D.C., 1943.
Desai, Walter S. *India and Burma, A Study*, Calcutta, 1954.
Desai, Walter S. "The Karens of Burma," *India Quarterly*, *6* (July-September, 1950), 276-282.
Donnison, F. S. V. *Public Administration in Burma, A Study of Development during the British Connexion*, London, 1953.
Fairbairn, Geoffrey. "Aspects of the Burmese Political Scene," *Pacific Affairs*, *29* (September, 1956), 211-222.
Fairbairn, Geoffrey, "Burma and the Cold War," *Australian Outlook*, *6* (September, 1952), 145-152.
Fairbairn, Geoffrey. "Some Minority Problems in Burma," *Pacific Affairs*, *30* (December, 1957), 299-311.
Fifield, Russell H. "New States in the Indian Realm," *American Journal of International Law*, *46* (July, 1952), 450-463.
Fitzgerald, Patrick. "The Yunnan-Burma Road," *The Geographical Journal*, *95* (March, 1940), 161-174.
Furnivall, J. S. *Colonial Policy and Practice*, New York, 1948, new printing, 1956.
Furnivall, J. S. *An Introduction to the Political Economy of Burma*, 2d ed., rev. by J. Russell Andrus, Rangoon, 1938.
Furnivall, J. S. "Twilight in Burma, Reconquest and Crisis," *Pacific Affairs*, *22* (March, 1949), 3-20.
Furnivall, J. S. "Twilight in Burma, Independence and After," *Pacific Affairs*, *22* (June, 1949), 155-172.

Furnivall, J. S. "Burma, Past and Present," *Far Eastern Survey, 22* (February 25, 1953), 21-26.

Furnivall, J. S. "Communism and Nationalism in Burma," *Far Eastern Survey, 18* (August 24, 1949), 193-197.

Furnivall, J. S., and May Oung, U. "The Dawn of Nationalism in Burma," *Journal of the Burma Research Society, 33* (April, 1950), 1-7.

Gledhill, Alan. "The Burmese Constitution," *The Indian Year Book of International Affairs, 1953.*

Griffiths, Sir Percival. "Burma and Her Neighbours Today," *Asiatic Review, 46* (July, 1950), 1063-1079.

Hagen, Everett E. *The Economic Development of Burma*, Washington, D.C., 1956.

Hall, D. G. E. *Burma*, 2d ed., London, 1956.

Hall, D. G. E. *Europe and Burma; A Study of European Relations with Burma from the Earliest Times to the Annexation of Thibaw's Kingdom in 1886*, London, 1945.

Harvey, Godfrey E. *British Rule in Burma, 1824-1942*, London, 1946.

Harvey, Godfrey E. *Outline of Burmese History*, Bombay, 1947.

Hobbs, Cecil. "Nationalism in British Colonial Burma," *Far Eastern Quarterly, 6* (February, 1947), 113-121.

Huke, Robert E. *Economic Geography of a North Burma Kachin Village*, Hanover, N.H., 1954.

Insurgent Atrocities in Burma, Rangoon, 1952.

Ireland, Alleyne. *The Province of Burma*, 2 vols., Boston, 1907.

Is It a People's Liberation? Rangoon, 1952.

"Kautilya," "The Naga Challenge," *India Quarterly, 12* (October-December, 1956), 426-435.

Knappen, Tippetts, Abbett, McCarthy, Engineers. *Comprehensive Report; Economic and Engineering Development of Burma*, 2 vols., Aylesbury, England, 1953.

Kozicki, Richard J. "The Sino-Burmese Frontier Problem," *Far Eastern Survey, 26* (March, 1957), 33-38.

Kuomintang Aggression Against Burma, Ministry of Information, Rangoon, 1953.

Law Yone, Edward M., and Mandelbaum, David G. "Pacification in Burma," *Far Eastern Survey, 19* (October 11, 1950), 182-187.

Law Yone, Edward M., and Mandelbaum, David G. "The New Nation of Burma," *Far Eastern Survey, 19* (October 25, 1950), 189-194.

Leach, E. R. *Political Systems of Highland Burma*, London, 1954.

Leach, F. Burton. "Burma and Her Land Communications," *Journal of the Royal Central Asian Society, 27* (January, 1940), 6-20.

MacDougal, Sir Raibeart M. "Burma Stands Alone," *Foreign Affairs, 26* (April, 1948), 542-553.

Marshall, Harry I. *The Karens of Burma*, London, 1945.

Maung Maung. *Burma in the Family of Nations*, Amsterdam, 1956.

Maung Maung. "Portrait of the Burmese Parliament," *Parliamentary Affairs, 10* (Spring, 1957), 204-209.

Maung Maung. "Burma Looks Ahead," *Pacific Affairs, 25* (March, 1952), 40-48.

Maung Maung. "Pyidawtha Comes to Burma," *Far Eastern Survey, 22* (August, 1953), 117-119.

Moscotti, Albert D. *British Policy in Burma, 1917-1941: A Study in the Development of Colonial Self-Rule and Independence.* Unpublished dissertation, Political Science Department, Yale University, 1950.

"New Hope for Burma: Politics and Prospects," *The World Today, 6* (September, 1950), 379-386.

Nu, Thakin. *Towards Peace and Democracy*, Rangoon, 1949.

Nu, Thakin. *From Peace to Stability*, Rangoon, 1951.

Nu, U. *The People Win Through*, Rangoon, 1952.

Nu, U. *Burma under the Japanese*, London, 1954.

Nu, U. *Towards a Welfare State*, Rangoon, 1952.

Nu, U. *Forward with the People*, Rangoon, 1955.

Nu, U. *Burma Looks Ahead*, Rangoon, 1953.

Nu, U. "Burma's Neutral Policy," *Burma, 5* (January, 1955), 1-15.

Pearn, B. R. *The Indian in Burma*, Ledbury, England, 1946.

Rance, Sir Hubert. "Burma Today," *Asian Review, 52* (July, 1956), 180-191.

Report of the First Asian Socialist Conference, Rangoon, 1953.

"The Second Congress of the Asian Socialist Conference," *Information Bulletin* (Asian Socialist Conference), *1* (November, 1956).

Seagrave, Gordon S. *Burma Surgeon*, New York, 1943.

Seagrave, Gordon S. *Burma Surgeon Returns*, New York, 1946.

Seagrave, Gordon S. *My Hospital in the Hills*, New York, 1955.

Silverstein, Joseph. "Politics, Parties, and National Elections in Burma," *Far Eastern Survey, 25* (December, 1956), 177-184.

Socialist Asia, Anniversary Number, 1954.

Spate, O. H. K. *Burma Setting*, London, 1943.

Stevenson, H. N. C. *The Hill Peoples of Burma*, London, 1944.

Story, Francis. *Buddhism Answers the Marxist Challenge*, Rangoon, 1952.

Sutton, Walter D., Jr. "U Aung San of Burma," *The South Atlantic Quarterly*, 47 (January, 1948), 1-16.

"The Burma-China Frontier Dispute," *The World Today, 13* (February, 1957), 86-92.

The Constitution of the Union of Burma, Rangoon, 1948.

The Pyidawtha Conference, Resolutions and Speeches, Rangoon, 1952.

"The Situation in Burma: Difficulties of Post-War Reconstruction," *The World Today, 2* (September, 1946), 430-439.

Thompson, Virginia. "The New Nation of Burma," *Far Eastern Survey, 17* (April 7, 1948), 81-84.

Thomson, John Seabury. "Burma: A Neutral in China's Shadow," *The Review of Politics, 19* (July, 1957), 330-350.

Thomson, John Seabury. "Burmese Neutralism," *Political Science Quarterly*, 72 (June, 1957), 261-283.

Those Fickle Communists! Rangoon, 1952.

Tinker, Hugh. *The Union of Burma: A Study of the First Years of Independence*, London, 1957.
Tinker, Hugh. "Burma's Northeast Borderland Problems," *Pacific Affairs, 29* (December, 1956), 324-346.
Tinker, Hugh. *The Foundations of Local Self-Government in India, Pakistan and Burma*, London, 1954.
Tinker, Hugh. "Nu, the Serene Statesman," *Pacific Affairs, 30* (June, 1957), 120-137.
Trager, Frank N. "Burma's Foreign Policy, 1948-56: Neutralism, Third Force, and Rice," *The Journal of Asian Studies, 16* (November, 1956), 89-102.
Trager, Frank N. *Towards a Welfare State in Burma; Economic Reconstruction and Development, 1948-1954*, New York, 1954.
Trager, Frank N., and Associates. *Burma*, New Haven, 1956.
Trager, Frank N., Wohlgemuth, Patricia, and Kiang, Lu-Yu. *Burma's Role in the United Nations, 1948-1955*, New York, 1956.
Tun Pe, U. *Sun Over Burma*, Rangoon, 1949.
U.S. Department of State. *The Union of Burma; Background*, Washington, D.C., 1955.
Welsh, Janet. "Burma's Development Problems," *Far Eastern Survey, 25* (August, 1956), 113-122.
Wolf, Charles, Jr. *Selected Economic Development Projects in Burma and Indonesia*, Ithaca, N.Y., 1954.

VII. THAILAND

Siam Rath Weekly Review.
The Bangkok Post.
The Siam Directory.
Adams, A. C. S. "Siam Since the War," *Journal of the Royal Central Asian Society, 36* (April, 1949), 114-123.
Andrews, James M. *Siam, 2nd Rural Economic Survey, 1934-1935*, Bangkok, 1935.
Benedict, Ruth. *Thai Culture and Behavior*, Ithaca, N.Y., 1952.
Chakrabongse, Chula. "The Political and Economic Background in Thailand," *Journal of the Royal Central Asian Society, 42* (April, 1955), 116-127.
Christian, John L., and Ike, Nobutake. "Thailand in Japan's Foreign Relations," *Pacific Affairs, 15* (June, 1942), 195-221.
Coast, John. *Some Aspects of Siamese Politics*, New York, 1953.
Coast, John. *Railroad of Death*, London, 1946.
Coughlin, Richard J. "The Status of the Chinese Minority in Thailand," *Pacific Affairs, 25* (December, 1952), 378-389.
Coughlin, Richard J. "The Pattern of the Chinese in Thailand," *Journal of the South Seas Society, 8* (June, 1952), 1-3.
Coughlin, Richard J. "The Chinese in Bangkok: A Commercial-orientated Minority," *American Sociological Review, 20* (June, 1955), 311-316.
Credner, Wilhelm. *Siam, das Land der Tai*, Stuttgart, 1935.

Crosby, Sir Josiah. *Siam: The Crossroads*, London, 1945.
Crosby, Sir Josiah. *Siam* (Foreign Office Handbook), London, 1920.
Crosby, Sir Josiah. "Siamese Imperialism and the Pan-Thai Movement," *The Fortnightly, 159* (May, 1943), 300-307.
Deignan, H. G. *Siam—Land of Free Men*, Washington, D.C., 1943.
de Young, John E. *Village Life in Modern Thailand*, Berkeley, Calif., 1955.
Dhaninivat, Prince (D. Sonakul). "The Old Siamese Conception of the Monarchy," *Journal of the Siam Society, 36* (1947), 91-106.
Fisher, Charles A. "The Thailand-Burma Railway," *Economic Geography, 23* (April, 1947), 85-97.
Graham, Walter Armstrong. *Siam*, 2 vols., London, 1924.
Hastain, Ronald E. W. *White Coolie*, London, 1947.
Ingram, James C. *Economic Change in Thailand Since 1850*, Stanford, Calif., 1955.
King, John Kerry. "Thailand's Bureaucracy and the Threat of Communist Subversion," *Far Eastern Survey, 23* (November, 1954), 169-173.
Landon, Kenneth P. *Siam in Transition*, Chicago, 1939.
Landon, Kenneth P. *The Chinese in Thailand*, New York, 1941.
Landon, Kenneth P. "Thailand's Quarrel with France in Perspective," *Far Eastern Quarterly, 1* (November, 1941), 25-42.
Landon, Kenneth P. "Thailand's Struggle for National Security," *Far Eastern Quarterly, 4* (November, 1944), 5-26.
Le May, Reginald. *An Asian Arcady, The Land and Peoples of Northern Siam*, Cambridge, England, 1926.
MacDonald, Alexander. *Bangkok Editor*, New York, 1949.
Martin, James V., Jr. *A History of the Diplomatic Relations between Siam and the United States of America, 1833-1929, 1929-1948*, 2 vols. Unpublished dissertation, Fletcher School of Law and Diplomacy, 1948.
Mueller, Wolfgang D. "Thailand in Politischen Kräftespiel Südostasiens," *Aussenpolitik, 3* (June, 1952), 395-400.
Muniswami, M. K. "Modern Siam," *The Indian Year Book of International Affairs, 1953.*
"Musical Chairs in Siam," *The World Today, 5* (September, 1949), 378-387.
Peterson, Alec. "Britain and Siam: The Latest Phase," *Pacific Affairs, 19* (December, 1946), 364-372.
Pickerell, Albert, and Moore, Daniel E. "Elections in Thailand," *Far Eastern Survey, 26* (June, 1957), 92-96 and *26* (July, 1957), 103-111.
"Political Alarms in Bangkok," *The World Today, 8* (February, 1952), 60-71.
Rawson, R. R. "Two New Railways in South-East Asia," *The Geographical Journal, 108* (July, 1946), 85-88.
Reeve, W. D. *Public Administration in Siam*, London, 1952.
Sayre, Francis B. *The Passing of Extraterritoriality in Siam*, Concord, N.H., 1928.

Sharp, Lauriston, ed. *Thailand*, New Haven, 1956.

Sharp, Lauriston, and Others. *Siamese Rice Village: A Preliminary Study of Bang Chan, 1948-1949*, Bangkok, 1953.

Sharp, Lauriston. "Peasants and Politics in Thailand," *Far Eastern Survey, 19* (September 13, 1950), 157-161.

Siam, International Acts, 1946-1947, Bangkok, 194-.

Siam's Case for Revision of Obsolete Treaty Obligations Admittedly Inapplicable to Present Conditions, 1919.

"Siam's Economic Problems, The Situation at the End of the War," *The World Today, 4* (April, 1948), 173-181.

Siam Treaties with Foreign Powers, 1920-1927, Norwood, 1928.

Skinner, G. William. "Chinese Assimilation and Thai Politics," *The Journal of Asian Studies, 16* (February, 1957), 237-250.

Skinner, G. William. *Chinese Society in Thailand: An Analytical History*, Ithaca, N.Y., 1957.

Skinner, G. William. *Leadership and Power in the Chinese Community of Thailand*, Ithaca, N.Y., 1958.

Stanton, Edwin F. *Brief Authority*, New York, 1956.

Stanton, Edwin F. "Spotlight on Thailand," *Foreign Affairs, 33* (October, 1954), 72-85.

Thailand, Department of Publicity. *How Thailand Lost Her Territories to France*, Bangkok, 1940.

Thailand, Department of Publicity. *The March of Thailand; A Survey of Various Aspects of Post-War Thailand*, Bangkok, 1950.

"The Siamese Elections of February, 1957," *The World Today, 13* (May, 1957), 220-226.

The Siam Society, *Fiftieth Anniversary Commemorative Publication*, 2 vols., Bangkok, 1954.

Thompson, Virginia. *Thailand, The New Siam*, New York, 1941.

Thompson, Virginia. "Siam and the Great Powers," *Foreign Policy Reports, 21* (March 1, 1946), 322-331.

Thompson, Virginia. "Governmental Instability in Siam," *Far Eastern Survey, 17* (August 25, 1948), 185-189.

Thompson, Virginia, and Adloff, Richard. "The State's Role in Thai Economy," *Far Eastern Survey, 21* (July 30, 1952), 123-127.

U.S. Department of State. *Thailand: Its People and Economy*, Washington, D.C., 1950.

U.S. Department of State. *Thailand*, Washington, D.C., 1956.

U.S. Office of Strategic Services, Research and Analysis Branch. *Territorial Conflicts Between Thailand and French Indochina*, Washington, D.C., 1945.

Vella, Walter F. *The Impact of the West on Government in Thailand*, Berkeley, Calif., 1955.

Wales, H. G. Quaritch. *Siamese State Ceremonies; Their History and Function*, London, 1931.

Wales, H. G. Quaritch. *Ancient Siamese Government and Administration*, London, 1934.

Wan Waithayakon, Prince. "Thai Culture," *Journal of the Thailand Research Society, 35* (1944), 135-145.

Wells, Kenneth Elmer. *Thai Buddhism, Its Rites and Activities*, Bangkok, 1939.

Wood, W. A. R. *A History of Siam, from the Earliest Times of the Year* A.D. *1781, with a Supplement Dealing with More Recent Events*, rev. ed., Bangkok, 1933.

VIII. VIETNAM, LAOS, CAMBODIA

Agence d'Information Télégraphique Vietnamienne, Viet-Nam Presse, *Bulletin Triquotidien d'Informations Télégraphiques*, Saigon.

News from Viet-Nam, Embassy of the Republic of Viet-Nam, Washington, D.C.

Secretariat of State for Foreign Affairs. *Vietnam in World Affairs*, Saigon, 1956.

Viet Nam Information Bulletin, News Service, Rangoon (Democratic Republic of Vietnam).

Viet-Nam Bulletin, Embassy of the Democratic Republic of Viet-Nam, Peking.

Lao Presse, *Bulletin Quotidien*, Vientiane.

Agence Khmère de Presse, *Bulletin Quotidien d'Information*, Phnom Penh.

The Times of Viet Nam.

Réalités Cambodgiennes.

Cambodge, Revue Illustrée Khmère.

Indochine, Sud Est Asiatique.

Annuaire des États-Associés; Cambodge, Laos, Vietnam, 1953, Paris, 1953.

Abadie, M. *Les Races du Haut-Tonkin*, Paris, 1924.

Accords Franco-Viêtnamiens du 8 Mars 1949, Conventions d'Application, Saigon, 1950.

Ambassade de France, Service de Presse et d'Information (New York). Treaty of Amity and Association Between the French Republic and the Kingdom of Laos and Conventions Annexed to the Treaty (Paris, October 22, 1953).

America's Stake in Vietnam, A Symposium, New York, 1956.

Ayme, G. *Monographie du Ve Territoire Militaire*, Hanoi, 1930.

Banerjee, Subrata. *Viet Nam Fights for Freedom*, Bombay, 1947.

Blanchet, M. T. *La Naissance de l'État Associé du Viet-Nam*, Paris, 1954.

Bodard, Lucien. "Où en Est le Nationalisme Viêtnamien?" *France-Asie, 6* (August, 1950), 360-368.

Briggs, Lawrence P. "A Sketch of Cambodian History," *Far Eastern Quarterly, 6* (August, 1947), 345-363.

Briggs, Lawrence P. "The Ancient Khmer Empire," Philadelphia, 1951.

Brodrick, Alan H. *Little China, The Annamese Lands*, New York, 1942.

Brodrick, Alan H. *Little Vehicle, Cambodia and Laos*, London, 1949.

Buu Loc. "Aspects of the Vietnamese Problem," *Pacific Affairs, 25* (September, 1952), 235-247.

"Cambodia [The Atlantic Report on the World Today]," *The Atlantic Monthly, 196* (October, 1955), 10, 12, 16, 18.
"Canadians in Indochina," *External Affairs*, 7 (February, 1955), 34-41.
Chatterji, Bijan Raj. *Indian Cultural Influence in Cambodia*, Calcutta, 1928.
Chesneaux, Jean. *Contribution à l'Histoire de la Nation Vietnamienne*, Paris, 1955.
Childs, Marquis W. *The Ragged Edge: The Diary of a Crisis*, Garden City, N.Y., 1955.
Clémentin, J. R. "The Nationalist Dilemma in Vietnam," *Pacific Affairs, 23* (September, 1950), 294-310.
Coedès, Georges. *Les États Hindouisés d'Indochine et d'Indonésie*, Paris, 1948.
Cole, Allan B., ed. *Conflict in Indochina and International Repercussions, A Documentary History, 1945-1955*, Ithaca, N.Y., 1956.
Condominas, Georges. "Aspects of a Minority Problem in Indochina," *Pacific Affairs, 24* (March, 1951), 77-82.
"Conflict in Indo-China," *Far East Spotlight*, New York.
Conférence de Genève sur l'Indochine, 8 Mai-21 Juillet 1954; Procès-Verbaux des Séances, Propositions, Documents Finaux, Paris, 1955.
Conférence Publique, Sisouk Nachampassak sur le "Pathet-Lao" et l'Application des Accords de Genève Donnée à la Salle des Fêtes le 27 Mars 1956 à 17H30 sous la Haute Présidence de S. A. Tiao Souvanna Phouma, Premier Ministre (mimeographed).
"Constitution du Royaume du Cambodge du 6 Mai 1947, Modifiée le 14 Janvier 1956," *Revue Internationale d'Histoire Politique et Constitutionnelle*, No. 23 (July-September, 1956), 218-231.
Conventions Inter-États, Saigon, 1951.
Coughlin, Richard J. "The Republic of Vietnam," *Far Eastern Survey, 19* (November, 1950), 203-207.
Crocker, H. E. "Cambodia," *Contemporary Review, 183* (April, 1953), 216-220.
Crozier, Brian. "The International Situation in Indochina," *Pacific Affairs, 29* (December, 1956), 309-323.
Crozier, Brian. "The Diem Regime in Southern Vietnam," *Far Eastern Survey, 24* (April, 1955), 49-56.
Dai, Shen-yu. "Peking and Indochina's Destiny," *The Western Political Quarterly*, 7 (September, 1954), 346-368.
Dam Bo. "Les Populations Montagnardes du Sud-Indochinois," *France-Asie, 5* (Spring, 1950).
Dang-Chân-Liêu. "Annamese Nationalism," *Pacific Affairs, 20* (March, 1947), 61-66.
Decoux, Jean. *À la Barre de l'Indochine*, Paris, 1949.
Devillers, Philippe. *Le Viêt-Nam Contemporain*, Paris, 1950.
Devillers, Philippe. *Histoire du Viêt-Nam de 1940 à 1952*, 3d ed., rev., Paris, 1952.
Devinat, Paul. "Un Renouveau Franco-Vietnamien Est-Il Possible?" *Politique Étrangère, 21* (July-August, 1956), 427-442.

Deydier, Henri. *Introduction à la Connaissance du Laos*, Saigon, 1952.
Dutt, V. P., and Singh, V. *Indian Policy and Attitudes Towards Indo-China and S.E.A.T.O.*, New York, 1954.
Eighty-fourth Congress, First Session. *Viet Nam, Cambodia, and Laos: Report by Senator Mike Mansfield*, October 6, 1955, Washington, D.C., 1955.
Eighty-third Congress, First Session. *Indochina: Report of Senator Mike Mansfield on a Study Mission to the Associated States of Indochina, Viet Nam, Cambodia, Laos*, October 27, 1953, Washington, D.C., 1953.
Eighty-third Congress, Second Session. *Report on Indochina: Report of Senator Mike Mansfield on a Study Mission to Vietnam, Cambodia, Laos*, October 15, 1954, Washington, D.C., 1954.
Embassy of Viet Nam, Washington, D.C. *Viet Minh Violations of the Geneva Armistice Agreement*, 1954.
Emerson, Rupert. "Indo-China," *Yale Review, 44* (Autumn, 1954), 51-63.
Ennis, Thomas E. *French Policy and Developments in Indochina*, Chicago, 1936.
Fall, Bernard B. *The Viet-Minh Regime; Government and Administration in the Democratic Republic of Viet-Nam*, rev. ed., New York, 1956.
Fall, Bernard B. "The International Relations of Laos," *Pacific Affairs, 30* (March, 1957), 22-34.
Fall, Bernard B. "Crisis in North Viet-Nam," *Far Eastern Survey, 26* (January, 1957), 12-15.
Fall, Bernard B. "Indochina Since Geneva," *Pacific Affairs, 28* (March, 1955), 3-25.
Fall, Bernard B. "Tribulations of a Party Line: The French Communists and Indochina," *Foreign Affairs, 33* (April, 1955), 499-510.
Fall, Bernard B. "La Politique Américaine au Viet-Nam," *Politique Étrangère, 20* (July, 1955), 298-322.
Fall, Bernard B. "The Political-Religious Sects of Viet-Nam," *Pacific Affairs, 28* (September, 1955), 235-253.
Fall, Bernard B. "Recent Publications on Indochina," *Pacific Affairs, 29* (March, 1956), 57-64.
Fischer, Ruth. "Ho Chi Minh: Disciplined Communist," *Foreign Affairs, 33* (October, 1954), 86-97.
Gauthier, Julien. *L'Indochine au Travail dans la Paix Française*, Paris, 1949.
Ginsburg, Norton S., ed. *Laos*, New Haven, 1955.
Gourou, Pierre. *Les Paysans du Delta Tonkinois, Étude de Géographie Humaine*, Paris, 1936.
Gourou, Pierre. *Land Utilization in French Indochina*, New York, 1945.
Great Britain. *Documents Relating to the Discussion of Korea and Indo-China at the Geneva Conference, April 29-June 15, 1954*, Cmd. 9186.
Great Britain. *Further Documents Relating to the Discussion of Indo-China at the Geneva Conference*, Cmd. 9239.

Great Britain. *French Indo-China* (Foreign Office Handbook), London, 1920.

Guillain, Robert. *La Fin des Illusions; Notes d'Indochine*, Paris, 1954.

Hall, Melvin. "Aspects of the Present Situation in Indo-China," *Journal of the Royal Central Asian Society, 40* (July-October, 1953), 204-216.

Hammer, Ellen J. *The Struggle for Indochina*, Stanford, Calif., 1954.

Hammer, Ellen J. *The Struggle for Indochina Continues, Geneva to Bandung*, Stanford, Calif., 1955.

Hammer, Ellen J. *The Emergence of Viet-Nam*, New York, 1947.

Hammer, Ellen J. "Blueprinting a New Indochina," *Pacific Affairs, 21* (September, 1948), 252-263.

Hanrahan, Gene Z. "Recent Chinese Communist Publications on Indochina and Malaya," *Pacific Affairs, 27* (December, 1954), 367-370.

Henderson, William. "South Viet Nam Finds Itself," *Foreign Affairs, 35* (January, 1957), 283-294.

Hertrich, Jean-Michel. *Doc-Lap! L'Indépendance ou la Mort!* Paris, 1946.

"Indo-China: The Unfinished Struggle," *The World Today, 12* (January, 1956), 17-26.

Indo-China, A Geographical Appreciation, Ottawa, 1953.

Ingber, David. "The Democratic Republic of Viet Nam," *Fortnightly, 179* (February, 1953), 92-96.

Institut Franco-Suisse d'Études Coloniales. *France and Viet-Nam, The Franco-Vietnamese Conflict According to Official Documents*, Geneva, 1947.

Issue on French Indochina, *Far Eastern Quarterly, 6* (August, 1947).

Ivens, Germaine Krull. "Error in Laos," *Far Eastern Survey, 16* (June 4, 1947), 121-124.

Janse, Olov R. T. *The Peoples of French Indochina*, Washington, D.C., 1944.

Jensen, Fritz. *Erlebtes Vietnam*, Berlin, 1955.

Julien, C. A. "From the French Empire to the French Union," *International Affairs, 26* (October, 1950), 487-502.

Jumper, Roy. "The Communist Challenge to South Viet Nam," *Far Eastern Survey, 25* (November, 1956), 161-168.

Karpikhin, A. "The United States Takes Over in South Viet-Nam," *International Affairs* (Moscow), April, 1956, 82-91.

Karpikhin, A. "The Interests of Peace Demand a Political Settlement in Viet-Nam and Laos," *International Affairs* (Moscow), January, 1956, 50-58.

Katay, Thao. *Le Laos, Pivot Idéal de la Lutte contre le Communisme dans le Sud-Est Asiatique*, Bangkok, 1949.

Katay, Thao. *Le Laos*, Bangkok, 1948.

Katzenbach, Edward L., Jr. "Indo-China: A Military-Political Appreciation," *World Politics, 4* (January, 1952), 186-218.

Kingdom of Laos. *Application of the Geneva Agreements in Laos*, Vientiane, 1955.

Langran, Gustave. *Vie Sociale et Religieuse en Annam,* Paris, 1947.
Lattre, J. de. "Indochine 1951, Ma Mission aux États-Unis," *Revue des Deux Mondes,* December 1, 1951, 385-394.
Le Laos. Panorama du Monde.
Le Thanh Khoi. *Le Viêt Nam, Histoire et Civilisation,* Paris, 1955.
Lévy, Roger. *L'Indochine et Ses Traités, 1946,* Paris, 1947.
Lévy, Roger. "Indochina: A Keystone in Asia—A French View," *India Quarterly, 8* (January-March, 1952), 31-38.
Lévy, Roger. "Die Entwicklung in Indochina seit den Genfer Abkommen vom Juli 1954," *Europa-Archiv, 11* (February 20, 1956), 8609-8618.
Lewis, Norman. *A Dragon Apparent,* New York, 1951.
Lin Wu-sun. "China and Cambodia: Friends," *People's China,* No. 5, March 1, 1956, 15-17.
Marchand, Jean Paul. *L'Indochine en Guerre,* Paris, 1954.
Marty, André. "La Guerre d'Indochine et les Traditions du Movement Ouvrier Français," *Cahiers du Communisme, 27* (March, 1950), 20-34.
Marty, André. "La Guerre au Viet-Nam, Contraire aux Intérêts Français," *Cahiers du Communisme, 28* (October, 1951), 1145-1158.
Masson, André. *Histoire de l'Indochine,* Paris, 1950.
Miller, E. Willard. "Industrial Resources of Indochina," *Far Eastern Quarterly, 6* (August, 1947), 396-408.
Ministry of Foreign Affairs. *Documents Related to the Implementation of the Geneva Agreements Concerning Viet-Nam,* Hanoi, 1956.
Moore, W. Robert. "War and Quiet on the Laos Frontier," *National Geographic Magazine, 105* (May, 1954), 665-680.
Mus, Paul. *Le Viet Nam Chez Lui,* Paris, 1946.
Mus, Paul. *Viêt-Nam, Sociologie d'une Guerre,* Paris, 1952.
Mus, Paul. "Viet-Nam: A Nation Off Balance," *Yale Review, 41* (Summer, 1952), 524-538.
Mus, Paul. "The Role of the Village in Vietnamese Politics," *Pacific Affairs, 22* (September, 1949), 265-272.
Navarre, Henri. *L'Agonie de l'Indochine,* Paris, 1956.
Newman, Bernard. *Report on Indo-China,* London, 1953.
Nguyen-Ai-Quoc. *Le Procès de la Colonisation Française,* Paris, 1926.
Nguyen-Dac-Khe. "L'Indépendance du Viêt-Nam et l'Union Française," *France-Asie, 9* (June-July, 1953), 573-588.
Norodom Sihanouk, Prince. "Étude Corrective de la Constitution Accordée par S.M. le Roi du Cambodge en 1947," *France-Asie, 11* (May, 1955), 654-663.
Pacificus. "Canada and Indochina," *International Journal, 11* (Autumn, 1956), 270-278.
Phan Quang Dan. "The Situation in Indochina," *Pakistan Horizon,* 7 (December, 1954), 177-188.
Pinto, Roger. *Aspects de l'Évolution Gouvernementale de l'Indochine Française,* Paris, 1946.
"Présence du Cambodge," *France-Asie, 10* (November-December, 1955).

"Présence du Royaume Lao," *France-Asie, 12* (March-April-May, 1956).

Press Office of the Royal Palace, *Modern Cambodia*, Saigon.

Purcell, Victor. "Indo-China and the Prospect in South-East Asia," *The Year Book of World Affairs, 1955*.

Reconnaissance Report, Lower Mekong River Basin, March, 1956 (prepared for International Coöperation Administration by United States Department of Interior, Bureau of Reclamation).

Reinach, L. de. *Le Laos*, Paris, 1911.

Reports: International Commission for Supervision and Control in Cambodia.
International Commission for Supervision and Control in Laos.
International Commission for Supervision and Control in Viet-Nam.

"Revolt of the Intellectuals in North Vietnam," *The World Today, 13* (June, 1957), 250-260.

Robequain, Charles. *The Economic Development of French Indo-China*, London, 1944.

Roberts, Chalmers M. "The Day We Didn't Go to War," *Reporter*, September 14, 1954, 31-35.

Roux, Henri. "Quelques Minorités Ethniques du Nord-Indochine," *France-Asie, 10* (January-February, 1954).

Royaume du Cambodge. *Plan d'Équipement Biennal, 1956-1957*, Phnom Penh, 1956.

Royaume du Laos. *Constitution Lao*, Saigon, 1952.

Sabattier, General G. *Le Destin de l'Indochine; Souvenirs et Documents, 1941-1951*, Paris, 1952.

Saint-Chamant, Jean de. "Der Internationale Krieg in Indochina," *Aussenpolitik, 3* (May, 1952), 310-317.

Sainteny, Jean. *Histoire d'une Paix Manquée*, Paris, 1953.

Sam Sary. *Conférence Publique sur les Accords de Genève et les Élections Générales au Cambodge*, Phnom Penh, 1955.

Sam Sary. *La Grande Figure de Norodom Sihanouk telle qu'Elle Est Dépeinte par les Documents de Valeur Historique Découverts dans les Archives du Palais Royal*, Phnom Penh, 1955.

Sasorith, Katay D. *Le Laos; Son Évolution Politique; Sa Place dans l'Union Française*, Paris, 1953.

Sasorith, Katay D. "Au Pays du Million d'Elephants: le 'Kh'lam,'" *France-Asie, 11* (April, 1955), 553-556.

Senger und Etterlin, F. von. "Die Kriegslehren von Dien Bien Phu," *Aussenpolitik, 5* (July, 1954), 423-428.

Shao Hsun-cheng. "Chinese Islands in the South China Sea," *People's China*, No. 13, July 1, 1956, 25-27.

Sharp, W. R. "Some Observations on Public Administration in Indochina," *Public Administration Review, 14* (Winter, 1954), 40-51.

Shepley, James. "How Dulles Averted War," *Life*, January 16, 1956, 70-80.

Shihchieh Chihshih (World Culture). *A Chronicle of Principal Events Relating to the Indo-China Question, 1940-1954*, Peking, 1954.

Singh, Vishal. "The Geneva Agreements and Developments in Viet Nam," *Foreign Affairs Reports*, September, 1955.
Soustelle, Jacques. "Indo-China and Korea: One Front," *Foreign Affairs, 29* (October, 1950), 56-66.
Stanley, George F. G. "Dien Bien Phu in Retrospect," *International Journal, 10* (Winter, 1954-1955), 38-50.
Starobin, Joseph R. *Eyewitness in Indo-China*, New York, 1954.
Steinberg, David J., and others. *Cambodia*, New Haven, 1957.
Stuchen, Philip. "Partitioned Indochina," *Queen's Quarterly, 64* (Autumn, 1957), 405-420.
Szaz, Zoltan M. "Cambodia's Foreign Policy," *Far Eastern Survey, 24* (October, 1955), 151-158.
Taboulet, Georges. *La Geste Française en Indochine*, 2 vols., Paris, 1955, 1956.
"The Independent State of Laos," *The World Today, 13* (October, 1957), 432-441.
"The Waning Power of France in Vietnam," *The World Today, 12* (February, 1956), 50-58.
Thomasset, René. "Les Viets au Laos," *Revue Politique et Parlementaire, 210* (May, 1953), 130-136.
Thompson, Virginia. *French Indo-China*, New York, 1937.
Thompson, Virginia. "The Vietnamese Community in France," *Pacific Affairs, 25* (March, 1952), 49-58.
Thompson, Virginia, and Adloff, Richard. "Cambodia Moves Toward Independence," *Far Eastern Survey, 22* (August, 1953), 105-111.
Ton That Thien. "The Influence of Indo-China on the Evolution of the French Union," *India Quarterly, 10* (October-December, 1954), 295-313.
Ton That Thien. "The Geneva Agreements and Peace Prospects in Vietnam," *India Quarterly, 12* (October-December, 1956), 375-388.
Topping, Seymour. "Indo-China on the Razor's Edge," *Foreign Affairs, 29* (April, 1951), 468-474.
Tran-Duc-Thao. "Vietnam and Eastern Asia," *Far Eastern Quarterly, 6* (August, 1947), 409-413.
U.S. Department of Commerce. *Basic Data on the Economy of the Republic of Viet-Nam*, Washington, D.C., 1956.
U.S. Department of Commerce. *Basic Data on the Economy of Laos*, Washington, D.C., 1955.
U.S. Department of Commerce. *Basic Data on the Economy of Cambodia*, Washington, D.C., 1955.
U.S. Information Service, Phnom Penh. *Background Information on Cambodia*, Phnom Penh, 1955.
U.S. Information Service, Vientiane. Laos (mimeographed).
U.S. Department of State. *Political Alignments of Vietnamese Nationalists*, Washington, D.C., 1949.
U.S. Department of State. *Outline of Basic Treaty Relationships between France and the Associated States of Indochina*, Washington, D.C., 1952.

U.S. Department of State. *Indochina: The War in Viet-Nam, Cambodia, and Laos, Background*, Washington, D.C., 1953.

Viêt Nam, A Nation on the March, 1953.

Vietnamese (A). "Recent Economic and Political Development in Viet Nam," *India Quarterly*, *5* (January-March, 1949), 60-71.

Vo-Nguyen-Giap. *On the Implementation of the Geneva Agreements*, Hanoi, 1955.

"What All Sides Say About Indo-China Truce," *U.S. News and World Report*, July 30, 1954, 85-94.

Woolsey, L. H. "The United States and Indo-China," *American Journal of International Law*, *48* (April, 1954), 276-281.

Yefimov, P. "The Democratic Republic of Viet-Nam Builds a New Life," *International Affairs* (Moscow), August, 1955, 44-56.

Zelinsky, Wilbur. "The Indochinese Peninsula: A Demographic Anomaly," *Far Eastern Quarterly*, *9* (February, 1950), 115-145.

IX. MALAYA

Federation of Malaya. *Annual Report.*

Colony of Singapore. *Annual Report.*

North Borneo. *Annual Report.*

State of Brunei. *Annual Report.*

Sarawak. *Annual Report.*

Public Relations Office, Singapore. *Singapore News Summary.*

Federation of Malaya Information Services. *The Federation of Malaya*, 2d ed., Kuala Lumpur, 1956.

The Straits Times.

Awbery, S. S., and Dalley, F. W. *Labour and Trade Union Organization in the Federation of Malaya and Singapore*, London, 1948.

Bartlett, Vernon. *Report from Malaya*, London, 1954.

Bauer, P. T. "Nationalism and Politics in Malaya," *Foreign Affairs*, *25* (April, 1947), 503-517.

Blythe, W. L. "An Historical Sketch of Chinese Labour in Malaya," *Journal of the Malayan Branch of the Royal Asiatic Society*, *20* (June, 1947), 64-114.

Brimmell, J. H. *A Short History of the Malayan Communist Party*, Singapore, 1956.

British Information Services. *Malaya—The Facts*, London, 1952.

British Information Services. *Malaya, The New Phase*, London, 1956.

British Information Services. "Malaya: General Templer Reviews Progress" [extract of text of speech to Federal Legislative Council, Kuala Lumpur], Washington, D.C., December 11, 1952.

Butwell, Richard. "A Chinese University for Malaya," *Pacific Affairs*, *26* (December, 1953), 344-348.

Calder, Ritchie. *Men Against the Jungle*, London, 1954.

Campbell, Arthur. *Jungle Green*, Boston, 1954.

Carnell, Francis G. "British Policy in Malaya," *Political Quarterly*, *23* (July-September, 1952), 269-281.

Carnell, Francis G. "Communalism and Communism in Malaya," *Pacific Affairs*, *26* (June, 1953), 99-117.

Carnell, Francis G. "Constitutional Reform and Elections in Malaya," *Pacific Affairs, 27* (September, 1954), 216-235.

Carnell, Francis G. "The Malayan Elections," *Pacific Affairs, 28* (December, 1955), 315-330.

Carnell, Francis G. "Political Ferment in Singapore," *Far Eastern Survey, 24* (July, 1955), 97-102.

Carnell, Francis G. "Malayan Citizenship Legislation," *International and Comparative Law Quarterly, 1* (October, 1952), 504-518.

Carnell, Francis G. "Closer Association in British South-East Asia," *Eastern World*, 7 (May, 1953), 12-14.

Cator, Sir Geoffrey. "Brunei," *Asiatic Review, 35* (October, 1939), 736-744.

Cator, Sir Geoffrey. "Labuan," *Asiatic Review, 43* (January, 1947), 84-88.

Chapman, F. Spencer. *The Jungle Is Neutral*, London, 1949.

Cheng-lock Tan. *Malayan Problems, from a Chinese Point of View*, Singapore, 1947.

Chief Minister and His Merdeka Motion (David Marshall), Public Relations Office, Singapore, 1956.

Chief Minister Reports (David Marshall), Public Relations Office, Singapore, 1956.

"Communism in Malaya, Background to the Fighting," *The World Today, 5* (August, 1949), 346-354.

Coupland, Sir Reginald. *Raffles of Singapore*, 3d ed., London, 1946.

del Tufo, M. V. *Malaya, A Report on the 1947 Census of Population*, London, 1949.

Department of Information, Federation of Malaya. *The Malayan Scene*, Kuala Lumpur, 1954.

Department of Information, Federation of Malaya, Public Relations Office, Singapore, and Regional Information Office for the United Kingdom in South-East Asia, Singapore. *Handbook to Malaya and the Emergency*, Singapore, 1955.

Digby, Kenelm. "Colony of Sarawak," *Eastern World*, 7 (December, 1953), 21-23.

Dobby, E. H. G. *Malaya and the Malayans*, London, 1948.

Dobby, E. H. G. *Malaya and South-East Asia*, London, 1948.

Dobby, E. H. G. "Singapore: Town and Country," *The Geographical Review, 30* (January, 1940), 84-109.

Dobby, E. H. G. "Settlement Patterns in Malaya," *The Geographical Review, 32* (April, 1942), 211-232.

Dobby, E. H. G. "Resettlement Transforms Malaya," *Economic Development and Cultural Change, 1* (October, 1952), 163-189.

Dobby, E. H. G. "Recent Settlement Changes in South Malaya," *The Malayan Journal of Tropical Geography, 1* (October, 1953), 1-8.

Dobby, E. H. G. "Malaya's Rice Problem," *Pacific Affairs, 27* (March, 1954), 58-60.

"Education in Malaya," *The World Today, 12* (September, 1956), 379-386.

Emerson, Rupert. *Malaysia: A Study in Direct and Indirect Rule*, New York, 1937.

Federation of Malaya Information Services. *The Constitutional Commission*, Kuala Lumpur, 1956.

Federation of Malaya Information Services. *Self-Government for the Federation of Malaya: Report of the Constitution Conference, London, January-February, 1956*, Kuala Lumpur, 1956.

Fenton, B. L. "British North Borneo, A Regional Geography," *Tijdschrift voor Economische en Sociale Geografie, 45* (November-December, 1954), 208-216.

Firth, Raymond. *Malay Fishermen: Their Peasant Economy*, London, 1946.

Gamba, Charles. "Trade Unionism in Malaya," *Far Eastern Survey, 23* (February, 1954), 28-30.

Geddes, W. R. *The Land Dayaks of Sarawak*, London, 1954.

Ginsburg, Norton S., ed. *Malaya*, New Haven, 1955.

Grenfell, Russell. *Main Fleet to Singapore*, London, 1951.

Hanrahan, Gene Z. *The Communist Struggle in Malaya*, New York, 1954.

Harris, George L., and others. *North Borneo, Brunei, Sarawak*, New Haven, 1956.

Harrisson, Tom. "Malaya and Borneo in Malaysia," *Malayan Historical Journal, 1* (December, 1954), 103-109.

Harrisson, Tom. "Explorations in Central Borneo," *The Geographical Journal, 114* (December, 1949), 129-150.

Harrisson, Tom. "The Chinese in Borneo, 1942-1946," *International Affairs, 26* (July, 1950), 354-362.

Hawkins, Gerald. "Marking Time in Malaya," *International Affairs, 24* (January, 1948), 76-88.

Hawkins, Gerald. "First Steps in Malayan Local Government," *Pacific Affairs, 26* (June, 1953), 155-158.

Henniker, Mark C. A. *Red Shadow Over Malaya*, Edinburgh, 1955.

Hodder, B. W. "Racial Groupings in Singapore," *The Malayan Journal of Tropical Geography, 1* (October, 1953), 25-36.

Indians in the Malayan Economy, New Delhi, 1950.

Interim Report of the Joint Coördination Committee, Government Printing Office, Singapore, 1955.

International Bank for Reconstruction and Development. *The Economic Development of Malaya*, Baltimore, 1955.

Irwin, Graham. *Nineteenth-Century Borneo*, Singapore, 1955.

Jones, Arthur Creech. "The Asian Crisis and the Malay Peninsula," *International Journal, 6* (Winter, 1950-1951), 29-42.

Jones, L. W. *North Borneo: A Report on the Census of Population Held on 4th June, 1951*, London, 1953.

Jones, S. W. *Public Administration in Malaya*, London, 1953.

Kahin, George McT. "The State of North Borneo, 1881-1946," *Far Eastern Quarterly*, 7 (November, 1947), 43-65.

Kanwar, H. I. S. "Malaya's Cultural Contacts with India," *Asia, Asian*

Quarterly of Culture and Synthesis, 12 (March, 1954), 536-543.
King, Frank H. H. *The New Malayan Nation*, New York, 1957.
King, John Kerry. "Malaya's Resettlement Problem," *Far Eastern Survey, 23* (March, 1954), 33-40.
Meek, John Paul. *Malaya: A Study of Governmental Response to the Korean Boom*, Ithaca, N.Y., 1955.
Miller, Harry. *The Communist Menace in Malaya*, New York, 1954.
Mills, Lennox A. *British Rule in Eastern Asia*, London, 1942.
Morrison, Ian. "Local Self-Government in Sarawak," *Pacific Affairs, 22* (June, 1949), 178-185.
Morrison, Ian. "Aspects of the Racial Problem in Malaya," *Pacific Affairs, 22* (September, 1949), 239-253.
Nim Chee Siew. *Labour and Tin Mining in Malaya*, Ithaca, N.Y., 1953.
Noakes, J. L. *Sarawak and Brunei: A Report on the 1947 Population Census*, Kuching, 1950.
Parkinson, C. Northcote. *A Short History of Malaya*, Singapore, 1956.
Parmer, J. Norman. "Trade Unions and Politics in Malaya," *Far Eastern Survey, 24* (March, 1955), 33-39.
Parmer, J. Norman. "Constitutional Change in Malaya's Plural Society," *Far Eastern Survey, 26* (October, 1957), 145-152.
Pelzer, Karl J. "Resettlement in Malaya," *Yale Review, 41* (Spring, 1952), 391-404.
Peterson, A. D. C. "The Birth of the Malayan Nation," *International Affairs, 31* (July, 1955), 311-316.
Purcell, Victor. *Malaya: Outline of a Colony*, London, 1946.
Purcell, Victor. "The Position of the Chinese Community in Malaya," *Journal of the Royal Central Asian Society, 40* (January, 1953), 70-81.
Purcell, Victor. "The Crisis in Malayan Education," *Pacific Affairs, 26* (March, 1953), 70-76.
Purcell, Victor. *Malaya: Communist or Free?* London, 1954.
Purcell, Victor. *The Chinese in Modern Malaya*, Singapore, 1956.
Pye, Lucian W. *Guerrilla Communism in Malaya; Its Social and Political Meaning*, Princeton, 1956.
Raghavan, N. *India and Malaya: A Study*, Bombay, 1954.
Rees-Williams, David R. "The Constitutional Position in Malaya," *Pacific Affairs, 20* (June, 1947), 174-178.
Rees-Williams, David R., and Others. *Three Reports on the Malayan Problem*, New York, 1949.
Report by the Chief Minister of the Federation of Malaya on the Baling Talks, Government Press, Kuala Lumpur, 1956.
Robequain, Charles. *Malaya, Indonesia, Borneo, and the Philippines; A Geographical, Economic, and Political Description of Malaya, the East Indies, and the Philippines*, London, 1954.
Robinson, J. B. P. *Transformation in Malaya*, London, 1956.
Royal Institute of International Affairs. *Problems of the Post-War Settlement in the Far East: E. North Borneo, Sarawak and Brunei*, London, 1942.

Rutter, Owen. *British North Borneo*, London, 1922.
Sansom, Sir George. "The Story of Singapore," *Foreign Affairs, 22* (January, 1944), 279-297.
Seitelman, Max. "Malaya in Transition," *Far Eastern Survey, 16* (May 21, 1947), 109-111.
Seitelman, Max. "Political Thought in Malaya," *Far Eastern Survey, 16* (June 4, 1947), 128-130.
Seitelman, Max. "The Cession of Sarawak," *Far Eastern Survey, 17* (February 11, 1948), 35-37.
Silcock, T. H. "Forces for Unity in Malaya," *International Affairs, 25* (October, 1949), 453-465.
Silcock, T. H. "Policy for Malaya, 1952," *International Affairs, 28* (October, 1952), 445-451.
Sington, Derrick. *Malayan Perspective*, London, 1953.
Smith, T. E. *Population Growth in Malaya*, London, 1952.
Spector, Stanley. "Students and Politics in Singapore," *Far Eastern Survey, 25* (May, 1956), 65-73.
Swettenham, Sir Frank A. *British Malaya*, rev. ed., London, 1948.
"The Emergency in Malaya," *The World Today, 10* (November, 1954), 477-487.
Thompson, Virginia. *Postmortem on Malaya*, New York, 1943.
T'ien Ju-Kang. *The Chinese of Sarawak*, London, 1953.
Tinker, Irene. "Malayan Elections: Electoral Pattern for Plural Societies?" *Western Political Quarterly, 9* (June, 1956), 258-282.
"Transition in South-East Asia: The Future of Malaya and Singapore," *Round Table, 46* (March, 1956), 125-131.
Tregonning, K. "Malaya, 1955," *Australian Quarterly, 28* (June, 1956), 20-35.
Tregonning, K. "American Activity in North Borneo, 1865-1881," *Pacific Historical Review, 23* (November, 1954), 357-372.
U.S. Department of State. *Malaya: Trouble Spot in Southeast Asia*, Washington, D.C., 1953.
U.S. Department of State. *Political and Economic Changes Effected by the Japanese in Malaya*, Washington, D.C., 1943.
Winstedt, Sir Richard O. *Britain and Malaya, 1786-1941*, London, 1944.
Winstedt, Sir Richard O. *Malaya and Its History*, London, 1948.
Winstedt, Sir Richard O. *The Malays: A Cultural History*, rev. ed., London, 1950.
Winstedt, Sir Richard O. "Kingship and Enthronement in Malaya," *Journal of the Malayan Branch of the Royal Asiatic Society, 20* (June, 1947), 129-139.

INDEX